New Perspectives on
Creating Web Pages
with **HTML**

COMPREHENSIVE

Patrick Carey

Carey Associates, Inc.

COURSE
TECHNOLOGY

ONE MAIN STREET, CAMBRIDGE, MA 02142

an International Thomson Publishing company I(T)P®

Cambridge • Albany • Bonn • Boston • Cincinnati • London • Madrid • Melbourne • Mexico City
New York • Paris • San Francisco • Singapore • Tokyo • Toronto • Washington

New Perspectives on Creating Web Pages with HTML—Comprehensive
is published by Course Technology.

Associate Publisher	Mac Mendelsohn
Series Consulting Editor	Susan Solomon
Senior Product Manager	Donna Gridley
Developmental Editor	Kathleen Finnegan
Production Editor	Nancy Shea
Text and Cover Designer	Ella Hanna
Cover Illustrator	Douglas Goodman

For more information contact:

Course Technology
One Main Street
Cambridge, MA 02142

ITP Europe
Berkshire House 168-173
High Holborn
London WCIV 7AA
England

Nelson ITP, Australia
102 Dodds Street
South Melbourne, 3205
Victoria, Australia

ITP Nelson Canada
1120 Birchmount Road
Scarborough, Ontario
Canada M1K 5G4

International Thomson Editores
Seneca, 53
Colonia Polanco
11560 Mexico D.F. Mexico

ITP GmbH
Königswinterer Strasse 418
53227 Bonn
Germany

ITP Asia
60 Albert Street, #15-01
Albert Complex
Singapore 189969

ITP Japan
Hirakawacho Kyowa Building, 3F
2-2-1 Hirakawacho
Chiyoda-ku, Tokyo 102
Japan

ISBN 0-7600-6484-9

Printed in the United States of America

2 3 4 5 6 7 8 9 10 BM 02 01 00 99

At **Course Technology** we have one foot in education and the other in technology. We believe that technology is transforming the way people teach and learn, and we are excited about providing instructors and students with materials that use technology to teach about technology.

Our development process is unparalleled in the higher education publishing industry. Every product we create goes through an exacting process of design, development, review, and testing.

Reviewers give us direction and insight that shape our manuscripts and bring them up to the latest standards. Every manuscript is quality tested. Students whose backgrounds match the intended audience work through every keystroke, carefully checking for clarity and pointing out errors in logic and sequence. Together with our own technical reviewers, these testers help us ensure that everything that carries our name is error-free and easy to use.

We show both how and why technology is critical to solving problems in college and in whatever field you choose to teach or pursue. Our time-tested, step-by-step instructions provide unparalleled clarity. Examples and applications are chosen and crafted to motivate students.

As the New Perspectives Series team at Course Technology, our goal is to produce the most timely, accurate, creative, and technologically sound product in the entire college publishing industry. We strive for consistent high quality. This takes a lot of communication, coordination, and hard work. But we love what we do. We are determined to be the best. Write to us and let us know what you think. You can also e-mail us at newperspectives@course.com.

The New Perspectives Series Team

Joseph J. Adamski	Jessica Evans	Scott MacDonald
Judy Adamski	Kathy Finnegan	Mac Mendelsohn
Roy Ageloff	Dean Fossella	William Newman
Tim Ashe	Marilyn Freedman	Dan Oja
David Auer	Robin Geller	David Paradice
Daphne Barbas	Kate Habib	June Parsons
Dirk Baldwin	Donna Gridley	Harry Phillips
Rachel Bunin	Roger Hayen	Sandra Poindexter
Joan Carey	Cindy Johnson	Mark Reimold
Patrick Carey	Charles Hommel	Ann Shaffer
Sharon Caswell	Janice Jutras	Karen Shortill
Barbara Clemens	Chris Kelly	Susan Solomon
Rachel Crapser	Mary Kemper	Susanne Walker
Kim Crowley	Stacy Klein	John Zeanchock
Melissa Dezotell	Terry Ann Kremer	Beverly Zimmerman
Michael Ekedahl	John Leschke	Scott Zimmerman

Preface The New Perspectives Series

What is the New Perspectives Series?

Course Technology's **New Perspectives Series** is an integrated system of instruction that combines text and technology products to teach computer concepts and microcomputer applications. Users consistently praise this series for innovative pedagogy, creativity, supportive and engaging style, accuracy, and use of interactive technology. The first New Perspectives text was published in January of 1993. Since then, the series has grown to more than 100 titles and has become the best-selling series on computer concepts and microcomputer applications. Others have imitated the New Perspectives features, design, and technologies, but none have replicated its quality and its ability to consistently anticipate and meet the needs of instructors and students.

What is the Integrated System of Instruction?

New Perspectives textbooks are part of a truly Integrated System of Instruction: text, graphics, video, sound, animation, and simulations that are linked and that provide a flexible, unified, and interactive system to help you teach and help your students learn. Specifically, the *New Perspectives Integrated System of Instruction* includes a Course Technology textbook in addition to some or all of the following items: Course Labs, Course Test Manager, Online Companions, and Figures on CD-ROM. These components—shown in the graphic on the back cover of this book—have been developed to work together to provide a complete, integrative teaching and learning experience.

How is the New Perspectives Series different from other microcomputer concepts and applications series?

The **New Perspectives Series** distinguishes itself from other series in at least four substantial ways: sound instructional design, consistent quality, innovative technology, and proven pedagogy. The applications texts in this series consist of two or more tutorials, which are based on sound instructional design. Each tutorial is motivated by a realistic case that is meaningful to students. Rather than learn a laundry list of features, students learn the features in the context of solving a problem. This process motivates all concepts and skills by demonstrating to students *why* they would want to know them.

Instructors and students have come to rely on the high quality of the **New Perspectives Series** and to consistently praise its accuracy. This accuracy is a result of Course Technology's unique multi-step quality assurance process that incorporates student testing at at least two stages of development, using hardware and software configurations appropriate to the product. All solutions, test questions, and other supplements are tested using similar procedures. Instructors who adopt this series report that students can work through the tutorials independently with minimum intervention or "damage control" by instructors or staff. This consistent quality has meant that if instructors are pleased with one product from the series, they can rely on the same quality with any other New Perspectives product.

The **New Perspectives Series** also distinguishes itself by its innovative technology. This series innovated Course Labs, truly *interactive* learning applications. These have set the standard for interactive learning.

How do I know that the New Perspectives Series will work?

Some instructors who use this series report a significant difference between how much their students learn and retain with this series as compared to other series. With other series, instructors often find that students can work through the book and do well on homework and tests, but still not demonstrate competency when asked to perform particular tasks outside the context of the text's sample case or project. With the **New Perspectives Series**, however, instructors report that students have a complete, integrative learning experience that stays with them. They credit this high retention and competency to the fact that this series incorporates critical thinking and problem-solving with computer skills mastery.

How does this book I'm holding fit into the New Perspectives Series?

New Perspectives applications books are available in the following categories:

Brief books are typically about 150 pages long, contain two to four tutorials, and are intended to teach the basics of an application.

Introductory books are typically about 300 pages long and consist of four to seven tutorials that go beyond the basics. These books often build out of the Brief editions by providing two or three additional tutorials.

Comprehensive books are typically about 600 pages long and consist of all of the tutorials in the Introductory books, plus a few more tutorials covering higher-level topics. Comprehensive books typically also include two Windows tutorials and three or four Additional Cases. The book you are holding is a Comprehensive book.

Advanced books cover topics similar to those in the Comprehensive books, but go into more depth. Advanced books present the most high-level coverage in the series.

Office books are typically 800 pages long and include coverage of each of the major components of the Office suite. These books often include tutorials introducing the suite, exploring the operating system, and integrating the programs in the suite.

Custom Books The New Perspectives Series offers you two ways to customize a New Perspectives text to fit your course exactly: *CourseKits*™, two or more texts packaged together in a box, and *Custom Editions*®, your choice of books bound together. Custom Editions offer you unparalleled flexibility in designing your concepts and applications courses. You can build your own book by ordering a combination of titles bound together to cover only the topics you want. Your students save because they buy only the materials they need. There is no minimum order, and books are spiral bound. Both CourseKits and Custom Editions offer significant price discounts. Contact your Course Technology sales representative for more information.

New Perspectives Series Microcomputer Applications				
■ **Brief Titles or Modules**	■ **Introductory Titles or Modules**	■ **Intermediate Tutorials**	■ **Advanced Titles or Modules**	■ **Other Modules**
Brief	**Introductory**	**Comprehensive**	**Advanced**	**Custom Editions**
2 to 4 tutorials	6 or 7 tutorials, or Brief + 2 or 3 more tutorials	Introductory + 4 or 5 more tutorials. Includes Brief Windows tutorials and Additional Cases	Quick Review of basics + in-depth, high-level coverage	Choose from any of the above to build your own Custom Editions® or CourseKits™

In what kind of course could I use this book?

This book can be used in any course in which you want students to learn the most important topics of HTML, including creating an HTML document; viewing an HTML file in a Web browser; working with tag text elements, including headings, paragraphs, and lists; inserting special characters, lines, and graphics; creating hypertext links; working with color and images; creating text and graphical tables; using tables to enhance page design; creating and working with frames; controlling the behavior of hyperlinks on a page with frames; learning about CGI scripts; creating an online form; creating a JavaScript function; working with JavaScript objects and events; creating a JavaScript program; and creating a multimedia Web page. It is particularly recommended for a full-semester course on HTML. This book assumes that students have learned basic Windows 95 or Windows NT navigation and file management skills from Course Technology's *New Perspectives on Microsoft Windows 95—Brief*, *New Perspectives on Microsoft Windows NT Workstation 4.0—Introductory*, or an equivalent book.

How do the Windows 95 editions differ from the Windows 3.1 editions?

Sessions We've divided the tutorials into sessions. Each session is designed to be completed in about 45 minutes to an hour (depending, of course, upon student needs and the speed of your lab equipment). With sessions, learning is broken up into more easily assimilated portions. You can more accurately allocate time in your syllabus, and students can better manage the available lab time. Each session begins with a "session box," which quickly describes the skills students will learn in the session. Furthermore, each session is numbered, which makes it easier for you and your students to navigate and communicate about the tutorial. Look on page HTML 1.4 for the session box that opens Session 1.1.

Quick Checks Each session concludes with meaningful, conceptual Quick Check questions that test students' understanding of what they learned in the session. Answers to the Quick Check questions in this book are provided on pages HTML 2.35 through HTML 2.37, pages HTML 5.39 through HTML 5.40, and pages HTML 9.41 through HTML 9.45.

New Design We have retained the best of the old design to help students differentiate between what they are to *do* and what they are to *read*. The steps are clearly identified by their shaded background and numbered steps. Furthermore, this new design presents steps and screen shots in a larger, easier to read format. Some good examples of our new design are pages HTML 1.16 and HTML 1.17.

What features are retained in the Windows 95 editions of the New Perspectives Series?

"Read This Before You Begin" Page This page is consistent with Course Technology's unequaled commitment to helping instructors introduce technology into the classroom. Technical considerations and assumptions about software are listed to help instructors save time and eliminate unnecessary aggravation. See pages HTML 1.2, HTML 3.2, and HTML 6.2 for the "Read This Before You Begin" pages in this book.

Tutorial Case Each tutorial begins with a problem presented in a case that is meaningful to students. The problem turns the task of learning how to use an application into a problem-solving process. The problems increase in complexity with each tutorial. These cases touch on multicultural, international, and ethical issues—so important to today's business curriculum. See page HTML 1.3 for the case that begins Tutorial 1.

**1.
2.
3.**

Step-by-Step Methodology This unique Course Technology methodology keeps students on track. They enter data, click buttons, or press keys always within the context of solving the problem posed in the tutorial case. The text constantly guides students, letting them know where they are in the course of solving the problem. In addition, the numerous screen shots include labels that direct students' attention to what they should look at on the screen. On almost every page in this book, you can find an example of how steps, screen shots, and labels work together.

TROUBLE?

TROUBLE? Paragraphs These paragraphs anticipate the mistakes or problems that students are likely to have and help them recover and continue with the tutorial. By putting these paragraphs in the book, rather than in the Instructor's Manual, we facilitate independent learning and free the instructor to focus on substantive conceptual issues rather than on common procedural errors. Some representative examples of TROUBLE? paragraphs appear on page HTML 1.14.

Reference Windows Reference Windows appear throughout the text. They are succinct summaries of the most important tasks covered in the tutorials. Reference Windows are specially designed and written so students can refer to them when doing the Tutorial Assignments and Case Problems, and after completing the course. Page HTML 1.24 contains the Reference Window for Creating Lists.

Tutorial Assignments, Case Problems, and Lab Assignments Each tutorial concludes with Tutorial Assignments, which provide students with additional hands-on practice of the skills they learned in the tutorial. See page HTML 3.45 for examples of Tutorial Assignments. The Tutorial Assignments are followed by four Case Problems that have approximately the same scope as the tutorial case. In the Windows 95 applications texts, the last Case Problem of each tutorial typically requires students to solve the problem independently, either "from scratch" or with minimum guidance. See page HTML 3.46 for examples of Case Problems. Finally, if a Course Lab accompanies a tutorial, Lab Assignments are included after the Case Problems. See page HTML 1.40 for examples of Lab Assignments.

Exploration Exercises The Windows environment allows students to learn by exploring and discovering what they can do. Exploration Exercises can be Tutorial Assignments or Case Problems that challenge students, encourage them to explore the capabilities of the program they are using, and extend their knowledge using the Help facility and other reference materials. Page HTML 4.47 contains Exploration Exercises for Tutorial 4.

What supplements are available with this textbook?

Course Labs: Now, Concepts Come to Life Computer skills and concepts come to life with the New Perspectives Course Labs—highly-interactive tutorials that combine illustrations, animations, digital images, and simulations. The Labs guide students step-by-step, present them with Quick Check questions, let them explore on their own, test their comprehension, and provide printed feedback. Lab icons at the beginning of the tutorial and in the tutorial margins indicate when a topic has a corresponding Lab. Lab Assignments are included at the end of each relevant tutorial. The Labs available with this book and the tutorials in which they appear are:

TUTORIAL 1	TUTORIAL 9	ADDITIONAL CASES

The Internet World Wide Web	Multimedia	Web Pages & HTML

Course Test Manager: Testing and Practice at the Computer or on Paper Course Test Manager is a powerful testing and assessment package that enables instructors to create and print tests from Testbanks designed specifically for Course Technology titles. In addition, instructors with access to a networked computer lab (LAN) can administer, grade, and track tests on-line. Students can also take on-line practice tests, which generate customized study guides that indicate where in the text students can find more information on each question.

Figures on CD-ROM: This lecture presentation tool allows instructors to create electronic slide shows or traditional overhead transparencies using the figure files from the book. Instructors can customize, edit, save, and display figures from the text in order to illustrate key topics or concepts in class.

Online Companions: Dedicated to Keeping You and Your Students Up-To-Date When you use a New Perspectives product, you can access Course Technology's faculty sites and student sites on the World Wide Web. You can browse this text's password-protected Faculty Online Companion to obtain an online Instructor's Manual, Solution Files, Student Files, and more by visiting Course Technology's Online Resource Center at **www.course.com**. Please see your Instructor's Manual or call your Course Technology customer service representative for more information. Students can access this text's Student Online Companion, which contains student files and additional coverage of selected topics in the text.

Instructor's Manual New Perspectives Series Instructor's Manuals contain instructor's notes and solutions for each tutorial. Instructor's notes provide tutorial overviews and outlines, technical notes, lecture notes, and extra Case Problems. Solutions include answers to Tutorial Assignments, Case Problems, Additional Cases, and Lab Assignments.

Student Files Student Files contain all of the data that students will use to complete the tutorials, Tutorial Assignments, Case Problems, and Additional Cases. A Readme file includes technical tips for lab management. See the inside front cover of this book and the "Read This Before You Begin" pages for more information on Student Files.

Solution Files Solution Files contain every file students are asked to create or modify in the tutorials, Tutorial Assignments, Case Problems, and Additional Cases.

CD in the back of this book A special feature of this book! The CD contains the following:

- Java applets
- HTML 4.0 Tag Reference
- Additional coverage
- Other multimedia elements

The following supplements are included in the Instructor's Resource Kit that accompanies this textbook:

- Electronic Instructor's Manual
- Solution Files
- Student Files
- Course Labs
- Course Test Manager Testbank
- Course Test Manager Engine
- Figures on CD-ROM
- HTML files of the Faculty Online Companion

Some of the supplements listed above are also available over the World Wide Web through Course Technology's password-protected Faculty Online Companion for this text. Please see your Instructor's Resource Kit or call your Course Technology customer service representative for more information.

Acknowledgments

This book would not have been started without the support and enthusiasm of Mac Mendelsohn, Associate Publisher, and Mark Reimold, Senior Product Manager, who initially proposed the project. Special thanks to Kathy Finnegan, who improved the book with her editorial skill and valuable ideas, and to Donna Gridley, Senior Product Manager, who kept the project on track and on time and provided useful input. Other people at Course Technology who deserve credit are Karen Shortill, Editorial Assistant; Nancy Shea, Production Editor; Devra Kunin and Jeri Freedman, copyeditors; and John McCarthy, Alex White, and Seth Freeman, QA testers. Feedback is an important part of writing any book, and thanks go to the following reviewers for their ideas and comments: John Chenoweth, East Tennessee State University; Ramona Coveny, Patrick Henry Community College; Joseph Farrelly, Palomer College; Ralph Hooper, University of Alabama; Stuart Varden, Pace University; and Dr. Ahmed Zaki, College of William & Mary. Finally, I want to thank my wife Joan for her encouragement, suggestions and photographs (which I liberally used in creating my sample Web pages!) and my four sons: John Paul, Thomas, Peter, and Michael, to whom this book is dedicated.

Patrick Carey

Table of **Contents**

Design Windows

Reference Windows

NEW
PERSPECTIVES
SERIES

Creating Web Pages with **HTML**

LEVEL I

TUTORIALS

Read This **Before You Begin**

STUDENT DISK

To complete HTML Tutorials 1–2 and end-of-tutorial assignments in this book, you need a Student Disk. Your instructor will either provide you with a Student Disk or ask you to make your own.

If you are supposed to make your own Student Disk, you will need one blank, formatted high-density disk. You will need to copy a set of folders from a file server or standalone computer onto your disk. Your instructor will tell you which computer, drive letter, and folders contain the files you need. See the inside front or inside back cover of this book for more information on Student Disk files, or ask your instructor or technical support person for assistance.

COURSE LAB

Tutorial 1 features an Interactive Course Lab to help you understand Internet World Wide Web concepts. There are Lab Assignments at the end of the tutorial that relate to this Lab. To start the Lab, click the Start button on the Windows 95 Taskbar, point to Programs, point to Course Labs, point to New Perspectives Applications, and click the Internet World Wide Web.

USING YOUR OWN COMPUTER

If you are going to work through this book using your own computer, you need:

■ **Computer System** A text editor and a Web browser (preferably Netscape Navigator or Internet Explorer, versions 3.0 or above) must be installed on your computer. If you are using a non-standard browser, it must support frames and HTML 3.2 or above. Most of the tutorials can be completed with just a text editor and a Web browser. However, to complete the last sections of Tutorial 2, you will need software that connects you to the Internet and an Internet connection.

■ **Student Disk** Ask your instructor or lab manager for details on how to get the Student Disk. You will not be able to complete the tutorials or end-of-tutorial assignments in this book using your own computer until you have a Student Disk. The Student Files may also be obtained electronically over the Internet. See the inside front or inside back cover of this book for more details.

VISIT OUR WORLD WIDE WEB SITE

Additional materials designed especially for you are available on the World Wide Web. Go to **http://www.course.com**. For example, see our Student Online Companion that contains additional coverage of selected topics in the text. These topics are indicated in the text by an online companion icon located in the left margin.

To complete HTML Tutorials 1–2 and end-of-tutorial assignments in this book, your students must use a set of files on one Student Disk. These files are included in the Instructor's Resource Kit, and they may also be obtained electronically over the Internet. See the inside front or inside back cover of this book for more details. Follow the instructions in the Readme file to copy the files to your server or standalone computer. You can view the Readme file using WordPad.

Once the files are copied, you can make a Student Disk for the students yourself, or you can tell students where to find the files so they can make their own Student Disks. Make sure the files get correctly copied onto the Student Disk by following the instructions in the Student Disk section above, which will ensure that students have enough disk space to complete all the tutorials and end-of-tutorial assignments.

COURSE LAB SOFTWARE

The Course Lab software is distributed on a CD-ROM included in the Instructor's Resource Kit. To install the Course Lab software, follow the setup instructions in the Readme file on the CD-ROM. Refer also to the Readme file for essential technical notes related to running the Lab in a multi-user environment. Once you have installed the Course Lab software, your students can start the Lab from the Windows 95 desktop by following the instructions in the Course Lab section above.

COURSE TECHNOLOGY STUDENT FILES

You are granted a license to copy the Student Files to any computer or computer network used by students who have purchased this book.

Creating a Web Page

Web Fundamentals and HTML

OBJECTIVES

In this tutorial you will:

- Explore the structure of the World Wide Web
- Learn the basic principles of Web documents
- Get to know the HTML language
- Create an HTML document
- View an HTML file in a Web browser
- Tag text elements, including headings, paragraphs, and lists
- Insert character tags
- Add special characters
- Insert horizontal lines
- Insert an inline graphic image

LAB

The Internet
World Wide Web

CASE

Creating an Online Resume

Mary Taylor just graduated from Colorado State with a master's degree in telecommunications. Now she has to find a job. Mary wants to explore as many employment avenues as possible, so she decides to post a copy of her resume on the World Wide Web. Creating an online resume offers Mary several advantages. The Web's skyrocketing popularity gives Mary the potential of reaching a large and varied audience. She can continually update an online resume, offering details on her latest projects and jobs. An online resume also gives a prospective employer the opportunity to look at her work history in more detail than is normal with a paper resume, because she can include links to other relevant documents. Mary asks you to help her create an online resume. You're happy to agree because it's something you wanted to learn anyway. After all, you'll be creating your own resume soon enough.

SESSION

1.1

In this session you will learn the basics of how the World Wide Web operates. Then you will begin to explore the code used to create Web documents.

Introducing the World Wide Web

The **Internet** is a structure made up of millions of interconnected computers whose users can communicate with each other and share information. The physical structure of the Internet uses fiber-optic cables, satellites, phone lines, and other telecommunications media that send data back and forth, as Figure 1-1 shows. Computers that are linked together form a **network**. Any user whose computer can be linked to a network that has Internet access can join the worldwide Internet community.

Figure 1-1 ◀
Structure of the
Internet

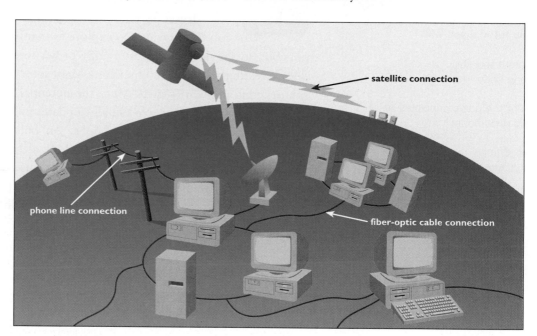

For years, anyone with Internet access could take advantage of the opportunities the Internet offered but not without some problems. New users often found their introduction to the Internet an unpleasant one. Many Internet tools required you to master a bewildering array of terms, acronyms, and commands before you could begin navigating the Internet. Navigation itself was a hit-and-miss proposition. A computer in Bethesda might have information on breast cancer, but if you didn't know that computer existed and how to reach it, the Internet offered few tools to help you get there. What Internet users needed was a tool that would be easy to use and would allow quick access to any computer on the Internet, regardless of its location. This tool would prove to be the World Wide Web.

The Development of the World Wide Web

The **World Wide Web** organizes the Internet's vast resources to give you easy access to information. In 1989, Timothy Berners-Lee and other researchers at the CERN nuclear research facility near Geneva, Switzerland, laid the foundation of the World Wide Web, or the Web. They wanted to create an information system that made it easy for researchers to share data and that required minimal training and support. They developed a system of hypertext documents that made it very easy to move from one source of information to another. A **hypertext document** is an electronic file that contains elements that you can select, usually by clicking a mouse, to open another document.

Hypertext offers a new way of progressing through a series of documents. When you read a book you follow a linear progression, reading one page after another. With hypertext, you progress through pages in whatever way is best suited to your goals. Hypertext lets you skip from one topic to another, following a path of information that interests you. Figure 1-2 shows how topics could be related in a hypertext fashion as opposed to a linear fashion.

Figure 1-2 ◀
Linear vs.
hypertext
documents

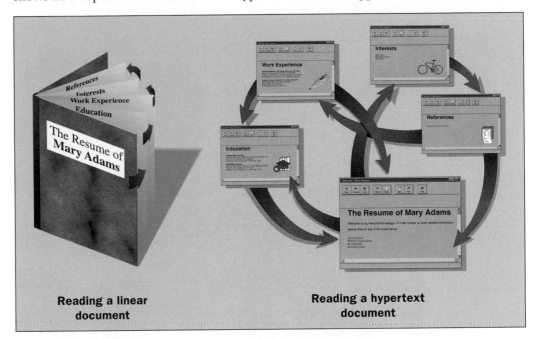

**Reading a linear
document**

**Reading a hypertext
document**

You might already be familiar with two common sources of hypertext: Windows Help files and Macintosh HyperCard stacks. In these applications, you move from one topic to another by clicking or highlighting a phrase or keyword known as a **link**. Clicking a link takes you to another section of the document or it might take you to another document entirely. Figure 1-3 shows how you might navigate a link in a Help file.

Figure 1-3 ◀
Clicking a link
in a Help file

when you click link, a
new document appears

Quicken 4 for Windows Help
File   Edit   Bookmark   Options   Help
Contents | Search | Back | Print | Glossary

**Create a logo for your
checks**

You can print your own logo on your
checks. To do this, you need to create
the artwork and store it as a bitmap file
(that is, a file with a .BMP extension). You
can use Paintbrush (or a similar
application) to create the bitmap.

Print a logo on your checks
Create a logo for your checks
Print a logo on your checks

hypertext
links

point at link
then click

Hypertext as implemented by the CERN group involves jumping from one document to another on computers scattered all over the world. In Figure 1-4, you are working at a computer in Canada that shows a hypertext document on traveling in the United States. This document contains a link to another document located on a computer in Washington D.C. on the National Park Service. That document in turn contains a link to a document located in California on Yosemite National Park.

Figure 1-4 ◄
Navigating
hypertext
documents on
the Web

You move from document to document (and computer to computer) by simply clicking links. This approach makes navigating the Internet easy. It frees you from knowing anything about the document's location. The link could open a document on your computer or a document on a computer in South Africa. You might never notice the difference.

Your experience with the Web is not limited to reading text. Web documents, also known as **pages**, can contain graphics, video clips, sound clips, and, more recently, programs that you can run directly from the page. Moreover, as Figure 1-5 shows, Web pages can display text in a wide variety of fonts and formats. A Web document is not only a source of information, it can also be a work of art.

Figure 1-5 ◀
Web page
featuring
interesting
fonts, graphics
and layout

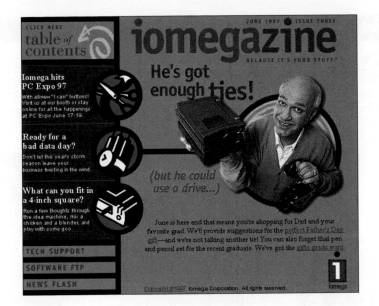

A final feature that contributes to the Web's popularity is that it gives users the ability to easily create their own Web documents. This is in marked contrast to other Internet tools, which often required the expertise of a computer systems manager. Figure 1-6 illustrates the Web's explosive growth: in 1993 there were only a couple hundred Web sites worldwide; by the beginning of 1997 there were almost 650,000. Even more impressively, the number of sites doubled in less than six months, according to estimates from Matthew Gray of the Massachusetts Institute of Technology. The Web has grown so fast, that it is almost impossible to estimate its current size. Is there any doubt why Mary sees the Web as a dynamic place to post a resume?

Figure 1-6 ◀
Growth of the
World Wide
Web

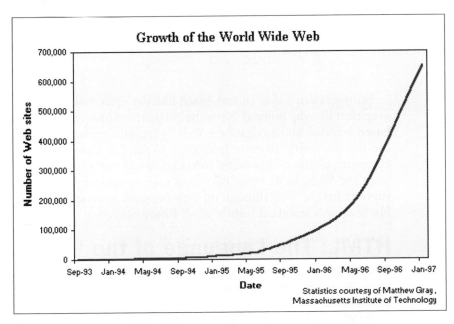

Web Servers and Web Browsers

The World Wide Web has the two components shown in Figure 1-7. The **Web server** is the computer that stores the Web document that users access. The **Web browser** is the software program that accesses the Web document and displays its contents on the user's computer. The browser can locate a document on a server anywhere in the world and display it for you to see.

Figure 1-7 ◀
Using a browser
to view a Web
document on a
server

Netscape Navigator
browser

browser in California
locates and displays
document stored on
server in Florida

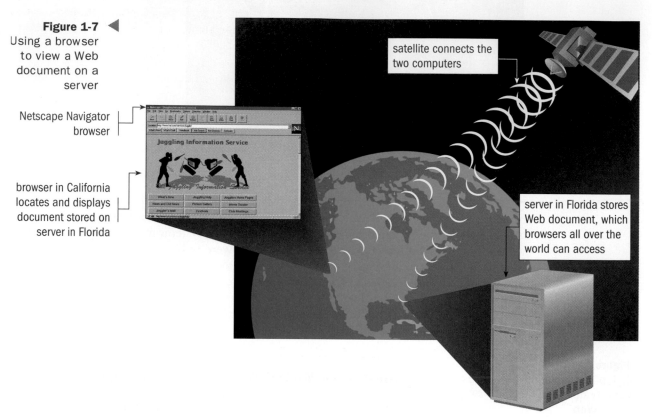

satellite connects the
two computers

server in Florida stores
Web document, which
browsers all over the
world can access

Browsers can either be text-based like the Lynx browser found on UNIX machines or graphical like the popular Netscape Navigator browser shown in Figure 1-7. With a text-based browser you navigate the Web by typing commands; with a graphical browser you can use the mouse to move from page to page. Browsers are available for virtually every computer platform. No matter what computer you have, you can probably use it to navigate the Web. In its latest operating system upgrade, Windows 95, Microsoft includes support for the Web through its Web browser, Internet Explorer. Web access will probably become a standard feature of all future operating systems.

HTML: The Language of the Web

When a browser locates a Web document on a server, it needs a way to interpret what it finds. To create a Web document, you use a special language that browsers can read called a **markup language**. The most common markup language is the **Hypertext Markup Language** or **HTML**. HTML is one example of a more general markup language called **Standard Generalized Markup Language (SGML)**. SGML encompasses several types of markup languages called **Document Type Definitions (DTD)**. So if you want to engage in a little acronym overload, you can tell your friends that HTML is an SGML DTD used on the WWW.

HTML was designed to describe the contents of a Web page in a very general way. As you've seen in previous figures, a browser can display a Web page with a variety of fonts and styles. If you've used a word processor you know that you can specify the appearance of text in terms of a font type such as Arial or Times Roman, or an attribute such as bold or italic. HTML doesn't describe how text looks. Instead it uses a **code** that describes the function the text has in the document. Text appearing in the document heading is marked with a heading code. Text appearing in a bulleted list is marked with a list code. A Web browser interprets these codes to determine the text's appearance. Different browsers might make different choices. One browser might apply a Times Roman font to text in the document heading, while another browser might use an Arial font. Figure 1-8 shows how the same HTML file might appear on two different browsers.

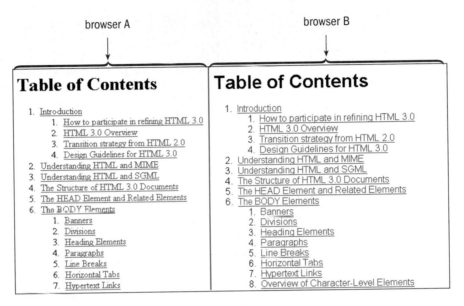

Figure 1-8 ◀
Two different browsers displaying the same HTML file

There are a couple reasons for this. The Web must work across computer platforms, a feature known as **portability**. Because each computer differs in terms of what, if any, fonts it can display, the browser determines how text is to be displayed. Portability frees Web page authors from worrying about making their pages compatible with the large variety of computers and operating systems on the Internet. HTML works with a wide range of devices, from clunky teletypes to high-end workstations. It also works with nonvisual media such as speech and Braille.

Another advantage of HTML is speed. While it might be possible to include exact specifications on how to display each character within the Web document, doing so would dramatically increase both file size and the time required to retrieve it. It is much quicker to render the document on the local computer using local specifications. The downside of this approach is that you cannot be sure exactly how every browser will display the text on your page. Some Web authors therefore test their code on several different browsers before posting their pages on the Internet.

Versions of HTML

The language HTML uses to mark text has a grammar or set of rules under which it operates, called its **syntax**. There must be a consensus on the syntax used in HTML files. If there were not, you would have no guarantee that other browsers on the Internet will recognize the code in your Web document. It wouldn't do Mary much good to create a stunning online resume that her potential employers cannot read. This consensus is referred to as the **specifications** or **standards** that have been developed by a consortium of Web authors, software companies, and interested users.

Figure 1-9 lists four versions of HTML; each follows a defined set of standards.

Figure 1-9 ◀
Versions of
HTML

Version	Description
HTML 1.0	The first public version of HTML, which included browser support for inline images and text controls.
HTML 2.0	The version supported by all graphical browsers, including Netscape Communicator, Internet Explorer and Mosaic. It supported interactive form elements such as option buttons and text boxes. A document written to follow 2.0 specifications would be readable by most browsers on the Internet.
HTML 3.2	This version included more support for creating and formatting tables and expanded the options for interactive form elements. It also allows for the creation of complex mathematical equations.
HTML 4.0	This version adds support for style sheets to give Web authors greater control over page layout. It adds new features to tables and forms and provides support for international features. This version also expands HTML's scripting ability and support for multimedia elements.

For detailed information on HTML standards and any updates, see the Web page at http://www.w3.org/MarkUp/.

Some browsers also support **extensions**, features that add new possibilities to HTML. The most well-known extensions were created for the Netscape Navigator browser. Because only Netscape Navigator browsers can interpret these extensions, many people argue that Netscape Navigator has undermined a fundamental advantage of the World Wide Web: the ability of a Web document to work on different platforms and browsers. On the other hand, Web authors clearly want the additional functions the Netscape Navigator extensions offer. These extensions foreshadowed many of the enhancements added in HTML 3.2. Moreover, the Netscape Navigator extensions didn't alter existing features. If you plan to use extensions in your Web documents, you should indicate this on your page and identify the browsers that support those extensions.

Tools for Creating HTML Documents

HTML documents are simple text files. The only software package you need to create them is a basic text editor like the Windows Notepad application. If you want a software package to do some of the work of creating an HTML document, you can use an HTML converter or an HTML editor.

An **HTML converter** takes text in one format and converts it to HTML code. For example, you can create the source document with a word processor like Microsoft Word and then have the converter save the document as an HTML file. Converters have several advantages. They free you from the occasionally laborious task of writing HTML code, and, because the conversion is automated, you do not have to worry about typographical errors ruining your code. Finally, you can create the source document using a software package that you might be more familiar with. Be aware that a converter has some limitations. As HTML specifications are updated and new extensions created, you will have to wait for the next version of the converter to take advantage of these features. Moreover, no converter can support all HTML features, so for anything but the simplest Web page, you still have to work with HTML.

An **HTML editor** helps you create an HTML file by inserting HTML codes for you as you work. HTML editors can save you a lot of work, but they have many of the same advantages and limitations as converters. They do let you set up your Web page quickly, but to create the finished document, you probably still have to work directly with the HTML code. You can read reviews of popular HTML editors on the Web page located at http://www.webcommando.com/editrev/index.html.

Quick Check

1 What is hypertext?

2 What are a Web server and a Web browser? Describe how they work together.

3 What is HTML?

4 How do HTML documents differ from documents created with a word processor like Word or WordPerfect?

5 What are the advantages of letting Web browsers determine the appearance of Web pages?

6 What are HTML extensions? What are some advantages and disadvantages of using extensions?

7 What software program do you need to create an HTML document?

SESSION

1.2

In this session you begin entering the text that will form the basis of your Web page. You will insert the appropriate HTML codes and create a simple Web page detailing Mary's work experience and qualifications.

Creating an HTML Document

It's always a good idea to plan the appearance of your Web page before you start writing code. In her final semester Mary developed a paper resume that she distributed at campus job fairs. Half her work is already done, because she can use the paper resume as her model.

Figure 1-10 shows Mary's hardcopy resume.

Figure 1-10
Mary's paper resume

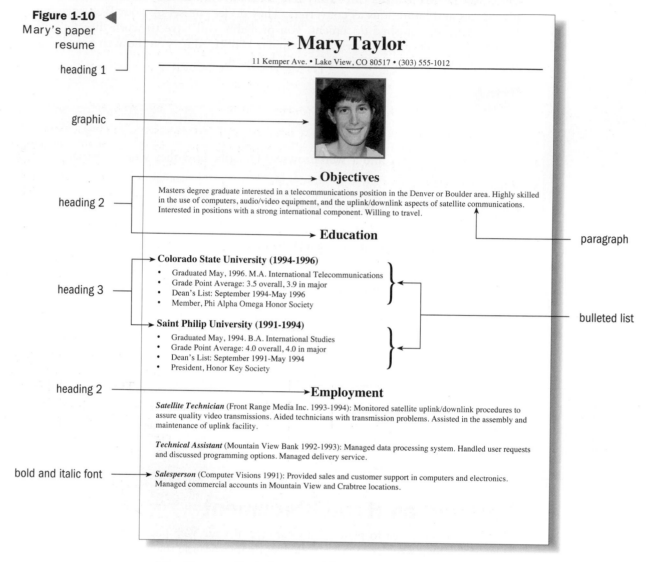

Mary Taylor

11 Kemper Ave. • Lake View, CO 80517 • (303) 555-1012

Objectives

Masters degree graduate interested in a telecommunications position in the Denver or Boulder area. Highly skilled in the use of computers, audio/video equipment, and the uplink/downlink aspects of satellite communications. Interested in positions with a strong international component. Willing to travel.

Education

Colorado State University (1994-1996)
- Graduated May, 1996. M.A. International Telecommunications
- Grade Point Average: 3.5 overall, 3.9 in major
- Dean's List: September 1994-May 1996
- Member, Phi Alpha Omega Honor Society

Saint Philip University (1991-1994)
- Graduated May, 1994. B.A. International Studies
- Grade Point Average: 4.0 overall, 4.0 in major
- Dean's List: September 1991-May 1994
- President, Honor Key Society

Employment

Satellite Technician (Front Range Media Inc. 1993-1994): Monitored satellite uplink/downlink procedures to assure quality video transmissions. Aided technicians with transmission problems. Assisted in the assembly and maintenance of uplink facility.

Technical Assistant (Mountain View Bank 1992-1993): Managed data processing system. Handled user requests and discussed programming options. Managed delivery service.

Salesperson (Computer Visions 1991): Provided sales and customer support in computers and electronics. Managed commercial accounts in Mountain View and Crabtree locations.

heading 1 — graphic — heading 2 — paragraph — heading 3 — bulleted list — heading 2 — bold and italic font

Mary's resume includes several features that she would like you to implement in the online version. A heading at the top prominently displays her name in a large font. Beneath the heading is her photo. Mary's resume is divided into three sections: Objectives, Education, and Employment. Within the Objectives section, a paragraph describes Mary's interests and future goals. Within the Education section, two smaller headings name the two universities she attended. Under each of these headings, a bulleted list details her accomplishments. The Employment section describes each position she's held, with the official title bolded and italicized. Mary's paper resume has three heading levels, bulleted lists, formatted characters, and graphics. When she creates her online resume with HTML, she wants to include these features. As you help Mary create this document for the World Wide Web, you will probably want to refer to Figure 1-10 periodically as the page develops.

HTML Syntax

The HTML syntax for creating the kinds of features that Mary wants in her page follow a very basic structure. An HTML document has two elements: document content and tags. **Document content** are those parts of the document that you want the user to see, such as text and graphics. **Tags** are the HTML codes that indicate the document content. You apply a tag to document content using the syntax:

```
<Tag Name Properties> Document Content </Tag Name>
```

You can always identify a tag by the brackets (<>) that enclose the tag name. Some tags can include **properties**, or additional information placed within the brackets that defines the tag's appearance. Tags usually come in pairs: the **opening tag** is the first tag, which tells the browser to turn on the feature and apply it to the document content that follows. The browser applies the feature until it encounters the **closing tag**, which turns off the feature. Note that closing tags are identified by the slash (/) that precedes the tag name. Not every tag has an opening and closing tag. Some tags are known as **one-sided tags** because they require only the opening tag. **Two-sided tags** require both opening and closing tags.

Look at the first line of Mary's resume, the name "Mary Taylor," in Figure 1-10. HTML uses the tag name <H1> for a heading 1. The HTML command that describes this line reads:

```
<H1 ALIGN=CENTER>Mary Taylor</H1>
```

Here the <H1 ALIGN=CENTER > opening tag tells the browser that the text that follows, "Mary Taylor," should appear as a heading 1. This tag also includes a property, the **alignment property** (ALIGN), which tells the browser how to align the text: in this case, centered. After the opening tag comes the content, Mary Taylor. The </H1> tag signals the browser to turn off the H1 heading. Remember that each browser determines the exact look of the H1 heading. One browser might apply a 14-point Times Roman bold font to Mary's text, whereas another browser might use 18-point italic Arial. Figure 1-11 shows how three different browsers might interpret this line of HTML code.

Figure 1-11 ◄
Examples of
how different
browsers might
interpret the
HTML<H1> tag

Browser interpreting the <H1> tag	Appearance of the document content
Browser A	**Mary Taylor**
Browser B	Mary Taylor
Browser C	*Mary Taylor*

Tags are not case sensitive. That means typing "<H1>" has the same effect as typing "<h1>." Many Web authors like to use only uppercase for tags to distinguish tags from document content. We'll follow that convention in the examples that follow.

Creating Basic Tags

When you start entering HTML code, it's best to identify the document's main components. First you enter tags that indicate the language in which Mary's document is written, identify the document's key sections, and give it a title. For now, type the text exactly as you see it. The text after the steps explains each line. To start entering code you need a text editor.

To start creating an HTML file:

1. Place your Student Disk in drive A.

   TROUBLE? If you don't have a Student Disk, you need to get one. Your instructor will either give you one or ask you to make your own. See the "Read This Before You Begin" page at the beginning of the tutorials for instructions.

   TROUBLE? If your Student Disk won't fit in drive A, try drive B. If it fits in drive B, substitute "drive B" for "drive A" in every tutorial.

2. Open a text editor on your system, and start a new document.

   TROUBLE? If you don't know how to locate, start, or use the text editor on your system, ask your instructor for help.

3. Type the following lines of code into your document. Press **Enter** after each line (twice for a blank line).

   ```
   <HTML>
   <HEAD>
   <TITLE>The Resume of Mary Taylor</TITLE>
   </HEAD>

   <BODY>
   </BODY>

   </HTML>
   ```

4. Save the file as **Resume.htm** in the Tutorial.01 folder on your Student Disk, but do not exit your text editor. If you are working with Windows 95, UNIX, or a Macintosh, you can save it with the more conventional **html** file extension. The text you typed should look something like Figure 1-12.

   TROUBLE? If you don't know how to save a file on your Student Disk, ask your instructor for assistance.

   TROUBLE? Don't worry if your screen doesn't look exactly like Figure 1-12. The text editor shown in the figures is the Windows 95 Notepad editor. Your text editor might look very different. Just make sure you entered the text correctly.

   TROUBLE? If you are using the Windows 95 Notepad text editor to create your HTML file, make sure you don't save the file as a text document type. Notepad automatically adds the .txt extension to the filename. This renders the file unreadable to the Netscape Navigator browser, which expects an htm or html file extension. Instead, save the file as type, All Files=(*.*), and add the htm or html extension to the filename yourself.

Figure 1-12 ◀
HTML codes
entered in text
editor

HTML tags
indicate code is
written in HTML

<HEAD> tags
surround information
about Web page

<BODY> tags
surround the portion
of the document
that appears
in the browser

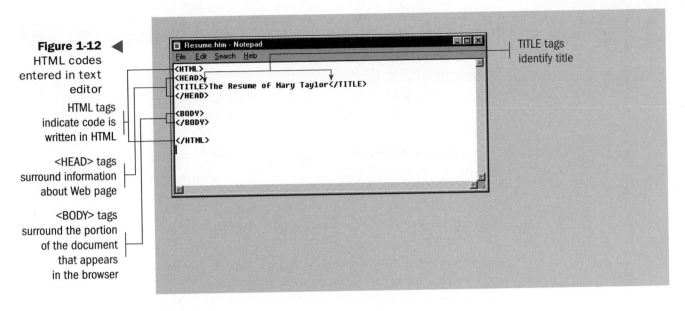

TITLE tags
identify title

The opening and closing HTML tags bracket all the remaining code in the document. This indicates to a browser that the page is written in HTML. While you don't have to include this tag, it is necessary if the file is to be read by another SGML application. Moreover, it is considered "good style" to include it.

The <HEAD> tag is where you enter information about the Web page. One such piece of information is the title of the page. The <TITLE> tag includes a title that names Mary's page "The Resume of Mary Taylor." This title will appear in the title bar of the Web browser window displaying Mary's page.

Finally, the portion of the document that Web users will see is contained within the <BODY> tags. At this point, the page is blank with no text or graphics. You'll add those later. The HEAD and BODY tags are also not strictly required, but you should include them to better organize your document and make its code more readable to others. The extra space before and after the BODY tags is also not required, but it will make your code easier to view as you add more features to it.

Displaying Your HTML Files

The file you are creating is the HTML file. A browser, of course, will not display the HTML file but will display the formatted page. As you continue adding to Mary's HTML file you should occasionally display the formatted page with your Web browser to verify that there are no syntax errors or other problems. You might even want to view the results on several browsers to check for differences between one browser and another. In the steps and figures that follow, the Netscape Navigator browser is used to display Mary's resume page as it gradually unfolds. If you are using a different browser, ask your instructor how to access local files.

To view the beginnings of Mary's resume page:

1. Start your browser. You do not need to be connected to the Internet to access a file loaded on your computer.

   TROUBLE? If you try to start your browser and are not connected to the Internet, you might get a warning message. Netscape Navigator, for example, gives a warning message telling you that it was unable to create a network socket connection. Click OK to ignore the message and continue.

2. After your browser loads its home page, click **File** then click **Open File**.

   TROUBLE? You use the Open File command to view an HTML document in Netscape Navigator 3.0. The Netscape Navigator 3.0 Gold command is Open File in Browser. If you are using a different browser, look for a similar command. In Internet Explorer, for example, you click Open on the File menu, and then click the Open File button.

3. Locate the **Resume.htm** file that you saved in the Tutorial.01 folder on your Student Disk, then click **Open**. Your browser displays Mary's file as shown in Figure 1-13. Note that the page title appears in the Netscape Navigator title bar.

   TROUBLE? If your browser displays something different, compare the code in your file to the code shown in Figure 1-12, and correct any errors.

title contains the text you entered between the <TITLE> tags

indicates the Resume.htm page is displayed

Figure 1-13 ◀
Mary's page displayed in the Netscape Navigator 3.0 browser

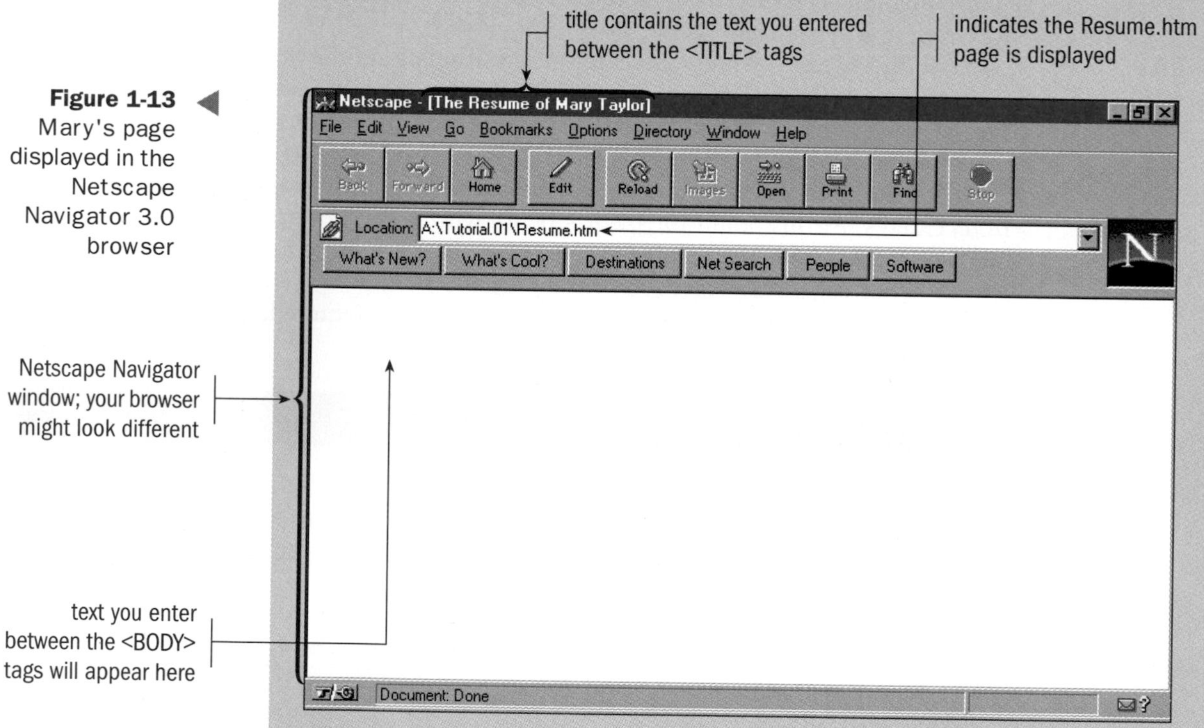

Netscape Navigator window; your browser might look different

text you enter between the <BODY> tags will appear here

4. Return to your text editor. You can leave your browser open.

Creating Headings, Paragraphs, and Lists

Now that the basic structure of Mary's page is set, you turn to filling in the details. The best place to start is with the headings for the various sections of her document. Her document needs a heading for the entire page and headings for each of three sections: Objectives, Education, and Employment. The Education section has two additional headings that provide information about the two universities she attended. You can create all these headings using HTML heading tags.

Creating Heading Tags

HTML has six levels of headings, numbered 1 through 6, with 1 being the most prominent. Headings appear in a larger font than normal text. Some headings are also bolded. The general syntax for a heading tag is:

```
<Hy>Heading Text</Hy>
```

where y is a heading numbered 1 through 6.

Figure 1-14 illustrates the general appearance of the six heading styles. Your browser might use slightly different fonts and sizes.

Figure 1-14 ◄
Six heading
levels

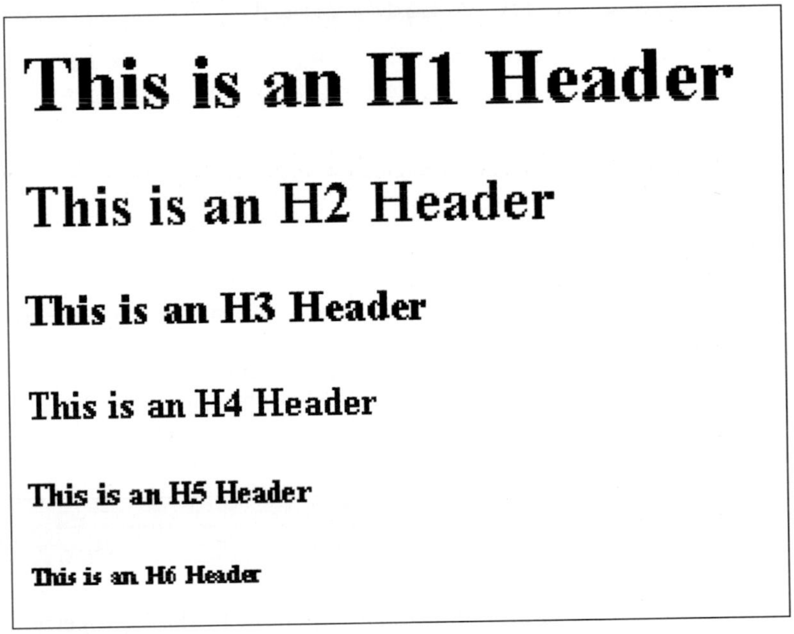

This is an H1 Header

This is an H2 Header

This is an H3 Header

This is an H4 Header

This is an H5 Header

This is an H6 Header

REFERENCE
window

CREATING A HEADING TAG

- Open the HTML file with your text editor.
- Type <H*n*> where *n* is the heading number you want to use.
- Specify the alignment property setting after *n* and before > if you want to use a special alignment.
- Type the text that you want to appear in the heading.
- Type </H*n*> to turn off the heading tag.

Starting with HTML 3.2, the heading tag can contain additional properties, one of which is the alignment property. Mary wants some headings centered on the page, so you take advantage of this property. Although Mary's address is not really heading text, you decide to format it with a heading 5 tag, because you want it to stand out a little from normal paragraphed text.

To add headings to the resume file:

1. Return to your text editor, and open the **Resume.htm** file, if it is not already open.

2. Type the following text between the <BODY> and </BODY> tags (type the address and phone number all on one line, as shown in Figure 1-15):

```
<H1 ALIGN=CENTER>Mary Taylor</H1>
<H5 ALIGN=CENTER>11 Kemper Ave. Lake View, CO 80517
   (303) 555-1012</H5>
<H2 ALIGN=CENTER>Objectives</H2>
<H2 ALIGN=CENTER>Education</H2>
<H3>Colorado State University (1994-1996)</H3>
<H3>Saint Philip University (1991-1994)</H3>
<H2 ALIGN=CENTER>Employment</H2>
```

The revised code is shown in Figure 1-15. In order to make it easier to follow the changes to the HTML file, new and altered text is highlighted in red.

3. Save the revised Resume.htm file into the Tutorial.01 folder on your Student Disk. You can leave the text editor open.

Figure 1-15 ◀
Entering HTML
code to mark
headings

enter the new code
between the
<BODY> tags

code you just
entered specifies
the headings
in Mary's resume

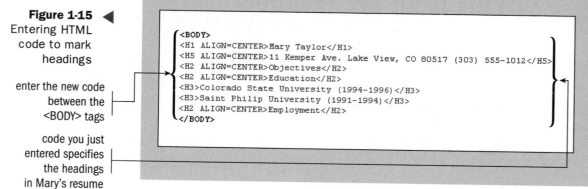

```
<BODY>
<H1 ALIGN=CENTER>Mary Taylor</H1>
<H5 ALIGN=CENTER>11 Kemper Ave. Lake View, CO 80517 (303) 555-1012</H5>
<H2 ALIGN=CENTER>Objectives</H2>
<H2 ALIGN=CENTER>Education</H2>
<H3>Colorado State University (1994-1996)</H3>
<H3>Saint Philip University (1991-1994)</H3>
<H2 ALIGN=CENTER>Employment</H2>
</BODY>
```

The section headings all use the ALIGN=CENTER property to center the text on the page. The tags for the two university headings, however, do not include that property and will be left-justified because that is the default alignment setting. If a browser that displays Mary's page does not support HTML 3.2 (or above) or does not support the alignment property through an extension, the headings will appear but all of them will be left-justified.

To display the revised Resume.htm file:

1. Return to your Web browser.

2. If the previous version of the file still appears in the browser window, click **View** then click **Reload** if you are using Netscape Navigator to reload the file. Otherwise open the file using the techniques you learned earlier.

The updated Resume.htm file looks like Figure 1-16.

Figure 1-16
Headings as
they appear
in the browser

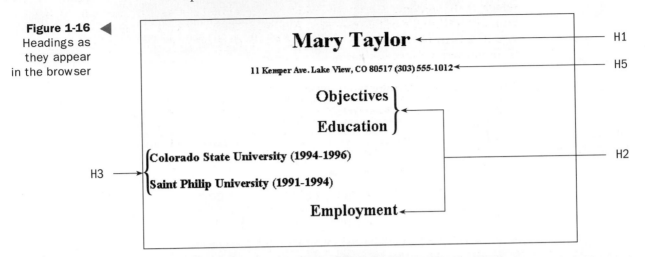

Mary Taylor — H1

11 Kemper Ave. Lake View, CO 80517 (303) 555-1012 — H5

Objectives

Education — H2

H3 — Colorado State University (1994-1996)

Saint Philip University (1991-1994)

Employment

Entering Paragraph Text

The next thing that you have to do is enter information for each section. If your paragraph does not require any formatting, you can enter the text without tags.

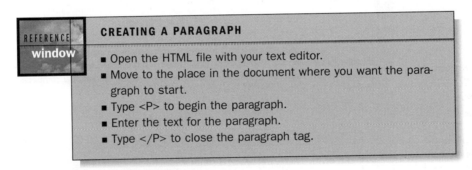

REFERENCE window

CREATING A PARAGRAPH

- Open the HTML file with your text editor.
- Move to the place in the document where you want the paragraph to start.
- Type <P> to begin the paragraph.
- Enter the text for the paragraph.
- Type </P> to close the paragraph tag.

Mary's career objective, which appears just below the Objectives heading, does not require formatting.

To enter paragraph text:

1. Return to your text editor, and reopen the **Resume.htm** file, if it is not already open.

2. Type the following text directly after the line of code that specifies the Objectives heading:

   Masters degree graduate interested in a telecommunications position in the Denver or Boulder area. Highly skilled in the use of computers, audio/video equipment and the uplink/downlink aspects of satellite communications. Interested in positions with a strong international component. Willing to travel.

   Your text should be placed between the Objectives head and the Education head as shown in Figure 1-17. Check your work for mistakes, and edit the file as necessary.

TROUBLE? If you are using a text editor like Notepad, the text might not wrap automatically. You might need to select the Word Wrap command on the Edit menu, or a similar command, to force the text to wrap so you can see it all on your screen.

Figure 1-17 ◀
Entering
paragraph text

enter Objectives
paragraph here

```
<BODY>
<H1 ALIGN=CENTER>Mary Taylor</H1>
<H5 ALIGN=CENTER>11 Kemper Ave. Lake View, CO 80517 (303) 555-1012</H5>
<H2 ALIGN=CENTER>Objectives</H2>
Masters degree graduate interested in a telecommunications position in the
Denver or Boulder area. Highly skilled in the use of computers, audio/video
equipment and the uplink/downlink aspects of satellite communications.
Interested in positions with a strong international component. Willing to
travel.
<H2 ALIGN=CENTER>Education</H2>
```

3. Save the changes you made to the Resume.htm file.

4. Return to your Web browser, and reload the **Resume.htm** file to view the text you've added. See Figure 1-18.

Figure 1-18 ◀
Paragraph text
as it appears
in the browser

Mary Taylor

11 Kemper Ave. Lake View, CO 80517 (303) 555-1012

Objectives

Objectives text

Masters degree graduate interested in a telecommunications position in the Denver or Boulder area. Highly skilled in the use of computers, audio/video equipment and the uplink/downlink aspects of satellite communications. Interested in positions with a strong international component. Willing to travel.

Education

5. Now enter the Employment paragraph text by returning to your text editor and reopening the **Resume.htm** file if needed.

6. Go to the end of the file, and, in the line before the final </BODY> tag, enter the following text:

Satellite Technician (Front Range Media Inc. 1993-1994): Monitored satellite uplink/downlink procedures to assure quality video transmissions. Aided technicians with transmission problems. Assisted in the assembly and maintenance of uplink facility.

Technical Assistant (Mountain View Bank 1992-1993): Managed data processing system. Handled user requests and discussed programming options. Managed delivery service.

Salesperson (Computer Visions 1991): Sales and customer support in computers and electronics. Managed commercial accounts in Mountain View and Crabtree locations.

Figure 1-19 shows the new code in Mary's resume file.

Figure 1-19
Entering
Employment
paragraph text

enter employment
descriptions here

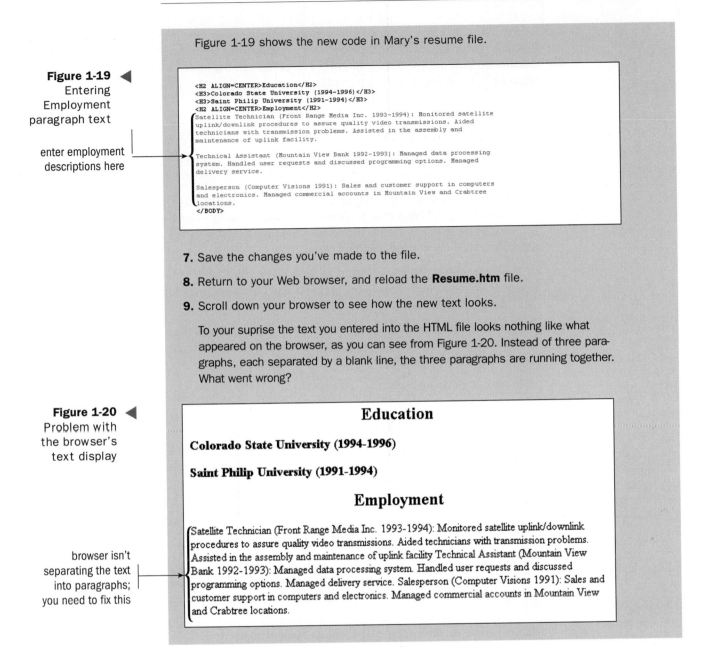

```
<H2 ALIGN=CENTER>Education</H2>
<H3>Colorado State University (1994-1996)</H3>
<H3>Saint Philip University (1991-1994)</H3>
<H2 ALIGN=CENTER>Employment</H2>
Satellite Technician (Front Range Media Inc. 1993-1994): Monitored satellite
uplink/downlink procedures to assure quality video transmissions. Aided
technicians with transmission problems. Assisted in the assembly and
maintenance of uplink facility.

Technical Assistant (Mountain View Bank 1992-1993): Managed data processing
system. Handled user requests and discussed programming options. Managed
delivery service.

Salesperson (Computer Visions 1991): Sales and customer support in computers
and electronics. Managed commercial accounts in Mountain View and Crabtree
locations.
</BODY>
```

7. Save the changes you've made to the file.

8. Return to your Web browser, and reload the **Resume.htm** file.

9. Scroll down your browser to see how the new text looks.

To your suprise the text you entered into the HTML file looks nothing like what appeared on the browser, as you can see from Figure 1-20. Instead of three paragraphs, each separated by a blank line, the three paragraphs are running together. What went wrong?

Figure 1-20
Problem with
the browser's
text display

browser isn't
separating the text
into paragraphs;
you need to fix this

Education

Colorado State University (1994-1996)

Saint Philip University (1991-1994)

Employment

Satellite Technician (Front Range Media Inc. 1993-1994): Monitored satellite uplink/downlink procedures to assure quality video transmissions. Aided technicians with transmission problems. Assisted in the assembly and maintenance of uplink facility Technical Assistant (Mountain View Bank 1992-1993): Managed data processing system. Handled user requests and discussed programming options. Managed delivery service. Salesperson (Computer Visions 1991): Sales and customer support in computers and electronics. Managed commercial accounts in Mountain View and Crabtree locations.

The problem here is that HTML formats text through the use of tags. HTML ignores such things as extra blank spaces, blank lines, or tabs. As far as HTML is concerned, the following three lines of code are identical, so a browser interprets and displays each line just like the others, ignoring the extra spaces and lines:

```
<H1>To be or not to be. That is the question.</H1>

<H1>To be or not to be.        That is the question.</H1>

<H1>To be or not to be.
        That is the question.</H1>
```

At first glance the Employment section seemed not to need formatting; however, each job description needs to be separated by a blank line. To add a blank line to an HTML document, you use the paragraph tag. The **paragraph tag** adds an extra line before text to separate it from any text that precedes it.

To incorporate paragraph tags into the resume file:

1. Return to your text editor.

2. Modify the Employment text, bracketing each paragraph between a **<P>** and **</P>** tag, so that the lines read:

<P>Satellite Technician (Front Range Media Inc. 1993-1994): Monitored satellite uplink/downlink procedures to assure quality video transmissions. Aided technicians with transmission problems. Assisted in the assembly and maintenance of uplink facility.</P>

<P>Technical Assistant (Mountain View Bank 1992-1993): Managed data processing system. Handled user requests and discussed programming options. Managed delivery service. </P>

<P>Salesperson (Computer Visions 1991): Sales and customer support in computers and electronics. Managed commercial accounts in Mountain View and Crabtree locations.</P>

3. Save the revised text file.

4. Return to your Web browser, and reload the **Resume.htm** file. The text in the Employment section is properly separated into distinct paragraphs as shown in Figure 1-21.

Figure 1-21 ◀
Paragraphs with paragraph tags inserted

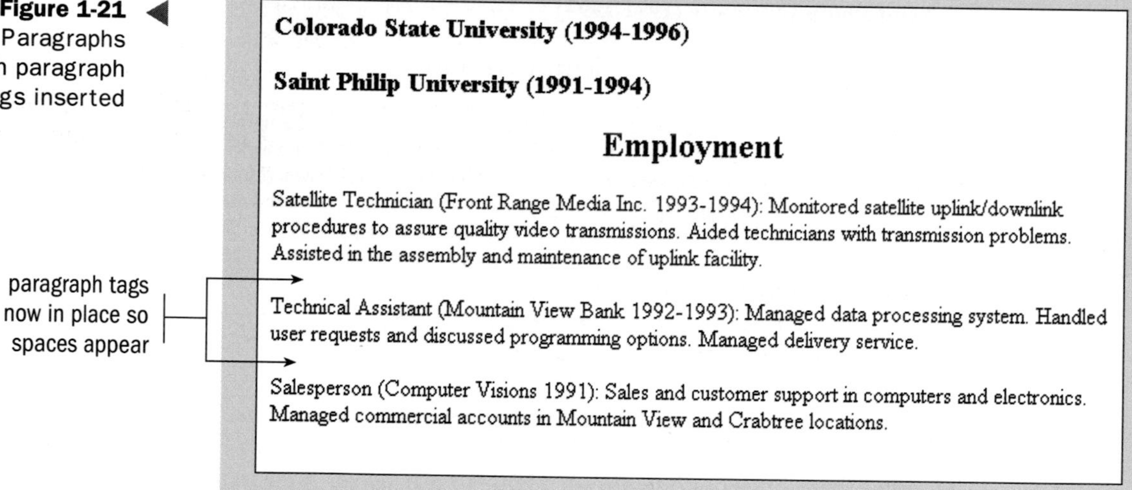

paragraph tags now in place so spaces appear

> **Colorado State University (1994-1996)**
>
> **Saint Philip University (1991-1994)**
>
> ## Employment
>
> Satellite Technician (Front Range Media Inc. 1993-1994): Monitored satellite uplink/downlink procedures to assure quality video transmissions. Aided technicians with transmission problems. Assisted in the assembly and maintenance of uplink facility.
>
> Technical Assistant (Mountain View Bank 1992-1993): Managed data processing system. Handled user requests and discussed programming options. Managed delivery service.
>
> Salesperson (Computer Visions 1991): Sales and customer support in computers and electronics. Managed commercial accounts in Mountain View and Crabtree locations.

If you start examining the HTML code for pages that you encounter on the Web, you might notice that the <P> tag is used in different ways on other pages. In the original version of HTML, the <P> tag inserted a blank line into the page. In HTML 1.0, <P> was placed at the end of each paragraph; no </P> tag was required. In versions 2.0 and 3.2, the paragraph tag is two-sided: both the <P> and </P> tags are used. Moreover, the <P> tag is placed at the beginning of the paragraph, not the end. Starting with HTML 3.2, you can specify the alignment property in a paragraph tag. In HTML 1.0 and 2.0, you cannot—paragraphs are always assumed to be left-justified. For the Web documents that you intend to create today, you should use the style convention shown in this example.

Creating Lists

You still need to enter the lists describing Mary's achievements at Colorado State and Saint Philip University. HTML provides tags for such lists. HTML supports three kinds of lists: ordered, unordered, and definition.

An **ordered list** is a list in numeric order. HTML adds the numbers. If you remove an item from the list, HTML automatically updates the numbers. For example, Mary might want to list her education awards in order from the most important to the least important. To do so, you could enter the following code into her HTML document:

```
<H3>Education Awards</H3>
<OL>
<LI>Enos Mills Scholarship
<LI>Physics Expo blue ribbon winner
<LI> Honor Key Award semi-finalist
</OL>
```

A Web browser might display this code as:

```
Education Awards

1. Enos Mills Scholarship

2. Physics Expo blue ribbon winner

3. Honor Key Award semi-finalist
```

This example shows the basic structure of an HTML list. The list text is bracketed between the <OL> and </OL> tags, where OL stands for ordered list. This tells the browser to present the text between the tags as an ordered list. Each list item is identified by a single <LI> tag, where LI stands for list item. There is no closing tag for list items.

An **unordered list** is one in which list items have no particular order. Browsers usually format unordered lists by inserting a bullet symbol before each list item. The entire list is bracketed between the <UL> and </UL> tags, where UL stands for unordered list. If Mary wants to display her awards without regard to their importance, you could enter the following code:

```
<H3>Education Awards</H3>
<UL>
<LI>Enos Mills Scholarship
<LI>Physics Expo blue ribbon winner
<LI>Honor Key Award semi-finalist
</UL>
```

A Web browser might display this code as:

```
Education Awards

■ Enos Mills Scholarship

■ Physics Expo blue ribbon winner

■ Honor Key Award semi-finalist
```

The third type of list that HTML can display is a definition list. A **definition list** is a list of terms, each followed by a definition line, usually indented slightly to the right. The <LI> tag used in ordered and unordered lists for individual items is replaced by two tags: the <DT> tag used for each term in the list and the <DD> tag used for each term's definition. As with the <LI> tag, both of these tags are one-sided. The entire list is bracketed by the <DL> and </DL> tags indicating to the browser that the list is a definition list. If Mary wants to create a list of her educational awards and briefly describe each, she could use a definition list. To create a definition list for her awards, you could enter this code into her HTML file:

```
<H3>Education Awards</H3>
<DL>
<DT>Enos Mills Scholarship<DD>Awarded to the outstanding
   student in the senior class
<DT>Physics Expo blue ribbon winner<DD>Awarded for a research
   project on fiberoptics
<DT>Honor Key Award semi-finalist<DD>Awarded for an essay on
   the information age
</DL>
```

A Web browser might display this code as:

Education Awards

Enos Mills Scholarship
   Awarded to the outstanding student in the senior class

Physics Expo blue ribbon winner
   Awarded for a research project on fiberoptics

Honor Key Award semi-finalist
   Awarded for an essay on the information age

REFERENCE
window

CREATING LISTS

- Open the HTML file with your text editor.
- Move to the place in the document where you want the list to appear.
- Type <OL> to start an ordered list or <UL> to start an unordered list.
- For each item in the list, type <LI> followed by the text for the list item.
- To turn off the list, type </OL> for an ordered list or </UL> for an unordered list.
- To create a definition list, type <DL> and </DL> as brackets, then within each bracket type <DT> before the term and <DD> before the definition.

On her paper resume (Figure 1-10) Mary's educational accomplishments are in a bulleted list. You can include this feature in Mary's online resume by using an unordered list.

To add an unordered list to the resume file:

1. Return to your text editor, and reopen the **Resume.htm** file if it is not still open.

2. Type these lines of code between the headings "Colorado State University" and "Saint Philip University":

   <UL>
   <LI>Graduated May, 1996. M.A. International Telecommunications
   <LI>Grade Point Average: 3.5 overall, 3.9 in major
   <LI>Dean's List: September 1994-May 1996
   <LI>Member, Phi Alpha Omega Honor Society
   </UL>

3. Type these lines of code after the heading "Saint Philip University":

   <UL>
   <LI>Graduated May, 1994. B.A. International Studies
   <LI>Grade Point Average: 4.0 overall, 4.0 in major
   <LI>Dean's List: September 1991-May 1994
   <LI>President, Honor Key Society
   </UL>

   The new lines in the resume file should look like Figure 1-22.

Figure 1-22 ◀
Entering
unordered lists

unordered lists ────

```
<H2 ALIGN=CENTER>Education</H2>
<H3>Colorado State University (1994-1996)</H3>
<UL>
<LI>Graduated May, 1996. M.A. International Telecommunications
<LI>Grade Point Average: 3.5 overall, 3.9 in major
<LI>Dean's List: September 1994-May 1996
<LI>Member, Phi Alpha Omega Honor Society
</UL>
<H3>Saint Philip University (1991-1994)</H3>
<UL>
<LI>Graduated May, 1994. B.A. International Studies
<LI>Grade Point Average: 4.0 overall, 4.0 in major
<LI>Dean's List: September 1991-May 1994
<LI>President, Honor Key Society
</UL>
<H2 ALIGN=CENTER>Employment</H2>
```

4. When you are sure that the revised resume matches the code in Figure 1-22, save the file as **Resume.htm**.

5. Switch to your Web browser and reload the **Resume.htm** file.

   Mary's resume file now includes lists formatted much like those on her paper resume. If your browser does not create a page that looks like Figure 1-23, return to the HTML file, and check for inconsistencies.

Figure 1-23 ◀
Unordered lists
as they appear
in the browser

browser formats
unordered lists
with bullets

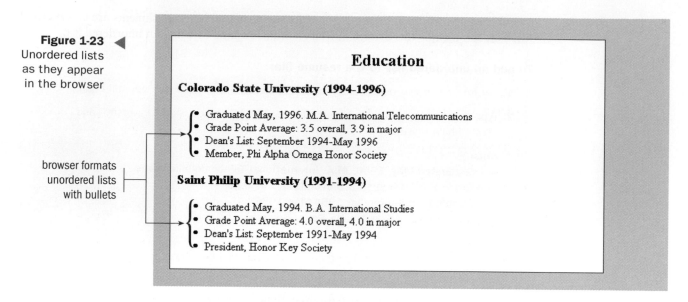

Education

Colorado State University (1994-1996)

- Graduated May, 1996. M.A. International Telecommunications
- Grade Point Average: 3.5 overall, 3.9 in major
- Dean's List: September 1994-May 1996
- Member, Phi Alpha Omega Honor Society

Saint Philip University (1991-1994)

- Graduated May, 1994. B.A. International Studies
- Grade Point Average: 4.0 overall, 4.0 in major
- Dean's List: September 1991-May 1994
- President, Honor Key Society

Creating Character Tags

Until now you've worked with tags that affect either the entire document or individual lines. HTML also lets you modify the characteristics of individual characters. A tag that you apply to an individual character is called a **character tag**. You can use two kinds of character tags: logical and physical. **Logical character tags** indicate how you want to use text, not necessarily how you want it displayed. Figure 1-24 lists some common logical character tags.

Figure 1-24 ◀
Common logical
character tags

Tag	Description
<EM>	Indicates that characters should be emphasized in some way. Usually displayed with italics.
<STRONG>	Emphasizes characters more strongly than <EM>. Usually displayed in a bold font.
<CODE>	Indicates a sample of code. Usually displayed in a Courier font or a similar font that allots the same width to each character.
<KBD>	Used to offset text that the user should enter. Often displayed in a Courier font or a similar font that allots the same width to each character.
<VAR>	Indicates a variable. Often displayed in italics or underlined.
<CITE>	Indicates short quotes or citations. Often italicized by browsers.

Figure 1-25 shows examples of how these tags might appear in a browser. Note that you can combine tags, allowing you to create bolded and italicized text by using both the <EM> and the <STRONG> tags.

Figure 1-25
Logical
character tags
as they appear
in the browser

examples of
individual logical
character tags

combined logical
character tags

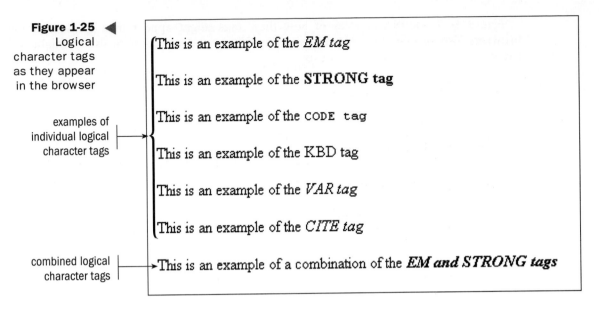

This is an example of the *EM tag*

This is an example of the **STRONG tag**

This is an example of the `CODE tag`

This is an example of the KBD tag

This is an example of the *VAR tag*

This is an example of the *CITE tag*

This is an example of a combination of the ***EM and STRONG tags***

HTML authors can also use **physical character tags** to indicate exactly how characters are to be formatted. Figure 1-26 shows common examples of physical character tags.

Figure 1-26
Common
physical
character tags

Tag	Description
<B>	Indicates that the text should be bold
<I>	Indicates that the text should be italic
<TT>	Indicates that the text should be used with a font like Courier that allots the same width to each character
<BIG>	Indicates that the text should be displayed in a big font. Available only in HTML 3.0 and above.
<SMALL>	Indicates that the text should be displayed in a small font. Available only in HTML 3.0 and above.
<SUB>	The text should be displayed as a subscript, in a smaller font if possible. Available only in HTML 3.0 and above.
<SUP>	The text should be displayed as a superscript, in a smaller font if possible. Available only in HTML 3.0 and above.

Figure 1-27 shows examples of how these tags might appear in a browser. Some browsers also support the <U> tag for underlining text, but other browsers might not show underlining, so use it cautiously.

Figure 1-27 ◀

Physical
character tags
as they appear
in the browser

This is an example of the **B tag**

This is an example of the *I tag*

This is an example of the TT tag

This is an example of the **BIG tag**

This is an example of the SMALL tag

This is an example of the SUB tag

This is an example of the SUP tag

Given the presence of both logical and physical character tags, which should you use to display some text in an italicized font: <EM> or <I>? The answer depends on who will view your Web page. Some browsers, like the UNIX browser Lynx, are text-based and cannot display italics. These browsers ignore the <I> tag, so emphasis you want to place on a certain piece of text is lost. In this case you would use a logical tag. On the other hand, if you decide that only graphical browsers such as Netscape Navigator or Internet Explorer will access your page, you might want to use a physical tag since it more explicitly defines what the resulting text looks like on the browser.

Because Mary is not certain who will access her online resume, you decide to use logical tags so the formatting appears on the widest range of browsers. Only one part of her resume requires character tags: the Employment section, where Mary wants to emphasize the title of each job she has held. You decide to use a combination of the <EM> and <STRONG> tags.

To add character tags to the resume file:

1. Return to your text editor, and reopen the **Resume.htm** file if necessary.

2. Type the **<EM>** and **<STRONG>** tags around the job titles in the Employment section of the resume (just after the <P> tags), so that they read:

   <EM><STRONG>Satellite Technician</STRONG></EM>
   <EM><STRONG>Technical Assistant</STRONG></EM>
   <EM><STRONG>Salesperson</STRONG></EM>

   Adjust any word wrapping in your editor to make the code easier to follow. See Figure 1-28.

Figure 1-28 ◀
Applying
character tags

character tags

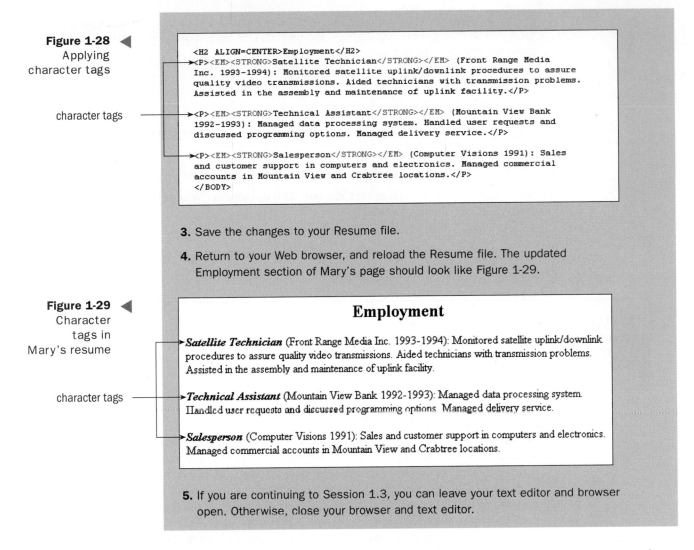

```
<H2 ALIGN=CENTER>Employment</H2>
<P><EM><STRONG>Satellite Technician</STRONG></EM> (Front Range Media
Inc. 1993-1994): Monitored satellite uplink/downlink procedures to assure
quality video transmissions. Aided technicians with transmission problems.
Assisted in the assembly and maintenance of uplink facility.</P>
<P><EM><STRONG>Technical Assistant</STRONG></EM> (Mountain View Bank
1992-1993): Managed data processing system. Handled user requests and
discussed programming options. Managed delivery service.</P>
<P><EM><STRONG>Salesperson</STRONG></EM> (Computer Visions 1991): Sales
and customer support in computers and electronics. Managed commercial
accounts in Mountain View and Crabtree locations.</P>
</BODY>
```

3. Save the changes to your Resume file.

4. Return to your Web browser, and reload the Resume file. The updated Employment section of Mary's page should look like Figure 1-29.

Figure 1-29 ◀
Character
tags in
Mary's resume

character tags

Employment

▶ **_Satellite Technician_** (Front Range Media Inc. 1993-1994): Monitored satellite uplink/downlink procedures to assure quality video transmissions. Aided technicians with transmission problems. Assisted in the assembly and maintenance of uplink facility.

▶ **_Technical Assistant_** (Mountain View Bank 1992-1993): Managed data processing system. Handled user requests and discussed programming options. Managed delivery service.

▶ **_Salesperson_** (Computer Visions 1991): Sales and customer support in computers and electronics. Managed commercial accounts in Mountain View and Crabtree locations.

5. If you are continuing to Session 1.3, you can leave your text editor and browser open. Otherwise, close your browser and text editor.

When you apply two character tags to the same text you should place one set of tags completely within another. You combine the <EM> and <STRONG> tags like this:

<EM><STRONG>Satellite Technician</STRONG></EM>

not like this:

<EM><STRONG>Satellite Technician</EM></STRONG>

Although many browsers interpret both sets of code the same way, nesting tags within each other rather than overlapping them makes your code easier to read and interpret.

Quick Check

1. Why should you include the <HTML> tag in your Web document?

2. Describe the syntax for creating a centered heading 1.

3. Describe the syntax for creating a paragraph.

4. If you want to display several paragraphs, why can't you simply type an extra blank line in the HTML file?

5. Describe the syntax for creating an ordered list, an unordered list, and a definition list.

6. Give two ways of italicizing text in your Web document. What are the advantages and disadvantages of each method?

You have finished adding text to Mary's online resume. In Session 1.3, you will add special formatting elements such as lines and graphics.

SESSION 1.3

In this session you will insert three special elements into Mary's online resume: a special character, a line separating Mary's name and address from the rest of her resume, and a photograph of Mary.

Adding Special Characters

Occasionally you will want to include special characters in your Web page that do not appear on your keyboard. For example, a math page might require mathematical symbols such as ß or µ. HTML supports several character symbols that you can insert into your page. Each character symbol is identified by a code number or name. To create a special character, type an ampersand (&) followed either by the code name or the code number. Code numbers must be preceded by a pound symbol (#). Figure 1-30 shows some HTML symbols and the corresponding code numbers or names. A fuller list of special characters is included in Appendix B.

Figure 1-30 ◀
Common special characters

Symbol	Code	Description
©	&#169	Copyright symbol
®	&#174	Registered trademark
•	&#183	Middle dot
°	&#186	Masculine ordinal
TM	&#153	Trademark symbol
		Non-breaking space, useful when you want to insert several blank spaces one after another
<	&lt	Less than sign
>	&gt	Greater than sign
&	&amp	Ampersand

As Mary views her resume file, she notices a place where she could use a special symbol. In the address information under her name, she finds that the street address, city, and phone numbers all flow together. She cannot add extra spaces because HTML will ignore the blank spaces and run the text together anyway. She decides instead to insert a bullet (•) between the street address and the city and another bullet between the zip code and the phone number.

To add a character code to the resume file:

1. Make sure the **Resume.htm** file is open in your text editor.

2. Revise the address line at the beginning of the file, inserting the code for a middle dot, &#183, between the street address and the city, and between the zip code and the phone number so that the line reads:

   <H5 ALIGN=CENTER>11 Kemper Ave. &#183 Lake View, CO 80517 &#183 (303) 555-1012</H5>

   TROUBLE? In your text editor this line probably appears as a single line.

3. Save the changes to your Resume file.

4. Return to your Web browser, and reload the Resume file. Figure 1-31 shows Mary's resume with the bullets separating the address elements.

Figure 1-31 ◀
Special
characters as
they appear in
the browser

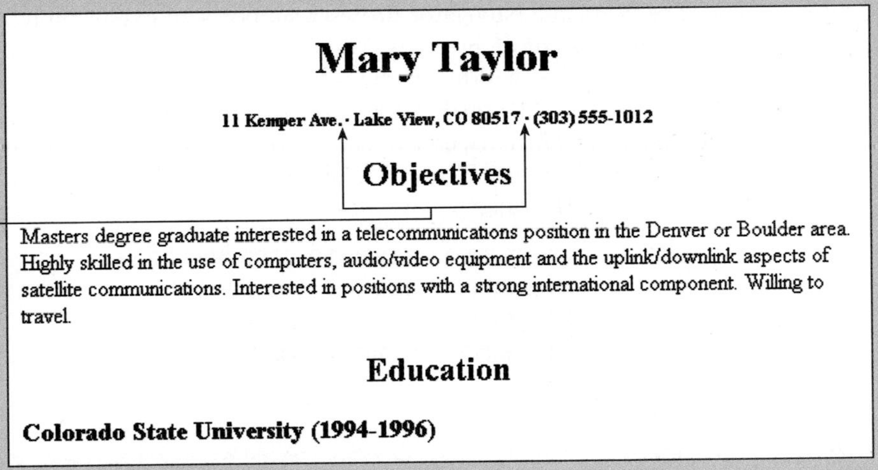

bullets now appear
in the address line

Mary Taylor

11 Kemper Ave. · Lake View, CO 80517 · (303) 555-1012

Objectives

Masters degree graduate interested in a telecommunications position in the Denver or Boulder area. Highly skilled in the use of computers, audio/video equipment and the uplink/downlink aspects of satellite communications. Interested in positions with a strong international component. Willing to travel.

Education

Colorado State University (1994-1996)

Inserting Horizontal Lines

The horizontal line after Mary's name and address lends shape to the appearance of her paper resume. She'd like you to duplicate that in the online version. You use the <HR> tag to create a horizontal line, where HR stands for horizontal rule. The <HR> tag is one-sided. When a text-based browser encounters the <HR> tag, it inserts a line by repeating an underline symbol across the width of the page.

To add a horizontal line to the Resume file:

1. Return to your text editor, and reopen the **Resume.htm** file if necessary.

2. At the end of Mary's address line, press **Enter** to insert a new blank line.

3. In the new line, type **<HR>**.

4. Save the changes to your Resume file.

5. Return to your Web browser, and reload the Resume file. The Resume file with the new horizontal line appears in Figure 1-32.

Figure 1-32
Horizontal line
as it appears
in the browser

horizontal line

Mary Taylor

11 Kemper Ave. · Lake View, CO 80517 · (303) 555-1012

Objectives

Masters degree graduate interested in a telecommunications position in the Denver or Boulder area. Highly skilled in the use of computers, audio/video equipment and the uplink/downlink aspects of satellite communications. Interested in positions with a strong international component. Willing to travel.

Education

The Netscape Navigator browser supports an extension to the <HR> tag that lets you define line size more precisely. You use the WIDTH property to tell the browser what percentage of the width of the display area the line should occupy. For example, WIDTH=50% tells the browser to place the line so that its length covers half the screen. You use the SIZE property to specify the line's width in pixels. A **pixel**, short for picture element, is ½" wide. Figure 1-33 shows how Netscape Navigator interprets the following lines of HTML code:

```
<HR ALIGN=CENTER SIZE=12 WIDTH=100%>
<HR ALIGN=CENTER SIZE=6 WIDTH=50%>
<HR ALIGN=CENTER SIZE=3 WIDTH=25%>
<HR ALIGN=CENTER SIZE=1 WIDTH=10%>
```

Figure 1-33
Experimenting
with different
line styles

SIZE=12
WIDTH=100%

SIZE=6
WIDTH=50%

SIZE=3
WIDTH=25%

SIZE=1
WIDTH=10%

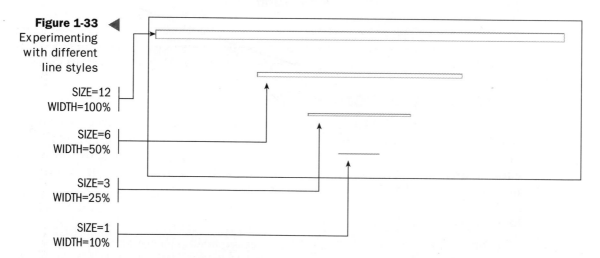

Other extensions allow you to use a graphic image for the line. As always, you should remember that using extensions might produce wildly different results on browsers that do not support the extension.

Inserting a Graphic

One feature of Web pages that has made the World Wide Web so popular is the ease of displaying a graphic image. The Web supports two methods for displaying a graphic: as an inline image and as an external image.

An **inline image** appears directly on the Web page and is loaded when the page is loaded. The Web only supports two graphic types for inline images: GIF (Graphics Interchange Format) and JPEG (Joint Photographic Experts Group). Of these, the GIF file format is the more common on the Web and not all browsers support JPEG files. Before you display a graphic image, your best bet is to convert it to a GIF file format. For example, if you create a graphic in an application like the Windows 95 Paint accessory, which supports only BMP files, you need to locate a graphics converter to convert your BMP file to a GIF file.

An **external image** is not displayed with the Web page. Instead the browser must have a **file viewer**, an application that the browser loads automatically whenever it encounters the image file and displays the image. You can find file viewers at several Internet Web sites. Most browsers make it easy to set up viewers for use with the Web. External images have one disadvantage: you can't actually display them on the Web page. Instead they are represented by an icon that a user clicks to view the image. However, external images are not limited to the GIF or JPEG formats. You can set up virtually any image format as an external image on a Web page, including video clips and sound files.

REFERENCE
window

INSERTING AN INLINE IMAGE

- Open the HTML file with your text editor.
- Move to the place in the document where you want the inline image to appear.
- Type <IMG SRC="*filename*"> where *filename* is the name of the graphics file (in GIF or JPEG format).

Mary is more interested in using an inline image than an external image. <IMG> is the tag for an inline image. You can place inline images on a separate line in your document, or you can place the image within a line of text (hence the term "inline"). To access the image file you need to include the filename within the tag. You do this using the SRC property, short for "source." The general syntax for an inline image is:

```
<IMG SRC="filename">
```

If the image file is located in the same directory as the HTML file, you do not need to include any directory information. However, if the image file is located in another directory or on another computer, you need to include the full path with the SRC property. Tutorial 2 discusses directory paths and filenames in more detail. For now, assume that Mary's image file is placed in the same directory as the HTML file. The image file that Mary has created is a photograph of herself in GIF format named Taylor.gif.

You'd like to center the image on the page. You can nest the image tag <IMG SCR="Taylor.gif"> within a paragraph tag and then set the ALIGN property to CENTER in the opening paragraph tag <P ALIGN=CENTER>. Note that the ALIGN property was introduced in HTML 3.2; in browsers that do not support this convention, Mary's image may be left-justified. Verify that the image file is in the same directory as your Resume.htm file, and then add the necessary code to your HTML file.

To add Mary's photo to the online resume:

1. Look in the Tutorial.01 folder on your Student Disk, and verify that both the **Resume.htm** file and **Taylor.gif** file are there.

2. Return to your text editor with the **Resume.htm** file open.

3. At the end of the line with the <HR> tag that you just entered, press **Enter** to create a new line.

4. Type **<P ALIGN=CENTER><IMG SRC="Taylor.gif"></P>** then save the changes to the Resume file.

5. Print a copy of your completed Resume.htm file, and then close your text editor unless you are continuing to the Tutorial Assignments.

6. Return to your Web browser, and reload the Resume file. Mary's online resume now includes an inline image. See Figure 1-34.

Figure 1-34 ◀
The final version of Mary's resume page

inline graphic appears directly on the Web page →

Mary Taylor

11 Kemper Ave. · Lake View, CO 80517 · (303) 555-1012

Objectives

Masters degree graduate interested in a telecommunications position in the Denver or Boulder area. Highly skilled in the use of computers, audio/video equipment and the uplink/downlink aspects of satellite communications. Interested in positions with a strong international component. Willing to travel.

Education

Colorado State University (1994-1996)

- Graduated May, 1996. M.A. International Telecommunications
- Grade Point Average: 3.5 overall, 3.9 in major
- Dean's List: September 1994-May 1996
- Member, Phi Alpha Omega Honor Society

Saint Philip University (1991-1994)

- Graduated May, 1994. B.A. International Studies
- Grade Point Average: 4.0 overall, 4.0 in major
- Dean's List: September 1991-May 1994
- President, Honor Key Society

Employment

Satellite Technician (Front Range Media Inc. 1993-1994): Monitored satellite uplink/downlink procedures to assure quality video transmissions. Aided technicians with transmission problems. Assisted in the assembly and maintenance of uplink facility.

Technical Assistant (Mountain View Bank 1992-1993): Managed data processing system. Handled user requests and discussed programming options. Managed delivery service.

Salesperson (Computer Visions 1991): Sales and customer support in computers and electronics. Managed commercial accounts in Mountain View and Crabtree locations.

7. Use your browser to print a copy of Mary's online resume. In Netscape Navigator, use the Print command on the File menu.

Compare the printout of the code, shown on the following page, to the online resume on your browser. When you finish, you can exit your browser unless you're continuing to the Tutorial Assignments.

```
<HTML>
<HEAD>
<TITLE>The Resume of Mary Taylor</TITLE>
</HEAD>

<BODY>
<H1 ALIGN=CENTER>Mary Taylor</H1>
<H5 ALIGN=CENTER>11 Kemper Ave. &#183 Lake View, CO 80517
  &#183 (303) 555-1012</H5>
<HR>
<P ALIGN=CENTER><IMG SRC="Taylor.gif"></P>
<H2 ALIGN=CENTER>Objectives</H2>
Masters degree graduate interested in a telecommunications
  position in the Denver or Boulder area. Highly skilled in
  the use of computers, audio/video equipment and the
  uplink/downlink aspects of satellite communications.
  Interested in positions with a strong international
  component. Willing to travel.
<H2 ALIGN=CENTER>Education</H2>
<H3>Colorado State University (1994-1996)</H3>
<UL>
<LI>Graduated May, 1996. M.A. International
  Telecommunications
<LI>Grade Point Average: 3.5 overall, 3.9 in major
<LI>Dean's List: September 1994-May 1996
<LI>Member, Phi Alpha Omega Honor Society
</UL>
<H3>Saint Philip University (1991-1994)</H3>
<UL>
<LI>Graduated May, 1994. B.A. International Studies
<LI>Grade Point Average: 4.0 overall, 4.0 in major
<LI>Dean's List: September 1991-May 1994
<LI>President, Honor Key Society
</UL>
<H2 ALIGN=CENTER>Employment</H2>
<P><EM><STRONG>Satellite Technician</STRONG></EM>
  (Front Range Media Inc. 1993-1994): Monitored satellite
  uplink/downlink procedures to assure quality video
  transmissions. Aided technicians with transmission
  problems. Assisted in the assembly and maintenance of
  uplink facility.</P>

<P><EM><STRONG>Technical Assistant</STRONG></EM> (Mountain
  View Bank 1992-1993): Managed data processing system.
  Handled user requests and discussed programming options.
  Managed delivery service. </P>
<P><EM><STRONG>Salesperson</STRONG></EM> (Computer Visions
  1991): Sales and customer support in computers and
  electronics. Managed commercial accounts in Mountain
  View and Crabtree locations.</P>
</BODY>

</HTML>
```

You show the completed online resume file to Mary; she thinks it looks great. You tell her that the next step is adding hypertext links to other material about herself for interested employers. You take a break while she heads to her desk to start thinking about what material she'd like to add. You'll learn about hypertext links in Tutorial 2.

Quick Check

1. How would you insert a copyright symbol, ©, into your Web page?

2. What is the syntax for inserting a horizontal line into a page?

3. Using the Netscape Navigator extension, what is the syntax for creating a horizontal line that is 70% of the display width of the screen and 4 pixels high?

4. What is an inline image?

5. What is an external image?

6. What is the syntax for inserting a left-aligned graphic named "mouse.jpg" into a Web document as an inline image?

7. What graphic file formats can you use with inline images?

Tutorial Assignments

After thinking some more about her online resume, Mary Taylor decides that she wants you to add a few more items. In the Education section, she wants you to add that she won the Enos Mill Scholarship contest as a senior at St. Philip University. She also wants to add that she worked as a climbing guide for The Colorado Experience touring company from 1989 to 1991. She would like to add her e-mail address, mtaylor@tt.gr.csu.edu, in italics at the bottom of the page. You tell her that adding a horizonal line to separate it from the rest of the resume might look nice. She agrees, so you get to work.

1. Open the Resume.htm file located in the Tutorial.01 folder on your Student Disk. This is the file you created over the course of this tutorial.

2. Save the file on your Student Disk with a new name: Resume2.htm.

3. After the HTML line reading "President, Honor Key Society," enter a new line, "Winner of the Enos Mills Scholarship."
   Use the <LI> tag to format this line as an addition to the existing list.

4. Move to the Employment section of the Resume2 file.

5. After the paragraph describing Mary's experience as a salesperson, insert the text, "Guide (The Colorado Experience 1989-1991): Climbing guide for private groups and schools."

   Make sure you mark the text with the correct code for a two-sided paragraph tag.

6. Using the <EM> and <STRONG> tags, bracket the word "Guide" in the line you just entered to make it both bold and italic.

7. After the paragraph on Mary's climbing guide experience, insert a horizontal line using the <HR> tag.

8. After the horizontal line, insert a new line with her e-mail address.

9. Use the <CITE> tag to format her e-mail address as a citation:

   <CITE>mtaylor@tt.gr.csu.edu</CITE>

10. Save the changes to your Resume2.htm file and print it.

11. View the file with your Web browser.

12. Print a copy of the page as viewed by your browser.

13. Hand in both printouts to your instructor.

Case Problems

1. Creating a Web Page at the University Music Department You are an assistant to a professor in the Music Department who is trying to create Web pages for topics in classical music. He wants to create a page showing the different sections of the fourth movement of Beethoven's Ninth symphony. The page should appear as shown in Figure 1-35.

Figure 1-35 ◀

Beethoven's Ninth Symphony

The Fourth Movement

Sonata-Concerto Form

1. Open Ritornello
2. Exposition
    1. Horror/Recitative
    2. Joy Theme
    3. Turkish Music
3. Development
4. Recapitulation
    1. Joy Theme
    2. Awe Theme
5. Codas Nos. 1 2 3

The page needs three headings and a list of the fourth movement's different sections. Several of the sections also have sublists. For example, the Recapitulation section contains both the Joy and Awe themes. You can create lists of this type with HTML by inserting one list tag within another. The HTML code for this is simply:

```
<OL>
<LI>Recapitulation
      <OL>
      <LI>Joy Theme
      <LI>Awe Theme
      </OL>
</OL>
```

1. Open a text editor on your computer.

2. Enter the <HTML>, <HEAD>, and <BODY> tags to identify different sections of the page.

3. Within the HEAD section, insert a <TITLE> tag with the text: "Beethoven's Ninth Symphony, 4th Movement."

4. Within the BODY section, create an H1 heading with the text "Beethoven's Ninth Symphony," center the heading on the page with the ALIGN property.

5. Below the H1 heading, create an H2 heading with the text "The Fourth Movement," and then center the heading on the page.

6. Below the H2 heading, create an H3 heading with the text "Sonata-Concerto Form," but this time do not center the heading.

7. Create an ordered list using the <OL> tag with the list items "Open Ritornello," "Exposition," "Development," "Recapitulation," and "Codas Nos. 1 2 3."

8. Within the Exposition list, create an ordered list with the items "Horror/Recitative," "Joy Theme," and "Turkish Music."

9. Within the Recapitulation list, create an ordered list with the items "Joy Theme" and "Awe Theme."

10. Save the code in a file named Ludwig.htm in the Cases folder of the Tutorial.01 folder on your Student Disk, print it, then close your text editor.

11. View the file with your Web browser, print it, then close your browser.

12. Hand in the printouts to your instructor.

2. Sports Page Info, Inc. You work for a sports information company, Sports Page Info, Inc., that publishes sports information on the Internet. You have been asked to create a Web page that describes the final standings for the NFL season. The standings follow.

Team	Wins	Losses	%
Packers	11	5	0.6875
Lions	10	6	0.6250
Bears	9	7	0.5625
Vikings	8	8	0.5000
Buccaneers	7	9	0.4375

Unfortunately if you type the text "as is" into your HTML file, browsers remove all blank spaces when displaying the document. You can overcome the inability of HTML to display extra blank spaces or extra blank lines by using the <PRE> tag, where PRE stands for preformatted. Browsers format text entered with <PRE> tags exactly as it appears within the HTML file, including extra spaces and blank lines. The <PRE> tag's limitation is that it forces all text to display in a monospace font like Courier. Still, the <PRE> tag is often used as a quick way to present table text.

1. Open a text editor on your computer.

2. Enter the <HTML>, <HEAD>, and <BODY> tags to identify different sections of the page.

3. Within the HEAD section, insert a <TITLE> tag with the text "NFL Info Page."

4. Within the BODY section, create an H1 heading with the text "Central Division Final Standings" and center the heading on the page with the ALIGN property.

5. Below the H1 heading, enter a new line and type <PRE> to turn on the pre-formatted feature, then press the Enter key.

6. Enter the NFL statistics. Press the Spacebar as necessary to align the columns properly. Don't use the Tab key because browers interpret tabs differently. Press the Enter key after the last line of the table.

7. Type </PRE> to turn off the preformatted feature.

8. Save the code in a file named NFL.htm in the Cases folder of the Tutorial.01 folder on your Student Disk, then print your file and close your text editor.

9. Using your Web browser, view the NFL.htm file.

10. View the file with your Web browser, print it, then close your browser.

11. Hand in the printouts to your instructor.

3. Chester the Jester A friend of yours who performs as a clown named "Chester the Jester" wants to advertise his services on the World Wide Web. He wants his Web page to be bright and colorful. One way of doing this is to create a colorful background for the page. You create a background using a graphic image. Such backgrounds are called **tile-image backgrounds** because the graphic image is repeated over and over again like tiles until it covers the entire page. Not all browsers support tile-image backgrounds. This feature is part of HTML 3.0 and above and is included in extensions for some browsers like Netscape Navigator and Internet Explorer. To create a tile-image background, you must have a graphic image in either GIF or JPEG file format. You insert the file in the background by adding the background property to the <BODY> tag with the syntax:

`<BODY BACKGROUND="Filename.gif">`

Your friend gives you a GIF file named Diamonds.gif that contains the pattern he uses in his clown costume. He also has a GIF file named Chester.gif that shows him in his clown outfit. You already wrote the text for his Web page, and you need only add links to his graphics files.

1. Open the file Chester.htm from the Cases folder of the Tutorial.01 folder on your Student Disk in your computer's text editor.

2. Modify the <BODY> tag to read:

   `<BODY BACKGROUND="Diamonds.gif">`

3. After the <HR> tag, insert the line:

   `<P ALIGN=CENTER><IMG SRC="Chester.gif"></P>`

4. Save the file as Chester2.htm file in the Cases folder of the Tutorial.01 folder on your Student Disk, then print it and close your text editor. The Diamonds.gif and Chester.gif files should already be in the Cases folder, but make sure of this before proceeding. The HTML file and all graphics to which it refers should be in the same folder.

5. Open the Chester2.htm file with your Web browser to verify that the graphic image file, Diamonds.gif, fills the background of the page and that the photo of Chester the Jester is displayed properly. Compare your image to Figure 1-36.

Figure 1-36 ◄

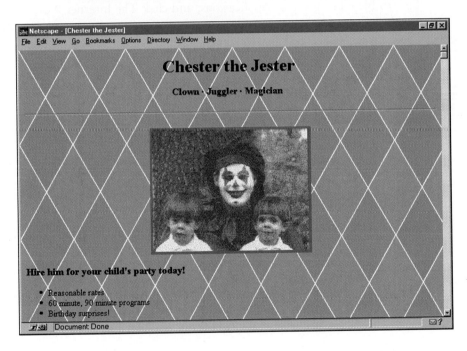

 6. Print the Chester2 page from your browser, and hand them in.

4. Create Your Own Resume After completing Mary Taylor's resume, you are eager to make your own. Using the techniques from this tutorial, design and create a resume for yourself. Make sure to include these features: section headers; bulleted or numbered lists; bold and/or italic fonts; paragraphs; inline graphic images; horizontal lines.

1. Create a file called MyResume.htm in the Cases folder of the Tutorial.01 folder on your Student Disk and enter the appropriate HTML code.

2. Add any other tags you think will improve your document's appearance.

3. You could take a picture of yourself to a local office services business and have them scan it. If you do, ask them to save it as a GIF file. Then place the GIF file in the Cases folder of the Tutorial.01 folder on your Student Disk. Add the appropriate code in your MyResume.htm file. If you don't have your own GIF file, use the file Kirk.gif, located in the Cases folder of the Tutorial.01 folder on your Student Disk.

4. You could use a graphics package that can store images in GIF format to create a background image that you could insert as you did in Case Problem 3. If you do, use light colors so the text you place on top is readable. Add the appropriate code to your MyResume.htm file using the steps in CP 3.

5. Test your code as you develop your resume by viewing MyResume.htm in your browser.

6. When you finish entering the code, save and print the MyResume.htm file.

7. View the final version in your browser, and print the Web page, then close your browser.

Lab Assignment

This Lab Assignment is designed to accompany the interactive Course Lab called The Internet World Wide Web. To start the Internet World Wide Web Course Lab, click the Start button on the Windows 95 taskbar, point to Programs, point to Course Labs, point to New Perspectives Applications, and click The Internet World Wide Web. If you do not see Course Labs on your Programs menu, see you instructor or technical support person.

The Internet World Wide Web Lab Assignment One of the most popular services on the Internet is the World Wide Web. This Lab is a Web simulator that teaches you how to use Web browser software to find information. You can use this Lab whether or not your school provides you with Internet access.

1. Click the Steps button to learn how to use Web browser software. As you proceed through the Steps, answer all of the Quick Check questions that appear. After you complete the Steps, you will see a Quick Check Summary Report. Follow the instructions on the screen to print this report.

2. Click the Explore button on the Welcome screen. Use the Web browser to locate a weather map of the Caribbean Virgin Islands. What is its URL?

3. A scuba diver named Wadson Lachouffe has been searching for the fabled treasure of Greybeard the pirate. A link from the Adventure Travel Web site leads to a Wadson's Web page called "Hidden Treasure." In Explore, locate the Hidden Treasure page and answer the following questions:
   a. What was the name of Greybeard's ship?
   b. What was Greybeard's favorite food?
   c. What does Wadson think happened to Greybeard's ship?

4. In the Steps, you found a graphic of Jupiter from the photo archives of the Jet Propulsion Laboratory. In the Explore section of the Lab, you can also find a graphic of Saturn. Suppose one of your friends wanted a picture of Saturn for an astronomy report. Make a list of the blue, underlined links your friend must click to find the Saturn graphic. Assume that your friend will begin at the Web Trainer home page.

5. Enter the URL *http://www.atour.com* to jump to the Adventure Travel Web site. Write a one-page description of this site. In your paper include a description of the information at the site, the number of pages the site contains, and a diagram of the links it contains.

6. Chris Thomson is a student at UVI and has his own Web pages. In Explore, look at the information Chris has included on his pages. Suppose you could create your own Web page. What would you include? Use word processing software to design your own Web pages. Make sure you indicate the graphics and links you would use.

Adding Hypertext Links to a Web Page

Developing an Online Resume with Hypertext Links

In this tutorial you will:

- Create hypertext links between elements within a document

- Create hypertext links between one document and another

- Review some basic Web page structures

- Create hypertext links to pages on the Internet

- Use and understand the difference between absolute and relative pathnames

- Learn to create hypertext links to various Internet resources, including FTP servers and newsgroups

Creating an Online Resume, continued

In Tutorial 1 you created the basic structure and content of an online resume for Mary Taylor. Since then Mary has made a few changes to the resume, and she has ideas for more content. The two of you sit down and discuss her plans. Mary notes that although the page contents reflect the paper resume, the online resume has one disadvantage: prospective employers must scroll around the document window to view pertinent facts about Mary. Mary wants to make it as easy to jump from topic to topic in her online resume as it is to scan through topics on a paper resume.

Mary also has a few references and notes of recommendation on file that she wants to make available to interested employers. She didn't include all this information on her paper resume because she wanted to limit that resume to a single page. With an online resume, Mary can still be brief, but at the same time she can make additional material readily available.

In this session you will create anchors on a Web page that let you jump to specific points in the document. After creating those anchors, you will create and then test your first hypertext link to another document.

Creating a Hypertext Document

In Tutorial 1 you learned that a hypertext document contains links that you can select, usually by clicking a mouse, to instantly view another topic or document, often called the **destination** of the link. In addition to making access to other documents easy, hypertext links provide some important organizational benefits. They indicate what points or concepts you think merit special attention or further reading. You can take advantage of these features by adding hypertext links to Mary's online resume.

At the end of Tutorial 1, the resume had three main sections: Objectives, Education, and Employment. You and Mary have made some additions and changes since then, including adding a fourth section, Other Information, that points to additional information about Mary. However, due to the document window's limited size, the opening screen does not show any of the main sections of Mary's resume. The browser in Figure 2-1 shows Mary's name, address, and photograph, but nothing about her education or employment history. Employers have to scroll through the document to find this information.

Figure 2-1 ◀
Opening screen
of Mary's
online resume

You can do little to show more of Mary's resume in the browser except remove the image file or move it to the end of the resume, which Mary doesn't want you to do. However, you could place text for the four headings (Objectives, Education, Employment, and Other Information) at the top of the document and then turn the text into hypertext links. When readers click or highlight one of the headings, they jump to that section of the document. The hypertext links that you create here point to sections within the same document. You do this in three steps:

1. Type the headings into the HTML file.

2. Mark each section in the HTML file using an anchor. (You'll learn what this is shortly.)

3. Link the text you added in Step 1 to the marks you added in Step 2.

You can accomplish the first step using techniques you learned in Tutorial 1. You need to open the Resume.htm text file in your text editor and then enter the text. You want the text to appear on the same line as Mary's photo in the browser, as in Figure 2-2.

Figure 2-2 ◀
Adding text for links to later sections in resume

Objectives · Education ·   · Employment · Other Info

you'll add text here ——

To achieve this, you place the text within the paragraph tags that already encompass the Taylor.gif graphics file. You could type all the text into the HTML file on the same line, but to keep the HTML file as legible as possible, add the text in two lines instead. This way, when you add more tags to the text later, it will still be easy to interpret. Because you format with markup tags in HTML, putting the text on different lines does not affect its appearance in the browser.

To add text to the document describing the different sections of the resume:

1. Open your text editor.

2. Open the file **ResumeMT.htm** from the Tutorial.02 folder on your Student Disk, then save the file in the same folder as **Resume.htm** so you still have a copy of the original.

   TROUBLE? If you can't locate the ResumeMT.htm file in the Tutorial.02 folder in your text editor's Open dialog box, you might need to set the file type to All Files.

3. Before "<IMG SRC="Taylor.gif">," type **Objectives &#183 Education &#183** then press **Enter** so this new entry is on its own line.

4. Create a new line directly after "<IMG SRC="Taylor.gif">," then type **&#183 Employment &#183 Other Info** so this new entry is on its own line. See Figure 2-3. The new lines include the special character code, &#183, which inserts a bullet into the text to separate section headings.

Figure 2-3 ◀
Text that points to each of the section headings

new lines ——

```
<BODY>
<H1 ALIGN=CENTER>Mary Taylor</H1>
<H5 ALIGN=CENTER>11 Kemper Ave. &#183 Lake View, CO 80517 &#183 (303) 555-10
<HR>

<P ALIGN=CENTER>
Objectives &#183 Education &#183
<IMG SRC="Taylor.gif">
&#183 Employment &#183 Other Info
</P>

<H2 ALIGN=CENTER>Objectives</H2>
Masters degree graduate interested in a telecommunications position in the D
```

5. Save the changes to the Resume.htm file, but leave the text editor open. You will revise this document throughout this tutorial.

6. Open your Web browser (you do not have to connect to the Internet), and view Resume.htm. See Figure 2-4.

Figure 2-4 ◀
New text with
special
characters

new text ———

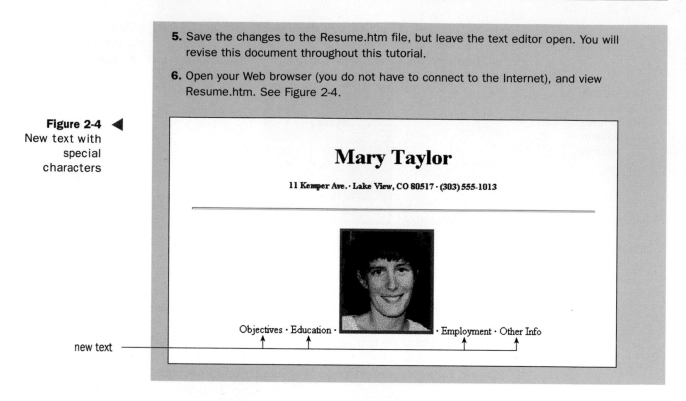

You've inserted the four headings on the same line next to Mary's photo.

Creating Anchors

Now that you've created the text describing the resume's different sections, you need to locate each heading and mark the heading text in the document using the <A> tag. The **<A> tag** creates an **anchor**, text that is specially marked so you can link to it from other points in the document. You assign each anchor its own anchor name using the NAME property. For example, if you want the text "Employment" to be an anchor, you could assign it the anchor name "EMP":

```
<A NAME="EMP">Employment</A>
```

The text "Employment" becomes an anchor named "EMP." Later, when you create a link from the beginning of Mary's resume to this anchor, the link will point to this particular place in the document using the anchor name "EMP." Figure 2-5 illustrates how the anchor you create will work as a reference point to a link.

Figure 2-5 ◀
Anchoring text

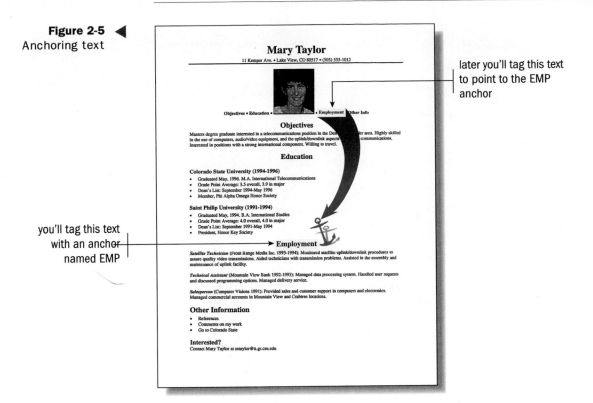

later you'll tag this text
to point to the EMP
anchor

you'll tag this text
with an anchor
named EMP

An anchor doesn't have to be just text. You can also mark an inline image using the same syntax:

```
<A NAME="PHOTO"><IMG SRC="Taylor.gif"></A>
```

In this example, you anchor a photo. You can create a link to this photo from other points in the document by using the anchor name "PHOTO."

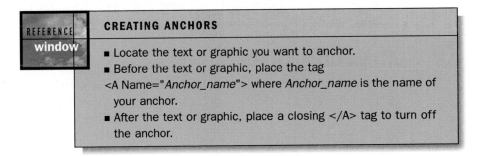

REFERENCE window

CREATING ANCHORS

■ Locate the text or graphic you want to anchor.
■ Before the text or graphic, place the tag
<A Name="*Anchor_name*"> where *Anchor_name* is the name of your anchor.
■ After the text or graphic, place a closing </A> tag to turn off the anchor.

As you'll see, adding an anchor does not change your document's appearance in any way. For Mary's resume file, you decide to create four anchors named "OBJ," "ED," "EMP," and "OTHER" for the Objectives, Education, Employment, and Other Information sections.

To add anchors to the resume's section headings:

1. Return to your text editor, and open the **Resume.htm file**, if it is not already open.

2. Locate the H2 heading for the Objectives section. This line currently reads:

```
<H2 ALIGN=CENTER>Objectives</H2>
```

3. Add an anchor tag around the Objectives heading so that it reads:

`<H2 ALIGN=CENTER><A NAME="OBJ">Objectives</A></H2>`

4. Locate the H2 heading for the Education section. This line currently reads:

`<H2 ALIGN=CENTER>Education</H2>`

5. Add an anchor tag around the Education heading so that it reads:

`<H2 ALIGN=CENTER><A NAME="ED">Education</A></H2>`

6. Locate the H2 heading for the Employment section, which reads:

`<H2 ALIGN=CENTER>Employment</H2>`

and add an anchor tag so that it reads:

`<H2 ALIGN=CENTER><A NAME="EMP">Employment</A></H2>`

7. Locate the H2 heading for the Other Information section, which reads:

`<H2>Other Information</H2>`

and add an anchor tag so that it reads:

`<H2><A NAME="OTHER"> Other Information</A></H2>`

8. Save the changes you made to the Resume file.

9. Open your Web browser, reload the Resume.htm file, then scroll through Resume.htm to confirm that the Resume file appears unchanged. Remember that the marks you placed in the document are reference points and should not appear in your browser.

TROUBLE? If you see a change in the document, check to make sure that you used the NAME property of the <A> tag.

You created four anchors in the Web page. The next step is to create links to those anchors from the text you added around Mary's picture.

Creating Links

After you anchor the text that will be the destination for your links, you create the links themselves. For Mary's resume, you want to link the text you entered around her photograph to the four sections in her document. Figure 2-6 shows the four links you want to create.

Figure 2-6
Links you need
to create

links

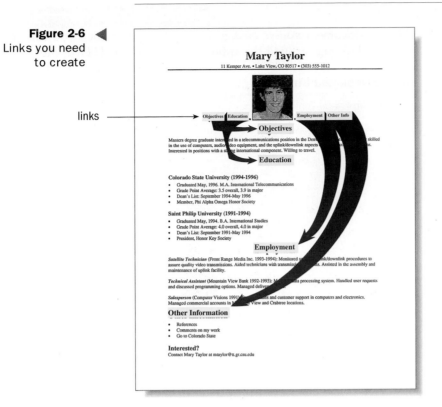

To create a link to an anchor, you use the same tag you used to create the anchor. The difference is that instead of using the NAME property to define the anchor, you use the HREF property, short for Hypertext Reference, to indicate the location to jump to. HREF can refer to an anchor that you place in the document, or, as you'll see later, a different HTML file on the Internet.

If you set up an anchor in the document with the anchor name *anchor_name*, you refer to that anchor with a pound (#) symbol. The entire reference looks like "*#anchor_name.*" For example, to create a link to a location in the current document with the anchor name "EMP," you enter this HTML command:

```
<A HREF="#EMP">Employment</A>
```

In this example, the entire text, "Employment," becomes a hypertext link. Selecting any part of that text within your Web browser jumps you to the location of the EMP anchor. The pound symbol has an important role in the hypertext anchor name, as you'll see later in this tutorial. You can also designate an inline image as a hypertext link. To turn an inline image into a hypertext link, place it within link tags, as in:

```
<A HREF="#OTHER"><IMG SRC="Taylor.gif"></A>
```

Tags that create links are called **link tags**.

REFERENCE
window

LINKING TO TEXT WITHIN A DOCUMENT

- Mark the destination text with an anchor.
- Locate the text or graphic you want to designate as the link.
- Before the text or graphic, place the tag
  <A HREF="#*Anchor_name*"> where *Anchor_name* is the name of the anchor.
- Close the link tag with the </A> closing tag.

In the current HTML document you've created four anchors to which you can link. You're ready to place the link tags around the appropriate text in the HTML file.

To add link tags to the Resume.htm file:

1. Return to your text editor, and make sure the Resume.htm file is open.

2. Locate the paragraph containing the four section titles and Mary's photograph at the top of the page. Within that paragraph you need to bracket each occurrence of a section title within a link tag.

3. Change the line reading "Objectives &#183 Education &#183" to

`<A HREF="#OBJ">Objectives</A> &#183 <A HREF="#ED">Education</A> &#183`

4. Change the line reading "&#183 Employment &#183 Other Info" to

`&#183 <A HREF="#EMP">Employment</A> &#183 <A HREF="#OTHER">Other Info</A>`

5. Compare your HTML file to Figure 2-7.

Figure 2-7 ◀
Adding link
tags

link tags ———

```
<BODY>
<H1 ALIGN=CENTER>Mary Taylor</H1>
<H5 ALIGN=CENTER>11 Kemper Ave. &#183 Lake View, CO 80517 &#183 (303) 555-10
<HR>

<P ALIGN=CENTER>
<A HREF="#OBJ">Objectives</A> &#183 <A HREF="#ED">Education</A> &#183
<IMG SRC="Taylor.gif">
&#183 <A HREF="#EMP">Employment</A> &#183 <A HREF="#OTHER">Other Info</A>
</P>

<H2 ALIGN=CENTER><A NAME="OBJ">Objectives</A></H2>
Masters degree graduate interested in a telecommunications position in the D
```

6. Save the changes you made to Resume.htm.

7. Open your Web browser and reload the Resume.htm file. Text links appear around Mary's photo. See Figure 2-8.

TROUBLE? If text links do not appear, check your code and make sure that you are using the <A> tag around the text and the HREF property within the tag.

Figure 2-8 ◀
Text links as
they appear in
the browser

link tags usually
appear as underlined
text in a different
color

Mary Taylor

11 Kemper Ave.· Lake View, CO 80517 · (303) 555-1013

Objectives · Education ·   · Employment · Other Info

Before continuing, you should verify that the links work properly. To test a link, you click it.

To test your links:

1. Click each link. You should jump to the section of the document indicated by the link. If not, check your code for errors by comparing it to Figure 2-7.

2. If you are continuing to Session 2.2, you can leave your browser and text editor open. Otherwise, close them.

Sometimes a link does not work as you expect. One common source of trouble is the case of the anchor. The HREF property is case-sensitive. An anchor name "EMP" is not evaluated the same as "emp." You should also remember to make each anchor name unique within a document. If you use the same anchor name for different text, your links won't go where you expect.

If you still have problems, make sure you coded the anchor and link tags correctly. When you add an anchor to a large section of text like a section heading, make sure to place the anchor within the heading tags. For example, you should write your tag as:

```
<H2><A NAME="EMP">Employment</A></H2>
```

not as:

```
<A NAME="EMP"><H2>Employment</H2></A>
```

The latter could confuse some browsers. The general rule is to always place anchors within other tag elements. Do not insert any tag elements within an anchor, except for tags that create document objects such as inline graphics.

You show the new links to Mary. She is excited to see how they work. She thinks they will quickly inform interested employers about her resume's contents, and help them quickly find the information they want.

Quick Check

1. What is the HTML code for marking the text "Colorado State University" with the anchor name "CSU"?

2. What is the HTML code for linking the text "Universities" to an anchor with the name "CSU"?

3. What is wrong with this statement?

```
<A NAME="INFO"><H3>For more information</H3></A>
```

4. What is the HTML code for marking an inline image, Photo.jpg, with the anchor name "PHOTO"?

5. What is the HTML code for linking the inline image, Button.jpg, to an anchor with the name "LINKS"?

6. True or false: Anchor names are case-insensitive.

In the next session, you'll add links to other HTML documents.

In Session 2.1 you created hypertext links to other points within the same document. In this session you create links to other HTML documents.

Mary wants to add two more pages to her online resume: a page of references and a page of comments about her work from former employers and teachers. She then wants to add links to her resume that point to both these pages. Figure 2-9 shows what she has in mind.

Figure 2-9 ◀
Mary's three
Web documents

Mary wants you to
create links from her
resume to her
Comments page and
her References page

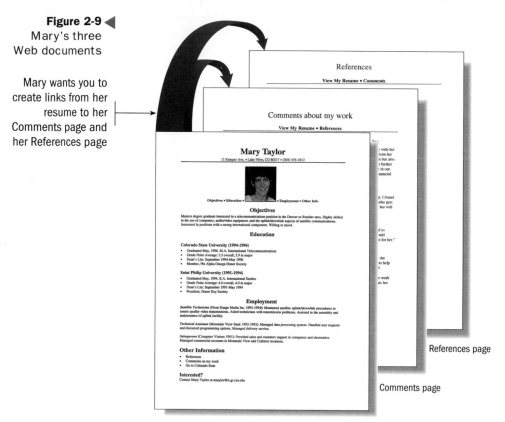

Resume page

Comments page

References page

You tell Mary that her ideas are good, but that before she starts thinking about how the documents will link to each other, she should understand the basics of Web page structures.

Web Page Structures

The three pages that will make up Mary's online resume—Resume, Comments, and References—are part of a system of Web pages. A **system** is a set of pages, usually created by the same person or group, that treat the same topic and that have the same look and feel. Before you set up links in a system of Web pages, it's worthwhile to map out exactly how you want the pages to relate, using a technique known as storyboarding. **Storyboarding** your Web pages before you create links helps you determine which structure works best for the type of information you're presenting. You want to make sure readers can navigate easily from page to page, without getting lost.

Linear Structures

You'll encounter several Web structures as you navigate the Web. Examining these structures can help you decide how to design your own system of Web pages. Figure 2-10 shows one common structure, the **linear structure**, in which each page is linked to the next and previous pages in an ordered chain of pages.

Figure 2-10 ◀
Linear
structure

in this structure you
can jump only from
one page to the next
or previous page

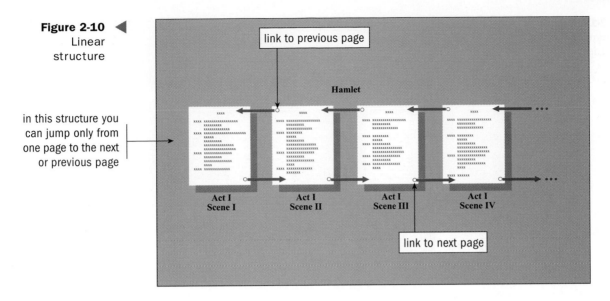

You might use this type of structure in Web pages that have a defined order. For example, you might work for a troupe that wants a single Web page for each scene from Shakespeare's *Hamlet*. If you use a linear structure for these pages, you assume that users want to progress through the scenes in order. You might, however, want to make it easier for users to return immediately to the opening scene rather than backtrack through several scenes. Figure 2-11 shows how you could include a link in each page that jumps directly back to the first page. This kind of storyboarding can reveal defects of the original structure that might otherwise be hidden.

Figure 2-11 ◀
Augmented
linear
structure

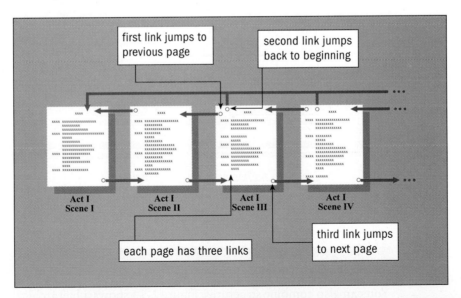

Hierarchical Structures

Another popular structure is the hierarchical structure of Web pages shown in Figure 2-12. A **hierarchical structure** starts with a general topic that includes links to more specific topics. Each specific topic includes links to yet more specialized topics, and so on. In a hierarchical structure, users can move easily from the general to the specific and back.

Figure 2-12 ◀
Hierarchical
structure

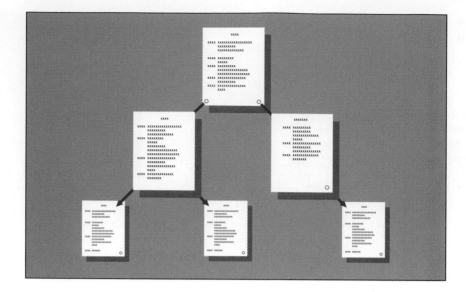

As with the linear structure, including a link to the top of the structure on each page gives users an easy path back to the beginning. Subject catalogs such as the Yahoo directory of Web pages often use this structure. Figure 2-13 shows this site, located at http://www.yahoo.com.

Figure 2-13 ◀
Hierarchical
structure on
Yahoo Web
page

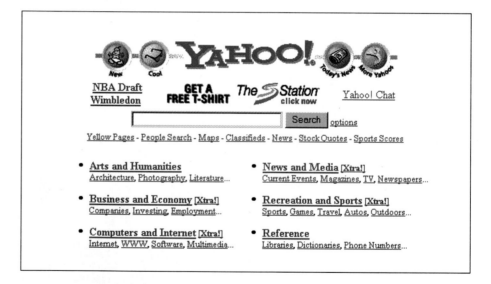

Mixed Structures

You can also combine structures. Figure 2-14 shows a hierarchical structure in which each level of pages is related in a linear structure. You might use this system for the Hamlet Web site to let the user move from scene to scene linearly, or from a specific scene to the general act to the overall play.

Figure 2-14
Combination of
linear and
hierarchical
structures

overall structure
is hierarchical

the scenes

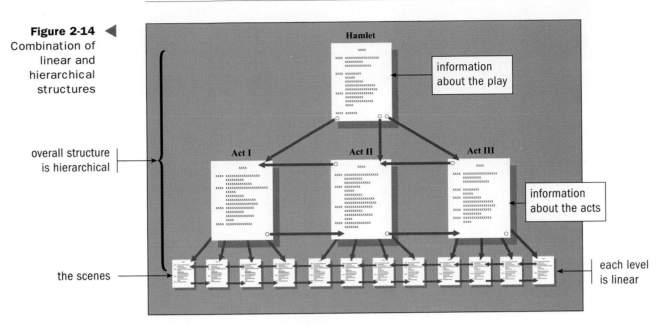

As these examples show, a little foresight can go a long way toward making your Web pages easier to use. The best time to organize a structure is when you first start creating multiple pages and those pages are small and easy to manage. If you're not careful, your structure might look like Figure 2-15.

Figure 2-15
Multi-page
document
with no
coherent
structure

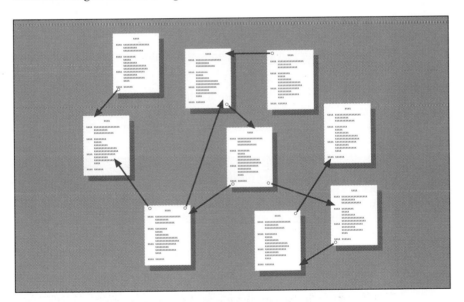

This structure is confusing because it gives users no idea of what content to expect when jumping from one link to another. Nor are users ever sure if they have viewed all possible pages.

Creating Links Between Documents

Mary and you discuss the type of structure that will work best for her online resume. She wants employers to move effortlessly between the three documents. Because there are only three pages, all focused on the same topic, you decide to include links within each document to the other two. If Mary later adds other pages to her resume, she will need to create a more formal structure involving some principles discussed in the previous sections.

For her simple three-page system, the structure shown in Figure 2-16 works just fine.

Figure 2-16 ◄
Structure of
Mary's Web
pages

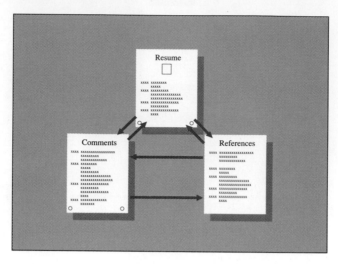

Mary has given you the information to create two additional HTML files: ReferMT.htm, a page with the names and addresses of previous employers or professors; and ComMT.htm, a page with comments from previous employers and teachers. You suggest that Mary include a graphic—a checkmark—on the Comments page. You have just the file for her, Check.gif. These three files are in the Tutorial.02 folder on your Student Disk. Save these files with new names: Refer.htm and Comments.htm.

To rename the ReferMT.htm and ComMT.htm files:

1. Using your text editor, open ReferMT.htm from the Tutorial.02 folder on your Student Disk and save it as **Refer.htm.**

2. With your text editor, open the file ComMt.htm in the Tutorial.02 folder and save it as **Comments.htm**.

Linking to a Document

You begin by linking Mary's Resume page to the References and Comments pages. You use the same <A> tag that you used earlier. For example, let's say you wanted a user to be able to click the phrase "Comments on my work" to jump back to the Comments.htm file. You could enter this HTML command in your current document:

`<A HREF="Comments.htm">Comments on my work</A>`

In this example, the entire text, "Comments on my work," is linked to the HTML file, Comments.htm. The only requirement is that Comments.htm must be in the same folder as the document containing the links.

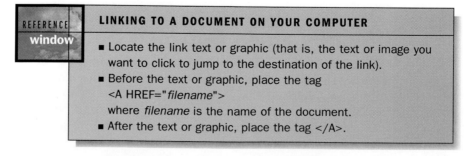

REFERENCE
window

LINKING TO A DOCUMENT ON YOUR COMPUTER

■ Locate the link text or graphic (that is, the text or image you want to click to jump to the destination of the link).
■ Before the text or graphic, place the tag
<A HREF="*filename*">
where *filename* is the name of the document.
■ After the text or graphic, place the tag </A>.

Unlike creating hypertext links between elements on the same page, you do not need to set an anchor in a file to link to it.

To add links in the Resume page to the References and Comments pages:

1. If you closed your text editor, reopen it and retrieve the Resume.htm file that you worked on in Session 2.1 of this tutorial.

2. Scroll down to the Other Information section of the file near the bottom of the page. Three items are listed; you want the first, References, to link to the References page, and the second, Comments on my work, to link to the Comments page.

3. Change the line reading "<LI>References" to:

   `<LI><A HREF="Refer.htm">References</A>`

4. Change the line reading "<LI> Comments on my work" to read:

   `<LI><A HREF="Comments.htm">Comments on my work</A>`

   See Figure 2-17.

Figure 2-17 ◀
Text you want
designated
as links to
other files

these two lines will
link to other pages

```
<H2><A NAME="OTHER">Other Information</A></H2>
<UL>
<LI><A HREF="Refer.htm">References</A>
<LI><A HREF="Comments.htm">Comments on my work</A>
<LI>Go to Colorado State
</UL>

<H3> Interested? </H3>
Contact Mary Taylor at mtaylor@tt.gr.csu.edu

</BODY>
```

5. Save the changes to the Resume file.

6. Open your Web browser, if it is not open already, and view Resume.htm. The items in the Other Information section now appear as the text links shown in Figure 2-18.

Figure 2-18 ◀
New links

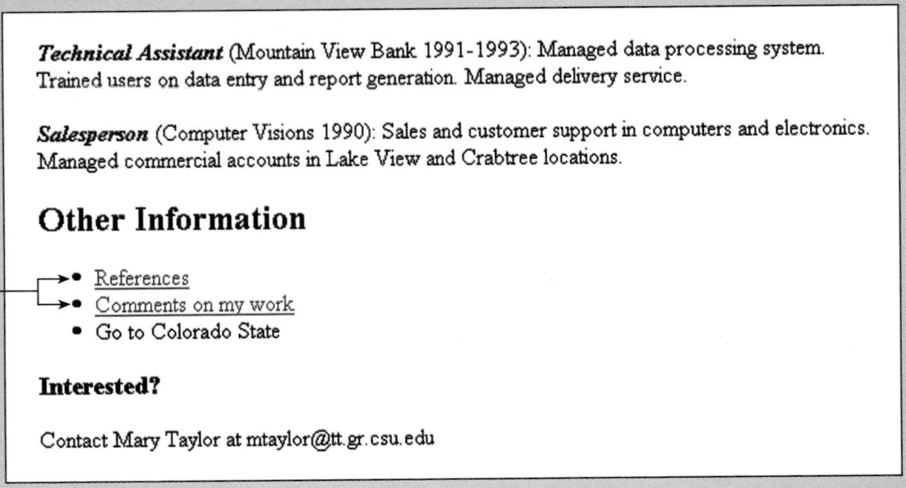

Technical Assistant (Mountain View Bank 1991-1993): Managed data processing system. Trained users on data entry and report generation. Managed delivery service.

Salesperson (Computer Visions 1990): Sales and customer support in computers and electronics. Managed commercial accounts in Lake View and Crabtree locations.

Other Information

links you just created

- References
- Comments on my work
- Go to Colorado State

Interested?

Contact Mary Taylor at mtaylor@tt.gr.csu.edu

7. Click the **References** link to verify that you jump to the References page shown in Figure 2-19.

TROUBLE? If the link doesn't work, check to see that Resume.htm and Refer.htm are in the same folder.

Figure 2-19 ◄
References
page

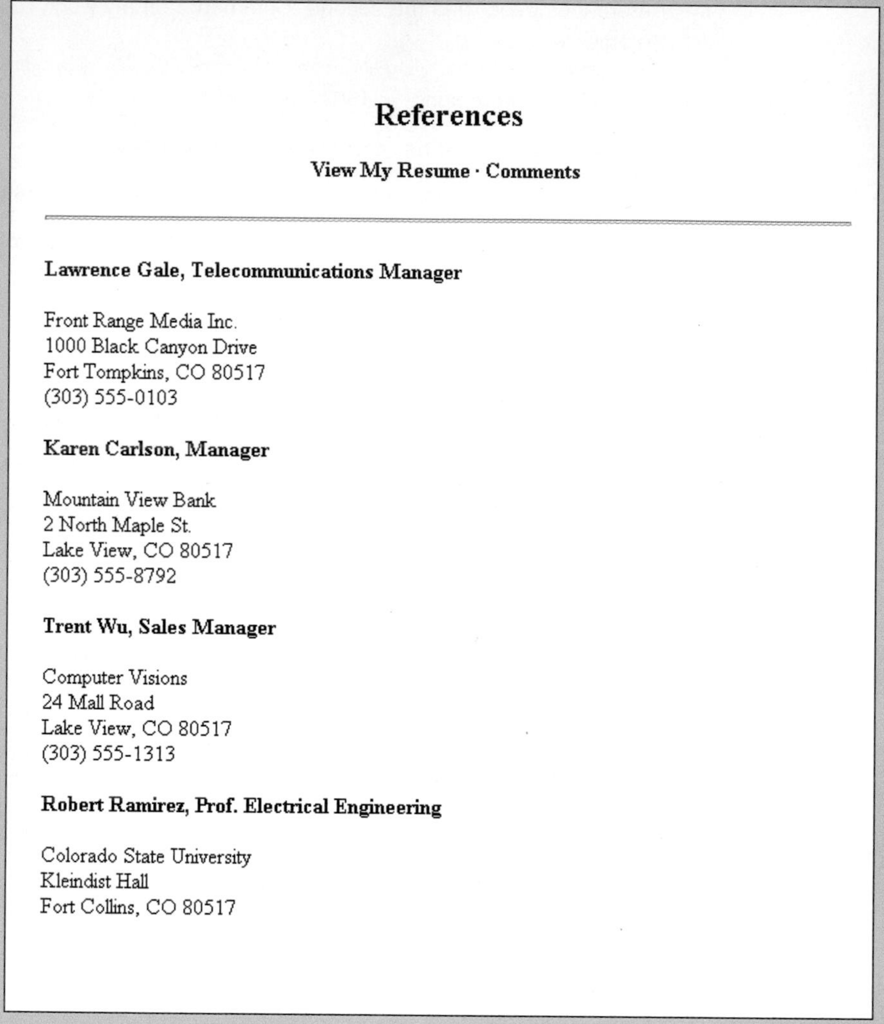

References

View My Resume · Comments

Lawrence Gale, Telecommunications Manager

Front Range Media Inc.
1000 Black Canyon Drive
Fort Tompkins, CO 80517
(303) 555-0103

Karen Carlson, Manager

Mountain View Bank
2 North Maple St.
Lake View, CO 80517
(303) 555-8792

Trent Wu, Sales Manager

Computer Visions
24 Mall Road
Lake View, CO 80517
(303) 555-1313

Robert Ramirez, Prof. Electrical Engineering

Colorado State University
Kleindist Hall
Fort Collins, CO 80517

8. Go back to the Resume page (usually by clicking a Back button), then click the **Comments on my work** link to verify that you jump to the Comments page shown in Figure 2-20.

Figure 2-20 ◀
Comments
page

notice inline
image, Check.gif

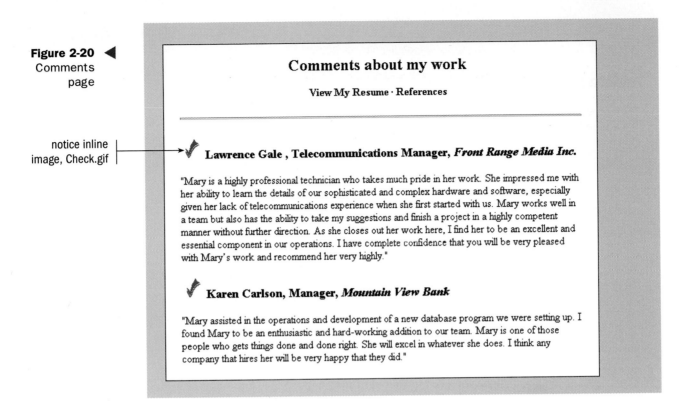

Next you want to add similar links to the Refer.htm and Comments.htm files. Each page should contain links that point to the other two pages.

To add links in the References page to the Resume and Comments pages:

1. Return to your text editor, and open the file **Refer.htm** from the Tutorial.02 folder on your Student Disk.

2. Locate the H4 heading at the top of the page.

3. Change the text "View my resume" to read:

   ```
   <A HREF="Resume.htm">View my resume</A>
   ```

4. Locate the text "Comments" on the same line. Change "Comments" to read:

   ```
   <A HREF="Comments.htm">Comments</A>
   ```

5. Compare your code to Figure 2-21.

Figure 2-21 ◀
Adding links to
the References
page

new links

```
<BODY>
<H2 ALIGN=CENTER> References</H2>

<H4 ALIGN=CENTER> <A HREF="Resume.htm">View My Resume</A> &#183
<A HREF="Comments.htm">Comments</A> </H4>
<HR>

<H4>Lawrence Gale, Telecommunications Manager</H4>
Front Range Media Inc.<BR>
1000 Black Canyon Drive<BR>
Fort Tompkins, CO 80517<BR>
(303) 555-0103
```

6. Save the changes to Refer.htm.

7. Open your Web browser, if it is not open already, and view Refer.htm. Your links should now look like Figure 2-22.

Figure 2-22 ◀
Links on
References
page

new links

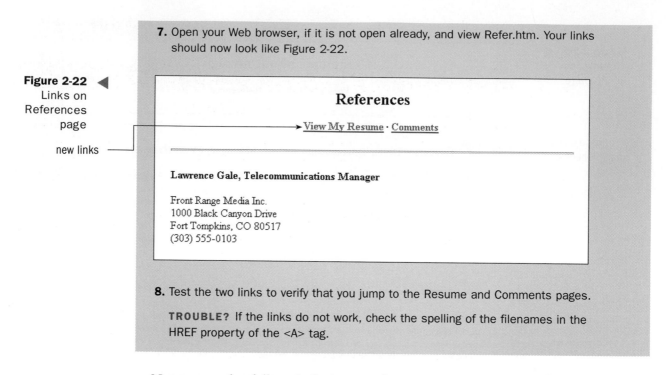

8. Test the two links to verify that you jump to the Resume and Comments pages.

TROUBLE? If the links do not work, check the spelling of the filenames in the HREF property of the <A> tag.

Now you need to follow similar steps so the Comments page links to the two other pages.

To add links in the Comments page to the Resume and References pages:

1. Return to your text editor, then open the file **Comments.htm** from the Tutorial.02 folder on your Student Disk.

2. Locate the H4 heading at the top of the page.

3. Change the text "View my resume" to read:

```
<A HREF="Resume.htm">View my resume</A>
```

4. Locate the text "References" on the same line. Change "References" to read:

```
<A HREF="Refer.htm">References</A>
```

5. Save the changes to Comments.htm.

6. Open your Web browser, if it is not open already, and view Comments.htm. You should see the links shown in Figure 2-23.

Figure 2-23 ◀
Links on the
Comments
page

new links

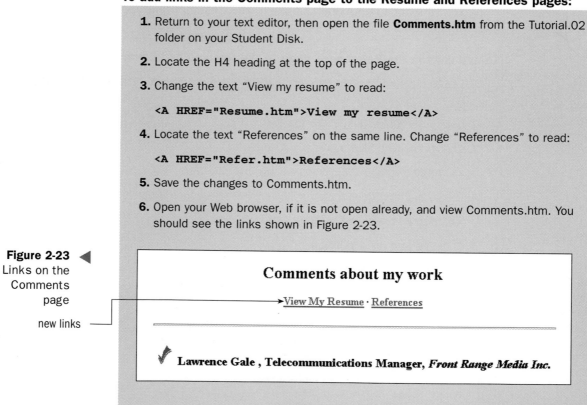

7. Click the two links to verify that you jump to the Resume and References pages.

Now that all the links between the three pages are set up, you can easily move between the three documents.

Linking to a Section of a Document

You might have noticed in testing your links that you always jump to the top of the destination page. What if you'd like to jump to a specific location later in a document, rather than the beginning? To do this, you can set anchors as you did in Session 2.1 and link to the anchor within the document. For example, to create a link to a section in the file Home.htm marked with an anchor name of "Interests," you could enter this HTML code in your current document:

```
<A HREF="Home.htm#interests">View my interests</A>
```

In this example, the entire text, "View my interests," is linked to the Interests section in the Home.htm file. Note that the pound (#) symbol in this tag distinguishes the filename from the anchor name.

Mary wants to link the positions listed in the Employment section of her resume to specific comments from employers on the Comments page. The Comments.htm file already has these anchors in place:

- "GALE" for comments made by Lawrence Gale, Mary's telecommunications manager
- "CARLSON" for comments made by Karen Carlson, manager of Mountain View Bank
- "WU" for comments made by Trent Wu of Computer Visions

Now you need to link the positions listed in the Resume file to these three anchors.

To add links to the Resume page that jump to anchors on the Comments page:

1. With your text editor, reopen the **Resume.htm** file.

2. Locate the Employment section in the middle of the Resume file. You need to bracket each job title within link tags with the reference pointing to the appropriate comment in the Comments page. Leave in place any tags that format the text such as the <P>, <EM>, and <STRONG> tags.

3. Move to the first job description, and replace the title "Satellite Technician" with:

```
<A HREF="Comments.htm#GALE">Satellite Technician</A>
```

4. Move to the next job description, and replace the title "Technical Assistant" with:

```
<A HREF="Comments.htm#CARLSON">Technical Assistant </A>
```

5. Move to the final job description, and replace the title "Salesperson" with:

```
<A HREF="Comments.htm#WU">Salesperson</A>
```

6. Save the changes to the Resume file.

7. Open your Web browser and load **Resume.htm**. The job titles in the Employment section should appear with text links as shown in Figure 2-24.

Figure 2-24 ◀
Links to
specific
locations within
the Comments
page

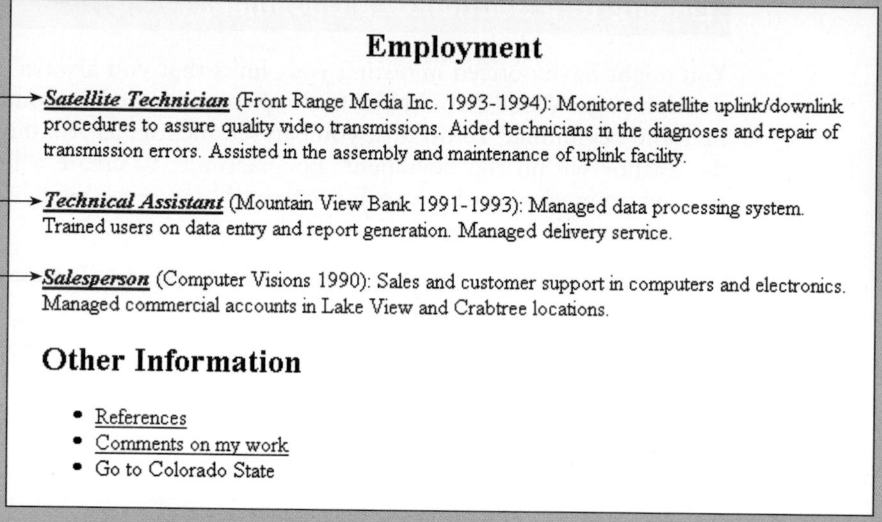

new links ———

Employment

→ *Satellite Technician* (Front Range Media Inc. 1993-1994): Monitored satellite uplink/downlink procedures to assure quality video transmissions. Aided technicians in the diagnoses and repair of transmission errors. Assisted in the assembly and maintenance of uplink facility.

→ *Technical Assistant* (Mountain View Bank 1991-1993): Managed data processing system. Trained users on data entry and report generation. Managed delivery service.

→ *Salesperson* (Computer Visions 1990): Sales and customer support in computers and electronics. Managed commercial accounts in Lake View and Crabtree locations.

Other Information

- References
- Comments on my work
- Go to Colorado State

8. Click the three links to verify that you jump to the appropriate place in the Comments page.

TROUBLE? If you have a problem with your links, remember that anchors are case-sensitive. Make sure you typed GALE, CARLSON, and WU in all uppercase letters.

9. If you are continuing to Session 2.3, you can leave your browser and text editor open. Otherwise, close them.

With these last hypertext links in place, you have given readers of Mary's online resume access to additional information.

Quick Check

1. What is storyboarding? Why is it important in creating a Web page system?

2. What is a linear structure? Draw a picture of a linear structure, and give an example how to use it.

3. What is a hierarchical structure? Draw a picture of a hierarchical structure, and give an example how to use it.

4. You are trying to create a system of Web pages for the play *Hamlet* in which each scene has a Web page. On each page you want to include links to the previous and next scenes of the play, as well as to the first scene of the play and the first scene of the current act. Draw a diagram of this multi-page document. (Just draw enough acts and scenes to make the structure clear.)

5. What HTML code would you enter to link the text "Sports info" to the HTML file Sports.htm?

6. What HTML code would you enter to link the text "Basketball news" to the HTML file Sports.htm at a place in the file with the anchor name "BBALL"?

In the next session, you learn how to point your hypertext links to documents and resources on the Internet.

SESSION

2.3

In Session 2.2 you created links to other documents within the same folder as the Resume.htm file. In this session you learn to create hypertext links to documents located in other folders and in other computers on the Internet.

Mary wants to add a link to her Resume page that points to the Colorado State University home page. The link gives potential employers an opportunity to learn more about the school and the courses it offers. Before creating this link for Mary, you need to review how HTML references files in different folders and computers.

Linking to Documents in Other Folders

Until now you've worked with documents that were all in the same folder. When you created links to other files in that folder, you specified the filename in the link tag but not its location. Browsers assume that if no folder information is given, the file is in the same folder as the current document. In some situations you might want to place different files in different folders, particularly when working with large multi-document systems that span several topics, each topic with its own folder.

When referencing files in different folders in the link tag, you must include each file's location, called its **path**. HTML supports two kinds of paths: absolute paths and relative paths.

Absolute Pathnames

The **absolute path** shows exactly where the file is on the computer. In HTML you start every absolute pathname with a slash (/). Then you type the folders' names on the computer, starting with the topmost folder in the folder hierarchy and progressing through the different levels of subfolders. You separate each folder name from the next with a slash. The pathname, from left to right, leads down through the folder hierarchy to the folder that contains the file. After you type the name of the folder that contains the file, you type a final slash and then the filename.

For example, consider the folder structure shown in Figure 2-25.

Figure 2-25 ◀
Folder tree

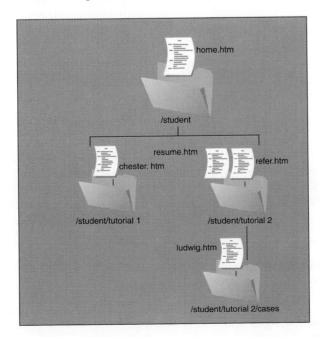

Figure 2-25 shows five HTML files scattered among four folders. The topmost folder is the student folder. Beneath the student folder are the tutorial1 and tutorial2 folders, and beneath the tutorial2 folder is the cases folder. Figure 2-26 shows absolute pathnames for the five files.

Figure 2-26 ◀
Absolute path names

Absolute pathname	Interpretation
/student/home.htm	The home.htm file in the student folder
/student/tutorial1/chester.htm	The chester.htm file in the tutorial folder, a subfolder of the student folder
/student/tutorial2/resume.htm	The resume.htm file in the tutorial2 folder, another subfolder of the student folder
/student/tutorial2/refer.htm	The refer.htm file in the same folder as the resume.htm file
/student/tutorial2/cases/ludwig.htm	The ludwig.htm file in the cases folder, a subfolder of the /student/tutorial2 folder

Even the absolute pathnames of files located on different hard disks begin with a slash. To differentiate these files, HTML requires you to include the drive letter followed by a vertical bar (|). For example, a file named "resume.htm" in the student folder on drive A of your computer has the absolute pathname "/A|/student/resume.htm."

Relative Pathnames

If a computer has many folders and subfolders, absolute pathnames can be long, cumbersome, and confusing. For that reason, most Web authors use relative pathnames in their hypertext links. A **relative path** gives a file's location in relation to the current Web document. As with absolute pathnames, folder names are separated by slashes. Unlike absolute pathnames, a relative pathname does not begin with a slash. To reference a file in a folder above the current folder in the folder hierarchy, relative pathnames use two periods(..).

For example, if the current file is resume.htm from the /student/tutorial2 folder shown in Figure 2-25, the relative pathnames and their interpretations for the other four files in the folder tree appear as in Figure 2-27.

Figure 2-27 ◀
Relative path names

Relative pathname	Interpretation
../home.htm	The home.htm file in the folder one level up in the folder tree from the current file
../tutorial1/chester.htm	The chester.htm file in the tutorial1 subfolder of the folder one level up from the current file
refer.htm	The refer.htm file in the same folder as the current file
cases/ludwig.htm	The ludwig.htm file in the cases subfolder, one level down from the current folder

A second reason to use relative pathnames is that they make your hypertext links portable. If you have to move your files to a different computer or server, you can move the entire folder structure and still use the relative pathnames in the hypertext links. If you use absolute pathnames, you need to painstakingly revise each and every link.

Linking to Documents on the Internet

Now you can turn your attention to creating the link on Mary's resume to Colorado State University. To create a hypertext link to a document on the Internet, you need to know its URL. A **URL**, or Uniform Resource Locator, gives a file's location on the Web. The URL for Colorado State University, for example, is http://www.colostate.edu/index.html. You can find the URL of a web page in the Location box of your browser's document window. You'll learn about the parts of a URL in the next section.

After you know a document's URL, you are ready to add the code that creates the link, again the <A> code with the HREF property that creates links to documents on your computer. For example, to create a link to a document on the Internet with the URL http://www.mwu.edu/course/info.html, you use this HTML code:

```
<A HREF="http://www.mwu.edu/course/info.html">Course Information</A>
```

This example links the text "Course Information" to the Internet document located at http://www.mwu.edu/course/info.html. As long as your computer is connected to the Internet, clicking the text within the tag should make your browser jump to that document.

REFERENCE window

LINKING TO A DOCUMENT ON THE INTERNET

- Locate the text or graphic you want to designate as the link.
- Before the text or graphic, place the tag <A HREF="*URL*"> where *URL* is the URL of the Web page you want to link to.
- Close the link tag with the </A> closing tag.

In the Other Information section of Mary's resume, she wants to link the text "Colorado State University" to the CSU home page. You're ready to add that link.

To add a link to the Colorado State University page from Mary's Resume page:

1. If necessary, open your text editor, then open the **Resume.htm** file that you worked on in Session 2.2 of this tutorial.

2. Locate the **Other Information** section of the file near the bottom of the page.

3. Change the line <LI>Go to Colorado State to read:

   ```
   <LI><A HREF="http://www.colostate.edu/index.html"> Go to
       Colorado State</A>
   ```

4. Save the changes to the Resume file.

5. If necessary, open the Web browser and connect to the Internet.

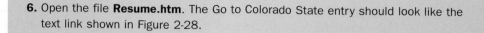

6. Open the file **Resume.htm**. The Go to Colorado State entry should look like the text link shown in Figure 2-28.

Figure 2-28 ◀
Link to
another page
on the Web

link to another
Web site

Other Information

- References
- Comments on my work
- Go to Colorado State

Interested?

Contact Mary Taylor at mtaylor@tt.gr.csu.edu

7. Click the **Go to Colorado State** link. The Colorado State University home page shown in Figure 2-29 appears.

TROUBLE? If the CSU home page doesn't appear right away, it might just be loading slowly on your system because it contains a large graphic. If the CSU home page still doesn't appear, verify that your computer is connected to the Internet.

Figure 2-29 ◀
Colorado State
University
home page

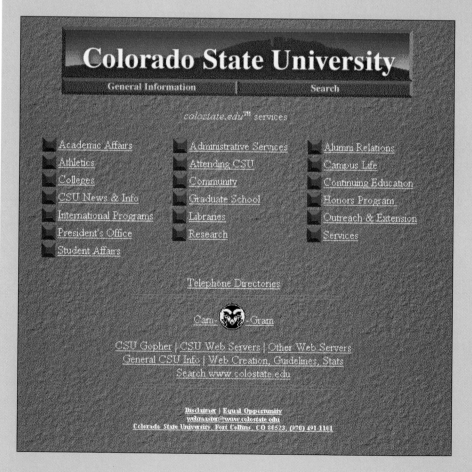

8. Click the **Back** button in your browser to return to Mary's resume.

Linking to Other Internet Objects

Occasionally you see a URL for an Internet object other than a Web page. Recall that part of the World Wide Web's success is that it lets users access several types of Internet resources using the same application. The method you used to create a link to the Colorado State University home page is the same method you use to set up links to other Internet resources, ranging from FTP servers to Usenet newsgroups. Only the proper URL for each object is required.

Each URL follows the same basic format. The first part identifies the **communication protocol**, the set of rules governing how information is exchanged. Web pages use the communication protocol **HTTP**, short for Hypertext Transfer Protocol. All Web page URLs begin with the letters "http." Other Internet resources use different communication protocols. After the communication protocol there is usually a separator, like a colon followed by a slash or two (://). The exact separator depends on the Internet resource. The rest of the URL identifies the location of the document or resource on the Internet. Figure 2-30 interprets a Web page with the URL:

```
http://www.mwu.edu/course/info.html#majors
```

Figure 2-30 ◀
Interpreting
parts of a URL

Part of URL	Interpretation
http://	The communication protocol
www.mwu.edu	The Internet host name for the computer storing the document
/course/info.html	The pathname and filename of the document on the computer
#majors	An anchor in the document

Before you walk Mary through the task of creating her final link, you take a quick detour to show her how to create links to other Internet resources if needed. You might not be familiar with all the Internet resources discussed in these next sections. This tutorial doesn't try to teach you about these resources; it just shows you how to reference them in your HTML file. Many books offer detailed information on these resources, among them CT's *The Internet Illustrated*.

Linking to FTP Servers

FTP servers store files that Internet users can download, or transfer, to their computers. **FTP,** short for File Transfer Protocol, is the communications protocol these file servers use to transfer information. URLs for FTP servers follow the same format as for Web pages, except they use the FTP protocol rather than the HTTP protocol: ftp://*FTP_Hostname*. For example, to create a link to the FTP server located at ftp.microsoft.com, you could use this HTML code:

```
<A HREF="ftp://ftp.microsoft.com">Microsoft FTP server</A>
```

In this example, clicking the text "Microsoft FTP server" jumps the user to the Microsoft FTP server page shown in Figure 2-31.

Figure 2-31 ◄
FTP server at
ftp.microsoft
.com

files and folders on
the FTP server

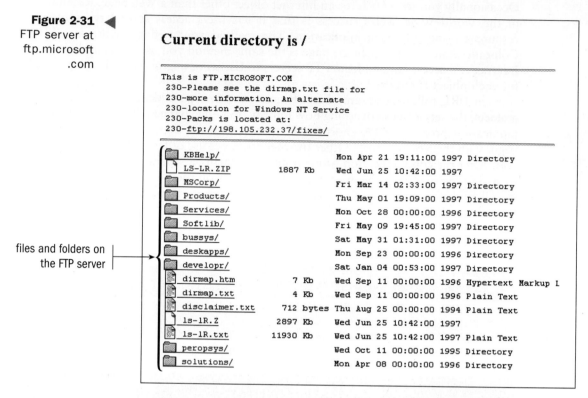

Linking to Gopher Servers

Before use of the World Wide Web became widespread, **Gopher servers** were popular tools that organized the Internet's resources. Gopher does this using hierarchical menus, from which you select the Internet resource that you want to access. The URL for a Gopher server is gopher://Host_name. To set up a hypertext link to the Gopher server at gopher.wisc.edu, you enter this code on your Web page:

```
<A HREF="gopher://gopher.wisc.edu">Go to the Wisconsin Gopher</A>
```

When a user clicks Go to the Wisconsin Gopher, the browser loads the page shown in Figure 2-32.

Figure 2-32 ◀
Gopher server
at gopher.wisc
.edu

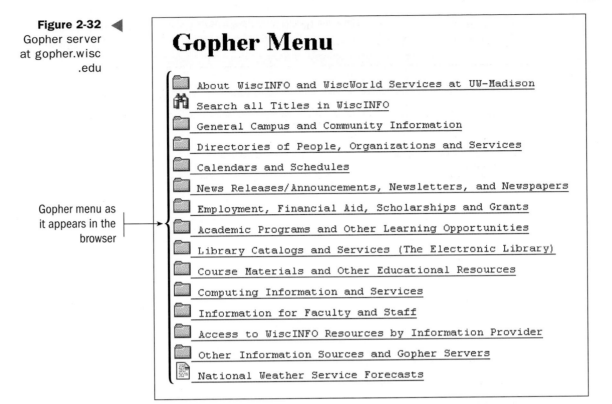

Gopher Menu

📁 About WiscINFO and WiscWorld Services at UW-Madison
🔍 Search all Titles in WiscINFO
📁 General Campus and Community Information
📁 Directories of People, Organizations and Services
📁 Calendars and Schedules
📁 News Releases/Announcements, Newsletters, and Newspapers
📁 Employment, Financial Aid, Scholarships and Grants
📁 Academic Programs and Other Learning Opportunities
📁 Library Catalogs and Services (The Electronic Library)
📁 Course Materials and Other Educational Resources
📁 Computing Information and Services
📁 Information for Faculty and Staff
📁 Access to WiscINFO Resources by Information Provider
📁 Other Information Sources and Gopher Servers
📄 National Weather Service Forecasts

Gopher menu as
it appears in the
browser →

Linking to Usenet News

Usenet is a collection of discussion forums, called **newsgroups**, that lets users send and retrieve messages on a wide variety of topics. The URL for a newsgroup is news:*newsgroup*. To access the surfing newsgroup, alt.surfing, you place this line in your HTML file:

```
<A HREF="news:alt.surfing">Go to the surfing newsgroup</A>
```

Not all browsers support the newsgroup URL. Even if your browser does, you still might need to configure your browser to access a news server that supports the newsgroup. If a user clicks the Go to the surfing newsgroup link in the Netscape Navigator browser, for example, Netscape Navigator loads its newsreader, shown in Figure 2-33. The user then works with the Netscape Navigator newsreader, not the browser, to view the latest messages from alt.surfing.

Netscape Navigator displays a newsreader when
it tries to access a newsgroup URL

Figure 2-33
Accessing
alt.surfing
newsgroup

newsgroups →

alt.surfing newsgroup

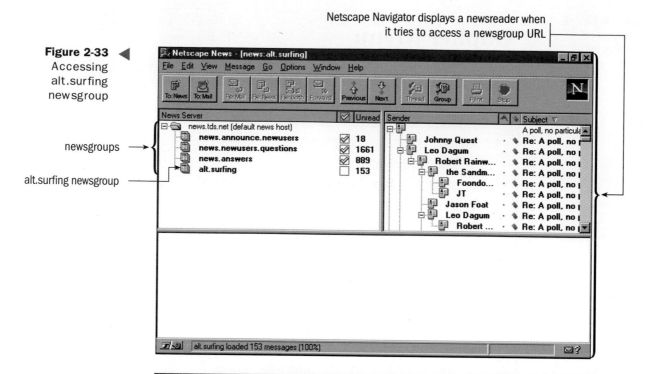

Linking to E-mail

Many Web authors include their e-mail addresses on their Web pages so users who access these pages can send feedback. Some browsers let these e-mail addresses act as hypertext links. When a user clicks the e-mail address, the browser runs a mail program and automatically inserts the author's e-mail address into the outgoing message. The user then edits the body of the message and, with a single mouse click, mails it. The URL for an e-mail address is mailto:*e-mail_address*. To create a link to the e-mail address davis@mwu.edu, for example, you enter the following into your Web document:

```
<A HREF="mailto:davis@mwu.edu">davis@mwu.edu</A>
```

If you click this link with the Netscape Navigator browser, for example, Netscape Navigator loads the Netscape mail program shown in Figure 2-34.

Netscape Navigator displays a mail program
when it tries to open a mailto URL

Figure 2-34
Sending mail to
davis@mwu
.edu

e-mail address

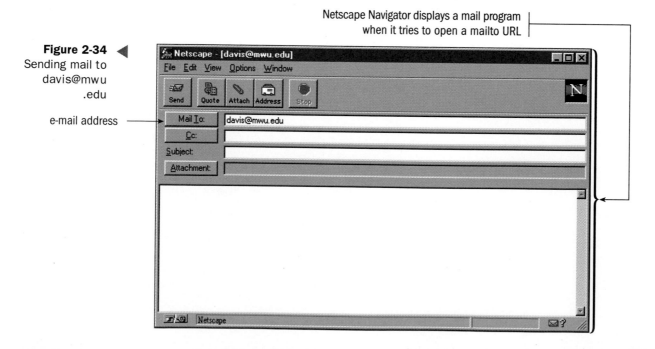

As with newsgroups, not all browsers support the e-mail hypertext link, although most popular ones like Netscape Navigator and Internet Explorer do.

Adding an E-mail Link to Mary's Resume

Mary wants a final addition to her resume: a link to her e-mail address. With this link, an interested employer can quickly send Mary a message through the Internet. Mary placed her e-mail address at the bottom of the Resume page. Now you need to designate that text as a link.

To add an e-mail link to Mary's resume:

1. Return to the **Resume.htm** file in your text editor.

2. Go to the bottom of the page.

3. Change the text "mtaylor@tt.gr.csu.edu" to

   `<A HREF="mailto:mtaylor@tt.gr.csu.edu">mtaylor@tt.gr.csu.edu</A>`

4. Save the changes to the Resume file.

5. Return to your Web browser.

6. Reload **Resume.htm**.

7. Move to the bottom of the page. Mary's e-mail address should look like the hypertext link shown in Figure 2-35.

   TROUBLE? Some browsers do not support the mailto URL. If you use a browser other than Netscape Navigator or Internet Explorer, check to see if it supports this feature.

Figure 2-35 ◀
Mary Taylor's
e-mail address
as a text link

Interested?

Contact Mary Taylor at <u>mtaylor@tt.gr.csu.edu</u>

Mary's e-mail address ⎯⎯⎯⎯⎯

8. Click the hypertext link to Mary's e-mail address. If you are using the Netscape Navigator browser, you should see the Netscape Mail program with Mary's e-mail address inserted in the Mail To box. See Figure 2-36.

Figure 2-36 ◀
Netscape Mail
program with
Mary Taylor's
e-mail address
automatically
inserted

Mary's e-mail address ⎯⎯⎯⎯⎯

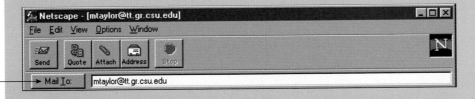

9. Cancel the mail message. Mary's e-mail address is fictional, so you can't send her mail anyway.

10. Close your Web browser and text editor.

You show Mary the final form of her online resume. She's really thrilled with the result. You tell her the next thing she needs to do is contact an Internet Service Provider and transfer the files to an account on their machine. When that's done, Mary's resume becomes available online to countless employers across the Internet.

Quick Check

1. What's the difference between an absolute path and a relative path?

2. Refer to the diagram in Figure 2-25: If the current file is ludwig.htm in the /student/tutorial2/cases folder, what are the relative pathnames for the four other files?

3. What HTML tag would you enter to link the text "Washington" to the FTP server at ftp.uwash.edu?

4. What HTML tag would you enter to link the text "Minnesota" to the Gopher server at gopher.umn.minn.edu?

5. What HTML tag would you enter to link the text "Boxing" to the newsgroup, rec.sports.boxing.pro?

6. What HTML tag would you enter to link the text "President" to the e-mail address president@whitehouse.com?

Tutorial Assignments

Mary Taylor decides that she wants you to add a few more items to her resume. She wants to add a link at the bottom of her resume page that returns readers to the top. In the Employment section, she wants to add that she worked as a tutor for Professor Ramirez at Colorado State University and link that to comments Professor Ramirez made about her in the Comments page. Finally she wants to add a link to the Colorado State University Gopher server.

1. Open the Resume.htm file located in the Tutorial.02 folder on your Student Disk. You worked with this file over the course of this tutorial.

2. Save the file on your Student Disk in the TAssign folder with the same name, Resume.htm.

3. Add an anchor tag around the page heading. Change the line

   ```
   <H1 ALIGN=CENTER>Mary Taylor</H1>
   ```

   to read:

   ```
   <H1 ALIGN=CENTER><A NAME="TOP">Mary Taylor</A> </H1>
   ```

4. After the HTML line at the bottom of the page containing Mary's e-mail address and before the </BODY> tag, enter a new line:

   ```
   <P><A HREF="#TOP">Go to the top of the page</A></P>
   ```

5. Move to the Employment section.

6. After the paragraph describing Mary's experience as a salesperson, insert this line: Tutor (Colorado State): "Tutored students in electrical engineering and mathematics."

7. Mark the text you entered in Step 6 with the correct code for a two-sided paragraph tag. Add the <EM> and <STRONG> tags used in other job descriptions.

8. Make "Tutor" a hypertext link to the RAMIREZ anchor in the Comments page using the tag:

   ```
   <A HREF="comments.htm#RAMIREZ">Tutor</A>
   ```

9. Move to the Other Information section.

10. Add a new list item to the unsorted list: "Go to Colorado State Gopher."

11. Make the list item you entered in Step 10 a hypertext link by adding the tag:

    ```
    <A HREF="gopher://gopher.colostate.edu/">Go to Colorado
       State Gopher</A>
    ```

12. Save the changes to your Resume.htm file, then print this file and close your text editor.

13. View the file with your Web browser. Make sure you open Resume.htm in the TAssign folder of the Tutorial.02 folder.

14. Print a copy of the page as viewed by your browser, then close your browser.

15. Give both printouts to your instructor.

Case Problems

1. Creating Links to Federal Departments As a librarian at the city library, you are creating a Web page to help people access the home pages for several federal government departments. Figure 2-37 lists each department's URL.

Figure 2-37 ◀

Department	URL
Department of Agriculture	http://www.fie.com/www/agri.htm
Department of Commerce	http://www.fie.com/www/commerce.htm
Department of Defense	http://www.fie.com/www/defense.htm
Department of Education	http://www.fie.com/www/educ.htm
Department of Energy	http://www.fie.com/www/energy.htm
Department of Health and Human Services	http://www.fie.com/www/hhs.htm
Department of Housing and Urban Development	http://www.fie.com/www/hud.htm
Department of Interior	http://www.fie.com/www/inter.htm
Department of Justice	http://www.fie.com/www/justice.htm
Department of Labor	http://www.fie.com/www/labor.htm
Department of State	http://www.fie.com/www/state.htm
Department of Transportation	http://www.fie.com/www/trans.htm
Department of Treasury	http://www.fie.com/www/treas.htm
Department of Veteran Affairs	http://www.fie.com/www/veteran.htm

Create an unsorted list containing department names. Make each name a text link to the department's home page.

1. Open the text editor on your computer and open a new document.

2. Enter the <HTML>, <HEAD>, and <BODY> tags to identify different sections of the page.

3. Within the HEAD section, insert a <TITLE> tag with the text, "Federal Government Departments."

4. Within the BODY section, create an H1 heading with the text, "A list of federal departments," and then center the heading on the page with the ALIGN property.

5. Create an unordered list using the <LI> tag for each department name in Figure 2-37. You can save yourself a lot of typing by using the Copy and Paste commands in your text editor.

6. Surround each department name in the list with a hypertext tag. For example, for the Department of Agriculture, enter the line:

```
<LI><A HREF="http://www.fie.com/www/agri.htm"> Department
   of Agriculture</A>
```

7. Save the code in a file named Depart.htm in the Cases folder of the Tutorial.02 folder on your Student Disk, then print the file and close your text editor.

8. View the file with your Web browser, and create a printout, then close your browser.

9. Give the printouts to your instructor.

2. Using Graphics as Hypertext Links You are an assistant to a professor in the Music Department who is trying to create Web pages for topics in classical music. Previously you created a Web page for her showing the different sections of the fourth movement of Beethoven's Ninth symphony. Now that you've learned to link multiple HTML files together, you have created pages for all four movements.

The four pages are in the Cases folder of the Tutorial.02 folder on your Student Disk. Their names are: Move1A.htm, Move2A.htm, Move3A.htm and Move4A.htm. You'll rename them Move1.htm, Move2.htm, Move3.htm, and Move4.htm, so you have the originals if you want to work on them later. Figure 2-38 shows the page for the third movement.

Figure 2-38 ◀
Web page for
third movement
of Beethoven's
Ninth
Symphony

You now need to link the pages. You've already placed graphic elements—the hands pointing to the previous or next movement of the symphony—in each file. You decide to mark each graphic image as a hypertext link that jumps the user to the previous or next movement.

1. Open the text editor on your computer.

2. Open the Move1A.htm file in the Cases folder of the Tutorial.02 folder on your Student Disk, and save it as Move1.htm in the same folder.

3. Change the image tag <IMG SRC="LEFT.GIF"> to read:

```
<A HREF="move2.htm"><IMG SRC="LEFT.GIF"></A>
```

4. Save the Move1.htm file.

5. Open the Move2A.htm file in the Cases folder of the Tutorial.02 folder on your Student Disk, and save it as Move2.htm in the same folder. Add hypertext links to the graphics as you did in Step 3 (this time to Move1 and Move3 using the Left and Right graphics), then save the Move2.htm file.

6. Open the Move3A.htm file in the Cases folder of the Tutorial.02 folder on your Student Disk, and save it as Move3.htm in the same folder. Add hypertext links to the graphics as you did in Step 3 (this time to Move2 and Move4 using the Left and Right graphics), then save the Move3.htm file.

7. Open the Move4A.htm file in the Cases folder of the Tutorial.02 folder on your Student Disk, and save it as Move4A.htm in the same folder. Add hypertext links to the graphics as you did in Step 3 (this time to Move3), then save the Move4A.htm file.

8. Print all four HTML files, then close your text editor.

9. Open the file Move1.htm in your Web browser.

10. Verify that you can move forward and backward through the four movements of the Ninth Symphony using the graphic images on the page.

11. Print each page in the Web browser, then close your browser.

12. Give the printouts to your instructor.

3. Creating a List of FTP Servers You maintain a Web site for a small college. One of your jobs is to create a list of FTP servers for students who want to download Internet files. Figure 2-39 lists the "popular" FTP sites you've identified.

Figure 2-39 ◀

Location	Description
archive.umich.edu	Software archives for UNIX, PC, and Macintosh computers
ftp.cica.indiana.edu	Software archives for UNIX machines and PCs
ftp.cwru.edu	Full text of U.S. Supreme Court decisions
ftp.microsoft.com	Device drivers and technical support for Microsoft products
ftp.sura.net	Software archives specializing in Internet tools
nic.funet.fi	Archive of electronic documents and works of literature
rtfm.mit.edu	Internet document archives—includes tutorials about using the Internet
wuarchive.wustl.edu	Software archives for UNIX, PC, and Macintosh computers.

To make the information in Figure 2-39 more accessible to students, you decide to place it on a Web page, making each FTP server's location a hypertext link that calls the server when clicked. To make the page more readable, format it using the definition list tag discussed in Tutorial 1.

1. Open the text editor on your computer to a new document.

2. Enter the <HTML>, <HEAD>, and <BODY> tags to identify different sections of the page.

3. Within the HEAD section, insert a <TITLE> tag with the text: "Popular FTP Servers."

4. Within the BODY section, create an H1 heading with the text, "A list of popular FTP servers," and then center the heading on the page with the ALIGN property.

5. Create a definition list using the <DT> tag for each FTP servers location and the <DD> tag for each servers description.

6. For each FTP server address listed, insert a hypertext tag. For example, for the server at ftp.microsoft.com, enter the line:

```
<DT><A HREF="ftp://ftp.microsoft.com">ftp://ftp.microsoft.com</A>
```

7. Save the code in a file named FTP.htm in the Cases folder of the Tutorial.02 folder on your Student Disk, then print the file and close your text editor.

8. View the file with your Web browser, and create a printout, then close your browser.

9. Give the printouts to your instructor.

4. Create Your Own Home Page Now that you've completed this tutorial, you are ready to create your own home page. The page should include information about you and your interests. If you like, you can create a page devoted entirely to one of your favorite hobbies. Include the following elements:

- section headers
- bold and/or italic fonts
- paragraphs
- an ordered, unordered, or definition list
- an inline graphic image
- links to some of your favorite Internet pages
- a hypertext link that moves the user from one object on your page to another

1. Create a file called Myhome.htm in the Cases folder of the Tutorial.02 folder on your Student Disk, and enter the appropriate HTML code.

2. Add any other tags you think will improve your document's appearance.

3. Insert any graphic elements you think will enhance your document.

4. Use your Web browser to explore other Web pages. Record the URLs of pages that you like, and list them in your document.

5. Test your code as you develop your resume by viewing Myhome.htm in your browser.

6. When you finish entering your code, save and print the Myhome.htm file, then close your text editor.

7. View the final version in your browser, and print the Web page, then close your browser.

8. Hand in any printouts to your instructor.

Answers to Quick Check Questions

SESSION 1.1

1 Hypertext refers to text that contains points called links that allow the user to move to other places within the document, or to open other documents, by activating the link.

2 A Web server stores the files used in creating World Wide Web documents. The Web browser retrieves the files from the Web server and displays them. The files stored on the Web server are described in a very general way; it is the Web browser that determines how the files will eventually appear to the user.

3 HTML, which stands for Hypertext Markup Language, is used to create Web documents.

4 HTML documents do not exactly specify the appearance of a document; rather they describe the purpose of different elements in the document and leave it to the Web browser to determine the final appearance. A word processor like Word exactly specifies the appearance of each document element.

5 Documents are transferred more quickly over the Internet and are available to a wider range of machines.

6 Extensions are special formats supported by a particular browser, but not generally accepted by all browsers. The advantage is that people who use that browser have a wider range of document elements to work with. The disadvantage is that the document will not work for users who do not have that particular browser.

7 All you need is a simple text editor.

SESSION 1.2

1 The <HTML> tag identifies the language of the file as HTML to packages that support more than one kind of generalized markup language.

2 `<H1 ALIGN=CENTER> Heading Text </H1>`

3 `<P> Paragraph Text </P>`

4 HTML does not recognize the blank lines as a format element. A Web browser will ignore blank lines and run the paragraphs together on the page.

5 Unordered list:
```
              <UL>
                  <LI> List item
                  <LI> List item
              </UL>
```
Ordered list:
```
              <OL>
                  <LI> List item
                  <LI> List item
              </OL>
```
Definition list:
```
              <DL>
                  <DT> List term <DD> Term definition
                  <DT> List term <DD> Term definition
              </DL>
```

6 `<EM> Italicized text </EM>` and `<I> Italicized text </I>`
The advantage of using the EM tag is that it will be recognized even by browsers that do not support italics (such as a terminal connected to a UNIX machine), and those browsers will still emphasize the text in some way. The I tag, on the other hand, will be ignored by those machines. Using the I tag has the advantage of explicitly describing how you want the text to appear.

SESSION 1.3

1 &#169

2 `<HR>`

3 `<HR WIDTH=70% SIZE=4>`

4 An inline image is a GIF or JPEG file that appears on a Web document. A browser can display it without a file viewer.

5 An external image is a graphic that requires the use of a software program, called a viewer, to be displayed.

6 `<IMG ALIGN=LEFT SRC="mouse.jpg">`

7 GIFs and JPEGs

SESSION 2.1

1 `<A NAME="CSU"> Colorado State University </A>`

2 `<A HREF="#CSU"> Universities </A>`

3 Anchor tags should be placed within style tags such as the H3 heading tag.

4 `<A NAME="PHOTO"> <IMG SRC="Photo.jpg"> </A>`

5 `<A HREF="#LINKS"> <IMG SRC="Button.jpg"> </A>`

6 False. Anchor names are case-sensitive.

SESSION 2.2

1 Storyboarding is diagramming a series of related Web pages, taking care to identify all hypertext links between the various pages. Storyboarding is an important tool in creating Web presentations that are easy to navigate and understand.

2 A linear structure is one in which Web pages are linked from one to another in a direct chain. Users can go to the previous page or next page in the chain, but not to a page in a different section of the chain.

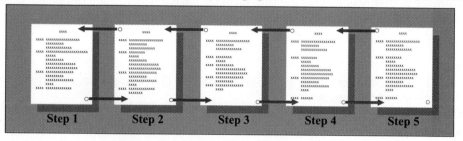

You could use a linear structure in a Web page presentation that included a series of steps that the user must follow, such as in a recipe or instructions to complete a task.

3 A hierarchical structure is one in which Web pages are linked from general to specific topics. Users can move up and down the hierarchy tree.

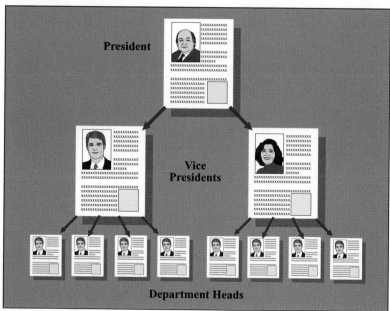

A company might use such a structure to describe the management organization.

4

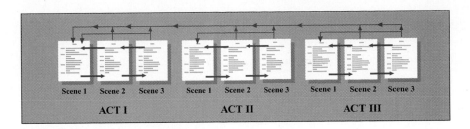

Scene 1 Scene 2 Scene 3   Scene 1 Scene 2 Scene 3   Scene 1 Scene 2 Scene 3
ACT I   **ACT II**   **ACT III**

5 `<A HREF="Sports.htm"> Sports info </A>`

6 `<A HREF="Sports.htm#BBALL"> Basketball news </A>`

SESSION 2.3

1 An absolute path gives the location of a file on the computer's hard disk. A relative path gives the location of a file relative to the active Web page.

2 ../../home.htm
   ../../tutorial1/chester.htm
   ../resume.htm
   ../refer.htm

3 `<A HREF= "ftp://ftp.uwash.edu> Washington </A>`

4 `<A HREF="gopher://gopher.umn.minn.edu> Minnesota </A>`

5 `<A HREF="news:rec.sports.boxing.pro"> Boxing </A>`

6 `<A HREF="mailto:president@whitehouse.com"> President </A>`

Creating Web Pages
with **HTML**

LEVEL II

TUTORIALS

Read This **Before You Begin**

STUDENT DISKS

To complete HTML Tutorials 3–5 and end-of-tutorial assignments in this book, you need two Student Disks. Your instructor will either provide you with Student Disks or ask you to make your own.

If you are supposed to make your own Student Disks, you will need two blank, formatted high-density disks. You will need to copy a set of folders from a file server or standalone computer onto your disks. Your instructor will tell you which computer, drive letter, and folders contain the files you need. The following table shows you which folders go on each of your disks, so that you will have enough disk space to complete all the tutorials, Tutorial Assignments, and Case Problems:

Student Disk	Write this on the disk label	Put these folders on the disk
1	Student Disk 1: Tutorials 3 and 4	Tutorial.03 and Tutorial.04
2	Student Disk 2: Tutorial 5	Tutorial.05

When you begin each tutorial, be sure you are using the correct Student Disk. See the inside front or inside back cover of this book for more information on Student Disk files, or ask your instructor or technical support person for assistance.

USING YOUR OWN COMPUTER

If you are going to work through this book using your own computer, you need:

■ **Computer System** A text editor and a Web browser (preferably Netscape Navigator or Internet Explorer, versions 3.0 or above) must be installed on your computer. If you are using a non-standard browser, it must support frames and HTML 3.2 or above.

■ **Student Disks** Ask your instructor or lab manager for details on how to get the Student Disks. You will not be able to complete the tutorials or end-of-tutorial assignments in this book using your own computer until you have the Student Disks. The Student Files may also be obtained electronically over the Internet. See the inside front or inside back cover of this book for more details.

VISIT OUR WORLD WIDE WEB SITE

Additional materials designed especially for you are available on the World Wide Web. Go to **http://www.course.com**. For example, see our Student Online Companion that contains additional coverage of selected topics in the text. These topics are indicated in the text by an online companion icon located in the left margin.

To complete HTML Tutorials 3–5 and end-of-tutorial assignments in this book, your students must use a set of student files on two Student Disks. These files are included in the Instructor's Resource Kit, and they may also be obtained electronically over the Internet. See the inside front or inside back cover of this book for more details. Follow the instructions in the Readme file to copy the files to your server or standalone computer. You can view the Readme file using WordPad.

Once the files are copied, you can make Student Disks for the students yourself, or you can tell students where to find the files so they can make their own Student Disks. Make sure the files get correctly copied onto the Student Disks by following the instructions in the Student Disks section above, which will ensure that students have enough disk space to complete all the tutorials and end-of-tutorial assignments.

COURSE TECHNOLOGY STUDENT FILES

You are granted a license to copy the Student Files to any computer or computer network used by students who have purchased this book.

Designing a Web Page

Working with Color and Graphics

OBJECTIVES

In this tutorial you will:

- Learn how HTML handles color
- Create a color scheme for a Web page
- Insert a background image into a Web page
- Create spot color
- Learn about different image formats
- Learn how to control the placement and appearance of images on a Web page
- Work with client-side image maps

CASE

Announcing the 1999 Space Expo

MidWest University has one of the top departments in the country for the study of astronomy and astrophysics. The university is also home to the Center for Space Science and Engineering, which works with the government and with industry to create products to be used on the Space Shuttle, space probes, and communications and weather satellites. Tom Calloway is the director of public relations for the center.

One of the major events of the year is the Space Expo, held in late April, at which professors and graduate students showcase their research. The purpose of the Expo is to allow representatives from industry, academia, and the government to meet and discuss new ideas and emerging trends. In recent years, the Expo has caught the imagination of the general public, and Tom has made a major effort to schedule events for schools and families to attend. The Expo has become not only an important public relations event, but also an important fund-raiser for the department and the center.

It is early March, less than two months before the Expo, and Tom would like you to create a page advertising the Space Expo on the World Wide Web. The page should provide all the necessary information about Expo events, and it should also catch the eye of the reader through the use of interesting graphics and color.

SESSION

3.1

In this session you will explore how HTML handles and defines color. You'll learn how to add color to a Web page's background and text. You'll also see how to liven up your page with a background image.

Working with Color in HTML

The time of the 1999 Space Expo is drawing close, and Tom has called you to discuss the appearance of the Web page advertising the event. Tom has already written the text of the page, as shown in Figure 3-1.

Figure 3-1 ◀
The 1999
Space Expo
Web page

> ## The 1999 Space Expo
>
> **More than 60 exhibits and events await visitors at the 1999 Space Expo,**
> ***Looking Towards the Future***
> **Friday-Sunday, April 24-26**
>
> The 1999 Space Expo is an annual, student-run event that showcases recent developments in astronomy and space sciences and demonstrates how these developments can be applied to everyday life. The event includes student, government and industrial exhibits, and features presentations from NASA, Ball Aerospace, Rockwell, and IBM.
>
> The 1999 Space Expo will feature activities for the kids, including *Creating a Comet, Building a Model Rocket,* and *The Inter-Galactic Scavenger Hunt.* Friday is Students' Day, with school children in grades K-8 displaying astronomy and space science projects and competing for individual and school achievement awards.
>
> Professor Greg Stewart's famous astronomy show is also coming to the Space Expo. Professor Stewart will show the wonders of the night sky and discuss the nature of quasars, exploding stars, and black holes. Presentations will be at the Brinkman Planetarium at 1 p.m. and 3 p.m., Friday through Sunday.
>
> Please check out these other events:
>
> - <u>Bryd Hall</u>   Rockwell representatives and graduate students will display some of the latest advances in robotics for use in the Space Shuttle missions.
> - <u>Mitchell Theatre</u>   Famous astronomer and popular science writer, Kathy White, will present a talk, "Forward to Mars and Beyond," on Saturday at 7 p.m. Tickets for this very special event are $12. Seating is limited.
> - <u>Astronomy Classrooms</u>   Graduate students and professors display the results of their research in atmospherics, satellite technology, climatology, and space engineering.
>
> The 1999 Space Expo is located on the engineering and physics campus, north of Granger Stadium, and is open to the public on April 24 (Students' Day) from 10 a.m.-5 p.m., April 25 from 9 a.m.-7 p.m. and April 26 from 11 a.m.-5 p.m. Admission is $4.00 for the general public and $3.00 for senior citizens and students. Children four and under will be admitted free.
>
> **Sponsored by the Department of Astronomy and the Center for Space Science and Engineering.**

Tom is satisfied with the page's content, but he wants you to work on the design of the page. For example, he'd like you to add a colorful background or background image to the page for visual interest, and modify the appearance of some of the text as well. He also would like you to add some graphics to the document, including the official logo of this year's Expo, as well as photographs of the Space Center. As the public relations director, he wants the Web page to be as visually appealing as possible so that it catches the viewer's eye.

Tom leaves you with a list of files, images, and photos to work with. You'll begin working on a color scheme for the page. But before doing that, you must first learn how to handle color within HTML.

Using Color Names

If you've worked with color in a graphics or desktop publishing program, you've probably selected and identified your color choices without much difficulty, because those packages usually have graphical interfaces. When working with color in HTML files, however, you have to create color schemes using text-based HTML tags. Trying to describe a color in textual terms can be a challenge.

HTML identifies a color in one of two ways: either by the color's name or by a description of the color's appearance. Both methods have their advantages and disadvantages. You'll first learn about color names.

There are 16 color names that are recognized by all versions of HTML. These color names are shown in Figure 3-2.

Figure 3-2 ◀
The 16 basic
color names

Aqua	Gray	Navy	Silver
Black	Green	Olive	Teal
Blue	Lime	Purple	White
Fuchsia	Maroon	Red	Yellow

As you can see, the list of color names is fairly basic: red, blue, green, black, white, and so forth. As long as you keep to simple color combinations, you can rely solely upon these color names to set up color schemes for your Web pages, and those color schemes will be understood by all graphical browsers.

However, a list of 16 color names is limiting, so some browsers (Netscape Navigator and Internet Explorer) now support an extension to this list of color names. Figure 3-3 shows a partial list of these additional color names. The extended color name list allows you to create color schemes with greater color variation. A fuller list is provided in the appendices.

Figure 3-3 ◀
Partial list
of extended
color names

Blueviolet	Gold	Orange	Seagreen
Chocolate	Hotpink	Paleturquoise	Sienna
Darkgoldenrod	Indigo	Peachpuff	Snow
Firebrick	Mintcream	Salmon	Tan

One problem with using a color name list is that, while it's easy to specify a blue background, "blue" might not be specific enough for your purposes. How do you specify a "light blue background with a touch of green"? To do so, you would have to look through a long list of color names before finding that Paleturquoise is close to the color you want. Even so, some users might try to access your page with older browsers that do not support the long list of color names. In that situation you would lose control over your page's appearance, and it might end up being unreadable on those browsers.

In cases where you want to have more control and more choices over the colors in your Web page, you must use a color value.

Using Color Values

A **color value** is a numerical expression that exactly describes a color's appearance. To understand how HTML uses numbers to represent colors, you have to examine some of the basic principles of color theory.

In classical color theory, any color can be thought of as a combination of three primary colors: red, green, and blue. You are probably familiar with the color diagram shown in Figure 3-4, in which the colors yellow, magenta, cyan, and white are produced by combining the three primary colors. By varying the intensity of each primary color, you can create any color and any shade of color that you want. This principle allows your computer monitor to combine pixels of red, green, and blue light to create the array of colors you see on your screen.

Figure 3-4 ◀
Combining
the three
primary colors

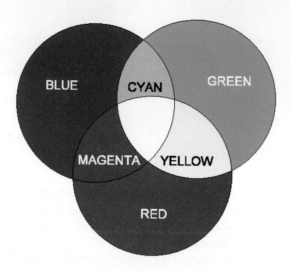

Software programs, like your Web browser, use a mathematical approach to define color. The intensity of each of the three primary colors is assigned a number from 0 (absence of color) to 255 (highest intensity). In this way, 255^3, or more than 16.7 million, distinct colors can be defined—more combinations than the human eye can distinguish. Each color is represented by a triplet of numbers, called an **RGB triplet**, based on its **R**ed, **G**reen, and **B**lue components. For example, white has a triplet of (255,255,255), indicating that red, green, and blue are equally mixed at the highest intensity. Gray is defined with the triplet (192,192,192), indicating an equal mixture of the primary colors with less intensity than white. Yellow has the triplet (255,255,0) because it is an equal mixture of red and green with no presence of blue. In most programs, you make your color choices with visual clues, usually without being aware of the underlying RGB triplet. Figure 3-5 shows a typical Colors dialog box in which you would make color selections based on the appearance of the color, rather than on the RGB values.

Figure 3-5 ◀
A typical Colors
dialog box

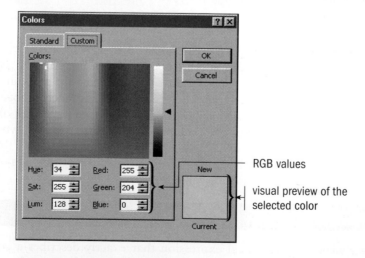

RGB values

visual preview of the
selected color

It is these RGB triplets that you have to enter into your HTML code if you want to express the exact appearance of a color. HTML requires that such color values be entered as hexadecimals. A **hexadecimal** is a number that is represented using 16 as a base rather than 10. In base 10 counting, you use combinations of 10 characters (0 through 9) to represent all of the integers, whereas hexadecimals include 6 extra characters: A (for 10), B (for 11), C (for 12), D (for 13), E (for 14), and F (for 15). For values above 15, you use a combination of the 16 characters; 16 is expressed as "10," 17 is expressed as "11," and so forth. To represent a number in hexadecimal, you convert the value to multiples of 16 plus a remainder. For example, twenty-one is equal to (16 x 1) + 5, so its hexadecimal representation is 15. The number 255 is equal to (16 x 15) + 15, or FF in hexadecimal format (remember that F=15 in hexadecimal). In the case of the number 255, the first F represents the number of times 16 goes into 255 (which is 15), and the second F represents the remainder of 15.

Once you know the RGB triplet of a color you want to use in your Web page, you need to convert that triplet to hexadecimal format and express it in a single string of six characters. For example, the color yellow has the RGB triplet (255,255,0), which is represented by the hexadecimal string FFFF00. Figure 3-6 shows the RGB triplets and hexadecimal equivalents for the 16 basic color names presented earlier.

Figure 3-6 ◄
Color names,
RGB triplets,
and
hexadecimal
values

Color Name	RGB Triplet	Hexadecimal	Color Name	RGB Triplet	Hexadecimal
Aqua	(0,255,255)	00FFFF	Navy	(0,0,128)	000080
Black	(0,0,0)	000000	Olive	(128,128,0)	808000
Blue	(0,0,255)	0000FF	Purple	(128,0,128)	800080
Fuchsia	(255,0,255)	FF00FF	Red	(255,0,0)	FF0000
Gray	(128,128,128)	808080	Silver	(192,192,192)	C0C0C0
Green	(0,128,0)	008000	Teal	(0,128,128)	008080
Lime	(0,255,0)	00FF00	White	(255,255,255)	FFFFFF
Maroon	(128,0,0)	800000	Yellow	(255,255,0)	FFFF00

At this point you might be wondering if you have to become a math major before you can even start adding color to your Web pages. In practice, Web authors rely on several tools to generate HTML code for specific colors. Some of the resources you can use on the World Wide Web are shown in Figure 3-7. You might also choose to create your initial code with an HTML editor, defining your color scheme with a Colors dialog box similar to the one shown earlier. Once that code is generated, you can further modify it within your text editor.

Figure 3-7 ◄
Color selection
resources
available on the
World Wide Web

Title	URL	Description
The Color Center	http://www.hidaho.com/colorcenter/	A Web page that allows you to interactively select page colors and textures and fragments of HTML code
Thalia's Color Page	http://www.sci.kun.nl/thalia/guide/color/	A Web page containing color databases, an application to interactively select your color scheme, and additional information on HTML and color issues
Color Browser	http://www.maximized.com/shareware/colorbrowser/	A Windows program to view and select colors
HTML-Color Pickers	http://tucows.hunterlink.net.au/mac/colormac.html	An overview of various color pickers for Windows and Macintosh computers.

However you decide to work with color in your Web pages, it's important to understand how HTML handles color, if for no other reason than to be able to interpret the source code of HTML files you'll find on the Web.

Specifying a Color Scheme for Your Page

After reviewing the issues surrounding color and HTML, you are ready to add color to the Web page that Tom has given you. Web browsers have a default color scheme that they apply to the background and text of the pages they retrieve. In most cases this scheme will involve black text on a white or gray background, with hypertext highlighted in purple and blue. You can override the default color scheme of the browser by specifying one of your own for your Web page. To do this, you'll need to modify the properties of the page using the <BODY> tag.

REFERENCE window	**DEFINING A COLOR SCHEME**
	■ Locate the <BODY> tag in your HTML file.
	■ Edit the <BODY> tag to read:
	<BODY BGCOLOR=*color* TEXT=*color* LINK=*color* VLINK=*color*>
	where BGCOLOR is the background color property, TEXT is the text color property, LINK is the color of hypertext links, and VLINK is the color of hypertext links that have been previously visited.
	For *color*, enter either the color name or the hexadecimal value formatted as "#hexadecimal_number".

In your work with HTML, you've used the <BODY> tag to identify the section of the HTML file containing the content that users would see in their browsers. At that point, the <BODY> tag had no purpose other than to separate the content of the Web page from other items such as the page's title and file heading. But the <BODY> tag can also be used to indicate the colors on your page. The syntax for controlling a page's color scheme through the <BODY> tag is:

```
<BODY BGCOLOR=color TEXT=color LINK=color VLINK=color>
```

Here, the BGCOLOR property sets the background color, the TEXT property controls text color, the LINK property defines the color of hypertext links, and the VLINK property defines the color of links that have been previously visited by the user. The value of *color* will be either one of the accepted color names or the color's hexadecimal value. If you use the hexadecimal value, you must preface the hexadecimal string with the pound symbol (#) and enclose the string in double quotation marks. For example, the HTML tag to create a background color with the hexadecimal value FFCO88 is:

```
<BODY BGCOLOR="#FFCO88">
```

After viewing various color combinations, Tom has decided that he'd like you to use a color scheme of white text on a dark green background. He also wants the hypertext links to appear in red, with previously visited links appearing in turquoise. Using color values he retrieved from a graphics program, Tom has learned that the RGB triplet for the dark green background is (0,102,0), which you'll enter as "#006600" in the <BODY> tag.

To change the color scheme of the Expo Web page:

1. Open your text editor.

2. Open the file **Expotext.htm** from the Tutorial.03 folder on your Student Disk, and then save the file in the same folder as **Expo1999.htm**.

3. Within the <BODY> tag at the top of the file, type **BGCOLOR="#006600" TEXT=WHITE LINK=RED VLINK=TURQUOISE**.

   Your file should appear as displayed in Figure 3-8.

Figure 3-8 ◀
Modified
<BODY> tag

background color

text color

hypertext color

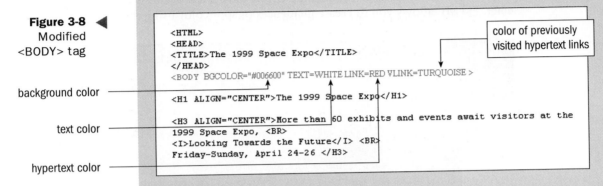

```
<HTML>
<HEAD>
<TITLE>The 1999 Space Expo</TITLE>
</HEAD>
<BODY BGCOLOR="#006600" TEXT=WHITE LINK=RED VLINK=TURQUOISE >

<H1 ALIGN="CENTER">The 1999 Space Expo</H1>

<H3 ALIGN="CENTER">More than 60 exhibits and events await visitors at the
1999 Space Expo, <BR>
<I>Looking Towards the Future</I> <BR>
Friday-Sunday, April 24-26 </H3>
```

color of previously
visited hypertext links

4. Save the changes to the Expo1999.htm file, but leave the text editor open. You'll be revising this file throughout this session.

5. Open your Web browser and view the Expo1999.htm file. See Figure 3-9.

Figure 3-9 ◀
The 1999
Space Expo
page with the
new color
scheme

white text

dark green
background

hypertext links
appear in red

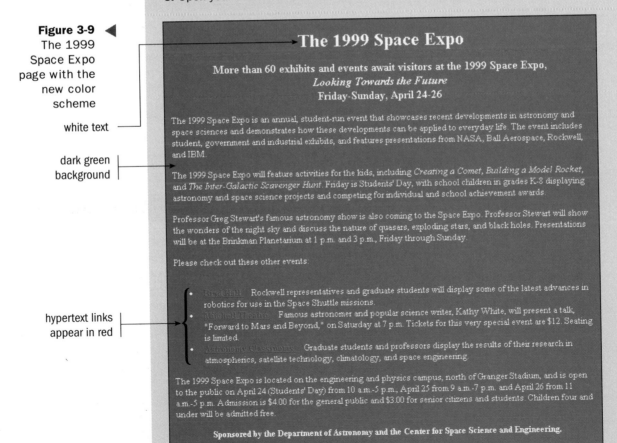

The Expo page now appears with white text on a dark green background. Hypertext links will show up in red and turquoise (you'll need to scroll the window to see the hypertext links). By adding the color scheme to the <BODY> tag of the HTML file, you've superceded the browser's default color scheme with one of your own.

Modifying Text with the <FONT> Tag

Specifying the text color in the <BODY> tag of your Web page changed the color of all the text on the page. Occasionally you will want to change the color of individual words or characters within the page. Color that affects only a few sections of a page is called **spot color**. HTML allows you to create incidences of spot color using the <FONT> tag.

REFERENCE window

MODIFYING TEXT APPEARANCE WITH THE <FONT> TAG

- In your Web page, locate the text whose appearance you want to modify.
- Place the text within the <FONT> tag as follows:
  <FONT SIZE=*sizevalue* COLOR=*color* FACE=*fontname*> Revised Text </FONT>
  where SIZE is the actual size of the text or the amount by which you want to increase or decrease the size of the text, in points; COLOR is the color name or color value you want to apply to the text; and FACE is the name of the font you want to use for the text.

You've already worked with some character tags that allow you to bold or italicize individual characters. The <FONT> tag gives you even more control by allowing you to specify the color, the size, and even the font to be used for the text on your page. The syntax for the <FONT> tag is:

```
<FONT SIZE=size COLOR=color FACE=font> Revised Text </FONT>
```

The <FONT> tag has three properties: size, color, and face. Your only concern right now is to use the <FONT> tag to change text color, but it's worthwhile exploring the other properties of the tag at this time.

Changing the Font Size

The SIZE property allows you to specify the font size of the revised text. The SIZE value can be expressed in either absolute or relative terms. For example, if you want your text to have a size of 2 points, you enter SIZE=2 in the <FONT> tag. On the other hand, if you want to increase the font size by 2 points relative to the surrounding text, you enter SIZE=+2 in the tag. Figure 3-10 shows the various point sizes as they appear in the browser.

Figure 3-10 ◀
Examples
of different
point sizes

This is 1 point text
This is 2 point text
This is 3 point text
This is 4 point text
This is 5 point text
This is 6 point text
This is 7 point text

For comparison, text formatted with the <H1> tag corresponds by default to bold, 6 point text; the <H2> tag is equivalent to bold, 5-point text, and so forth. Figure 3-11 presents a complete comparison of header tags and point sizes.

Figure 3-11 ◀
Header tags
and point sizes

Tag	Format
<H1>	6 point, bold
<H2>	5 point, bold
<H3>	4 point, bold
<H4>	3 point, bold
<H5>	2 point, bold
<H6>	1 point, bold
Normal text (no <H*i*> tag)	3 point, not bold

So, if you use the property SIZE=+1 to increase the size of text enclosed within an <H3> tag, the net effect will be to produce text that is 5 points in size and bold. Note that the largest font size supported by browsers is 7 points.

Changing the Font Color

The COLOR property allows you to change the color of individual characters or words. As when creating a color scheme, you specify the color by using either an accepted color name or the color value. For example, to change the color of the word "Expo" to the color value 8000C0, you would enter the following HTML tag:

```
<FONT COLOR="#8000C0"> Expo </FONT>
```

The text surrounding the word "Expo" would still be formatted in the color scheme specified in the <BODY> tag, or in the default scheme used by the Web browser.

Changing the Font Face

The final property of the <FONT> tag is the FACE property. You use the FACE property to indicate the font the text should be displayed in. This property is a bit of a departure from earlier versions of HTML, in which the browser alone determined the font used in the Web page. With the FACE property you can override the browser's choice. For this to work, you must specify a font that is installed on the user's computer. But, because you have no way of knowing which fonts have been installed, the FACE property allows you to specify a list of potential font names. The browser will attempt to use the first font in the list; if that fails, it will try the second font, and so on to the end of the list. If none of the fonts listed matches a font installed on the user's computer, the browser will ignore this property and use the default font. For example, to display the word "Expo" in a font without serifs, you could enter the following HTML tag:

```
<FONT FACE="ARIAL, HELVETICA, SANS SERIF"> Expo </FONT>
```

In this example, each of the three specified fonts is a non-serif font. The browser will first attempt to display the word "Expo" in the Arial font. If that fails, it will try the Helvetica font, and after that it will try the Sans Serif font. If none of these fonts are installed on the user's computer, the browser will use the default font.

DESIGN
window

WORKING WITH TEXT

- Do not overwhelm your page with different font sizes, colors, and font faces. Using a minimal number of font styles gives your page a uniform appearance that is easy to read.
- Avoid using the same color for normal text as you do for hypertext links, so that you do not confuse the reader.
- If you use a particular font face for your text, specify a list of alternate font names to accommodate different operating systems.

Using the <FONT> Tag for Spot Color

As you can see, the <FONT> tag gives you a lot of control over the appearance of individual blocks of text. At this point, though, you are only interested in using the <FONT> tag for spot color. Tom wants the name of this year's event, "Looking Towards the Future," to stand out on the page. To accomplish this, you'll format the line of text so that the title appears in yellow.

To change the appearance of the Expo title:

1. Return to your text editor and the Expo1999.htm file.

2. Enclose the title within the <FONT> tag as follows:

   <FONT COLOR=YELLOW> Looking Towards the Future </FONT>

The Expo1999.htm file should now appear as shown in Figure 3-12.

Figure 3-12 ◀
Using the
<FONT> tag
to create
spot color

text will appear
in yellow

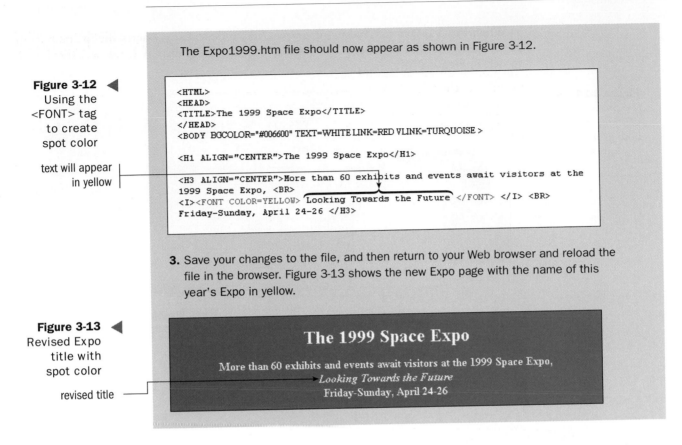

```
<HTML>
<HEAD>
<TITLE>The 1999 Space Expo</TITLE>
</HEAD>
<BODY BGCOLOR="#006600" TEXT=WHITE LINK=RED VLINK=TURQUOISE >

<H1 ALIGN="CENTER">The 1999 Space Expo</H1>

<H3 ALIGN="CENTER">More than 60 exhibits and events await visitors at the
1999 Space Expo, <BR>
<I><FONT COLOR=YELLOW> Looking Towards the Future </FONT> </I> <BR>
Friday-Sunday, April 24-26 </H3>
```

3. Save your changes to the file, and then return to your Web browser and reload the file in the browser. Figure 3-13 shows the new Expo page with the name of this year's Expo in yellow.

Figure 3-13 ◀
Revised Expo
title with
spot color

revised title

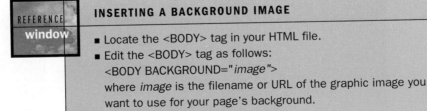

The 1999 Space Expo

More than 60 exhibits and events await visitors at the 1999 Space Expo,
Looking Towards the Future
Friday-Sunday, April 24-26

You show the revised page to Tom. He likes the use of color in the page and the spot color, but feels that the background needs work. He's seen Web pages that have graphic images used for backgrounds, and he'd like you to try something similar.

Inserting a Background Image

Another property of the <BODY> tag is the BACKGROUND property. With this property you can use a graphic file as a background image for your page. The syntax for inserting a background image is:

```
<BODY BACKGROUND="image">
```

Here, *image* is the name or URL of the graphic file you want to use. For example, to use a graphic file named "Bricks.gif" as your background image, you would enter:

```
<BODY BACKGROUND="Bricks.gif">
```

REFERENCE window	**INSERTING A BACKGROUND IMAGE**
	■ Locate the <BODY> tag in your HTML file. ■ Edit the <BODY> tag as follows: 　<BODY BACKGROUND="*image*"> 　where *image* is the filename or URL of the graphic image you 　want to use for your page's background.

When the browser retrieves your graphic file, it repeatedly inserts the image into the page's background, in a process called **tiling**, until the entire display window is filled up, as shown in Figure 3-14.

Figure 3-14
The process of tiling the background image

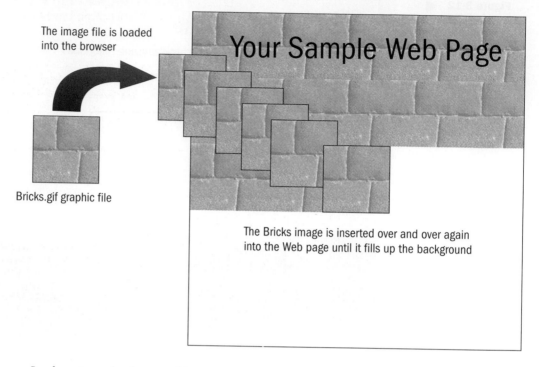

The image file is loaded into the browser

Your Sample Web Page

Bricks.gif graphic file

The Bricks image is inserted over and over again into the Web page until it fills up the background

In choosing a background image, you should remember the following:

- Use an image that will not detract from your page's text, making it hard to read.

- Do not use a large image file (more than 20 kilobytes). Large and complicated backgrounds will cause your page to take a long time to load, and no matter how attractive the page's background is, it won't impress people who won't wait around to see it.

- The background should appear seamless to the user. Use images that will not show boundaries and grids when tiled.

Figure 3-15 shows examples of well-designed and poorly designed Web page backgrounds.

Figure 3-15
Examples of Web page backgrounds

Background overwhelms the text in the foreground

Background shows distracting seams between image tiles

Background does not show seams or overwhelm the foreground text

Finding the right background image is a process of trial and error. You won't know for certain whether a background image works well until you actually view it in a browser. There are numerous collections of background images available on the Web. You can copy many of these and use them on your own pages for free. The only restriction is that you cannot sell or distribute the images in a commercial product. Figure 3-16 provides a short list of these collections.

Figure 3-16 ◀
Places on the Web to get background images

Title	URL	Description
3D Netscape Backgrounds	http://www.sonic.net/~lberlin/new/3dnscape.html	A collection of heavily textured and colored backgrounds
Founder's Background Samplers	http://www.mei-web.de/backgrounds/back_main.shtml	A collection of background images from around the world
Netscape's Background Sampler	http://www.netscape.com/assist/net_sites/bg/backgrounds.html	A collection of backgrounds from Netscape
SBN Image Gallery	http://www.microsoft.com/gallery/images/default.asp	A collection of images and backgrounds from the Microsoft Site Builder Network
Cool Archive	http://www.coolarchive.com/	An archive of images, backgrounds, buttons and icons
The Design Shoppe	http://www.thedesign-shoppe.com/	Free, original graphics for Web pages

After searching, Tom has found a graphic he thinks will work well for the Expo. The image, named Space.jpg, is shown in Figure 3-17.

Figure 3-17 ◀
Space.jpg background image

Next, you'll add this image to the 1999 Space Expo background.

To add the Space.jpg graphic file to the background:

1. Return to your text editor and the Expo1999.htm file.

2. Modify the <BODY> tag, replacing the BGCOLOR property with:
   BACKGROUND="Space.jpg"

The revised <BODY> tag should now appear as shown in Figure 3-18.

Figure 3-18 ◀
Specifying the
Space.jpg
graphic as a
background
image

the background
image property

```
<HTML>
<HEAD>
<TITLE>The 1999 Space Expo</TITLE>
</HEAD>
<BODY BACKGROUND="Space.jpg" TEXT=WHITE LINK=RED VLINK=TURQUOISE >

<H1 ALIGN="CENTER">The 1999 Space Expo</H1>

<H3 ALIGN="CENTER">More than 60 exhibits and events await visitors at the
1999 Space Expo, <BR>
<I><FONT COLOR=YELLOW> Looking Towards the Future </FONT> </I> <BR>
Friday-Sunday, April 24-26 </H3>
```

3. Save your changes to Expo1999.htm, and then view the page in your Web browser. Figure 3-19 shows the new background for the Expo page.

Figure 3-19 ◀
Space Expo
Web page with
the background
image

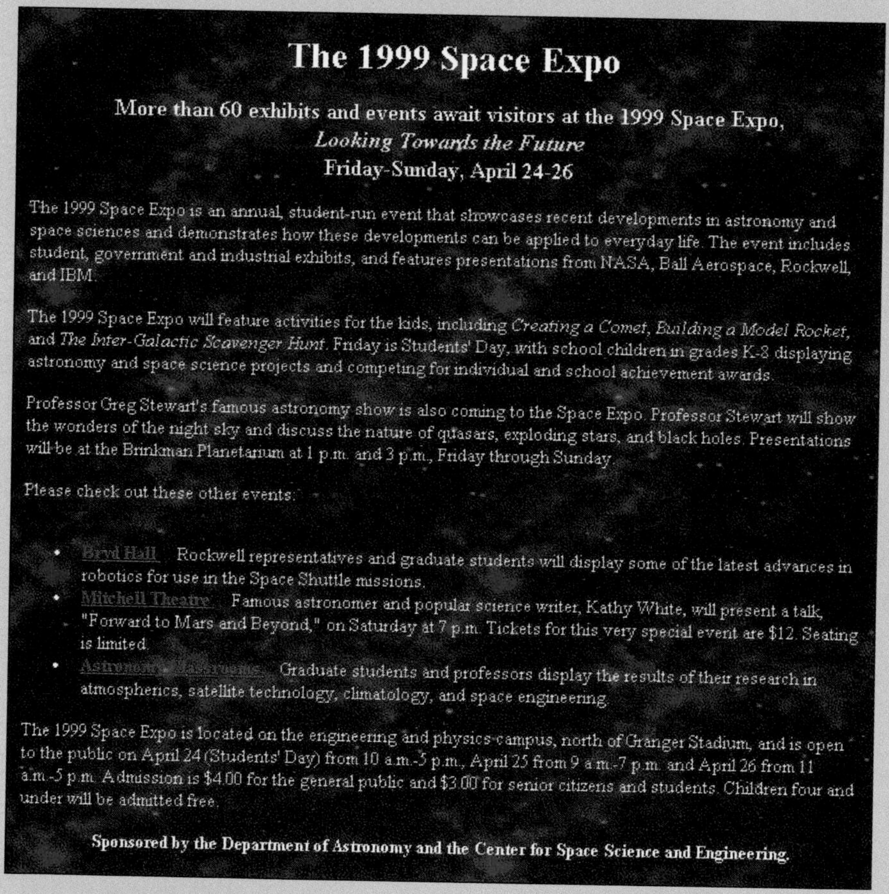

Tom is pleased with the impact of the new page background. He notes that the size of the image file is not too large (only 6 kilobytes) and that it does not show any obvious seams between the image tiles. Also, the background does not overwhelm the content of the Web page, and it fits in well with the theme of the Space Expo.

Quick Check

1. What are the two ways of specifying a color in an HTML file? What are the advantages and disadvantages of each?

2. What tag would you enter in your HTML file to use a color scheme of red text on a gray background, with hypertext links displayed in blue, and previously visited hypertext links displayed in yellow?

3. What is spot color?

4. What tag would you enter to format the words "Major Sale" in red, with a font size 5 points larger than the surrounding text?

5. What tag would you enter to display the text "Major Sale" in the Times New Roman font and, if that font is not available, in the MS Serif font?

6. What tag would you enter to use the graphic file "Stars.gif" as the background image for a Web page?

7. Name three things you should avoid when using a background image for your Web page.

In the next session, you'll learn more about handling graphics with HTML as you add inline images to the Expo1999.htm file.

SESSION 3.2

In this session you will learn about different graphic file formats and how you can use them to add special effects to your Web page. You'll explore the advantages and disadvantages of each format. Finally, you'll learn how to control the size, placement, and appearance of your page's inline images.

Understanding Image Formats

Having finished adding color to the Expo Web page, you now turn to the task of adding graphics. The two image formats supported by most Web browsers are GIF and JPEG. Choosing the appropriate image format for your graphics is an important part of Web page design. You have to balance the goal of creating an interesting and attractive page against the need to keep the size of your page small and easy to retrieve. Each graphic format has its advantages and disadvantages, and you will probably use a combination of both in your Web page designs. First you'll look at the advantages and disadvantages of GIF image files.

Working with GIF Files

GIF (Graphics Interchange Format) is the most commonly used image format on the Web. Web pages with GIF image files should be compatible with any graphical browser users have. GIF files are limited to displaying 256 colors, so they are more often used for graphics requiring fewer colors, such as clip art images, line art, logos, and icons. Images that require more color depth, such as photographs, often appear grainy when saved as GIFs. There are actually two GIF file formats: GIF87 and GIF89a. The GIF89a format, the newer standard, includes enhancements such as interlacing, transparent colors, and animation. You'll explore these enhancements now, and learn how to use them in your Web page design. First you'll look at interlacing.

Interlaced and Noninterlaced GIFs

Interlacing refers to the way the GIF file is saved by the graphics software. Normally, with a **noninterlaced** GIF the image is saved one line at a time, starting from the top of the graphic and moving downward. The graphic image is retrieved as it was saved: starting from the top of the image and moving down. Figure 3-20 shows how a noninterlaced GIF appears as it is slowly retrieved by the Web browser. If the graphic is large, it might take several minutes for the entire image to appear. People who access your page might find this annoying if the part of the image that interests them is located at the bottom.

Figure 3-20 ◀
Noninterlaced
image as
the browser
retrieves it

top appears first

image appears one
line at a time

entire image is
retrieved

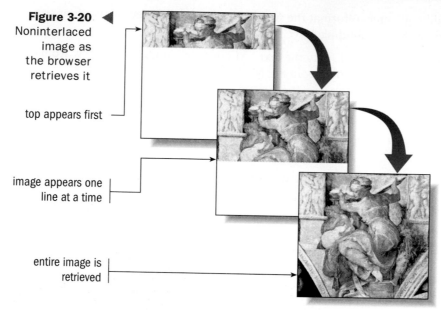

With **interlaced** GIFs, the image is saved and retrieved "stepwise." For example, every fifth line of the image might appear first, followed by every sixth line, and so forth through the remaining rows. As shown in Figure 3-21, the effect of interlacing is that the graphic starts out as a blurry representation of the final image, then gradually comes into focus—unlike the noninterlaced graphic, which is always a sharp image as it's being retrieved, although an incomplete one.

Figure 3-21 ◀
Interlaced
image as
the browser
retrieves it

a rough image
appears first

image starts to show
more detail

final image is crisp
and detailed

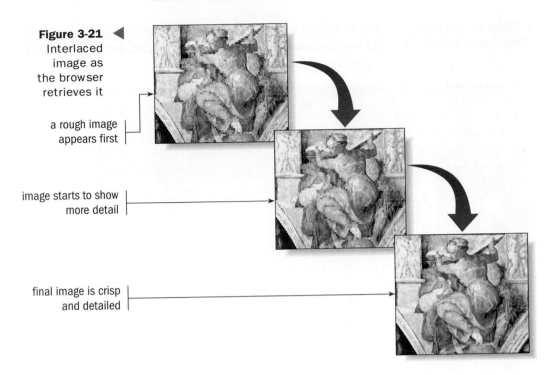

Interlacing is an effective format if you have a large graphic and want to give users a preview of the final image. They get an idea of what the image looks like and can decide whether to wait for it to come into focus. The downside of interlacing is that it increases the size of the GIF file—anywhere from 3 to 20 kilobytes, depending on the image.

Transparent GIFs

Another enhancement of the GIF89a format is the ability to create transparent colors. A **transparent color** is a color from the image that is not displayed when the image appears in the browser. In place of that color, the browser will display whatever happens to appear on the page background. This effect integrates inline images with the page background. The process by which you create a transparent color depends on your graphics software. Many packages include extra options you can select when saving images in GIF89a format. One of these is to designate a particular color from the image as transparent. Other packages include a transparent color tool, which you use to click the color from the image that you want saved as transparent.

Tom has a graphic created in the GIF89a format that displays the official logo for the 1999 Space Expo. He wants you to replace the text heading from the Expo1999.htm file with the graphic image. The logo is shown in Figure 3-22.

Figure 3-22 ◀
The 1999
Space Expo
logo

the red background
color will appear
transparent when
displayed in
the browser

When the graphic was created, the red background color was designated as transparent. This means that when you insert the graphic into your Web page, the background image you inserted in the previous session will show through in places where red now appears. To see how this works, you'll replace the text heading with the logo.

To insert the logo in your HTML file:

1. If you took a break after the previous session, start your text editor and reopen the Expo1999.htm file from the Tutorial.03 folder of your Student Disk.

2. Go to the top of the page and replace the text within the <H1> tag with the following <IMG> tag:

   <IMG SRC="Logo.gif">

   Figure 3-23 shows the modified section of the Expo1999.htm file.

Figure 3-23 ◀
Inserting the
logo image into
the page
heading

the logo image file ——

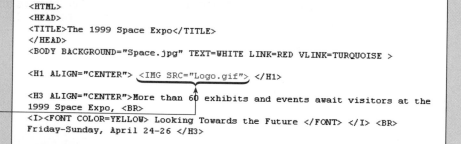

```
<HTML>
<HEAD>
<TITLE>The 1999 Space Expo</TITLE>
</HEAD>
<BODY BACKGROUND="Space.jpg" TEXT=WHITE LINK=RED VLINK=TURQUOISE >

<H1 ALIGN="CENTER"> <IMG SRC="Logo.gif"> </H1>

<H3 ALIGN="CENTER">More than 60 exhibits and events await visitors at the
1999 Space Expo, <BR>
<I><FONT COLOR=YELLOW> Looking Towards the Future </FONT> </I> <BR>
Friday-Sunday, April 24-26 </H3>
```

3. Save your changes, and then load the file in your Web browser. The browser displays the revised page with the logo, as shown in Figure 3-24.

Figure 3-24 ◀
Space Expo
logo in the
Web page

logo background
is transparent

Note that the background image is visible beneath the graphic in those locations
where red text appeared in the original image.

Animated GIFs

One of the most popular uses of GIF files in recent years has been to create animated
images. Compared to video clips, animated GIFs are easier to create and smaller in size.
An animated GIF is composed of several graphic images, each one slightly different. When
the GIF image is displayed in the Web browser, the images are displayed one after another
in rapid succession, creating the animated effect. To create animated GIFs, you need special software. Figure 3-25 provides a list of such programs available on the Web.

Figure 3-25 ◀
Software to
create
animated GIFs

Title	URL	Platform
GifBuilder	http://iawww.epfl.ch/Staff/ Yves.Piguet/clip2gif-home/ GifBuilder.html	Macintosh
Gif.glf.giF	http://www.cafe.net/peda/ggg/	Windows, Macintosh
GIF Construction Set	http://www.mindworkshop.com/ alchemy/gifcon.html	Windows
AniMagic	http://rtlsoft.com/ animagic/	Windows

Animated GIF software allows you to control the rate at which the animation plays (in
number of frames per second) and to determine the number of times the animation will be
repeated before halting. You can also set the animation to loop continuously. Most of these
packages will import and combine individual GIF files, but some also provide tools to create special transitions between one GIF image and another. For example, you could use the
software to gradually fade from one image into another, in a process called **morphing**.

If you don't want to take the time to create your own animated GIFs, many animated GIF collections are available on the Web. Figure 3-26 lists a few of them.

Figure 3-26 ◄
Animated GIF
collections

Title	URL
Netscape Animated GIFs	http://www.netscape.com/assist/net_sites/starter/samples/animate.html
Yahoo! List of Animated GIF Collections	http://dir.yahoo.com/Arts/Visual_Arts/Animation/Computer_Animation/Animated_GIFs/
Gallery of GIF Animation	http://members.aol.com/royalef1/galframe.htm
GIF World	http://www.gifworld.com/

Because an animated GIF is much larger than the corresponding static GIF image, overusing animated GIFs can greatly increase the size of your page. You should also be careful not to overwhelm the user with animated images. Animated GIFs can quickly become a source of irritation to the user once the novelty has worn off, especially because there is no way for the user to turn them off! As with other GIF files, animated GIFs are limited to 256 colors, which makes them ideal for small icons and logos, but not for larger images.

To see whether an animated GIF will enhance the appearance of your Web page, you'll replace the existing Space 1999 Expo logo with an animated version of the logo.

To insert the animated logo in your HTML file:

1. Return to your text editor and the Expo1999.htm file.

2. Replace "Logo.gif" in the <IMG> tag at the top of the document with the filename **"LogoAnim.gif"**.

3. Save your changes, and then reload the file in your Web browser.

   As shown in Figure 3-27, the revised logo now shows a spinning Earth superimposed on the Space Expo title. Note as well that animated GIFs, like static GIFs, can use transparent colors.

Figure 3-27 ◄
Animated
GIF logo

animated globe

transparent
background

Not all Web browsers support animated GIFs. If a user tries to access your page with an older browser, only a static image of the first frame of the animation will be displayed.

Tom likes the new animated logo you've added. The next image you'll add to the page is a photo in the JPEG format.

Working with JPEG Files

The other important image format supported by most Web browsers is the JPEG format. **JPEG** stands for **Joint Photographic Experts Group**. The JPEG format differs from the GIF format in several ways. With JPEG files you can create graphics that use the full 16.7 million colors available in the color palette. Because of this, JPEG files are most often used for photographs and images that cover a wide spectrum of color.

Another feature of JPEG files is that they can be compressed, yielding image files that are usually (though not always) smaller than their GIF counterparts. For example, in the previous session you used the JPEG file Space.jpg as your background image. The file itself is only 6 Kb; however, if that image is converted to a GIF file, the size increases to 23 Kb. There are also situations in which the GIF format creates a smaller and better-looking image, such as when the image has large sections covered with a single color.

Compressing a graphic reduces the file size, but it might do so at the expense of image quality. Figure 3-28 shows the effect of increasing a compression on a JPEG file. As you can see, the increased compression cuts the file size to one-sixth of the original, but leaves much of the image blurry.

Figure 3-28 ◀
The effects of compression on JPEG file size and image quality

Minimal compression
File size=23 kb

Moderate compression
File size=11 kb

Medium compression
File size=7 kb

Heavy compression
File size=4 kb

By testing different compression levels with your graphics software, you can reduce the size of your JPEG files while maintaining an attractive image. Note that a smaller file size does not always mean that your page will load faster. The browser has to decompress the JPEG image when it retrieves it, and for a heavily compressed image this can take more time than retrieving and displaying a less-compressed file.

There are some other differences between JPEGs and GIFs. You cannot use transparent colors or animation with JPEG files, and standard JPEG files are not interlaced, which means that they do not "fade in" gradually as do interlaced GIFs. In recent years a new format called **Progressive JPEG** has been introduced, which allows for interlacing without increasing the size of the graphic file. Not all graphics programs and Web browsers support progressive JPEGs, however.

Tom wants you to add a photograph of the Center for Space Science and Engineering to the Expo Web page. The photo has been saved as a JPEG file named Center.jpg on your Student Disk. You will insert the image directly below the Expo logo.

To insert the Center photograph into your Web page:

1. Return to your text editor and the Expo1999.htm file.

2. Locate the paragraph that begins "The 1999 Space Expo is an annual, student-run event …" and then insert the following <IMG> tag after the paragraph's <P> tag:

```
<IMG SRC="Center.jpg">
```

Figure 3-29 shows the revised HTML code.

Figure 3-29 ◄
Adding the
Center JPEG
image to the
Expo Web page

```
<H1 ALIGN="CENTER"> <IMG SRC="LogoAnim.gif"> </H1>

<H3 ALIGN="CENTER">More than 60 exhibits and events await visitors at the
1999 Space Expo, <BR>
<I><FONT COLOR=YELLOW> Looking Towards the Future </FONT> </I> <BR>
Friday-Sunday, April 24-26 </H3>

<P> <IMG SRC="Center.jpg"> The 1999 Space Expo is an annual, student-run eve:
developments in astronomy and space sciences and demonstrates how these
developments can be applied to everyday life. The event includes student,
government and industrial exhibits, and features presentations from NASA,
Ball Aerospace, Rockwell, and IBM.</P>
```

image tag for the
Center JPEG file

3. Save your changes, and then reload the Expo1999.htm file in your Web browser. Figure 3-30 shows the revised page with the newly inserted JPEG graphic.

Figure 3-30 ◄
Space Center
inline image

the Space
Center photo

TROUBLE? If the graphic appears blurry or grainy, it could be because your monitor is capable of displaying only 256 colors and not the full palette of 16.7 million colors.

CHOOSING GRAPHIC IMAGE TYPES

DESIGN
window

Use GIF images when you want to:
- create animated graphics
- use transparent colors
- display logos or clip art containing up to 256 colors

Use JPEG images when you want to:
- display photographs
- use images that contain more than 256 colors
- reduce the size of your images through file compression

Using the ALT Property

One of the properties available with the <IMG> tag is the ALT property. The ALT property allows you to specify text that will appear in place of your inline images. Alternate image text is important because it allows users who have nongraphical browsers to learn the content of your graphics. Alternate image text also appears as a placeholder for the graphic while the page is loading. This is particularly important for users accessing your page through a slow dial-up connection.

SPECIFYING ALTERNATE TEXT FOR AN INLINE IMAGE

REFERENCE
window

- Locate the <IMG> tag for the inline image.
- Edit the <IMG> tag as follows:
  <IMG SRC="*image*" ALT="*alternate text*">
  where *image* is the filename or URL of the graphic image and *alternate text* is the text you want to have displayed in place of the image.

The syntax for specifying alternate text is:

```
<IMG SRC="image" ALT="alternate text">
```

You'll add the ALT property to the two <IMG> tags in your Expo Web page now.

To insert alternate image text into your Web page:

1. Return to the Expo1999.htm file in your text editor.

2. Within the <IMG> tag for the Expo logo, insert the text: **ALT="The 1999 Space Expo"**.

3. After the <IMG> tag for the Center photograph, insert the text: **ALT="The MWU Center for Space Science and Engineering"**.

Figure 3-31 shows the revised <IMG> tags for the Expo1999.htm file.

Figure 3-31 ◀
Specifying
alternate text
for the inline
images

alternate text

```
<HTML>
<HEAD>
<TITLE>The 1999 Space Expo</TITLE>
</HEAD>
<BODY BACKGROUND="Space.jpg" TEXT=WHITE LINK=RED VLINK=TURQUOISE >

<H1 ALIGN="CENTER"> <IMG SRC="LogoAnim.gif" ALT="The 1999 Space Expo" > </H1>

<H3 ALIGN="CENTER">More than 60 exhibits and events await visitors at the
1999 Space Expo, <BR>
<I><FONT COLOR=YELLOW> Looking Towards the Future </FONT> </I> <BR>
Friday-Sunday, April 24-26 </H3>

<P> <IMG SRC="Center.jpg" ALT="The MWU Center for Space Science and Engineering" >
The 1999 Space Expo is an annual, student-run event that showcases recent
developments in astronomy and space sciences and demonstrates how these
developments can be applied to everyday life. The event includes student,
government and industrial exhibits, and features presentations from NASA,
Ball Aerospace. Rockwell. and IBM.</P>
```

4. Save your changes to the file. Figure 3-32 shows the appearance of your Web page with the alternate text replacing the image. (You can create this effect by turning off the display of inline images within your browser, or by interrupting the retrieval of the Expo page before the two images are rendered.)

Figure 3-32 ◀
Alternate text
as it appears in
the Web page

alternate text

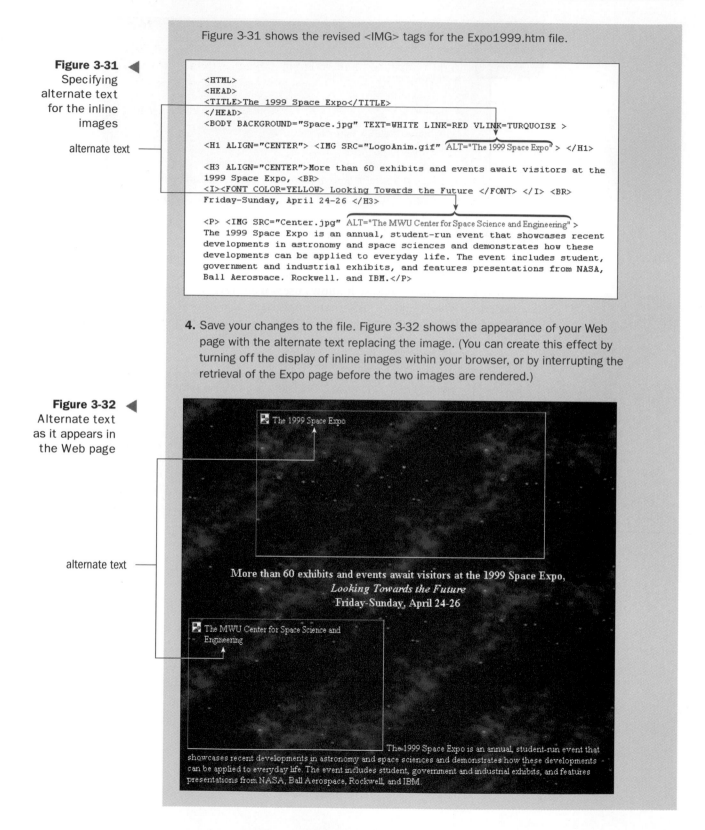

Now that you've entered the images on the page, your next task is to control their placement and appearance.

Controlling Image Placement and Size

You show Tom the progress you've made on the Web page. Although he's pleased with the graphic image of the Center, he wants you to modify the placement of the image on the page. With the image's current placement, the page now has a large blank space to the upper right of the image. Tom wonders if you could control the way text flows around the image so that there is less blank space. You can, using the ALIGN property of the <IMG> tag.

REFERENCE
window

ALIGNING TEXT AROUND AN IMAGE

- Locate the <IMG> tag for the inline image.
- Edit the <IMG> tag as follows:
  <IMG SRC="*image*" ALIGN=*alignment*>
  where *image* is the filename or URL of the graphic image, and *alignment* specifies how surrounding text should be aligned with the graphic (top, middle, bottom, left, or right).

Controlling Image Alignment

As you know, the ALIGN property can be used to control the alignment of paragraph tags. The ALIGN property fulfills a similar function in the <IMG> tag. The syntax for the ALIGN property is:

```
<IMG SRC="image"ALIGN=alignment>
```

Here, *alignment* is a value that indicates how you want the image aligned with the surrounding text. Different versions of HTML support different values for the ALIGN property. The three values for the ALIGN property accepted in all versions of HTML are Top, Middle, and Bottom. With ALIGN set to Top, the surrounding text aligns with the top of the image; the Middle setting aligns the text with the middle of the image; and the Bottom setting aligns the text with the bottom of the image.

Figure 3-33 shows the effect of each of these on text surrounding the Space Center image.

Figure 3-33 ◄
Effects of the
ALIGN property

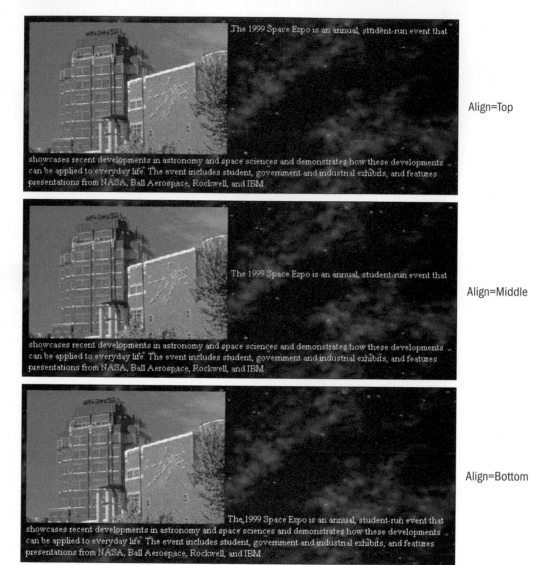

Align=Top

Align=Middle

Align=Bottom

Inserting an image works fine if you have only one line of text, or if the image itself is very small. However, if you are trying to integrate a large image with several lines, you will invariably create a lot of blank space, as illustrated in Figure 3-33.

Versions of HTML 3.0 and above, as well as the Netscape Navigator and Internet Explorer browsers, support an extension to the <IMG> tag that aligns the image with either the left or right margin of the page and wraps text around the image. By using the values LEFT and RIGHT for the ALIGN property, you can remove the blank space problem that Tom was concerned about.

Next, you'll align the Center image with the left side of the page, wrapping the surrounding text around the image.

To align the Center photograph on the left side of the page:

1. In the <IMG> tag for the Center photograph, insert the following text after the ALT property: **ALIGN=LEFT**.

Your revised <IMG> tag should appear as shown in Figure 3-34.

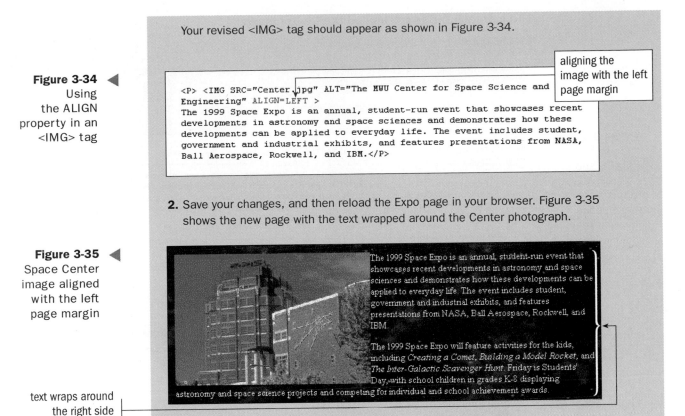

Figure 3-34 ◀
Using
the ALIGN
property in an
<IMG> tag

aligning the
image with the left
page margin

```
<P> <IMG SRC="Center.jpg" ALT="The NWU Center for Space Science and
Engineering" ALIGN=LEFT >
The 1999 Space Expo is an annual, student-run event that showcases recent
developments in astronomy and space sciences and demonstrates how these
developments can be applied to everyday life. The event includes student,
government and industrial exhibits, and features presentations from NASA,
Ball Aerospace, Rockwell, and IBM.</P>
```

2. Save your changes, and then reload the Expo page in your browser. Figure 3-35 shows the new page with the text wrapped around the Center photograph.

Figure 3-35 ◀
Space Center
image aligned
with the left
page margin

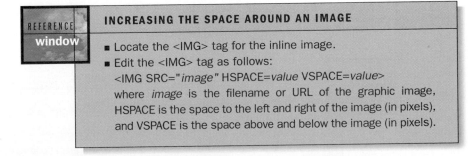

The 1999 Space Expo is an annual, student-run event that showcases recent developments in astronomy and space sciences and demonstrates how these developments can be applied to everyday life. The event includes student, government and industrial exhibits, and features presentations from NASA, Ball Aerospace, Rockwell, and IBM.

The 1999 Space Expo will feature activities for the kids, including *Creating a Comet, Building a Model Rocket,* and *The Inter-Galactic Scavenger Hunt.* Friday is Students' Day, with school children in grades K-8 displaying astronomy and space science projects and competing for individual and school achievement awards.

text wraps around
the right side

Because the LEFT and RIGHT alignment values are not supported by all browsers, some older browsers might not display your page correctly. However, almost all of the newer browsers should be able to render the page properly.

Controlling Vertical and Horizontal Space

Wrapping the text around the image has solved one problem: the large blank space has been removed. A second problem now exists, however—there's not enough space separating the image and the surrounding text, which makes the page appear crowded. You can increase the horizontal and vertical space around the image with the HSPACE and VSPACE properties, as follows:

`<IMG SRC="`*image*`"VSPACE=`*value*` HSPACE=`*value*`>`

The HSPACE property increases the space to the left and right of the image, and the VSPACE property increases the space above and below the image. The value of the VSPACE and HSPACE properties is measured in pixels. As with the ALIGN property, the HSPACE and VSPACE properties might not be supported by older browsers, but all new browsers should support them.

REFERENCE
window

INCREASING THE SPACE AROUND AN IMAGE

■ Locate the <IMG> tag for the inline image.
■ Edit the <IMG> tag as follows:
    <IMG SRC="*image*" HSPACE=*value* VSPACE=*value*>
    where *image* is the filename or URL of the graphic image,
    HSPACE is the space to the left and right of the image (in pixels),
    and VSPACE is the space above and below the image (in pixels).

You need to use the VSPACE and HSPACE properties to increase the space between the Center image and the surrounding text.

To increase the space around the Center image:

1. Return to the Expo1999.htm file in your text editor.

2. Within the <IMG> tag for the Center image, add the following properties and values: **VSPACE=5 HSPACE=10**.

   Your revised <IMG> tag should appear as shown in Figure 3-36.

Figure 3-36 ◄
Using the
HSPACE and
VSPACE
properties to
increase space
around the
image

```
<P> <IMG SRC="Center.jpg" ALT="The MWU Center for Space Science and
Engineering" ALIGN=LEFT VSPACE=5 HSPACE=10 >
The 1999 Space Expo is an annual, student-run event that showcases recent
developments in astronomy and space sciences and demonstrates how these
developments can be applied to everyday life. The event includes student,
government and industrial exhibits, and features presentations from NASA,
Ball Aerospace, Rockwell, and IBM.</P>
```

properties to increase
the vertical and
horizontal space

These property values will increase the gap to the left and right of the image to 10 pixels, and the gap above and below to 5 pixels.

3. Save your changes, and then reload the Expo page in your browser. The revised page shows an increased gap between the image and the surrounding text. See Figure 3-37. The page does not seem so crowded now.

Figure 3-37 ◄
Increased
vertical and
horizontal
space around
the Space
Center image

more space
around the image

Controlling Image Size

The final properties you'll be setting for the image are the HEIGHT and WIDTH properties, which tell the browser how large to make the image. You can use these properties to increase or decrease the size of the image on your page. Generally, if you want to decrease the size of an image, you should do so in a graphics package, because then you will also be reducing the size of the graphics file. Changing the size of the image within the <IMG> tag does not affect the file size. The syntax for setting the HEIGHT and WIDTH properties is:

    <IMG SRC="image" HEIGHT=value WIDTH=value>

REFERENCE
window

SPECIFYING THE SIZE OF AN INLINE IMAGE

- Locate the <IMG> tag for the inline image.
- Edit the <IMG> tag as follows:
  <IMG SRC="image" HEIGHT=value WIDTH=value>
  where "image" is the filename or URL of the graphic image, and
  HEIGHT and WIDTH are the dimensions of the image (in pixels).

Specifying the height and width of an image is a good idea, even if you're not trying to change the image's dimensions. Why? Because of the way browsers work with inline images. When a browser encounters an inline image, it has to calculate the image size, and then use this information to format the page. If you include the dimensions of the image, the browser does not have to perform that calculation, and the page will be displayed that much faster. To determine the size of an image, use your graphics software and record the dimension of each graphic on your page in pixels.

The LogoAnim image is 414 pixels wide by 209 pixels high, and the Space Center image is 280 pixels wide by 186 pixels high. You'll enter this information into the <IMG> tags for each image.

To specify the width and height of the two images:

1. Return to your text editor.

2. Within the <IMG> tag for the LogoAnim image, add the following properties and values: **WIDTH=414 HEIGHT=209**.

3. Within the <IMG> tag for the Space Center image, add the following properties and values: **WIDTH=280 HEIGHT=186**.

The revised Expo1999.htm file should appear as shown in Figure 3-38.

Figure 3-38 ◀
Specifying the
width and
height of the
inline images

width and
height properties

```
<H1 ALIGN="CENTER"> <IMG SRC="LogoAnim.gif" ALT="The 1999 Space Expo"
WIDTH=414 HEIGHT=209, > </H1>

<H3 ALIGN="CENTER">More than 60 exhibits and events await visitors at the
1999 Space Expo, <BR>
<I><FONT COLOR=YELLOW> Looking Towards the Future </FONT> </I> <BR>
Friday-Sunday, April 24-26 </H3>

<P> <IMG SRC="Center.jpg" ALT="The MWU Center for Space Science and
Engineering" ALIGN="LEFT" VSPACE=5 HSPACE=10 WIDTH=280 HEIGHT=186 >
The 1999 Space Expo is an annual, student-run event that showcases recent
developments in astronomy and space sciences and demonstrates how these
developments can be applied to everyday life. The event includes student,
government and industrial exhibits, and features presentations from NASA,
Ball Aerospace, Rockwell, and IBM.</P>
```

4. Save your changes, and then reload the Expo page in your browser. Confirm that the layout is the same as the last time you viewed the page, because you have not changed the dimensions of the inline images—you've simply included their dimensions in the HTML file.

General Tips for Working with Color and Images

You've completed much of the layout of the 1999 Space Expo page. When working with color and images in your Web page, keep in mind that the primary purpose of the page is to convey information. "A picture is worth a thousand words," and if an image can convey an idea quickly, by all means use it. If an image adds visual interest to your page and makes the user interested in what you have to say, include it. However, always be aware that overusing graphics can make your page difficult to read and cumbersome to display. With that in mind, this section provides some tips to remember as you work with color and images in your Web pages.

Reduce the Size of Your Pages

You should strive to make your page quick and easy to retrieve. If users will be accessing your page over a dial-up connection, the amount of material they can retrieve in a given time will be limited. For example, a user with a 14.4 kbps modem can retrieve information at a rate of about 1 kilobyte per second. If you have more than 30k of graphics on your page, that user will wait, on average, half a minute to see it. If you have more than 100k of graphics, the user might have to wait from 1½ to 2 minutes. Even with a 28.8 kbps modem, such a page could take a minute to load. A general rule of thumb is that the total amount of graphics on your Web page should be no more than 40 to 50 kilobytes. There are several ways to achieve this:

- Reduce the size of the images using your graphics software (not by simply changing the WIDTH and HEIGHT properties in the <IMG> tag).

- Reduce the number of colors used. Instead of saving an image in a 16.7 million color format, reduce it to 256 colors.

- Experiment with different graphic format types. Is the file size smaller with the JPEG format or the GIF? Can you compress the JPEG graphic without losing image quality?

- Use **thumbnails**—pictures that are reduced versions of your graphic images. Place the thumbnail image within a hypertext link to the larger, more detailed image, so that clicking the reduced image loads the better image. This gives users who really want to view the more well-defined image the option to do so.

- Reuse your images. If you are creating a Web presentation covering several pages, consider using the same background image for each page. Once a browser has retrieved the image file, it will store the image locally on the user's computer and will be able to retrieve it quickly to display it again, if necessary.

Finally, you should provide an alternate, text-only version of your Web page for those users who are either using a text-based browser or want to quickly load the information stored on your page without viewing inline images.

Manage Your Colors

Color can add a lot to your page, but it can also detract from it. Make sure that you have enough contrast between the text and the background. In other words, don't put dark text on a dark background or light text on a light background. Avoid clashing colors. A green text on a red background is not only difficult to read, it's an eyesore. Color is handled differently on different browsers, so you should try to view your page in most of the popular browsers. Certainly you should check to see how Netscape Navigator and Internet Explorer render your page.

You should also check to see how your page appears under different color depths. Your monitor might be capable of displaying 16.7 million colors, but users viewing your page might not be so lucky. View your page with your display set to 256 colors to see how it is rendered. When a 16.7 million color image is displayed at 256 colors, the browser must go through a process called **dithering**, in which the appearance of increased color depth is approximated. As shown in Figure 3-39, dithered images can sometimes appear grainy. Even if your computer is capable of displaying full-color images, you might want to consider creating all your images in 256 colors to control the effect of dithering.

Figure 3-39 ◀
Image dithering

original image

dithered image

To completely eliminate dithering, some Web authors recommend that you use the Safety Palette. The **Safety Palette** is a palette of 211 colors that are guaranteed to be displayed accurately on all browsers without dithering.

By limiting your color selections to the colors of the Safety Palette, you can be assured that your images will appear the same in the users' Web browsers as they do in your graphics software. You can learn more about the Safety Palette at http://www.microsoft.com/workshop/design/default.asp.

Quick Check

1. Discuss three reasons for using the GIF image format instead of the JPEG format.

2. Discuss three reasons for using the JPEG image format instead of the GIF format.

3. What HTML tag would you enter to display the alternate text "MidWest University" in place of the graphic image mwu.jpg?

4. What tag would you enter to align the mwu.jpg image with the top of the surrounding text?

5. What tag would you enter to wrap the surrounding text around the left side of the mwu.jpg image? For which browsers would this tag not work?

6. What tag would you enter to increase the horizontal and vertical space around the mwu.jpg image to 10 pixels?

7. The mwu.jpg image is 120 pixels wide by 85 pixels high. Using this information, what would you enter into your HTML file to increase the speed at which the page is rendered by the browser?

8. What is dithering? What is the Safety Palette?

You're finished working with the inline images on your Web page. You've learned about the different image formats supported by most browsers and their advantages and disadvantages. You've also seen how to control the appearance and placement of images on your Web page. In the next session you'll learn how to create an image that links to other Web pages.

SESSION 3.3

In this session you will learn about different types of image maps, and you'll create an image map and test it for the Space Expo Web page.

Introducing Image Maps

Tom has reviewed your Space Expo Web page and is pleased with the progress you're making. He's decided that the page should also include a map of the center's floor plan (shown in Figure 3-40) so that visitors will know where to go for different exhibits.

Figure 3-40 ◀
Map of
the Center
for Space
Science and
Engineering

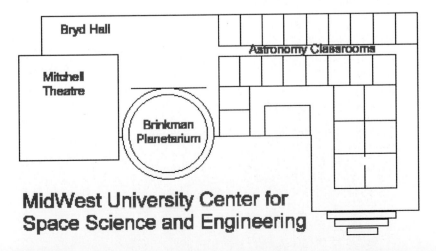

Tom wants the graphic of the map to be interactive, so that when a user clicks Mitchell Theatre on the floor plan, a page displaying events at the theatre will appear. If a user clicks the Brinkman Planetarium, a page about the planetarium will be displayed, and so forth. Figure 3-41 shows how these links will work on the map.

Figure 3-41 ◀
Linking the
map to
different
Web pages

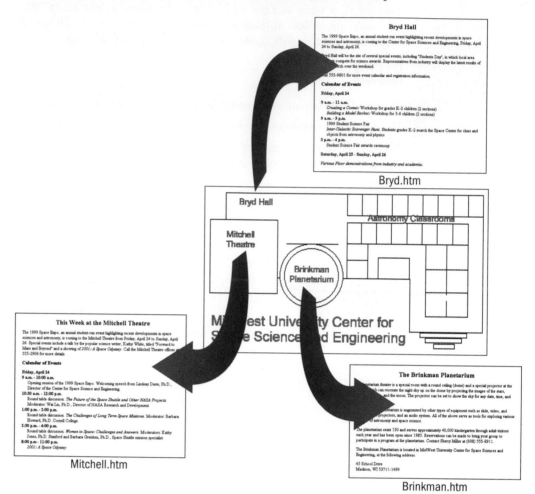

To use a single graphic to access multiple targets, you must set up hotspots within the image. A **hotspot** is a defined area of the image that acts as a hypertext link. One such hotspot for the floor plan of the Space Center would be the circular area that defines the location of the Brinkman Planetarium.

You define hotspots through the use of image maps. **Image maps** list the coordinates on the image that define the boundaries of the hotspots. Anytime a user clicks inside those boundaries, the hyperlink is activated. As a Web author, you can use two types of image maps: server-side image maps and client-side image maps. Each has advantages and disadvantages.

Server-Side Image Maps

In a **server-side image map**, the server, which is the computer that stores the Web page, controls the image map. As shown in Figure 3-42, the Web author includes the coordinates of the hotspots within the Web page, these coordinates are sent to a program running on the server whenever a user clicks the inline image, and the program uses them to activate the appropriate hyperlink.

Figure 3-42 ◄
Server-side
image map

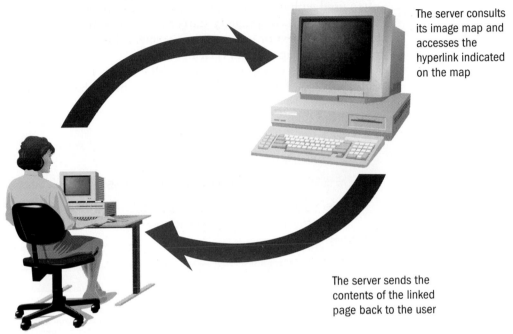

The server consults
its image map and
accesses the
hyperlink indicated
on the map

The server sends the
contents of the linked
page back to the user

The user clicks a hotspot on
the image

Server-side image maps are supported by most, if not all, graphical browsers. There are limitations to server-side image maps. Because a program on the server must process the image map, you cannot test your HTML code using local files. Also, server-side image maps can be slow to operate, because every time a user clicks the inline image, the request has to be processed by the Web server. On most Web browsers the target of a hyperlink is indicated in the browser's status bar, giving valuable feedback to the user but this is not done with the hotspots of a server-side image map. Because it is the server and not the Web browser that handles the hotspots, no feedback is given to the user regarding the location of the hotspots and their targets. These limitations can be overcome through the use of client-side image maps.

Client-Side Image Maps

In a **client-side image map**, you insert the image map into the HTML file, and the image map is processed locally by the Web browser. Because all of the processing is done locally, and not on the Web server, you can easily test your Web pages using the HTML files stored on your computer. Another advantage of client-side image maps is that they tend to be more responsive than server-side maps, because the information does not have to be sent over the network or dial-up connection. Finally, when a user moves the pointer over the inline image, the browser's status bar will display the target of each hotspot. The downside of client-side image maps is that older browsers do not support them.

As you become more experienced with HTML, you will probably want to support both server-side and client-side image maps in your Web pages. For now, however, you will concentrate solely on working with client-side image maps.

Before creating the image map, you'll add the floor plan graphic to the Expo1999.htm file. In addition to the graphic, you'll add a note that describes what the user should do to activate hyperlinks within the graphic's image map. This note should appear directly above the image. To achieve this, you can use the <BR> tag, which creates a line break and forces the following image or text to appear on its own line. The CLEAR property is often used within the <BR> tag to create the effect of starting a paragraph below the inline image. The CLEAR property starts the next line at the first point at which the page margin is clear of text or images. For example, using <BR CLEAR=LEFT> starts the next line when the left page margin is clear.

In this case, you'll use just the <BR> tag to force the floor plan graphic to appear directly below the text describing how to activate the hyperlinks in the graphic.

To add the floor plan graphic:

1. If you took a break after the previous session, open the Expo1999.htm file in your text editor.

2. At the bottom of the file, directly above the <H5> tag, enter the following HTML code:

```
<H5 ALIGN=CENTER> Click each location for a list of events <BR>
<IMG SRC="Layout.gif"> </H5>
```

The <BR> tag creates a line break, causing the Layout.gif image to appear directly below the explanatory text. Your revised file should appear as shown in Figure 3-43.

Figure 3-43 ◀
Inserting the floor plan image

```
<P>The 1999 Space Expo is located on the engineering and physics campus,
north of Granger Stadium, and is open to the public on April 24 (Students'
Day) from 10 a.m.-5 p.m., April 25 from 9 a.m.-7 p.m. and April 26 from
11 a.m.-5 p.m. Admission is $4.00 for the general public and $3.00 for
senior citizens and students. Children four and under will be admitted
free. </P>

<H5 ALIGN=CENTER > Click each location for a list of events <BR>
<IMG SRC="Layout.gif"> </H5>

<H5 ALIGN="CENTER">Sponsored by the Department of Astronomy and the Center
for Space Science and Engineering.</H5>

</BODY>
</HTML>
```

creates a new line below the text

center floor plan

3. Save your changes to the Expo1999.htm file, and then open the file in your Web browser. Figure 3-44 shows the Layout image as it appears in the Web page.

Figure 3-44 ◀
Center floor plan as it appears in the Web page

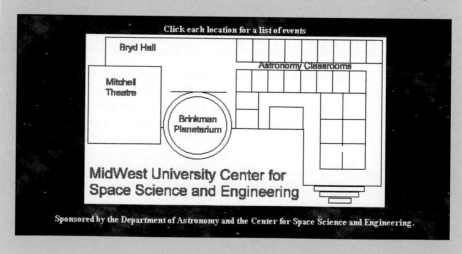

Now that you've inserted the floor plan image into the Web page, your next task is to turn this image into an image map.

Defining Image Map Hotspots

To create the image map, you could open the image in a graphics program and record the coordinates of the points corresponding to the hotspot boundaries. In practice, this is difficult and time-consuming, so you'll typically use a special program to create image map coordinates for you. There are several different programs available for this purpose, some of which are listed in Figure 3-45.

Figure 3-45 ◀
Software to create image maps

Title	URL	Platform
Web Hotspots 3.0 S Edition	http://www.concentric.net/~automata/hotspots.shtml	Windows
LiveImage	http://www.mediatec.com/	Windows
Mac-ImageMap	http://weyl.zib-berlin.de/imagemap/Mac-ImageMap.html	Macintosh
Mapedit	http://www.boutell.com/mapedit/	Windows, UNIX
MapServe	http://www.spub.ksu.edu/other/machttp_tools/ mapserve/mapserve.html	Macintosh

Most image map programs generate the coordinates for hotspots as well as the necessary HTML tags. To help you understand the syntax of image maps better, you'll be given the coordinates and then use that information to create your own HTML code.

REFERENCE window

DEFINING A CLIENT-SIDE IMAGE MAP

- Create the <MAP> tag that defines the different hotspots on the image as follows:
  <MAP NAME="*mapname*">
  <AREA SHAPE="*shape*" COORDS=*coordinates* HREF=*URL*>
  ...
  </MAP>
  where *mapname* is the name of the image map, *shape* is the type of hotspot (rectangle, circle, or polygon), *coordinates* are the locations of points that define the shape, and *URL* is the target of the hypertext link. You can have multiple <AREA> tags for each image map.
- Once the image map is created, add the USEMAP property to the <IMG> tag for the inline image as follows:
  <IMG SRC="*image*" USEMAP="#*mapname*">
  where *image* is the filename of the graphic, and *mapname* is the name of the image map defined in the <MAP> tag.

The general syntax for an image map tag is:

```
<MAP NAME="mapname">
<AREA SHAPE=shape COORDS="coordinates" HREF="URL">
</MAP>
```

The <MAP> tag gives the name of the image map. You can create different image maps for each inline image in your HTML file. Within the <MAP> tag, you use the <AREA>

tag to specify the areas of the image that will act as hotspots. You can include as many <AREA> tags as you need for the image map.

The <AREA> tag has three properties: SHAPE, COORDS, and HREF. The SHAPE property refers to the shape of the hotspot: RECT for a rectangular hotspot, CIRCLE for a circular hotspot, and POLY for irregular polygons.

In the COORDS property you enter coordinates to specify the hotspot's location. The values you enter depend on the shape of the hotspot. As you'll see, you need to enter different coordinates for a rectangular hotspot than you would for a circular one. Coordinates are expressed as a point's distance in pixels from the left and the top edges of the image. For example, the coordinates (123,45) refer to a point 123 pixels from the left edge and 45 pixels down from the top. If the coordinates of your <AREA> tags overlap, the browser uses the first tag in the list.

In the HREF parameter, you enter the URL for the hypertext link that the hotspot points to. You can use the value "NOHREF" in place of a URL if you do not want the hotspot to activate a hypertext link. This is a useful technique when you are first developing your image map, without all the hypertext links in place. The <AREA> tag then acts as a placeholder until the time when you have the hypertext links ready for use.

 REFERENCE window

DEFINING IMAGE MAP HOTSPOTS

- Locate the <MAP> tag that defines the hotspots on the image.
- Within the <MAP> tag, enter the code for the type of hotspot(s). The syntax for a rectangular hotspot is:
  <AREA SHAPE=RECT COORDS="*x_left, y_upper, x_right, y_lower*"HREF="*URL*">
  where *x_left, y_upper* are the coordinates of the upper-left corner of the rectangle, and *x_right,y_lower* are the coordinates of the lower-right corner.
  The syntax for a circular hotspot is:
  <AREA SHAPE=CIRCLE COORDS="*x_center, y_center, radius*" HREF="*URL*">
  where *x_center, y_center* is the center of the circle, and *radius* is the circle's radius.
  The syntax for a polygonal hotspot is:
  <AREA SHAPE=POLY COORDS="*x1, y1, x2, y2, x3, y3, ...* " HREF="*URL*" >
  where *x1, y1, x2, y2, x3, y3, ...* are the coordinates of the vertices of the polygon.

Before creating your <AREA> tags, you'll add the <MAP> tag to the Expo1999.htm file and assign the name "Layout" to the image map.

To insert the <MAP> tag:

1. Return to the Expo1999.htm file in your text editor.

2. Go to the bottom of the file and enter the following directly above the </BODY> tag:

```
<MAP NAME="Layout">
</MAP>
```

With the <MAP> tag in place, you must next determine what kinds of areas the image map will require. Tom wants the image to include hotspots for the Mitchell Theatre, the Brinkman Planetarium, and Bryd Hall. The locations of these three hotspots are shown in Figure 3-46.

Figure 3-46 ◀
Hotspots
for the floor
plan image

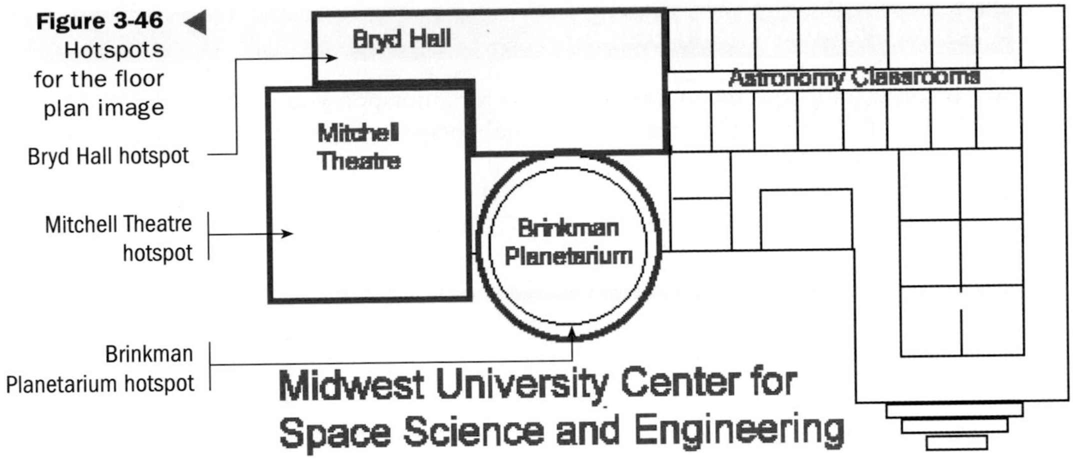

Bryd Hall hotspot

Mitchell Theatre
hotspot

Brinkman
Planetarium hotspot

You'll define the hotspot for the Mitchell Theatre first. The hotspot for the Mitchell Theatre will be a rectangle.

Creating a Rectangular Hotspot

Two points define a rectangular hotspot: the upper-left corner and the lower-right corner. These points for the Mitchell Theatre hotspot are located at (5,45) and (108,157). In other words, the upper-left corner is 5 pixels to the left and 45 pixels down from the left and top edges of the image, respectively, and the lower-right corner is 108 pixels to the left and 157 pixels down. The hotspot will link to the file Mitchell.htm, a page with information on events at the Mitchell Theatre.

To insert the Mitchell Theatre <AREA> tag:

1. Insert a new blank line between the opening and closing <MAP> tags you just entered.
2. Type the following in the new blank line:

   `<AREA SHAPE=RECT COORDS="5,45,108,157" HREF="Mitchell.htm">`

   Note that the coordinates are entered as a series of four numbers separated by commas. Because this is a rectangular hotspot, HTML expects that the first two numbers represent the coordinates for the upper-left corner of the rectangle, and the second two numbers indicate the location of the lower-right corner.

Next you'll enter the <AREA> tag for the Brinkman Planetarium, a circular hotspot.

Creating a Circular Hotspot

The coordinates required for a circular hotspot differ from those of a rectangular hotspot. A circular hotspot is defined by the locations of its center and its radius. The circle representing the Brinkman Planetarium is centered at the coordinates (161,130), and it has a radius of 49 pixels. The hotspot will link to the file Brinkman.htm. You need to enter this <AREA> tag into the Expo1999.htm file.

To insert the Brinkman Planetarium <AREA> tag:

1. Insert a new blank line directly below the Mitchell Theatre <AREA> tag.
2. Type the following in the new blank line:

   `<AREA SHAPE=CIRCLE COORDS="161,130,49" HREF="Brinkman.htm">`

The final hotspot you have to define is for Bryd Hall. Because of its irregular shape, you have to create a polygonal hotspot.

Creating a Polygonal Hotspot

When you want to specify an irregular shape for a hotspot, you must use the POLY value for the SHAPE property. To create a polygonal hotspot, you enter the coordinates for each vertex in the shape.

The coordinates for the vertices of the Bryd Hall hotspot are (29,4), (29,41), (111,41), (111,78), (213,78), and (213,4). See Figure 3-47. The HREF for this hotspot is the file Bryd.htm.

Figure 3-47 ◄
Coordinates for
the Bryd Hall
hotspot

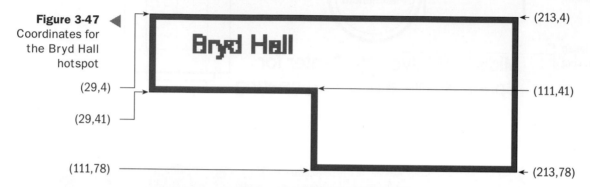

With the coordinate information in hand, you can create the final <AREA> tag for your image map.

To insert the Bryd Hall <AREA> tag:

1. Insert a new blank line directly below the Brinkman Planetarium <AREA> tag.

2. Type the following in the new blank line:

   ```
   <AREA SHAPE=POLY COORDS="29,4,29,41,111,41,111,78,213,78,213,4"
   HREF="Bryd.htm">
   ```

   Figure 3-48 shows the completed list of <AREA> tags for the Layout image map. Compare these values with the ones you've entered, to confirm that you entered them correctly.

Figure 3-48 ◄
Layout image
map and
hotspots

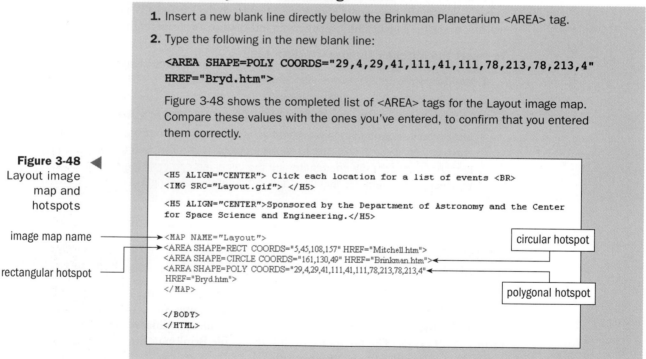

With all of the <AREA> tags in place, you're finished defining the image map. Your next task is to instruct the browser to use the Layout image map with the Layout inline image. Then you'll test the image to confirm that it works properly.

Using an Image Map

The final step in adding an image map to a Web page is to add the USEMAP property to the <IMG> tag for the image map graphic. The USEMAP property tells the browser the name of the image map to associate with the inline image. The syntax for accessing an image map is:

```
<IMG SRC="image" USEMAP="#mapname">
```

Here, *mapname* is the name assigned to the NAME property in the <MAP> tag. Note that you have to place a pound sign (#) before the image map name. You named your image map "Layout" and you inserted the Layout.gif into your Web page. Now you have to add the USEMAP property to the <IMG> tag to associate Layout.gif with the Layout image map.

To assign the Layout image map to the Layout graphic and test the image map:

1. Locate the Layout.gif <IMG> tag in the Expo1999.htm file.

2. Add the following property to the tag: **USEMAP="#Layout"**.

   The completed <IMG> tag should appear as shown in Figure 3-49.

Figure 3-49 ◄
the image map
specified

the image
map specified

```
<H5 ALIGN=CENTER> Click each location for a list of events <BR>
<IMG SRC="Layout.gif" USEMAP="#Layout"> </H5>

<H5 ALIGN="CENTER">Sponsored by the Department of Astronomy and the Center
for Space Science and Engineering.</H5>

<MAP NAME="Layout">
<AREA SHAPE=RECT COORDS="5,45,108,157" HREF="Mitchell.htm">
<AREA SHAPE=CIRCLE COORDS="161,130,49" HREF="Brinkman.htm">
<AREA SHAPE=POLY COORDS="29,4,29,41,111,41,111,78,213,78,213,4"
 HREF="Bryd.htm">
</MAP>

</BODY>
</HTML>
```

3. Save the changes to the Expo1999.htm file.

   Now that you've created the image map, you're ready to test it in your Web browser.

4. Reload the Space Expo Web page in your Web browser.

5. Scroll down to the Layout graphic and place the pointer over the graphic. Note that the pointer changes to a hand 🖑 when it is positioned over a hotspot. Note as well that the status bar displays the URL for that particular hotspot. See Figure 3-50.

Figure 3-50 ◄
Placing the
pointer over the
Mitchell
Theatre
hotspot

pointer changes to a
hand as it passes
over a hotspot

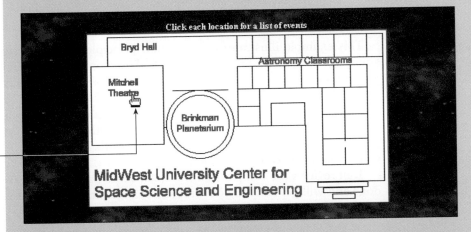

TROUBLE? If your image does not have a red border around it, don't worry. The border is created by Netscape Navigator and will be discussed in the section that follows.

6. Click within the Mitchell Theatre hotspot in the floor plan graphic. Your Web browser displays the page listing the events at the Mitchell Theatre over the Expo weekend.

7. Click the **Back** button in your Web browser to return to the 1999 Space Expo page.

8. Test the other hotspots in the graphic and confirm that they jump to the appropriate page of events. When you're finished working with those pages, return to the Expo page.

If you are using Netscape Navigator, you will notice that the floor plan image is surrounded by a red border that is not displayed when you view the image in a graphics program. Where did this border come from? The border is placed around the image by the Netscape Navigator browser to identify the image as a hyperlink to other Web pages. (*Note:* If you are using Internet Explorer, you will not see this border.) The border color is red because that is the color you specified earlier for hyperlinks. You can remove the border with the BORDER property.

Using the BORDER Property

The BORDER property allows you to create a border to surround your inline images. The syntax for changing the border width is:

```
<IMG SRC="image" BORDER=value>
```

where *value* is the width of the border in pixels. An inline image that does not contain hyperlinks to other documents will, by default, not contain a border. However, if the image does contain hyperlinks to other documents, Netscape Navigator will create a border 2 pixels wide (Internet Explorer will not). If you want to either create a border (for an image that does not have one) or remove a border, you can do so by specifying the appropriate border width.

Tom thinks that the floor plan image would look better without a border, so you'll remove it from the floor plan by specifying a border width of 0 pixels. (*Note:* You should complete the following steps even if you're not using Netscape Navigator, to ensure that your page would look good if a user accessed it using Netscape Navigator.)

To remove the border from the layout graphic:

1. Return to the Expo1999.htm file in your Web browser.

2. Go to the <IMG> tag for the Layout.gif inline image.

3. Insert the property **BORDER=0** within the <IMG> tag.

4. Save your changes to the file, and then reload it in your Web browser.

   If you are running Netscape Navigator, you should see that the border has been removed. If you are running Internet Explorer, you won't notice a difference in your page.

This example illustrates an important principle of page design: you should examine your page in different browsers. If you had used only Internet Explorer to view your page, you would not have learned of the border issue for Netscape Navigator.

The BORDER property works for both Internet Explorer and Netscape Navigator, although it is used differently with Internet Explorer. In the case of Internet Explorer, applying the BORDER property to an image without hyperlinks will create an invisible border around the image, whereas for images that contain hyperlinks, the border color will be the same as the link color.

Tom reviews the completed 1999 Space Expo page. He's pleased with the work you've done and will get back to you with any changes he wants you to make. For now you can close your browser and text editor.

To close your work:

1. Close your Web browser.

2. Return to your text editor, and then close the Expo1999.htm file.

Figure 3-51 shows the finished Web page, and Figure 3-52 shows the complete text of the Expo1999.htm file.

Figure 3-51 ◀
Completed
1999 Space
Expo Web page

More than 60 exhibits and events await visitors at the 1999 Space Expo,
Looking Towards the Future
Friday-Sunday, April 24-26

The 1999 Space Expo is an annual, student-run event that showcases recent developments in astronomy and space sciences and demonstrates how these developments can be applied to everyday life. The event includes student, government and industrial exhibits, and features presentations from NASA, Ball Aerospace, Rockwell, and IBM.

The 1999 Space Expo will feature activities for the kids, including *Creating a Comet*, *Building a Model Rocket*, and *The Inter-Galactic Scavenger Hunt*. Friday is Students' Day, with school children in grades K-8 displaying astronomy and space science projects and competing for individual and school achievement awards.

Professor Greg Stewart's famous astronomy show is also coming to the Space Expo. Professor Stewart will show the wonders of the night sky and discuss the nature of quasars, exploding stars, and black holes. Presentations will be at the Brinkman Planetarium at 1 p.m. and 3 p.m., Friday through Sunday.

Please check out these other events:

- Bryd Hall   Rockwell representatives and graduate students will display some of the latest advances in robotics for use in the Space Shuttle missions.
- Mitchell Theatre   Famous astronomer and popular science writer, Kathy White, will present a talk, "Forward to Mars and Beyond," on Saturday at 7 p.m. Tickets for this very special event are $12. Seating is limited.
- Astronomy Classrooms   Graduate students and professors display the results of their research in atmospherics, satellite technology, climatology, and space engineering.

The 1999 Space Expo is located on the engineering and physics campus, north of Granger Stadium, and is open to the public on April 24 (Students' Day) from 10 a.m.-5 p.m., April 25 from 9 a.m.-7 p.m. and April 26 from 11 a.m.-5 p.m. Admission is $4.00 for the general public and $3.00 for senior citizens and students. Children four and under will be admitted free.

Click each location for a list of events

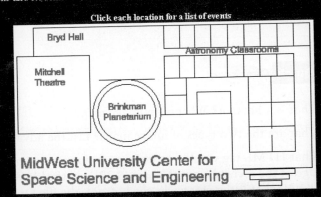

Sponsored by the Department of Astronomy and the Center for Space Science and Engineering.

Figure 3-52 ◄
Complete
Expo1999.htm
file

```
<HTML>
<HEAD>
<TITLE>The 1999 Space Expo</TITLE>
</HEAD>
<BODY BACKGROUND="Space.jpg" TEXT=WHITE LINK=RED VLINK=TURQUOISE>

<H1 ALIGN="CENTER"><IMG SRC="LogoAnim.gif" ALT="The 1999 Space Expo"
 WIDTH=414 HEIGHT=209></H1>

<H3 ALIGN="CENTER">More than 60 exhibits and events await visitors at the
1999 Space Expo, <BR>
<I><FONT COLOR=YELLOW>Looking Towards the Future</FONT></I> <BR>
Friday-Sunday, April 24-26 </H3>

<P><IMG SRC="Center.jpg" ALT="The MWU Center for Space Science and
Engineering" ALIGN=LEFT VSPACE=5 HSPACE=10 WIDTH=280 HEIGHT=186>
The 1999 Space Expo is an annual, student-run event that showcases recent
developments in astronomy and space sciences and demonstrates how these
developments can be applied to everyday life. The event includes student,
government and industrial exhibits, and features presentations from NASA,
Ball Aerospace, Rockwell, and IBM.</P>

<P>The 1999 Space Expo will feature activities for the kids, including
<I>Creating a Comet</I>, <I>Building a Model Rocket</I>, and <I>The
Inter-Galactic Scavenger Hunt</I>. Friday is Students' Day, with school
children in grades K-8 displaying astronomy and space science projects and
competing for individual and school achievement awards.</P>

<P>Professor Greg Stewart's famous astronomy show is also coming to the
Space Expo. Professor Stewart will show the wonders of the night sky and
discuss the nature of quasars, exploding stars, and black holes.
Presentations will be at the Brinkman Planetarium at 1 p.m. and 3 p.m.,
Friday through Sunday. </P>

<P>Please check out these other events:</P>

<UL>
<B><LI> <A HREF="Bryd.htm"> Bryd Hall </A> </B>     Rockwell
representatives and graduate students will display some of the latest
advances in robotics for use in the Space Shuttle
missions.</LI>

<B><LI> <A HREF="Theatre.htm"> Mitchell Theatre </A> </B>    
Famous astronomer and popular science writer, Kathy White, will present a
talk, "Forward to Mars and Beyond," on Saturday at 7 p.m. Tickets for this
very special event are $12. Seating is limited.</LI>

<B><LI> <A HREF="Classes.htm"> Astronomy Classrooms </A> </B>    
Graduate students and professors display the results of their research in
atmospherics, satellite technology, climatology, and space engineering.</LI>
</UL>

<P>The 1999 Space Expo is located on the engineering and physics campus,
north of Granger Stadium, and is open to the public on April 24 (Students'
Day) from 10 a.m.-5 p.m., April 25 from 9 a.m.-7 p.m. and April 26 from
11 a.m.-5 p.m. Admission is $4.00 for the general public and $3.00 for
senior citizens and students. Children four and under will be admitted
free. </P>

<H5 ALIGN=CENTER> Click each location for a list of events <BR>
<IMG SRC="Layout.gif" USEMAP="#Layout" BORDER=0> </H5>

<H5 ALIGN="CENTER">Sponsored by the Department of Astronomy and the Center
for Space Science and Engineering.</H5>

<MAP NAME="Layout">
<AREA SHAPE=RECT COORDS="5,45,108,157" HREF="Mitchell.htm">
<AREA SHAPE=CIRCLE COORDS="161,130,49" HREF="Brinkman.htm">
<AREA SHAPE=POLY COORDS="29,4,29,41,111,41,111,78,213,78,213,4"
 HREF="Bryd.htm">
</MAP>

</BODY>
</HTML>
```

Quick **Check**

1. What is a hotspot? What is an image map?

2. What are the two types of image maps? List the advantages and disadvantages of each.

3. What HTML tag would you enter to define a rectangular hotspot with the upper-left edge of the rectangle at the point (5,20) and the lower-right edge located at (85,100)? Assume that if the user clicks the hotspot, the file Oregon.htm will be displayed.

4. What tag would you enter for a circular hotspot centered at (44,81), with a radius of 23 pixels, and linked to the LA.htm file?

5. What tag would you enter for a hotspot that connects the points (5,10), (5,35), (25,35), (30,20), and (15,10) and is linked to the Hawaii.htm file?

6. What HTML tag would you enter to assign an image map named States to the graphics file WestCoast.gif?

7. What HTML tag would you enter to increase the border around the WestCoast graphic to 5 pixels?

You've finished enhancing the 1999 Space Expo page with graphics. You've seen how to create an image map so that a single graphic can link to several different Web pages. You've also learned about some of the design issues involved in adding graphics to a Web page, and how to choose the correct graphic type for a particular image. Using the knowledge you've gained, you're ready to work on new design challenges that Tom has for you.

Tutorial Assignments

After reviewing the finished 1999 Space Expo Web page, Tom made a few changes to its contents. He also has a few additional suggestions for you to implement. He would like you to add a hotspot to the Layout image that points to a page listing the talks given in various classrooms. He also would like you to work with the other Web pages to improve their appearance.

To implement Tom's suggestions:

1. In your text editor, open the Mitchtxt.htm file in the TAssign folder of the Tutorial.03 folder on your Student Disk, and then save the file as Mitchell.htm in the same folder.

2. Use the Stars.jpg file as your background image for this page. Change the color of the text on the page to white.

3. Change the font of the heading "This Week at the Mitchell Theatre" to use the hexadecimal color value 00CC00. Use the Arial font to display the heading. In case a user's computer does not have Arial, specify that Helvetica and then, finally, Sans Serif should be used instead.

4. Change the color of the "Calendar of Events" line to the hexadecimal color value 00CC00.

5. Change the color of the day and date lines (for example Friday, April 24) to the RGB triplet (255,0,0).

6. Save your changes to the Mitchell.htm file.

7. Repeat Steps 2 through 5 for the Brydtxt.htm file in the TAssign folder, saving the file as Bryd.htm in the same folder.

8. Open the Brinktxt.htm file in the TAssign folder of the Tutorial.03 folder on your Student Disk, and then save the file as Brinkman.htm in the same folder.

9. Change the background color value to (0,153,204). (*Hint:* You will have to convert this RGB triplet to hexadecimal, using one of the resources mentioned in Figure 3-7.) Change the text color value to white.

10. Change the color of the heading "The Brinkman Planetarium" to (255,255,204).

11. Insert an inline image from the Equip.jpg file at the beginning of the first paragraph. Align the image with the right edge of the page. Increase the horizontal and vertical space to 5 pixels. Enter "The Planetarium Projector" as alternate text for the image.

12. The inline image is 326 pixels wide by 201 pixels high. With this information, how could you increase the speed at which your Web browser loads this page? Implement your response to increase the speed. Save your changes to the file.

13. Open the Expotxt.htm file in the TAssign folder of the Tutorial.03 folder on your Student Disk, and then save the file as Expo1999.htm in the same folder.

14. Add a polygonal hotspot to the Layout image map that connects to the Class.htm file. The coordinates of the hotspot are (215,4), (215,132), (311,132), (311,213), (424,213), and (424,4).

15. Load the Expo1999.htm file into your Web browser and confirm that the hotspot to the Class.htm file works correctly. Examine the appearances of the other Web pages for any errors.

16. Save your work, and then close your Web browser and text editor.

Case Problems

1. Creating a New Products Page for Jackson Electronics Paul Reichtman is a sales manager at Jackson Electronics in Seattle, Washington. He wants you to create a Web presentation that advertises three new products released in the last month: the ScanMaster scanner, the LaserPrint 5000 printer, and the Print/Scan 150 combination printer-scanner-copier.

The press releases for the three products and the general announcement have already been put into HTML files for you. The general announcement is shown in Figure 3-53.

Figure 3-53 ◀

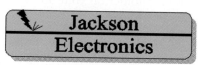

Jackson Electronics Introduces a New Line of Products

Jackson Electronics announced this month a new line of small business printers, copiers and scanners. Designed to meet the growing need for economical scanning and printing solutions, the new products do not sacrifice quality or dependability.

The ScanMaster continues Jackson Electronics' leadership in the field of flatbed scanners. With the patented "Single-Pass" technology, the ScanMaster is fast, with image quality better than multiple-pass scanners.

Building on its popular line of laser printers, Jackson Electronics introduces the LaserPrint 5000. The LaserPrint 5000 prints b&w text at 12 ppm. and its memory expands up to 24 megabytes for graphic-intensive print jobs.

The new Print/Scan 150 combines the benefits of a printer, copier and scanner - all in one! And all without sacrificing quality. Save money (and space) with this three-in-one product.

Interested? Click one of the product names to the left for more information.

Paul would like you to enhance the appearance of this page and the other pages with special color and graphics. The pages should also be linked through an image map. A preview of the page you'll create is shown in Figure 3-54.

Figure 3-54 ◀

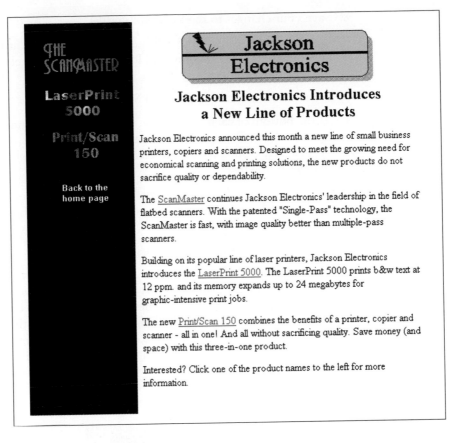

You'll create the left bar effect shown in the figure by using a background image consisting of a single line that is 1 pixel high and 1600 pixels wide. The first 180 pixels of the line are black, and the remainder of the line is white. The browser repeatedly inserts this image into the page background, but because the image is so wide, the bar is not repeated across the width of the page, only down the length of it. An inline image with a black background is placed on the left edge of the page to complete the effect. You'll use this background and image combination for all four of the documents that Paul gives you.

To create Paul's Web presentation:

1. In your text editor, open the Newtext.htm file in the Cases folder of the Tutorial.03 folder on your Student Disk, and then save the file as Jackson.htm in the same folder.

2. Change the background image to the Bars.gif file.

3. Insert the file Product.gif as an inline image at the top of the page. Align the image with the left edge of the page. Increase the space around the image to 5 pixels in all directions. Set the border width of the inline image to 0 pixels.

4. Create an image map named "Product_List."

5. Add four rectangular hotspots to the Product_List image map. The first rectangle has the coordinates (4,2) and (143,66) and is linked to the Scanner.htm file. The second has the coordinates (4,68) and (143,137) and is linked to the Printer.htm file. The third has coordinates at (4,139) and (143,208) and is linked to the PS150.htm file. The final hotspot has the coordinates (4,210) and (143,278) and is linked to the Jackson.htm file.

6. Add to the Product.gif <IMG> tag the property that uses the Product_List image map.

7. Link the first occurrences of the words "ScanMaster," "LaserPrint 5000," and "Print/Scan 150" in the body of the press release to the files Scanner.htm, Printer.htm, and PS150.htm, respectively.

8. Save your changes to the Jackson.htm file.

9. Open the files Scantext.htm, Printext.htm, and PStext.htm, and then save them as Scanner.htm, Printer.htm, and PS150.htm, respectively, in the Cases folder of the Tutorial.03 folder.

10. For each of the three files, repeat Steps 2 through 6.

11. At the bottom of each of the three files, insert a single line with the text "Return to the Jackson Electronics home page." in the <H5> heading tag. Specify that the line of text should be centered and linked to the Jackson.htm file. Save your changes to the file.

12. Load the Jackson.htm file in your Web browser and confirm that the hypertext links in the image map work properly. Confirm that the hypertext links in the main text also work correctly.

13. Close your Web browser and your text editor.

2. Announcing the SFSF '99 You are in charge of publicity for the 1999 San Francisco Science Fiction Convention (also known as SFSF '99). One of your jobs is to create a Web presentation announcing the three guests of honor for the convention. You've decided to create a home page with three thumbnail photos of the guests combined into a single image map, which will then be linked to separate biography pages for each person. The biography pages will also contain the photos, but in a larger and more detailed format. A preview of the home page is shown in Figure 3-55, and a preview of one of the biography pages is shown in Figure 3-56.

Figure 3-55 ◀

**Welcome to the 1999 San Francisco
Science Fiction Convention**

The SFSF '99 committee welcomes you to the annual San Francisco Science Fiction convention. The convention starts Thursday, August 19th at 8 p.m. with the Get-Together party in Derleith Hall. The fun doesn't stop until Sunday morning on August 22nd. Be sure to attend Friday's costume party and *"You Don't Know Jack* trivia contest.

The guests of honor at this year's convention are: <u>Philip Forrest</u>, famous fan and fiction follower; <u>Karen Charnas</u>, author of the award-winning novel *The Unicorn Express* , and <u>Jeffrey Unwin</u>, critic and editor of *The Magazine of Speculative Fiction.*

Click the images above for guest biographies

Registration is $35 at the door, $30 in advance. It's worth it!

For more information and a calendar of events, contact:

*SFSF '99
301 Howlitze Lane
San Francisco, CA 94201
(311)555-2989*

Figure 3-56 ◄

Biography

Name: Philip Forrest

Age: 68

Occupation: Professional fan and editor of *Horizons*

Favorite Fish: Huh? What? Fried, I guess.

Comments: I'm thrilled to be selected fan guest of honor. I look forward to seeing everyone at SFSF '99

Phil has been a fan favorite for forty years. His knowledge of science fiction is legendary and anyone who has seen his immense magazine collection knows where that knowledge came from! As editor of *Horizons*, Phil has won two Tucker awards for best fanzine of year.

To create the SFSF '99 Web presentation:

1. In your text editor, open the Forsttxt.htm file in the Cases folder of the Tutorial.03 folder on your Student Disk, and then save the file as Forrest.htm in the same folder.

2. Change the background color to the RGB triplet (255, 255, 204).

3. At the top of the page, before the <H2> Biography heading, insert the Forrest.jpg inline image aligned with the left margin. Specify 10 pixels of horizontal space and 5 pixels of vertical space.

4. After the Comments line, change the <BR> tag so that it starts the next line below the inline image you inserted in Step 3. What would happen if you left the <BR> tag in its original condition?

5. Save your changes.

6. Open the file Charntxt.htm in the Cases folder of the Tutorial.03 folder, and then repeat Steps 2 through 5. Save the file as Charnas.htm in the same folder. Then open the file Unwintxt.htm in the Cases folder and repeat Steps 2 through 5. Save the file as Unwin.htm.

7. Open the SFSFtxt.htm file in the Cases folder of the Tutorial.03 folder on your Student Disk, and then save the file as SFSF.htm in the same folder.

8. Change the background color value to (255, 255, 204).

9. Within the <H2> heading at the top of the page, insert the inline image SFSF.gif. Place a <BR> tag after the image so that it resides on its own line. Color the heading text blue.

10. After the description of the guests of honor, insert a centered <H4> tag with the inline image Guests.jpg on one line, followed by a <BR> tag and then the text "Click the images above for guest biographies" on the second line. Color the text blue.

11. Create an image map named "Guests" with three rectangular hotspots. The first hotspot has the coordinates (0,0) and (70,70) and points to the Forrest.htm file; the second has coordinates at (71,0) and (140,70) and points to the Charnas.htm file; and the third has coordinates at (141,0) and (210,70) and points to the Unwin.htm file. Apply this image map to the Guests.jpg inline image.

12. For the first occurrences of the names of the guests of honor, create hypertext links that point to their biography pages.

13. Save your changes.

14. Open the SFSF.htm file in your Web browser and check all hypertext links to verify that they work properly.

15. Close your Web browser and your text editor.

3. Creating an Online Menu for Kelsey's Diner You've been asked to create an online menu for Kelsey's Diner, a well-established restaurant in Worcester, Massachusetts, so that patrons can order carry-out dishes from the Web. The manager, Cindy Towser, shows you a text file with the current carry-out breakfast menu, displayed in Figure 3-57. She wants you to spice it up with colors and graphics. She also wants you to create hyperlinks to the lunch and dinner carry-out menus. A preview of the page that you'll create is shown in Figure 3-58.

Figure 3-57 ◀

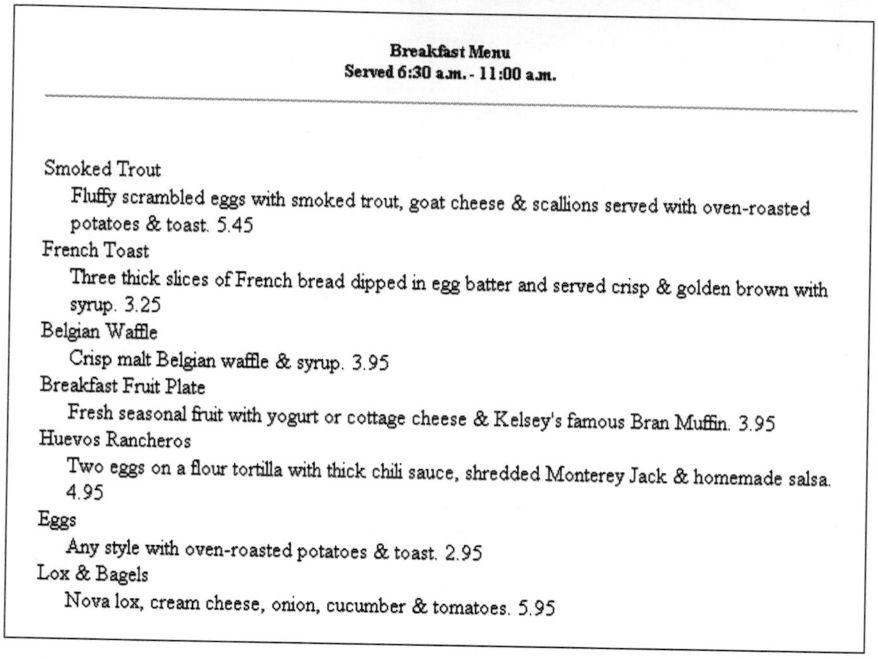

Figure 3-58 ◀

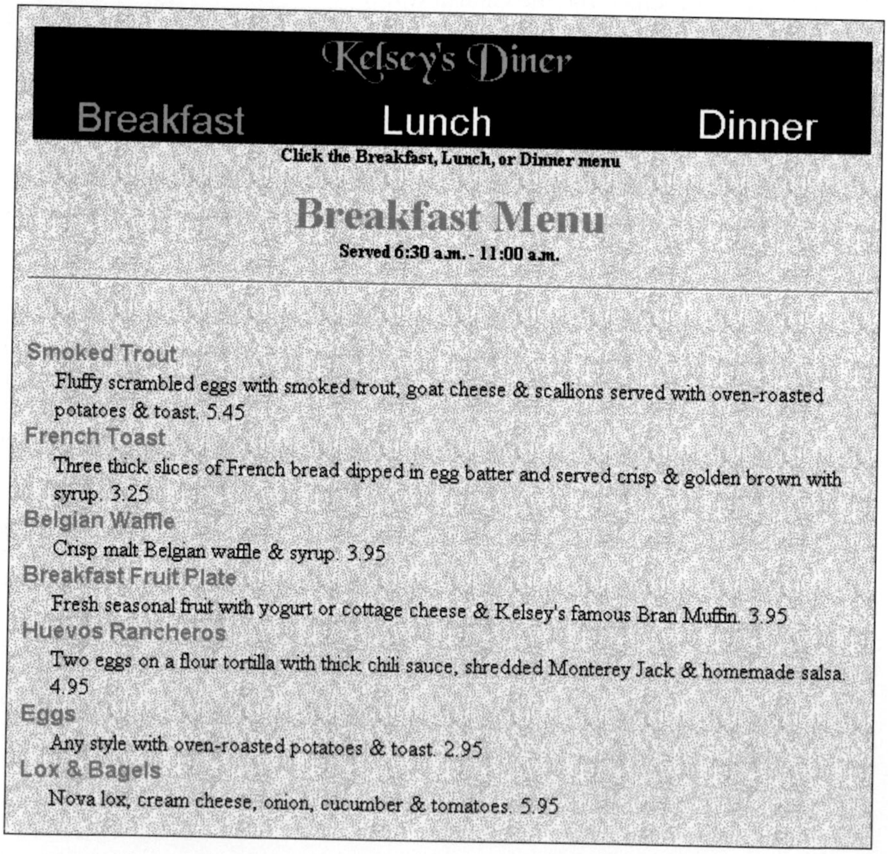

To create the Web menu for Kelsey's Diner:

1. In your text editor, open the Breaktxt.htm file in the Cases folder of the Tutorial.03 folder on your Student Disk, and then save the file as Breakfst.htm in the same folder.

2. Use the graphic file Tan.jpg as a background image for this page.

3. Insert the graphic Breakfst.gif at the top of the page within a set of <H5> tags. Center the image on the page. Directly below the image, after a line break, insert the text "Click the Breakfast, Lunch, or Dinner menu" (within the <H5> tags used for the inline image).

4. Change the text of the title "Breakfast Menu" to green and increase the point size of the text by three points.

5. For the name of each dish in the menu, bold the text, change the color of the text to green, and specify that the text should appear in either the Arial, Helvetica, or Sans Serif font (in that order).

6. At the bottom of the page, insert an image map named "Menu." The image map should have three rectangular hotspots. The first hotspot has the coordinates (20,40) and (156,77) and points to the Breakfst.htm file; the second has coordinates at (241,40) and (336,77) and points to the Lunch.htm file; the third has coordinates at (464,40) and (568,77) and points to the Dinner.htm file. Apply this image map to the Breakfst.gif inline image.

7. Repeat Steps 2 through 6 with the Lunchtxt.htm file in the Cases folder of the Tutorial.03 folder, but place the Lunch.gif image at the top of the page, and save the file as "Lunch.htm."

8. Repeat Steps 2 through 6 with the Dinnrtxt.htm file in the Cases folder of the Tutorial.03 folder, but place the Dinner.gif image at the top of the page, and save the file as "Dinner.htm."

9. Open the Breakfst.htm file in your browser and test the hyperlinks. Verify that the pages look correct and that the inline image changes to reflect the change in the menu.

10. Print a copy of the Breakfast menu, and then print the source code for all three files.

11. Close your Web browser and your text editor.

4. Creating a Listing for Tri-State Realty Tri-State Realty is in the process of putting their listings on the World Wide Web. You've been asked to create some pages for their Web site. You've been given the following information for your first page, a listing describing property located at 22 Northshore Drive:

"This is a must see. Large waterfront home overlooking Mills Lake. It comes complete with three bedrooms, a huge master bedroom, hot tub, family room, large office or den, and three-car garage. Wood boat ramp. Great condition!"

In addition, the owners of the property have included the following main points they want to be emphasized in the Web page:

- 2900 sq. feet

- 15 years old

- updated electrical, plumbing, and heating systems

- central air conditioning

- near school, park, and shopping center

- nice, quiet neighborhood

- asking price: $280,000

Finally, you've been given the following files (in the Cases folder of the Tutorial.03 folder on your Student Disk):

- House.jpg, which contains a photo of the property; size is 243 × 163
- Tristate.gif, the company logo; size is 225 × 100
- Listings.gif, a graphic image showing the various listing categories; size is 600 × 100
- TSBack.gif, the background texture used on all Tri-State Web pages

Using this information, you'll create a Web page for the property at 22 Northshore Drive. The design of the page is up to you, but it should include the following:

- an appropriately titled heading
- a paragraph describing the house
- a bulleted list of the main points of interest
- the photo of the house, the company logo, and the graphic of the different listing categories (use the company background file as your page's background)
- at least one example of spot color
- at least one example of a font displaying a different face and size from the surrounding text
- alternative text for the logo and house photo images
- height and width information for all inline images
- the listings graphic converted to an image map, with the following hotspots (target files are not included):
  - rectangular hotspot at (5,3) (182,44) that points to the Newhome.htm file
  - rectangular hotspot at (12,62) (303,95) that points to the Mansions.htm file
  - rectangular hotspot at (210,19) (374,60) that points to the Business.htm file
  - rectangular hotspot at (375,1) (598,44) that points to the Family.htm file
  - rectangular hotspot at (378,61) (549,96) that points to the Apartmnt.htm file
- appropriately labeled hypertext links that point to the same files as indicated in the image map
- your name, as Web page author, in italics

Save the page as Tristate.htm in the Cases folder of the Tutorial.03 folder on your Student Disk, and then print a copy of your page and the HTML code. Close your Web browser and your text editor when finished.

Designing a Web Page with Tables

Creating a Products Page

CASE

Middle Age Arts

Middle Age Arts is a company that creates and sells replicas of historic European works of art for home and garden use. The company specializes in sculpture, tapestries, prints, friezes, and busts that evoke the artistic styles of the Middle Ages and the Renaissance.

Nicole Swanson, an advertising executive at Middle Age Arts, is directing the effort to create Web pages for the company. She hopes that a Web page can improve the company's visibility, as well as make it easier for customers to place orders. The type of information she wants to provide on the Web includes a description of the company, contact information for individuals who want to place an order over the phone, a list of stores that distribute Middle Age Arts products, and a display of the company's merchandise.

Nicole has asked you to work on creating Web pages for the Gargoyle Collection, a new line of Middle Age Arts products featuring gargoyles recreated from the walls and towers of Gothic buildings and churches. The page should display the product name, item number, description, and price. Information of this type is best displayed in a table, so to create the page, you'll have to learn how to work with tables in HTML.

SESSION 4.1

In this session you will learn how to add tables to a Web page, starting with simple text tables and then moving to graphical tables, and you'll learn the advantages of each approach. You'll also learn how to define table rows, cells, and headings with HTML tags. Finally, you'll add a caption to your table and learn how to control the caption's placement on the page.

Tables on the World Wide Web

Nicole has been considering the prototype page she wants you to create for the Gargoyle Collection. She wants you to start out small. The page will eventually have to display more than 50 separate items, but for now she is only interested in a small sample of that number. With that in mind, Nicole has selected three products, shown in a table format in Figure 4-1, that she wants you to place on the Web page.

Figure 4-1 ◀
Nicole's products table

Name	Item #	Type	Finish	Price
Bacchus	48059	Wall Mount	Interior Plaster	$95
Praying Gargoyle	48159	Garden Figure	Gothic Stone	$125
Gargoyle Judge	48222	Bust	Interior Plaster	$140

There are two ways to insert a table of information on a Web page: you can create either a text table or a graphical table. A **text table**, like the one shown in Figure 4-2, contains only text, evenly spaced out on the page in rows and columns. Text tables use only standard typewriter characters, so that even a line in a text table is created by repeating a typographical character, such as a hyphen, underline, or equals sign.

Figure 4-2 ◀
A text table

all table elements are
created using
typewriter characters

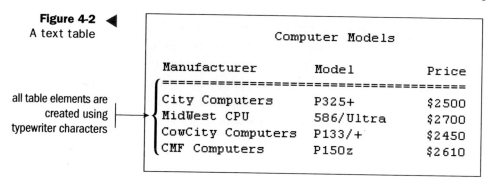

```
                    Computer Models

Manufacturer            Model           Price
========================================================
City Computers          P325+           $2500
MidWest CPU             586/Ultra       $2700
CowCity Computers       P133/+          $2450
CMF Computers           P150z           $2610
```

A **graphical table**, as shown in Figure 4-3, appears as a graphical element on the Web page. A graphical table allows you to include design elements such as color, shading, and borders in a table. Because of this, you have greater control over the table's appearance. You can control the size of individual table cells and text alignment. You can even create cells that span several rows or columns.

Figure 4-3 ◄
A graphical
table

color background

a table cell

graphical borders
and shading

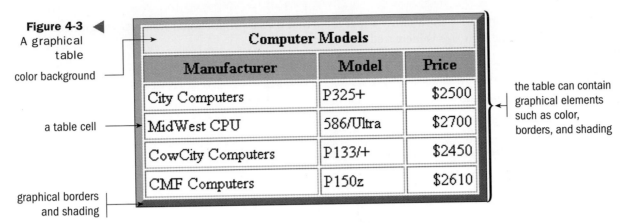

the table can contain
graphical elements
such as color,
borders, and shading

Graphical tables are more flexible than text tables and are more attractive. However, there are some situations in which you will want to use a text table. Some browsers, such as the text-based Lynx browser used on many UNIX systems, can display only text characters. Also, working with the tags for graphical tables can be complicated and time-consuming. For these reasons, you might want to create two versions of your Web page: one that uses only text elements and text tables, and another that takes advantage of graphical elements. This is the approach Nicole suggests that you take. First you'll create a text table of the products in the Gargoyle Collection, and then you'll start to work on the graphical version of the table.

Creating a Text Table

The beginning of the file you'll use for the text table version of the products page has already been created for you and is stored on your Student Disk as MAA.htm. To begin, you'll open this file and save it with a new name.

To open the MAA.htm file and then save it with a new name:

1. Start your text editor.

2. Open the file **MAA.htm** from the Tutorial.04 folder on your Student Disk, and then save the file in the same folder as **MAAtext.htm**.

The page consists of two headings formatted with the <H1> and <H3> tags followed by a paragraph of text that describes the Gargoyle Collection. You'll add the text table below the paragraph.

Using Fixed-Width Fonts

To create a text table you have to control the type of font that is used. A text table relies on spaces and the characters that fill those spaces to create its column boundaries. You have to use a font that allots the same amount of space to each character and to the empty spaces between characters. This type of font is called a **fixed-width font** or a **typewriter font**.

Most typeset documents (such as the one you're reading now) use **proportional fonts**—that is, fonts in which the width of each character differs with the character's shape. For example, the character "m" is wider than the character "l."

Proportional fonts are more visually attractive than fixed-width fonts, so you might be tempted to use them for your text tables. The distinction between the fixed-width and proportional font is important, however, because if you use a proportional font in a text table, the varying width of the characters and the spaces between characters might cause errors when the page is rendered in the user's browser.

Figure 4-4 shows how a text table that uses a proportional font loses alignment when the font size is increased or decreased.

Figure 4-4 ◀
Column alignment problems with proportional font

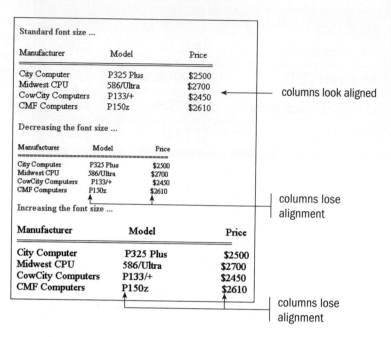

By contrast, the table shown in Figure 4-5 uses fixed-width fonts. Note that the columns remain aligned regardless of font size.

Figure 4-5 ◀
Column alignment with fixed-width font

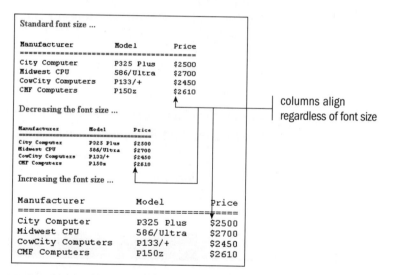

Different browsers use different font sizes to display text, so you should always use a fixed-width font to ensure that the columns in your text tables remain in alignment. You can accomplish this using the <PRE> tag.

Using the <PRE> Tag

The <PRE> tag is used to display preformatted text, which is text formatted in ways that you want retained in your Web page. HTML ignores extra blank spaces, blank lines, or tabs unless you've inserted a tag or special character for those features. Any text formatted with the <PRE> tag retains those extra blank spaces and blank lines. The <PRE> tag also displays text using a fixed-width font, which is what you want for your text table.

REFERENCE window	**CREATING A TEXT TABLE USING THE <PRE> TAG**
	■ Type <PRE> to use the preformatted text tag.
	■ Enter the table text, aligning the columns of the table by inserting blank spaces as appropriate.
	■ Type </PRE> to turn off the preformatted text tag.

You'll use the <PRE> tag to enter the table data from Figure 4-1 into the MAAtext.htm file. When you use this tag, you insert blank spaces by pressing the spacebar to align the columns of text in the table.

To create the text table with the <PRE> tag:

1. Place the insertion point in the blank line directly above the </BODY> tag.

2. Type **<PRE>** and then press the **Enter** key to create a new blank line.

3. Type **Name** and then press the **spacebar** 15 times.

4. Type **Item #** and then press the **spacebar** 5 times.

5. Type **Type** and then press the **spacebar** 15 times.

6. Type **Finish** and then press the **spacebar** 15 times.

7. Type **Price** and then press the **Enter** key.

   Next you'll enter a series of equals signs to create an underline that will separate the column headings from the text of the table.

8. Type a line of = signs to underline the column headings you just entered. End the line below the "e" in "Price," and then press the **Enter** key.

9. Complete the table by entering the following text aligned with the left edge of the column headings:

```
Bacchus              48059 Wall Mount     Interior Plaster $95

Praying Gargoyle 48159 Garden Figure  Gothic Stone        $125

Gargoyle Judge    48222 Bust           Interior Plaster $140
```

10. Press the **Enter** key after entering the last row of table text, and then type **</PRE>** to turn off the preformatted text tag. Figure 4-6 shows the complete preformatted text as it appears in the file.

Figure 4-6 ◀
Text table
created with
the <PRE> tag

text appears in
the browser as it
appears here

```
<P>Throughout Europe, countless gargoyles peer down from the towers and
parapets of medieval cathedrals. In honor of these fascinating creations,
Middle Age Arts presents an exclusive line of gargoyle replicas. Choose
representations from the most famous cathedrals in the world, including
the popular gargoyles of Notre Dame. Select from the following list of
our most popular gargoyles.</P>
<PRE>
Name               Item #     Type            Finish           Price
==================================================================
Bacchus            48059      Wall Mount      Interior Plaster $95
Praying Gargoyle   48159      Garden Figure   Gothic Stone     $125
Gargoyle Judge     48222      Bust            Interior Plaster $140
</PRE>
</BODY>
</HTML>
```

11. Save your changes, and then close the MAAtext.htm file.

12. Open the MAAtext.htm file in your Web browser. Figure 4-7 displays the page as it appears in the browser.

Figure 4-7 ◄
Text table as it appears in the Web browser

text appears in a fixed-width font

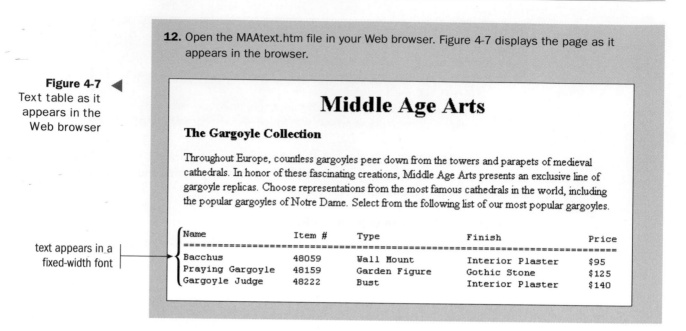

By using the <PRE> tag, you've created a text table that can be displayed by all browsers, and you've ensured that the columns will retain their alignment no matter what font the browser is using.

You show the completed table to Nicole. She's pleased with your work and would like you to create a similar page using a graphical table. To create that table, you'll start by learning how HTML defines table structures.

Defining a Table Structure

Creating tables with HTML can be a complicated process because you have to enter a lot of information to define the layout and appearance of your table. The first step is to specify the table structure: the number of rows and columns, the location of column headings, and the placement of a table caption. Once you have the table structure in place, you can start populating the cells of the table with text and data.

As with the text table page, the beginning of the page for the graphical table has already been created and stored on your Student Disk as MAA2.htm. You need to open that file in your text editor and save it with a new name.

To open the MAA2.htm file and then save it with a new name:

1. Return to your text editor.

2. Open the file **MAA2.htm** from the Tutorial.04 folder on your Student Disk, and then save the file in the same folder as **MAAtable.htm**.

Using the <TABLE>, <TR>, and <TD> Tags

To create a graphical table with HTML, you start with the <TABLE> tag. The <TABLE> tag identifies where the table structure begins, and the </TABLE> tag indicates where the table ends. After you've identified the location of the table, you identify the number of rows in the table by inserting a <TR> (for table row) tag at the beginning of each table row, starting with the top row of the table and moving down. The end of the table row is indicated by a </TR> tag. Finally, within the <TR> tags you must indicate the location of each table cell with <TD> (for table data) tags.

HTML does not provide a means of specifying the number and placement of table columns. Columns are determined by how many cells are inserted within each row. For example, if you have four <TD> tags in each table row, that table has four columns. So if you want to make sure that the columns in your table line up correctly, you must be careful about the placement and number of <TD> tags within each row. The general syntax of a graphical table is:

```
<TABLE>
     <TR>
             <TD> First Cell </TD>
             <TD> Second Cell </TD>
     </TR>
     <TR>
             <TD> Third Cell </TD>
             <TD> Fourth Cell </TD>
     </TR>
</TABLE>
```

This example creates a table with two rows and two columns, displaying a total of four cells. Figure 4-8 shows the layout of a table with this HTML code.

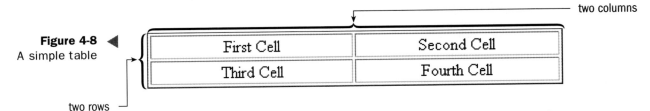

Figure 4-8
A simple table

two columns

two rows

Strictly speaking, the </TR> tag is not necessary, because the presence of the next <TR> tag will signal the browser to go to the next table row. However it is good practice to use the </TR> tag, at least until you become comfortable with the way HTML creates tables.

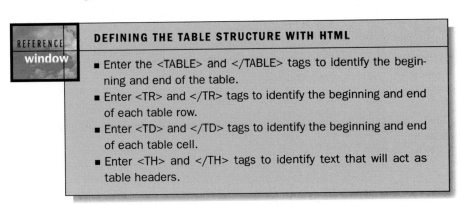

REFERENCE window

DEFINING THE TABLE STRUCTURE WITH HTML

- Enter the <TABLE> and </TABLE> tags to identify the beginning and end of the table.
- Enter <TR> and </TR> tags to identify the beginning and end of each table row.
- Enter <TD> and </TD> tags to identify the beginning and end of each table cell.
- Enter <TH> and </TH> tags to identify text that will act as table headers.

Look at the table that Nicole outlined in Figure 4-1. Notice that the table requires four rows and five columns. However, one of the rows consists of column titles, called **table headers**. HTML provides a special tag for table headers, which you'll learn about shortly, leaving three rows and five columns for the body of the table. You'll create the basic table structure first and then enter the table text.

To create the structure for the products table:

1. Place the insertion point in the blank line directly above the </BODY> tag.

2. Press the **Enter** key, type **<TABLE>** to identify the beginning of the table structure, and then press the **Enter** key again.

3. Type the entries for the first row of the table as follows:

```
<TR>
  <TD></TD>
  <TD></TD>
  <TD></TD>
  <TD></TD>
  <TD></TD>
</TR>
```

Note that you do not need to indent the <TD> tags, but you might find it easier to interpret your code if you do indent them and place them on separate lines.

4. Press the **Enter** key, and then repeat Step 3 twice to create the final two rows of the table. You might want to use the copy and paste functions of your text editor to save time.

5. Press the **Enter** key, and then type **</TABLE>** to complete the code for the table structure. See Figure 4-9.

Figure 4-9 ◀
Structure of the products table in HTML

beginning of the table structure

beginning of the first table row

five table cells per table row

end of the first table row

end of the table structure

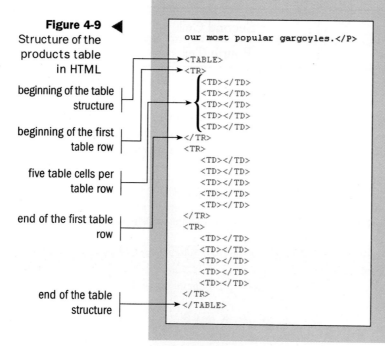

With the table structure in place, you're ready to add the text for each cell, inserted within the <TD> tags in each table row.

To insert the table text:

1. Go to the first <TD> tag in the table structure.

2. Within the first set of <TD> tags, type **Bacchus**.

3. Within the next four <TD> tags, enter the remaining entries for the first row of the table as follows:

<TD> 48059 </TD>
<TD> Wall Mount </TD>
<TD> Interior Plaster </TD>
<TD> $95 </TD>

4. Continue entering the text for the cells in the remaining two rows of the table. Figure 4-10 shows the completed text for the body of the table.

Figure 4-10 ◄
Completed
table text

text for the first
cell in the first row
of the table

```
<TABLE>
<TR>
    <TD>Bacchus</TD>
    <TD>48059</TD>
    <TD>Wall Mount</TD>
    <TD>Interior Plaster</TD>
    <TD>$95</TD>
</TR>
<TR>
    <TD>Praying Gargoyle</TD>
    <TD>48159</TD>
    <TD>Garden Figure</TD>
    <TD>Gothic Stone</TD>
    <TD>$125</TD>
</TR>
<TR>
    <TD>Gargoyle Judge</TD>
    <TD>48222</TD>
    <TD>Bust</TD>
    <TD>Interior Plaster</TD>
    <TD>$140</TD>
</TR>
</TABLE>
```

With the text for the body of the table entered, you'll next add the table headers.

Creating Headers with the <TH> Tag

HTML provides a special tag for cells that will act as table headers (or column headings): the <TH> tag. Like the <TD> tag, the <TH> tag is used with cells within the table. The difference between the <TH> and <TD> tags is that text formatted with the <TH> tag is centered within the cell and displayed in a boldface font. A table can have several rows of table headers. In fact, because the <TH> tag is a replacement for the <TD> tag, you can use the <TH> tag for any cell containing text that you want to be displayed in centered boldfaced type.

In the gargoyle products table, Nicole has specified a single row of table headers. You'll enter them now using the <TH> tag.

To insert the table headers:

1. Go to the <TABLE> tag line and press the **Enter** key to create a new blank line below it.

2. Type the following:

<TR>
<TH> Name </TH>
<TH> Item # </TH>
<TH> Type </TH>
<TH> Finish </TH>
<TH> Price </TH>
</TR>

Figure 4-11 shows the <TH> tags as they appear in your file.

Figure 4-11 ◀
Creating table
headers with
<TH> tags

table headers

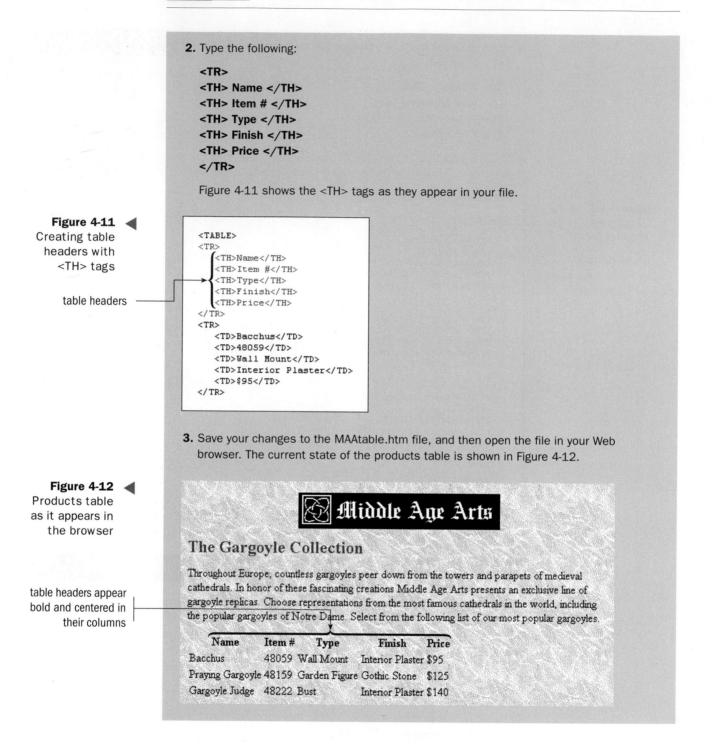

3. Save your changes to the MAAtable.htm file, and then open the file in your Web
browser. The current state of the products table is shown in Figure 4-12.

Figure 4-12 ◀
Products table
as it appears in
the browser

table headers appear
bold and centered in
their columns

Note that the cells formatted with the <TH> tag appear in boldface and centered above
each table column. Your next task is to add a table caption.

Creating a Table Caption

You create a table caption using the <CAPTION> tag. The syntax for the <CAPTION> tag is:

   <CAPTION ALIGN=*value*>*caption text*</CAPTION>

where *value* indicates the caption placement—either TOP (above the table) or BOTTOM (below the table). In either case, the caption will be centered in relation to the table. Because the <CAPTION> tag works only with tables, the tag must be placed within the <TABLE> tags.

REFERENCE
window

CREATING A TABLE CAPTION

- Within the <TABLE> tags enter the following tag:
  <CAPTION ALIGN=*value*>*caption text*</CAPTION>
  where *value* can be either TOP (to place the caption directly above the table) or BOTTOM (to place the caption directly below the table).

   Nicole asks you to add the caption "Here is a sample of our products" centered above the table.

To add the caption to the products table:

1. Return to the MAAtable.htm file in your text editor.

2. Insert a blank line below the <TABLE> tag.

3. In the new line type **<CAPTION ALIGN=TOP>Here is a sample of our products</CAPTION>**. See Figure 4-13.

Figure 4-13 ◀
Inserting a
caption above
the table

caption will be placed
above the table

<CAPTION> tag

```
<TABLE>
<CAPTION ALIGN=TOP>Here is a sample of our products</CAPTION>
<TR>
    <TH>Name</TH>
    <TH>Item #</TH>
    <TH>Type</TH>
    <TH>Finish</TH>
    <TH>Price</TH>
</TR>
```

4. Save your changes to the MAAtable.htm file, and then reload the file in your Web browser. Figure 4-14 shows the table with the newly added caption.

Figure 4-14 ◀
Products table
with the table
caption

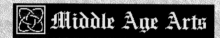

The Gargoyle Collection

Throughout Europe, countless gargoyles peer down from the towers and parapets of medieval cathedrals. In honor of these fascinating creations Middle Age Arts presents an exclusive line of gargoyle replicas. Choose representations from the most famous cathedrals in the world, including the popular gargoyles of Notre Dame. Select from the following list of our most popular gargoyles.

table caption ⟶ Here is a sample of our products

Name	Item #	Type	Finish	Price
Bacchus	48059	Wall Mount	Interior Plaster	$95
Praying Gargoyle	48159	Garden Figure	Gothic Stone	$125
Gargoyle Judge	48222	Bust	Interior Plaster	$140

Captions are shown as normal text without special formatting. As with other tags in your HTML file, you can format table text by embedding the text within the appropriate tags. For example, placing the caption text within a pair of <B> and <I> tags will cause the caption to appear in a bold italicized font.

Quick Check

1 What are the two kinds of tables you can place in a Web page? What are the advantages and disadvantages of each?

2 What is the difference between a proportional font and a fixed-width font? Which should you use in a text table, and why?

3 What tag can you use to create a text table?

4 Name the purpose of the following tags in defining the structure of a table:

<TABLE>
<TR>
<TD>
<TH>

5 How do you determine the number of rows in a graphical table? How do you determine the number of columns?

6 How does the <TH> tag differ from the <TD> tag?

7 What HTML code would you enter to place the caption "Product Catalog" below a table? Where must this code be placed in relation to the <TABLE> and </TABLE> tags?

You've completed your work with the initial structure of the products table. Overall, Nicole is pleased with your progress, but she would like you to make some improvements in the table's appearance. In the next session, you'll learn how to control the appearance and placement of your table and the text in it.

In this session you will learn how to create table and cell borders and how to control the width of each. You'll learn how to specify the space between table text and the surrounding table. You'll also work with the placement and size of the table on your Web page. Finally, you'll learn how to specify a table background color.

Modifying the Appearance of a Table

After viewing the products table in the browser, Nicole notes that the text is displayed with properly aligned columns, but that the format of the table could be improved. Nicole asks you to enhance the table's appearance with borders and color. She also wants you to control the placement of the table on the page as well as the table size. HTML provides tags and properties to do all of these things.

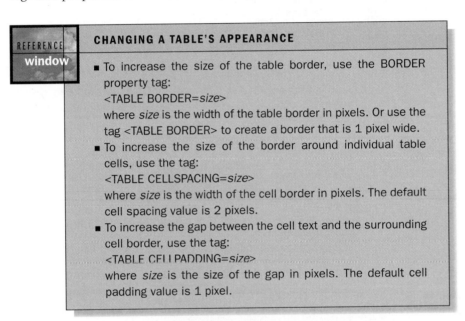

REFERENCE
window

CHANGING A TABLE'S APPEARANCE

- To increase the size of the table border, use the BORDER property tag:
  <TABLE BORDER=*size*>
  where *size* is the width of the table border in pixels. Or use the tag <TABLE BORDER> to create a border that is 1 pixel wide.
- To increase the size of the border around individual table cells, use the tag:
  <TABLE CELLSPACING=*size*>
  where *size* is the width of the cell border in pixels. The default cell spacing value is 2 pixels.
- To increase the gap between the cell text and the surrounding cell border, use the tag:
  <TABLE CELLPADDING=*size*>
  where *size* is the size of the gap in pixels. The default cell padding value is 1 pixel.

You'll begin enhancing the products table by adding a table border.

Adding a Table Border

By default, your browser displays tables without table borders. You can create a table border with the BORDER property. The syntax for creating a table border is:

    <TABLE BORDER=*size*>

where *size* is the width of the border in pixels. The size value is optional; if you don't specify a size, but simply enter BORDER, the browser creates a border 1 pixel wide around the table. Figure 4-15 shows the effect of varying the border size on a table's appearance.

Figure 4-15 ◀
Tables with different values for the BORDER property

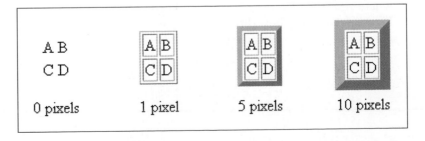

Nicole wants a good-sized border around the products table, so you'll format the table with a 10-pixel-wide border.

To insert a table border:

1. If you took a break after the previous session, start your text editor and open the MAAtable.htm file.

2. Go to the <TABLE> tag and within the tag, type **BORDER=10**. See Figure 4-16.

Figure 4-16 ◄
Adding a
10-pixel border
to the products
table

BORDER property

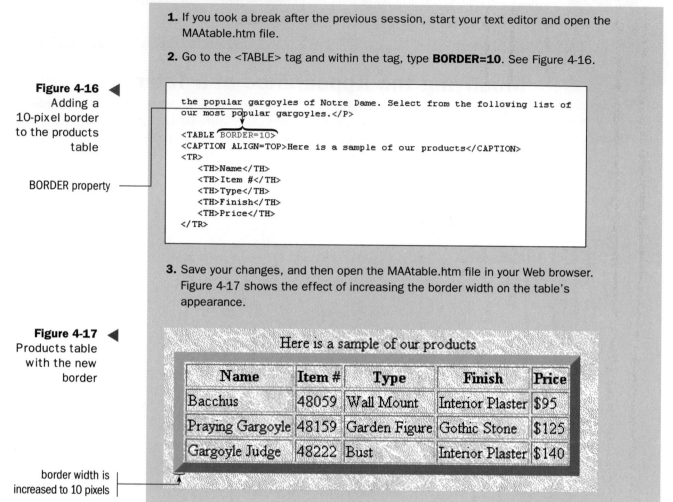

```
the popular gargoyles of Notre Dame. Select from the following list of
our most popular gargoyles.</P>

<TABLE BORDER=10>
<CAPTION ALIGN=TOP>Here is a sample of our products</CAPTION>
<TR>
    <TH>Name</TH>
    <TH>Item #</TH>
    <TH>Type</TH>
    <TH>Finish</TH>
    <TH>Price</TH>
</TR>
```

3. Save your changes, and then open the MAAtable.htm file in your Web browser. Figure 4-17 shows the effect of increasing the border width on the table's appearance.

Figure 4-17 ◄
Products table
with the new
border

Here is a sample of our products

Name	Item #	Type	Finish	Price
Bacchus	48059	Wall Mount	Interior Plaster	$95
Praying Gargoyle	48159	Garden Figure	Gothic Stone	$125
Gargoyle Judge	48222	Bust	Interior Plaster	$140

border width is
increased to 10 pixels

You've modified the outside border of the table, but Nicole would also like you to change the width of the *inside* border, between individual table cells. She feels that the table would look better if the interior borders were less prominent. This is done using the CELLSPACING property.

Controlling Cell Spacing

The CELLSPACING property controls the amount of space inserted between table cells. The syntax for specifying the cell spacing is:

```
<TABLE CELLSPACING=size>
```

where *size* is the width of the interior borders in pixels. The default cell spacing is 2 pixels. Figure 4-18 shows how different cell spacing values affect a table's appearance.

Figure 4-18
Tables with
different values
for the
CELLSPACING
property

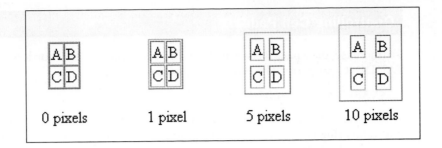

Nicole has decided that she wants the width of the borders between individual table cells to be as small as possible, so you'll decrease the width to 0 pixels. This will not remove the border between the cells (as long as you have a border around the entire table, you will always have a line separating individual table cells), but it will decrease the interior border width to a minimal size. This is because the interior border includes a drop shadow. Even if the cell spacing is set to 0, the drop shadow remains to give the effect of an interior border.

To change the cell spacing:

1. Return to the MAAtable.htm file in your text editor.

2. Go to the <TABLE> tag and type **CELLSPACING=0** within the tag, as shown in Figure 4-19.

Figure 4-19 ◀
Changing the
CELLSPACING
property to
0 pixels

CELLSPACING
property

```
<TABLE BORDER=10 CELLSPACING=0>
<CAPTION ALIGN=TOP>Here is a sample of our products</CAPTION>
<TR>
    <TH>Name</TH>
    <TH>Item #</TH>
    <TH>Type</TH>
    <TH>Finish</TH>
    <TH>Price</TH>
</TR>
```

3. Save your changes, and then reload the MAAtable.htm file in your Web browser. The new cell spacing is shown in Figure 4-20. Note that the line separating the cells has been slightly reduced, but has not totally disappeared (compare Figure 4-17 with Figure 4-20).

Figure 4-20 ◀
Products table
with decreased
cell spacing

interior borders are
now thinner

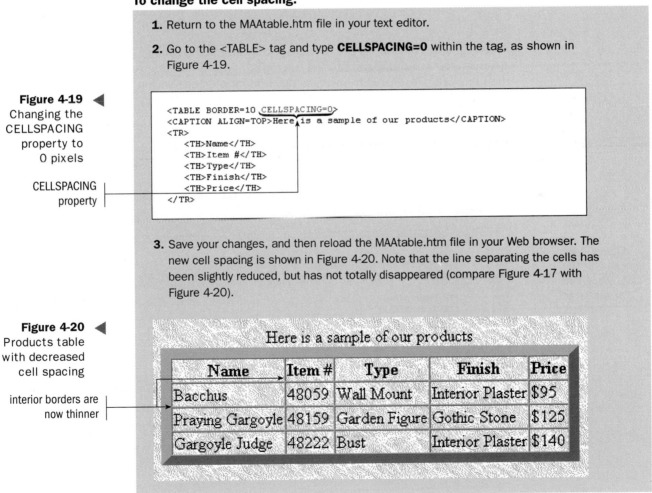

Here is a sample of our products

Name	Item #	Type	Finish	Price
Bacchus	48059	Wall Mount	Interior Plaster	$95
Praying Gargoyle	48159	Garden Figure	Gothic Stone	$125
Gargoyle Judge	48222	Bust	Interior Plaster	$140

After viewing the modified table, Nicole points out that it now appears crowded. She would like you to increase the space between the table text and the surrounding cell borders. You can do this by increasing the amount of cell padding in the table.

Controlling Cell Padding

To increase the space between the table text and the cell borders, you use the CELL-PADDING property. The syntax for this property is:

```
<TABLE CELLPADDING=size>
```

where *size* is the distance from the table text to the cell border in pixels. The default cell padding value is 1 pixel. Figure 4-21 shows the effect of changing the cell padding value on a sample table.

Figure 4-21 ◀
Tables with different values for the CELLPADDING property

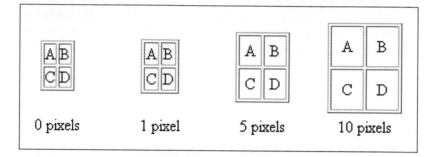

You might confuse the terms cell spacing and cell padding. Just remember that cell spacing refers to the space *between* the cells, and cell padding refers to the space *within* the table cells. You need to increase the amount of space within your table cells because the default 1-pixel gap is too small and causes the cell borders to crowd the cell text. You'll increase the cell padding to 4 pixels.

To increase the amount of cell padding:

1. Return to the MAAtable.htm file in your text editor.

2. Go to the <TABLE> tag and type **CELLPADDING=4** within the tag, as shown in Figure 4-22.

Figure 4-22 ◀
Increasing the CELLPADDING property to 4 pixels

CELLPADDING property |

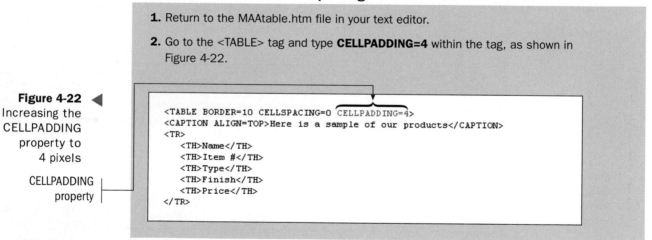

```
<TABLE BORDER=10 CELLSPACING=0 CELLPADDING=4>
<CAPTION ALIGN=TOP>Here is a sample of our products</CAPTION>
<TR>
    <TH>Name</TH>
    <TH>Item #</TH>
    <TH>Type</TH>
    <TH>Finish</TH>
    <TH>Price</TH>
</TR>
```

3. Save your changes, and then reload the MAAtable.htm file in your Web browser. Figure 4-23 shows the table with the increased amount of cell padding.

Figure 4-23 Products table with increased cell padding

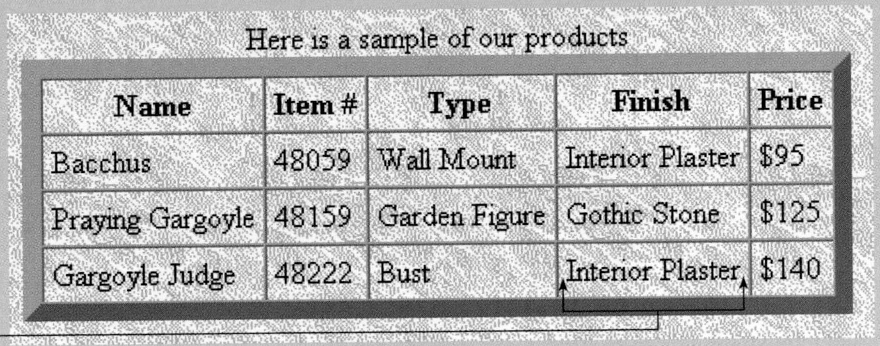

Here is a sample of our products

Name	Item #	Type	Finish	Price
Bacchus	48059	Wall Mount	Interior Plaster	$95
Praying Gargoyle	48159	Garden Figure	Gothic Stone	$125
Gargoyle Judge	48222	Bust	Interior Plaster	$140

cells now include more space around the text

By increasing the cell padding, you added needed space to the table. Next you'll work with the alignment of the table on the page and the text within the table.

Controlling Table and Text Alignment

By default, the browser places a table on the page's left margin, with surrounding text placed either above or below the table. You can change this placement by using the ALIGN property. The syntax for this property is:

```
<TABLE ALIGN=alignment>
```

where *alignment* equals either left or right. The ALIGN property is similar to the ALIGN property used with the <IMG> tag, except that images have more alignment options. As with inline images, using left or right alignment places the table on the page's margin and wraps surrounding text to the side, as illustrated in Figure 4-24.

Figure 4-24 Tables with different ALIGN values

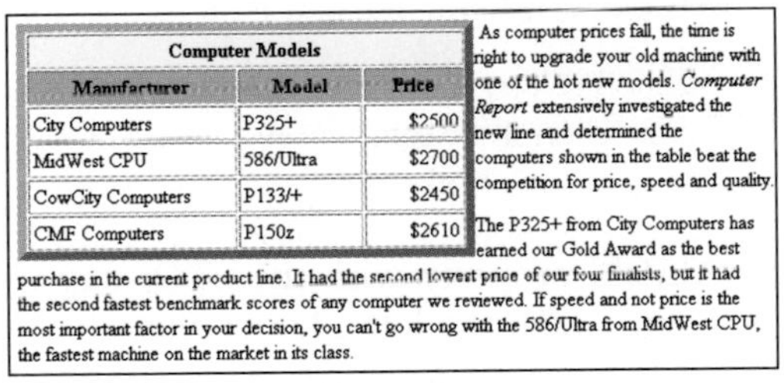

Computer Models		
Manufacturer	Model	Price
City Computers	P325+	$2500
MidWest CPU	586/Ultra	$2700
CowCity Computers	P133/+	$2450
CMF Computers	P150z	$2610

As computer prices fall, the time is right to upgrade your old machine with one of the hot new models. *Computer Report* extensively investigated the new line and determined the computers shown in the table beat the competition for price, speed and quality.

The P325+ from City Computers has earned our Gold Award as the best purchase in the current product line. It had the second lowest price of our four finalists, but it had the second fastest benchmark scores of any computer we reviewed. If speed and not price is the most important factor in your decision, you can't go wrong with the 586/Ultra from MidWest CPU, the fastest machine on the market in its class.

ALIGN=LEFT

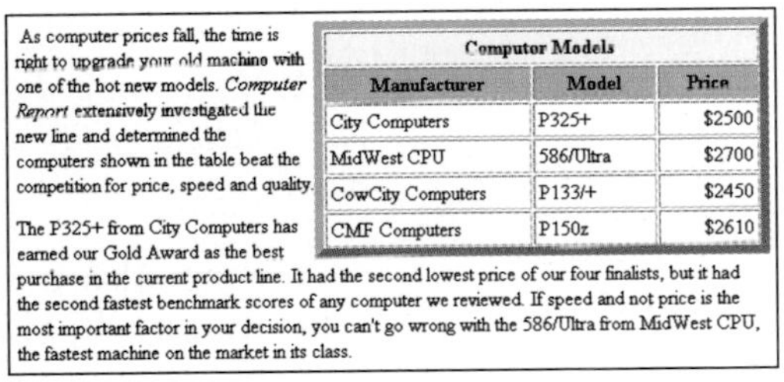

As computer prices fall, the time is right to upgrade your old machine with one of the hot new models. *Computer Report* extensively investigated the new line and determined the computers shown in the table beat the competition for price, speed and quality.

Computor Models		
Manufacturer	Model	Price
City Computers	P325+	$2500
MidWest CPU	586/Ultra	$2700
CowCity Computers	P133/+	$2450
CMF Computers	P150z	$2610

The P325+ from City Computers has earned our Gold Award as the best purchase in the current product line. It had the second lowest price of our four finalists, but it had the second fastest benchmark scores of any computer we reviewed. If speed and not price is the most important factor in your decision, you can't go wrong with the 586/Ultra from MidWest CPU, the fastest machine on the market in its class.

ALIGN=RIGHT

The ALIGN property is a recent addition to HTML and is available only with Netscape Navigator, Internet Explorer, or browsers that support HTML 3.2. Earlier browsers will ignore the ALIGN property and leave the table on the left margin without wrapping text around it.

ALIGNING A TABLE ON THE PAGE

- To align the table with the left page margin, wrapping text to the right of the table, enter:
  <TABLE ALIGN=LEFT>
- To align the table with the right page margin, wrapping text to the left, enter:
  <TABLE ALIGN=RIGHT>
- To center the table on the page, enclose the <TABLE> tags within <CENTER> tags as follows:
  <CENTER>
  　　<TABLE>
  ....
  　　</TABLE>
  </CENTER>

Another possible value for the ALIGN property is CENTER, which centers the table on the page. However, this option is not supported by all browsers. To ensure that your table is centered, you should instead enclose the entire table structure within <CENTER> tags. The <CENTER> tag can be used to center any text, table, or graphic on the page.

Nicole wants the products table to be centered, to better balance the layout of the page. You'll use the <CENTER> tag to accomplish this.

To center the products table:

1. Return to the MAAtable.htm file in your text editor.

2. Insert a blank line *above* the <TABLE> tag.

3. Type **<CENTER>** in the new line.

4. Insert a blank line *below* the </TABLE> tag, and then type **</CENTER>**.

5. Save your changes, and then reload the file in your Web browser. The products table should now be centered on the page.

You can also use the ALIGN property with the <TD> tag to align text within table cells. By default, text is aligned with the left edge of the table cell, but you can use the ALIGN property to center the text within the cell or to align it with the cell's right edge. Another property, VALIGN, allows you to control the vertical placement of text within the table cell. By default, text is placed at the top of the cell, but with the VALIGN property you can align text with the top, middle, or bottom of the cell. Figure 4-25 shows how the combination of the ALIGN and VALIGN properties affects the placement of text within a table cell.

Figure 4-25 ◀
Values of the
ALIGN and
VALIGN
properties

ALIGN=LEFT VALIGN=TOP	ALIGN=LEFT VALIGN=MIDDLE	ALIGN=LEFT VALIGN=BOTTOM
ALIGN=CENTER VALIGN=TOP	ALIGN=CENTER VALIGN=MIDDLE	ALIGN=CENTER VALIGN=BOTTOM
ALIGN=RIGHT VALIGN=TOP	ALIGN=RIGHT VALIGN=MIDDLE	ALIGN=RIGHT VALIGN=BOTTOM

Looking over the table, Nicole decides that the values in the Price column should be right-aligned so that the numbers align properly. Because of the way HTML works with table columns, if you want to align the text for a single column, you must apply the ALIGN property to every cell within that column.

To right-align the Price column values:

1. Return to the MAAtable.htm file in your text editor.

2. For each <TD> tag in the Price column, insert the text **ALIGN=RIGHT**. Figure 4-26 shows the revised HTML code in your file.

Figure 4-26 ◀
Right-aligning
the values in
the Price
column

ALIGN property

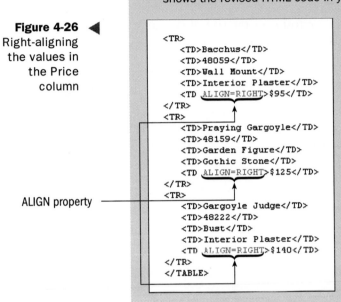

```
<TR>
    <TD>Bacchus</TD>
    <TD>48059</TD>
    <TD>Wall Mount</TD>
    <TD>Interior Plaster</TD>
    <TD ALIGN=RIGHT>$95</TD>
</TR>
<TR>
    <TD>Praying Gargoyle</TD>
    <TD>48159</TD>
    <TD>Garden Figure</TD>
    <TD>Gothic Stone</TD>
    <TD ALIGN=RIGHT>$125</TD>
</TR>
<TR>
    <TD>Gargoyle Judge</TD>
    <TD>48222</TD>
    <TD>Bust</TD>
    <TD>Interior Plaster</TD>
    <TD ALIGN=RIGHT>$140</TD>
</TR>
</TABLE>
```

3. Save your changes, and then reload the page in your Web browser. The prices are now right-aligned. See Figure 4-27.

Figure 4-27 ◀
Right-aligned
prices in the
products table

prices are aligned
with the right edge of

Here is a sample of our products

Name	Item #	Type	Finish	Price
Bacchus	48059	Wall Mount	Interior Plaster	$95
Praying Gargoyle	48159	Garden Figure	Gothic Stone	$125
Gargoyle Judge	48222	Bust	Interior Plaster	$140

You can also use the ALIGN and VALIGN properties with the <TR> tag if you want to align all the text within a single row in the same way. Your next task will be to work with the size of your table and table cells.

Working with Table and Cell Size

The size of a table is determined by the text it contains. By default, HTML places text on a single line. If you insert additional text in a cell, the width of the column and the table will increase up to the page edge, still keeping the text confined to a single line (unless you've inserted a break, paragraph, or header tag within the cell). Once the page edge is reached, the browser will reduce the size of the remaining columns to keep the text to a single line. The browser will wrap the text to a second line within the cell only when it can no longer increase the size of the column and table or decrease the size of the remaining columns. As more text is added, the height of the table automatically expands to accommodate the additional text.

If you want to have greater control over the size of the table and table cells, you can explicitly define the width and height of these elements.

DESIGN window	**CHOOSING TABLE AND CELL SIZE**
	■ Do not specify a table size beyond about 610 pixels (roughly), or else the table will extend beyond the display area of most monitors set at resolutions of 640 x 480. ■ Specify a cell width (either absolute or relative) for all of your table cells, so that you can be sure that the table will be rendered accurately in the browser. ■ Test the appearance of your table under several different monitor resolutions, from 640 x 480 on up.

Defining the Table Size

The syntax for specifying the table size is:

```
<TABLE WIDTH=size HEIGHT=size>
```

Here *size* is the width and height of the table either in pixels or as a percentage of the display area. If you want your table to fill the entire width of the display area, regardless of the resolution of the user's monitor, you would set the WIDTH property to 100%. Note that the percent value should be placed within double quotation marks (use WIDTH="100%" *not* WIDTH=100%). Similarly, to create a table whose height is equal to the height of the display area, enter the property HEIGHT="100%".

On the other hand, you must specify the size of a table exactly, so that its absolute size remains constant, regardless of the browser used. If you use this approach, remember that some monitors will display your page at a resolution of 640 by 480 pixels. If it's important that the table not exceed the browser's display area, you should specify a table width of less than 610 pixels (roughly) to allow space for other window elements such as scroll bars.

REFERENCE window	**SPECIFYING THE TABLE SIZE**
	■ To create a table of a specific size, enter the following tag: <TABLE WIDTH=*size* HEIGHT=*size*> where *size* is the table's height or width either in pixels or as a percentage of the browser's display area. Percentages must be enclosed in quotation marks (for example, WIDTH="70%").

You'll set the width of the products table to 550 pixels. This will ensure that the table will not extend beyond the display area, but will also provide more room in the table cells if you want to insert additional text. You don't need to specify the height of the table, because the table's height will expand as additional products are added.

To increase the width of the products table:

1. Return to the MAAtable.htm file in your text editor and move to the <TABLE> tag.

2. Within the <TABLE> tag, type **WIDTH=550**, as shown in Figure 4-28.

Figure 4-28 ◀
Increasing the
width of the
products table
to 550 pixels

WIDTH property

```
<CENTER>
<TABLE BORDER=10 CELLSPACING=0 CELLPADDING=4 WIDTH=550>
<CAPTION ALIGN=TOP>Here is a sample of our products</CAPTION>
<TR>
    <TH>Name</TH>
    <TH>Item #</TH>
    <TH>Type</TH>
    <TH>Finish</TH>
    <TH>Price</TH>
</TR>
```

3. Save your changes, and then reload the file in your Web browser. Figure 4-29 shows the revised page with the table width increased to 550 pixels.

Figure 4-29 ◀
Products table
with its width
increased

The Gargoyle Collection

Throughout Europe, countless gargoyles peer down from the towers and parapets of medieval cathedrals. In honor of these fascinating creations Middle Age Arts presents an exclusive line of gargoyle replicas. Choose representations from the most famous cathedrals in the world, including the popular gargoyles of Notre Dame. Select from the following list of our most popular gargoyles.

Here is a sample of our products

Name	Item #	Type	Finish	Price
Bacchus	48059	Wall Mount	Interior Plaster	$95
Praying Gargoyle	48159	Garden Figure	Gothic Stone	$125
Gargoyle Judge	48222	Bust	Interior Plaster	$140

table width increased
to 550 pixels

Now that you've set the width of the table, you need to set the width of individual cells.

Defining Cell and Column Sizes

The <TH> and <TD> tags support the WIDTH property as well. To set the size of an individual cell, you enter the HTML code:

```
<TD WIDTH=size>
```

where *size* once again can be expressed either in pixels or as a percentage of the table width. For example, a width value of 30% displays a cell that is 30% of the total width of the table (whatever that might be). To create a cell that is 35 pixels wide, you would enter WIDTH=35 within the <TD> tag. Whether you enter the pixel value or the percentage depends on whether you're trying to create a table that will fill a specific space or a relative space.

Specifying a width for an individual cell does not guarantee that the cell will take that width when displayed in the browser. The problem is that the cell is part of a column containing other cells. If one of those other cells is set to a different width or expands because of the text entered into it, the widths of all cells in the column change accordingly. Setting a width for one cell guarantees only that the cell width will not be *less* than that value. If you want to ensure that the cells do not change in size, neither increasing nor decreasing from the value you set, you must set the WIDTH property of *all* the cells in the column to the same value.

Internet Explorer also supports the HEIGHT property for individual cells. Like the WIDTH property, the HEIGHT property can be expressed either in pixels or as a percentage of the height of the table. If you include more text than can be displayed within that height value, the browser will expand to display the additional text.

Nicole decides that the widths of both the Item # and Price columns can be reduced. Reducing these columns will make more space available to the remaining three columns, in which she expects that additional text might be entered. A width of 60 pixels for the Item # column and 50 pixels for the Price column should work well for the products table.

To set the column widths for the Item # and Price columns:

1. Return to the MAAtable.htm file in your text editor.

2. For the <TH> and <TD> tags in the Item # column, enter the property **WIDTH=60**.

3. For the <TH> and <TD> tags in the Price column, enter the property **WIDTH=50**.

   Figure 4-30 shows the revised HTML code in your file. Check your code carefully because it's easy to place the properties in the wrong columns.

Figure 4-30 ◄
Increasing the width of the Item # and Price columns

WIDTH property —

```
<TR>
   <TH> Name </TH>
   <TH WIDTH=60> Item # </TH>
   <TH> Type </TH>
   <TH> Finish </TH>
   <TH WIDTH=50> Price </TH>
</TR>
<TR>
   <TD>Bacchus</TD>
   <TD WIDTH=60>48059</TD>
   <TD>Wall Mount</TD>
   <TD>Interior Plaster</TD>
   <TD ALIGN=RIGHT WIDTH=50>$95</TD>
</TR>
<TR>
   <TD>Praying Gargoyle</TD>
   <TD WIDTH=60>48159</TD>
   <TD>Garden Figure</TD>
   <TD>Gothic Stone</TD>
   <TD ALIGN=RIGHT WIDTH=50>$125</TD>
</TR>
<TR>
   <TD>Gargoyle Judge</TD>
   <TD WIDTH=60>48222</TD>
   <TD>Bust</TD>
   <TD>Interior Plaster</TD>
   <TD ALIGN=RIGHT WIDTH=50>$140</TD>
</TR>
```

4. Save your changes, and then reload the page in your Web browser to verify that the column widths for the Item # and Price columns have been decreased.

You've completed your work with the layout, and now Nicole would like you to turn your attention to the table color. By default, the table background color matches the page background color, but some browsers allow you to change that.

Modifying the Table Background

One of the extensions supported by both Internet Explorer and Netscape Navigator is the ability to define the background color or image for a table. To change the background color, insert the BGCOLOR property in the <TABLE>, <TR>, <TH>, and/or <TD> tags. You can use either the color name or the RGB color value. Your color choices might not show up on other browsers, so you should make sure that any design decisions you make work with the background color either on or off.

Setting color for the table follows a hierarchy. Using the BGCOLOR property for the <TABLE> tag sets the background color for all cells in the table. You can override this color choice for a single row by using the BGCOLOR property in the <TR> tag. You can also override the table or row color choices for a single cell by inserting the BGCOLOR property in a <TD> or <TH> tag. To set the background color for a column, you must define the background color for each cell in that column.

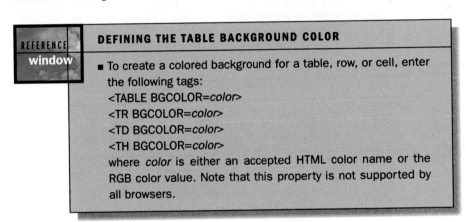

REFERENCE window

DEFINING THE TABLE BACKGROUND COLOR

■ To create a colored background for a table, row, or cell, enter the following tags:
<TABLE BGCOLOR=*color*>
<TR BGCOLOR=*color*>
<TD BGCOLOR=*color*>
<TH BGCOLOR=*color*>
where *color* is either an accepted HTML color name or the RGB color value. Note that this property is not supported by all browsers.

After considering many different colors, Nicole decides that she would like to have the background color of the header row set to green, the rows of the table set to white, and the background of the names of the products set to yellow. She asks you to make these changes now. You'll start by setting the table background color.

To define the table background color:

1. Return to the MAAtable.htm file in your text editor and go to the <TABLE> tag.

2. Type **BGCOLOR=WHITE** within the <TABLE> tag.

Now that you've set the background color of each cell to white, you'll override this option for the header row, setting the background for cells in that row to a shade of green. The RGB color value is (51,204,102), which translates to 33CC66.

To define the background color for the header row:

1. Go to the first <TR> tag in the products table (the row containing the <TH> tags).

2. Type **BGCOLOR="#33CC66"** within the <TR> tag.

Finally you'll change the background color of the three product names to yellow.

To define the background color for the cells in the first column:

1. Go to the <TD> tag for the Bacchus cell.

2. Type **BGCOLOR=YELLOW** within the <TD> tag.

3. Insert the BGCOLOR=YELLOW property within the remaining two cells for the first column (the Praying Gargoyle cell and the Gargoyle Judge cell). Figure 4-31 shows the revised HTML code for your page.

Figure 4-31 ◀
Setting background colors for the table, the header row, and individual table cells

background color for the table

background color for the header row

background color for an individual table cell

```
<TABLE BORDER=10 CELLSPACING=0 CELLPADDING=4 WIDTH=550 BGCOLOR=WHITE>
<CAPTION ALIGN=TOP>Here is a sample of our products</CAPTION>
<TR BGCOLOR="#33CC66">
    <TH> Name </TH>
    <TH WIDTH=60> Item # </TH>
    <TH> Type </TH>
    <TH> Finish </TH>
    <TH WIDTH=50> Price </TH>
</TR>
<TR>
    <TD BGCOLOR=YELLOW>Bacchus</TD>
    <TD WIDTH=60>48059</TD>
    <TD>Wall Mount</TD>
    <TD>Interior Plaster</TD>
    <TD ALIGN=RIGHT WIDTH=50>$95</TD>
</TR>
<TR>
    <TD BGCOLOR=YELLOW>Praying Gargoyle</TD>
    <TD WIDTH=60>48159</TD>
    <TD>Garden Figure</TD>
    <TD>Gothic Stone</TD>
    <TD ALIGN=RIGHT WIDTH=50>$125</TD>
</TR>
<TR>
    <TD BGCOLOR=YELLOW>Gargoyle Judge</TD>
    <TD WIDTH=60>48222</TD>
    <TD>Bust</TD>
    <TD>Interior Plaster</TD>
    <TD ALIGN=RIGHT WIDTH=50>$140</TD>
</TR>
</TABLE>
```

4. Save your changes, and then reload the file in your Web browser. Figure 4-32 shows the revised table with the new color scheme.

Figure 4-32 ◀
Products table with the new background colors

Here is a sample of our products				
Name	**Item #**	**Type**	**Finish**	**Price**
Bacchus	48059	Wall Mount	Interior Plaster	$95
Praying Gargoyle	48159	Garden Figure	Gothic Stone	$125
Gargoyle Judge	48222	Bust	Interior Plaster	$140

TROUBLE? If your page looks different from the one shown in Figure 4-32, it could be because of your browser. The Internet Explorer browser applies the table background color to the caption. The Netscape Navigator browser does not. Also the Netscape Navigator browser might align the table text differently.

Spanning Rows and Columns

Nicole has reviewed your table and would like to make a few more changes. She notes that the Gargoyle Judge item comes in two finishes, interior plaster and gothic stone. The gothic stone version has item number 48223, and Nicole wants this information added to the table. You can add the information by inserting a new row in the table, but that would leave you with two rows with the same item name. Is there a way that you can use the cell containing the item name in both rows? Yes, with a spanning cell.

A **spanning cell** is a cell that occupies more than one row or column in a table. Figure 4-33 shows a table of opinion poll data in which some of the cells span several rows and/or columns.

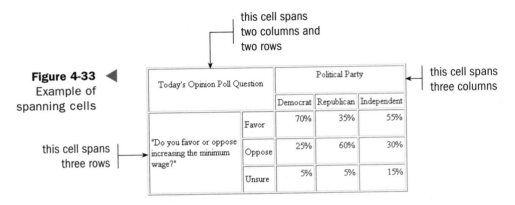

Figure 4-33
Example of
spanning cells

Nicole wants to include similar spanning cells in the products table. She sketches how she expects the table to appear with the new Gargoyle Judge entry (Figure 4-34). She has indicated two new spanning cells: the Gargoyle Judge entry will span two rows, and the Type and Finish columns will be combined into a single cell spanning two columns.

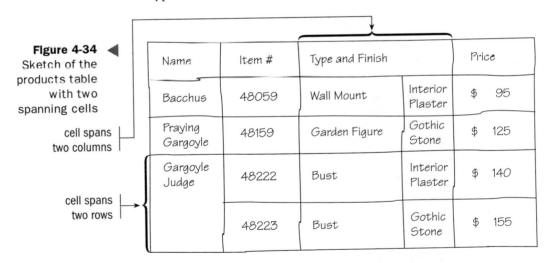

Figure 4-34
Sketch of the
products table
with two
spanning cells

You can create spanning cells in HTML using the ROWSPAN and COLSPAN properties in a <TD> or <TH> tag. The syntax for the <TD> tag is:

```
<TD ROWSPAN=value COLSPAN=value> Cell Text </TD>
```

where *value* is the number of rows or columns that the cell will span within the table. Spanning is always downwards and to the right of the cell containing the ROWSPAN and COLSPAN properties. For example, to create a cell that spans two columns in the table, you would enter a <TD COLSPAN=2> tag. For a cell that spans two rows, the tag is <TD ROWSPAN=2>, and to span two rows and two columns, the tag is <TD ROWSPAN=2 COLSPAN=2>.

The important thing to remember when you have a cell that spans several rows or columns is that you must adjust the number of cell tags used in the table row. If a row has five columns, but one of the cells in the row spans three columns, you would only need to have three <TD> tags: two <TD> tags for the cells that occupy a single column, and the third for the <TD> spanning three rows.

When a cell spans several rows, the rows below the spanning cell must also be adjusted. Consider a table with three rows and four columns. The first cell in the first row is a spanning cell that spans three rows. You would need four <TD> tags for the first row, but only three <TD> tags for rows two and three. This is because the spanning cell from row one occupies the cells that would normally appear in rows two and three (Figure 4-35).

Figure 4-35 ◀
Table structure
with a
row-spanning
cell

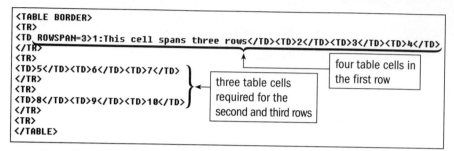

HTML code

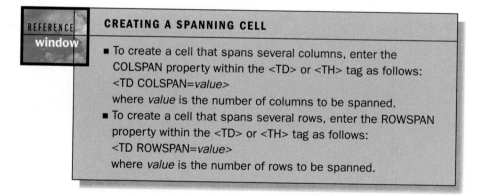

resulting table

REFERENCE window

CREATING A SPANNING CELL

■ To create a cell that spans several columns, enter the COLSPAN property within the <TD> or <TH> tag as follows:
<TD COLSPAN=*value*>
where *value* is the number of columns to be spanned.

■ To create a cell that spans several rows, enter the ROWSPAN property within the <TD> or <TH> tag as follows:
<TD ROWSPAN=*value*>
where *value* is the number of rows to be spanned.

To make the changes Nicole requested, you must first change the cell containing the text "Gargoyle Judge" to a spanning cell covering two rows, and then you need to add a new row to the bottom of the table.

To create a cell that spans two rows:

1. Return to the MAAtable.htm file in your text editor and locate the <TD> tag for the Gargoyle Judge cell in the last row of the table.

2. Type **ROWSPAN=2** within the <TD> tag.

3. Go to the </TR> tag at the end of the row, and then press the **Enter** key to create a new blank line below it.

4. Enter the following text, starting at the new line you just inserted:

<TR>
  <TD WIDTH=60>48223</TD>
  <TD>Bust</TD>
  <TD>Gothic Stone</TD>
  <TD ALIGN=RIGHT WIDTH=50>$155</TD>
</TR>

Note that this new row has four cell tags, and not five like the other rows in the table, because one of the cell tags is being replaced by the spanning cell you created in the previous row. Figure 4-36 shows the revised HTML code.

Figure 4-36 ◀
Creating a
row-spanning
cell in the
products table

ROWSPAN property ———

new table row ———

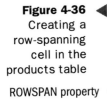

```
<TR>
    <TD BGCOLOR=YELLOW ROWSPAN=2>Gargoyle Judge</TD>
    <TD WIDTH=60>48222</TD>
    <TD>Bust</TD>
    <TD>Interior Plaster</TD>
    <TD ALIGN=RIGHT WIDTH=50>$140</TD>
</TR>
<TR>
    <TD WIDTH=60>48223</TD>
    <TD>Bust</TD>
    <TD>Gothic Stone</TD>
    <TD ALIGN=RIGHT WIDTH=50>$155</TD>
</TR>
</TABLE>
```

5. Save your changes, and then reload the file in your Web browser. The Gargoyle Judge cell now spans two rows in the first column. See Figure 4-37.

Figure 4-37 ◀
Row-spanning
cell in the
products table

cell spans two rows ———

Here is a sample of our products				
Name	**Item #**	**Type**	**Finish**	**Price**
Bacchus	48059	Wall Mount	Interior Plaster	$95
Praying Gargoyle	48159	Garden Figure	Gothic Stone	$125
Gargoyle Judge	48222	Bust	Interior Plaster	$140
	48223	Bust	Gothic Stone	$155

The text in the spanning cell is centered vertically, but it would look better if it were placed at the top of the cell. You can do this using the VALIGN property mentioned earlier.

To align the text with the top of the spanning cell:

1. Return to the MAAtable.htm file in your text editor.

2. Within the <TD> tag for the spanning cell you just created, type **VALIGN=TOP**.

Your next task is to merge the Type and Finish header cells into one cell. To do this, you can create a spanning cell to span across the Type and Finish columns.

To span a cell across the two columns:

1. Go to the <TH> tag in the first row of the table for the word "Type."

2. Within the <TH> tag, type **COLSPAN=2**.

3. Change the table header "Type" to **Type and Finish**.

Because this cell now spans two columns, you have to remove the Finish cell from the header row.

4. Delete the <TH> tags and enclosed text for the Finish table header. Figure 4-38 shows the revised HTML code.

Figure 4-38 ◀
Creating a column-spanning cell in the products table

the old Finish table header has been removed

column-spanning cell

```
<TABLE BORDER=10 CELLSPACING=0 CELLPADDING=4 WIDTH=550 BGCOLOR=WHITE>
<CAPTION ALIGN=TOP>Here is a sample of our products</CAPTION>
<TR BGCOLOR="#33CC66">
    <TH> Name </TH>
    <TH WIDTH=60> Item # </TH>
    <TH COLSPAN=2> Type and Finish </TH>
    <TH WIDTH=50> Price </TH>
</TR>
```

5. Save your changes, and then reload the file in your browser. Figure 4-39 shows the final layout of the gargoyle products table.

Figure 4-39 ◀
Final version of the gargoyle products table

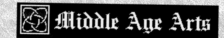

Middle Age Arts

The Gargoyle Collection

Throughout Europe, countless gargoyles peer down from the towers and parapets of medieval cathedrals. In honor of these fascinating creations Middle Age Arts presents an exclusive line of gargoyle replicas. Choose representations from the most famous cathedrals in the world, including the popular gargoyles of Notre Dame. Select from the following list of our most popular gargoyles.

Here is a sample of our products

Name	Item #	Type and Finish		Price
Bacchus	48059	Wall Mount	Interior Plaster	$95
Praying Gargoyle	48159	Garden Figure	Gothic Stone	$125
Gargoyle Judge	48222	Bust	Interior Plaster	$140
	48223	Bust	Gothic Stone	$155

Quick Check

1. What HTML code would you enter to create a table that has a 5-pixel-wide border with a 3-pixel border between table cells and 4 pixels between the cell text and the surrounding cell border?

2. What HTML code would you enter to align text with the top of a table header cell?

3. What HTML code would you enter to center *all* of the text within a given row?

4. What are the two ways of expressing table width? What are the advantages and disadvantages of each?

5. What HTML code would you enter to create a table that fills up half the width of the browser's display area, regardless of the resolution of the user's monitor?

6. What HTML code would you enter to set the width of a cell to 60 pixels? Will this keep the cell from exceeding 60 pixels in width? Will this keep the cell from being less than 60 pixels wide? How would you guarantee that the cell width will be exactly 60 pixels?

7. What HTML code would you enter to set the background color of your table to yellow? What are the limitations of this code?

8. What HTML code would you enter to create a cell that spans three rows and two columns?

You've completed your work on the appearance of the products table. You've learned how to control table size, alignment, border style, and color. You've also seen how to create cells that span several rows or columns in your table. In the next session you'll learn how to use tables to enhance the layout of an entire Web page.

SESSION

4.3

In this session you will work with tables to create a newspaper-style layout for a Web page. You'll create nested tables to enhance the page's design. Finally, you'll learn about some extensions supported by Internet Explorer that you can use on your tables.

Creating a Page Layout with Tables

In the first two sessions you've used the <TABLE> tag to create a table of products. In practice, however, the table features of HTML are most often used to control the layout of the page. If you want to design a page that displays text in newspaper-style columns, or separates the page into different topical areas, you'll find tables a handy tool. One of the most useful features of tables is that within each table cell you can use any of the HTML layout tags you've learned so far. For example, you can insert an <H1> header within a cell, or you can insert an ordered list of items. You can even nest one table inside another.

Nicole is satisfied with your prototype page of Middle Age Arts products. She now wants you to create a home page for the Gargoyle Collection product line. The page will contain a list of links to other Middle Age Arts pages, a message from the company president, a few notes about the uses of gargoyles, and a profile of one of Middle Age Arts' artists.

Nicole sketches a layout for the home page (Figure 4-40).

Figure 4-40
Nicole's sketch
of the Gargoyle
Collection
Home Page

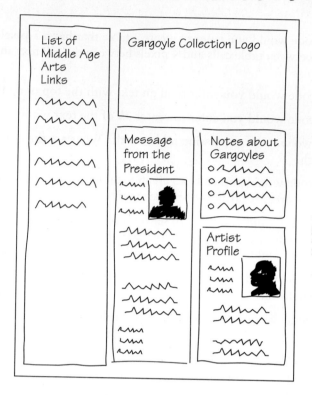

To create the layout specified in Nicole's sketch, you will create two tables, one nested inside the other. The first table, shown in Figure 4-41, consists of one row with two columns. The first column will contain the list of hypertext links. The second column will contain the nested table along with the rest of the page material. You'll create this outer table first.

Figure 4-41
Outer table of
the Gargoyle
Collection
Home Page

1 row x 2 columns

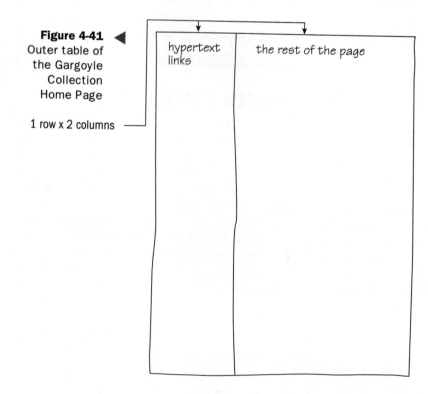

Designing the First Half of the Page

When designing a page that contains tables and other elements within tables, it's best to begin with the outer table and work inward. In the case of the Gargoyle Collection Home Page, you'll start by creating the outer table, which has one row and two columns. Because you want to control the layout exactly, you'll specify a width of 610 pixels for the table. This will preserve the layout of the various page elements and allow users with monitor resolutions of 640 × 480 to view the page correctly. You'll set the width of the first column to 165 pixels and the width of the second column to 445 pixels. As you design Web pages, you'll decide on column widths like these through trial and error, and whatever "looks right." In this case, you've been given the values beforehand.

The HTML code for pages like the one you're about to create can be long and complicated. One aid for you and for others who will be viewing the source code of your page is to include comments that describe the different sections of the page. The text entered into comments will not appear on the Web page. The format for a comment tag is:

```
<! comment text >
```

Any text appearing within the tag after the exclamation point is ignored by the browser.

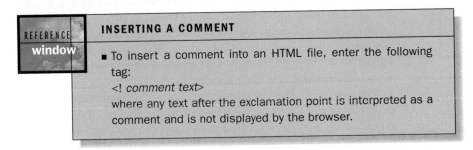

REFERENCE window

INSERTING A COMMENT

- To insert a comment into an HTML file, enter the following tag:
  `<! comment text>`
  where any text after the exclamation point is interpreted as a comment and is not displayed by the browser.

The initial file that you'll use for the Gargoyle Collection Home Page has been created for you. The file, named GHome.htm, contains no text but does have a page title and a background image consisting of a single maroon-colored stripe. Now you need to open the file and create the outer table structure. You'll include comments along with the <TABLE> tags to help you document the different elements of the page layout.

To create the outer table and comments:

1. If you took a break after the previous session, start your text editor.

2. Open the file **GHome.htm** in the Tutorial.04 folder of your Student Disk.

3. Save the file as **Gargoyle.htm**.

4. Between the <BODY> tags, enter the following:

```
<TABLE WIDTH=610 CELLPADDING=0 CELLSPACING=0>
<TR>
   <!- -List of Hypertext Links- ->
   <TD WIDTH=165 VALIGN=TOP>
   </TD>
   <!- -Articles about the Gargoyle Collection- ->
   <TD WIDTH=445 VALIGN=TOP>
   </TD>
</TR>
</TABLE>
```

The Gargoyle.htm file should look like Figure 4-42.

Figure 4-42
Tags for the
outer table and
comments
in the
Gargoyle.htm
file

comment tags

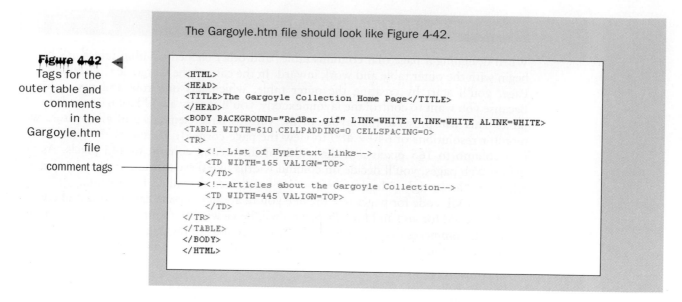

```
<HTML>
<HEAD>
<TITLE>The Gargoyle Collection Home Page</TITLE>
</HEAD>
<BODY BACKGROUND="RedBar.gif" LINK=WHITE VLINK=WHITE ALINK=WHITE>
<TABLE WIDTH=610 CELLPADDING=0 CELLSPACING=0>
<TR>
<!--List of Hypertext Links-->
<TD WIDTH=165 VALIGN=TOP>
</TD>
<!--Articles about the Gargoyle Collection-->
<TD WIDTH=445 VALIGN=TOP>
</TD>
</TR>
</TABLE>
</BODY>
</HTML>
```

Note that in both cells of this outer table, you've set the vertical alignment to top, rather than using the default value of middle. This is because the cells in this table will act as newspaper columns, with text flowing from the cell top down. You'll follow this practice with other table cells on the page. You've also set the cell padding and cell spacing values to 0. This allows any text entered into those cells to use the full cell width. You won't be creating any table borders in this layout.

Leaving aside the contents of the second cell of the outer table until later, you'll concentrate on the first cell, which will contain the list of Middle Age Arts hypertext links. A page has already been created with this information, shown in Figure 4-43.

Figure 4-43
Page with the
list of
hypertext links

hypertext links

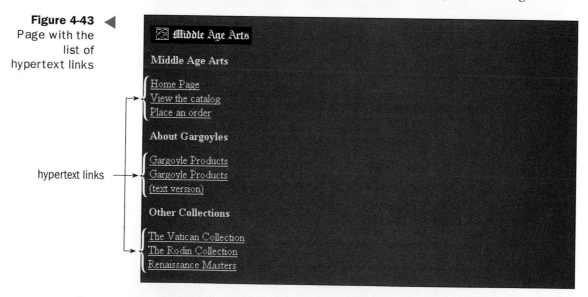

To create the contents for the table's first column, you'll copy the information contained in the document shown in Figure 4-43 and paste it between the table cell tags. (If you don't know how to copy and paste with your text editor, ask your instructor or technical support person for assistance.)

To insert the first column's contents:

1. Insert a blank line between the first set of <TD> and </TD> tags in the Gargoyle.htm file.

2. Open the file **Links.htm** from the Tutorial.04 folder of your Student Disk.

   TROUBLE? You might have to close your text editor if your operating system does not permit you to have multiple copies of the editor running at the same time. If so, save the changes to the Gargoyle.htm file before opening Links.htm.

3. Copy the HTML code within the <BODY> tags of the Links.htm file, but do *not* include the <BODY> tags themselves. Note that all the code you need to copy is indented in the file.

4. Return to the Gargoyle.htm file in your text editor.

5. Paste the HTML code you copied from Links.htm in the blank space you created between the first set of <TD> and </TD> tags. See Figure 4-44.

Figure 4-44 ◀
HTML code for
the list of
hypertext links

```
<TR>
    <!--List of Hypertext Links-->
    <TD WIDTH=165 VALIGN=TOP>
        <IMG SRC="MAA2.gif" WIDTH=144 HEIGHT=25 ALT="Middle Age Arts">
        <H4><FONT COLOR=YELLOW>Middle Age Arts</FONT></H4>
        <FONT COLOR=WHITE>
        <A HREF="Index.htm">Home Page</A><BR>
        <A HREF="Catalog.htm">View the catalog</A><BR>
        <A HREF="Orders.htm">Place an order</A><BR>
        </FONT>
        <H4><FONT COLOR=YELLOW>About Gargoyles</FONT></H4>
        <FONT COLOR=WHITE>
        <A HREF="MAAtable.htm">Gargoyle Products</A><BR>
        <A HREF="MAAtext.htm">Gargoyle Products<BR>(text version)</A><BR>
        </FONT>
        <H4><FONT COLOR=YELLOW>Other Collections</FONT></H4>
        <FONT COLOR=WHITE>
        <A HREF="Vatican.htm">The Vatican Collection</A><BR>
        <A HREF="Rodin.htm">The Rodin Collection</A><BR>
        <A HREF="Masters.htm">Renaissance Masters</A><BR>
        </FONT>
    </TD>
```

6. Save your changes, and then open the Gargoyle.htm file in your Web browser. Figure 4-45 shows the current state of the Gargoyle Collection Home Page.

Figure 4-45 ◀
Initial Gargoyle
Collection
Home Page

TROUBLE? Note that not all of the links on this page point to existing files.

Notice that the contents of the original Links.htm file are contained within the boundaries of the first column of the outer table. You've completed the first half of the page. Now you'll turn your attention to the second half.

Designing the Second Half of the Page

The material in the second column will be organized inside another table. This inner, or nested, table has three rows and three columns, as shown in Figure 4-46. The first row contains a single cell with the Gargoyle Collection logo spanning the three columns. The first cell in the second row contains the president's message spanning the second and third rows of the table. The second cell in that row will act as a **gutter**, which is a blank space separating the material between columns (in this case, between the first and third columns). The gutter will also span the second and third rows. Finally, the third cell in the second row contains the notes about gargoyles, and the third cell in the last row contains the artist's profile.

Figure 4-46
Inner table of the Gargoyle Collection Home Page

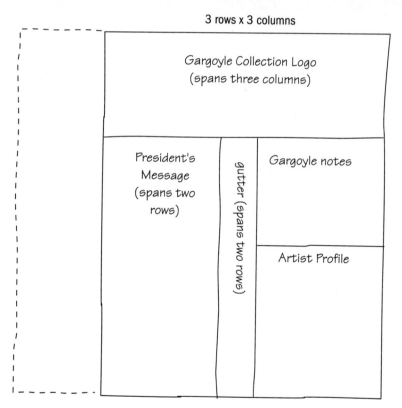

As with previous tables, you'll first enter the table structure and then enter the table text. Nested tables work in the same way as regular tables, except that they must be inserted within <TD> tags.

To create the nested table:

1. Return to the Gargoyle.htm file in your text editor.

2. Insert a blank line between the second set of <TD> and </TD> tags.

3. Enter the following text, indented three spaces in from the <TD> tag:

```
<TABLE WIDTH=445 CELLSPACING=0 CELLPADDING=0>
<TR>
   <!- The Gargoyle Collection Logo->
   <TD COLSPAN=3 VALIGN=TOP ALIGN=CENTER>
   </TD>
</TR>
<TR>
   <!-A message from the company president->
   <TD ROWSPAN=2 WIDTH=220 VALIGN=TOP>
   </TD>
   <!-The table gutter->
   <TD ROWSPAN=2 WIDTH=5></TD>
   <!-Notes about gargoyles->
   <TD WIDTH=220 VALIGN=TOP>
   </TD>
</TR>
<TR>
   <!-Profile of an artist->
   <TD WIDTH=220 VALIGN=TOP>
   </TD>
</TR>
</TABLE>
```

Your file should appear as shown in Figure 4-47. Note that by indenting the text for the nested table three spaces, you have improved the readability of the HTML code without affecting the code itself.

Figure 4-47 ◀
HTML code for
the inner table

```
<!--Articles about the Gargoyle Collection-->
<TD WIDTH=445 VALIGN=TOP>
   <TABLE WIDTH=445 CELLSPACING=0 CELLPADDING=0>
   <TR>
      <!-- The Gargoyle Collection Logo-->
      <TD COLSPAN=3 VALIGN=TOP ALIGN=CENTER>
      </TD>
   </TR>
   <TR>
      <!--A message from the company president-->
      <TD ROWSPAN=2 WIDTH=220 VALIGN=TOP>
      </TD>
      <!--The table gutter-->
      <TD ROWSPAN=2 WIDTH=5></TD>
      <!--Notes about gargoyles-->
      <TD WIDTH=220 VALIGN=TOP>
      </TD>
   </TR>
   <TR>
      <!--Profile of an artist-->
      <TD WIDTH=220 VALIGN=TOP>
      </TD>
   </TR>
   </TABLE>
</TD>
```

Before proceeding, you should study the HTML code you just entered and compare it to Figure 4-46. Make sure that you understand the purpose of each tag in the nested table.

The first item you'll enter in the nested table is an inline image, GLogo.jpg, which you'll place in the table's first row.

To insert the Gargoyle Collection logo:

1. Insert a blank line below the first <TD> tag in the nested table.

2. Type the following in the blank line, indented three spaces in from the <TD> tag, to make the code more readable:

   <IMG SRC="GLogo.jpg" WIDTH=440 HEIGHT=220>

   Figure 4-48 shows the revised HTML code.

Figure 4-48 ◀
Inserting the
Gargoyle
Collection logo

```
<TD WIDTH=445 VALIGN=TOP>
   <TABLE WIDTH=445 CELLSPACING=0 CELLPADDING=0>
   <TR>
     <!-- The Gargoyle Collection Logo-->
     <TD COLSPAN=3 VALIGN=TOP ALIGN=CENTER>
        <IMG SRC="GLogo.jpg" WIDTH=440 HEIGHT=220>
     </TD>
   </TR>
```

With the logo in place, you'll insert the message from the company president next. The message has already been saved for you in the file Oneil.htm. This page is shown in Figure 4-49.

Figure 4-49 ◀
Message from
the company
president

From the President

This month Middle Age Arts introduces the Gargoyle Collection. I'm really excited about this new set of classical figures.

The collection contains faithful reproductions of gargoyles from some of the famous cathedrals of Europe, including Notre Dame, Rheims and Warwick Castle. All reproductions are done to exacting and loving detail.

The collection also contains original works by noted artists such as Susan Bedford and Antonio Salvari. Our expert artisans have produced some wonderful and whimsical works, perfectly suited for home or garden use.

Don't delay, order your gargoyle today.

Irene O'Neil
President,
Middle Age Arts

As you did with the list of hypertext links, you'll copy and paste the contents of the page body into a table cell. The pasted text needs to be placed in the first column of the second row of the nested table.

To insert the message from the company president:

1. Insert a blank line below the first <TD> tag in the second row of the nested table.

2. Open the file **Oneil.htm** from the Tutorial.04 folder of your Student Disk.

3. Copy the HTML code between, but not including, the <BODY> tags. All of the code you need to copy is already indented.

4. Return to the Gargoyle.htm file in your text editor.

5. Paste the HTML code you copied from Oneil.htm in the blank line you created in Step 1. See Figure 4-50.

Figure 4-50 ◀
HTML code for the president's message

table cell from the second row, first column of the nested table

```
<TR>
  <!--A message from the company president-->
  <TD ROWSPAN=2 WIDTH=220 VALIGN=TOP>
    <H4 ALIGN=CENTER><FONT COLOR=GREEN>From the President</FONT></H4>
    <IMG SRC="Oneil.jpg" ALIGN=RIGHT WIDTH=86 HEIGHT=111>
    <P>This month Middle Age Arts introduces the Gargoyle
    Collection. I'm really excited about this new set of classical
    figures.</P>
    <P>The collection contains faithful reproductions of gargoyles
    from some of the famous cathedrals of Europe, including Notre
    Dame, Rheims and Warwick Castle. All reproductions are done to
    exacting and loving detail.</P>
    <P>The collection also contains original works by noted artists
    such as Susan Bedford and Antonio Salvari. Our expert artisans
    have produced some wonderful and whimsical works, perfectly
    suited for home or garden use.</P>
    <P>Don't delay, order your gargoyle today.</P>
    <I>Irene O'Neil</I><BR>
    <B>President,<BR>
    Middle Age Arts</B>
  </TD>
```

6. Save your changes, and then reload the file in your browser. The page now displays the column from the company president, as well as the Gargoyle Collection logo. See Figure 4-51.

Figure 4-51 ◄
Logo and president's message as they appear on the page

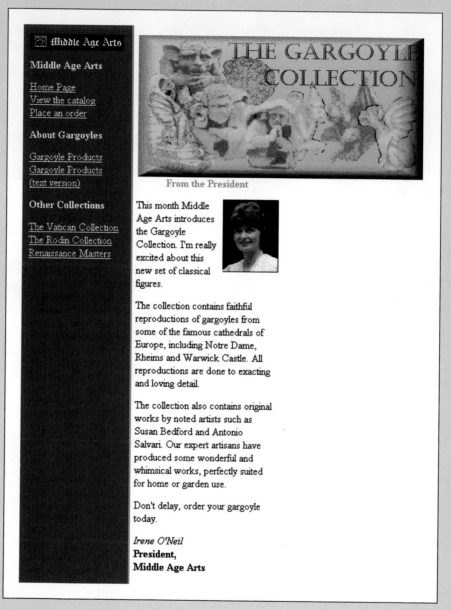

The next cell in the nested table creates a space (gutter) between the first and third columns. You do not have to enter any text into this cell, but you should leave a blank space between the <TD> and </TD> tags. The blank space ensures that the cell occupies the 5-pixel width set aside for it. Without anything in the table cell, some browsers will not display the cell, even if you have specified a width for it.

To insert a blank space into the gutter:

1. Return to the Gargoyle.htm file in your text editor.

2. Go to the <TD> tag after the table gutter comment tag.

3. Insert a blank space between the <TD> and </TD> tags.

The blank space you inserted will help ensure that the column retains its 5-pixel width. The next cell in the table will include a whimsical list describing the "uses" of gargoyle products. The contents of the list have been saved in the GNotes.htm file, shown in Figure 4-52.

Figure 4-52 ◀
List of gargoyle
"uses"

> ### What do I do with a gargoyle?
>
> Don't think you need a gargoyle? Think again. Gargoyles are useful as:
>
> - Bird baths
> - Wind chimes
> - Pen holders
> - Paperweights
> - Bookends

Note that the background of this page is yellow. This is a feature you'll want to keep when you transfer the contents of this page into the table cell. You'll accomplish this using the BGCOLOR property of the cell.

To insert the gargoyle notes:

1. Make sure the Gargoyle.htm file is displayed in your text editor.

2. Insert a blank line below the <TD> tag located in the second row of the nested table.

3. Open the file **GNotes.htm** from the Tutorial.04 folder of your Student Disk.

4. Copy the HTML code between the <BODY> tags. Once again, do *not* include the <BODY> tags themselves.

5. Return to the Gargoyle.htm file.

6. Paste the HTML code in the blank line you created in Step 1.

   Next, you'll change the color of the cell background to yellow.

7. Type **BGCOLOR=YELLOW** within the <TD> tag for the cell. The revised code is shown in Figure 4-53.

Figure 4-53 ◀
HTML code for
the list of
gargoyle uses

table cell from the
second row,
third column of
the nested table

table cell background
color changed to yellow

```
<!--The table gutter-->
<TD ROWSPAN=2 WIDTH=5> </TD>
<!--Notes about gargoyles-->
<TD WIDTH=220 VALIGN=TOP BGCOLOR=YELLOW>
   <FONT COLOR="#800000">
   <H4 ALIGN=CENTER>What do I do with a gargoyle?</H4>
   Don't think you need a gargoyle? Think again. Gargoyles are
   useful as:
   <UL>
      <LI>Bird baths
      <LI>Wind chimes
      <LI>Pen holders
      <LI>Paperweights
      <LI>Bookends
   </UL>
   </FONT>
</TD>
</TR>
```

8. Save your changes, and then reload the file in your browser. The revised Gargoyle Collection page is shown in Figure 4-54.

Figure 4-54 ◀
Gargoyle
notes on the
Web page

TROUBLE? The space between the columns might look different in your browser from what is shown in Figure 4-54. Different browsers handle column spaces and gutters in slightly different ways.

The last component of the page is the profile of the artist, Michael Cassini. The contents of this profile can be found in the Cassini.htm file, shown in Figure 4-55.

Figure 4-55
Artist profile
page

Profile of the Artist

This month's artist is Michael Cassini. Michael has been a professional sculptor for ten years. He has won numerous awards, including the prestigious *Reichsman Cup* and an Award of Merit at the 1997 Tuscany Arts Competition.

Michael specializes in recreations of gargoyles from European cathedrals. You'll usually find Michael staring intently at the church walls in northern France. His work is represented by the *Turin Gargoyle*, a great entry to our Gargoyle Collection.

You need to place the text for the profile in the last cell in the third row. Remember that the first two cells of the third row have been already filled in, being merely extensions of the spanning cells created in the table's second row.

To insert the profile of Michael Cassini:

1. Return to the Gargoyle.htm file in your text editor.

2. Insert a blank line below the final <TD> tag, located in the third row of the nested table.

3. Open the file **Cassini.htm** from the Tutorial.04 folder of your Student Disk. Again, the HTML code is already indented.

4. Copy the HTML code between the <BODY> tags.

5. Return to the Gargoyle.htm file.

6. Paste the HTML code in the blank line you created earlier. See Figure 4-56.

Figure 4-56
HTML code
for the artist
profile

table cell from the
third row,
third column of
the nested table

```
<TR>
  <!--Profile of an artist-->
  <TD WIDTH=220 VALIGN=TOP>
    <H4 ALIGN=CENTER><FONT COLOR=GREEN>Profile of the Artist</FONT></H4>
    <IMG SRC="Cassini.jpg" ALIGN=RIGHT WIDTH=64 HEIGHT=74>
    <P>This month's artist is Michael Cassini. Michael has been a
    professional sculptor for ten years. He has won numerous awards,
    including the prestigious <I>Reichsman Cup</I> and an Award of
    Merit at the 1997 Tuscany Arts Competition.</P>
    <P>Michael specializes in recreations of gargoyles from European
    cathedrals. You'll usually find Michael staring intently at the
    church walls in northern France. His work is represented by the
    <I>Turin Gargoyle</I>, a great entry to our Gargoyle
    Collection.</P>
  </TD>
</TR>
</TABLE>
```

7. Save your changes, and then reload the file in your browser. Figure 4-57 shows the final version of the page.

Figure 4-57 ◀
Final version of
the Gargoyle
Collection
Home Page

You've completed the design of the Gargoyle Collection Home Page. By using tables, you managed to create an interesting and attractive layout. This process illustrated several principles that you should keep in mind when creating such layouts in the future:

- Diagram the layout before you start writing the HTML code.

- Create the text for various columns and cells in separate files, which you'll insert later.

- Create the table structure for the outer table first, and then gradually work inward.

- Insert comment tags to identify the different sections of the page.

- Indent the various levels of nested tables, to make your code easier to follow.

- Test and review your code as you proceed, in order to catch errors early.

DESIGN window

CREATING A PAGE LAYOUT WITH TABLES

- Create gutters and use cell padding to keep your columns from crowding each other.
- Add background colors to columns to provide visual interest and variety.
- Use the VALIGN=TOP property in cells containing articles, to ensure that the text flows from the top down.
- Use row spanning to vary the size and starting point of articles within your columns. Having all articles start and end within the same row creates a static layout that is difficult to read.
- Avoid having more than three columns of text, if possible. Inserting additional columns could make the column widths too narrow and make the text hard to read.

You show the final version of the page to Nicole. She's pleased that you were able to create a page to match her sketch. She'll look over the page you created and get back to you with any additional changes. As you wait for her feedback, you can learn a little more about tables and HTML tags.

Extensions to Tables

If you want to enhance the appearance of your tables, Internet Explorer supports several additional tags, not supported by all other browsers. These additional tags, or **extensions**, allow you to specify table border colors and control the appearance of cell boundaries. Although you won't apply them to any of the tables you've created so far, you might want to use them in tables you create in the future.

Specifying the Table Border Color

By default, a table's borders are displayed in two shades of gray, creating a three-dimensional effect. Both Internet Explorer and Netscape Navigator support an extension that allows you to choose the border color. The syntax of this extension is:

```
<TABLE BORDERCOLOR=color>
```

where *color* is either the color name or color value. Figure 4-58 shows examples of tables using the BORDERCOLOR property.

Figure 4-58 ◄
Applying
Internet
Explorer's
BORDERCOLOR
property to
table borders

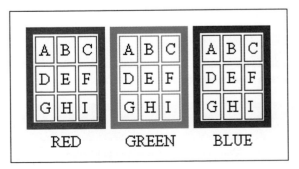

Note that this tag applies the color to the entire border, which eliminates the three-dimensional effect of the default color scheme. What if you want to keep the 3-D effect, but you want to use a different set of colors? Only Internet Explorer provides two additional properties—the BORDERCOLORLIGHT and BORDERCOLORDARK properties—which make this possible. The syntax for specifying the light and dark border colors is:

```
<TABLE BORDERCOLORDARK=color BORDERCOLORLIGHT=color>
```

Figure 4-59 shows an example of the use of the BORDERCOLORDARK and BORDERCOLORLIGHT properties to create a 3-D border effect with shades of blue.

Figure 4-59 ◀
Applying the
BORDER-
COLORLIGHT
and BORDER-
COLORDARK
properties

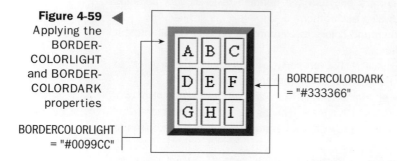

BORDERCOLORDARK
= "#333366"

BORDERCOLORLIGHT
= "#0099CC"

When using these extensions, be sure to view your page in browsers other than Internet Explorer, to verify that the table still looks good even when the color extensions are not supported.

Creating Frames and Rules

Two additional properties introduced in HTML 4.0, which may not be supported by older browsers, are the FRAME and RULE properties. As you've seen, when borders are displayed, they surround the entire table on all four sides. The FRAME property allows you to control which sides of the table will have borders. The syntax for the FRAME property is:

```
<TABLE FRAME=value>
```

where *value* is either BOX (the default), ABOVE, BELOW, HSIDES, VSIDES, LHS, RHS, or VOID. Figure 4-60 describes each of these values.

Figure 4-60 ◀
Values of
Internet
Explorer's
FRAME
property

FRAME Value	Description
BOX	Draws borders around all four sides
ABOVE	Draws only the top border
BELOW	Draws only the bottom border
HSIDES	Draws both the top and bottom borders (the horizontal sides)
LHS	Draws only the left-hand side
RHS	Draws only the right-hand side
VSIDES	Draws both the left and right borders (the vertical sides)
VOID	Does not draw borders on any of the four sides

Figure 4-61 shows the effect of each of these values on the table grid.

Figure 4-61 ◀
Effect of
different
FRAME values

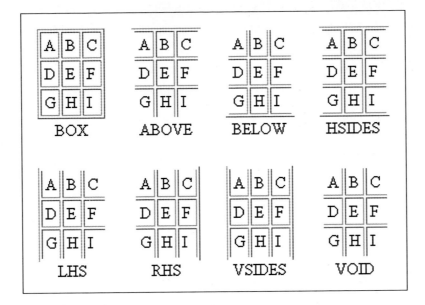

By default, borders are drawn around each cell in the table. The RULES property lets you control this by specifying how you want the table grid to be drawn. The syntax of the RULES property is:

```
<TABLE RULES=value>
```

where *value* is either ALL, ROWS, COLS, or NONE. The ALL value causes all cell borders to be drawn. The ROWS and COLS values cause borders to be drawn around only the table rows and columns, respectively. NONE suppresses the display of any cell borders. Figure 4-62 shows the effect of different RULES property values on a table's appearance.

Figure 4-62 ◀
Effect of
different
RULES values

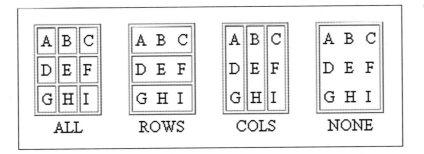

Once again, remember that when you use these Internet Explorer extensions, the effects you see will not be duplicated in other Web browsers, which will display tables with the usual grid layout. Therefore, you should always test under different Web browsers.

You've finished your work on the Web page and can now close your browser and text editor.

To close your work:

1. Close your Web browser.

2. Return to your text editor, and then close the Gargoyle.htm file.

Quick Check

1 What HTML code would you enter to create two 2 × 2 tables, one nested inside the upper-left cell of the other?

2 What HTML code inserts the comment "Nested table starts here"?

3 What code would you enter to change the border color of your table to yellow?

4 What code would you enter to use red for the light border color and blue for the dark border color?

5 What code would you enter to display only the top border of your table?

6 What code would you enter to create dividing lines around your table columns only?

7 What is the limitation of the code you created for Quick Checks 3 through 6?

You've completed your work with HTML tables. You've learned how to create text tables and graphical tables. You've seen how to control the appearance of your table and the text it contains, and you've seen how tables can help you create attractive page designs.

Tutorial Assignments

Nicole has finished reviewing the pages you created for her. She has made a few changes and has a few additional suggestions that she wants you to implement. These involve updating the text table you created to reflect the changes made to the graphical table, altering the appearance of the products table, and making some changes to the Gargoyle Collection Home Page.

To implement Nicole's suggestions:

1. In your text editor, open the MAA4.htm file in the TAssign folder of the Tutorial.04 folder on your Student Disk, and then save the file as Gtable.htm in the same folder.

2. Align the Name header with the left edge of its cell.

3. Increase the size of the table border to 10 pixels. Increase the size of the cell spacing to 3 pixels.

4. Change the Bust cell in the third row of the table body to a spanning cell that spans two rows.

5. Align the text "Bust" in the spanning cell with the cell's top edge.

6. Add the following new item to the bottom of the products table: Item Name— Spitting Gargoyle, Item #—49010, Type—Garden Figure, Finish—Gothic Stone, Price—$110.

7. Change the color of the header row to a greenish-blue. The color value (in hexadecimal) is 33FFFF. Save the changes to the Gtable.htm file.

8. Open the MAA3.htm file in the TAssign folder of the Tutorial.04 folder on your Student Disk, and then save the file as Gtext.htm in the same folder.

9. Add a fourth and fifth row to the text table body to match the items listed in the graphical table. Save your changes.

10. Open the GHome2.htm file in the TAssign folder of the Tutorial.04 folder on your Student Disk, and then save the file as Gcollect.htm in the same folder.

11. Add a fourth row at the bottom of the nested table. The row should have one cell that spans three columns.

12. Within the cell, insert the text "View a table of gargoyle products". Format the text as a hypertext link to the Gtable.htm file.

13. Align the text in the cell with the top and center of the cell.

14. Change the background color of the table cell to the hexidecimal value #800000. Save your changes.

15. Print both the page and the HTML code for the Gtext.htm, Gtable.htm, and GCollect.htm files.

16. Close your Web browser and your text editor.

Case Problems

1. Creating a Calendar of Activities at Avalon Books You've been asked to create a Web page that displays a calendar of activities at the Avalon Books bookstore for the month of May, 1999. Updating the calendar is a monthly activity, so a page has already been created containing a graphical table of the days of the month. Your job will be to update this table with the May activities. You will also add a caption and title to the table and format it.

The calendar should include the following activities:

- Every Monday: Noon storytime with Susan Sheridan
- Every Friday: Noon storytime with Doug Evans
- May 1st: Young authors' workshop from 1 to 4 p.m.
- May 5th: Ecology workshop with Nancy Fries from 9 to 11 a.m.
- May 15th: Ms. Frizzle teaches about science from 2 to 3 p.m.
- May 19th: Origami with Rita Davis from 2 to 3 p.m.
- May 22nd: Making a model of the solar system from 2 to 3 p.m.
- May 29th: Spenser Brown's Clown Show from 1 to 2 p.m.

To create the Avalon Books calendar:

1. In your text editor, open the Avalon.htm file in the Cases folder of the Tutorial.04 folder on your Student Disk, and then save the file as May_List.htm in the same folder.

2. Set the table width to use 100% of the display area.

3. Modify each cell in the table, changing the cell for Sundays to 16% of the table width, and make the width of each of the remaining days 14% of the table width. Align the text in each cell with the top of the cell border.

4. At the beginning of the table, insert a new row that spans the seven table columns. Set the width of this cell to 100% of the width of the table.

5. Within the spanning cell, insert the text "Children's Events in May, 1999". Center this text within the spanning cell and format it as an <H3> header.

6. Insert the days of the week in the cells of the table header row, starting with Sunday.

7. Enter the activities listed earlier. Note that some of the activities are repeated throughout the month.

8. Insert the table caption "For more information call Debbie at 555-4892" aligned with the bottom of the table.

9. Increase the width of the table border to 5 pixels.

10. Save your changes, and then view the page in your Web browser. If your monitor allows it, view the table at different screen resolutions (you might need to ask your instructor how to modify your monitor's resolution). How does the appearance of the table change under different resolutions?

11. Print the HTML code for the calendar page. Print the page itself; if you change your monitor resolution, print the page at the 640 × 480 and 800 × 600 screen resolutions.

12. Close your Web browser and your text editor.

2. Creating a Television Schedule at WMTZ You're in charge of creating Web pages for WMTZ in Atlanta. One of these pages contains the weekly prime-time television schedule from 7:00 p.m to 10 p.m. You'll create this schedule with a table broken down in half-hour installments. Because some programs in the schedule last longer than 30 minutes, you will have to include spanning cells to cover those time periods. Figure 4-63 shows the completed table.

Figure 4-63 ◀

Day	7:00	7:30	8:00	8:30	9:00	9:30
Mon.	The Nanny	Fred's Place	Old Friends	Cybill	Emergency Center	
Tue.	Babylon 5		Tonite!	911 Stories	Mission Impossible	
Wed.	Special: The Budget Crisis		Perfume		48 Hours	
Thu.	Mel's Diner	Alien World	Movie: Wayne's World III			
Fri.	Movie Special: Schindler's List					
Sat.	Dr. Quinn		Murder for Hire		New York Streets	
Sun.	Hey Dogs!	Wild Life	Movie: The Lost World			

To create the television schedule table:

1. In your text editor, open the WMTZ.htm file in the Cases folder of the Tutorial.04 folder on your Student Disk, and then save the file as TVList.htm in the same folder.

2. Create a table that has seven columns and eight rows, one of the rows consisting of table headers.

3. Set the table border width to 5 pixels, the cell spacing to 3 pixels, and the cell padding to 5 pixels.

4. Using the Internet Explorer extensions, change the color of the dark part of the table border to the color value 0000FF and the color of the light part of the table border to CCCCFF.

5. Set the width of each cell in the first column to 50 pixels.

6. Set the width of the table header cells (aside from the first column) to 90 pixels.

7. Enter the table text. Create spanning cells as indicated in Figure 4-63.

8. For each half-hour program, set the cell width to 90 pixels; set the cell width of hour programs to 180 pixels, of two-hour programs to 360 pixels, and of three-hour programs to 540 pixels.

9. Set the background color of the first row and first column of the table to yellow.

10. Center the table on the page.

11. Save your changes to the file.

12. View the page. What would be the difference between the way the page appears in the Netscape Navigator browser and the Internet Explorer browser?

13. Print a copy of your HTML code and the finished Web page.

14. Close your Web browser and your text editor.

3. Creating the Dunston Retreat Center Home Page The Dunston Retreat Center, located in northern Wisconsin, offers weekends of quiet and solitude for all who visit. The center, started by a group of Trappist monks, has grown in popularity over the last few years as more people have become aware of its services. The director of the center, Benjamin Adams, wants to advertise the center on the Internet and has asked you to create a home page. The page will include a welcoming message from Benjamin Adams, a list of upcoming events, a letter from one of the center's guests, and a description of the current week's events. The home page you'll create is shown in Figure 4-64.

Figure 4-64 ◀

Welcome

Welcome to the Dunston Retreat Center. Whether you are planning to attend one of our many conferences or embarking on a private retreat, we're sure that you will enjoy your stay.

Located in the northern woods of Wisconsin, the Dunston Retreat Center provides comfortable and attractive accommodations while you enjoy the rustic setting available just outside your door. The Retreat Center has 32 beds, large meeting rooms, a chapel, and kitchen facilities. If you want to get out, there are ample opportunities for hiking, canoeing and horseback riding in the surrounding area.

Throughout the year the center staff conducts retreats to accommodate the needs of various groups. We offer retreats for men, for women, and for couples. Please call about special needs retreats.

If you prefer, an individually directed retreat is possible. The retreat includes a time of daily sharing and guidance by a retreat director to supplement your private time of solitude and meditation.

At the Dunston Retreat Center we make everything as easy as possible, providing meals, towels, bedding - everything you need. Just bring yourself.

Benjamin Adams
Director,
Dunston Retreat Center

Next week at the Dunston Retreat Center

The annual meeting of the Midwest Marriage Encounter occurs at the Dunston Retreat Center, June 11-13. Registration is $50 and includes room and board. A boating trip on Lake Superior is planned for Saturday night ($10 fee).

Contact Maury Taylor at 555-2381 for reservation information.

Upcoming Events

June 11-13 Marriage Encounter

June 18-20 Recovering Alcoholics

June 25-27 Spirituality Workshop

July 2-4 Lutheran Brotherhood

July 9-11 Recovering Alcoholics

July 16-18 Duluth Fellowship

July 23-25 Special Needs Children

August 6-8 St. James Men's Group

August 13-15 St. James Women's Group

August 20-22 Recovering Alcoholics

August 27-29 Knights of Columbus

A letter from one of our guests

I'm writing to tell you how much I enjoyed my retreat at Dunston. I came to your center haggard and worn out from a long illness and job difficulties. I left totally refreshed. I especially want to thank Father Thomas Holloway for his support.

I've enthusiastically told all of my friends about the wonderful place you have. Some of us are hoping to organize a group retreat. Rest assured that you'll see me again. Going to Dunston will become a yearly event for me.

Sincerely,

Doris Patterson

To create this home page, you'll use tables and nested tables to organize the page design elements.

To create the Dunston Retreat Center Home Page:

1. In your text editor, open the DRCtext.htm file in the Cases folder of the Tutorial.04 folder on your Student Disk, and then save the file as Dunston.htm in the same folder.

2. Create a table that has three columns and one row. The width of the first column should be 200 pixels, the second column 5 pixels, and the third column 395 pixels.

3. Above the first column, insert the comment "Welcoming Message"; above the second column, insert the comment "Gutter"; and, above the third column, insert the comment "Nested Table."

4. Specify that any text within the three cells should be vertically aligned with the top of the cell.

5. Insert the contents (but not the <BODY> tags or information within the <HEAD> tags) of the Welcome.htm file (from the Cases folder) into the first column of the table. Format the background of this cell using the same background color found in the Welcome.htm file.

6. Within the third cell, insert a nested table with the following dimensions: four rows by three columns. Both the first and second rows of the table should contain a single cell that spans three columns. The third row of the table should have a single nonspanning cell with a width of 210 pixels, followed by a cell that spans two rows and is 5 pixels wide, and then a third cell that is 180 pixels wide and also spans two rows. The fourth row of the table should contain a single cell 210 pixels in width—making a total of six cells in the table.

7. Insert comments into the nested table. Label the first cell "Dunston Logo," the second cell "Dunston Photo," the third cell "Midwest Marriage Encounter," the fourth cell "Nested Table Gutter," the fifth cell "Letter," and the sixth cell "List of upcoming events."

8. Vertically align the contents of the nested table cells with the cell top.

9. Insert the inline image DLogo.gif (from the Cases folder) into the first cell of the nested table. Specify that the dimensions of the image should be 390 pixels wide by 75 pixels high.

10. Insert the inline image Dunston.jpg (from the Cases folder) into the second cell of the nested table. Enter a dimension of 390 pixels by 170 pixels for the image's width and height.

11. Insert the body contents of the Nextweek.htm file (from the Cases folder) into the third cell of the nested table.

12. Insert a blank space into the fourth cell of the table.

13. Insert the body contents of the Letter.htm file (from the Cases folder) into the fifth cell of the table.

14. Insert the body contents of the Upcoming.htm file (from the Cases folder) into the sixth cell of the table.

15. Save your changes to the Dunston.htm file.

16. Print the HTML code and the resulting Web page.

17. Close your Web browser and your text editor.

4. Creating the TravelWeb E-Zine Magazines on the Web, sometimes called e-zines, provide useful material to subscribers online. You have joined the staff of an e-zine called *TravelWeb*, which publishes travel information and tips. You've been asked to work on the layout for the e-zine's front page. You've been given files that you should use in creating the page. Figure 4-65 lists and describes these files.

Figure 4-65 ◀

File	Description
LuxAir.htm	Article about LuxAir reducing airfares to Europe
Photo.htm	Article about the Photo of the Week
PPoint.jpg	Image file of the Photo of the Week (320 × 228)
PPoint2.jpg	Small version of the Photo of the Week image (180 × 128)
Toronto.htm	Article about traveling to Toronto
TWLinks.htm	Links to other TravelWeb pages (list version)
TWLinks2.htm	Links to other TravelWeb pages (table version)
TWLogo.gif	Image file of the TravelWeb logo (425 × 105)
Yosemite.htm	Article about limiting access to Yosemite National Park
Yosemite.jpg	Image file of Yosemite National Park (112 × 158)

To create the TravelWeb e-zine front page:

1. Use the files listed in Figure 4-65 to create a newspaper-style page. All of these files are stored in the Cases folder of the Tutorial.04 folder on your Student Disk. The page should include several columns, but the number, size, and layout of the columns are up to you.

2. Use all of the files on the page, with the following exceptions: use only one of the two files TWLinks.htm and TWLinks2.htm, and use only one of the two image files PPoint.jpg and PPoint2.jpg. (*Note*: Not all of the links on this page point to existing files.)

3. Use background colors and spot color to give your page an attractive and interesting appearance.

4. Include comment tags to describe the different parts of your page layout.

5. Save your page as TW.htm in the Cases folder of the Tutorial.04 folder on your Student Disk.

6. Print a copy of the page and the HTML code.

7. Close your Web browser and your text editor.

TUTORIAL 5

Using Frames in a Web Page

Creating a Framed Presentation Containing Multiple Pages

OBJECTIVES

In this tutorial you will:

- Create frames for a Web presentation

- Control the appearance and placement of frames

- Control the behavior of hyper-links on a page with frames

- Use magic target names to specify the target for a hypertext link

- Create a page that is viewable both by browsers that support frames and by those that do not

- Work with Netscape Navigator extensions that change the appearance of frames

CASE

Advertising for The Colorado Experience

One of the most popular climbing schools and backcountry touring agencies in Colorado is The Colorado Experience. Located in Vale Park, outside of Rocky Mountain National Park, The Colorado Experience specializes in teaching beginning and advanced climbing techniques. The school also sponsors several tours, leading individuals to some of the most exciting, challenging, and picturesque climbs in the Vale Park area. The school has been in existence for 15 years and, in that time, it has helped thousands of people experience the mountains in ways they never thought possible.

The Colorado Experience has stiff competition in the area from other climbing schools and touring groups. The owner, Debbie Chen, is always looking for ways to improve the visibility of the school. Early on, she decided to use the Internet and the World Wide Web as a means of advertising the school's services. She has already created an extensive number of Web pages to highlight the company's offerings.

Debbie has seen other Web pages that use frames, which are windows that allow the browser to display several HTML files within its display window. She feels that this would be a good way of showcasing the Web pages she has already created within an easy-to-use page design. She asks you to help her modify the company's Web presentation to take advantage of frames.

SESSION 5.1

In this session you will create a page that contains frames. You will learn about the HTML tags that control the placement and appearance of frames. You'll also learn how to specify a source document for each frame, and how to nest one set of frames inside another.

Introducing Frames

When Web presentations contain several pages, each page is usually dedicated to a particular subject or set of topics. One page might contain a list of hypertext links; another page might display contact information for the company or school; and another page might describe the company's history and philosophy. As more pages are created, you might start wishing that there were some way in which the user could view information from two or more pages simultaneously. One solution would be to repeat the information on several pages, but such a solution presents problems as well. For example, it would require a great deal of time and effort to type (or copy and paste) the same information over and over again. Also, if you had to change the information on one page, you would need to ensure that you changed the same information on all other pages in the presentation.

Such considerations led Netscape to create the <FRAME> tag. **Frames** are windows appearing within the browser's display area, each capable of displaying the contents of a different HTML file. An example of a page with frames is shown in Figure 5-1. In this example, a page consisting of hypertext links appears in a frame on the left, while the Products Home Page appears in a frame on the right.

Figure 5-1
Example of
a frame

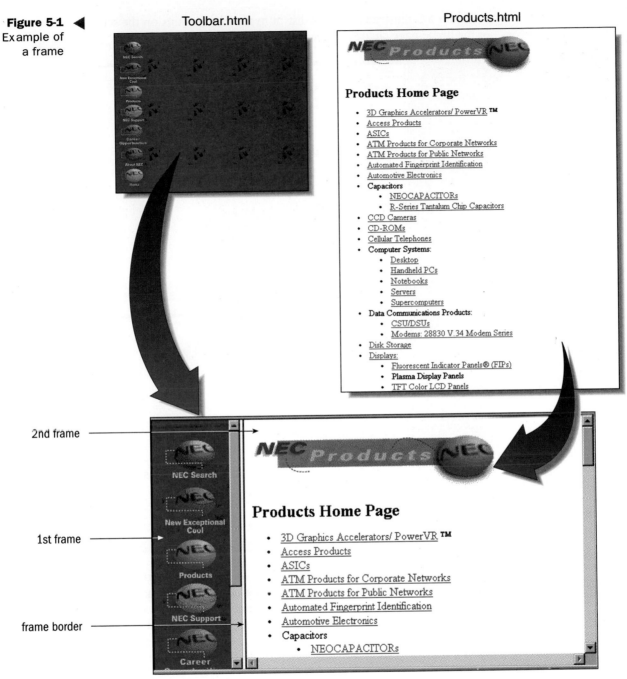

Both files are joined into a single page using frames

Frames can be set up to be permanent, allowing users to move through the contents of the Web presentation while always being able to see an overall table of contents.

Figure 5-2 illustrates how the list of hyperlinks remains on the screen while the contents of the home page change, depending on which hyperlink is clicked.

Figure 5-2 ◀
Activating a
hyperlink with
frames

When the user clicks
the Support
hyperlink ...

... the frame
containing the
document page is
updated, but the list
of hyperlinks remains
unchanged.

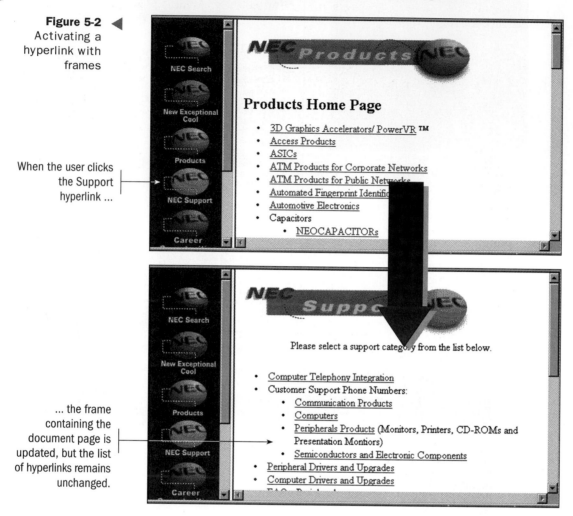

One downside to using frames is that you are causing the browser to load multiple HTML files rather than a single one, which could result in a longer delay for users. Also, not all browsers are able to display a framed page. Some earlier versions of Netscape Navigator and other non-Netscape browsers do not support frames. With the increasing popularity of frames, this is less of an issue, but you should still try to create both framed and nonframed versions of your Web presentations to accommodate all users and browsers.

Planning Your Frames

Before you start creating your frames, you should first plan their appearance and use. There are several issues to consider:

■ What information will be displayed in each of the frames?

■ How do you want the frames placed on the Web page? What is the size of each frame?

■ Which frames will be **static**—that is, always showing the same content?

■ Which frames will change in response to hyperlinks being clicked?

■ What Web pages will users see first when they access the site?

■ Do you want to allow users to resize the frames and change the layout of the page?

As you proceed in designing the Web page for The Colorado Experience, you'll consider each of these questions. Debbie has already thought about what information should be displayed on some of the pages in The Colorado Experience's Web site. Figure 5-3 lists the files for these pages.

Figure 5-3 ◀
Some of the files at The Colorado Experience's Web site

Topic	Filename	Content
Biographies	Staff.htm	Links to biographical pages of The Colorado Experience staff
Home page	TCE.htm	The Colorado Experience Home Page
Lessons	Lessons.htm	Climbing lessons offered by The Colorado Experience
Logo	Head.htm	A page containing the company logo
Philosophy	Philosph.htm	Statement of The Colorado Experience's business philosophy
Table of contents	Links.htm	Links to The Colorado Experience Web pages
Tours	Diamond.htm	Description of the Diamond climbing tour
Tours	Eldorado.htm	Description of the Eldorado Canyon climbing tour
Tours	Grepon.htm	Description of the Petit Grepon climbing tour
Tours	Kieners.htm	Description of the Kiener's Route climbing tour
Tours	Lumpy.htm	Description of the Lumpy Ridge climbing tour
Tours	Nface.htm	Description of the North Face climbing tour

The files are organized into various topic areas such as pages devoted to tour descriptions, climbing lessons, and company philosophy. Two of the files, Links.htm and Staff.htm, do not cover topics but rather contain hyperlinks to other Colorado Experience Web pages. How should this kind of material be organized on the Web page, and what should the user see first?

Debbie has considered these questions and has sketched a layout detailing how she would like the frames organized on the company's Web page (Figure 5-4).

Figure 5-4 ◀
Layout for the
Colorado
Experience
Web page

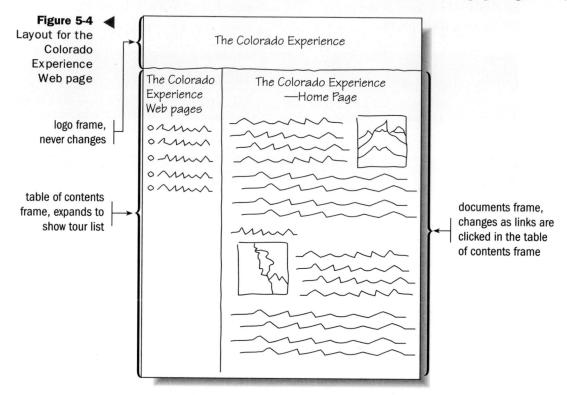

logo frame,
never changes

table of contents
frame, expands to
show tour list

documents frame,
changes as links are
clicked in the table
of contents frame

Debbie would like to have three frames in the presentation. The top frame will display the company logo and will always be visible to the user (that is, static). She has already created this information in the Head.htm file listed earlier in Figure 5-3. The frame on the left will display the table of contents page, Links.htm, with each item in the list acting as a hyperlink to a specific page. Finally, the frame on the right will display different Colorado Experience documents, depending on which hyperlink the user clicks in the table of contents frame. The Colorado Experience Home Page should be the first page that the user sees in this frame. This is a standard layout and a typical use for frames.

Your first task will be to insert the HTML code that creates the type of layout Debbie has in mind.

Creating a Frame Layout

Frame layout is defined using the <FRAMESET> tag. The general syntax for the <FRAMESET> tag in your HTML file is:

```
<HTML>
<HEAD>
<TITLE>Page Title</TITLE>
</HEAD>

<FRAMESET>
    Frame Definitions
</FRAMESET>
</HTML>
```

Notice that this code does not include the <BODY> tags. When you use the <FRAMESET> tag, you omit the <BODY> tag. Upon reflection, the reason for this should be clear: a page with frames displays the content of *other* pages. There is no page body to speak of. There is one situation in which you'll use the <BODY> tag in your page—when you are creating a page that can be displayed whether the browser supports frames or not. This situation is discussed later in the tutorial.

Specifying Frame Size and Orientation

The <FRAMESET> tag has two properties: ROWS and COLS. You use the ROWS property when you want to create frames that are laid out in rows, and you use the COLS property to lay the frames out in columns (Figure 5-5). You choose only one layout for a single <FRAMESET> tag, either rows or columns. You cannot use both properties at once.

Figure 5-5 ◄

Frames defined in either rows or columns

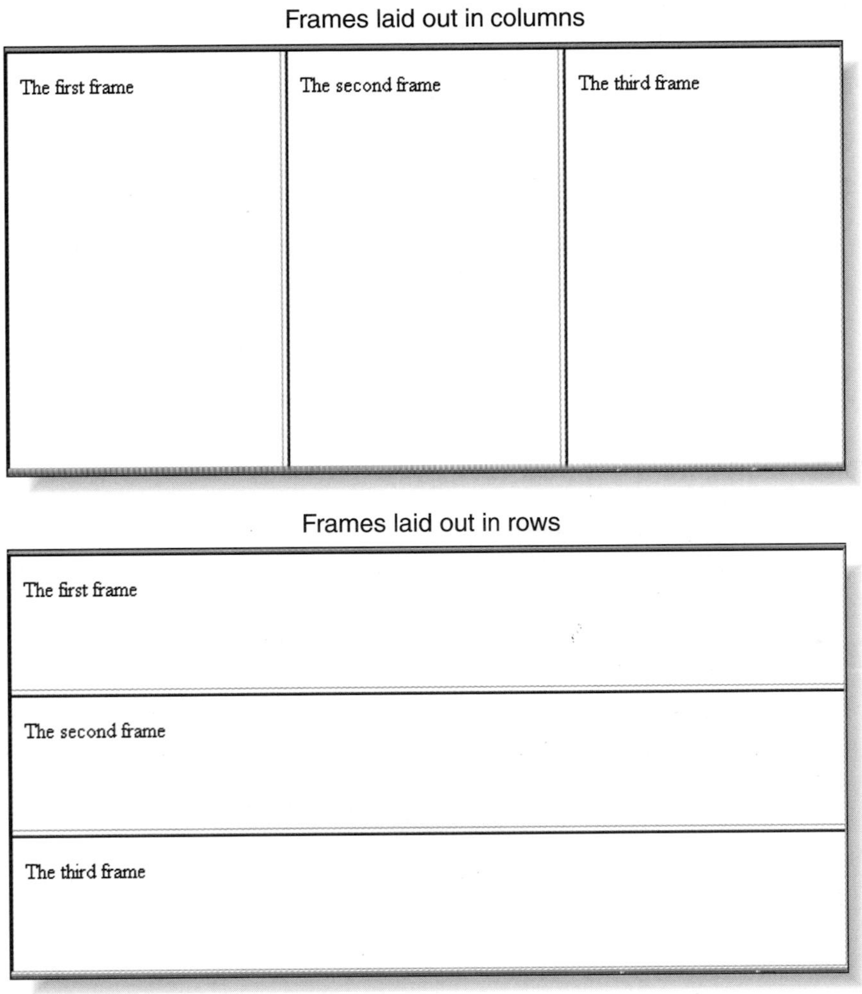

Frames laid out in columns

The first frame	The second frame	The third frame

Frames laid out in rows

The first frame
The second frame
The third frame

The syntax for specifying the row or column layout for the <FRAMESET> tag is:

`<FRAMESET ROWS="row height, row height, row height, …">`

or

`<FRAMESET COLS="column width, column width, column width, …">`

where *row height* is the height of each row, and *column width* is the width of each column. There is no limit to the number of rows or columns you can specify for a frameset.

Row and column sizes are specified in three ways: in pixels, as a percentage of the total size of the frameset, or by an asterisk (*). The asterisk tells the browser to allocate any unclaimed space in the frameset to the particular row or column. For example, the tag <FRAMESET ROWS="160,*"> creates two rows of frames. The first row has a height of 160 pixels, and the height of the second row is equal to whatever space remains in the display area. For a display area that is 400 pixels high, this would be 240 pixels.

You can use all three ways of specifying row or column size in a single <FRAMESET> tag. The tag <FRAMESET COLS="160,25%,*"> creates the series of columns shown in Figure 5-6. The first column is 160 pixels wide, the second column is 25% of the width of the display area, and the third column covers whatever space is left.

Figure 5-6 ◀
Frames with
different sizes

160 pixels wide

25% of the width of
the display area

whatever space is left

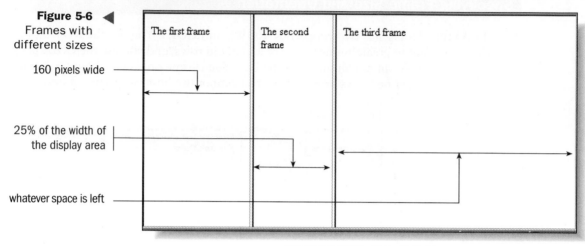

< FRAMESET COLS ="160,25%,*" >

Invariably at least one of the rows or columns of your <FRAMESET> tag will be specified with an asterisk to guarantee that the frames fill up the screen regardless of the user's monitor resolution. You can also include multiple asterisks. For example, the tag <FRAMESET ROWS="*,*,*"> creates three rows of frames with equal heights.

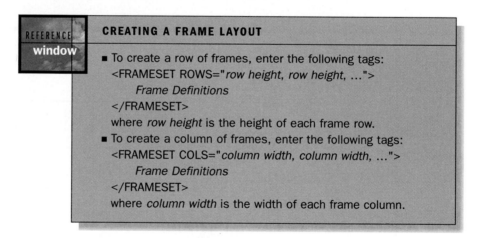

REFERENCE window

CREATING A FRAME LAYOUT

■ To create a row of frames, enter the following tags:
   <FRAMESET ROWS="*row height, row height, ...*">
      Frame Definitions
   </FRAMESET>
   where *row height* is the height of each frame row.
■ To create a column of frames, enter the following tags:
   <FRAMESET COLS="*column width, column width, ...*">
      Frame Definitions
   </FRAMESET>
   where *column width* is the width of each frame column.

An initial file for use in setting up the frames for the Colorado Experience Web page has been created for you and saved as COLtext.htm in the Tutorial.05 folder of your Student Disk. You'll open that file now and save it with a new name.

To open the COLtext.htm file and save it with a new name:

1. Start your text editor.

2. Open the file **COLtext.htm** from the Tutorial.05 folder on your Student Disk, and then save the file in the same folder as **Colorado.htm**.

The first set of frames you'll create for the Colorado Experience page will have two rows. The top row will be used for the company logo (saved in the Head.htm file), and the second row will be used for the rest of the page's content. A frame that is 60 pixels high should be tall enough to display the logo. The rest of the browser's display area will be taken up by the second row.

To create the first set of frames:

1. Create a new blank line directly below the </HEAD> tag in the Colorado.htm file.

2. Insert the following code:

```
<FRAMESET ROWS="60,*">
</FRAMESET>
```

This code specifies a height of 60 pixels for the top row and allocates the remaining space to the second row. Figure 5-7 shows the revised Colorado.htm file.

Figure 5-7 ◀
Creating two
rows of frames
in the
Colorado.htm
file

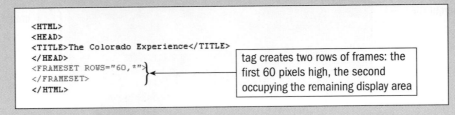

```
<HTML>
<HEAD>
<TITLE>The Colorado Experience</TITLE>
</HEAD>
<FRAMESET ROWS="60,*">
</FRAMESET>
</HTML>
```
tag creates two rows of frames: the
first 60 pixels high, the second
occupying the remaining display area

The initial frame layout is now defined. You'll be augmenting this layout later to include the third frame, following Debbie's design. For now, you need to specify the source for the two frame rows.

Specifying a Frame Source

The tag used to specify the page that will be inserted into a frame is the <FRAME> tag. The syntax for this tag is:

```
<FRAME SRC=document>
```

where *document* is the URL or filename of the page that you want to load. You must insert the <FRAME> tag between the <FRAMESET> and </FRAMESET> tags.

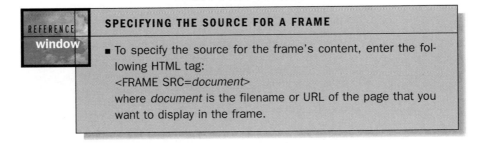

REFERENCE
window

SPECIFYING THE SOURCE FOR A FRAME

■ To specify the source for the frame's content, enter the following HTML tag:
  <FRAME SRC=document>
  where *document* is the filename or URL of the page that you want to display in the frame.

The top frame displays the Head.htm file, which contains the company logo. Figure 5-8 previews the contents of this file and its placement on the page.

Figure 5-8 ◀
Head.htm file containing the Colorado Experience logo

transparent GIF

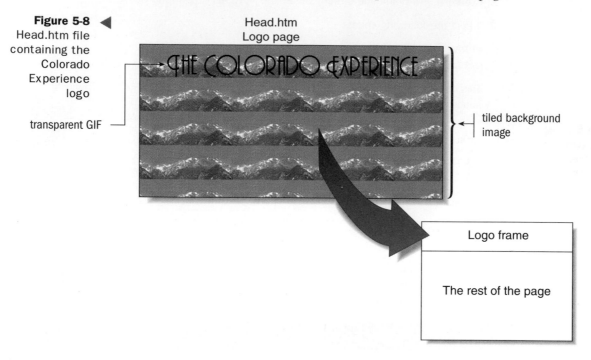

Head.htm
Logo page

THE COLORADO EXPERIENCE

tiled background image

Logo frame

The rest of the page

Note that the logo consists of the company name, formatted as a transparent GIF and then placed on a tiled background of mountain images. Using a tiled background is a common technique for frames that display company logos. In this case, the advantage of this approach is that it guarantees that the mountain images will fill the frame under any monitor resolution.

To insert the Head.htm frame source:

1. Go to the end of the <FRAMESET> tag line, and then press the **Enter** key.

2. Type the following code (indent the code three spaces):

```
<!--- Company Logo --->
<FRAME SRC="Head.htm">
```

Figure 5-9 shows the inserted code.

Figure 5-9 ◀
Specifying the source for the first frame row

source file for the frame in the first row

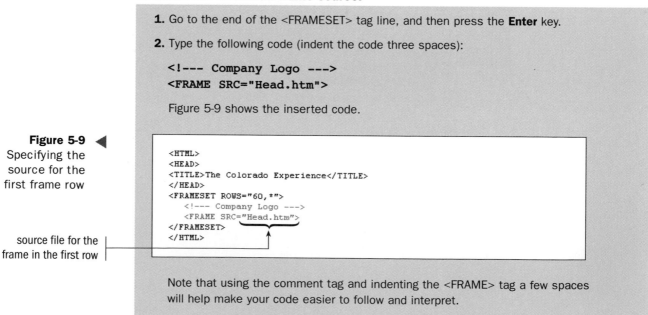

```
<HTML>
<HEAD>
<TITLE>The Colorado Experience</TITLE>
</HEAD>
<FRAMESET ROWS="60,*">
   <!--- Company Logo --->
   <FRAME SRC="Head.htm">
</FRAMESET>
</HTML>
```

Note that using the comment tag and indenting the <FRAME> tag a few spaces will help make your code easier to follow and interpret.

You've specified the source for the first row of the layout, but what about the second row? Looking back at Debbie's sketch in Figure 5-4, notice that this row will contain two additional frames. So rather than specify a source for the second row, you have to create another set of frames. To do this, you have to nest a second set of <FRAMESET> tags within the first.

Nesting <FRAMESET> Tags

Because a <FRAMESET> tag can include either a ROWS property or a COLS property, but not both, you have to nest <FRAMESET> tags if you want to create a grid of frames on your Web page. When you do this, the meaning of the ROWS or COLS property for the nested <FRAMESET> tag changes slightly. For example, a row height of 25% does not mean 25% of the display area, but rather 25% of the height of the frame into which that row has been inserted (or nested).

The second row of your current frame layout consists of two columns. The first column will display a table of contents, and the second column will display various Colorado Experience documents. You'll specify a width of 140 pixels for the first column, and whatever remains in the display area will be allotted to the second column.

To create the second set of frames:

1. Go to the end of the <FRAME> tag line that you just inserted, and then press the **Enter** key to create a blank line below it.

2. Type the following code (indent the text three spaces to make the code easier to follow):

```
<!--- Nested frames --->
<FRAMESET COLS="140,*">
</FRAMESET>
```

Your file should appear as shown in Figure 5-10.

Figure 5-10 ◀
Creating a
nested set of
frames in
the second
frame row

```
<HTML>
<HEAD>
<TITLE>The Colorado Experience</TITLE>
</HEAD>
<FRAMESET ROWS="60,*">
   <!--- Company Logo --->
   <FRAME SRC="Head.htm">
   <!--- Nested frames --->
   <FRAMESET COLS="140,*">
   </FRAMESET>
</FRAMESET>
</HTML>
```

two columns of
frames nested in the
second frame row

Next you'll specify the sources for the two frames in this row. The frame in the first column will display the contents of the Links.htm file. The Colorado Experience Home Page, stored in the TCE.htm file, will appear in the second frame. Figure 5-11 shows the content of these two pages and their placement on the Web page.

Figure 5-11 ◄
Links.htm and
TCE.htm pages

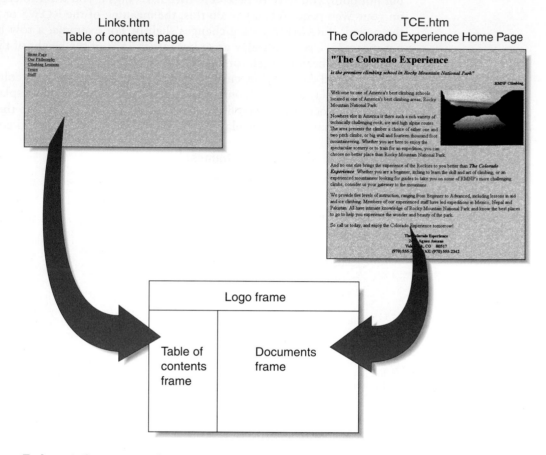

To insert the sources for the two frames:

1. Insert a blank line below the nested <FRAMESET> tag you just created.

2. Type the following code, indented six spaces:

```
<!--- List of Colorado Experience hyperlinks --->
<FRAME SRC="Links.htm">
<!--- Colorado Experience Web pages --->
<FRAME SRC="TCE.htm">
```

Figure 5-12 shows the code for the two new frames.

Figure 5-12 ◄
Sources for the
two frames in
the second row

table of
contents page

The Colorado
Experience
Home Page

```
<HTML>
<HEAD>
<TITLE>The Colorado Experience</TITLE>
</HEAD>
<FRAMESET ROWS="60,*">
   <!--- Company Logo --->
   <FRAME SRC="Head.htm">
   <!--- Nested frames --->
   <FRAMESET COLS="140,*">
      <!--- List of Colorado Experience hyperlinks --->
      <FRAME SRC="Links.htm">
      <!--- Colorado Experience Web pages --->
      <FRAME SRC="TCE.htm">
   </FRAMESET>
</FRAMESET>
</HTML>
```

3. Save your changes to the Colorado.htm file.

4. Open the file in your Web browser. Figure 5-13 shows the page's current appearance.

Figure 5-13 ◀
Colorado
Experience
Web page
with frames

text extends beyond
the frame border

logo

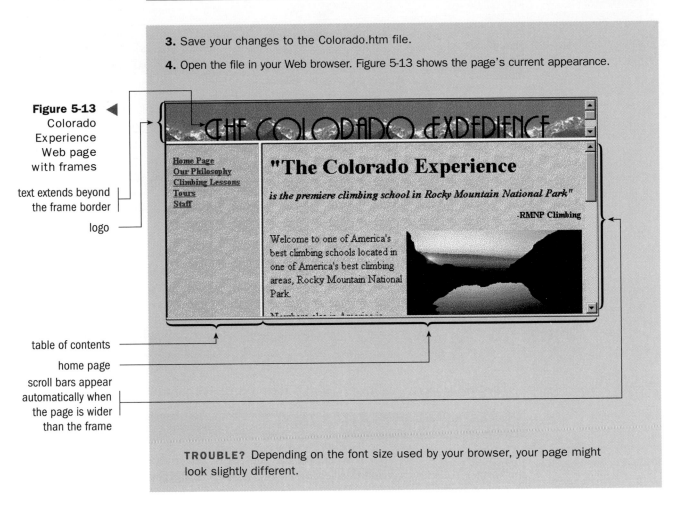

table of contents

home page

scroll bars appear
automatically when
the page is wider
than the frame

TROUBLE? Depending on the font size used by your browser, your page might look slightly different.

The page shows the three HTML files that Debbie wants on the page. However, the page's appearance needs some improvement. The company name is cut off in the logo frame, which also causes a scroll bar to appear. Scroll bars appear whenever the content of a page overflows the size of the frame. For example, scroll bars do not appear in the links frame, because the entire list of links is visible, but they do appear in the home page frame, because its contents are not completely visible. You can use the scroll bars to see the rest of the home page, but do not click any hypertext links yet. You will be working with hyperlinks and frames in the next session. For now, your task is to control how each frame appears on the page.

Controlling the Appearance of Frames

You can control three properties of a frame's appearance: the frame's scroll bars, the size of the margin between the source document and the frame border, and whether or not the user is allowed to change the frame's width or height.

CHANGING THE APPEARANCE OF FRAMES
■ To control the appearance of a frame's scroll bars, use the SCROLLING property as follows: <FRAME SRC=*document* SCROLLING=*value*> where *value* can be either YES (to display scroll bars) or NO (to remove scroll bars). If you do not specify the SCROLLING property, scroll bars will appear only when the content of the frame source cannot fit within the frame's boundaries.
■ To control the amount of space between the frame source and the frame boundary, enter the following tag: <FRAME SRC=*document* MARGINWIDTH=*value* MARGIN-HEIGHT=*value*> where *value* is expressed in pixels. The margin width is the space to the left and right of the frame source. The margin height is the space above and below the frame source. If you do not specify a margin height or width, the browser will assign dimensions based on the content of the frame source.
■ To keep users from resizing frames, enter the tag: <FRAME SRC=*document* NORESIZE>

The first property you'll work with is the property for controlling scroll bars.

Controlling the Appearance of Scroll Bars

By default, scroll bars appear whenever the content of the source page cannot fit within the frame. You can override this setting using the SCROLLING property. The syntax for this property is:

```
<FRAME SRC=document SCROLLING=value>
```

where *value* can either be YES (to always display scroll bars) or NO (to never display scroll bars). If you don't specify a setting for the SCROLLING property, the browser will display scroll bars whenever it needs to.

Because the logo is not centered vertically within its frame and, therefore, is not entirely visible, scroll bars appear on the right side of the logo frame. Debbie feels that scroll bars are inappropriate for the logo frame, and wants to make sure that it never displays them. Therefore, you need to add the SCROLLING=NO property to the logo <FRAME> tag. However, Debbie does want scroll bars to appear for the other two frames, as needed, so you won't specify this property for their <FRAME> tags.

Note that when you are making changes to a framed Web page with Netscape Navigator, you will have to reopen the file to view the changes. If you simply click the Reload button, you will not see the results of your modifications. This is not the case with Internet Explorer 3.0 and above, in which you can view changes to the page by clicking the Refresh button.

To remove the scroll bars from the logo frame:

1. Return to the Colorado.htm file in your text editor.

2. Within the <FRAME> tag for the logo frame, enter the property **SCROLLING=NO** as shown in Figure 5-14.

Figure 5-14
Removing the
scroll bars from
the logo frame

removes the
scroll bars

```
<FRAMESET ROWS="60,*">
    <!--- Company Logo --->
    <FRAME SRC="Head.htm" SCROLLING=NO>
    <!--- Nested frames --->
    <FRAMESET COLS="140,*">
        <!--- List of Colorado Experience hyperlinks --->
        <FRAME SRC="Links.htm">
        <!--- Colorado Experience Web pages --->
        <FRAME SRC="TCE.htm">
    </FRAMESET>
</FRAMESET>
```

3. Save your changes, and then view the file in your Web browser. You might have to reopen the Colorado.htm file to see the effects of your code changes.

Note that although the scroll bars for the logo frame have been removed, the logo itself is still not centered vertically within the frame. (You'll correct this problem next.)

When designing your Web pages, keep in mind that you should remove scroll bars from a frame only when you are convinced that all the contents of the frame source are displayed in the frame. To do this, you should view your page using several different monitor resolutions. A particular frame's contents might be displayed correctly in 800×600 resolution or higher, but this might not be the case with a resolution of 640×480. Few things are more irritating to users than to discover that some content is missing from a frame with no scroll bars available to display the missing content.

With that in mind, your next task is to solve the problem of the off centered logo. To do so, you have to modify the internal margins of the frame.

Controlling Frame Margins

When your browser retrieves a Web page to display inside a frame, it automatically determines the amount of space between the page's content and the frame border. Sometimes the browser makes the margin between the border and the content too large. Generally you want the margin to be big enough to keep the source's text or images from running into the frame's borders; however, you do not want the margin to take up too much space, because you usually want to display as much of the source as possible.

The margin height for the logo frame is too large and has caused part of the logo's text to be pushed down beyond the frame's border. To fix this problem, you need to specify a smaller margin for the frame. This should cause the logo to move up in the frame and allow the entire text to be displayed.

The syntax for specifying the frame's margin is:

```
<FRAME SRC=document MARGINHEIGHT=value MARGINWIDTH=value>
```

Here, MARGINHEIGHT is the amount of space (in pixels) that appears above and below the content of the page in the frame, and MARGNWIDTH is the amount of space that appears to the page's left and right. You do not have to specify both the margin height and width; however, if you specify only one, the browser will assume that you want to use the same value for both. In general you will want to have margin sizes of 0 or 1 pixels for frames that display only an inline image (like the logo frame), and 5 to 10 pixels for frames that display text (such as the frame that is displaying the Colorado Experience Home Page). Setting margin values is a process of trial and error, as you try to determine what combination of margin sizes looks best.

To correct the problem with the logo frame, you'll decrease its margin size to 0 pixels. This setting should allow the complete logo to be displayed within the frame. Also, Debbie would like users to be able to view more of the home page without scrolling, so she asks you to decrease the margin height for the home page frame to 0 pixels. To keep the home page text from running into the frame borders, you'll also specify a margin width of 10 pixels for its frame. The links frame margin does not require any changes.

Figure 5-17 shows the files that each of these hyperlinks points to. The Home Page link points to the TCE.htm file; the Our Philosophy link points to Philsph.htm; Climbing Lessons points to Lessons.htm; Tours points to Tours.htm; and Staff points to the Staff.htm file.

Figure 5-17 ◄

Hyperlinks in the Colorado Experience Web page

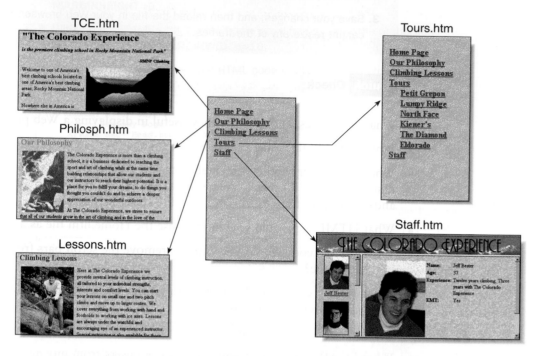

By default, clicking a hyperlink within a frame will open the linked file inside the same frame. However, this is not the way Debbie wants each of the hyperlinks to work. She wants the Home Page, Our Philosophy, and Climbing Lessons pages to open in the frame currently occupied by the home page. She wants the Tours page to replace the current table of contents, and finally she wants the Staff page to replace the entire frame structure.

When you want to control the behavior of hyperlinks in a framed page, you have to do two things: give each frame on the page a name and then point each hyperlink to one of those named frames.

REFERENCE window

RETRIEVING A PAGE IN A SPECIFIC FRAME

- Assign a name to the frame by editing the <FRAME> tag as follows:

  <FRAME SRC=*document* NAME=*frame_name*>

  where *frame_name* is a single word used to describe the content and purpose of the frame.
- Edit the <A> tag for the hyperlink, specifying a target for the link as follows:

  <A HREF=*document* TARGET=*frame_name*>

  where *frame_name* is the name you assigned to the frame.
- To use the same target for all links in a page, insert the <BASE> tag between the file's <HEAD> and </HEAD> tags as follows:

  <BASE TARGET=*frame_name*>

  All links on the page will direct their output to the frame specified by *frame_name*.

Assigning a Name to a Frame

To assign a name to a frame, you use the NAME property. The syntax for this property is:

```
<FRAME SRC=document NAME=frame_name>
```

where *frame_name* is any single word you want to assign to the frame. Case is important in assigning names. A frame named "information" is different from one named "INFORMATION."

You'll name the three frames in the Colorado Experience page "Logo," "Links," and "Documents."

To assign names to the frames:

1. If you took a break after the previous session, start your text editor and open the Colorado.htm file.

2. Within the tag for the logo frame, enter the property **NAME=Logo**.

3. Within the tag for the links frame, enter the property **NAME=Links**.

4. Within the tag for the home page frame, enter the property **NAME=Documents**. Figure 5-18 shows the revised code for the Colorado.htm file.

Figure 5-18 ◀
Assigning
a name to
each frame

```
<FRAMESET ROWS="60,*">
    <!--- Company Logo --->
    <FRAME SRC="Head.htm" SCROLLING=NO MARGINHEIGHT=0 NORESIZE NAME=Logo>
    <!--- Nested frames --->
    <FRAMESET COLS="140,*">
        <!--- List of Colorado Experience hyperlinks --->
        <FRAME SRC="Links.htm" NORESIZE NAME=Links>
        <!--- Colorado Experience Web pages --->
        <FRAME SRC="TCE.htm" MARGINHEIGHT=0 MARGINWIDTH=10 NORESIZE NAME=Documents>
    </FRAMESET>
</FRAMESET>
```

5. Save your changes to the Colorado.htm file.

Now that you've named the frames, your next task is to specify the Documents frame as the target for the Home Page, Our Philosophy, and Climbing Lessons pages, so that each of these will open in the home page frame.

Specifying a Link Target

To display a page within a specific frame, you add the TARGET property to the <A> tag of the hyperlink. The syntax for this property is:

```
<A HREF=document TARGET=frame_name>
```

where *name* is the name you've assigned to a frame on your page. In this case the target name for the frame you need to specify is "Documents." To change the targets for the links, you have to edit the <A> tags in the Links.htm file. You'll start by editing only the <A> tags pointing to the Home Page, Our Philosophy, and Climbing Lessons pages. You'll work with the other hyperlinks later.

To specify the targets for the hypertext links:

1. In your text editor, open the **Linktext.htm** file from the Tutorial.05 folder on your Student Disk.

2. Within the <A> tag for the Home Page, Our Philosophy, and Climbing Lessons hyperlinks, enter the property **TARGET=Documents**. The revised code is shown in Figure 5-19.

Figure 5-19 ◄
Assigning a
target to
hyperlinks

the target is the
Documents frame on
the Web page

```
<A HREF="TCE.htm" TARGET=Documents>Home Page</A><BR>
<A HREF="Philosph.htm" TARGET=Documents>Our Philosophy</A><BR>
<A HREF="Lessons.htm" TARGET=Documents>Climbing Lessons</A><BR>
<A HREF="Tours.htm">Tours</A><BR>
<A HREF="Staff.htm">Staff</A>
```

3. Save the modified file as **Links.htm**. If you are prompted to overwrite the current version of Links.htm, click the **Yes** button.

TROUBLE? If you need to return to the original version of the file, you can use the Linktext.htm file.

Now test the first three hyperlinks in the list.

4. Open the **Colorado.htm** file in your Web browser.

5. Click the **Our Philosophy** link in the Links frame. The Our Philosophy Web page appears in the Documents frame. See Figure 5-20.

TROUBLE? If the Our Philosophy page appears in the left frame, you either have to reload or reopen the Colorado.htm file.

Figure 5-20 ◄
Our Philosophy
page in the
Documents
frame

6. Click the **Home Page** and **Climbing Lessons** links to verify that the links are working properly.

Sometimes a table of contents frame will contain several such hyperlinks. It would be tedious to create TARGET properties for each link. Fortunately, HTML gives you a way to specify a target for all the hyperlinks in your file.

Using the <BASE> Tag

The <BASE> tag appears within the <HEAD> tags of your HTML file and is used to specify global options for the page. One of the properties of the <BASE> tag is the TARGET property, which identifies a default target for all of the page's hyperlinks. The syntax for this property is:

```
<BASE TARGET=name>
```

where *name* is the name of the target. The <BASE> tag is useful when your page contains a lot of hypertext links that all point to the same target. Rather than adding the TARGET property to each <A> tag, you can enter the information only once with the <BASE> tag.

If your file contains a few links that you do not want pointing to the target in the <BASE> tag, you can specify a different target for them. When the <BASE> tag points to one target, and an individual <A> tag points to a different target, the target in the <A> tag takes precedence.

To see how the <BASE> tag works, you'll use it to specify the Documents frame as the default target for all hyperlinks in the Links.htm file. In the process you'll remove the TARGET properties you've just entered.

To specify a default target with the <BASE> tag:

1. Return to the Links.htm file in your text editor.

2. Delete from the three <A> tags the TARGET=Documents properties you entered previously.

3. Insert the line **<BASE TARGET=Documents>** directly above the </HEAD> tag, as shown in Figure 5-21.

Figure 5-21 ◀
Specifying a
default target
for all
hyperlinks

default target

```
<HTML>
<HEAD>
<TITLE>The Colorado Experience Hypertext Links</TITLE>
<BASE TARGET=Documents>
</HEAD>
<BODY BACKGROUND="Wall2.gif">
<FONT SIZE=2><B>
<A HREF="TCE.htm">Home Page</A><BR>
<A HREF="Philosph.htm">Our Philosophy</A><BR>
<A HREF="Lessons.htm">Climbing Lessons</A><BR>
<A HREF="Tours.htm">Tours</A><BR>
<A HREF="Staff.htm">Staff</A>
</B></FONT>
</BODY>
</HTML>
```

4. Save your changes, and then reload the Colorado.htm file in your Web browser. You might have to reopen the file to see the changes.

5. Test the hypertext links for the Home Page, Our Philosophy, and Climbing Lessons pages to verify that the pages appear within the Documents frame. Do not test the other hyperlinks yet.

TROUBLE? If any hyperlinks do not work correctly, check the frame name and target name to verify that they match exactly, both in spelling and use of uppercase and lowercase letters.

You've so far worked with only the first three hyperlinks in the list. The remaining two links require different methods to display.

3. Within the <A> tag that points to the Links.htm file, enter the property **TARGET=_self**. This will redisplay the Links.htm file, containing the original table of contents. See Figure 5-25.

Figure 5-25
Revised
Tours.htm file

the default target
for hyperlinks on
this page

clicking this link
displays the
Links.htm file

```
<HTML>
<HEAD>
<TITLE>The Colorado Experience Hypertext Links</TITLE>
<BASE TARGET=Documents>
</HEAD>
<BODY BACKGROUND="Wall2.gif">
<FONT SIZE=2 COLOR=BLUE><B>
<A HREF="TCE.htm">Home Page</A><BR>
<A HREF="Philosph.htm">Our Philosophy</A><BR>
<A HREF="Lessons.htm">Climbing Lessons</A><BR>
<A HREF="Links.htm" TARGET=_self>Tours</A><BR>
      <A HREF="Grepon.htm">Petit Grepon</A><BR>
      <A HREF="Lumpy.htm">Lumpy Ridge</A><BR>
      <A HREF="NFace.htm">North Face</A><BR>
      <A HREF="Kieners.htm">Kiener's</A><BR>
      <A HREF="Diamond.htm">The Diamond</A><BR>
      <A HREF="Eldorado.htm">Eldorado</A><BR>
<A HREF="Staff.htm">Staff</A>
</B></FONT>
</BODY>
</HTML>
```

4. Save your changes to the Tours.htm file.

TROUBLE? The original version of the Tours.htm file is stored in the Tutorial.05 folder of your Student Disk as Tourtext.htm, if you need to return to the original file for some reason.

5. Return to your Web browser and reopen the Colorado.htm file. (You might have to restart your browser and reload the page.)

6. Click the **Tours** link and verify that the tours list appears to be alternately expanded and contracted as you click it. Also click the individual tour pages and verify that they appear in the Documents frame. See Figure 5-26.

Figure 5-26
Viewing a
tour page

list of tours

currently selected tour

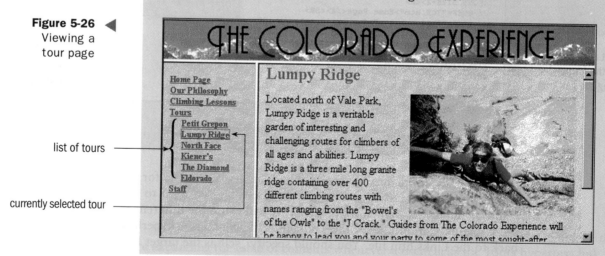

The technique employed here is a common one for tables of contents that double as hypertext links. Clicking the Tours hyperlink gives the effect that the list is expanding and contracting, but what is actually happening is that one table of contents is being replaced by another. You'll see this technique used on other pages on the Web.

The last link in the list points to a page of staff biographies, stored in the Staff.htm file. Debbie asked another employee to produce the contents of the page. The results are shown in Figure 5-27.

Figure 5-27 ◀
Staff Web page

As you can see, this page also uses frames. How should this page be displayed within your frame layout? If you use the Documents frame as the target, you'll end up with the series of nested frame images shown in Figure 5-28.

Figure 5-28 ◀
One frame
image
appearing
inside another

This is not what Debbie wants. She wants the Staff page to load into the full display area, replacing the frame layout with its own layout. To target a link to the full display area, you use the _top magic target name. The _top target is often used when one framed page is accessing another. It's also used when you are linking to pages that lie outside your Web presentation, such as pages on the World Wide Web. For example, a link to the Colorado Tourism Board Web site should not appear within a frame on the Colorado Experience page for two reasons. First, once you go outside your Web presentation, you lose control of content, and you could easily end up with a nested frame layout problem. The second reason is that such a setup could confuse users, making it appear as if the Colorado Tourism Board is another component of the Colorado Experience climbing school, which would create an inaccurate impression.

Next, you'll add the _top magic target name for the Staff link to the link's <A> tag.

To use the _top magic target name to specify the target for the Staff link:

1. Open the **Links.htm** file in your text editor.

2. Within the <A> tag for the Staff link, enter the property **TARGET=_top**. See Figure 5-29.

Figure 5-29 ◀
Revised
Links.htm file
using the _top
magic target
name

target is the top of
the document
window, replacing the
current frame layout

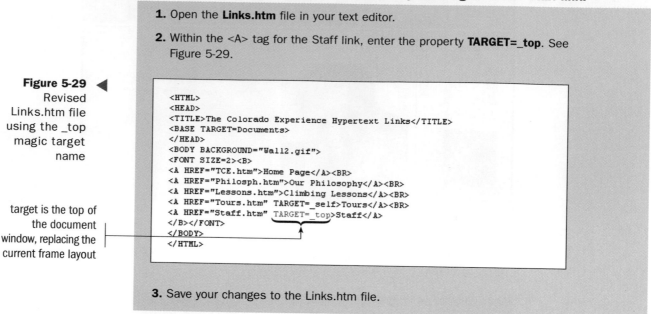

```
<HTML>
<HEAD>
<TITLE>The Colorado Experience Hypertext Links</TITLE>
<BASE TARGET=Documents>
</HEAD>
<BODY BACKGROUND="Wall2.gif">
<FONT SIZE=2><B>
<A HREF="TCE.htm">Home Page</A><BR>
<A HREF="Philosph.htm">Our Philosophy</A><BR>
<A HREF="Lessons.htm">Climbing Lessons</A><BR>
<A HREF="Tours.htm" TARGET=_self>Tours</A><BR>
<A HREF="Staff.htm" TARGET=_top>Staff</A>
</B></FONT>
</BODY>
</HTML>
```

3. Save your changes to the Links.htm file.

Because the Tours.htm file also acts as a table of contents (with the added references to the tour pages), you should also edit the hyperlink to the Staff page in that file. In this way, a user can click the Staff hyperlink from both the table of contents with the expanded list of tours and from the original table of contents.

To edit the Tours.htm file:

1. Open the **Tours.htm** file in your text editor.

2. Within the <A> tag for the Staff link, enter the property **TARGET=_top**.

3. Save your changes to the Tours.htm file.

4. Reopen the Colorado Experience page in your Web browser and verify that the Staff link now opens the Staff page and replaces the existing frame layout with its own. Be sure to test the Staff link from both the original table of contents and the table of contents with the expanded list of tours.

   TROUBLE? If the Staff link does not work properly, verify that you used lower-case letters for the magic target name.

Debbie has viewed all the hypertext links on the Colorado Experience page and is satisfied with the results. However, she wonders what would happen if a user with an older browser encountered the page. Is there some way to accommodate browsers that don't support frames? Yes, using the <NOFRAMES> tag.

Using the <NOFRAMES> Tag

In most cases you do not need to include the <BODY> tags for pages containing frames. However, if you want your page to be viewable by browsers that do not support frames, as well as by those that do, you need to use the <BODY> tags. The difference is that the <BODY> tags must be placed within a pair of <NOFRAMES> tags. The <NOFRAMES> tag identifies a section of your HTML file that contains code to be read by frame-blind browsers. The general syntax for the <NOFRAMES> tag is:

```
<HTML>
<HEAD>
<TITLE>Page Title</TITLE>
</HEAD>
<FRAMESET>
    Frame Definitions
</FRAMESET>
<NOFRAMES>
<BODY>
    Page Layout
</BODY>
</NOFRAMES>
</HTML>
```

By examining this syntax, you can determine how the <NOFRAMES> tag works. If a browser that supports frames retrieves this code, it knows that it should ignore everything within the <NOFRAMES> tags and concentrate solely on the code within the <FRAME-SET> tags. If a browser that doesn't support frames retrieves this code, it doesn't know what to do with the <FRAMESET> and <NOFRAMES> tags, so it just ignores them. However it does know that it's supposed to render whatever appears within the <BODY> tags on the page. In this way, both types of browsers are supported within a single HTML file.

REFERENCE window

SUPPORTING FRAME-BLIND BROWSERS

- Create a version of your page that does not use frames.
- In the framed version of the page, insert the following tags.
  <NOFRAMES>
  </NOFRAMES>
- Copy the HTML code between the <BODY> tags, including both the <BODY> and </BODY> tags, from the nonframed version of the page.
- Paste the copied code between the <NOFRAMES> and </NOFRAMES> tags in the framed version of the page.

The Colorado Experience has been using a nonframed version of its home page for some time now. This page is shown in Figure 5-30.

Figure 5-30 ◀
Nonframed
version of the
Colorado
Experience
Web page

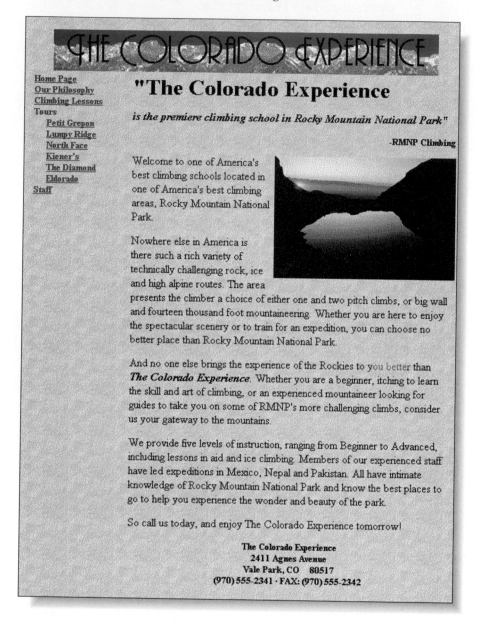

To display this page for frame-blind browsers, you need to copy the HTML code, including the <BODY> tags, and place it within a pair of <NOFRAMES> tags in the Colorado.htm file.

To insert support for frame-blind browsers:

1. Open the **Colorado.htm** file in your text editor.

2. Insert a blank line above the </HTML> tag.

3. Enter the following HTML code:

```
<!- - - Frameless version of this page - - ->
<NOFRAMES>
</NOFRAMES>
```

4. Save your changes to the Colorado.htm file.

Next you'll copy the code from the nonframed page into the Colorado.htm file.

5. In your text editor, open the **Noframes.htm** file from the Tutorial.05 folder on your Student Disk.

6. Copy the HTML code beginning with the <BODY> tag and down to the </BODY> tag. Be sure to include *both* the opening and closing <BODY> tags in your selection.

7. Open the **Colorado.htm** file in the text editor.

8. Insert a blank line below the <NOFRAMES> tag.

9. Paste the text you copied from the Noframes.htm file in the blank line below the <NOFRAMES> tag. Figure 5-31 shows a portion of the revised code.

Figure 5-31 ◀
Inserting the
NOFRAMES
code into the
Colorado.htm
file

```
<NOFRAMES>
<BODY BACKGROUND="Wall.gif">
<TABLE WIDTH=610>
<TR>
    <!--- Company Logo --->
    <TD ALIGN=CENTER COLSPAN=2>
        <IMG SRC="Logo.jpg" WIDTH=550 HEIGHT=60 ALT="The Colorado Experience">
    </TD>
</TR>
<TR>
```

```
    2411 Agnes Avenue<BR>
    Vale Park, CO     80517<BR>
    (970) 555-2341 &#183 FAX: (970) 555-2342
    </B></FONT></CENTER>
    </TD>
</TR>
</TABLE>

</BODY>
</NOFRAMES>
```

10. Save the file in your text editor.

To test your page, you should try to locate a browser that does not support frames (you can retrieve early versions of Netscape Navigator and Internet Explorer at their Web sites). Note that the table structure of the frameless page closely matches the frame layout you created. In this case, the first row is a single cell that spans two columns and displays the company logo, and the second row contains the list of links in the first cell and the home page text in the second cell.

Not all HTML editors support frames. If you try to use an HTML editor to edit a Web page, rather than working with the HTML code directly, you might find that the editor will only load the code between the <NOFRAMES> tags. The HTML editors that do not support frames, such as Netscape Gold, for example, will go directly to the first <BODY> tag they find. In these situations, you'll have to edit any code related to frames directly with a text editor.

DESIGN
window

TIPS FOR USING FRAMES

- Create framed and nonframed versions of your Web page to accommodate all browsers.
- Do not turn off vertical or horizontal scrolling unless you are certain that all the content will appear within the frame borders.
- Assign names to all of your frames to make your HTML code easier to interpret.
- Simplify your HTML code by using the <BASE> tag when most of the hyperlinks in your framed page point to the same target.
- Never display pages that lie outside your Web presentation (such as pages created by other authors on the World Wide Web) within a frame.

You're finished working with the Colorado Experience page. There are some additional features you can add to this page, which are not supported by all browsers. You'll investigate them next.

Using Frame Extensions

Netscape Navigator and Internet Explorer both support extensions to the <FRAME> tag that allow you to change border size and appearance. For example, you can remove borders from your frames to free up more space for text and images, or you can change the color of the frame border so that it matches your color scheme more closely. As with other extensions, you should use care when implementing these extensions, because they might not be supported by all browsers.

REFERENCE
window

USING ENHANCEMENTS TO THE <FRAME> AND <FRAMESET> TAGS

(Netscape Navigator users only)
- To define a color for your frame borders, use the following tags:
  <FRAMESET BORDERCOLOR=*color*>
  or
  <FRAME BORDERCOLOR=*color*>
  where *color* is either the color name or color value. Enter the BORDERCOLOR property in the <FRAMESET> tag to change all of the frame border colors in a set of frames. Enter the property in the <FRAME> tag to change the color of a single frame border.
- To change the width of your frame borders, use the tag:
  <FRAMESET BORDER=*value*>
  where *value* is the width of the border in pixels. You cannot change the width of individual frame borders.

Setting the Border Color

One of the extensions supported by Netscape Navigator is the ability to change the color of a frame's border. The BORDERCOLOR property can be applied either to an entire set of frames (within the <FRAMESET> tag) or to individual frames (within the <FRAME> tag). The syntax for this property is:

```
<FRAMESET BORDERCOLOR=color>
or
<FRAME BORDERCOLOR=color>
```

where *color* is either a color name or a color value. Applying the BORDERCOLOR property to a set of frames colors all of the frames and nested frames within the set.

Debbie asks you to test the BORDERCOLOR property on the Colorado Experience page by changing the color of the Logo frame border to blue. You'll leave the colors of the rest of the frame borders as they are.

To change the Logo frame border color:

1. Return to the Colorado.htm file in your text editor.

2. Within the <FRAME> tag for the Logo frame, enter the property **BORDERCOLOR=BLUE**.

3. Save your changes to the file, and then reopen the file in the Netscape Navigator browser. Figure 5-32 shows the Logo frame with a blue border.

Figure 5-32 ◀
Logo frame
with a blue
border

blue frame border ────

TROUBLE? If you don't have the Netscape Navigator browser, or if your browser does not support the BORDERCOLOR property for frames, you will not be able to view the results of this set of steps. Continue reviewing the steps, however.

Another way of modifying frame borders is to change their widths.

Setting the Border Width

Netscape Navigator also supports the BORDER property, an extension that allows you to specify the width of the frame borders. Unlike the BORDERCOLOR property, this property can be used only in the <FRAMESET> tag, and not in individual <FRAME> tags. The syntax for the BORDER property is:

```
<FRAMESET BORDER=value>
```

where *value* is the width of the frame borders in pixels.

To see how this property affects the appearance of your page, Debbie asks you to use it to remove the frame borders by setting the width to 0 pixels. Once again, you can view the results of this property in the Netscape Navigator browser, version 3.0 or above.

To change the size of the frame borders:

1. Return to the Colorado.htm file in your text editor.

2. Locate the Logo <FRAME> tag and delete the BORDERCOLOR property that you entered in the previous set of steps. You don't need this property because you're going to remove the frame borders entirely.

3. Within the first <FRAMESET> tag, enter the property **BORDER=0**. See Figure 5-33.

Figure 5-33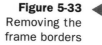
Removing the frame borders

width of each frame border is 0 pixels

```
<HTML>
<HEAD>
<TITLE>The Colorado Experience</TITLE>
</HEAD>
<FRAMESET ROWS="60,*" BORDER=0>
    <!--- Company Logo --->
```

4. Save your changes, and then reopen the Colorado.htm file in the Netscape Navigator browser. As shown in Figure 5-34, the frame borders have been removed from the page.

Figure 5-34
The Colorado Experience Web page without frame borders

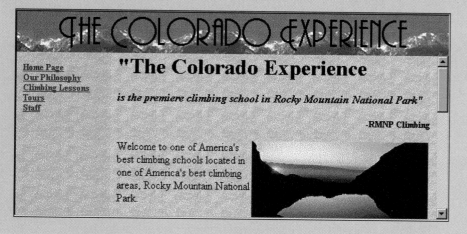

By removing the borders, you created more space for the text and images in each of the pages. You've also created the impression of a "seamless" Web page. Some Web authors prefer to eliminate frame borders, in order to give the illusion of having a single Web page rather than three separate ones.

You can create a similar effect by using the FRAMEBORDER property. This is another property that is supported by both Netscape Navigator and Internet Explorer. Specifying FRAMEBORDER=NO in a <FRAMESET> tag removes the borders from the frames in your page.

Quick Check

1. When you click a hyperlink inside of a frame, what frame will the page appear in by default?

2. What HTML code would you enter to assign the name "Address" to a frame whose document source is Address.htm?

3. What HTML code would you enter to direct a hyperlink to a frame named "News"?

4. What HTML code would you enter to point a hyperlink to the document "Sales.htm" with the result that the Sales.htm file is retrieved into the entire display area, overwriting any frames in the process?

5. What tag would you enter to direct all hyperlinks in a document to the "News" target?

6. Describe what you would do to make your page readable by both browsers that support frames and those that do not.

7. What tag would you enter to set the frame border color of every frame on the page to red?

8. What tag would you enter to set the frame border width to 5 pixels?

9. What is the limitation of the tags you created in Quick Checks 7 and 8?

You've completed your work with the Web page for The Colorado Experience. Using frames, you created an interesting presentation that is easy to navigate and attractive to the eye. Debbie looks over your work and will get back to you with any changes.

Tutorial Assignments

Debbie has some suggestions for modifications to the Web presentation for The Colorado Experience. Recall that the Staff page already uses frames. Debbie would like you to make a few changes to the design of this page. Specifically, she wants you to:

- create a new frame containing a hyperlink pointing back to the Colorado.htm file
- remove any scroll bars from the frame and keep it from being resized by the user
- remove the frame borders for users of Netscape Navigator
- insert HTML code to support users with frame-blind browsers

To implement Debbie's suggestions:

1. Start your text editor and open the Stafftxt.htm file in the TAssign folder of the Tutorial.05 folder on your Student Disk, and then save the file as Staff.htm in the same folder.

2. Replace the <FRAME> tag and the corresponding comment tag in the first column of the second row with a <FRAMESET> tag to create two rows of nested frames. The height of the first row should be 25 pixels. The height of the second row should be whatever space is left.

3. Specify the file Return.htm as the source for the frame in the first row. Do not allow users to resize this frame, and remove any scroll bars. Set the width of the frame margins to 1 pixel. Name the frame "Return."

4. Specify the file Photos.htm as the source for the frame in the second row. Turn off frame resizing, but allow the browser to display scroll bars when needed. Set the margin height of this frame to 1 pixel, and set the margin width to 10 pixels. Name the frame "Photos."

5. Close off the two <FRAME> tags with a </FRAMESET> tag.

6. Insert an opening and closing <NOFRAME> tag below the last </FRAMESET> tag.

7. Copy the HTML code from the StaffNF.htm file (in the TAssign folder), including the <BODY> tags, and paste the code between the <NOFRAMES> tags in the Staff.htm file.

8. Change the border width of the frames in the Staff.htm file to 0 pixels.

9. Insert comment tags that document the different frames you created in the file.

10. Save your changes to the Staff.htm file.

11. Open the Retrntxt.htm file in the TAssign folder of the Tutorial.05 folder on your Student Disk, and then save the file as Return.htm in the same folder.

12. Change the text "Go to home page" to a hyperlink pointing to the Colorado.htm file. Set up the hyperlink so that it loads Colorado.htm into the full display window when clicked.
13. Save your changes to the Return.htm file.
14. Open the Staff.htm file from the TAssign folder in your Web browser and verify that the frames appear correctly and all hyperlinks are working properly. Figure 5-35 shows the finished appearance of the page.

Figure 5-35 ◀

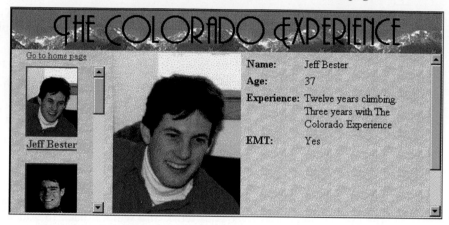

15. Print your Web page and the corresponding HTML code for the Staff.htm and Return.htm files.
16. Close your Web browser and your text editor.

Case Problems

1. Creating a Sales Report for Doc-Centric Copiers Doc-Centric Copiers, located in Salt Lake City, is one of the nation's leading manufacturers of personal and business copiers. The annual shareholders' convention in Chicago is approaching, and the general manager, David Edgars, wants you to create an online report for the convention participants. The report will run off a computer located in the convention hall and will be accessible to everyone. David feels that creating a Web presentation to run locally on the computer is the best way of presenting the sales data. Using hyperlinks between various reports will enable Doc-Centric Copiers to make a wealth of information available to shareholders in an easy-to-use format. Most of the Web pages have already been created for you. Your job is to combine the information into a single page using frames. A preview of the page you'll create is shown in Figure 5-36.

Figure 5-36 ◀

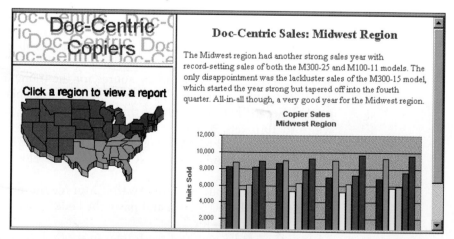

To create the Doc-Centric Copiers sales report page:
1. Open the file DCCtxt.htm in the Cases folder of the Tutorial.05 folder on your Student Disk, and then save the file as DCC.htm in the same folder.

2. Create a frame layout. The layout should consist initially of two columns. The left column should be 240 pixels wide, and the right column should fill up the rest of the display area.

3. Within the first frame column, insert two rows of nested frames. The frame in the first row should be 75 pixels high, and the second row should fill up the remaining space. The source for the first frame row is the Head.htm file, which contains the company logo. The source for the second frame row is the Map.htm file, which contains a map showing the different sales regions for the company. Name the first frame "Logo" and the second frame "USMap."

4. The source for the frame in the second column is the file Report.htm. This frame will contain the various sales reports that David wants displayed. Name the frame "Reports."

5. Complete the tags required for the frame layout and add comment tags describing each frame. Save your changes.

6. Open the file Maptxt.htm in the Cases folder of the Tutorial.05 folder on your Student Disk, and then save the file as Map.htm in the same folder.

EXPLORE

7. The Map.htm file contains an image map of the different sales regions. For each hyperlink in the Map.htm file, direct the link to the Reports target, so that the pages appear in the Reports frame. Save your changes.

8. View the DCC.htm file in your Web browser. What improvements could be made to the page? What things should be removed?

9. Return to the DCC.htm file in your text editor and reduce the margin for the Logo frame to 1 pixel. Reduce the margin width for the USMap frame to 1 pixel, and change the margin height to 30 pixels.

10. Remove scroll bars from both the Logo and USMap frames.

11. View the page again to verify that the problems you identified in Step 8 have been resolved.

12. Return to the DCC.htm file and lock the size of the frames to prevent users from inadvertently changing the frame sizes.

13. Reopen the Doc-Centric Copiers sales report page and test the image map in the USMap frame. Verify that each of the four sales reports is correctly displayed in the Reports frame.

14. Print a page displaying one of the sales reports. Print a copy of both the DCC.htm and Map.htm files.

15. Close your Web browser and your text editor.

2. Creating a Tour Page for Travel Scotland! You've been asked to create a Web presentation for a touring agency called Travel Scotland!, which organizes tours to Scotland and the British Isles. The page will display an itinerary and photo for four popular tours: the Lake District tour, the Castles of Scotland tour, a tour of the Scottish Highlands, and, finally, a tour of the Hebrides. A page with a frame layout has been created for each tour. Your task is to create a page that ties the four separate Web pages into a single presentation. A preview of the completed Web page is shown in Figure 5-37.

Figure 5-37 ◄

To create the Travel Scotland! page:

1. Open the file Scottxt.htm in the Cases folder of the Tutorial.05 folder on your Student Disk, and then save the file as Scotland.htm in the same folder.
2. Create a frame layout for the Scotland.htm page that consists of three rows of frames. The size of the first row should be 45 pixels, the third row should be 70 pixels, and the middle row should occupy whatever space is left.
3. Specify the file TSLogo.htm—a file containing the company logo—as the source for the first frame. The source for the second frame is Laketour.htm, a file describing the Lake District tour. Finally, the source for the third frame is TSList.htm, a page containing a graphic with the four tour names.
4. Assign the following names to the frames: Logo, Tours, and TourList, respectively.
5. Save your changes to the Scotland.htm file.
6. The TourList frame refers to a file that contains an inline image with titles for the four main tours offered by Travel Scotland! Change this graphic to an image map:
   a. Open the file TSLtxt.htm in the Cases folder of the Tutorial.05 folder on your Student Disk, and then save the file as TSList.htm in the same folder.
   b. Assign an image map named "TourList" to the inline image with the following hotspots:
      - a rectangular hotspot at (17,0) (158,59) that points to Laketour.htm
      - a rectangular hotspot at (159,0) (306,59) that points to Casttour.htm
      - a rectangular hotspot at (307,0) (454,59) that points to Hightour.htm
      - a rectangular hotspot at (455,0) (593,59) that points to Hebdtour.htm
   c. For each hotspot in the graphic, specify the Tours frame as the target.
   d. Save your changes to TSList.htm.
7. Open the Scotland.htm file in your Web browser. What problems do you see? Reopen Scotland.htm in your text editor and fix the problems.
8. Reopen Scotland.htm in your browser. Is the problem fixed? If so, return to the file in your text editor and lock the size and position of the frame borders by preventing users from resizing the frames. Reopen the page in the browser.

9. Test the hyperlinks in the image map. Note that when you click a hyperlink, two frames are updated in the page. This is because the source for the frame in the middle row is itself a framed page. This is one way you can have two frames updated with a single click of a hyperlink.
10. Print the Travel Scotland! Web page and the source code in the Scotland.htm and TSList.htm files.

11. Trace the code for the series of hyperlinks and framed pages in this Case Problem and create a diagram showing how all of the files are connected.
12. Close your Web browser and your text editor.

3. Creating a Sonnets Page for English 220 Professor Sherry Lake is teaching a course on 16th and 17th century poetry. She's asked you to help her create a Web presentation of a section of her course dealing with sonnets. She has collected ten sonnets written by John Donne, William Shakespeare, and Edmund Spenser, that she wants the students to learn and has placed them in HTML files. She has also created a page that shows the title of the course and a list of the ten sonnets. She wants you to organize this material using frames. A preview of the page you'll create is shown in Figure 5-38.

Figure 5-38 ◄

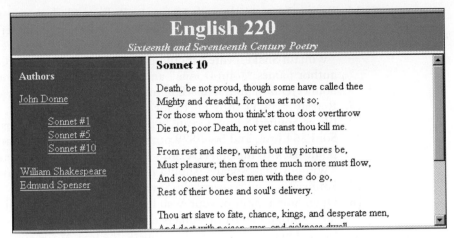

The table of contents for this page appears in the leftmost frame. Sherry wants the links in the table of contents frame to work as follows:

- If a user clicks the name of an author, a list of sonnets by that author alternately expands and contracts in the table of contents frame.
- If a user clicks the name of a sonnet, the sonnet appears in the rightmost frame.

Sherry doesn't want the layout of the page to be locked in; that is, she wants to give students the ability to resize the frames when they're viewing the page.

To create the sonnets page:

1. Open the file Sontxt.htm in the Cases folder of the Tutorial.05 folder on your Student Disk, and then save the file as Sonnet.htm in the same folder.

2. Create a frame layout in which the first frame row is 65 pixels high, and the height of the second frame row is whatever space remains on the page.

3. Within the second frame row, create a nested frame layout of two columns. The first column should be 220 pixels wide, and the second column should cover the rest of the page.

4. The source for the first frame is Eng220.htm. The source for the second frame is SonTOC.htm, and the source for the third frame is Blank.htm.

5. Name the first frame "Head," the second frame "List," and the third frame "Sonnet."

6. Set the margin height for the Head and Sonnet frames to 1 pixel. Set the margin width for the Sonnet frame to 10 pixels.

7. Save your changes to Sonnet.htm, and then close the file.

8. Open the SnTOCtxt.htm file in the Cases folder of the Tutorial.05 folder on your Student Disk, and then save the file as SonTOC.htm in the same folder.

9. Set the base target for all hyperlinks in this file to the magic target name that loads the document into the same frame that contains the hyperlink tag.

10. Convert the names of the three authors to hypertext links: "John Donne" should point to the SonnetJD.htm file, "William Shakespeare" to SonnetWS.htm, and "Edmund Spenser" to SonnetES.htm. Save your changes to SonTOC.htm, and then close the file.

11. Open the John Donne file, JDtxt.htm, in the Cases folder of the Tutorial.05 folder on your Student Disk, and then save the file as SonnetJD.htm in the same folder.

12. Convert the author names and sonnet names to hypertext links. The sonnets should point to the files SonJD1.htm, SonJD5.htm, and SonJD10.htm, respectively. The author name "John Donne" should point back to the SonTOC.htm file, and the author names "William Shakespeare" and "Edmund Spenser" should point to the files SonnetWS.htm and SonnetES.htm, respectively.

13. Set the Sonnet frame as the base target for hyperlinks in this document. Set the target for each author name to the magic target name that loads the document into the same frame that contains the hyperlink tag. Save your changes.

14. Repeat Steps 11 through 13 for the William Shakespeare file, WStxt.htm. Save the file as SonnetWS.htm. Create hyperlinks to the sonnet files SonWS12.htm, SonWS18.htm, SonWS116.htm, and SonWS130.htm. The author name "William Shakespeare" should point back to the SonTOC.htm file, and the author names "John Donne" and "Edmund Spenser" should point back to SonnetJD.htm and SonnetES.htm, respectively. Save your changes.

15. Repeat Steps 11 through 13 for the Edmund Spenser file, EStxt.htm. Save the file as SonnetES.htm. Create hyperlinks to the sonnet files SonES54.htm, SonES64.htm, and SonES79.htm. The author name "Edmund Spenser" should point back to the SonTOC.htm file, and the author names "John Donne" and "William Shakespeare" should point back to SonnetJD.htm and SonnetWS.htm, respectively. Save your changes.

16. Open Sonnet.htm in your Web browser. Verify that by clicking the names of the authors, the list of sonnets is alternately expanded and contracted, and that by clicking the names of the sonnets, the text of the sonnet appears in the rightmost frame.

17. Print a copy of the Web page and the code for the following files: Sonnet.htm, SonTOC.htm, SonnetJD.htm, SonnetWS.htm, and SonnetES.htm.

18. Close your Web browser and your text editor.

4. Creating a Web Presentation for Warner Peripherals Warner Peripherals, a company located in Tucson, makes high-quality peripherals for computers. The company leads the industry in disk drives and tape drives. Its most popular products include the SureSave line of tape drives and the SureRite line of disk drives. You've been asked to consolidate several Web pages describing these products into a single Web presentation that uses frames. The files shown in Figure 5-39 are available for your use.

Figure 5-39

File	Contents
Drive15L.htm	Description of the 15L SureRite hard drive
Drive20M.htm	Description of the 20M SureRite hard drive
Drive30M.htm	Description of the 33M SureRite hard drive
Drive60M.htm	Description of the 60M SureRite hard drive
Tape800.htm	Description of the 800 SureSave tape backup drive
Tape3200.htm	Description of the 3200 SureSave tape backup drive
Tape9600.htm	Description of the 9600 SureSave tape backup drive
WLogo.htm	Web page containing the Warner Peripherals logo

To create the Warner Peripherals Web presentation:

1. Create a table of contents page that includes hyperlinks to the files listed in Figure 5-39. The layout and appearance of this page are up to you. Save this page as WTOC.htm in the Cases folder of the Tutorial.05 folder on your Student Disk.

2. Create a file named Warner.htm that consolidates the logo page, table of contents page, and product description pages into a single page using frames. The layout of the frames is up to you. Include comment tags in the file describing each element of the page. Save the Warner.htm file in the Cases folder of the Tutorial.05 folder on your Student Disk.

3. Test your page and verify that each link works properly and appears in the correct frame.

4. Print a copy of the page and the HTML code.

5. Close your Web browser and your text editor.

Answers to Quick Check Questions

SESSION 3.1

1 Color names and color values. Color names are easier to work with but the color name may not exist for exactly the color you want to use. Also your color name may not be supported by all browsers. Color values allow you to exactly describe a color, but they can be difficult to work with.

2 <BODY BGCOLOR=GRAY TEXT=RED LINK=BLUE VLINK=YELLOW>

3 Spot color is color that affects only a few sections of a page such as a single character, word or phrase.

4 <FONT COLOR=red SIZE=+5>Major Sale</FONT>

5 <FONT FACE="Times New Roman, MS Serif">Major Sale</FONT>

6 <BODY BACKGROUND="Stars.gif">

7 overwhelming the page's text, using a large image file that will make the page take longer to load, and using an image that displays visible seams

SESSION 3.2

1 when you want to use transparent colors, when you want to use an animated image, and when your image has only 256 colors or less

2 for photographic images, for images that contain more than 256 colors, and to reduce file size through compression

3 <IMG SRC="mwu.jpg" ALT="MidWest University">

4 <IMG SRC="mwu.jpg" ALIGN=TOP>

5 <IMG SRC="mwu.jpg" ALIGN=RIGHT> This tag will not work for browsers that don't support the LEFT align property such as versions of Netscape Navigator and Internet Explorer prior to 3.0.

6 <IMG SRC="mwu.jpg" HSPACE=10 VSPACE=10>

7 <IMG SRC="mwu.jpg" HEIGHT=85 WIDTH=120>

8 When an image with many colors is displayed on a monitor that does not support all those colors, the monitor will attempt to approximate the appearance of those colors. The Safety Palette is a palette of 211 colors that is guaranteed to be displayed on all browsers without resorting to dithering.

SESSION 3.3

1 A hotspot is a defined area of the image that acts as a hypertext link. An image map lists the coordinates on the image that define the boundaries of the hotspots.

2 Server-side and client-side. The server-side is the older, more accepted method of creating image maps and relies on the Web server to interpret the image map and create the hypertext jump. The client-side image map is newer and is not supported by all browsers (though this is rapidly changing). Because the user's machine interprets the image map, the image map is interpreted more quickly, it can be tested on the local machine, and information about the various hotspots appears in the status bar of the Web browser.

3 <AREA SHAPE=RECT COORDS="5,20,85,100" HREF="Oregon.htm">

4 <AREA SHAPE=CIRCLE COORDS="44,81,23" HREF="LA.htm">

5 <AREA SHAPE=POLY COORDS="5,10,5,35,25,35,30,20,15,10" HREF="Hawaii.htm">

6 <IMG SRC="WestCoast.gif" USEMAP="#States">

7 <IMG SRC="WestCoast.gif" BORDER=5>

SESSION 4.1

1 Text tables and graphical tables. The text table is supported by all browsers and is easier to create. The graphical table is more difficult to create but provides the user with a wealth of formatting options. Graphical tables are also more flexible and attractive since the text tables have to be created in a fixed width font.

2 A proportional font assigns different widths to each character based on the character's shape. A fixed-width font assigns the same width to each character regardless of shape.

3 the <PRE> tag

4 The <TABLE> tag identifies the beginning of a table. The <TR> tag identifies the beginning of a table row. The <TD> tag identifies individual table cells, and the <TH> tag identifies table cells that will act as table headers.

5 The number of rows in a table is determined by the number of <TR> tags. The number of columns is equal to the largest number of <TD> or <TH> tags within a single table row.

6 Text within the <TH> tag is automatically bolded and centered within the table cell.

7 <CAPTION ALIGN=BOTTOM>Product Catalog</CAPTION> Place this tag anywhere between the <TABLE> and </TABLE> tags.

SESSION 4.2

1 <TABLE BORDER=5 CELLSPACING=3 CELLPADDING=4>

2 <TD VALIGN=TOP> or <TH VALIGN=TOP>

3 <TR ALIGN=CENTER>

4 In pixels or as a percentage of the display area. Use pixels if you want to exactly control the size of the table. Use percentages if you want your table to adapt itself to the user's monitor resolution.

5 <TABLE WIDTH="50%">

6 <TD WIDTH=60> or <TH WIDTH=60>. This will not keep the cell from exceeding 60 pixels in width. The only way to do that is to set the width of *all* cells in that table column to 60 pixels.

7 <TABLE BGCOLOR=YELLOW> This property is not supported by earlier browsers.

8 <TD ROWSPAN=3 COLSPAN=2> or <TH ROWSPAN=3 COLSPAN=2>

SESSION 4.3

1 <TABLE>
<TR><TD>
<TABLE><TR><TD></TD><TD></TD></TR><TR><TD></TD><TD></TD></TR></TABLE>
</TD>
<TD></TD>
</TR>
<TR>
<TD></TD>
<TD></TD>
</TR>
</TABLE>

2 <! Nested table starts here>

3 <TABLE BORDERCOLOR=YELLOW>

4 <TABLE BORDERCOLORDARK=BLUE BORDERCOLORLIGHT=RED>

5 <TABLE FRAME=ABOVE>

6 <TABLE RULES=COLS>

7 It works for browsers that support HTML 4.0. It may not work for older browsers that support the earlier HTML specifications.

SESSION 5.1

1 Frames are windows appearing within the browser's display area, each capable of displaying the contents of a different HTML file.

2 Because there is no page body. Instead the browser displays the <BODY> tags from other pages.

3 <FRAMESET ROWS="200,50%,*">

4 <FRAME SRC="Home.htm">

5 <FRAME SRC="Home.htm" SCROLLING=NO>

6 <FRAME SRC="Home.htm" MARGINHEIGHT=3>

7 3 pixels

8 <FRAME SRC="Home.htm" NORESIZE>

SESSION 5.2

1 the frame containing the hyperlink

2 <FRAME SRC="Address.htm" NAME=Address>

3 <A HREF=*URL* TARGET=News>

4 <A HREF="Sales.htm" TARGET=_top>

5 Place the tag, <BASE TARGET=News>, in the <HEAD> section of the HTML file.

6 Create a section starting with the <NOFRAMES> tag. After the <NOFRAMES> tag enter a <BODY> tag to identify the text and images you want frame-blind browsers to display. Complete this section with a </BODY> tag followed by a </NOFRAMES> tag.

7 <FRAMESET BORDERCOLOR=RED>

8 <FRAMESET BORDERWIDTH=5>

9 They cannot be used by all browsers.

NEW PERSPECTIVES SERIES

Creating Web Pages with **HTML**

LEVEL III

TUTORIALS

Read This **Before You Begin**

STUDENT DISKS

To complete HTML Tutorials 6–9, end-of-tutorial assignments, and the Additional Cases in this book, you need six Student Disks. Your instructor will either provide you with Student Disks or ask you to make your own.

If you are supposed to make your own Student Disks, you will need six blank, formatted high-density disks. You will need to copy a set of folders from a file server or standalone computer onto your disks. Your instructor will tell you which computer, drive letter, and folders contain the files you need. The following table shows you which folders go on each of your disks, so that you will have enough disk space to complete everything:

Student Disk	Write this on the disk label	Put these folders on the disk
1	Student Disk 1: Tutorials 6, 7, and 8	Tutorial.06, Tutorial.07, and Tutorial.08
2	Student Disk 2: Tutorial 9 (Tutorial files and Tutorial Assignment files)	Tutorial.09 and the TAssign folder of the Tutorial.09 folder
3	Student Disk 3: Tutorial 9 (Case Problem 1)	Case1 folder of the Tutorial.09 folder
4	Student Disk 4: Tutorial 9 (Case Problem 2)	Case2 folder of the Tutorial.09 folder
5	Student Disk 5: Tutorial 9 (Case Problems 3 and 4)	Case3 folder and Case4 folder of the Tutorial.09 folder
6	Student Disk 6: Additional Cases	Case1 folder, Case2 folder, Case3 folder of the Tutorial.add folder

When you begin each tutorial, be sure you are using the correct Student Disk. See the inside front cover of this book for more information on Student Disk files, or ask your instructor or technical support person for assistance.

COURSE LABS

Tutorial 9 and the Additional Cases feature interactive Course Labs. Refer to the Lab Assignments at the end of those tutorials for instructions on starting the Labs.

ADDITIONAL RESOURCE: CD IN THE BACK OF THIS BOOK

Take advantage of this special feature of *New Perspectives on Creating Web Pages with HTML—Comprehensive*. By using the CD in the back of this book you can access Java applets, an HTML 4.0 Tag Reference, additional coverage, and other multimedia elements. Use any or all of these items to enhance your learning process.

USING YOUR OWN COMPUTER

If you are going to work through this book using your own computer, you need:

■ **Computer System** A text editor and a Web browser (preferably Netscape Navigator or Internet Explorer, versions 3.0 or above) must be installed on your computer. If you are using a non-standard browser, it must support frames and HTML 3.2 or above. The ability to run sound clips and video clips is preferable.

■ **Student Disks** Ask your instructor or lab manager for details on how to get the Student Disks. You will not be able to complete the tutorials, end-of-tutorial assignments, or Additional Cases in this book using your own computer until you have the Student Disks. The Student Files may also be obtained electronically over the Internet.

VISIT OUR WORLD WIDE WEB SITE

Additional materials designed especially for you are available on the World Wide Web. Go to **http://www.course.com**. For example, see our Student Online Companion that contains additional coverage of selected topics in the text. These topics are indicated in the text by an online companion icon located in the left margin.

To complete HTML Tutorials 6–9, end-of-tutorial assignments, and the Additional Cases in this book, your students must use a set of files on six Student Disks. These files are included in the Instructor's Resource Kit, and they may also be obtained electronically over the Internet. See the inside front cover of this book for more details. Follow the instructions in the Readme file to copy the files to your server or standalone computer. You can view the Readme file using WordPad.

Once the files are copied, you can make Student Disks for the students yourself, or you can tell students where to find the files so they can make their own Student Disks. Make sure the files get correctly copied onto the Student Disks by following the instructions in the Student Disks section above, which will ensure that students have enough disk space to complete all the tutorials, end-of-tutorial assignments, and Additional Cases.

COURSE TECHNOLOGY STUDENT FILES

You are granted a license to copy the Student Files to any computer or computer network used by students who have purchased this book.

TUTORIAL 6

Creating Web Page Forms with HTML

Designing a Customized Registration Form

OBJECTIVES

In this tutorial you will:

- Learn about CGI scripts

- Review the various parts of an online form

- Create form elements using HTML tags

- Create a hidden field on a form

- Work with form properties

- Learn how to send data from a form to a CGI script

- Learn how to send form information without using CGI scripts

---

CASE

Creating a Registration Form for Jackson Electronics

Jackson Electronics, located in Seattle, is one of the leading manufacturers of imaging equipment such as printers, copiers, and flatbed scanners. The company has already established a presence on the World Wide Web with pages that describe the company's products and its corporate philosophy. Now, Jackson Electronics would like to improve upon that presence by creating interactive pages that will allow customers to give feedback about the company's products online.

Lisa Clemente, the director of customer support for Jackson Electronics, would like to have a page for customer registration. She's aware that fewer than 10% of the registration cards included with the product packaging are ever returned to the company, and she feels that this low response could be improved if product registration could be accomplished on the Web. Customers could fill out the registration form online and then send the information via e-mail to one of Lisa's assistants, who would enter the information into the company's database.

Lisa has asked you to help her create such a registration page. To do so, you'll have to learn how to create HTML forms and how to use those forms to record information for the company.

In this session you will learn some of the fundamentals of creating forms with HTML. You'll learn how forms interact with CGI scripts to transfer information from the Web browser to the Web server. You'll also create your first form element, an input box.

Working with CGI Scripts

Lisa has been considering how she wants the product registration form to appear, keeping in mind that the company plans to use the form to record customer information. Lisa decides to model the form on the registration cards already packaged with Jackson Electronics' products. Because a long form would discourage customers from completing it, Lisa wants the form kept brief and focused on the information the company is most interested in. She sketches out the form she would like you to create (Figure 6-1).

Figure 6-1 ◀
Lisa's proposed registration form

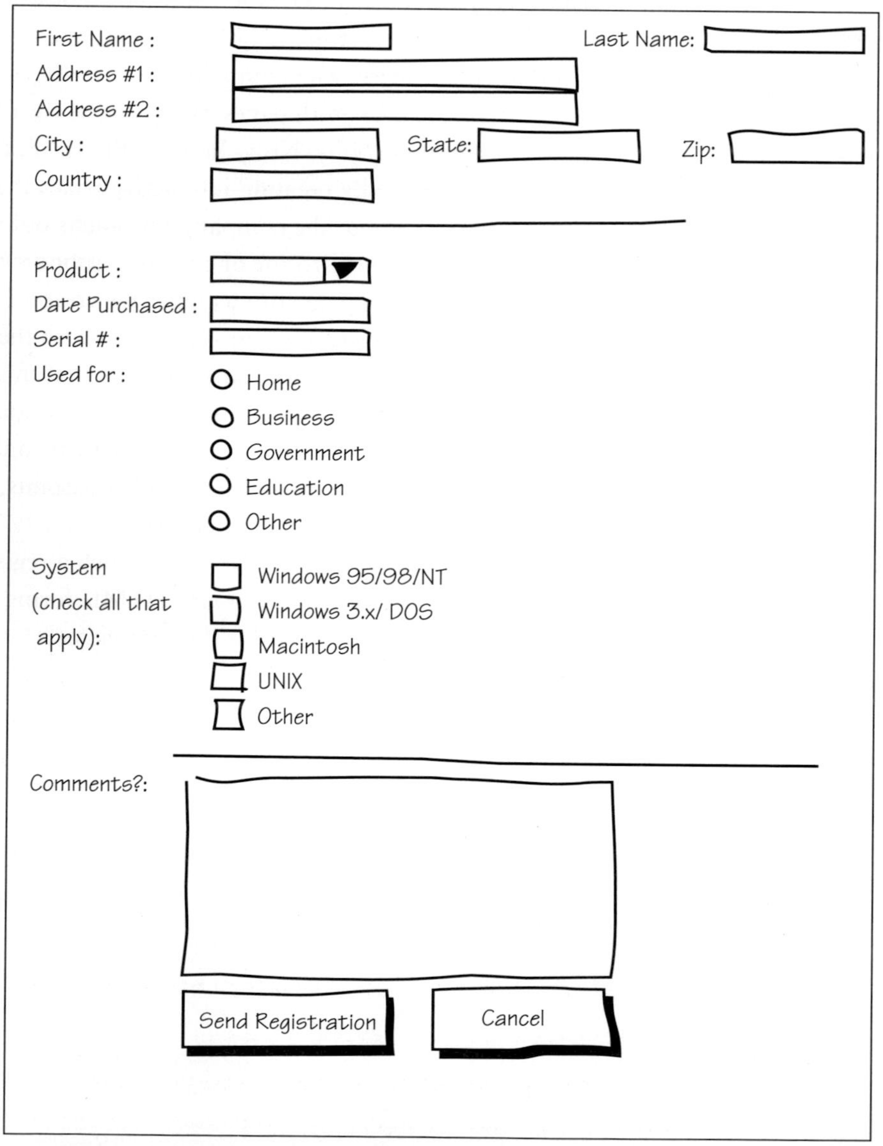

The form collects contact information for each customer as well as information on which product the customer purchased, what operating system the customer uses, and how the customer will use the product. There is also a place for customers to enter comments about the product or Jackson Electronics. With this registration form, Lisa hopes to collect information that will help Jackson Electronics better understand its customers and their needs.

Before you begin to create the form, you need to understand how such forms are interpreted and processed on the Web. Although HTML supports tags that allow you to create forms like the one shown in Figure 6-1, it does not have the ability to process that information. One way of processing information is to send it to a program running on the Web server, called a CGI script. A **CGI (Common Gateway Interface) script** is any program or set of commands running on the Web server that receives data from the Web page and then acts on that data to perform a certain task. Figure 6-2 illustrates how a Web page form interacts with a CGI script.

Figure 6-2 ◀
The interaction
between a Web
page form and
a CGI script

The Web page form is
completed and sent to the
Web server ...

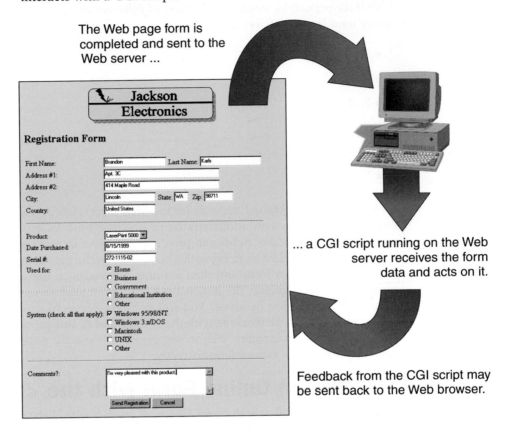

... a CGI script running on the Web
server receives the form
data and acts on it.

Feedback from the CGI script may
be sent back to the Web browser.

The introduction of CGI scripts represented a dramatic change in how the Web was perceived and used. By giving users access to programs that react to user input, the Web became an environment in which companies could interact with customers in ways that go beyond simple static Web documents. One example is the ability to maintain customer databases, which Lisa wants to do for Jackson Electronics. More importantly, CGI scripts made it possible for commerce to enter the Web, through the introduction of pages in which customers could locate and purchase merchandise online. Software manufacturers have also used CGI scripts to provide better support for their products by allowing users to access their customer support databases. In addition to working with data, CGI scripts have also been used for:

- reporting the number of times a Web page has been accessed
- creating server-side image maps
- creating message boards for online discussion forums
- managing e-mail for discussion groups

Because CGI scripts run on the Web server, you, as a Web page author, might not have the ability to create or edit them. In some cases, another programmer will create the scripts offered by the Web server and provide you with their specifications, indicating what input the scripts expect and what output they create.

Internet Service Providers and universities often provide CGI scripts that their customers and students are free to access from their Web pages, but which they cannot directly access or modify.

There are several good reasons to restrict direct access to a CGI script. The main reason is that when you run a CGI script, you are actually running a program directly on the server. Mindful of the dangers that computer hackers can present and the drain on system resources caused by large numbers of programs running simultaneously, system administrators are understandably anxious to control access to their servers.

CGI scripts can be written in a variety of different computer languages. The most commonly used languages are:

- AppleScript
- C/C++
- Perl
- the UNIX shell
- TCL
- Visual Basic

Which language is used depends on the Web server. Check with your Internet Service Provider or your system administrator to find out how CGI scripts are used on your server and what kinds of rights and privileges you have in working with them.

In this case, you'll be working with a script that performs the task of retrieving the data from the registration form and then mailing the results to one of Lisa's assistants. The assistant will then extract the information from an e-mail message and enter it into the company's registration database. You will not have access to the CGI scripts on the Web server, so you'll just be working with the HTML end of this process. Later, once the page is installed on the company's Web server, others will test the page and the script to verify that the information is passed on correctly.

Starting an Online Form with the <FORM> Tag

Now that you're familiar with how CGI scripts interact with Web page forms, you can begin to work on the registration form that Lisa wants you to create. As shown in Figure 6-3, the form contains the following elements, which are commonly used in Web page forms:

- **input boxes** for text and numerical entries
- **radio buttons**, also called **option buttons**, to select a single option from a predefined list
- **selection lists** for long lists of options, usually in a drop-down list box
- **check boxes** to specify an item as either being present or absent
- **text areas** for extended entries that might include several lines of text
- **Submit** and **Reset buttons** to either submit the form to the CGI script or to reset the form to its original state

Figure 6-3 ◀
Parts of a form

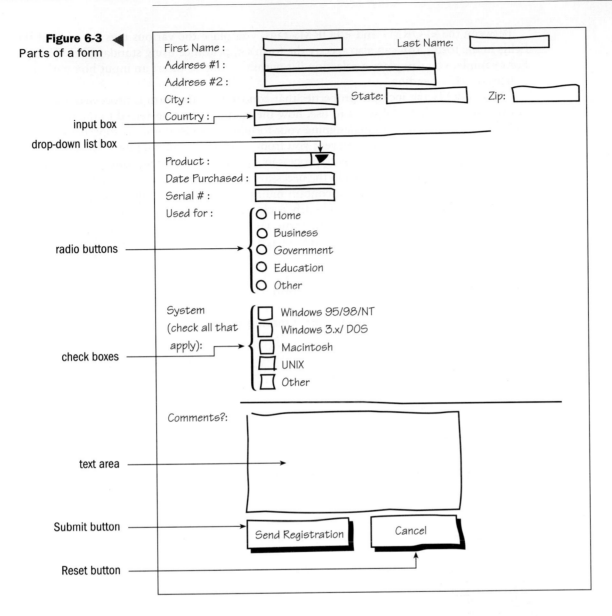

Each element in which the user can enter information is called a **field**. Information entered into a field is called the **field value**, or simply the **value**. In some fields, users are free to enter anything they choose. Other fields, like selection lists, confine their values to a predefined list of possible options.

Before you can create any fields, you must first indicate to the browser that the page will contain fields. You do this using the <FORM> tag. The <FORM> tag identifies the beginning and end of a form, like the <TABLE> tag, which defines the beginning and end of a graphical table. A single page can include several different forms, one after another, but you cannot nest one form inside another, as you can with tables. The general syntax of the <FORM> tag is:

```
<FORM Properties>
        Form elements and layout tags
</FORM>
```

Between the <FORM> and </FORM> tags, you place the various tags for each of the fields in the form. You can also specify the form's appearance using standard HTML tags. For example, you can place a selection list within a table or insert an input box within an italicized <H2> heading.

The <FORM> tag includes properties that control how the form is processed, including information on what CGI script to use, how the data is to be transferred to the script, and so forth. When you first begin designing your form, you can leave these properties out. One good reason for doing so is to prevent you from accidentally running the CGI script on an unfinished form, causing the script to process incomplete information. After you've finalized the form's appearance, you can add the necessary properties to access the CGI script.

Because a single Web page can contain multiple forms, the <FORM> tag includes the NAME property, allowing you to identify each form on the page. Although this property is not required for a page with a single form, you'll include the property for Lisa's page in case she decides to add other forms to the page in the future. You'll name the form REG, for registration.

Lisa has already prepared an HTML file for you, named Regtext.htm. You'll open this page and start to create the registration form.

To open the Regtext.htm file and start creating your form:

1. Start your text editor.

2. Open the file **Regtext.htm** from the Tutorial.06 folder on your Student Disk, and then save the file as **Register.htm** in the same folder.

3. Directly above the </BODY> tag, insert the following two lines:

```
<FORM NAME=REG>
</FORM>
```

Figure 6-4 shows the updated Register.htm file.

Figure 6-4 ◀
Adding the
<FORM> tag
to the
Register.htm
file

form tags ⎯⎯⎯

name of form ⎯⎯⎯

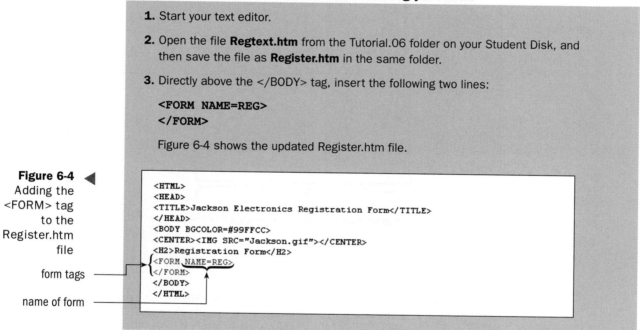

```
<HTML>
<HEAD>
<TITLE>Jackson Electronics Registration Form</TITLE>
</HEAD>
<BODY BGCOLOR=#99FFCC>
<CENTER><IMG SRC="Jackson.gif"></CENTER>
<H2>Registration Form</H2>
<FORM NAME=REG>
</FORM>
</BODY>
</HTML>
```

With the <FORM> tags in place, you can start creating the form layout. Look again at Lisa's plan for the form, shown in Figure 6-3. Notice that input boxes and other form elements are aligned on the page. This makes the form easier to read than if the elements were scattered across the width of the form. You can achieve this effect by using a table to control the layout of form objects. Figure 6-5 shows the simple two-column table that you'll use to create the form. Notice that some table cells in the second column contain several different form fields.

Figure 6-5
Placing a form
within a table

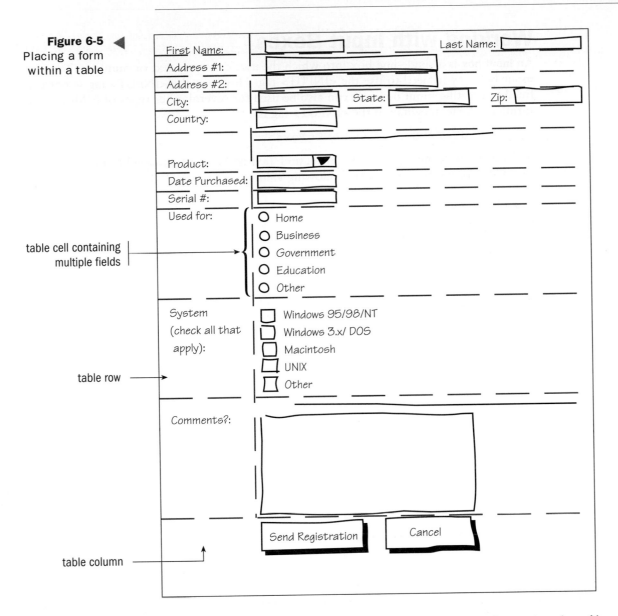

table cell containing
multiple fields

table row

table column

Next, you'll add the tags for the two-column table to the Register.htm file.

To insert the table tags:

1. Go to the <FORM> tag in the Register.htm file.

2. Insert the following two lines between the <FORM> and </FORM> tags:

<TABLE>
</TABLE>

3. Save your changes to the Register.htm file.

With the <FORM> and <TABLE> tags in place, you can now start to insert tags for each field in the form. You'll begin by learning how to create input boxes.

Working with Input Boxes

An **input box** is a single-line box into which the user can enter text or numbers. To create input boxes, you need to use the <INPUT> tag. However, the <INPUT> tag is not confined to creating input boxes; it can also be used for several other types of fields on your form. The general syntax of the <INPUT> tag is:

<INPUT TYPE=*Option* NAME=*Text*>

where *Option* is the type of input field, and *Text* is the name assigned to the input field. The TYPE property can have the following values:

- BUTTON
- CHECKBOX
- HIDDEN
- IMAGE
- PASSWORD
- RADIO
- RESET
- SUBMIT
- TEXT
- TEXTAREA

You'll learn about all these types as you progress with Lisa's registration form. The field you want to create now is an input box, which you create using TEXT as the value for the TYPE property. In fact, TEXT is the TYPE property's default value, so in most cases Web authors will simply leave out the TYPE property when they want to create an input box.

The NAME property is required with the <INPUT> tag. When information from the form is sent to the CGI script, field names are used to identify what values have been entered in each field. As shown in Figure 6-6, when the form data is sent, the CGI script receives the name of each field in the form paired with whatever value the user entered into the field. The script will then process the information according to each name/value pair.

Figure 6-6 ◀
Name/value
pairs sent from
the Web form
to the CGI
script

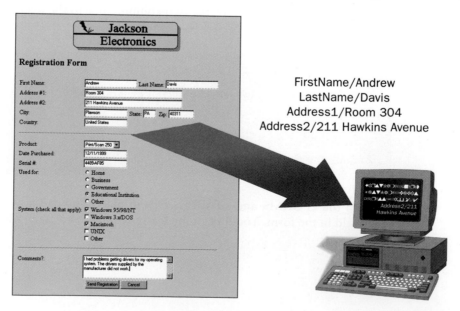

FirstName/Andrew
LastName/Davis
Address1/Room 304
Address2/211 Hawkins Avenue

Some CGI scripts will require that your form contain a particular field. For example, a CGI script whose purpose is to mail the form results to another user might require a field named "email" that contains the e-mail address of the recipient. Before using a CGI script, you should check with your Internet Service Provider or system administrator to see whether there are any such required fields. Be aware that case is important in field names. A field named "email" might not be interpreted by the CGI script in the same way as a field named "EMAIL".

REFERENCE window

CREATING AN INPUT BOX

- To create an input box, use the following tag:
  <INPUT NAME=*text* VALUE=*value* SIZE=*value*
  MAXLENGTH=*value*>
  where the NAME property sets the field name, the VALUE property assigns a default value to the input box, the SIZE property defines the width of the input box in number of characters, and the MAXLENGTH property defines the maximum number of characters allowed in the field.

The first part of the registration form deals with contact information for the customer. Each of the fields in this section is an input box. Because input boxes are blank boxes without any accompanying text, you have to insert a text description next to each box so that the user knows what to enter. In Lisa's form you are also using a table to control the form's layout, so you'll have to add the appropriate row and cell tags as well.

To insert the input boxes on the form:

1. Between the <TABLE> and </TABLE> tags in the Register.htm file, enter the following lines (you can make your code easier to follow by indenting the lines as shown):

```
<TR>
   <TD>First Name:</TD>
   <TD><INPUT NAME=FirstName>
       Last Name: <INPUT NAME=LastName></TD>
</TR>
<TR>
   <TD>Address #1:</TD>
   <TD><INPUT NAME=Address1></TD>
</TR>
<TR>
   <TD>Address #2:</TD>
   <TD><INPUT NAME=Address2></TD>
</TR>
<TR>
   <TD>City:</TD>
   <TD><INPUT NAME=City> State: <INPUT NAME=State>
       Zip: <INPUT NAME=ZIP></TD>
</TR>
<TR>
   <TD>Country:</TD>
   <TD><INPUT NAME=Country></TD>
</TR>
```

2. Save your changes to the Register.htm file.

3. Open the Register.htm file in your browser. Figure 6-7 shows the registration page as it appears in the Internet Explorer browser. Note that by using a table, you've caused the leftmost input boxes in each row to be vertically aligned, giving a uniform appearance to the registration form.

Figure 6-7 ◀
Contact fields
in the
registration
form

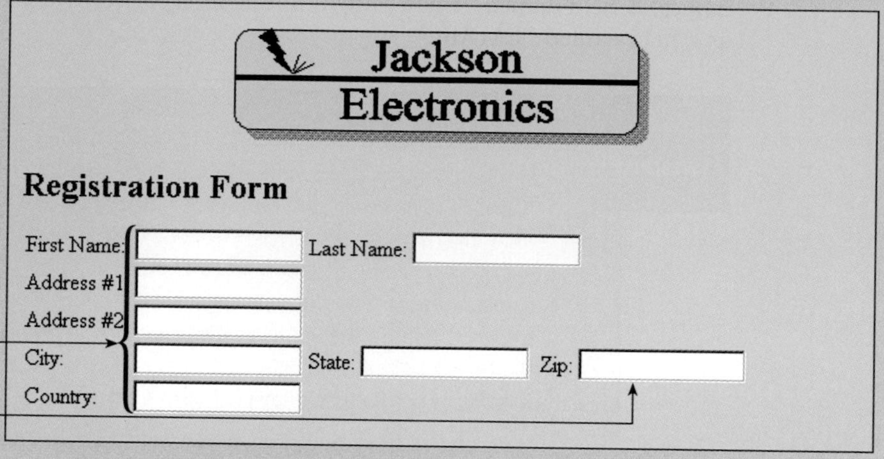

all input boxes are
the same size

input box

TROUBLE? If you are using the Netscape Navigator or Communicator browser, your form will look different from the one shown in Figure 6-7. You'll handle this problem shortly.

Note that even though forms appear to use graphical elements, these elements can also be displayed on text-based browsers, such as Lynx, using text characters.

Different browsers will display form elements in slightly different ways, so you should always test your form on the various popular browsers and, if possible, under different operating systems. For example, the Register.htm form shown in Figure 6-7 will appear in Netscape Navigator or Communicator as shown in Figure 6-8. In this case, the browser has used a larger font to render the input boxes and form elements, causing the field for the Zip code to be placed on the next line in the form.

Figure 6-8 ◀
The registration
form as it
appears in
Netscape

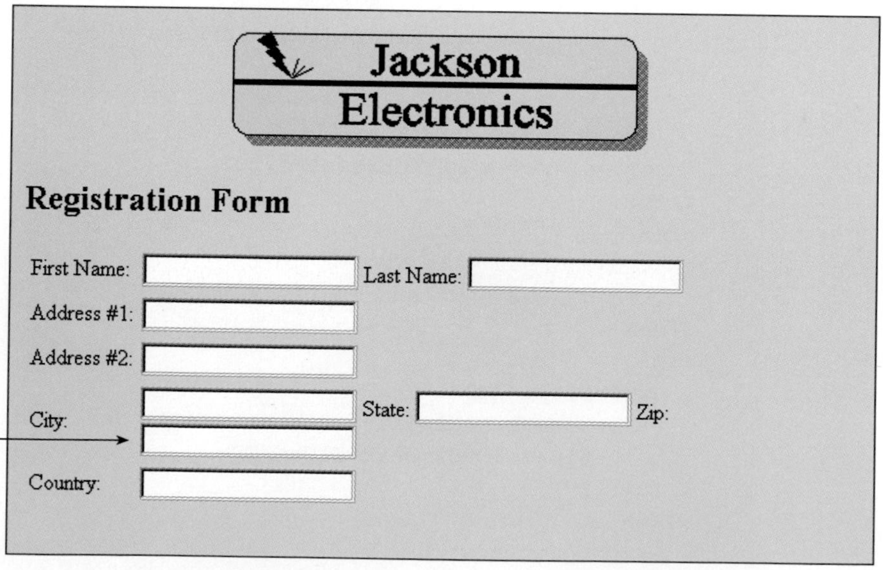

input box for Zip code

A user accessing the form with the Netscape Navigator or Communicator browser at this screen resolution will not see the attractive form layout you designed. You can take care of this problem by reducing the size of some of the input boxes on the form.

Controlling the Size of an Input Box

By default, the browser made all of the input boxes in the registration form the same size—20 characters wide. You can specify a different size. The syntax for changing the size of an input box is:

```
<INPUT SIZE=value>
```

where *value* is the size of the input box in number of characters.

After looking over the form, Lisa decides that the size of both the First Name field and the Last Name field should be increased to 25 characters, to allow for longer names. Similarly, the Address #1 and Address #2 fields should be increased to about 50 characters each, to allow for street numbers and street names. The State field can be reduced to a size of three characters for state abbreviations, and the size of the Zip field should be reduced to 10 characters. The City and Country fields can remain unchanged, with the default width of 20 characters each.

To specify the size of the input boxes:

1. Return to the Register.htm file in your text editor.

2. For the FirstName and LastName <INPUT> tags, insert the property **SIZE=25**.

3. For the Address1 and Address2 <INPUT> tags, insert the property **SIZE=50**.

4. For the State <INPUT> tag, insert the property **SIZE=3**.

5. For the ZIP <INPUT> tag, insert the property **SIZE=10**.

Figure 6-9 shows the revised Register.htm file.

Figure 6-9 ◀
Changing the size of the input boxes

```
<TR>                                                           ┌────────────────┐
    <TD>First Name:</TD>                                       │ size property  │
    <TD><INPUT NAME=FirstName SIZE=25>                         └────────────────┘
        Last Name: <INPUT NAME=LastName SIZE=25></TD>
</TR>
<TR>
    <TD>Address #1:</TD>
    <TD><INPUT NAME=Address1 SIZE=50></TD>
</TR>
<TR>
    <TD>Address #2:</TD>
    <TD><INPUT NAME=Address2 SIZE=50></TD>
</TR>
<TR>
    <TD>City:</TD>
    <TD><INPUT NAME=City>State: <INPUT NAME=State SIZE=3>
        Zip: <INPUT NAME=ZIP SIZE=10></TD>
</TR>
```

6. Save your changes, and then reload the file in your Web browser. Figure 6-10 shows the revised form, which should show the proper layout under all browsers.

Figure 6-10 ◀
Registration
form with
resized input
boxes

input boxes vary
in size

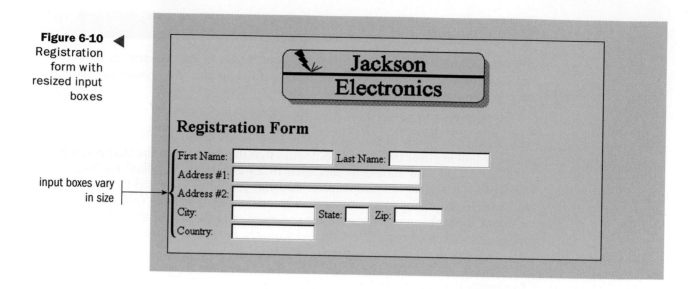

Setting the Maximum Length for Text Input

By setting the size of an input box, you are not putting limitations on the text that can be entered into that field. If a user tries to enter text longer than the input box, the text will automatically scroll to the left. The user will not be able to see all of the text at once, but all of the text will be sent to the CGI script.

Sometimes you might want to limit the number of characters the user enters, as a check to verify that the input is valid. For example, if you have a Social Security Number field, you know in advance that only nine characters are allowed. You can keep users from erroneously entering a 10-character value by setting the maximum length of the field to 9. The syntax for setting the maximum length of the input is:

    `<INPUT MAXLENGTH=value>`

where *value* is the maximum number of characters allowed. In the Social Security Number example, the <INPUT> tag might look like the following:

    `<INPUT NAME=SSNUM SIZE=9 MAXLENGTH=9>`

None of the fields in the registration form you are creating requires the maximum length property, but you should keep this property in mind for future Web forms.

Setting a Default Value for an Input Box

Another property you can use with the <INPUT> tag is the VALUE property. The VALUE property is the default value of the field and is also the value that appears in the input box when the form is initially displayed. The syntax for the VALUE property is:

    `<INPUT VALUE="value">`

where *value* is the default text or number that will appear in the field.

Lisa wants the Country field on the registration form to have a default value of "United States" because domestic sales account for over 80% of Jackson Electronics' income.

To set the default value for the Country field:

1. Return to the Register.htm file in your text editor.

2. Type **VALUE="United States"** in the Country <INPUT> tag, as shown in Figure 6-11.

Figure 6-11
Setting the
default value
for the
Country field

```
<TR>
    <TD>Country:</TD>
    <TD><INPUT NAME=Country VALUE="United States"></TD>
</TR>
</TABLE>
```

3. Save your changes, and then reload the file in your browser. Verify that "United States" is now automatically entered into the Country field.

TROUBLE? If you are using the Netscape Navigator browser, you might have to reopen the file in your browser rather than simply clicking the Reload button to see the changes to your Web form.

If customers from countries outside of the United States use this Web form, they can remove the default value by selecting the entire text string and pressing the Delete key.

Creating a Password Field

In some instances you will want to prevent the screen from displaying what the user enters into an input box. For example, one part of your form might prompt the user for a credit card number. If so, you would like to prevent the card number from being displayed on the computer monitor, as a security measure. You can accomplish this with a Password field. A **Password field** is identical to an input box except that the characters typed by the user are displayed as bullets or asterisks. The syntax for creating a Password field is:

```
<INPUT TYPE=PASSWORD>
```

As with input boxes, you can specify a size, maximum length, and name for your password. Using a Password field should not be confused with having a secure connection between the Web client and the Web server. The password itself is not encrypted, so it is still possible for someone to intercept the password as it is being sent from your Web browser to the CGI script. The Password field *only* acts as a mask for the field entry as it is displayed on the computer screen. You do not need to specify any Password fields for the registration form.

At this point, you've completed the first part of the registration form. In order to make a form easier to follow, some designers recommend separating different topical groups with a horizontal line. Because the first few fields you've entered so far deal solely with collecting contact information, Lisa suggests that you set them off with a horizontal line located below the Country field.

To add a horizontal line to your form:

1. Return to the Register.htm file in your text editor.

2. Directly above the </TABLE> tag, insert the following lines:

```
<TR>
    <TD COLSPAN=2><HR></TD>
</TR>
```

Note that the COLSPAN property will cause the horizontal line to span the two columns in the table.

3. Save your changes to Register.htm, and then reload the file in your browser. There should now be a horizontal line below the Country field.

Before going on to other tasks, you'll test the registration form by entering some test values in it. To move from one input box to the next, you press the Tab key. To move to the previous input box, press the Tab key while holding down the Shift key. Pressing the Enter key will submit the form, but because you have not created a Submit button for the form yet, pressing the Enter key will do nothing at this point.

To test your form:

1. Click the input box for the First Name field, type **Wayne**, press the **Tab** key to move to the Last Name field, and then type **Hollins**.

2. Continue entering the text shown in Figure 6-12, pressing **Tab** to move from one input box to the next.

Figure 6-12
Sample data for the registration form

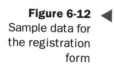

Jackson
Electronics

Registration Form

First Name: Wayne   Last Name: Hollins

Address #1: Apt. 5B

Address #2: 120 Thorpe Avenue

City: Oak Creek   State: WI   Zip: 53154

Country: United States

You might want to try other test values for the registration form. Try inserting extra text in an input box, and notice that the text automatically scrolls to the left when it exceeds the width of the box. This feature allows you to enter more text than can be displayed in the form.

Quick Check

1. What is a CGI script?

2. What is the purpose of the <FORM> tag?

3. What HTML tag would you enter to create a text input box with the name "Phone"?

4. What property would you enter to create a Phone input box that is 10 characters wide?

5. What property would you enter to limit entry to the Phone input box to no more than 10 characters?

6. What HTML tag would you enter to create an input box named "Subscribe" with a default value of "Yes"?

7. How would you prevent the contents of an input box from being displayed on the user's computer screen?

You've finished working on the first part of the registration form. You've learned how forms and CGI scripts work together to allow Web authors to collect information from users. You've also seen how to create simple text input boxes using the <INPUT> tag. In the next session, you'll learn other uses for the <INPUT> tag by adding new fields to the form, including a selection list field, radio buttons, and check boxes.

SESSION

6.2

In this session you will learn how to create selection lists to allow users to select single or multiple options from a drop-down list box. You'll also create radio buttons for selecting single option values, and check boxes for activating or deactivating fields. Finally, you'll create text areas, also known as text boxes, for extended comments and memos.

Creating a Selection List

The next section of the registration form is dedicated to collecting information about the product that the customer has purchased, and how it is intended to be used. The first field you'll create in this section records the product name. There are six Jackson Electronics products that the registration form covers:

- ScanMaster
- ScanMaster II
- LaserPrint 1000
- LaserPrint 5000
- Print/Scan 150
- Print/Scan 250

Because the products constitute a predefined list of values for the product name, Lisa wants this information displayed with a selection list. A **selection list** is a list box from which the user selects a particular value or set of values, usually by clicking the item or items with a mouse or other pointing device. Generally it's a good idea to use selection lists rather than input boxes when you have a fixed set of possible responses. By using a selection list, you can guard against spelling mistakes and erroneous entries.

REFERENCE
window

CREATING A SELECTION LIST

- To create a selection list, use the following set of HTML tags:
  ```
  <SELECT NAME=Text>
      <OPTION>Option 1
      <OPTION>Option 2
      .
      .
      .
  </SELECT>
  ```
  where the NAME property is the field name of the selection list, and each <OPTION> tag represents an entry in the list.
- To allow the user to select multiple items in the selection list, use the following tag:
  ```
  <SELECT MULTIPLE>
  ```
- To display several items in the selection list, or to change the selection list style from a drop-down list box to a fully displayed list box, use the following tag:
  ```
  <SELECT SIZE=Value>
  ```
  where Value is the number of items displayed in the list box.

Using the <SELECT> and <OPTION> Tags

You create a selection list using the <SELECT> tag, and you specify individual selection items with the <OPTION> tag. The general syntax for the <SELECT> and <OPTION> tags is:

```
<SELECT NAME=Text>
    <OPTION>Option 1
    <OPTION>Option 2
  .
  .
  .
</SELECT>
```

where *Text* is the name you've assigned to the selection field, and *Option 1*, *Option 2*, and so forth are the possible values displayed in the selection list. Note that the values for each option are entered *to the right* of the <OPTION> tag rather than inside the tag. The structure of the <SELECT> and <OPTION> tags is similar to that of the unordered list tags, <UL> and <LI>. Recall that the syntax of an unordered list is:

```
<UL>
    <LI>Item 1
    <LI>Item 2
  .
  .
  .
</UL>
```

Your next task is to add the product selection list to the registration form.

To add the selection list to the form:

1. If you took a break after the previous session, start your text editor and reopen the Register.htm file from the Tutorial.06 folder of your Student Disk.

2. Directly above the </TABLE> tag, insert the following lines:

```
<TR>
    <TD>Product:</TD>
    <TD><SELECT NAME=Product>
        <OPTION>ScanMaster
        <OPTION>ScanMaster II
        <OPTION>LaserPrint 1000
        <OPTION>LaserPrint 5000
        <OPTION>Print/Scan 150
        <OPTION>Print/Scan 250
        </SELECT></TD>
</TR>
```

Figure 6-13 shows the revised HTML code.

Figure 6-13 ◄
Creating a
selection list

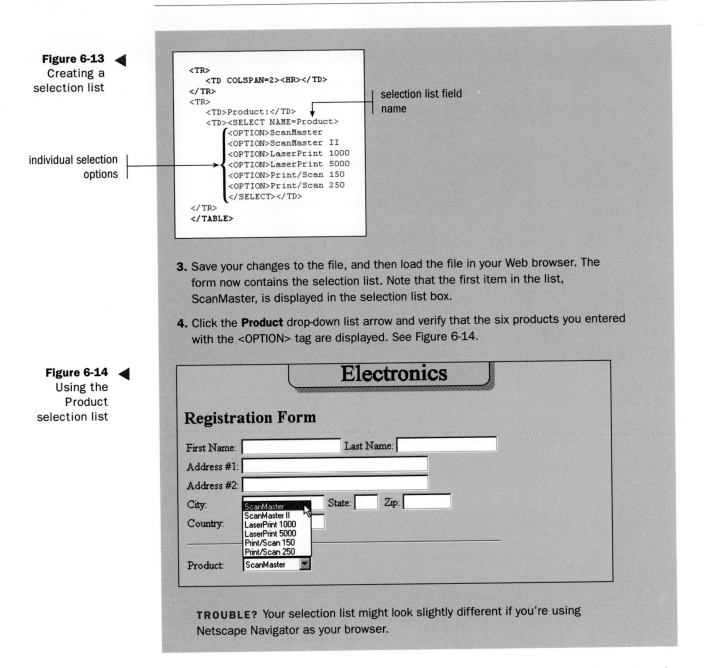

individual selection
options

```
<TR>
    <TD COLSPAN=2><HR></TD>
</TR>
<TR>
    <TD>Product:</TD>
    <TD><SELECT NAME=Product>
        <OPTION>ScanMaster
        <OPTION>ScanMaster II
        <OPTION>LaserPrint 1000
        <OPTION>LaserPrint 5000
        <OPTION>Print/Scan 150
        <OPTION>Print/Scan 250
        </SELECT></TD>
</TR>
</TABLE>
```

selection list field
name

3. Save your changes to the file, and then load the file in your Web browser. The form now contains the selection list. Note that the first item in the list, ScanMaster, is displayed in the selection list box.

4. Click the **Product** drop-down list arrow and verify that the six products you entered with the <OPTION> tag are displayed. See Figure 6-14.

Figure 6-14 ◄
Using the
Product
selection list

Electronics

Registration Form

First Name: [   ]   Last Name: [   ]

Address #1: [   ]

Address #2: [   ]

City: [ScanMaster]   State: [ ]   Zip: [   ]
      ScanMaster II
Country: LaserPrint 1000
      LaserPrint 5000
      Print/Scan 150
      Print/Scan 250

Product: [ScanMaster ▼]

TROUBLE? Your selection list might look slightly different if you're using Netscape Navigator as your browser.

There are two additional input boxes associated with the product information: the product serial number and the date the product was purchased. You'll add these fields to the registration form now.

To add the Date Purchased and Serial # fields to the form:

1. Return to the Register.htm file in your text editor.

2. Directly above the </TABLE> tag, insert the following lines:

```
<TR>
    <TD>Date Purchased:</TD>
    <TD><INPUT NAME=Date></TD>
</TR>
<TR>
    <TD>Serial #:</TD>
    <TD><INPUT NAME=Serial></TD>
</TR>
```

The revised HTML code is shown in Figure 6-15.

Figure 6-15 ◀
Adding two
input boxes to
the registration
form

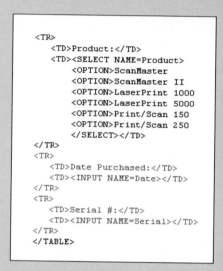

```
<TR>
    <TD>Product:</TD>
    <TD><SELECT NAME=Product>
        <OPTION>ScanMaster
        <OPTION>ScanMaster II
        <OPTION>LaserPrint 1000
        <OPTION>LaserPrint 5000
        <OPTION>Print/Scan 150
        <OPTION>Print/Scan 250
        </SELECT></TD>
</TR>
<TR>
    <TD>Date Purchased:</TD>
    <TD><INPUT NAME=Date></TD>
</TR>
<TR>
    <TD>Serial #:</TD>
    <TD><INPUT NAME=Serial></TD>
</TR>
</TABLE>
```

3. Save your changes to Register.htm, and then reopen the file in your Web browser. Figure 6-16 shows the registration form with the two new input boxes.

Figure 6-16 ◀
Date
Purchased and
Serial # input
boxes

Registration Form

First Name: [ ] Last Name: [ ]
Address #1: [ ]
Address #2: [ ]
City: [ ] State: [ ] Zip: [ ]
Country: [United States]

Product: [ScanMaster ▼]

new input boxes ——▶ Date Purchased: [ ]
——▶ Serial #: [ ]

Modifying the Appearance of a Selection List

HTML provides several properties to modify the appearance and behavior of selection lists and selection options. By default, the <SELECT> tag displays only one option from the selection list, along with a drop-down list arrow to allow you to view other selection options. You can change this by modifying the SIZE property. The syntax of the SIZE property is:

```
<SELECT SIZE=value>
```

where *value* is the number of items that the selection list will display in the form. By specifying a SIZE value greater than 1, you change the selection list from a drop-down list box to a list box with a scroll bar that allows the user to scroll through the various options. If you set the SIZE property to be equal to the number of options in the selection list, the scroll bar is either not displayed or is dimmed. See Figure 6-17.

Figure 6-17 ◀
Modifying the
format of a
selection list
with the SIZE
property

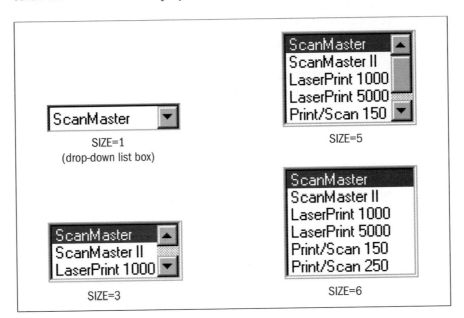

Lisa doesn't want to change the appearance of the product selection list, so you don't have to specify a different value for the SIZE property.

Making Multiple Selections

The user is not limited to making only a single selection from a selection list. You can modify your list to allow multiple selections by adding the MULTIPLE property to the <SELECT> tag. The syntax for this property is:

```
<SELECT MULTIPLE>
```

The most common way to make multiple selections from a selection list is to hold down a specific key while you click the selection items. With the Windows interface, you can make multiple selections in the following ways:

- For a noncontiguous selection, hold down the Ctrl key and click each item you want to choose in the selection list.

- For a contiguous selection, click the first item in the range of items you want to select, hold down the Shift key, and click the last item in the range of items. The two items you clicked, plus any items between them, will be selected.

If you decide to use a multiple selection list in one of your forms, you should be aware that the form will send a name/value pair to the CGI script for each option the user selects from the list. This means that the CGI script needs to be able to handle a single field with multiple values. You should check and verify that your CGI scripts are set up to handle this before using a multiple selection list.

Working with Option Values

By default, your form will send to the CGI script the values that appear in the selection list. In creating the Product field earlier, you assigned it such possible values as ScanMaster II, LaserPrint 5000, and so on. These are the values that will be sent to the CGI script. Sometimes you will want to display an option in the selection list with one string of text, but have a different text string sent to the CGI script. This occurs when you display long descriptive text for each option in the selection list, in order to help the user make an informed choice, but you need only a short abbreviated version of the user's selection for your records. You can specify the value that is sent to the CGI script with the VALUE property. For example, the following HTML code sends the value "1" to the CGI script if the ScanMaster is selected, "2" if the ScanMaster II is selected, and so forth:

```
<SELECT NAME=Product>
    <OPTION VALUE=1>ScanMaster
    <OPTION VALUE=2>ScanMaster II
    <OPTION VALUE=3>LaserPrint 1000
    <OPTION VALUE=4>LaserPrint 5000
    <OPTION VALUE=5>Print/Scan 150
    <OPTION VALUE=6>Print/Scan 250
</SELECT>
```

You can also specify which option in the selection list is initially selected (highlighted) when the form is displayed. By default, the first option in the list is selected; however, using the SELECTED property, you can specify a different value. For example, in the following HTML code, the LaserPrint 1000 will be the option that is initially selected when the user first encounters the Product field on the form:

```
<SELECT NAME=Product>
    <OPTION>ScanMaster
    <OPTION>ScanMaster II
    <OPTION SELECTED>LaserPrint 1000
    <OPTION>LaserPrint 5000
    <OPTION>Print/Scan 150
    <OPTION>Print/Scan 250
</SELECT>
```

You don't have to make any changes to the selection list at this point, because Lisa wants to follow the default settings of sending the text associated with each selection option to the CGI script, and leaving the first option in the selection list selected by default. Having finished your work with selection lists on the registration form, you'll next turn to creating fields using radio buttons.

Working with Radio Buttons

Radio buttons are similar to selection lists in that they display a list of choices from which the user makes a selection. Unlike the items in a selection list, only one radio button can be selected, and the act of selecting one option automatically deselects any previously selected option.

Radio buttons use the same <INPUT> tag as input boxes, except that the TYPE property is set to RADIO. The syntax for an individual radio button is:

```
<INPUT TYPE=RADIO NAME=text VALUE=value>
```

where *text* is the name assigned to the field containing the radio button, and *value* is the value of the radio button, which will be sent to the CGI script if that option is selected. The NAME property is important because it groups distinct radio buttons together, so that selecting one radio button in the group automatically deselects all of the other radio buttons in that group. Note that the <INPUT> tag does not create any text for the radio button. In order for users to understand the purpose of the radio button, you must insert descriptive text next to the <INPUT> tag, as you did with the input boxes. The value of the radio button does not have to match the accompanying text. Figure 6-18 shows an example of HTML code that creates radio buttons for party affiliations.

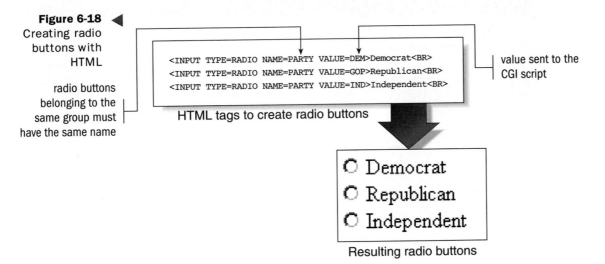

```
<INPUT TYPE=RADIO NAME=PARTY VALUE=DEM>Democrat<BR>
<INPUT TYPE=RADIO NAME=PARTY VALUE=GOP>Republican<BR>
<INPUT TYPE=RADIO NAME=PARTY VALUE=IND>Independent<BR>
```

value sent to the
CGI script

HTML tags to create radio buttons

○ Democrat
○ Republican
○ Independent

Resulting radio buttons

Note that in this sample code, the value sent to the CGI script does not match the text displayed with the radio button. If the user selects the Republican radio button, the value "GOP" is sent to the CGI script paired with the field name "PARTY."

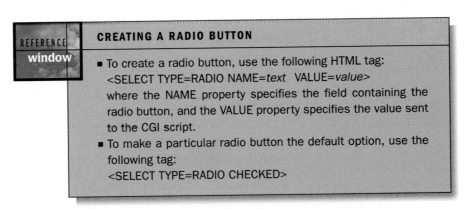

REFERENCE
window

CREATING A RADIO BUTTON

■ To create a radio button, use the following HTML tag:
  <SELECT TYPE=RADIO NAME=*text* VALUE=*value*>
  where the NAME property specifies the field containing the radio button, and the VALUE property specifies the value sent to the CGI script.
■ To make a particular radio button the default option, use the following tag:
  <SELECT TYPE=RADIO CHECKED>

On the registration form, Lisa has indicated that she would like you to create radio buttons for product usage. The name of the field that will contain the radio buttons is USE. There are five possible choices: Home, Business, Government, Educational Institution, and Other. You can enter the HTML code for this field now.

To add the USE field and radio buttons to the form:

1. Return to the Register.htm file in your text editor.

2. Directly above the </TABLE> tag, insert the following lines:

```
<TR>
   <TD VALIGN=TOP>Used for:</TD>
   <TD><INPUT TYPE=RADIO NAME=USE VALUE=HOME>Home<BR>
       <INPUT TYPE=RADIO NAME=USE VALUE=BUS>Business<BR>
       <INPUT TYPE=RADIO NAME=USE VALUE=GOV>Government<BR>
       <INPUT TYPE=RADIO NAME=USE VALUE=ED>Educational
          Institution<BR>
       <INPUT TYPE=RADIO NAME=USE VALUE=OTHER>Other</TD>
</TR>
```

Note that you use the <BR> tag in this code to start each radio button on a new line within the table cell. Your HTML code should appear as shown in Figure 6-19.

Figure 6-19 ◀
Adding radio buttons to the registration form

field value sent to the CGI script

<INPUT> tag type set to RADIO

name of field is "USE" for all radio buttons in the group

```
<TR>
    <TD>Serial #:</TD>
    <TD><INPUT NAME=Serial></TD>
</TR>
<TR>
    <TD VALIGN=TOP>Used for:</TD>
    <TD><INPUT TYPE=RADIO NAME=USE VALUE=HOME>Home<BR>
        <INPUT TYPE=RADIO NAME=USE VALUE=BUS>Business<BR>
        <INPUT TYPE=RADIO NAME=USE VALUE=GOV>Government<BR>
        <INPUT TYPE=RADIO NAME=USE VALUE=ED>Educational Institution<BR>
        <INPUT TYPE=RADIO NAME=USE VALUE=OTHER>Other</TD>
</TR>
</TABLE>
```

3. Save your changes to Register.htm, and then reload the file in your Web browser. Figure 6-20 shows the new registration form with the radio buttons for various product usage options. Note that the VALIGN=TOP property causes the table cell containing the text "Used for:" to be aligned with the top of the cell containing the radio buttons.

Figure 6-20 ◀
The "Used for" radio buttons

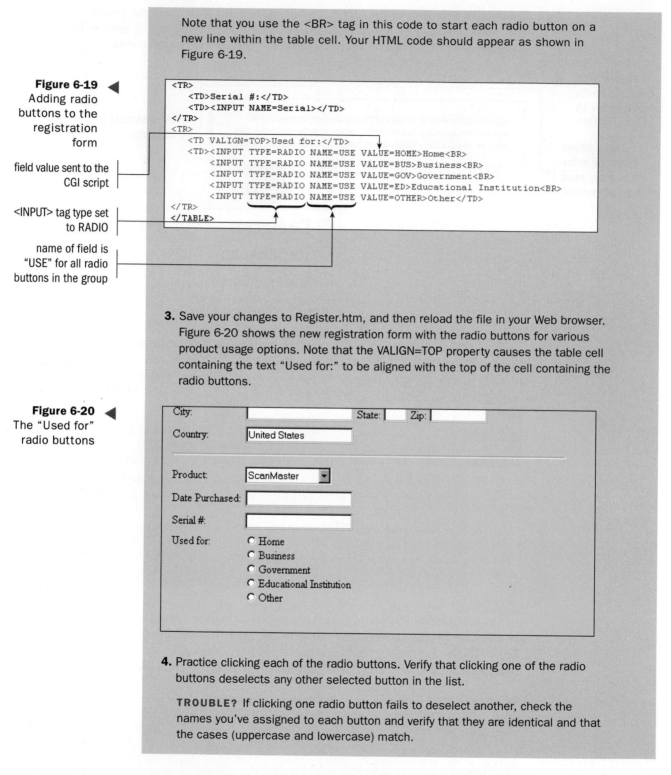

4. Practice clicking each of the radio buttons. Verify that clicking one of the radio buttons deselects any other selected button in the list.

TROUBLE? If clicking one radio button fails to deselect another, check the names you've assigned to each button and verify that they are identical and that the cases (uppercase and lowercase) match.

Notice that when you first open the registration form, none of the radio buttons is selected. In some cases you might want to designate one of the radio buttons as the default and have it already selected when the form opens. You can do this by adding the CHECKED property to the <INPUT> tag for that particular radio button. For example, to set the Business radio button as the default option in the registration form, you would enter the following tag:

```
<INPUT TYPE=RADIO NAME=USE VALUE=BUS CHECKED>Business
```

Lisa informs you that most Jackson Electronics products are used by businesses, and she would like to see this option set as the default in the Web page form.

To set Business as the default option in the USE field:

1. Return to the Register.htm file in your text editor.

2. Locate the <INPUT> tag for the Business radio button, and then type **CHECKED** within the tag.

3. Save your changes.

4. Return to your Web browser and reload or refresh the Web page. Verify that the Business radio button is selected automatically when the form opens in the browser.

   TROUBLE? If you are using Netscape Navigator or Communicator, you might have to reopen the Register.htm file in the browser to see this change.

When should you use radio buttons and when should you use a selection list? Generally, if you have a very long list of options that would be difficult or cumbersome to display within your form, you should use a selection list. If you want to allow users to select more than one option, you should use a selection list with the MULTIPLE property turned on. If you have a short list of possible options with only one option allowed at a time, you should use radio buttons.

Working with Check Boxes

The next type of input field you'll create in the registration form is the check box field. A check box is either selected or not, but unlike radio buttons, there is only one check box per field. You create check boxes using the <INPUT> tag, with the TYPE property set to CHECKBOX, as follows:

```
<INPUT TYPE=CHECKBOX NAME=text>
```

where *text* is the name of the field. A check box field has the value "on" if the check box is selected, and no value is assigned if the check box is left unselected. You can use the VALUE property to assign a different check box value from "on." For example, the following HTML code assigns the value "YES" to the DEMOCRAT field if the check box is selected:

```
<INPUT TYPE=CHECKBOX NAME=DEMOCRAT VALUE=YES>
```

As with radio buttons, the <INPUT> tag for the check box does not display any text. So you must add text next to the <INPUT> tag to describe the purpose of the check box.

By default, check boxes are unselected when the form opens. As with radio buttons, you can use the CHECKED property to automatically select a check box. The appropriate HTML code is:

```
<INPUT TYPE=CHECKBOX NAME=DEMOCRAT VALUE=YES CHECKED>
```

In this case, the DEMOCRAT check box field will be selected when the browser opens the form.

REFERENCE window

CREATING A CHECK BOX

- To create a check box, use the following HTML tag:
  <SELECT TYPE=CHECKBOX NAME=*Text* VALUE=*Value*>
  where the NAME property specifies the field containing the check box, and the VALUE property specifies the value sent to the CGI script if the check box is selected.
- To make a check box selected by default, use the following tag:
  <SELECT TYPE=CHECKBOX CHECKED>

Lisa has specified five check boxes for the registration form. Each one identifies a type of operating system, and customers can select one or more to indicate which systems they are using the product with. Even though you'll group these check boxes together on the form, each one belongs to a distinct field (unlike the radio buttons you just created, which are all associated with the USE field).

To add the check boxes to your form:

1. Return to your text editor and the Register.htm file.

2. Directly above the </TABLE> tag, insert the following lines:

```
<TR>
    <TD VALIGN=TOP>System (check all that apply):</TD>
    <TD><INPUT TYPE=CHECKBOX NAME=WIN9598NT>Windows 95/98/NT<BR>
        <INPUT TYPE=CHECKBOX NAME=WINDOS>Windows 3.x/DOS<BR>
        <INPUT TYPE=CHECKBOX NAME=MAC>Macintosh<BR>
        <INPUT TYPE=CHECKBOX NAME=UNIX>UNIX<BR>
        <INPUT TYPE=CHECKBOX NAME=OTHER_SYSTEM>Other</TD>
</TR>
```

Your HTML code should appear as shown in Figure 6-21.

Figure 6-21 ◀
Adding check boxes to the registration form

```
<TR>
    <TD VALIGN=TOP>Used for:</TD>
    <TD><INPUT TYPE=RADIO NAME=USE VALUE=HOME>Home<BR>
        <INPUT TYPE=RADIO NAME=USE VALUE=BUS CHECKED>Business<BR>
        <INPUT TYPE=RADIO NAME=USE VALUE=GOV>Government<BR>
        <INPUT TYPE=RADIO NAME=USE VALUE=ED>Educational Institution<BR>
        <INPUT TYPE=RADIO NAME=USE VALUE=OTHER>Other</TD>
</TR>
<TR>
    <TD VALIGN=TOP>System (check all that apply):</TD>
    <TD><INPUT TYPE=CHECKBOX NAME=WIN9598NT>Windows 95/98/NT<BR>
        <INPUT TYPE=CHECKBOX NAME=WINDOS>Windows 3.x/DOS<BR>
        <INPUT TYPE=CHECKBOX NAME=MAC>Macintosh<BR>
        <INPUT TYPE=CHECKBOX NAME=UNIX>UNIX<BR>
        <INPUT TYPE=CHECKBOX NAME=OTHER_SYSTEM>Other</TD>
</TR>
</TABLE>
```

field name

You've completed the fields on the form that deal with the product the customer purchased and how the customer plans to use it. As you did earlier with the contact information, you'll separate these fields from others on the form with a horizontal line.

To add a second horizontal line to your form:

1. Directly above the </TABLE> tag, insert the following tags:

```
<TR>
    <TD COLSPAN=2><HR></TD>
</TR>
```

2. Save your changes to Register.htm.

Next, view the registration form in your Web browser to confirm that the check boxes work properly.

To test your form:

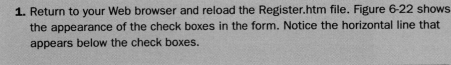

1. Return to your Web browser and reload the Register.htm file. Figure 6-22 shows the appearance of the check boxes in the form. Notice the horizontal line that appears below the check boxes.

Figure 6-22 ◄
Form with the operating system check boxes

check boxes

horizontal line

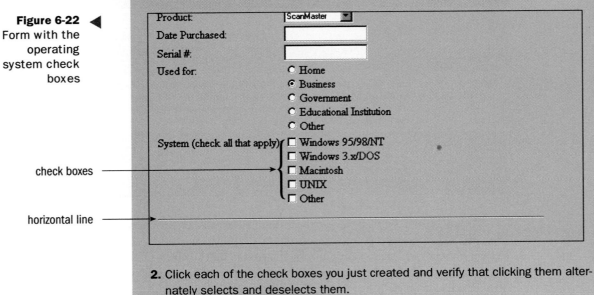

2. Click each of the check boxes you just created and verify that clicking them alternately selects and deselects them.

Creating a Text Area

The next section of the registration form allows users to enter comments about the products they purchased. Because these comments will probably consist of long text strings and sentences, an input box might be too small to display them. Instead you need to use the <TEXTAREA> tag. The <TEXTAREA> tag creates a text box, like the one shown in Figure 6-23, in which the user enters extended comments.

Figure 6-23 ◄
A sample text box

Enter comments here: | The Print/Scan 150 is a great addition to our small business. We've managed to increase productivity with this printer/scanner combination.

The syntax of the <TEXTAREA> tag is:

```
<TEXTAREA ROWS=Value COLS=Value NAME=Text>Default
    text</TEXTAREA>
```

where the ROWS and COLS properties define the number of rows and columns in the text box, and *Default text* is the text that appears in the text box when the form opens. Although it is not required, you could use default text to provide additional instructions to the user about what to enter in the text box, as in the following example:

```
<TEXTAREA ROWS=3 NAME=COMMENTS>Enter comments here</TEXTAREA>
```

Note that unlike the other field tags, <TEXTAREA> is a two-sided tag, which means that it has an opening tag, <TEXTAREA>, and a closing tag, </TEXTAREA>. You need to include the </TEXTAREA> tag even if you don't specify any default text.

The text you enter into a text box does not automatically wrap to the next row in the box. Instead, a text box acts like an input box in which the text is automatically scrolled to the left as additional text is typed. You can override this default behavior using the WRAP property. The values for the WRAP property are shown in Figure 6-24.

Figure 6-24 ◀
Values of the
<TEXTAREA>
WRAP property

Value	Description
OFF	All the text is displayed on a single line, scrolling to the left if the text extends past the width of the box. Text goes to the next row in the box only if the Enter key is pressed. The text is sent to the CGI script in a single line.
SOFT (or VIRTUAL)	Text wraps automatically to the next row when it extends beyond the width of the text box. The text is still sent to the CGI script in a single line without any information about how the text was wrapped within the text box.
HARD (or PHYSICAL)	Text wraps automatically to the next row when it extends beyond the width of the text box. When the text is sent to the CGI script, the line-wrapping information is included, allowing the CGI script to work with the text exactly as it appears in the text box.

You will probably want to set the value of the WRAP property to either VIRTUAL or PHYSICAL to allow the text to automatically wrap within the text box. The difference between these two options lies in how the text is sent to the CGI script. Setting the WRAP property to PHYSICAL preserves any line wrapping that takes place in the text box; the VIRTUAL option does not. You should check the documentation of the CGI script to see whether one method is preferred over the other.

REFERENCE window

CREATING A TEXT AREA

- To create a text area for extended text entry, use the following tag:
  <TEXTAREA>*Default Text*</TEXTAREA>
  where the *Default Text* is the text that initially appears in the text area (this is optional).
- To control how text is wrapped in a text area, use the following tag:
  <TEXTAREA WRAP=*Option*>
  where *Option* is OFF, SOFT (or VIRTUAL), or HARD (or PHYSICAL). OFF turns off text wrapping. SOFT (VIRTUAL) turns text wrapping on, but does not send text wrapping information to the Web server. HARD (PHYSICAL) turns text wrapping on and also sends this information to the Web server.

For the Comments field, you'll use the <TEXTAREA> tag with the WRAP property set to VIRTUAL so that the user's comments wrap automatically to the next row in the box. The size of the text area will be 3 rows high and 50 columns wide, which Lisa thinks should work well for the typed comments. You won't specify any default text for the Comments field.

To add a text box to the registration form:

1. Return to your text editor and the Register.htm file.

2. Directly above the </TABLE> tag, insert the following lines:

```
<TR>
   <TD VALIGN=TOP>Comments?:</TD>
   <TD>
   <TEXTAREA ROWS=3 COLS=50 NAME=Comments WRAP=VIRTUAL></TEXTAREA>
   </TD>
</TR>
```

3. Save your changes to Register.htm, and then reload the page in your Web browser.

4. Test the line-wrapping feature of the text box by typing the following text in the Comments field:

I'm very pleased with my purchase of the ScanMaster II. Is there equipment that would allow me to scan photo negatives and transparencies?

The text should wrap automatically, as shown in Figure 6-25.

Figure 6-25 ◀
Entering
comments into
the Comments
text box

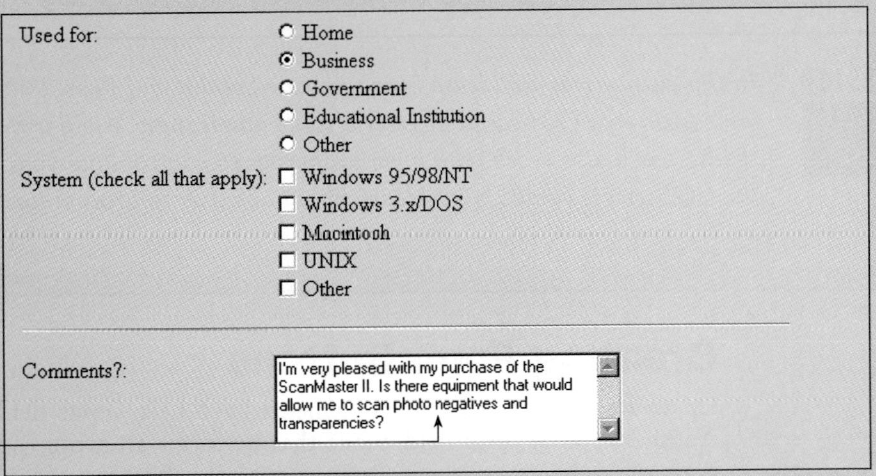

text wraps
automatically

Note that the text box includes a vertical scroll bar so that if the user enters more text than can be displayed within the area of the text box, the user can scroll to see the hidden text.

TROUBLE? If you are using Netscape Navigator or Communicator, your Comments text box will look slightly different from the one shown in Figure 6-25. The text box might also look different depending on what version of the Internet Explorer browser you are using.

Quick Check

1 What HTML tag would you enter to create a selection list with a field named "State" and with the options "California," "Nevada," "Oregon," and "Washington"?

2 How would you modify the tag in Quick Check 1 to allow more than one state to be selected from the list?

3 What HTML tag would make "Oregon" the default selection in Quick Check 1?

4 What HTML tag would you enter to create a series of radio buttons for a field named "State" with the options "California," "Nevada," "Oregon," and "Washington"?

5 How would you modify the tag in Quick Check 4 to send the number "1" to the CGI script if the user selects "California," "2" for "Nevada," "3" for "Oregon," and "4" for "Washington"?

6 What HTML tag would you enter to create a check box field named "California"? What value is sent to the CGI script if the check box is selected?

7 What HTML tag would you enter to create a text box field named "Memo" that is 5 rows high and 30 columns wide, and has the default text "Enter notes here."?

8 What property would you add to the tag in Quick Check 7 to cause the Memo text to automatically wrap to the next row, and to send that text-wrapping information to the CGI script?

You've created the last input field for the registration form. Using HTML you've added input boxes, a selection list, radio buttons, check boxes, and a text area to your form. In the next session, you'll learn how to set up your form to work with a CGI script.

SESSION

6.3

In this session you will learn how to create Submit and Reset buttons to either send your form to a CGI script or reset it to its initial state. You'll learn how to create image fields. You'll also work with form properties to control how your form is submitted to the CGI script. Finally, you'll learn about one way to process form data without using a CGI script.

Creating Form Buttons

Up to now, all of your form elements have been input fields of one kind or another. Another type of form field is one that performs an action when activated—as a button does when the user clicks it. Buttons can be used to run programs, submit forms, or reset the form to its original state.

REFERENCE window	**CREATING FORM BUTTONS**

	■ To create a button to submit the form to the CGI script, enter the following tag:
	`<INPUT TYPE=SUBMIT VALUE="text">`
	where the VALUE property defines the text that appears on the button and specifies the value that is sent to the CGI script to indicate which button on the form has been clicked.
	■ To create a button to cancel or reset the appearance of your form, use the TYPE property shown in the following tag:
	`<INPUT TYPE=RESET>`
	■ To create a button to perform an action within the Web page by running a program or script, use the following tag:
	`<INPUT TYPE=BUTTON>`

Creating Buttons that Perform Actions

If you want to include a button on your form that performs an action, such as calculating a value or validating the user's input on the form, you can create a button using the TYPE=BUTTON property. For example, the following tag creates a button with the label "Click to calculate total order":

```
<INPUT TYPE=BUTTON VALUE="Click to calculate total order">
```

You can insert programs into your Web page that will respond to this button being clicked and run the described calculations. You'll learn how to write and attach programs to your Web page in Tutorials 7 and 8.

Creating Submit and Reset Buttons

When the user finishes entering information into the form, that information can be submitted to the CGI script or, if the user made a mistake, the form can be reset to its original default values without submitting anything to the CGI script. This is accomplished through clicking a button on the form. You create Submit and Reset buttons using the same <INPUT> tag you've used for other form elements. The TYPE property is set to either SUBMIT or RESET. The syntax for the two buttons is:

```
<INPUT TYPE=SUBMIT>
<INPUT TYPE=RESET>
```

You can also specify NAME and VALUE properties for Submit and Reset buttons, although these properties are not required. You would use these properties when you have more than one Submit button and the CGI script performs a different action depending on which button is clicked. For example, a Web page advertising a shareware program might include three buttons: one used to download the program from the company's Web site, another used to retrieve additional information about the product, and the third used to cancel the form submission. The HTML tags for such buttons might appear as shown in Figure 6-26.

Figure 6-26 ◀
Creating form
buttons with
HTML

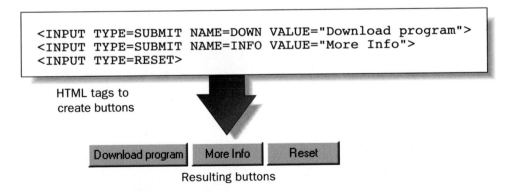

```
<INPUT TYPE=SUBMIT NAME=DOWN VALUE="Download program">
<INPUT TYPE=SUBMIT NAME=INFO VALUE="More Info">
<INPUT TYPE=RESET>
```

HTML tags to
create buttons

Download program | More Info | Reset

Resulting buttons

As shown in the figure, the VALUE property also changes the text that appears on the button from either "Submit" or "Reset" to whatever you choose.

Lisa wants the registration form to include two buttons: a Submit button and a Reset button. The Submit button, labeled "Send Registration," will send the form information to the CGI script. The Reset button, labeled "Cancel," will cancel the form, resetting all the fields to their default values. You'll place these buttons at the bottom of the form, centered within the table.

To add the Submit and Reset buttons to the registration form:

1. If you took a break after the previous session, start your text editor and reopen the Register.htm file from the Tutorial.06 folder of your Student Disk.

2. Directly above the </TABLE> tag, insert the following tags:

```
<TR>
    <TD COLSPAN=2 ALIGN=CENTER>
    <INPUT TYPE=SUBMIT VALUE="Send Registration">
    <INPUT TYPE=RESET VALUE="Cancel">
    </TD>
</TR>
```

Figure 6-27 shows the current code in the Register.htm file.

Figure 6-27 ◀
Adding Submit
and Reset
buttons to the
registration
form

```
<TR>
    <TD VALIGN=TOP>Comments?:</TD>
    <TD>
    <TEXTAREA ROWS=3 COLS=50 NAME=Comments WRAP=VIRTUAL></TEXTAREA>
    </TD>
<TR>
    <TD COLSPAN=2 ALIGN=CENTER>
    <INPUT TYPE=SUBMIT VALUE="Send Registration">
    <INPUT TYPE=RESET VALUE="Cancel">
    </TD>
</TR>
</TABLE>
```

button type ——————

button value and text ——————

3. Save your changes to the file, and then reload the file in your Web browser. Figure 6-28 shows the complete registration form, including the two buttons you just created, as rendered by the Internet Explorer and Netscape Navigator browsers. There are some differences in the form's appearance in the two browsers, but they're basically the same.

Figure 6-28 ◀
The completed
registration
form

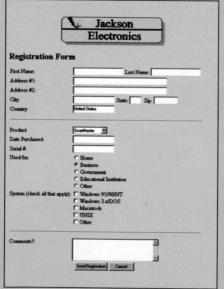

Internet Explorer   Netscape Navigator

TROUBLE? The Comments text box on your screen might look different from the text boxes shown in Figure 6-28, depending on which version of the browser you are using.

4. Test the Cancel button by entering test values into the form and then clicking the **Cancel** button. The form should be returned to its initial state.

TROUBLE? If the Cancel button doesn't work, check the HTML code for the button and verify that you've entered the code correctly. The Send Registration button will not do anything yet, because you have not identified the CGI script to receive the form data.

Creating Image Fields

Another form element that you can use in your Web pages is the inline image. Inline images can act like Submit buttons so that when the user clicks the image, the form is submitted. You create inline images using the <INPUT> tag, but with the TYPE property set to IMAGE. The syntax for this type of form element is:

```
<INPUT TYPE=IMAGE SRC="URL" NAME=text VALUE="text">
```

where *URL* is the filename or URL of the inline image, *text* is the name of the field, and the VALUE property assigns a value to the image. When the form is submitted to the CGI script, the coordinates corresponding to where the user clicked inside the image are attached to the image's name and value in the format: NAME.*x_coordinate*, VALUE.*y_coordinate*. For example, suppose your Web page contains the following inline image form element:

```
<INPUT TYPE=IMAGE SRC="USAMAP.gif" NAME=USA VALUE="STATE">
```

Assume that a user loads your page and clicks the inline image at the coordinates (15,30). In this case, the Web page will send the field name USA.15 paired with the field value STATE.30 to the script. Once the CGI script receives this information, it will perform different actions, depending on where the user clicked within the image. See Figure 6-29.

Figure 6-29 ◄
Using an image field with a CGI script

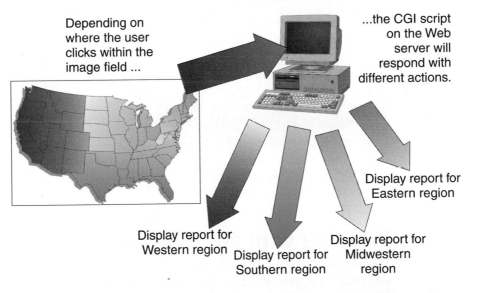

Depending on where the user clicks within the image field ...

...the CGI script on the Web server will respond with different actions.

Display report for Eastern region

Display report for Western region

Display report for Southern region

Display report for Midwestern region

You do not have to include any inline image fields in your Web page form.

Lisa is pleased with the final appearance of the registration form. She shows the form to Warren Kaughman, one of the programmers at Jackson Electronics and the person responsible for the CGI script that you'll be using. Warren notices only one thing missing from the form—the e-mail address of Lisa's assistant, who will receive the registration forms through e-mail. Warren's CGI script requires that the form include a field named EMAIL containing the recipient's e-mail address. You need to add an e-mail field to the form. To do so, you'll work with a hidden field.

Working with Hidden Fields

Unlike the other fields you've created, the e-mail field has a predefined value (the e-mail address of Lisa's assistant), which customers should not be able to change. In fact, the customers shouldn't even see the e-mail address of Lisa's assistant displayed on the form. You need a hidden field, one that is part of the form but not displayed on the Web page, to prevent the customers from seeing the address.

You create a hidden field using the <INPUT> tag with the TYPE property set to HIDDEN. The syntax for this tag is:

```
<INPUT TYPE=HIDDEN NAME=text VALUE=value>
```

You've already learned from Warren that the name of the e-mail field should be EMAIL, and you learn from Lisa that the e-mail address of her assistant is "adavis@Jkson_Electronics.com" (note that this is a fictional address used for the purposes of this tutorial). Now that you know both the field name and the field value, you can add the hidden field to the registration form.

Because the field is hidden, you can place it anywhere between the opening and closing <FORM> tags. A standard practice is to place all hidden fields in one location, usually at the beginning of the form, to make it easier to interpret your HTML code. You should also include a comment describing the purpose of the field.

To add the hidden field to the registration form:

1. Return to the Register.htm file in your text editor.

2. Directly below the <FORM> tag, insert the following two lines:

```
<!--- e-mail address of the person handling this form --->
<INPUT TYPE=HIDDEN NAME=EMAIL VALUE="adavis@Jkson_Electronics.com">
```

Figure 6-30 shows the revised HTML code.

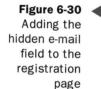

Figure 6-30
Adding the hidden e-mail field to the registration page

```
<H2>Registration Form</H2>
<FORM NAME=REG>
<!--- e-mail address of the person handling this form --->
<INPUT TYPE=HIDDEN NAME=EMAIL VALUE="adavis@Jkson_Electronics.com">
<TABLE>
```

3. Save your changes to the file.

With the recipient field now placed in the registration form, you'll return to the first tag you entered into this document, the <FORM> tag, and insert the properties needed for it to interact with the Jackson Electronics CGI script.

Working with Form Properties

You've added all the elements needed for the form. The final task is to specify where to send the form data and how to send it. To control how information entered into your form is processed, you must modify the properties of the <FORM> tag. There are three properties you'll work with: ACTION, METHOD, and ENCTYPE.

The **ACTION property** identifies the CGI script that will process your form. The syntax for this property is:

```
<FORM ACTION=URL>
```

where *URL* is the URL of the CGI script. Your Internet Service Provider or the person who wrote the CGI script will provide this information for you. Warren, the programmer responsible for the CGI script at Jackson Electronics, tells you that the CGI script used for e-mailing form information is located at the following URL:

    http://www.Jkson_electronics.com/cgi/mailer

(Remember that this is a fictional URL and that you cannot actually connect to a CGI script at this address.)

Now that you know where to send the form information, you next have to determine how to send that information. The **METHOD property** controls how your Web browser sends data to the Web server running the CGI script. The syntax for the METHOD property is:

    <FORM METHOD=*Type*>

where *Type* is either GET or POST. The distinction between the GET and POST methods is technical and extends beyond the scope of this book. In brief, the **GET method**, which is the default, packages the form data by appending it to the end of the URL specified in the ACTION property. The Web server then retrieves the modified URL and stores it in a text string for processing by the CGI script. The **POST method** sends form information in a separate data stream, allowing the Web server to receive the data through what is called "standard input." Because it is more flexible, the POST method is considered the preferred way of sending data to the Web server. It is also safer, because some Web servers limit the amount of data sent via the GET method and will truncate the URL, cutting off valuable information. Don't be concerned if you don't completely understand the difference between using GET and POST. Your Internet Service Provider will usually provide the necessary information about which of the two methods you should use in your <FORM> tag. If you start writing your own CGI scripts, this issue becomes more important. Warren informs you that his e-mail program uses the POST method to retrieve form data.

The final form property you might have to be concerned with is the ENCTYPE property. The **ENCTYPE property** specifies the format of the data when it is transferred from your Web page to the CGI script. The syntax of this property is:

    <FORM ENCTYPE=*Text*>

where *Text* is the data format. Once again, this is a complex technical issue that goes beyond the scope of this book. The default ENCTYPE value is "application/x-www-form-urlencoded," so if you do not specify an encoding value, this is the one the Web server will assume is used for your data. Another ENCTYPE value that is often used is "multipart/form-data," which allows the form to send files to the Web server along with any form data. Your Internet Service Provider will indicate any special values that you need to include with the ENCTYPE property. Warren's CGI script uses the default encoding value, so you do not have to enter it into the <FORM> tag.

A final possible property you might use with the <FORM> tag is the TARGET property. If your form is part of a framed presentation, you use the **TARGET property** to specify which frame receives output from the CGI script. If your page is not using frames, you do not need to be concerned with this property.

Now that you understand the issues involved in sending form data to a CGI script, you are ready to make some final modifications to the Register.htm file. You need to enter the ACTION property to specify what CGI script will receive the form data, and the METHOD property to specify that the POST method will be used for processing the form data.

To add the properties to the <FORM> tag:

1. Insert the following properties in the <FORM> tag:

   ACTION="http://www.Jkson_electronics.com/cgi/mailer" METHOD=POST

The revised file should appear as shown in Figure 6-31.

Figure 6-31 ◄
Specifying
where and how
to send the
form data

location of the
CGI script

how the form data
will be sent to the
CGI script

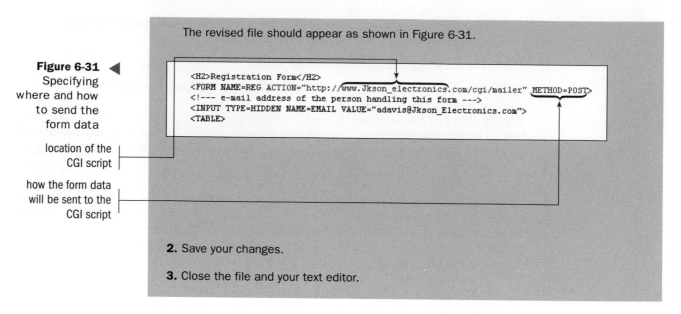

```
<H2>Registration Form</H2>
<FORM NAME=REG ACTION="http://www.Jkson_electronics.com/cgi/mailer" METHOD=POST>
<!--- e-mail address of the person handling this form --->
<INPUT TYPE=HIDDEN NAME=EMAIL VALUE="adavis@Jkson_Electronics.com">
<TABLE>
```

2. Save your changes.

3. Close the file and your text editor.

You've finished the registration form. Warren will take the Register.htm file and transfer it to a folder on the company's Web server. From there it can be fully tested to verify that the CGI script and the form work properly, and that the form data is mailed to Lisa's assistant.

To allow you to see how this form works in practice, a modified version of it has been placed on the Web at the URL: http://www.careys.com/Jkson_Electronics/Register.htm for you to work with. If you have a connection to the Web, you can open this page and test the form and the CGI script.

To test the registration form:

1. Open the URL **http://www.careys.com/Jkson_Electronics/Register.htm** in your Web browser.

A modified version of the page that you created in this tutorial is displayed.

2. Type your e-mail address in the E-mail input box in the first field of the form.

Note that unlike the form you created, this form will mail the form data to the e-mail address you enter.

3. Enter contact information for yourself in the appropriate fields.

4. Complete the rest of the form using test entries of your own choosing.

5. Click the **Click to register** button. Your Web browser presents the page, an example of which is shown in Figure 6-32, displaying the names of each field in the form and the values you've assigned to them.

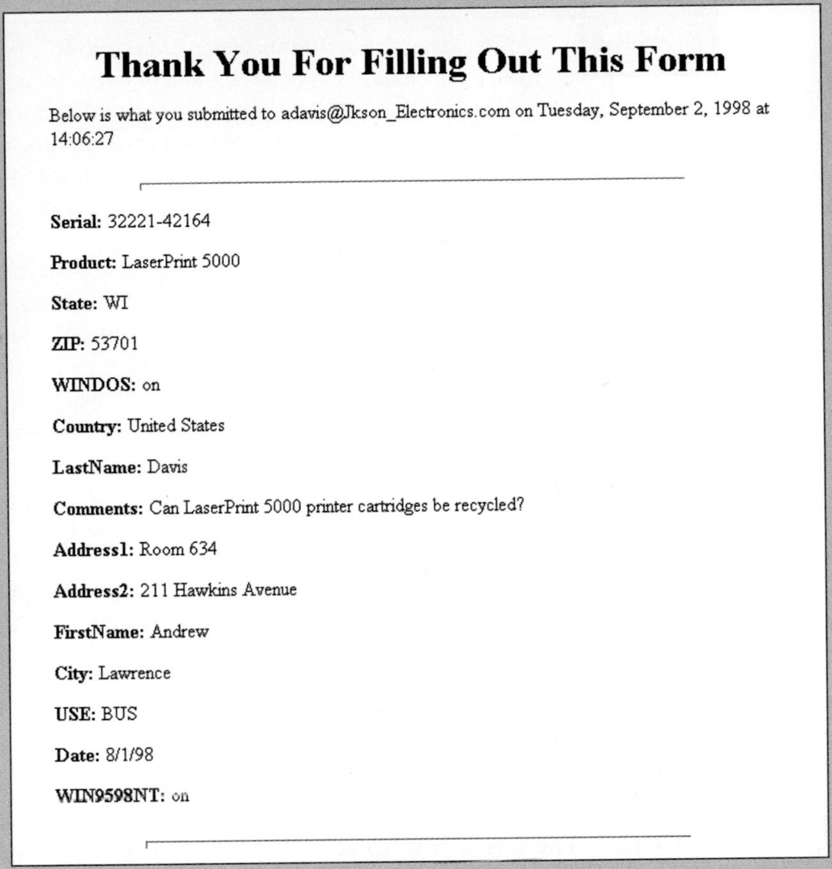

Figure 6-32
Response to
the registration
form

Thank You For Filling Out This Form

Below is what you submitted to adavis@Jkson_Electronics.com on Tuesday, September 2, 1998 at 14:06:27

Serial: 32221-42164

Product: LaserPrint 5000

State: WI

ZIP: 53701

WINDOS: on

Country: United States

LastName: Davis

Comments: Can LaserPrint 5000 printer cartridges be recycled?

Address1: Room 634

Address2: 211 Hawkins Avenue

FirstName: Andrew

City: Lawrence

USE: BUS

Date: 8/1/98

WIN9598NT: on

You should soon receive a message in your mail box like the page shown in Figure 6-32.

TROUBLE? If you don't receive an e-mail message within a few hours, either there is a problem with your mail server, causing a delay in the posting of the message, or you might have mistyped your e-mail address on the registration form. You should try again, carefully checking your e-mail address in the form.

DESIGN window

CREATING WEB PAGE FORMS

- Form elements will differ between browsers, so be sure to view your form on different browsers and different browser versions to make sure that the form looks correct in all situations.
- Label all input boxes with clear and concise directions.
- Use horizontal lines, tables, and line breaks to separate topical groups from one another. Number your elements to give your form an organized structure.
- Use radio buttons, check boxes, and selection lists whenever possible, to control the user's entries. Use input boxes only in situations where a specified list of options is unavailable.
- Let users know the correct format for the text in an input box by inserting default text (for example, insert the text string "mm/dd/yyyy" in a Date input box to indicate the date form that should be used).
- Use selection lists for items with several possible options. Use radio buttons for items with fewer options. Use check boxes for items with only two options (yes/no).
- Use Password fields for any input boxes that contain sensitive or confidential information (for example, credit card numbers, passwords, and so on).

Using the MAILTO Action

So far in working with Lisa's registration file, you have built a form to use Warren's e-mail CGI script. There is a way to send form information through e-mail without using a script. Starting with version 3.0, Netscape Navigator began supporting an ACTION property called MAILTO. This action accesses the user's own mail program and uses it to mail form information to a specified e-mail address, bypassing the need for using CGI scripts on a Web server. The syntax of the MAILTO action is:

```
<FORM ACTION="mailto:e-mail_address" METHOD=POST>
```

where *e-mail_address* is the e-mail address of the recipient of the form information. Because the MAILTO action does not require a CGI script, you can avoid some of the problems associated with coordinating your page with a program running on the Web server. One disadvantage of this action is that not all browsers support it. Internet Explorer 3.0 does not support it, for example, but Internet Explorer 4.0 does. Both Netscape Navigator 3.0 and Netscape Communicator 4.0 will support this action, but earlier versions of the browser do not.

When you click the Submit button on a form that uses the MAILTO action, the operating system invokes the mail program and receives the content for the mail message from your Web browser. Depending on how your system is configured, either you will have a chance to edit the mail message further, or it will be sent automatically without allowing you to intervene.

An e-mail message generated by the MAILTO action is full of special characters that must be interpreted either by you or by a special translation program before the message can be read. Figure 6-33 shows the e-mail message that the MAILTO action generated for the registration form you completed in this tutorial (filled in with some sample data).

Figure 6-33
Results of the
MAILTO action

field value

field name

Comments field

field value (spaces
represented by
"+" symbols)

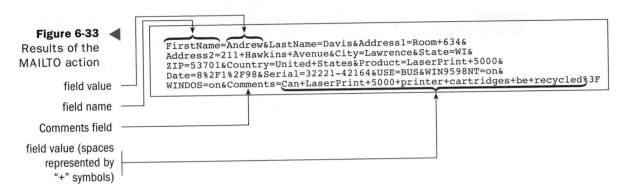

```
FirstName=Andrew&LastName=Davis&Address1=Room+634&
Address2=211+Hawkins+Avenue&City=Lawrence&State=WI&
ZIP=53701&Country=United+States&Product=LaserPrint+5000&
Date=8%2F1%2F98&Serial=32221-42164&USE=BUS&WIN9598NT=on&
WINDOS=on&Comments=Can+LaserPrint+5000+printer+cartridges+be+recycled%3F
```

The mail message shows each field name and field value pair. The field name is first, followed by an equals sign and then the field value. The next field name/field value pair is indicated by an ampersand (&). Because the mail message is one long continuous text string, no spaces are allowed. Spaces are replaced with plus symbols. Some of the other symbols used in messages generated by the MAILTO action are listed in Figure 6-34.

Figure 6-34
Special
characters
used by the
MAILTO action

MAILTO Character	Represents
+	Space
&	Line break or new field
%25	%
%2B	+
%2F	/
%5C	\
%7E	~

If you want to use a program to translate messages created by the MAILTO action into easily readable files, you can use one of the files listed in Figure 6-35.

Figure 6-35
Programs
to translate
MAILTO mail
messages

Operating System	Program	URL
Windows	WebForms	http://www.q-d.com/wf.htm
Macintosh	inFORMer	http://www.phoenix.net/~jacobson/hs.html

If you use the MAILTO action, keep in mind that some users might be working with browsers that do not support it. As this action becomes a more standard way of retrieving and sending form information, this should change. Because some browsers do not support the MAILTO action, Lisa decides not to use it in the registration form at this time and, instead, to continue using Warren's CGI script.

Quick Check

1 What HTML tag would you enter to create a Submit button with the label "Send Form"?

2 What HTML tag would you enter to create a Reset button with the label "Cancel Form"?

3 What HTML tag would you enter to create an image field named "Sites" for the graphic image "Sites.gif" with the VALUE property "GotoPage"?

4 If a user clicks the Sites image field from Quick Check 3 at the coordinates (42,21), what information will be sent to the Web server?

5 What HTML tag would you enter to create a hidden field named "Subject" with the field value "Form Responses"?

6 You need to have your form work with a CGI script located at http://www.j_davis.com/cgi-bin/post-query. The method the Web server uses is the GET method. What should the <FORM> tag be to correctly access this CGI script?

7 If your Web page gives users the option of sending files along with form information to the Web server, what type of encoding does it probably use?

8 You want to use the MAILTO action to send your form to the e-mail address walker@j_davis.com. What is the appropriate <FORM> tag to enter? What is a limitation of this Web page that you should be concerned about?

You're finished working with forms and form properties. The page you created for Lisa has been stored on the company's Web server. She is reviewing the page with her assistant and will inform you of any additional modifications required.

Tutorial Assignments

Lisa and her assistant have worked with your registration form and have decided on some changes they would like you to make to the form. Specifically, they want you to:

- Remove the Address1 and Address2 fields and replace them with a single text area field.

- Add the following items to the product list: PrintMaster 300, PrintMaster 600, and ColorPrinter Plus.

- Change the selection list from a drop-down list box to a list box displaying four items.

- Add OS/2 to the list of possible operating systems.

- Include a question asking whether the customer wants to be on the Jackson Electronics mailing list. Specify "Yes" as the default response to this question.

- Add an input field for the customer's e-mail address.

Warren also has some changes he'd like you to make to the form:

- Add a hidden field to the form with the field name "SUBJECT" and the value "Registration form response." The CGI script will insert this information in the subject line of the mail message sent to Lisa's assistant.

- Modify the form so that it uses a new CGI script located at http://www.Jkson_Electronics.com/cgi/formmail, using the POST method.

When finished, the modified form should appear as shown in Figure 6-36.

Figure 6-36 ◀

Jackson
Electronics

Registration Form

Register your Jackson Electronics product here

First Name: [   ]   Last Name: [   ]
Address:

City: [   ]   State: [ ]   Zip: [   ]
Country: [United States]

Product: [ScanMaster / ScanMaster II / LaserPrint 1000 / LaserPrint 5000]

Date Purchased: [   ]
Serial #: [   ]
Used for: ○ Home   ○ Educational Institutition
            ● Business   ○ Other
            ○ Government

System (check all that apply): ☐ Windows 95/98/NT ☐ UNIX
                               ☐ Windows 3.x/DOS ☐ OS2
                               ☐ Macintosh   ☐ Other

Comments?:

Add me to the mailing list: ● Yes ○ No
E-mail address: [   ]
[Click to register] [Click to cancel]

Lisa gives you a new file in which you'll make the suggested changes.

To implement the changes to the registration form:

1. Start your text editor and open the Regtext.htm file in the TAssign folder of the Tutorial.06 folder on your Student Disk, and then save the file as Register.htm in the same folder.

2. Insert a hidden field tag after the <FORM> tag with a field name of SUBJECT and a value of "Registration form response."

3. Remove the two rows from the table that contain the Address1 and Address2 fields. Insert a single row in their place with the following properties:

   ■ The first cell in the row should contain the text "Address:" vertically aligned with the top of the cell.
   ■ The second cell in the row should span two columns and contain a text area box. The size of the text area should be 4 rows by 50 columns. Assign the text area the field name "Address." Do not insert any default text into the text area.

4. Go to the selection list for the product field. Add options to the end of the list for PrintMaster 300, PrintMaster 600, and ColorPrinter Plus.

5. Increase the size of the selection list to 4.

6. Vertically align the text "Product:" located in the first cell of the row containing the selection list with the top of the cell.

7. Go to the table row containing check boxes for the various operating systems. Insert a check box for the OS/2 operating system in the same table cell containing the UNIX check box field. Name the new field "OS2."

8. Below the Comments text area field, insert a new row in the table with the following specifications:

- In the first cell, insert the text "Add me to the mailing list:".
- In the second cell, add a pair of radio buttons with the common field name "MLIST." Assign the radio buttons the values "Yes" and "No." Insert the text "Yes" directly to the right of the Yes button, and the text "No" directly to the right of the No button. Make the "Yes" radio button selected by default.

9. Below the row containing the mailing list radio buttons, insert another row with the following specifications:

- In the first cell of the row, insert the text "E-mail address:".
- The second cell of the row should span two columns and contain an input box with the field name "MAILADDRESS."

10. Modify the properties of the form so that it accesses the CGI script located at "http://www.Jkson_Electronics.com/cgi/formmail" using the POST method.

11. Save your changes to the Register.htm file, and then view it in your Web browser.

12. Print a copy of your form and the HTML code.

13. Close your Web browser and text editor.

Case Problems

1. Creating a Search Form for Gordon Media Gordon Media owns several newspapers in the Midwest. Recently Gordon Media has been moving towards online publishing. One of the company's ventures is to place classified ads online and to give customers the ability to search the classified listings from Gordon Media's many papers.

Tim Steward, the managing editor of the online publishing group, has contacted you about creating the search form for the classified ads page. The search form will allow customers to search in several different classified ad sections, to specify the newspapers they want to examine, and to indicate the time period they want to search in. Once this search form is completed, the form information will be sent to a CGI script for processing. The users will also have the option of viewing a helpful Web page containing search tips. A preview of the page you'll create is shown in Figure 6-37.

Figure 6-37 ◀

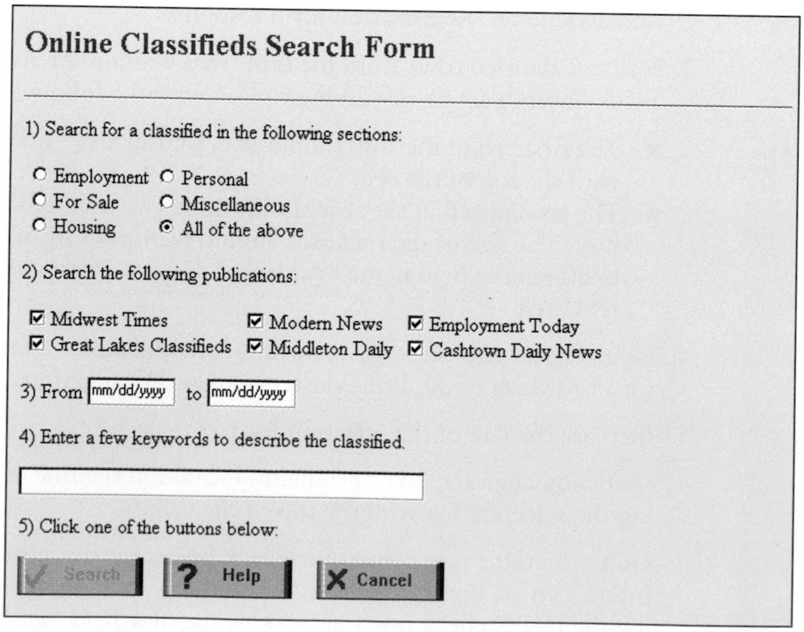

To create the Online Classifieds Search Form:

1. Start your text editor and open the file Adstext.htm in the Cases folder of the Tutorial.06 folder on your Student Disk, and then save the file as Ads.htm in the same folder.

2. Add an opening and closing <FORM> tag to the body of the page. Name the form "Ads."

3. Below the first question in the form, insert a table with one row and two columns. In the first table cell, insert on separate lines within the cell (using the <BR> tag) the following radio buttons and button descriptions (use the field name ADTYPE for each radio button and place the radio buttons before the text descriptions):

   ■ Employment (set the field value to EMP)
   ■ For Sale (set the field value to FORSALE)
   ■ Housing (set the field value to HOUSE)

4. In the second cell of the table, insert the following radio buttons and button descriptions, using the ADTYPE field name for each radio button. As before, place each radio button on a separate line within the table cell.

   ■ Personal (set the field value to PERSON)
   ■ Miscellaneous (set the field value to MISC)
   ■ All of the above (set the field value to ALL)

5. Make "All of the above" the default radio button.

6. Below the second question, insert a table with one row and three columns. In the first table cell, insert the following check boxes (place the check boxes on separate lines within the cell and put the text descriptions after the check boxes):

   ■ Midwest Times (field name=MWT)
   ■ Great Lakes Classifieds (field name=GLC)

7. In the second cell, create the following check boxes, on separate lines:

   ■ Modern News (field name=MN)
   ■ Middleton Daily (field name=MD)

8. In the third cell, add these two check boxes on separate lines:

   ■ Employment Today (field name=ET)
   ■ Cashtown Daily News (field name=CD)

9. Format all the check boxes so that they are selected by default.

10. Add two input boxes to the third form question, as shown in Figure 6-37. Make each input box 10 characters in width, and give each input box the default value of "mm/dd/yyyy." Name the first input box START and the second input box END.

11. Insert an input box after the fourth search form question. Set the width of the input box to 50 characters. Assign the input box the field name KEYWORDS.

12. Add three inline image fields at the bottom of the form. Use the file Search.gif to create the Search button, the file Help.gif to create the Help button, and the file Cancel.gif to create the Cancel button. Separate each inline image by two nonbreaking spaces.

13. Set the form to access a CGI script located at "http://www.gordonmed.com/cgi/fsearch.cgi" using the POST method.

14. Save your changes to the Ads.htm file.

15. View the file in your Web browser. Print a copy of the completed page and the corresponding HTML code.

16. Close your Web browser and text editor.

2. Creating a Travel Expense Form for DeLong Enterprises DeLong Enterprises, a manufacturer of computer components, is setting up a corporate intranet to put news and information online for company employees. One item that Dolores Crandall, a payroll manager, would like to put online is travel expense forms. Company employees fill out these forms after they attend conferences or business meetings. Dolores has contacted the company's computer service division for help, and they have assigned you the task of creating the travel expense form.

The travel expense form requires the employee to provide information about the business trip and to itemize various travel deductions. A preview of the form you'll create is shown in Figure 6-38.

Figure 6-38 ◀

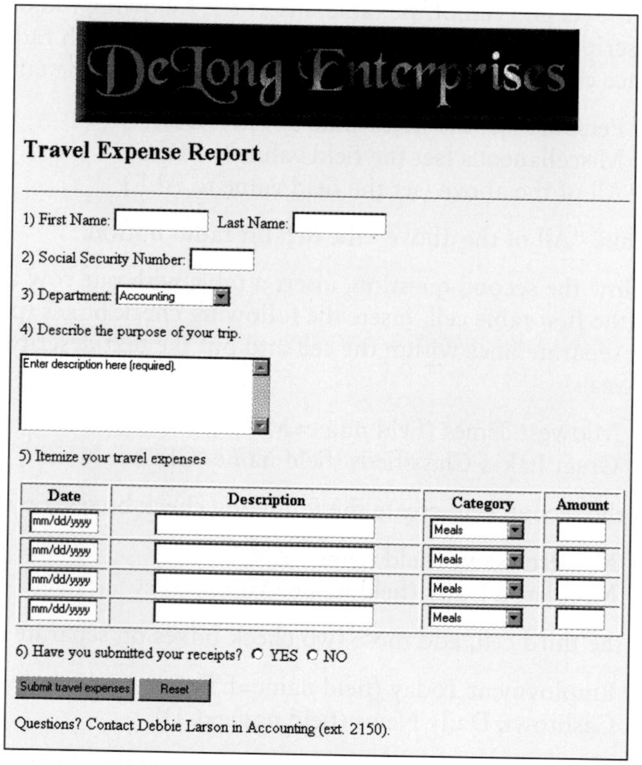

To create the travel expense form:

1. Start your text editor and open the file Travltxt.htm in the Cases folder of the Tutorial.06 folder on your Student Disk, and then save the file as Travel.htm in the same folder.

2. Add an opening and closing <FORM> tag to the body of the page. Name the form "Travel."

3. Insert input boxes for the employee's first name and last name in item #1 of the form. Assign these fields the names FIRST and LAST. Set the size of both input boxes to 15 characters.

4. Create a password input box for the Social Security number in item #2 of the form. Set the width and maximum length of the input box to 9 characters.

5. Create a drop-down list box for the list of departments in item #3. Insert the following options into the drop-down list box: Accounting, Advertising, Consumer Relations, Sales, Management, Payroll, Quality Control, and R & D. Set DEPT as the field name for the list box.

6. Create a text area field for the trip description in item #4. The text area field should be 4 rows high and 50 columns wide. Set DESC as the field name. Specify "Enter description here (required)." as the default text.

7. For each row (except the header row) of the expense itemization table (item #5), do the following:

   - In the first column, insert an input box with the field name DATE and a size of 10 characters. Specify "mm/dd/yyyy" as the default text.
   - In the second column, insert an input box that is 40 characters long and has the field name DESCRIPTION.
   - In the third column, insert a selection list with the field name CATEGORY, and include the following options in the list: Meals, Miscellaneous, Registration, and Transportation.
   - In the fourth column, insert an input box named AMOUNT that is 6 characters wide.

8. Create a pair of radio buttons for item #6, regarding submitting a receipt. Name both fields RECEIPT. Assign the first radio button the value YES and the second button the value NO. Insert the text "YES" next to the first radio button and the text "NO" next to the second button.

9. Below item #6 insert two form buttons. The first button should be a Submit button with the value "Submit travel expenses." The second button should be a Reset button.

10. Set the form to access the CGI script at the URL "http://www.DeLongEnt.com/cgi/Trvl.cgi" using the POST method.

11. Save your changes to the Travel.htm file.

12. View the file in your Web browser. Print a copy of the completed page and the corresponding HTML code.

13. Close your Web browser and text editor.

3. Registering Patients at St. Mary's of Northland Pines St. Mary's of Northland Pines is creating a system to register patients online using Web pages. You've been asked by Dr. Louise Mayer to create a registration form for newborn infants. The form should contain the infant's name, the name of the parents, the infant's medical record number, date of birth, birth weight, and 5-minute APGAR score. Dr. Mayer also wants you to include information about which physicians were involved in the birth. She has a list of seven physicians, and she wants the form to allow users to select multiple physicians in cases where more than one doctor was involved.

A preview of the form you'll create is shown in Figure 6-39.

Figure 6-39 ◀

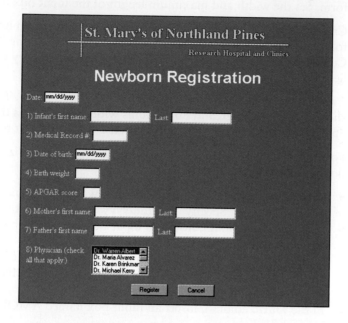

St. Mary's of Northland Pines

Research Hospital and Clinics

Newborn Registration

Date: mm/dd/yyyy

1) Infant's first name: [   ] Last: [   ]

2) Medical Record #: [   ]

3) Date of birth: mm/dd/yyyy

4) Birth weight: [   ]

5) APGAR score: [   ]

6) Mother's first name: [   ] Last: [   ]

7) Father's first name: [   ] Last: [   ]

8) Physician (check all that apply:)
Dr. Warren Albert
Dr. Maria Alvarez
Dr. Karen Brinkmar
Dr. Michael Kerry

[Register] [Cancel]

Dr. Mayer wants all results of the form mailed to Robert Brockton, whose e-mail address is brockton@StMarysNP.com. All browsers in the hospital can support the MAILTO action, so she wants you to use the MAILTO action in your form.

To create the newborn registration form:

 **EXPLORE**

1. Start your text editor and open the file NBtext.htm in the Cases folder of the Tutorial.06 folder on your Student Disk, and then save the file as Newborn.htm in the same folder.

2. Add an opening and closing <FORM> tag to the body of the page. Name the form "Newborn." Insert the MAILTO action in the <FORM> tag with the e-mail address brockton@StMarysNP.com (your instructor might ask you to insert your own e-mail address here). Use the POST method.

3. Insert an input box for the Date line at the top of the form. Set the size and maximum length of text in the input box to 10 characters, and set the default text to "mm/dd/yyyy." Assign the Date field the name FORMDATE.

4. Insert input boxes for the infant's first and last name. Use the field names FIRST and LAST.

5. Insert an input box for the medical record number. Use the field name MEDRECNO. Set the size and maximum length of data in this field to 10 characters.

6. Insert an input box for the infant's birth date named DOB. Set the size and maximum length of this input box to 10 characters. Set the default text to "mm/dd/yyyy."

7. Insert input boxes for the birth weight and APGAR score with the field names BWGT and APGAR. Set the size of the input boxes to 6 and 3 characters, respectively.

8. Create input boxes for the first and last name of the mother. Name the fields MFIRST and MLAST.

9. Create input boxes for the first and last name of the father. Name the fields FFIRST and FLAST.

10. Item #8 of the form should contain a selection box with the names of possible physicians. Assign the field name "DOCTOR" to the selection list. A table has already been created for you, and you should insert the selection box into the second cell of the table. The selection box should have the following options (the value for each option is shown in parentheses):

- Dr. Warren Albert (1)
- Dr. Maria Alvarez (2)
- Dr. Karen Brinkman (3)
- Dr. Michael Kerry (4)
- Dr. Chad Nichols (5)
- Dr. Karen Paulson (6)
- Dr. Tai Webb (7)
- Other (99)

Set up the selection box so that four options are shown within the box, and allow for multiple selections on the part of the user.

11. Insert a Submit button labeled "Register" and a Reset button labeled "Cancel" centered at the bottom of the form.

12. Save your changes to the Newborn.htm file.

13. View the file in your Web browser. Print a copy of the completed page and the corresponding HTML code.

14. If you used an e-mail address supplied by your instructor for the MAILTO action, complete the form in your Web browser with test data and mail the form to the address specified.

15. Close your Web browser and text editor.

4. Order Form for Millennium Computers You work at Millennium Computers, a discount mail-order company specializing in computers and computer components. You've been asked by your supervisor, Sandy Walton, to create an order form Web page for customers who want to purchase products online. Your order form will be for computer purchases only. There are several different options available to customers purchasing computers from Millennium; these are:

- Processor speed: 150 MHz, 200 MHz, 300 MHz, 400 MHz

- Memory: 8 meg, 16 meg, 32 meg, and 64 meg

- Drive size: 1 gigabyte, 2 gigabyte, 4 gigabyte

- Monitor size: 15 inch, 17 inch, 19 inch, 21 inch

- CD-ROM: 12x, 16x, 24x

Create Sandy's order form using the following guidelines (the layout and appearance of the page are up to you):

1. Create input boxes for the customer's first and last name, phone number, and credit card number and expiration date. Make sure the credit card information that the user enters is not displayed on the screen.

2. Using selection boxes or radio buttons, create fields in the form for the different component options listed previously.

3. Insert a check box asking whether the customer wants to be placed on the Millennium Computers mailing list.

4. Place three buttons on the form: a Submit button to send the order, a Reset button to reset the page, and a second Submit button to request that a Millennium Computers representative call the customer to process the order. Use the values "Send," "Cancel," and "Call Me" for the three buttons.

5. Assign the <FORM> tag the NAME property C_ORDER. Use the POST method and set up the form to use the CGI script located at http://www.mill_computers.com (a fictional URL).

6. Save your file as Computer.htm in the Cases folder of the Tutorial.06 folder on your Student Disk. Print a copy of your HTML code and the page as it appears in the Web browser.

7. Close your Web browser and text editor.

Programming with JavaScript

Creating a Programmable Web Page

OBJECTIVES

In this tutorial you will:

- Learn about the features of JavaScript

- Send output to a Web page

- Work with variables and data

- Work with expressions and operators

- Create a JavaScript function

- Work with arrays, program loops, and conditional statements

CASE

Calculating Shopping Days for North Pole Novelties

North Pole Novelties, located in Seton Grove, Minnesota, is a gift shop specializing in toys, decorations, and other items for the Christmas holiday season. Founded in 1948 by David Watkins, the company is one of the largest holiday stores in the country, with over 300 employees servicing loyal customers from around the world.

Because December 25th is the "red letter" day for North Pole Novelties, and 85% of its business occurs during the holiday season, the company is always aware of the number of shopping days remaining until Christmas—and wants its customers to be aware of this, too.

With this in mind, Andrew Savatini, the director of marketing, wants to include a reminder of the number of days remaining until Christmas on the company's home page. The Web page will have to be updated daily to reflect the correct number of days left. Although the company could assign someone the task of manually changing the Web page every morning, it would be much better if this task could be performed automatically by a program running on the Web page itself.

Andrew has asked you to create such a program. To do this, you'll have to learn how to write and run programs in JavaScript, a programming language designed for Web pages.

SESSION

7.1

In this session you will learn about the development and features of JavaScript. You'll learn how to insert a JavaScript program into an HTML file and how to hide that program from older browsers that don't support JavaScript. Finally, you'll write a simple JavaScript program to send customized output to a Web page.

Introduction to JavaScript

In your work with HTML so far, you've created only static Web pages, whose content and layout did not change. Beginning with this tutorial, you'll learn how to create Web pages that can change in response to user input. Using a program called JavaScript, you'll create a Web page that is programmable.

Server-side and Client-side Programs

In the previous tutorial, you learned about accessing programs involving forms and CGI scripts. In that example, the program was run off the Web server. There are some disadvantages to this approach: users had to be connected to the Web server to run the CGI script; only the programmer could alter the script itself; the system administrator of the Web server could place limitations on how users accessed the script, and so on. Such an approach also posed problems for the system administrator, who had to be concerned about users continually accessing the server, slowing it down, and potentially overloading the system. With the Web exploding in popularity, the prospect of even *more* users accessing the server could mean costly machine upgrades to handle the increased usage.

Issues like these led to the development of programs, or scripts, that could be run from the Web browser on the user's own computer (the client), as illustrated in Figure 7-1.

Figure 7-1 ◀
Server-side and
client-side
programming

Server-side programs

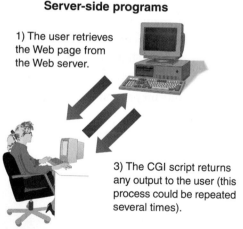

1) The user retrieves the Web page from the Web server.

2) The user works with the page to send information back to a CGI script running on the server.

3) The CGI script returns any output to the user (this process could be repeated several times).

Client-side programs

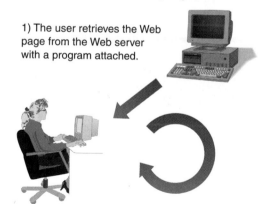

1) The user retrieves the Web page from the Web server with a program attached.

2) The user runs the program locally, receiving instant feedback.

Client-side programs solve many of the problems associated with CGI scripts. Computing is distributed over the Web so that no one server is overloaded with handling programming requests. Web pages containing client-side scripts can be tested locally without first uploading them to the Web server. The client-side program is likely to be more responsive to the user, because the user does not have to wait for data to be sent over the Internet to the Web server. However, client-side programs can never completely replace CGI scripts. For example, if you need to run a search form or process a purchase order, that type of job must be run from a central server, because the server will most likely contain the database needed to complete those operations.

The Development of Java and JavaScript

As with many innovations in the history of computing, client-side programming came from unexpected sources. In the early 1990s, before the development of the World Wide Web, programmers at Sun Microsystems foresaw the day when even common consumer devices such as refrigerators, toasters, and garage door openers, would all be networked and capable of being controlled by a single operating system. The programmers began to develop such an operating system and based it on a language called **Oak**. Oak was designed to be extremely reliable and flexible. Unfortunately the project did not succeed, but Oak was so useful that Sun Microsystems realized that it could be used on the Internet. Oak was modified in 1995 and renamed **Java**. Sun Microsystems also released a product called **HotJava**, which could run programs written in the Java language.

HotJava acted as a **Java interpreter**, which means that it was able to interpret a Java program and run it for the user. The idea was that Java programs would run inside Java interpreters, and because Java interpreters could be created for different operating systems, users could run Java in any environment, including the UNIX, Windows, DOS, and Macintosh operating systems. Just as Web pages are designed to be platform-independent, so was Java.

The advantages of Java were immediately apparent, and Netscape incorporated a Java interpreter into Netscape Navigator version 2.0, making HotJava unnecessary for Navigator users. Microsoft's Internet Explorer browser followed suit, beginning with version 3.0.

With Java the user downloads a program, called an **applet**, along with the Web page. The browser, with the built-in Java interpreter, is able to run the applet from the user's own machine, freeing up the Web server for other purposes (Figure 7-2).

Figure 7-2 ◀
Applets
and Java
interpreters

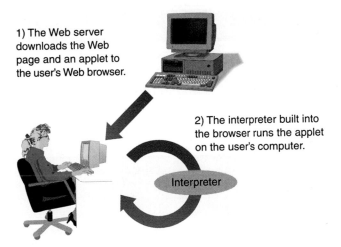

1) The Web server downloads the Web page and an applet to the user's Web browser.

2) The interpreter built into the browser runs the applet on the user's computer.

Interpreter

One problem with Java was that nonprogrammers found it difficult to learn and use. Users also needed access to the JDK (Java Developer's Kit) to first create the programs and then to **compile** them (a process by which a program is converted from a readable text file into an executable file). To simplify the process, a team of developers from Netscape and Sun Microsystems created JavaScript. **JavaScript** is a subset of Java with several differences. Users don't need to work with a developer's kit or to compile a JavaScript program, and JavaScript commands can be inserted directly into an HTML file rather than being placed in an applet. This saves the Web browser from having to download a separate file when the page is accessed, which speeds up the process. JavaScript is not as powerful a computing language as Java, but it is simpler to use, and it meets the needs of most users who want to create programmable Web pages.

Figure 7-3 highlights some of the differences between Java and JavaScript.

Figure 7-3 ◄
Comparison of
Java and
JavaScript

Java	JavaScript
Complicated	Easy to learn and use
Requires the JDK (Java Developer's Kit) to create applets	No developer's kit required
Programs must be saved as separate files and compiled before they can be run	Scripts are written directly into the HTML file and require no compiling
Powerful; used for complex tasks	Used for relatively simple tasks

Several versions of JavaScript have been developed, the most recent being version 1.3. Figure 7-4 lists the different versions and describes how they're supported by Netscape Navigator and Internet Explorer. Internet Explorer actually uses a variation of JavaScript called **JScript**. For all practical purposes, JScript is identical to JavaScript, but some JavaScript commands are not supported in JScript, and vice versa. You should, therefore, test your JavaScript programs on a variety of Web browsers. Although it is tempting to use commands available in the latest JavaScript or JScript version, doing so could make your page uninterpretable to many Web users.

Figure 7-4 ◄
Versions of
JavaScript

Version Number	Description
JavaScript v 1.0	Used in Netscape Navigator 2.0 and Internet Explorer 3.0
JavaScript v 1.1	Used in Netscape Navigator 3.0; parts, but not all, implemented in Internet Explorer 3.0
JavaScript v 1.2	Used in Netscape Navigator 4.0, Netscape Messenger, and Netscape Collabra
JavaScript v 1.3	Introduced in Netscape Communicator 4.06 and 4.5, featuring a major overhaul in the Date feature

Other client-side programming languages are available to the Web page author. You can use Internet Explorer's scripting language, VBScript, for example. Because of the nearly universal support of JavaScript, you'll use this language in your work for North Pole Novelties.

Running JavaScript

Now that you're familiar with JavaScript and its use, you're ready to start working with JavaScript. Your task is to create a page that calculates the remaining days until Christmas for North Pole Novelties. Andrew wants this information displayed on the company's home page, shown in Figure 7-5, so that customers know how long they have to make their holiday purchases.

Figure 7-5 ◀
North Pole
Novelties home
page

current date and
day count

The home page shows the number of days remaining until Christmas, but this information has been explicitly entered into the HTML file and, therefore, works only if the date is June 27th, 1999. Andrew wants this information to be calculated automatically for the current date, whatever that might be. Furthermore, if the current date is December 25th or later in the year, he wants the page to display the text "Happy Holidays from North Pole Novelties" instead of the day count.

Before you start to write a program, it's a good idea to outline the main tasks you have to perform. In this case, the tasks are as follows:

☐ 1) Learn how to send text to a Web page using JavaScript.

☐ 2) Display test date information on a Web page.

☐ 3) Calculate the difference between the test date and December 25th.

☐ 4) Make allowances for the presence of leap years in the calculation.

☐ 5) If the date is December 25th or later (through December 31st), display a greeting
      message; otherwise, display the number of days remaining until Christmas.

Your first task, therefore, is to create and run a simple JavaScript program that sends output to your Web page. A JavaScript program is run by the Web browser, either in the process of rendering the HTML file or in response to an event, such as the user clicking a Submit button or positioning the mouse on a hyperlink. In the case of North Pole Novelties, you'll create a JavaScript program that is run automatically when the browser loads the North Pole Novelties home page. In the next tutorial, you'll learn how to create JavaScript programs that run in response to user-initiated events.

There are two ways to create a JavaScript program. As noted earlier, you can place the JavaScript commands directly into the HTML file. You can also place the commands in an external file. Placing the program in an external file allows you to hide the program code from the user, whereas source code placed directly in the HTML file can be viewed by anyone. However, an external file must be stored on the Web server, which means that the server has the added task of transferring both the Web page and the JavaScript file to the user. Generally, the more complicated and larger the JavaScript program, the more likely you are to place it in an external file. In this tutorial you'll enter the code directly into the HTML file.

When you place JavaScript code directly into the HTML file, you need some way of distinguishing it from text that you want to appear on the Web page (otherwise your browser might start displaying your JavaScript commands on your page). You can do this with the <SCRIPT> tag.

Using the <SCRIPT> Tag

The <SCRIPT> tag is a two-sided tag that identifies the beginning and end of a client-side program. The general syntax for this tag is:

```
<SCRIPT SRC=URL LANGUAGE="Text">

    Script commands and comments

</SCRIPT>
```

where URL is the URL for an external document containing the program code, and Text is the language that the program is written in. The SRC property is required only if you place your program in a separate file. The LANGUAGE property is needed so that the browser knows which interpreter to use with the client-side program code. The default LANGUAGE value is "JavaScript." (Internet Explorer interprets "JavaScript" as being identical to "JScript.") Another possible value for the LANGUAGE property is "LiveScript," which was the original term for JavaScript, but this term is used only by older browsers and is not supported by Internet Explorer. If you omit the LANGUAGE property, the browser will assume that the program is written in JavaScript.

REFERENCE window

INSERTING A CLIENT-SIDE PROGRAM

- To insert a client-side program into your HTML file, use the following syntax:
  <SCRIPT SRC=URL LANGUAGE="Text">
      Script commands and comments
  </SCRIPT>
  where the URL is the file containing the programming commands (if you choose to store the program in an external file), and the LANGUAGE property is the programming language of the client-side program. To create a JavaScript program, set the LANGUAGE property to "JavaScript" or omit the LANGUAGE property, and the Web browser will assume that JavaScript is the programming language by default.

Your program can be placed anywhere within the HTML file, either within the <HEAD> tags or the <BODY> tags. Many programmers favor placing their programs between <HEAD> tags in order to separate the programming code from the page's content and layout. Others favor placing their programs within the page's body, at the location where output from the program is generated and displayed. In the example that follows, you'll do a little of both.

Hiding Your Script from Older Browsers

Older browsers that do not support JavaScript present a problem. If such browsers encounter JavaScript commands, they will attempt to display them on the page, treating them as part of the page's content. To avoid this problem, you can hide the script using comment tags.

You've already used comment tags in your HTML files to explain the purpose of your various HTML tags. JavaScript supports similar comment tags, using a set of double slashes (//) at the beginning of a line to tell the browser to ignore the line and not interpret it as a JavaScript command.

By combining the HTML comment tag and JavaScript comment symbols, you can hide your JavaScript program from browsers that don't support the <SCRIPT> tag. The syntax for doing this is as follows:

```
<SCRIPT LANGUAGE="JavaScript">

<!--- Hide this script from browsers that don't support JavaScript

    JavaScript commands

// Stop hiding from other browsers   -->

</SCRIPT>
```

When a browser that doesn't support scripts encounters this code, it first ignores the <SCRIPT> tag, because it doesn't recognize the tag and doesn't know what to do with it. The next line is the start of the HTML comment tag, which doesn't close until the > symbol in the second-to-last line. So, everything in the JavaScript program is ignored. The final </SCRIPT> tag is similarly ignored by the browser. The JavaScript comment (starting with the // symbol) in the second-to-last line is there to help other users understand and interpret your code. A browser that supports JavaScript recognizes the <SCRIPT> tag and will ignore any HTML tags found between the <SCRIPT> and </SCRIPT> tags. So it passes the comment tag in the second line and processes the JavaScript program as written.

Having seen the basic structure of a JavaScript program, you're ready to insert the necessary lines of code into the North Pole Novelties home page in order to hide the script from other browsers. The page is stored on your Student Disk in the file NPNtext.htm, which you'll rename as NPN.htm. You'll delete the HTML tags already present in the file that display the 6/27/99 date information because you'll eventually replace these with a program that works for *any* date.

To open the NPNtext.htm file and start creating your programmable Web page:

1. Start your text editor.

2. Open the file **NPNtext.htm** from the Tutorial.07 folder on your Student Disk, and then save the file as **NPN.htm** in the same folder.

3. Scroll down the file until you locate the HTML comment tag "<!-- Days until Christmas --->".

4. Delete the following two lines of code (but keep the formatting tags that occur before and after this text):

   Today is 6/27/99
   Only 181 days until Christmas

5. In place of the deleted lines, insert the following lines (indented to make your code easier to interpret):

   ```
   <SCRIPT LANGUAGE="JavaScript">
   <!--- Hide from non-JavaScript browsers
   // Stop hiding -->
   </SCRIPT>
   ```

Your file should appear as shown in Figure 7-6. At this point, no date information will be displayed on the page.

Figure 7-6 ◀
Inserting the
<SCRIPT> tag
into the
NPN.htm file

script language

beginning of script

end of script

comment tag to hide
code from older
browsers

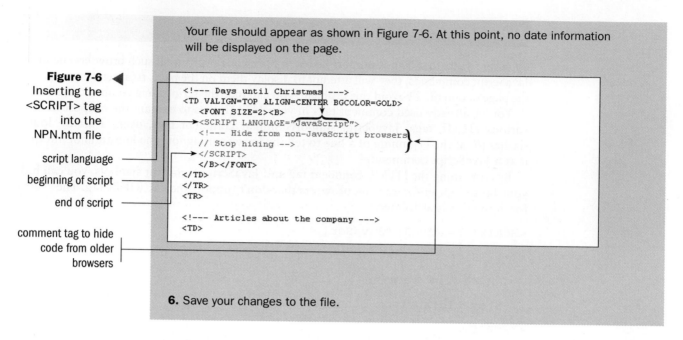

```
<!--- Days until Christmas --->
<TD VALIGN=TOP ALIGN=CENTER BGCOLOR=GOLD>
   <FONT SIZE=2><B>
   <SCRIPT LANGUAGE="JavaScript">
   <!--- Hide from non-JavaScript browsers
   // Stop hiding -->
   </SCRIPT>
   </B></FONT>
</TD>
</TR>
<TR>

<!--- Articles about the company --->
<TD>
```

6. Save your changes to the file.

With the <SCRIPT> tags and comments in place, your next task is to write a JavaScript program that sends output to the Web page. Because you haven't yet learned how to either determine the current date or calculate the number of days until Christmas, this program will display a simple text string.

Sending Output to a Web Page

JavaScript provides two commands to display text on a Web page: the document.write() and document.writeln() commands. The syntax of each is:

```
document.write("text");
```

```
document.writeln("text");
```

where *text* is a text string that you want sent to the Web page. For example, the following command will display the text *Only 45 days until Christmas* at the spot in the page where you placed the JavaScript program:

```
document.write("Only 45 days until Christmas");
```

The write() and writeln() commands work in the same way, except that writeln() attaches a carriage return at the end of the text string that it sends to the page. This becomes relevant only when the text string is preformatted with the <PRE> tag, in which case the browser recognizes the existence of carriage returns in rendering the text on the page. Otherwise there is no difference between the write() and writeln() commands. In the JavaScript program you'll be creating, you'll use the document.write() command to send text to the Web page.

SENDING OUTPUT TO A WEB PAGE

■ To display text on your Web page, use the following JavaScript command:

document.write("*text*");

or

document.writeln("*text*");

where *text* is the text and HTML tags that you want to send to your Web page. The document.write() and document.writeln() methods are identical, except that the document.writeln() method attaches a carriage return to the text. This is important only if you are using preformatted text, which recognizes the existence of carriage returns.

A text string created with the document.write() command is enclosed within double or single quotation marks. This allows you to include single or double quotation marks as part of your text string. Consider the following JavaScript command:

```
document.write("Come meet David 'Bud' Davis");
```

This command will display the text Come meet David 'Bud' Davis (including the single quotation marks) on the Web page. Similarly, you can display double quotation marks by enclosing your text string within single quotation marks.

You're not limited to displaying only text; you can also include HTML tags in the text string. For example the following command displays the text *News Flash!* formatted with the <H3> heading style:

```
document.write("<H3>News Flash!</H3>");
```

The document.write() and document.writeln() commands reflect the object-oriented nature of the JavaScript language. Here, "document" is an object (the page that your Web browser is accessing), and "write()" or "writeln()" are actions that can be applied to the document. JavaScript calls these actions "methods." You'll learn more about objects and methods in the next tutorial. For now, when the term "method" is used, it means an action that is applied to something existing on your Web page or in your Web browser.

As when working with HTML, there are some syntax issues you should be aware of in JavaScript. Most JavaScript commands and names are case-sensitive. Your Web browser will understand "document.write()" and apply the method correctly, but your browser will not recognize the method "Document.Write()" and will display an error message. Also note that each JavaScript command line ends with a semicolon to distinguish it from the next command in the program. In some situations, the semicolon is optional, but you should still use it to make your code easier to follow.

Now that you've learned a little about the document.write() method, you'll add it to the JavaScript program you just created in the NPN.htm file. Because this is your first JavaScript program, you'll create a simple program to display the date information you deleted in the previous set of steps.

To display text on your Web page with JavaScript:

1. Below the line "<!--- Hide from non-JavaScript browsers," insert the following two commands (indented to make your code easier to read):

**document.write("Today is 6/27/99
");**
document.write("Only 181 days until Christmas");

Note that the text you're sending to the Web page includes the <BR> tag to create a line break between the date and the number of days until Christmas. Figure 7-7 shows the revised file.

Figure 7-7
Using
JavaScript
to send text to
the Web page

HTML tag

text sent to the
Web page

```
<!--- Days until Christmas --->
<TD VALIGN=TOP ALIGN=CENTER BGCOLOR=GOLD>
  <FONT SIZE=2><B>
  <SCRIPT LANGUAGE="JavaScript">
  <!--- Hide from non-JavaScript browsers
  document.write("Today is 6/27/99<BR>");
  document.write("Only 181 days until Christmas");
  // Stop hiding -->
  </SCRIPT>
  </B></FONT>
</TD>
</TR>
<TR>
```

2. Save your changes to the file, and then open the NPN.htm file in your Web browser. The browser should display the two lines you created using JavaScript, and the two lines should appear exactly as they did earlier in Figure 7-5.

TROUBLE? If you receive a JavaScript error message, close the Error Message dialog box and return to your text editor. Check the code you entered against the code shown in the steps. Minor errors, such as omitting a quotation mark, can cause your program to fail.

DESIGN
window

TIPS FOR WRITING A JAVASCRIPT PROGRAM

- Use comments extensively to document your program and its features. Comments will help you and others better understand the program.
- Use indented text where appropriate to make your code easier to read and follow.
- Watch the use of uppercase and lowercase letters. Most JavaScript commands and names are case-sensitive.
- Include the HTML comment tag to hide your JavaScript code from older browsers that do not support JavaScript.
- Test your JavaScript program under a variety of browsers and browser versions. Some browsers might not support the commands you have written.

Quick Check

1 What is a client-side program? What is a server-side program?

2 Describe two differences between Java and JavaScript.

3 What are the two ways JavaScript can be run from a Web page?

4 What HTML tags do you enter to indicate the beginning and end of a JavaScript program?

5 Why should you place your JavaScript commands within an HTML comment tag?

6 What JavaScript command would you enter to place the text "Avalon Books" into your Web page, formatted with the <H1> heading style?

You've completed your first JavaScript program! True, the program does nothing more than display text you could have entered directly with HTML, but it's a program you'll build upon in the next sessions to perform the more sophisticated tasks required to meet Andrew's goals for the North Pole Novelties Web page.

SESSION

7.2

In this session you will learn some of the fundamentals of the JavaScript language. You'll learn how to create variables and how to work with different data types. You'll also learn about expressions and operators and how to use them to change the variable values. Finally, you'll create your own JavaScript function and use it in a program.

Working with Variables and Data

In the previous session you learned how to insert text onto your Web page using the document.write() method. You had to specify the text explicitly; therefore, the program did no more than what you could have accomplished by writing the HTML tag yourself. The next task on your list for the North Pole Novelties home page is to have your program determine the current date and then display that information (using a test date) on the page.

✓ 1) Learn how to send text to a Web page using JavaScript.

☐ 2) Display test date information on a Web page.

☐ 3) Calculate the difference between the test date and December 25th.

☐ 4) Make allowances for the presence of leap years in the calculation.

☐ 5) If the date is December 25th or later (through December 31st), display a greeting message; otherwise, display the number of days remaining until Christmas.

To do this, you have to create a JavaScript variable. A **variable** is a named element in a program, used to store and retrieve information. Variables are useful because they can store information created in one part of your program and use that information later on. For example, you could create a variable named "Year" to store the value of the current year, and then use the Year variable at different locations in your program.

Variables are given values through **assignment operators**, the most common being the equals sign. To assign the value 1999 to the variable "Year," you would enter the following JavaScript command:

```
Year=1999;
```

With the Year variable assigned a value, you can use the document.write() method to display this value on the Web page, as follows:

```
document.write(Year);
```

This code would cause the text "1999" to be displayed on the Web page. You can also combine text with the variable value by using a plus symbol (+), as in the following example:

```
document.write("The year is " + Year);
```

This command will display the text *The year is 1999* on the Web page. In the program you're creating for Andrew, you won't be explicitly entering the date information. Instead, your program will determine the current date and year for you and store that information in a variable so that you can use the date later in the program.

The following restrictions apply to names you assign to variables:

- The first character must be either a letter or an underscore (_).

- The rest of the characters can be letters, numbers, or underscores.

- Variable names cannot contain spaces.

- You cannot use words that JavaScript has reserved for other purposes. For example, you cannot name a variable "document.write."

Variable names are case-sensitive. A variable named "Year" is considered different from a variable named "YEAR." If your JavaScript program isn't working properly, switching uppercase and lowercase letters is often the source of the problem.

Data Types

JavaScript supports four different kinds of variable values, also called **data types**—numbers, strings, Boolean values, and null values. A **number** can be any numeric value, such as 13, 22.5, or −3.14159. Numbers can also be expressed in scientific notation: for example, 5.1E2 for the value 5.1×10^2, or 510. A **string** is any group of characters, such as "Hello" or "Happy Holidays!" Strings must be enclosed within double or single quotation marks, but you must be consistent. The string value "Hello" is acceptable, but the string value "Hello' is not. **Boolean variables** can take only one of two values, either true or false. You use Boolean variables in situations in which you want the program to act in a particular way, depending on whether a condition, represented by the Boolean variable, is either true or false. A **null value** is a variable that has no value at all. This will happen when you create a variable in the program, but have not assigned it a value yet.

Declaring a Variable

Before you can use a variable in your program, you have to create it. This is also known as **declaring a variable**. You declare a variable in JavaScript either by assigning it a value in a JavaScript command or by using the **var** command to create it without assigning it a value. Each of the following JavaScript commands will create a variable named "Month":

```
Month="December";

var Month;
```

You can also combine these two commands into a single one both to declare the variable and to assign it a value in the same operation:

```
var Month="December";
```

It's considered good programming style to include the var command when declaring your variables. Doing so helps you organize your program by keeping track of the variables the program will use. It also makes it easier for others to interpret your code. Many programmers place all of their variable declarations at the beginning of the program along with comments describing each variable's purpose and scope.

REFERENCE window

DECLARING A JAVASCRIPT VARIABLE

- You can create (declare) variables with any of the following three JavaScript commands:
  var *variable*;
  variable = *value*;
  var *variable* = *value*;
  where *variable* is the name of the variable, and *value* is the initial value of the variable. The first command creates the variable without assigning it a value; the second and third commands both create the variable and assign it a value.

Working with Dates

In your program for North Pole Novelties, you'll be working with dates as you try to calculate the number of days remaining until December 25th. JavaScript does not provide a date data type, as some other programming languages do; however, it allows you to create a **date object**, which is an object that contains date information. There are two forms of the command for creating date objects in JavaScript:

variable = new Date("*month, day, year, hours:minutes:seconds*")

variable = new Date(*year, month, day, hours, minutes,seconds*)

where *variable* is the name of the variable that will contain the date information, and *month*, *day*, *year*, *hours*, *minutes*, and *seconds* indicate the date and time. The keyword **new** in the above example is used to indicate to JavaScript that you're creating a new object. Note that in the first command form you specify the date using a text string, and in the second command form you use values. For example, each of the following commands will create a variable named "SomeDay" corresponding to a date of June 15th, 1999 and a time of 2:35 p.m.:

```
SomeDay = new Date("June, 15, 1999, 14:35:00");

SomeDay = new Date(1999, 5, 15, 14, 35, 0);
```

In this example, you might have noticed a couple of quirks in how JavaScript handles dates. First, when you specify the month with values rather than a text string, you must subtract 1 from the month number. This is because JavaScript numbers the months starting with 0 for January up through 11 for December. So, in the second command, the date for June 15th is expressed as (1999, 5, 15 ...) and *not* as (1999, 6, 15 ...). Also note that hours are expressed in military time (14:35 rather than 2:35 p.m.).

If you omit the time information, JavaScript assumes that the time is 0 hours, 0 minutes, and 0 seconds. If you omit *both* the date and time information, JavaScript returns the current date and time. For example, the following command creates a variable named "Today" that contains information about the current date and time:

```
Today = new Date();
```

This command is exactly what you will eventually want for your program, so that it will retrieve and display the current date.

CREATING A DATE AND TIME VARIABLE

- To create a date and time variable, use the following JavaScript command:
  variable = new Date("*month, day, year, hours:minutes: seconds*")
  or
  variable = new Date(*year, month, day, hours, minutes, seconds*)
  For example, the following two commands create a date and time variable with the same value:
  DayVariable = new Date("April, 4, 1999, 16:40:00");
  DayVariable = new Date(1999, 3, 4, 16, 40, 0);
- Use the following command to return the current date and time:
  DayVariable = new Date();

Extracting Day Information

Once you've created a variable such as Today, you have to extract date information from it. For example, you might not be interested in the current time down to the millisecond, but want only the current day of the month. To get just that information, you apply a method called the **getDate()** method. The general syntax of this method is:

```
DayValue = DateObject.getDate()
```

where *DayValue* is a variable that will contain the day of the month, and *DateObject* is a date object or a date variable that contains the complete date and time information.

EXTRACTING DATE AND TIME VALUES

- To extract the year value from a date and time variable named *DateVariable*, use the command:
  Year = *DateVariable*.getYear();
- To extract the month value from a date and time variable named *DateVariable*, use the command:
  Month = *DateVariable*.getMonth();
- To extract the day of the month value from a date and time variable named *DateVariable*, use the command:
  DayofMonth = *DateVariable*.getDate();
- To extract the day of the week value from a date and time variable named *DateVariable*, use the command:
  DayofWeek = *DateVariable*.getDay();

The following code shows how you could use JavaScript to create a variable containing the current day of the month:

```
Today = new Date();

DayofMonth = Today.getDate();
```

In this code, you first create a variable named "Today" that contains complete information about the current date and time. Then, in the second line of code, you apply the getDate() method to extract only the current day of the month from Today and place that information into the DayofMonth variable. For example, if the current date is June 28th 1999, the value of the DayofMonth variable would be 28.

Extracting Month Information

A similar method exists for extracting the value of the current month. This method is named **getMonth()**. There is one important point about this method: because JavaScript starts counting the months with 0 for January, you need to add 1 to the month number JavaScript produces. The following JavaScript code extracts the current month number, increases it by 1, and stores it in a variable named Month:

```
Today = new Date();

Month = Today.getMonth()+1;
```

If the current date is June 28th in this example, the value of the Month variable would be 6.

Extracting Year Information

The final date method you'll be using in your program is the getYear() method. As the name implies, the **getYear()** method extracts the year value from the date variable. The following code shows how you would create a variable containing the value of the current year:

```
Today = new Date();

Year = Today.getYear();
```

If the current date is June 28th 1999, the value of the Year variable will be 99, not 1999 as you might expect. The getYear() method works differently in Internet Explorer than in Netscape Navigator. Unfortunately, it also works inconsistently in both browsers. Figure 7-8 shows the year value returned by both browsers for various years.

Figure 7-8 ◄
Values of the
getYear()
method for the
two major Web
browsers

Year	Value returned by the getYear() method in Netscape Navigator	Value returned by the getYear() method in Internet Explorer
1998	98	98
1999	99	99
2000	2000	100
2001	2001	101

Both browsers have trouble with the year 2000. For example, Netscape Navigator uses 98 to represent 1998, but 2000 to represent the year 2000; therefore, if you use these values to calculate the number of years between 1998 and 2000, you will come up with the answer 1902! Performing this calculation in Internet Explorer returns the correct value, 2, but at the cost of identifying the year 2000 as the year 100. Such discrepancies will cause serious problems. You can avoid these problems using the getFullYear() method introduced in JavaScript 1.3 and supported by Netscape 4.5 and Internet Explorer 4.0. Older browsers will not support this method however. You can safely work with the getYear() method for dates in the twentieth century, but if you intend to work with dates in the twenty-first century you might have to make adjustments to the values returned by this method.

Some of the other date methods you can use with JavaScript are shown in Figure 7-9.

Figure 7-9 ◀
Date methods

Method	Description	Example
getDate()	Returns the day of the month	For the date object: Date("May, 5, 1999, 12:25:28"); getDate() = 5 getDay() = 3 (a Wednesday) getHours() = 12 getMinutes() = 25 getMonth() = 4 (May) getSeconds() = 28 getTime() = 925,925,128,000 getYear() = 99
getDay()	Returns the day of the week (0=Sunday, 1=Monday, 2=Tuesday, 3=Wednesday, 4=Thursday, 5=Friday, 6=Saturday)	
getHours()	Returns the hours	
getMinutes()	Returns the minutes	
getMonth()	Returns the month (0=January, 1=February,...)	
getSeconds()	Returns the seconds	
getTime()	Returns the complete time, expressed as the number of milliseconds since January 1st, 1970	
getYear()	Returns the number of years	

Now that you've learned how to use dates in a JavaScript program, you are ready to modify your JavaScript program to work with date variables. Eventually you'll set up the program to use whatever the current date is; for now, however, you'll use a specific date, October 15th, to test the program. You'll create the following five variables:

- Today, which will contain complete date and time information.

- ThisDay, which will contain the day of the month, extracted from the Today variable.

- ThisMonth, which will contain the value of the month, extracted from the Today variable.

- ThisYear, which will contain the year value extracted from the Today variable.

- DaysLeft, which will contain the number of days left until Christmas. Because you haven't calculated this value yet, you'll set this variable equal to 999 as a placeholder until you calculate the actual value.

Using these variables, you'll replace the commands you entered in the previous session, with commands based on variable values.

To insert the date information into the NPN.htm file:

1. If you took a break after the previous session, start your text editor and reopen the NPN.htm file from the Tutorial.07 folder of your Student Disk.

2. Scroll down to the "Days until Christmas" section of the file.

3. Delete the following command:

document.write("Today is 6/27/99
");

4. Replace the command you removed with the following lines:

//Get date information
var Today = new Date("October, 15, 1999");
var ThisDay = Today.getDate();
var ThisMonth = Today.getMonth()+1;
var ThisYear = Today.getYear();
document.write("Today is "+ThisMonth+"/"+ThisDay+"/"+ThisYear+"<BR>");

The first line is a comment line that documents what the following lines of code will do. The next four lines declare the date variables you'll use in the program and give them their initial values. These variables are then combined to display a text string (using the document.write method) with the current date.

5. Move one line down in your program and delete the command:

document.write ("Only 181 days until Christmas");

6. Replace the deleted command with the following lines:

//Get number of days until Christmas
var DaysLeft = 999;
document.write("Only " + DaysLeft + " days until Christmas");

These lines create the DaysLeft variable, which will eventually store the number of days remaining until Christmas, and then display that information on the Web page (using the document.write method).

When entering this code, be sure to carefully note the placement of the double quotation marks and uppercase and lowercase letters. Your complete code should appear as shown in Figure 7-10.

Figure 7-10 ◀
Inserting date
information into
your JavaScript
program

test date ─────

year ─────

days until Christmas
(test value)

```
<!--- Days until Christmas --->
<TD VALIGN=TOP ALIGN=CENTER BGCOLOR=GOLD>
   <FONT SIZE=2><B>
   <SCRIPT LANGUAGE="JavaScript">
   <!--- Hide from non-JavaScript browsers
   //Get date information
   var Today = new Date("October, 15, 1999");
   var ThisDay = Today.getDate();
   var ThisMonth = Today.getMonth()+1;
   var ThisYear = Today.getYear();
   document.write("Today is "+ThisMonth+"/"+ThisDay+"/"+ThisYear+"<BR>");
   //Get number of days until Christmas
   var DaysLeft = 999;
   document.write("Only " + DaysLeft + " days until Christmas");
   // Stop hiding -->
   </SCRIPT>
   </B></FONT>
</TD>
```

day of month

month number

7. Save your changes to the file.

8. Open the NPN.htm file in your Web browser. The revised page should appear as shown in Figure 7-11.

Figure 7-11 ◄
North Pole
Novelties home
page with new
date values

test date

output generated
by JavaScript

test value

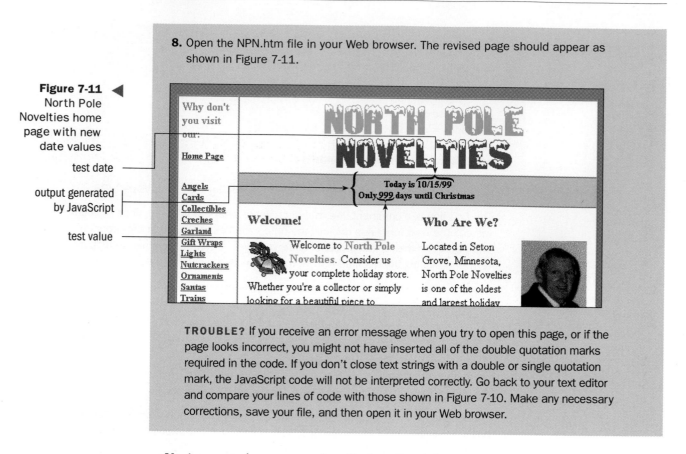

TROUBLE? If you receive an error message when you try to open this page, or if the page looks incorrect, you might not have inserted all of the double quotation marks required in the code. If you don't close text strings with a double or single quotation mark, the JavaScript code will not be interpreted correctly. Go back to your text editor and compare your lines of code with those shown in Figure 7-10. Make any necessary corrections, save your file, and then open it in your Web browser.

You've created a program that displays date information on your Web page, so you've completed the second item in your task list.

☑ 1) Learn how to send text to a Web page using JavaScript.

☑ 2) Display test date information on a Web page.

☐ 3) Calculate the difference between the test date and December 25th.

☐ 4) Make allowances for the presence of leap years in the calculation.

☐ 5) If the date is December 25th or later (through December 31st), display a greeting message; otherwise, display the number of days remaining until Christmas.

Your next step is to take that date information and use it to calculate the days remaining until December 25th. To do this you'll have to learn how to work with expressions, operators, and functions.

Working with Expressions and Operators

Expressions are JavaScript commands that assign values to your variables. You've already worked with several expressions in your JavaScript program. One expression, for example, assigned the value 999 to the DaysLeft variable. Expressions can also contain **operators**, which are elements that perform actions within the expression. A simple example is the **+ operator,** which performs the action of adding or combining two elements. You used the plus operator in your program with the following command:

```
var ThisMonth = Today.getMonth()+1;
```

This command uses the + operator to increase the value returned by the getMonth() method by 1. You also used the + operator to combine text strings:

document.write("Only " + DaysLeft + " days until Christmas");

In each of these examples, the plus operator combines two or more values or elements to create a single value or element.

Arithmetic Operators

The + operator belongs to a group of operators called the **arithmetic operators,** which perform simple mathematical calculations. Figure 7-12 lists some of the arithmetic operators and gives examples of how they work.

Figure 7-12 ◀
Arithmetic operators

Operator	Description	Example

+	Adds two values together	var Men = 20;
		var Women = 25;
		var TotalPeople = Men + Women;

−	Subtracts one value from another	var Price = 1000;
		var Expense = 750;
		var Profit = Price − Expense;

*	Multiplies two values together	var Width = 50;
		var Length = 25;
		var Area = Width*Length;

/	Divides one value by another	var People = 50;
		var TotalCost = 200;
		var CostperPerson = TotalCost/People;

%	Shows the remainder after dividing one value by another	var TotalEggs = 64;
		var CartonSize = 12;
		var EggsLeft = TotalEggs % CartonSize;

++	Increases a value by 1 (unary operator)	var Eggs = 12; var BakersDozen = Eggs++;
--	Decreases a value by 1 (unary operator)	var Eggs = 12; var EggsIfOneIsBroken = Eggs--;
−	Changes the sign of a value (unary operator)	var MyGain = 50; var YourLoss = − MyGain;

Some of the arithmetic operators in Figure 7-12 are also known as **binary operators** because they work on two elements in an expression. There are also **unary operators,** which work on only one variable. These include the increment (++), decrement (--), and negation (−) operators. The **increment operator** can be used to increase the value of a variable by 1. In the following code, the value of the x variable is 100, and the value of the y variable is 101:

```
x = 100;

y = x++;
```

The **decrement operator** has the opposite effect, reducing the value of a variable by 1. The following JavaScript code assigns the value 100 to the x variable and 99 to the y variable:

```
x = 100;

y = x--;
```

Finally, the **negation operator** simply assigns the opposite sign to a variable, as in the following example:

```
x = -100;

y = -x;
```

In this code, the value of the x variable is –100, and the value of the y variable is opposite that, or 100. You'll have a chance to use a unary operator later in this tutorial.

Logical and Comparison Operators

Arithmetic expressions are used for numbers. As you learned earlier, another data type in JavaScript is the Boolean data type, which can be either true or false. Specific operators called comparison and logical operators work with Boolean values. A **comparison operator** compares the value of one element with that of another, as in the following expressions:

```
x < 100;

y == 20;
```

In the first example, if x is less than 100, this expression returns the value "true"; however, if x is 100 or greater, the expression is "false." In the second example, the y variable must have an exact value of 20 for the expression to be true. Note that this comparison operator uses a double equals sign (==) rather than a single one. The single equals sign is an assignment operator and is not used for making comparisons. Figure 7-13 lists some of the other comparison operators used in JavaScript.

Figure 7-13 ◄
Comparison
operators

Operator	Description
==	Returns true if variables are equal (x = y)
!=	Returns true if variables are not equal (x != y)
>	Returns true if the variable on the left is greater than the variable on the right (x > y)
<	Returns true if the variable on the left is less than the variable on the right (x < y)
>=	Returns true if the variable on the left is greater than or equal to the variable on the right (x >= y)
<=	Returns true if the variable on the left is less than or equal to the variable on the right (x <= y)

A **logical** operator evaluates two or more Boolean expressions. One such operator is the **&& operator**, which returns a value of "true" only if all of the expressions are true. For example, the following expression will be true only if x is less than 100 *and* y is equal to 20:

```
(x < 100) && (y == 20);
```

Figure 7-14 lists some of the logical operators used by JavaScript.

Figure 7-14 ◀
Logical
operators

Operator	Description	Example
&&	Returns true only when both expressions are true	Var x = 20; Var y = 25;
||	Returns true when either expression is true	(x == 20) && (y == 25) returns true (x == 20) && (y == 20) returns false (x == 20) || (y == 20) returns true (x == 25) || (y == 20) returns false
!	Returns true if the expression is false, and false if the expression is true	! (x == 20) returns false ! (x == 25) returns true

You use logical and comparison operators when you want your program to act differently in response to different conditions, or when you want a certain group of commands to be executed repeatedly until a specific condition is met. You'll have a chance to work with both of these situations later in this tutorial.

Assignment Operators

Expressions assign values using **assignment operators**. You've already seen one example of an assignment operator, the equals (=) sign. JavaScript provides other assignment operators that manipulate elements in an expression and assign values within a single operation. One of these is the += operator. In JavaScript, the following two expressions create the same result:

```
x = x + y;

x += y
```

In both expressions, the value of the x variable is added to the value of the y variable and stored in x. An assignment operator can also be used with numbers to increase a variable by a specific amount. For example, to increase the value of the x variable by 2, you can use either of the following two expressions:

```
x = x + 2;

x += 2
```

Other assignment operators are shown in Figure 7-15.

Figure 7-15 ◀
Assignment
operators

Operator	Description
=	Assigns the value of the variable on the right to the variable on the left (x = y)
+=	Adds the two variables and assigns the result to the variable on the left (equivalent to x = x + y)
-=	Subtracts the variable on the right from the variable on the left and assigns the result to the variable on the left (equivalent to x = x − y)
*=	Multiplies the two variables together and assigns the result to the variable on the left (equivalent to x = x*y)
/=	Divides the variable on the left by the variable on the right and assigns the result to the variable on the left (equivalent to x = x/y)
%=	Divides the variable on the left by the variable on the right and assigns the remainder to the variable on the left (equivalent to x = x % y)

As you can see, once you master the syntax, assignment operators allow you to create expressions that are both efficient and compact. As you start learning JavaScript, you might prefer using the longer form for such expressions. However, if you study the code of other JavaScript programmers, you will certainly encounter programs that make substantial use of assignment operators to reduce program size.

Creating JavaScript Functions

When you begin creating more complicated programs with JavaScript, you might find that you are repeatedly using the same expressions or groups of expressions. To save time, you can place these expressions within a function. A **function** is a series of commands that either performs an action or calculates a value. A function consists of the **function name**, which identifies it; **parameters**, which are values sent to the function; and a set of commands that are run when the function is used. Not all functions require parameters. The general syntax of a JavaScript function is:

```
function function_name(parameters){

    JavaScript commands

}
```

where *function_name* is the name of the function, *parameters* are the values sent to the function, and *JavaScript commands* are the actual commands and expressions used by the function. Note that curly braces { } are used to mark the beginning and end of the commands in the function. The group of commands set off by the curly braces is called a **command block** and, as you'll see, command blocks exist for other JavaScript structures in addition to functions.

Function names, like variable names, are case-sensitive. XMASDAYS and XmasDays are considered different function names. The function name must begin with a letter or underscore (_) and cannot contain any spaces.

You are not limited in the number of function parameters a function contains. The parameters must be placed within parentheses (following the function name), and each parameter must be separated from the others with a comma.

REFERENCE window

CREATING AND USING A JAVASCRIPT FUNCTION

- To create a user-defined function in JavaScript, use the following syntax:
  function *function_name*(*parameters*){
      JavaScript commands
  }
  where *function_name* is the name of the function, *parameters* are the parameters of the function (a list of variable names separated by commas), and the opening and closing braces enclose the JavaScript commands used by the function.
- To run a user-defined function, use the following command:
  function_name(*values*);
  where *function_name* is the name of the function, and *values* are the values substituted for each of the function parameters.

Performing an Action with a Function

To see how a function works, consider the following function, which displays a message with the current date:

```
function ShowDate(date) {
document.write("Today is " + date + "<BR>");
}
```

In this example, the function name is ShowDate, and it has one parameter, date. There is one line in the function's command block, which displays the current date. To run a function, you insert a JavaScript command containing the function name and any parameters it requires. This process is known as **calling** a function. To call the ShowDate function, you could enter the following commands:

```
var Today = "3/25/99";
ShowDate(Today);
```

In this example, the first command creates a variable named "Today" and assigns it the text string "3/25/99." The second command runs the ShowDate function, using the value of the Today variable as a parameter. The result of calling the ShowDate function is that the text "Today is 3/25/99" is displayed on the Web page.

Returning a Value from a Function

You can also use a function to calculate a value. This process is also known as **returning a value**, and is achieved by placing a **return** command at the end of the function's command block. Consider the following Area function:

```
function Area(Width, Length) {
    var Size = Width*Length;
    return Size;
}
```

Here, the Area function calculates the area of a rectangular region, given its width and length, and places the value in a variable named "Size." The value of the Size variable is then returned by the function. A simple JavaScript program that uses this function might appear as follows:

```
var x=8;
var y=6;
var z=Area(x,y);
```

The first two commands assign the values 8 and 6 to the x and y variables, respectively. The values of both of these variables are then sent to the Area function, corresponding to the Width and Length parameters. The Area function uses these values to calculate the area, which it then returns, assigning that value to the z variable. The result of these commands is that 48 is assigned to the value of the z variable.

Placing a Function in an HTML File

Where you place a function in the HTML file is important. The function definition must be placed before the command that calls the function. If you try to call a function before it is defined, you might receive an error message from the browser. Although not a requirement, one programming convention is to place all of the function definitions used in the Web page between the <HEAD> and </HEAD> tags. This ensures that each function definition has been read and interpreted before being called by other JavaScript commands. When the browser loads the HTML file containing a function, the browser passes over the command block located in the function and does not execute it. The function and, therefore, the command block will be executed only when called by another JavaScript command.

Inserting the XmasDays Function

You're now going to start creating a function called XmasDays, which will calculate the number of days remaining until Christmas, given the current date. There are many ways to create such a function. You're going to use a method that will illustrate several aspects of JavaScript programming. To create this function, you'll break the task into two steps: first you'll create a function that will work for a few specific dates in the year, and then you'll create a function that will work for any date. Doing it this way will give you a chance to create a simple function before tackling a more difficult one.

☐ 3) Calculate the difference between the test date and December 25th.

☐ a) Create a function for a few specific dates in the year.

☐ b) Create a function that works for any day of the year.

Before creating the function, you'll want to consider how to calculate the number of days remaining until Christmas. One way is to break the problem up into two separate calculations. The first calculation will determine the number of days from the current date to the 25th day of the current month. The second calculation will determine the number of days from the 25th day of the current month to December 25th. The advantage to this approach is that the first calculation is simple, and the second calculation involves known values. For example, if the current date is November 11th, there are 14 days until November 25th. November has 30 days, which means that there are 30 days between November 25th and December 25th. Therefore, the number of days between November 11th and December 25th is 44 (14 + 30).

This method also works if the current date is past the 25th of the month. Suppose that the current date is November 28th; then the number of days until Christmas is (-3) + 30, or 27 days.

If the current date is earlier in the year, such as October 15th, you have to add the number of days in October and November to the total. October has 31 days, and November has 30 days. This means that the number of days between October 15th and December 25th is:

```
(25 — 15) + 31 + 30 = 10 + 61 = 71 days
```

Your simple version of the XmasDays function will handle only dates in October. The code for this reduced function is as follows:

```
function XmasDays(Month, Day, Year) {

  var DayCount=(25 — Day) + 31 + 30;

  return DayCount;

}
```

Notice that the parameters for this function include a Month parameter (corresponding to the month number of the current date), a Day parameter (the day of the month), and a Year parameter containing the current year. Although this version of the function uses only the Day parameter in its calculation, eventually you'll be using the Month and Year parameters as well. The number of days remaining until Christmas is calculated and stored in a variable named DayCount. The value of that variable is then returned by the function.

Now that you know the form of the simple XmasDays function, you'll insert it into the NPN.htm file. Following standard practice, you'll place the code for this function between the <HEAD> and </HEAD> tags.

To insert the XmasDays function into the NPN.htm file:

1. Return to your text editor and the NPN.htm file.

2. Below the <TITLE> tag at the beginning of the HTML file, insert the following lines:

```
<SCRIPT LANGUAGE="JavaScript">
<!--- Hide from non-JavaScript browsers
//This function calculates the number of days until Christmas
function XmasDays(Month, Day, Year) {
    var DayCount=(25 − Day) + 31 + 30;
    return DayCount;
}
// Stop hiding -->
</SCRIPT>
```

Figure 7-16 shows the revised HEAD section of the NPN.htm file.

Figure 7-16 ◀
The simple
XmasDays
function (for
days in October)

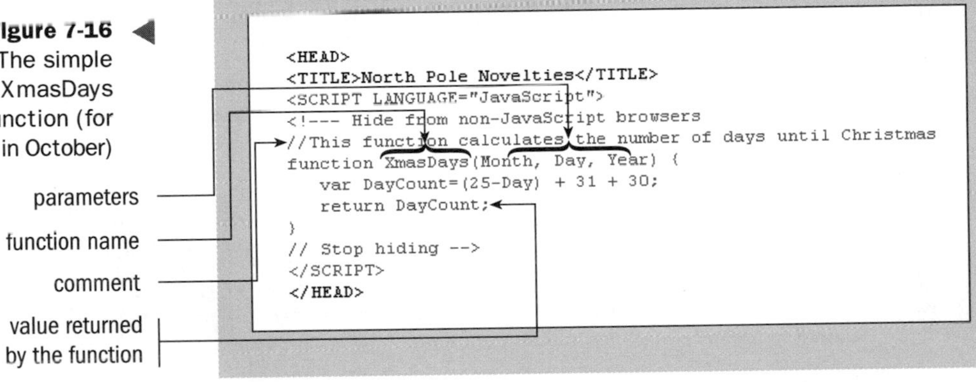

parameters

function name

comment

value returned
by the function

```
<HEAD>
<TITLE>North Pole Novelties</TITLE>
<SCRIPT LANGUAGE="JavaScript">
<!--- Hide from non-JavaScript browsers
//This function calculates the number of days until Christmas
function XmasDays(Month, Day, Year) {
    var DayCount=(25-Day) + 31 + 30;
    return DayCount;
}
// Stop hiding -->
</SCRIPT>
</HEAD>
```

Having created the first version of the XmasDays function, you next have to insert a command into the NPN.htm file to call the function. Recall that you previously created a variable named DaysLeft, which you set to the value 999 (a test value). Now you'll set the value of DaysLeft to whatever is returned by the XmasDays function. To do this you'll send the values of ThisDay (the day of the month), ThisMonth (the month of the year), and ThisYear (the year value) to the XmasDays function.

To call the XmasDays function:

1. Scroll down the NPN.htm file to the line "var DaysLeft = 999;" and replace this line with:

   var DaysLeft = XmasDays(ThisMonth, ThisDay, ThisYear);

Figure 7-17 shows the revised code. Note that the date used in this example is October 15th, which will work with your function, since it is designed only for dates in October at this point.

Figure 7-17 ◀
Calling the
simple
XmasDays
function

date used by
the function

statement that calls
the XmasDays
function

values sent to
the function

```
<SCRIPT LANGUAGE="JavaScript">
<!--- Hide from non-JavaScript browsers
//Get date information
var Today = new Date("October, 15, 1999");
var ThisDay = Today.getDate();
var ThisMonth = Today.getMonth()+1;
var ThisYear = Today.getYear();
document.write("Today is "+ThisMonth+"/"+ThisDay+"/"+ThisYear+"<BR>");
//Get number of days until Christmas
var DaysLeft = XmasDays(ThisMonth, ThisDay, ThisYear);
document.write("Only " + DaysLeft + " days until Christmas");
// Stop hiding -->
</SCRIPT>
```

2. Save your changes to the file, and then reload the file in your Web browser. As shown in Figure 7-18, the Web page now displays the date specified by the Today variable (10/15/99) and has correctly calculated that there are 71 days left until Christmas.

Figure 7-18 ◀
North Pole
Novelties page
showing the
results of the
XmasDays
function

result of the
XmasDays function

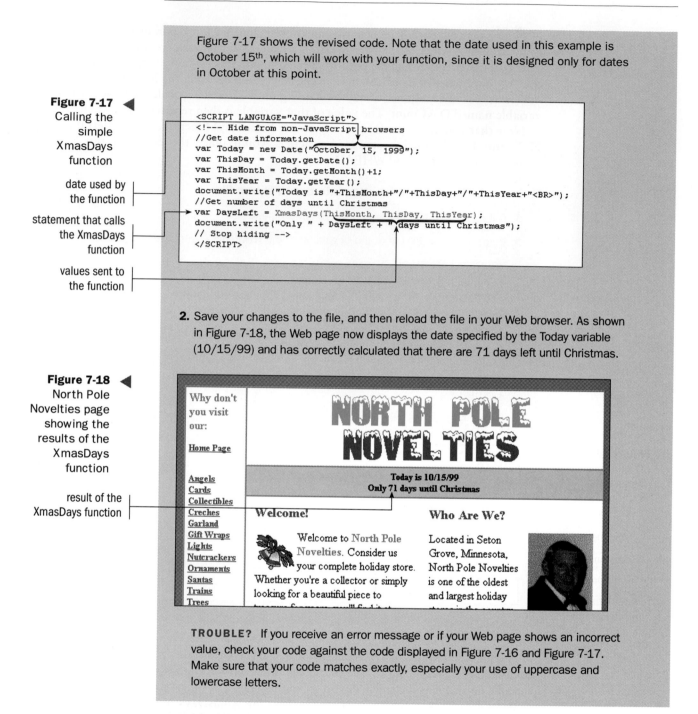

TROUBLE? If you receive an error message or if your Web page shows an incorrect value, check your code against the code displayed in Figure 7-16 and Figure 7-17. Make sure that your code matches exactly, especially your use of uppercase and lowercase letters.

You've seen how the XmasDays function works for the October 15th date. Andrew asks you to change the date to October 18th to verify that the function correctly updates the DaysLeft value.

To change the test date to October 18th:

1. Return to your text editor and change the date on the line "var Today = new Date("October, 15, 1999");" to:

   "October, 18, 1999"

2. Save your changes to the file, and then reload the file in your Web browser. Confirm that the number of days left has been changed to 68 days to reflect the new date.

Quick Check

1. What are the four data types supported by JavaScript?

2. What command would you enter to insert information about the current date into a variable named "Now"?

3. What command would you enter to extract and store the current day of the month from the Now variable in a variable called Tdate?

4. What issue should you be aware of when extracting the month value from the Now variable?

5. Define the following terms:

   Expression

   Operator

   Binary operator

   Unary operator

6. Give two commands you could use to take the variable x, increase its value by 1, and store the result in a variable named y.

7. What is the difference between the = operator and the == operator?

8. Provide the general syntax of a JavaScript function.

You've created the simple version of the XmasDays function, which was the first of your two tasks for calculating the days remaining until Christmas.

☐ 3) Calculate the difference between the test date and December 25th.

☑ a) Create a function for a few specific dates in the year.

☐ b) Create a function that works for any day of the year.

In the next session, you will finish the function, enabling it to work with any day of the year.

SESSION

7.3

In this session you will complete the XmasDays function. To do this you'll learn how to create and use arrays, and work with program loops to create groups of commands that are executed repeatedly. You'll also learn how to add decision-making capabilities to your JavaScript program through the use of conditional statements.

Creating Arrays

In your first version of the XmasDays function, you were limited to working with a single month, October. However, Andrew wants the XmasDays function to work for any month so that customers can see the number of days left until Christmas whenever they view the North Pole Novelties home page. For this to happen, you need a variable that can store multiple values. This variable will need to store the number of days in each of the 12 months of the year. This type of variable is called an array.

CREATING AND POPULATING AN ARRAY

- To create an array variable, use the command:
  var *variable* = new Array();
  where *variable* is the name of the array variable.
- To populate the array with values, use the command:
  variable[*i*]=*value*;
  where *variable* is the name of the array variable, *i* is the *i*th
  element of the array, and *value* is the value of the *i*th element.

An **array** is an ordered collection of values referenced by a single variable name. For example, you might have an array named "Weekday" that contains a list of the days of the week. The array could look like the following:

```
Weekday[1]="Monday"

Weekday[2]="Tuesday"

Weekday[3]="Wednesday"

Weekday[4]="Thursday"

Weekday[5]="Friday"

Weekday[6]="Saturday"

Weekday[7]="Sunday"
```

This array displays seven items, or elements. Each element is identified by its **index**, which is the number that appears between the brackets. For example, the element "Friday" has an index value of 5 in the Weekday array. The first element in any array is the zero index. In the Weekday array, there are actually eight total elements. The first element, Weekday[0], not shown, has the null value.

The syntax for creating an array variable is:

```
var variable = new Array(size);
```

where *variable* is the name of the array variable, and *size* is the number of elements in the array. Specifying a size for your array is optional. If you don't specify a size, JavaScript will dynamically increase the size of the array as you add more elements. The following JavaScript code shows how you would create an array named Month, and then populate one of the array elements with a value:

```
var Month = new Array();

Month[12]="December";
```

In this example, the size of the Month array is not initially specified, but JavaScript automatically increases the size of the array when it encounters the command to create the Month[12] element. At this point in the program, the Month array has 13 elements, ranging from Month[0] to Month [12] (recall that all arrays start with the zero index), but all except the Month[12] element have null values.

An array is a powerful programming tool that allows you to handle large lists of data with a single variable name. You can also use variables to represent index values. Consider the following code, in which the variable IndexNumber is used to display a single element from the Weekday array:

```
var Weekday = new Array();

Weekday[1]="Monday";

Weekday[2]="Tuesday";

Weekday[3]="Wednesday";

Weekday[4]="Thursday";

Weekday[5]="Friday";

Weekday[6]="Saturday";

Weekday[7]="Sunday";

var IndexNumber = 3;

document.write("Today is " + Weekday[IndexNumber]);
```

Because the variable IndexNumber has been assigned the value 3, and Weekday[3] = "Wednesday", the text *Today is Wednesday* is sent to the Web page.

Next, you'll add an array named "MonthCount" to the XmasDays function you created in the previous session. The array will store the number of days in each month of the year, except for December. Then you'll use values from the array in the XmasDays function to calculate the days remaining until Christmas.

To insert the MonthCount array into the XmasDays function:

1. If you took a break after the previous session, start your text editor and reopen the NPN.htm file from the Tutorial.07 folder of your Student Disk.

2. Below the function statement "function XmasDays(Month, Day, Year) {," insert the following lines (indented to make your program easier to read):

```
var MonthCount = new Array();
MonthCount[1]=31;
MonthCount[2]=28;
MonthCount[3]=31;
MonthCount[4]=30;
MonthCount[5]=31;
MonthCount[6]=30;
MonthCount[7]=31;
MonthCount[8]=31;
MonthCount[9]=30;
MonthCount[10]=31;
MonthCount[11]=30;
```

In the previous session, you explicitly entered the number of days in the months of October and November, so that the function could calculate the number of days left until Christmas from any date in October. Now you'll change the function so that it retrieves that same information from the MonthCount array.

3. Change the line "var DayCount=(25−Day) + 31 + 30;" to

```
var DayCount = (25 – Day) + MonthCount[10] + MonthCount[11];
```

Remember that MonthCount[10] is the number of days in October, and MonthCount[11] is the number of days in November. Figure 7-19 shows the current form of the XmasDays function.

Figure 7-19 ◀
Adding an array to the XmasDays function

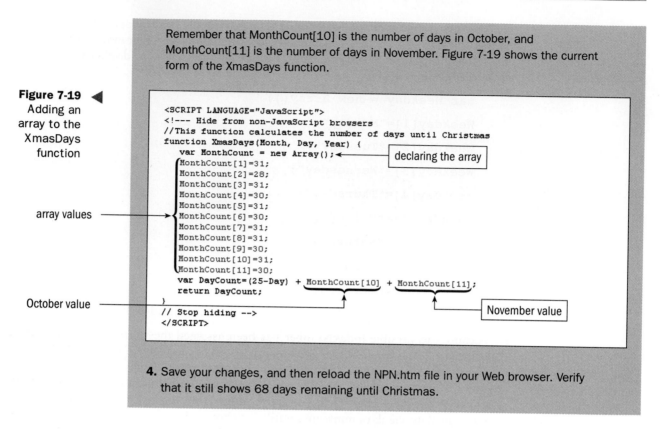

array values

October value

```
<SCRIPT LANGUAGE="JavaScript">
<!--- Hide from non-JavaScript browsers
//This function calculates the number of days until Christmas
function XmasDays(Month, Day, Year) {
   var MonthCount = new Array();        declaring the array
   MonthCount[1]=31;
   MonthCount[2]=28;
   MonthCount[3]=31;
   MonthCount[4]=30;
   MonthCount[5]=31;
   MonthCount[6]=30;
   MonthCount[7]=31;
   MonthCount[8]=31;
   MonthCount[9]=30;
   MonthCount[10]=31;
   MonthCount[11]=30;
   var DayCount=(25-Day) + MonthCount[10] + MonthCount[11];
   return DayCount;
}
// Stop hiding -->                      November value
</SCRIPT>
```

4. Save your changes, and then reload the NPN.htm file in your Web browser. Verify that it still shows 68 days remaining until Christmas.

Having created and tested an array for your function, your next step is to use that array to calculate XmasDays for any date in the year. To do this you'll have to work with program loops.

Working with Loops

Up to now each line of code in your JavaScript program has been run just once. However, programming often involves creating code that does not run just once, but is repeated an indeterminate number of times.

Consider the current state of the XmasDays function. As long as you limit the problem to working with October dates only, the solution is fairly simple: calculate the number of days until the 25th of the month, and then add the number of days in October and November. The problem arises when you don't limit the program to that single month. In this situation, the program must have the ability to continually add the number of days in each month from the current month until December.

To provide the program with this capability, you must use a program loop. A **loop** is a set of instructions that is executed repeatedly. There are two types of loops: loops that repeat a set number of times before quitting, and loops that repeat until a certain condition is met. You create the first type of loop using a For statement.

> **REFERENCE window**
>
> ## CREATING PROGRAM LOOPS
>
> - To create a For loop, use the following syntax:
>   ```
>   for(start; stop; update) {
>           JavaScript Commands
>   }
>   ```
>   where *start* is an expression defining the starting value of the For loop's counter, *stop* is an expression defining the condition under which the loop ends, and *update* is an expression defining how the counter changes as the For loop progresses.
> - To create a While loop, use the following syntax:
>   ```
>   while(condition) {
>           JavaScript Commands
>   }
>   ```
>   where *condition* is an expression that halts the While loop when its value is "false."

The For Loop

The **For loop** allows you to create a group of commands that will be executed a set number of times through the use of a **counter**, which tracks the number of times the command block has been run. You set an initial value for the counter, and each time the command block is executed, the counter changes in value. When the counter reaches a specified value, the loop ends. The general syntax of the For loop is:

```
for(start; stop; update) {

    JavaScript Commands

}
```

where *start* is the starting value of the counter, *stop* is the ending value of the counter or the condition under which the loop quits, and *update* specifies how the counter changes in value each time the command block is executed. Like a function, the command block in the For loop is set off by curly braces { }. The following is an example of a For loop that displays several lines of text:

```
for(Num=1; Num<4; Num++) {

    document.write("The value of Num is " + Num + "<BR>");

}
```

The counter in this example is the variable Num, which starts with an initial value of 1 and is increased by 1 each time the command group is run. When the value of Num reaches 4, the condition for running the loop is no longer met, and the loop stops. Note that the update expression used in this For loop is Num++. As you learned earlier in the discussion of arithmetic operators, this is an example of an increment operator, which increases the value of a variable by 1. When this For loop is run, the following lines will be generated on the Web page:

```
The value of Num is 1

The value of Num is 2

The value of Num is 3
```

The For loop is not limited to incrementing the value of the counter by 1. You can specify one of several different counting methods. Here are some other possible For loops:

```
for(i=10; i>0; i--)

for(i=0; i<=360; i+=15)

for(i=2; i<64; i*=2)
```

In the first example, the counter i starts with the value 10 and is decreased by 1 as long as it remains greater than 0. This update expression uses the decrement operator to decrease the value of the counter. In the second example, the counter starts at 0 and increases in value as long as it's less than or equal to 360. Note that the update expression for this example uses an assignment operator, which is equivalent to the expression i = i + 15, and so has the effect of increasing the value of the i counter by 15 each time the command block is run. In the third example, the counter starts with a value of 2 and is doubled in value as long it remains less than 64. Once again, an assignment operator, i*=2, which is equivalent to i = i*2, accomplishes the task of incrementing the counter.

The While Loop

Similar to the For loop is the **While loop**, which runs a command group as long as a specific condition is met. The general syntax of the While loop is:

```
while(condition) {

    JavaScript Commands

}
```

where *condition* is an expression using logical or comparison operators that can be either true or false. As long as the condition is true, the group of statements will be executed by JavaScript. The following is an example of a While loop:

```
var Num=1;

while(Num<4) {

    document.write("The value of Num is " + Num);

    Num++;

}
```

Note that this While loop produces the same results as the sample For loop discussed earlier. The Num variable starts with a value of 1 and is increased by 1 each time the command group is run. The loop ends once the condition that Num should be less than 4 is no longer true. For loops and While loops are similar. You would use a While loop instead of a For loop in situations where there is no counter variable, and you want more flexibility in halting the program loop.

Using a Loop in the XmasDays Function

With an understanding of program loops, you are ready to modify the XmasDays function so that it works for any day of the year. The following is the function you'll use to calculate the number of days until Christmas:

```
function XmasDays(Month, Day, Year) {
   var MonthCount = new Array();
   MonthCount[1]=31;
   MonthCount[2]=28;
   MonthCount[3]=31;
   MonthCount[4]=30;
   MonthCount[5]=31;
   MonthCount[6]=30;
   MonthCount[7]=31;
   MonthCount[8]=31;
   MonthCount[9]=30;
   MonthCount[10]=31;
   MonthCount[11]=30;
   var MonthTotal=0;
   for(i=Month;i<12;i++) {
        MonthTotal = MonthTotal+MonthCount[i];
   }
   var DayCount = (25 - Day) + MonthTotal;
   return DayCount;
}
```

Before entering this code into the NPN.htm file, you should pause to consider how it works. One of the key features of this function is the introduction of a new variable, MonthTotal. MonthTotal is equal to the number of days between the current month and December. The initial value of MonthTotal is set to 0. The final value of MonthTotal is determined by adding up the number of days in each month in the following For loop:

```
for(i=Month;i<12;i++) {
     MonthTotal = MonthTotal+MonthCount[i];
}
```

The counter in the For loop starts with the value of the current month and increments that value by 1 until it reaches a value of 12 (for December), at which point the loop stops. The command block inside the For loop takes the value of MonthTotal and increases it by the value of MonthCount[i]—the number of days in the ith month of the year.

Figure 7-20 illustrates how this For loop will work.

Figure 7-20 ◀
Running the For
loop for the
XmasDays
function

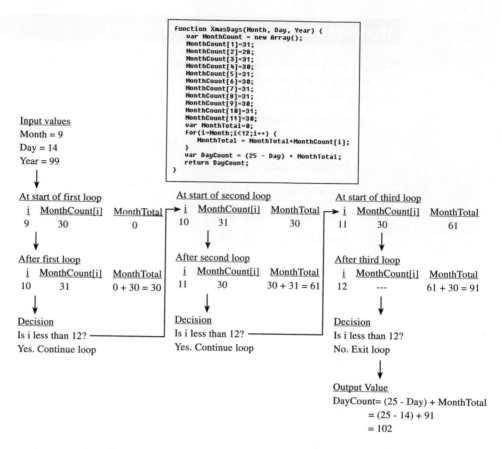

```
function XmasDays(Month, Day, Year) {
    var MonthCount = new Array();
    MonthCount[1]=31;
    MonthCount[2]=28;
    MonthCount[3]=31;
    MonthCount[4]=30;
    MonthCount[5]=31;
    MonthCount[6]=30;
    MonthCount[7]=31;
    MonthCount[8]=31;
    MonthCount[9]=30;
    MonthCount[10]=31;
    MonthCount[11]=30;
    var MonthTotal=0;
    for(i=Month;i<12;i++) {
        MonthTotal = MonthTotal+MonthCount[i];
    }
    var DayCount = (25 - Day) + MonthTotal;
    return DayCount;
}
```

Input values
Month = 9
Day = 14
Year = 99

At start of first loop

i	MonthCount[i]	MonthTotal
9	30	0

After first loop

i	MonthCount[i]	MonthTotal
10	31	0 + 30 = 30

Decision
Is i less than 12?
Yes. Continue loop

At start of second loop

i	MonthCount[i]	MonthTotal
10	31	30

After second loop

i	MonthCount[i]	MonthTotal
11	30	30 + 31 = 61

Decision
Is i less than 12?
Yes. Continue loop

At start of third loop

i	MonthCount[i]	MonthTotal
11	30	61

After third loop

i	MonthCount[i]	MonthTotal
12	---	61 + 30 = 91

Decision
Is i less than 12?
No. Exit loop

Output Value
DayCount= (25 - Day) + MonthTotal
= (25 - 14) + 91
= 102

Suppose that the current date is 9/14/99 (as shown in the figure). You want MonthTotal to be equal to the number of days in September, October, and November. As the For loop starts, MonthTotal equals 0, and the value of the Month variable is 9. The For loop's counter, therefore, starts with a value of 9 and will run the commands in the command block until the counter's value reaches 12. The first time through the loop, the following expression is run:

```
MonthTotal = MonthTotal+MonthCount[9];
```

Because MonthCount[9] equals 30, this is equivalent to:

```
MonthTotal = MonthTotal+30;
```

So, the value of MonthTotal is increased to 30 to account for the 30 days in September. The counter is then increased by 1 to a value of 10. This is less than 12, which meets the condition for the loop to continue, so the For loop runs the command block again. The next time through the loop, the expression is:

```
MonthTotal = MonthTotal+MonthCount[10];
```

Because MonthTotal = 30 and MonthCount[10] = 31, the value of MonthTotal is increased to 30 + 31, or 61, accounting for the number of days in both September and October. The counter increases in value to 11, which is still less than 12. The For loop runs the command block again, generating the following expression:

```
MonthTotal = MonthTotal+MonthCount[11];
```

MonthTotal = 61 and MonthCount[11] = 30. The new value of MonthTotal is increased to 61 + 30, or 91, which accounts for the number of days in September, October, and November. The counter is increased in value to 12, which causes the For loop to stop, because the condition that the counter be less than 12 is no longer met. The final MonthTotal value, therefore, is 91—there are 91 days between September 1st and December 1st.

Once out of the loop, JavaScript goes to the next expression and subtracts the current day of the month from 25, and then adds the result to the value of MonthTotal. In the case of September 14th, that expression is equal to $(25 - 14) + 91$, or 102. There are 102 days between September 14th and December 25th.

Refer to Figure 7-20 and study the For loop in the expression until you understand how it works. Once the method is clear to you, you're ready to add the loop to the XmasDays function. To verify that this new version of the XmasDays function works, you'll also change the test date to September 14th, 1999. As you've already seen, the function should calculate that there are 102 days between September 14th and December 25th.

To add the For loop to the XmasDays function:

1. Return to the NPN.htm file in your text editor.

2. Below the line: "MonthCount[11]=30;" insert the following lines:

   var MonthTotal=0;
   for(i=Month;i<12;i++) {
       MonthTotal = MonthTotal+MonthCount[i];
   }

3. Change the line "var DayCount = (25 – Day) + MonthCount[10] + MonthCount[11];" to:

   var DayCount = (25 – Day) + MonthTotal;

   The revised function is shown in Figure 7-21.

Figure 7-21 ◀
Adding a For
loop to the
XmasDays
function

ending condition ─────

starting value ─────

```
function XmasDays(Month, Day, Year) {
    var MonthCount = new Array();
    MonthCount[1]=31;
    MonthCount[2]=28;
    MonthCount[3]=31;
    MonthCount[4]=30;
    MonthCount[5]=31;
    MonthCount[6]=30;
    MonthCount[7]=31;
    MonthCount[8]=31;
    MonthCount[9]=30;
    MonthCount[10]=31;
    MonthCount[11]=30;
    var MonthTotal=0;            increment
    for(i=Month;i<12;i++) {
        MonthTotal = MonthTotal+MonthCount[i];    For loop
    }
    var DayCount=(25-Day) + MonthTotal;
    return DayCount;
}
```

4. Scroll down and change the date of the Today variable to **"September, 14, 1999"**.

5. Save your changes, and then reopen the file in your Web browser. The page should now show the correct day count, 102 days.

   TROUBLE? If you receive an error message, check the case of all your variables. They must always match in uppercase and lowercase. You cannot use the variable name "Month" in one part of your program and the variable name "month" in another.

You've completed the third major task on your list—calculating the difference between the test date and December 25th for any day of the year.

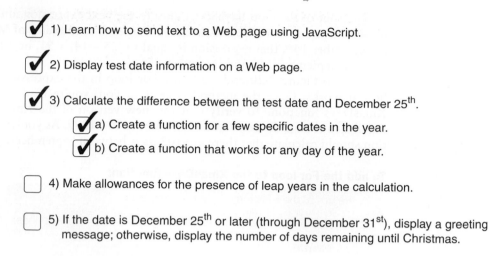

☑ 1) Learn how to send text to a Web page using JavaScript.

☑ 2) Display test date information on a Web page.

☑ 3) Calculate the difference between the test date and December 25th.

    ☑ a) Create a function for a few specific dates in the year.

    ☑ b) Create a function that works for any day of the year.

☐ 4) Make allowances for the presence of leap years in the calculation.

☐ 5) If the date is December 25th or later (through December 31st), display a greeting message; otherwise, display the number of days remaining until Christmas.

Your next task is to make the XmasDays function work for any year, which will involve making adjustments for leap years. To do this you have to create conditional statements.

Working with Conditional Statements

A **conditional statement** is one that runs only if certain conditions are met. You've seen this at work already with While loops in which a command block is run only under certain conditions. Another type of conditional statement is the If statement. Unlike a program loop, the If statement is a one-shot deal. If a certain condition is met, a command block is run; otherwise, the command block is not run.

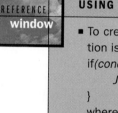

REFERENCE window	**USING CONDITIONAL STATEMENTS**

	▪ To create a command block that runs only if a certain condition is met, use the following syntax:
	if(*condition*) {
	    JavaScript Commands
	}
	where *condition* is an expression that is either true or false. If *condition* is true, the command block is run.
	▪ To choose between two command blocks, use the following syntax:
	if(*condition*) {
	    JavaScript Commands if true
	} else {
	    JavaScript Commands if false
	}
	where *condition* is an expression that is either true or false. The first command block is run if the expression is true; the second command block is run if the expression is false.

Using the If Statement

The If statement has the following general syntax:

```
if(condition){

    JavaScript Commands

}
```

where *condition* is an expression that is either true or false. The following is an example of an If statement that controls what text is sent to the Web page:

```
if(Day=="Friday"){

    document.write("Have a nice weekend!");

}
```

In this example, the value of the Day variable is tested. If the Day variable contains the text "Friday," then the text "Have a nice weekend!" is sent to the Web page. Note that the test is performed using the == operator, and not the = operator. The = operator is used only for assigning values, not for testing values.

You can create a similar If statement to handle the occurrence of leap years in the XmasDays function. Leap years occur in years that are evenly divisible by 4. One exception to this rule is a century year (1800, 1900, 2000, and so on), which must be divisible by 400 in order to be a leap year. However, as you saw earlier in Figure 7-8, JavaScript's handling of years is inconsistent beyond the year 1999. Given this problem, you'll ignore the exception to the rule and simply assume that all years divisible by 4 are leap years. This will cause problems in the year 2100, but the getYear method should be fixed before then.

You can determine whether a value is evenly divisible by 4 using the modulus operator (%). The **modulus operator** calculates the remainder after dividing one number by another. Consider the following expression:

```
Remainder = 25 % 8;
```

This expression assigns a value of 1 to the Remainder variable, because 8 divides into 25 three times with a remainder of 1. For leap years you need a remainder of 0 after dividing by 4, so the following expression must be true for the year to be considered a leap year:

```
Year % 4 == 0
```

If a year is a leap year, the number of days in February must be increased to 29. Putting together what you learned about the If statement with what you learned about the modulus operator, here is the conditional statement you need to add to the XmasDays function:

```
if(Year % 4 == 0){

MonthCount[2]=29;

}
```

The first expression determines whether the value of the Year variable is divisible by 4 and is, therefore, a leap year. If so, then the expression "MonthCount[2]=29;" is run. If not, the value of MonthCount[2] remains at 28. You'll add this statement to your XmasDays function now. Then you'll test to see whether the function works as expected by changing the date to February 14th in a non-leap year, and then changing the date to the same day in a leap year.

To insert the If statement into the XmasDays function and then test the function:

1. Return to the NPN.htm file in your text editor.

2. Below the line: "MonthCount[11]=30;" insert the following lines (indented to make your code easier to follow):

   if(Year % 4 == 0){
       MonthCount[2]=29;
   }

   Your revised function should appear as shown in Figure 7-22.

Figure 7-22 ◀
Increasing the number of days in February for leap years

if condition ⟶

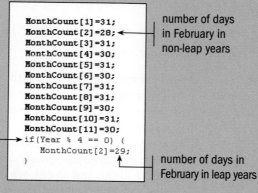

```
MonthCount[1]=31;
MonthCount[2]=28;      ◀──  number of days
MonthCount[3]=31;           in February in
MonthCount[4]=30;           non-leap years
MonthCount[5]=31;
MonthCount[6]=30;
MonthCount[7]=31;
MonthCount[8]=31;
MonthCount[9]=30;
MonthCount[10]=31;
MonthCount[11]=30;
if(Year % 4 == 0) {
    MonthCount[2]=29;
}                     ◀──  number of days in
                           February in leap years
```

3. Scroll down and change the date of the Today variable to **"February, 14, 1999"**.

4. Save your changes, and then reopen the file in your Web browser. The page should now show that there are 314 days until Christmas.

   Next you'll change the date in the Today variable to a leap year date.

5. Return to your text editor and change the date of the Today variable to **"February, 14, 1996"**.

6. Save your changes, and then reopen the file in your Web browser. Now the page should indicate that there are 315 days until Christmas. The program correctly calculated the number of days until Christmas by including the 29th day in February.

You've accounted for the existence of leap years in the XmasDays function. You now have only one task remaining on your list.

☑ 1) Learn how to send text to a Web page using JavaScript.

☑ 2) Display test date information on a Web page.

☑ 3) Calculate the difference between the test date and December 25th.

    ☑ a) Create a function for a few specific dates in the year.

    ☑ b) Create a function that works for any day of the year.

☑ 4) Make allowances for the presence of leap years in the calculation.

☐ 5) If the date is December 25th or later (through December 31st), display a greeting message; otherwise, display the number of days remaining until Christmas.

The final task is to change the message displayed on the Web page, based on the current date. Andrew wants one message displayed before Christmas and another message displayed directly after Christmas, through December 31st. You can accomplish this using a variation of the If statement called the If...Else statement.

Using the If ... Else Statement

The If statement you just entered runs a set of commands if the condition is true, but does nothing if the condition is false. Sometimes you want the If statement to run one set of commands if the condition is true and another set of commands if the condition is false. An **If ... Else** statement allows you to do this. The syntax for this statement is:

```
if(condition){

    JavaScript Commands if true

} else {

    JavaScript Commands if false

}
```

where *condition* is an expression that is either true or false, and one set of commands is run if the expression is true, and another is run if the expression is false. The following is an example of an If ... Else statement:

```
if(Day=="Friday"){

    document.write("Have a nice weekend!");

} else {

    document.write("Good morning").;

}
```

In this example the text "Have a nice weekend!" is generated if Day equals "Friday"; otherwise, the text "Good morning" is displayed.

If ... Else structures can also be nested, one within another. Here is an example of a nested structure:

```
if(Day=="Friday"){

  document.write("Have a nice weekend!");

} else {

  if(Day=="Monday") {

      document.write("Welcome back");

  } else {

      document.write("Good morning");

  }

}
```

In this example, the text "Have a nice weekend!" is displayed if the day is Friday. If the day is Monday, the text "Welcome back" is displayed. On other days the text "Good morning" is generated.

You have a similar situation in the North Pole Novelties home page. If the current date is December 25th or later (through December 31st), Andrew wants the page to display a holiday greeting; otherwise it should display the number of days until Christmas as calculated by the XmasDays function.

You can distinguish between the two situations by creating an If...Else statement that looks at the value returned by the XmasDays function. If that value is positive, then the current date is before December 25th, and the page should display the number of days left in the holiday season. On the other hand, if the value is 0 or negative, then the current date is December 25th or later in the year, and a holiday message should be generated. The code to perform this is as follows:

```
if(DaysLeft > 0) {

   document.write("Only " + DaysLeft + "  days until Christmas";

} else {

document.write("Happy Holidays from North Pole Novelties");

}
```

You need to insert these statements into the NPN.htm file, replacing the previous document.write() method you used to display the number of days until Christmas.

To insert the If...Else statement into the NPN.htm file:

1. Return to your text editor and the NPN.htm file.

2. Replace the line "document.write("Only " + DaysLeft + " days until Christmas");" with:

   //Display either the number of days until Christmas, or a holiday greeting
   if(DaysLeft > 0) {
   **   document.write("Only " + DaysLeft + " days until Christmas");**
   } else {
   document.write("Happy Holidays from North Pole Novelties");
   }

   Indent the various lines of your program to make it easier to read. The revised code should appear as shown in Figure 7-23.

Figure 7-23 ◀
Using an
If...Else
conditional
statement

expression if the
condition is true

expression if the
condition is false

```
<SCRIPT LANGUAGE="JavaScript">
<!--- Hide from non-JavaScript browsers
//Get date information
var Today = new Date("February, 14, 1996");
var ThisDay = Today.getDate();
var ThisMonth = Today.getMonth()+1;
var ThisYear = Today.getYear();
document.write("Today is "+ThisMonth+"/"+ThisDay+"/"+ThisYear+"<BR>");
//Get number of days until Christmas
var DaysLeft = XmasDays(ThisMonth, ThisDay, ThisYear);
//Display either the number of days until Christmas, or a holiday greeting
if(DaysLeft > 0) {
   document.write("Only " + DaysLeft + " days until Christmas");
} else {
   document.write("Happy Holidays from North Pole Novelties");
}
// Stop hiding -->
</SCRIPT>
```

3. Save your changes and then reopen NPN.htm in your Web browser. The page should still display the text "Only 315 days until Christmas" because the date specified in the Today variable is February 14, 1996.

4. Return to your text editor and the NPN.htm file.

5. Change the date of the Today variable to **"December, 28, 1999"**.

6. Save your changes, and then reload the file in your Web browser. As shown in Figure 7-24, the page should now display the Happy Holidays greeting.

Figure 7-24 ◀
North Pole
Novelties home
page with
special holiday
greeting

By successfully entering the If...Else statement, you've completed all of the tasks on your list.

☑ 1) Learn how to send text to a Web page using JavaScript.

☑ 2) Display test date information on a Web page.

☑ 3) Calculate the difference between the test date and December 25th.

    ☑ a) Create a function for a few specific dates in the year.

    ☑ b) Create a function that works for any day of the year.

☑ 4) Make allowances for the presence of leap years in the calculation.

☑ 5) If the date is December 25th or later (through December 31st), display a greeting message; otherwise, display the number of days remaining until Christmas.

Before showing the Web page to Andrew for his final approval, you need to remove the test date and allow the page to use the current date (whatever that might be). Recall that if you don't specify a date value, the current date and time are automatically used. You'll make this change to the NPN.htm file now.

To use the current date in the North Pole Novelties Web page:

1. Return to your text editor.

2. Change the line "var Today = new Date("December, 28, 1999");" to:

    var Today = new Date();

3. Save your changes to the file and close your text editor.

4. Open the file in your Web browser and verify that the correct date and days until Christmas are shown.

    You've completed your work with the JavaScript program.

5. Close your Web browser.

The complete code for the XmasDays function is shown in Figure 7-25, and the script to display the results is shown in Figure 7-26.

Figure 7-25 ◄
The complete
XmasDays
function

```
<SCRIPT LANGUAGE="JavaScript">
<!--- Hide from non-JavaScript browsers
//This function calculates the number of days until Christmas
function XmasDays(Month, Day, Year) {
    var MonthCount = new Array();
    MonthCount[1]=31;
    MonthCount[2]=28;
    MonthCount[3]=31;
    MonthCount[4]=30;
    MonthCount[5]=31;
    MonthCount[6]=30;
    MonthCount[7]=31;
    MonthCount[8]=31;
    MonthCount[9]=30;
    MonthCount[10]=31;
    MonthCount[11]=30;
    if(Year % 4 == 0) {
        MonthCount[2]=29;
    }
    var MonthTotal=0;
    for(i=Month;i<12;i++) {
        MonthTotal = MonthTotal+MonthCount[i];
    }
    var DayCount=(25-Day) + MonthTotal;
    return DayCount;
}
// Stop hiding -->
</SCRIPT>
```

Figure 7-26 ◄
The complete
script to display
the results

```
<SCRIPT LANGUAGE="JavaScript">
<!--- Hide from non-JavaScript browsers
//Get date information
var Today = new Date("December, 28, 1999");
var ThisDay = Today.getDate();
var ThisMonth = Today.getMonth()+1;
var ThisYear = Today.getYear();
document.write("Today is "+ThisMonth+"/"+ThisDay+"/"+ThisYear+"<BR>");
//Get number of days until Christmas
var DaysLeft = XmasDays(ThisMonth, ThisDay, ThisYear);
//Display either the number of days until Christmas, or a holiday greeting
if(DaysLeft > 0) {
    document.write("Only " + DaysLeft + " days until Christmas");
} else {
    document.write("Happy Holidays from North Pole Novelties");
}
// Stop hiding -->
</SCRIPT>
```

Quick Check

1. What is an array? What command would you enter to create an array named Colors?

2. The Colors array should contain five values: Red, Green, Blue, Black, and White. What commands would you enter to insert these values into the array? How many elements are in this array?

3. What is a program loop? Name the two types of program loops supported by JavaScript.

4. What code would you enter to run the command "document.write("News Flash!
");" five times?

5. What values will the counter variable "i" take in the following For loop?

```
for(i=5; i<=25; i+=5)
```

6. What commands would you enter to send the text "Welcome back to school!" to the Web page if the value of the Month variable is September?

7. What commands would you use to display the text "Welcome back to school!" on the Web page if the Month variable equals September, and to display the text "Today's headlines" otherwise?

8. What commands would you enter to display the text "Welcome back to school!" if the Month variable equals September; "Summer's here!" if the Month variable equals June; and "Today's headlines" otherwise?

Andrew has received the final version of your page and the JavaScript programs you wrote. He has viewed the page on his Web browser and is happy that it works so well. He'll review the page with his colleagues and get back to you with any modifications they suggest.

Tutorial Assignments

Andrew has worked with your Web page and shown it to other employees at North Pole Novelties. They would like you to make the following two changes to the page:

- Change the message for December 24th so that it reads "Last day for Christmas shopping." Keep the other messages the same.

- Change the appearance of the date so that it displays the name of the month and day, but not the year. In other words, instead of displaying "Today is 9/14/99," the page should display "Today is September 9."

To make these changes:

1. Start your text editor and open the NPNtext2.htm file in the TAssign folder of the Tutorial.07 folder on your Student Disk, and then save the file as NPN2.htm in the same folder.

2. After the XmasDays function (but before the "// Stop hiding -->" comment within the <SCRIPT> tags), create a new function named MonthText. The function will have one parameter named Month.

3. Within the MonthText function, create an array named MonthNames. Populate the elements of the MonthNames array with the names of each month; that is, MonthNames[1]="January" and so on.

4. Use the value of the Month parameter as the index and have the MonthText function return the value of MonthNames[Month].

5. Go to the section in the NPN2.htm file that displays the current date and holiday message. Revise the document.write() method that displays the date so that it displays the name of the current month, using the MonthText function, along with the day of the month.

6. Revise the document.write() method that displays either the day count or a holiday greeting so that it displays a different message on the day before Christmas. Do this by replacing the first condition of the current If ... Else statement (which tests whether the current date is before December 25th) with a nested If...Else statement that tests the following two conditions:

- If DayCount equals 1, the text "Last day for Christmas shopping" is displayed. (*Hint:* Be sure to use == and not = as your comparison operator.)
- If DayCount is greater than 1, the number of days until Christmas is displayed.

7. View your page with the following test dates and print a copy of each test. Verify that the correct message is displayed on each day.

   August 12, 1999
   December 24, 1999
   December 31, 1999

8. Print a copy of your JavaScript code for both the MonthText function and the revised script to display the daily messages.

9. Close your Web browser and your text editor.

Case Problems

1. Displaying the Daily Dinner Specials at Kelsey's Diner Kelsey's Diner has made its dinner menu available on the World Wide Web. The only item missing from the menu is the chef's nightly special. Each day of the week, there is a different special. Rather than having to update the page every day, or include a cumbersome list of all the specials, the manager would like you to use JavaScript to display the special that is available on the current day. The daily specials (shown in *italics*) and their descriptions are:

- Sunday: *Chicken Burrito Amigo.* Chicken with mushrooms, onions and Monterey Jack in flour tortilla. 9.95

- Monday: *Chicken Tajine.* Chicken baked with garlic, olives, capers and prunes. 8.95

- Tuesday: *Pizza Bella.* Large pizza with pesto, goat cheese, onions, and mozzarella. 8.95

- Wednesday: *Salmon Filet.* Grilled salmon with spicy curry sauce and baked potato. 9.95

- Thursday: *Greek-style Shrimp.* Shrimp, feta cheese and tomatoes simmered in basil and garlic. 9.95

- Friday: *All you can eat fish.* Deep-fried cod with baked potato and roll. 9.95

- Saturday: *Prime Rib.* 12-oz cut with baked potato, rolls and dinner salad. 12.95

You'll write a program that will create a variable with the current date, and extract from the date the day of the week, using the getDay() method (see Figure 7-9). Using the day of the week value, you'll create two functions, DishName and DishDesc, which will return the name of the nightly special and a description of the nightly special, respectively. You'll place these text strings in the appropriate places on the Web page. Your finished Web page should look like Figure 7-27 for Sunday's menu.

Figure 7-27

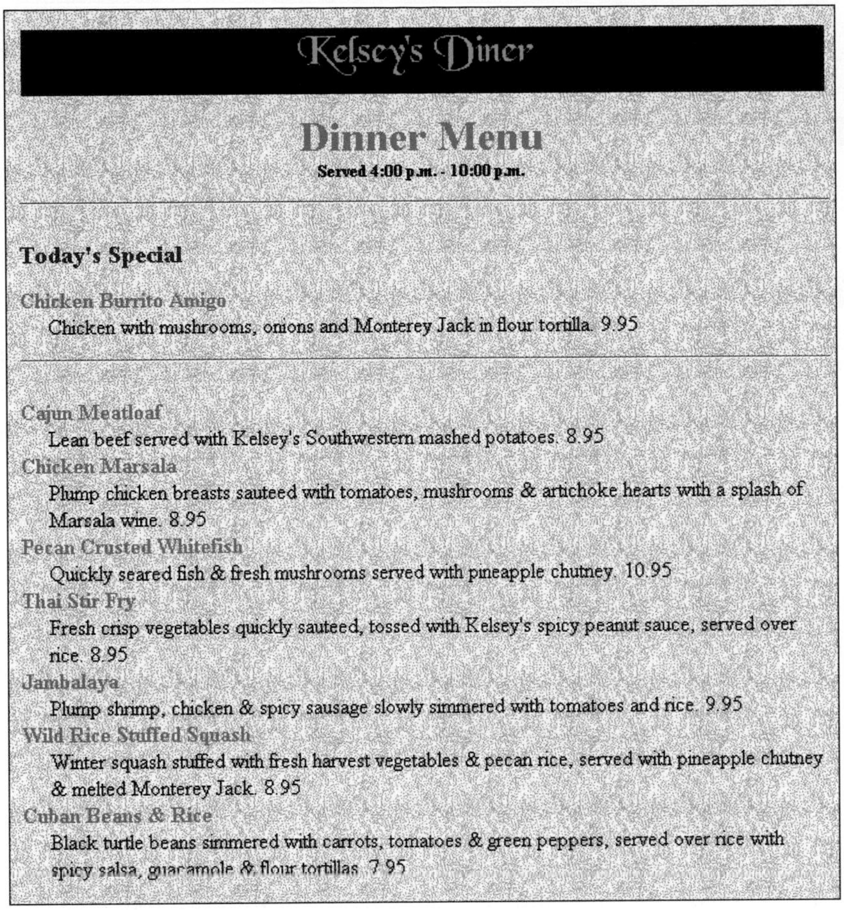
Kelsey's Diner

Dinner Menu

Served 4:00 p.m. - 10:00 p.m.

Today's Special

Chicken Burrito Amigo
Chicken with mushrooms, onions and Monterey Jack in flour tortilla. 9.95

Cajun Meatloaf
Lean beef served with Kelsey's Southwestern mashed potatoes. 8.95
Chicken Marsala
Plump chicken breasts sauteed with tomatoes, mushrooms & artichoke hearts with a splash of Marsala wine. 8.95
Pecan Crusted Whitefish
Quickly seared fish & fresh mushrooms served with pineapple chutney. 10.95
Thai Stir Fry
Fresh crisp vegetables quickly sauteed, tossed with Kelsey's spicy peanut sauce, served over rice. 8.95
Jambalaya
Plump shrimp, chicken & spicy sausage slowly simmered with tomatoes and rice. 9.95
Wild Rice Stuffed Squash
Winter squash stuffed with fresh harvest vegetables & pecan rice, served with pineapple chutney & melted Monterey Jack. 8.95
Cuban Beans & Rice
Black turtle beans simmered with carrots, tomatoes & green peppers, served over rice with spicy salsa, guacamole & flour tortillas. 7.95

To create the nightly dinner menu:

1. Start your text editor and open the file Menutext.htm in the Cases folder of the Tutorial.07 folder on your Student Disk, and then save the file as Menu.htm in the same folder.
2. In the HEAD section of the HTML file, insert <SCRIPT> tags for the functions that you'll be creating. Add an HTML comment tag and a JavaScript comment line to hide the script from older browsers.
3. Within the <SCRIPT> tags create a new function named DishName with a single parameter, Day.
4. Within the DishName function, create an array variable named DName. Populate the array with the names of the nightly dish specials (that is, for Sunday let DName[0]="Chicken Burrito Amigo" and so on).
5. Using the value of the Day parameter as the index variable, have the DishName function return the value of DName[Day].
6. Below the DishName function, create another function named DishDesc that contains a single parameter, Day.
7. Within the DishDesc function create an array variable named DDesc. Populate the array with the descriptions of the nightly dish specials. Use the same index numbering that you used for the DishName function (that is, for Sunday let DDesc[0]="Chicken with mushrooms, onions and Monterey Jack in flour tortilla. 9.95" and so on). Using the value of the Day parameter as the index variable, have the DishDesc function return the value of DDesc[Day].

8. Go to the <Script> tags already entered in the body of the document. Within the first set of <SCRIPT> tags enter a command line to retrieve the current date information and save it to a variable named Today.

9. Using the getDay() method, extract the day of the week number from the Today variable and save it as a variable named WeekDay.

10. Use the document.write() method to display the value of DishName(WeekDay) on your Web page.

11. Go to the second <SCRIPT> tag in the body of the Web page and enter another command line to retrieve the current date information and save it to a variable named Today. As before, extract the day of the week number from this variable and save it in the WeekDay variable.

12. Use the document.write() method to display the value of DishDesc(WeekDay) on your Web page.

13. Test your JavaScript program for these dates: September 12, 1999 through September 18, 1999.

14. Print the resulting Web page for each test date.

15. Restore your Web page to use the current date.

16. Save and print a copy of the Menu.htm file.

17. Close your Web browser and your text editor.

2. Displaying Random Quotes from Mark Twain Professor Stewart Templeton of the Humanities Department at Madison State College has created a Web site devoted to the works of Mark Twain. One of the pages in the site is dedicated to Mark Twain's quotations. Stewart would like you to help him with the Web page by creating a JavaScript program to display random Twain quotes. He has given you the Web page and a list of five quotes. You have to use these to create a function, MQuote, which will display one of these quotes on the page.

The latest release of JavaScript includes a random function, but because it might not be supported by all browsers, you'll simulate the behavior of a random function by using the getSeconds method along with the modulus operator. Your MQuote function will determine the current time, and then use the getSeconds command to extract the "seconds" portion of that time. Finally it will use the modulus operator to calculate the remainder of the Seconds value after dividing it by 5, and then return that value. You'll use that value to select which of the five quotes to display. The five Mark Twain quotes Stewart wants you to use are:

- "I smoke in moderation, only one cigar at a time."

- "Be careful of reading health books, you might die of a misprint."

- "Man is the only animal that blushes--or needs to."

- "Clothes make the man. Naked people have little or no influence on society."

- "One of the most striking differences between a cat and a lie is that a cat has only nine lives."

A preview of the page you'll create is shown in Figure 7-28.

Figure 7-28 ◀

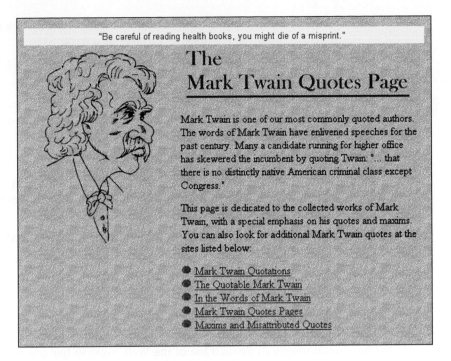

To create the Mark Twain random quotes function:

1. Start your text editor and open the file Twaintxt.htm in the Cases folder of the Tutorial.07 folder on your Student Disk, and then save the file as Twain.htm in the same folder.

2. Go to the <SCRIPT> tags located in the HEAD section of the document. Create a function named MQuote containing a single parameter, Qnum.

3. Within the MQuote function create an array named Quotes that contains five elements. The first element Quotes[0] should contain the text '"I smoke in moderation, only one cigar at a time."' (Note that the double quotation marks of the statement are enclosed within single quotation marks. This allows the double quotation marks to be part of the text displayed on the page.) Set the next four elements in the array equal to the remaining quotes in Stewart's list.

4. Using the value of the Qnum parameter as the index variable, have the MQuote function return the value of mQuotes[Qnum].

5. Directly below the MQuote function (but still within the <SCRIPT> tags), create a second function named Rand5. Do not include any parameters for the function. (You still must include the open and closing parentheses following the function name, however.)

6. Within the Rand5 function create a variable named "Time" that contains the current date and time information.

7. Using the getSeconds() method (see Figure 7-9) extract the current second from the Time variable and store it in a variable named "Seconds."

8. Using the modulus operator (%), calculate the remainder of the Seconds variable when divided by 5 and store the value in a variable named "Rnum." Have the Rand5 function return the value of the Rnum variable.

9. Scroll down the Twain.htm document until you locate the <SCRIPT> tags to insert a random Mark Twain quote into the Web page. Within the <SCRIPT> tags, create a variable named "RandValue" and set the value of the variable by calling the Rand5 function. What are the possible values of the RandValue variable?

10. Create a variable named "QuoteText" and set its value by calling the MQuote function using the RandValue variable as a parameter.

11. Using the document.write() method, display the value of QuoteText on your Web page.

EXPLORE

12. Using what you know about the MQuote and Rand5 functions, arrays, and the modulus operator, briefly describe how these functions combine to display one of the five Twain quotes.

13. Save your changes to the Twain.htm file.

14. Open Twain.htm in your Web browser. Click the Refresh or Reload button several times and verify that doing so allows you to see different quotations from the list of five Twain quotes.

15. Print a copy of the Twain.htm file as it appears in your Web browser.

16. Print a copy of the source code for the MQuote and Rand5 functions you created.

17. Close your Web browser and your text editor.

3. Displaying a Table of Trigonometric Functions Professor Karen Franklin of the Mathematics Department at Southern Missouri State University is creating a Web site for her trigonometry students. One of the Web pages in her site will deal with geometry and trigonometric functions. She would like to have a page that displays the sine and cosine values for various angles from 0 degrees up to 360 degrees. Karen would like to avoid typing this information in and would like you to write a program that automatically generates this table. Because JavaScript calculates sines and cosines in radians, and not degrees, you will have to convert the degree value to radians using the following command:

```
var Radian = Math.PI/180*d;
```

where d is the angle expressed in degrees. Once you have the angle expressed in radians, you can calculate the sine and cosine values, using the following two JavaScript commands:

```
var SineValue = Math.sin(Radian);

var CosineValue = Math.cos(Radian);
```

Using these three commands along with a For loop, you'll create a table of sine and cosine values from 0 to 360 degrees in increments of 15 degrees. A preview of part of the page you'll create is shown in Figure 7-29. Part of the page has already been created for you. Your job is to finish the JavaScript program.

Figure 7-29 ◀

Table of Sines and Cosines

Degrees	Sin(d)	Cos(d)
0	0	1
15	0.258819045102521	0.965925826289068
30	0.5	0.866025403784439
45	0.707106781186547	0.707106781186548
60	0.866025403784439	0.5
75	0.965925826289068	0.258819045102521
90	1	6.12303176911189e-017
105	0.965925826289068	-0.258819045102521

To create the table of trigonometric functions:

1. Start your text editor and open the file Trigtext.htm in the Cases folder of the Tutorial.07 folder on your Student Disk, and then save the file as Trig.htm in the same folder.

2. Within the <SCRIPT> tags create a For loop. The loop should use a counter variable named "d" which starts with a value of 0 and increases by 15 as long as it is less than or equal to 360. The variable "d" will contain the degree value.

3. Within the For loop's command block, use the document.write() method to send a <TR> tag to the Web page. This will start a new row in your trigonometry table.

4. Below the <TR> tag, insert a document.write() method that will display the value of "d" between <TD> and </TD> tags. This will cause the degree values to be displayed in the first column of your trigonometry table.

5. Convert "d" to radians and store the value in a variable named "Radian."

6. Calculate the value of sin(Radian) and store it in a variable named "SineValue."

7. Display the value of the SineValue variable in the second column of your table by using the document.write() method. (Remember that you must enclose the SineValue variable within <TD> and </TD> tags.) The sine values will go in the second column of your table.

8. Calculate the value of cos(Radian) and store it in a variable named "CosineValue."

9. Display the value of the CosineValue variable in the third column of the trigonometry table.

10. Finish the For loop's command block with a document.write() method to send a </TR> tag to the Web page. This will end the row in your table.

11. Open Trig.htm in your Web browser. Verify that the page displays a list of sines and cosines from 0 degrees up to 360 degrees in increments of 15 degrees.

12. The cos(90) should be equal to 0, but what value is displayed in your table? What would you tell Karen about the reliability of using JavaScript in calculating trigonometric functions?

13. Print a copy of the Trig.htm file as it appears in your Web browser.

14. Print a copy of the JavaScript program you wrote to create the trigonometry table.

15. Close your Web browser and your text editor.

4. Creating a List of Daily Events at Avalon Books   The Avalon Books bookstore sponsors several special events each month. You've been asked by store manager Liu Davis to create a Web page that will display a calendar of the current month's activities as well as a list of any events occurring that day. The following is a list of the special events for the upcoming month of April:

- Every Monday: Storytime with Susan Sheridan. 12 noon.

- Every Friday: Storytime with Doug Evans. 12 noon.

- First Saturday of the month: A Novel Idea: Discussion Group. 7 - 9 p.m.

- April 4th: Young Authors' Workshop. 1 - 4 p.m.

- April 14th: Meet author Jeff Farley. 7 - 8 p.m.

- April 24th: Meet author Karen Charnas. 7 - 8 p.m.

Figure 7-30 shows an example of a page you could create. The final layout and design of the page are up to you, however.

Figure 7-30 ◀

April Events at Avalon Books

Today's Events: 4/4/99
Young Authors' Workshop. 1 - 4 p.m.

Events in April, 1999						
Sunday	**Monday**	**Tuesday**	**Wednesday**	**Thursday**	**Friday**	**Saturday**
				1)	2)	3) A Novel Idea: Discussion Group. 7 - 9 p.m.
4) Young Authors' Workshop. 1 - 4 p.m.	5) 12:00 pm. Story time with Susan Sheridan	6)	7)	8)	9) 12:00 pm. Story time with Doug Evans	10)
11)	12) 12:00 pm. Story time with Susan Sheridan	13)	14) Meet author Jeff Farley. 7 - 8 p.m.	15)	16) 12:00 pm. Story time with Doug Evans	17)
18)	19) 12:00 pm. Story time with Susan Sheridan	20)	21)	22)	23) 12:00 pm. Story time with Doug Evans	24) Meet author Karen Charnas. 7 - 8 p.m.
25)	26) 12:00 pm. Story time with Susan Sheridan	27)	28)	29)	30) 12:00 pm. Story time with Doug Evans	

To create the daily events schedule for Avalon Books:

1. Create a file named Avalon.htm in the Cases folder of the Tutorial.07 folder on your Student Disk.

2. Copy the tags used to create the April Events calendar from the April.htm file (located in the Cases folder of the Tutorial.07 folder) and paste them in Avalon.htm.

3. Add title tags and descriptive text to Avalon.htm.

4. Use JavaScript to send the following output to your Web page:
   - Display the current date in the mm/dd/yy format.
   - If it is Monday, display the Susan Sheridan storytime event.
   - If it is Friday, display the Doug Evans storytime event.
   - If it is Saturday and the day of the month is less than or equal to 7, display the Novel Idea Discussion Group event.
   - If it is the 4th day of the month, display the Young Authors' Workshop event.
   - If it is the 14th day of the month, display the Meet Jeff Farley event.
   - If it is the 24th day of the month, display the Meet Karen Charnas event.

5. Use the following test dates to test Avalon.htm: 4/3/99, 4/4/99, 4/12/99, 4/14/99, 4/24/99, and 4/30/99.

6. Open Avalon.htm in your Web browser for each of the six test dates and confirm that the proper daily event is displayed on the page.

7. Print a copy of your Web page for the test date 4/30/99.

8. Print a copy of the HTML tags and JavaScript commands you used to create this Web page.

9. Close your Web browser and your text editor.

Working with JavaScript Objects and Events

Enhancing Your Forms with JavaScript

OBJECTIVES

In this tutorial you will:

■ Learn about form validation

■ Study the object-based nature of the JavaScript language

■ Work with objects, properties, methods, and events

■ Create programs that run in response to user actions

■ Create dialog boxes that prompt the user for input

■ Create message boxes that alert users to problems

CASE

Validating User Input in the Neonatal Feeding Study

St. Mary's hospital, located in the city of Northland Pines, is a large complex, serving the needs of the community and neighboring towns. St. Mary's is also a research hospital, which means that it is the home of several research institutions, including the Midwest Clinical Cancer Center and General Clinical Research Center.

One of the tasks involved in clinical research is enrolling patients in various studies. Each patient placed in a study must go through a registration process, including the completion of a registration form used to determine whether the patient is eligible to participate.

In past years, these forms were paper records, filled out by hand by the attending nurse or physician. Recently, however, the hospital has developed an intranet—a network similar to the World Wide Web, but with a scope limited to the confines of the hospital. Some researchers want to place registration forms on the hospital intranet, allowing them to be filled out online and automatically sent to a database for storage.

You've been asked to help develop one of the first online registration forms for a study run by Dr. Karen Paulson on the effects of different feeding strategies on newborn infants. The form will have to be interactive, in that it will have to calculate key items as well as check the user's entries for mistakes. To create this Web page form, you'll have to use JavaScript to control how users access and enter data into the form.

SESSION

8.1

In this session you will learn about the principle of form validation. You'll see how validation applies to the objects found on a Web page form. You'll learn about the object-based nature of the JavaScript language and explore the principles of objects, properties, and methods.

Understanding Form Validation

You meet with Dr. Paulson to discuss the online form she wants you to create for her clinical study. She brings with her a copy of the current registration form, which is already saved in HTML format as Studytxt.htm. This is the form that she wants you to modify. Although you won't be working with this form right away (you have to learn more about JavaScript first), you'll open the Studytxt.htm file now, save it with a different name, and view it in your Web browser.

To open Dr. Paulson's Web page form:

1. Start your text editor.

2. Open the file **Studytxt.htm** from the Tutorial.08 folder on your Student Disk, and then save the file as **Study.htm** in the same folder.

3. Close your text editor, and then open the Study.htm file in your Web browser. Figure 8-1 shows the current state of the Web page form.

Figure 8-1 ◀
Dr. Paulson's
registration
form

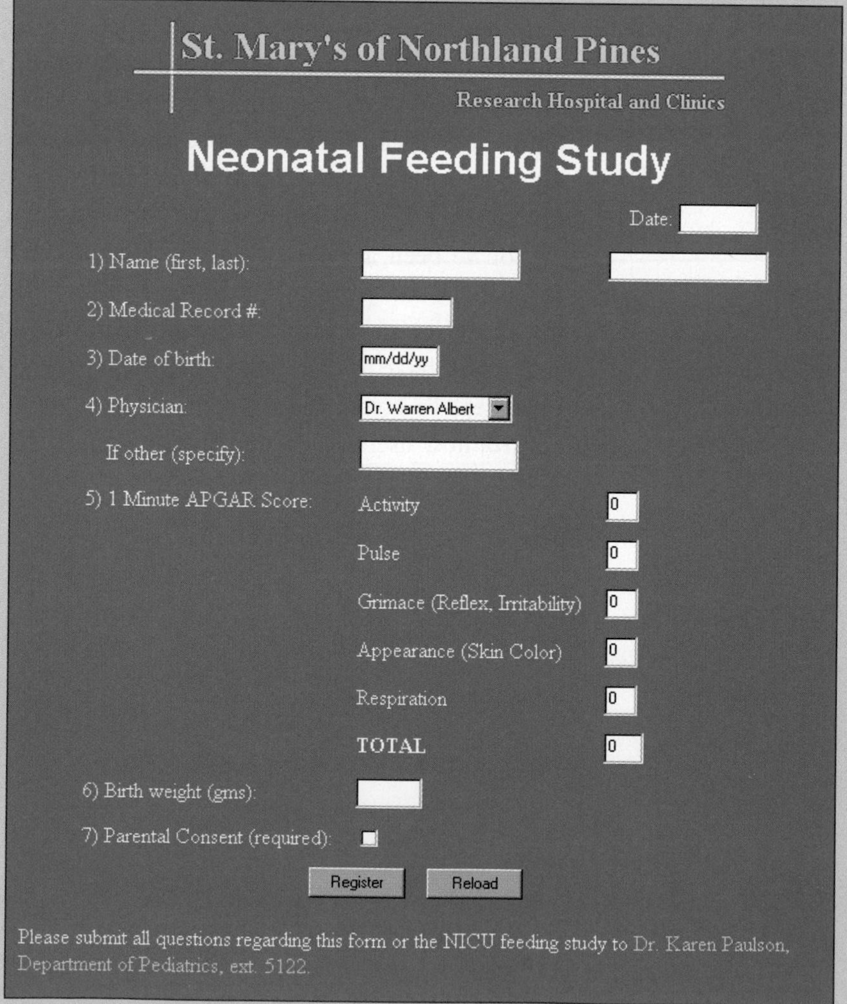

TROUBLE? If you're using Netscape Navigator or Netscape Communicator, your form will look slightly different from the form in the figure.

4. Scroll through the form and review its structure. Enter some test data to help you become familiar with the form's layout and content.

As you examine Dr. Paulson's form, notice that it collects basic information on newborns. The first field is used to record the date that the form was filled out. The next fields record the baby's name and medical record number (to easily tie in with the hospital database) and date of birth.

A selection list follows, containing the names of the physicians in the pediatric ward who might be participating in the study. The selection list also includes an option labeled "Other" for situations in which none of the seven primary physicians is involved in the birth. In such a case, the input field below the selection list should contain that physician's name.

Next, a series of boxes calculates the infant's 1-minute APGAR score, a measure of a newborn baby's health summed up from the evaluation of five criteria (activity, pulse, grimace, appearance, and respiration). Each component of the APGAR score should have a value of 0, 1, or 2.

The form concludes with a record of the newborn's birth weight and whether or not a parental consent form has been filled out, allowing the baby to be enrolled in Dr. Paulson's study. Figure 8-2 shows the names of each field in the registration form. The name of the form itself is "REG." Take time to review these field names now; you'll use them extensively later on when you modify Dr. Paulson's form.

Figure 8-2 ◀
Field names in the registration form

name of form = REG

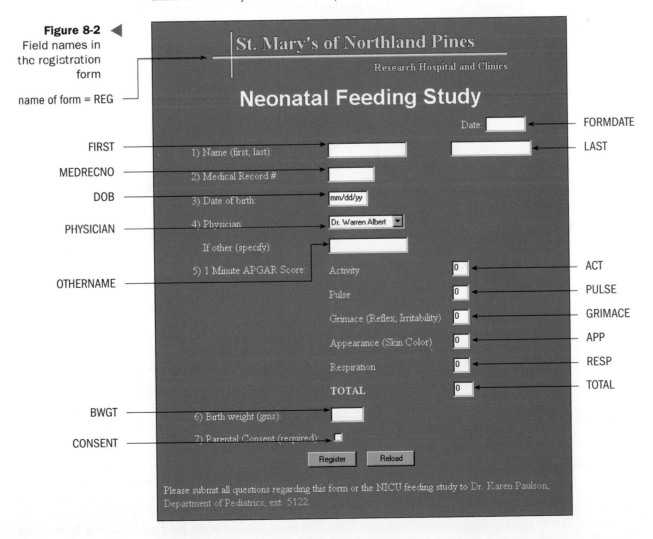

As the form is currently designed, almost any value could be entered into any of the input fields. This concerns Dr. Paulson, and she explains what she would like the online form to do automatically for the user, to address her concerns: 1) The Date field should be completed automatically for the user, to avoid the possibility of an incorrect date being entered. 2) If "Other" is selected from the Physician selection list, the user should be prompted for the physician's name. Otherwise, the user should go directly to the APGAR scores. 3) The 1-minute total APGAR score should be calculated automatically based on the value of its five component parts. 4) The value of each component of the APGAR score (activity, pulse, grimace, appearance, and respiration) can be only 0, 1, or 2. The form should reject all other values and alert the user that an improper value was entered. 5) No registration form should be submitted unless a parental consent form has been filled out, as indicated by a check in the Parental Consent check box on the registration form.

To meet Dr. Paulson's requirements, your Web page form must be able to react in different ways, depending on the user's input. The form must be able to skip certain fields if the user selects a certain item, but not if the user selects a different item. The form must also check the APGAR values that the user enters and either calculate a total score or, if necessary, inform the user that a mistake has been made.

Dr. Paulson's criteria are examples of **form validation**, a process by which the form entries are checked and, where possible, errors are eliminated. Form validation is a critical aspect of data entry. A properly designed form will reduce the possibility of the user entering faulty data. On the Web, form validation can occur on either the client side or the server side. As shown in Figure 8-3, in **server-side validation**, the form is sent to the Web server, which then checks the values. If a mistake is found, the user is notified and asked to resubmit the form. In **client-side validation**, the form is checked as the user enters the information, and immediate feedback is provided if the user makes a mistake. Dr. Paulson wants this type of validation for her form.

Figure 8-3 ◀
Server-side and
client-side
validation

Web server   **Web server**

Server-side validation

1) The user submits the form to the Web server.

2) The Web server validates the user's responses and, if necessary, returns the form to the user for correction.

3) After correcting any errors, the user resubmits the form to the Web server for another validation.

Client-side validation

1) The user submits the form, and validation is performed on the user's computer.

2) After correcting any errors, the user submits the form to the Web server.

One function of JavaScript is to provide this kind of client-side validation. With a script built into the Web page form, you can give immediate feedback to users as they enter data, which also reduces the amount of network traffic between users and the Web server. Before you can do this for Dr. Paulson's form, however, you must first learn how JavaScript can be used to manipulate elements on your Web page, not just when the page is initially loaded, but also in response to events initiated by the user. The first step in accomplishing this is to understand the object-based nature of the JavaScript language and how it can be used to control the behavior of the Web page, the form on the page, and even the Web browser itself.

Working with an Object-based Language

JavaScript is an **object-based language**, which means that the language is based on manipulating objects by either modifying their properties or applying methods to them. That definition might sound daunting, but the concept is simple. **Objects** are items that exist in a defined space. Each object has **properties** that describe its appearance, purpose, or behavior; furthermore an object can have **methods**, which are actions that can be performed with it or to it.

Consider the example of an oven in your kitchen. The oven is an object. It has certain properties, such as its model name, age, size, and color. There are certain methods you can perform with the oven object, such as turning on the grill or the self-cleaner. Some of these methods change the properties of the oven, such as the oven's current temperature. You modify the oven's temperature property through the method of turning the stove on or off.

Similarly, your Web browser has its own set of objects, properties, and methods. The Web browser itself is an object, and the page you're viewing is an object. If the page contains frames, each frame is an object, and if the page contains forms, each field on the form (as well as the form itself) is an object. These objects have properties. The browser object has the type property (Netscape Communicator or Internet Explorer), the version property (1.0, 2.0, 3.0, or 4.0), and so forth. There are some methods you can apply to your browser: you can open it, close it, reload the contents of the browser window, or move back and forth in your history list.

Now that you've been introduced to the concept of objects, properties, and methods, your next task is to learn how to work with these concepts in a JavaScript program.

Understanding JavaScript Objects and Object Names

An object is identified by its **object name**, a name that JavaScript reserves for referring to a particular object. Figure 8-4 lists some of the many objects available in JavaScript and their corresponding object names.

Figure 8-4 ◄
Some JavaScript objects and their object names

Object	JavaScript Object Name
The browser window	window
A frame within the browser window	frame
The history list containing the Web pages the user has already visited in the current session	history
The Web browser being run by the user	navigator
The URL of the current Web page	location
The Web page currently displayed in the browser window	document
A hyperlink on the current Web page	link
A target or anchor on the current Web page	anchor
A form on the current Web page	form

When you want to use JavaScript to manipulate the current window, for example, you have to use the object name "window." Operations that affect the current Web page use the "document" object name.

An object can also use a name that you've assigned to it. You've seen many HTML tags that include the NAME property, such as the <FORM>, <FRAME>, and <INPUT> tags. You can refer to objects created from those tags with the values specified in the NAME property. For example, in Dr. Paulson's registration form, the following tag starts the form:

```
<FORM NAME=REG>
```

You refer to this form using the object name (REG) in your JavaScript program.

It is helpful to visualize the object names shown in Figure 8-4 as part of a hierarchy of objects. Figure 8-5 shows the layout of this hierarchy.

Figure 8-5 ◀
JavaScript
object hierarchy

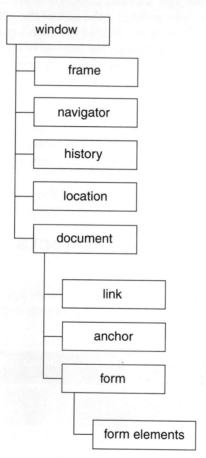

The topmost object in the hierarchy is the window object. The window object contains the other objects in the list, such as the current frame, history list, or document. The document contains its own set of objects, including links, anchors, forms, and within each form, form elements such as input boxes.

In some situations, you will need to specify this hierarchy when referring to an object. You can do that by separating each object by a period and including the objects in the object name, starting at the top of the hierarchy and moving down. For example, in Dr. Paulson's form, the MEDRECNO input box lies within the REG form, which lies within the application window. The complete object reference for the input box, including the other objects in the hierarchy, is:

```
window.document.REG.MEDRECNO
```

In most cases, you can omit the window object name from the hierarchy, and JavaScript will assume that it is there. In other words, JavaScript treats the previous object reference in the same way as the following reference:

```
document.REG.MEDRECNO
```

When working with objects on Web page forms, like the form you'll be developing for Dr. Paulson, you should include the entire hierarchy of object names (except for the window object). Some browsers cannot interpret the object names without the complete hierarchy.

Figure 8-6 illustrates how the hierarchy applies to other objects on Dr. Paulson's Web registration form. You'll need this information later when you start to work on the form.

Figure 8-6
Object references in the registration form

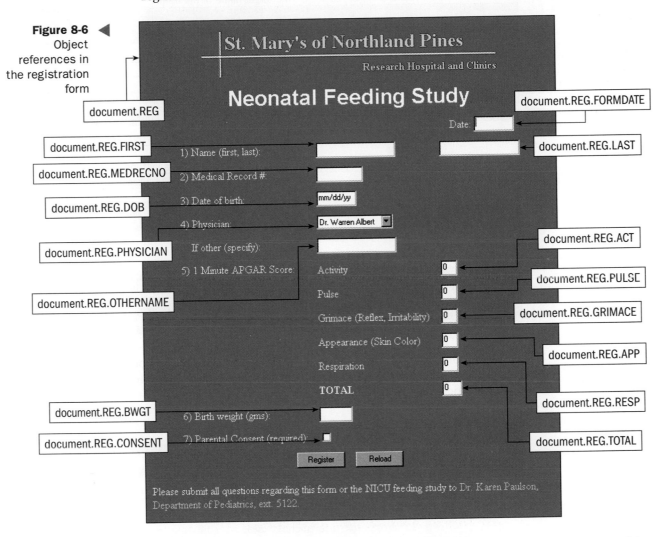

Now that you understand how JavaScript assigns object names to various objects, you'll next look at how JavaScript works with objects and their properties.

Working with Object Properties

Each object in JavaScript has properties associated with it. The number of properties varies depending on the particular object. Some objects have only a few properties, whereas others have dozens. As with object names, there are certain key names that identify these properties. A partial list of objects and their properties is shown in Figure 8-7.

Figure 8-7 ◄
JavaScript
objects and
their properties

Object Name	Property Name	Description
window	DefaultStatus	The default message displayed in the window's status bar
	frames	An array of all the frames in the window
	length	The number of frames in the window
	name	The target name of the window
	status	A priority or temporary message in the window's status bar
frame	document	The document displayed within the frame
	length	The number of frames within the frame
	name	The target name of the frame
history	length	The number of entries in the history list
navigator	appCodeName	The code name of the browser
	appName	The name of the browser
	appVersion	The version of the browser
location	href	The URL of the location
	protocol	The protocol (HTTP, FTP, etc.) used by the location
document	bgColor	The page's background color
	fgColor	The color of text on the page
	lastModified	The date the document was last modified
	linkColor	The color of hyperlinks on the page
	title	The title of the page
link	href	The URL of the hyperlink
	target	The target window of the hyperlink (if specified)
anchor	name	The name of the anchor
form	action	The ACTION property of the <FORM> tag
	length	The number of elements in the form
	method	The METHOD property of the <FORM> tag
	name	The name of the form

JavaScript gives you several ways of working with properties: you can change the value of a property, store the property's value in a variable, or test whether the property equals some specific value in an If...Then expression.

REFERENCE
window

WORKING WITH OBJECT PROPERTIES

- To change the value of a property, use the following JavaScript syntax:

  object.property = expression

  where *object* is the object name, *property* is the property name, and *expression* is a JavaScript expression that assigns a value.
- To assign an object property value to a variable, use the syntax:

  variable = object.property

  where *variable* is the name of the JavaScript variable.

Modifying a Property's Value

The syntax for changing the value of a property is:

```
object.property = expression
```

where *object* is the JavaScript object name of the object you want to manipulate, *property* is a property of that object, and *expression* is a JavaScript expression that assigns a value to the property. Figure 8-8 shows how you could use objects and properties to modify your Web page and Web browser.

Figure 8-8 ◄
Changing an
object's value

expressions ———
properties ———
objects ———

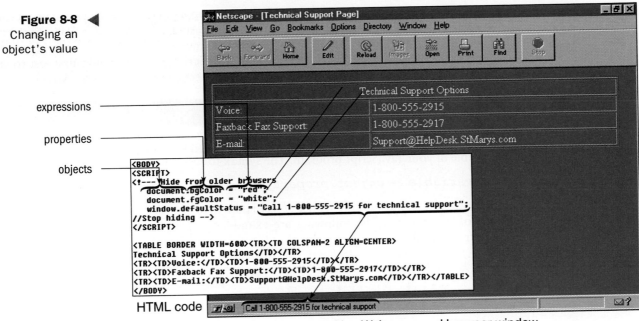

HTML code

resulting Web page and browser window

In this example, the first JavaScript command, document.bgColor="red", modifies the current Web page, changing the background color to red. Note that this will override the browser's default background color. Similarly, the second command, document.fgColor="white", changes the foreground color—the text color—to white. The final command uses the window.defaultStatus property to display the text "Call 1-800-555-2915 for technical support" in the window's status bar. This is the default status bar text, but it might be replaced by other text at certain times (such as the URL of a Web page when the user passes the mouse over a hyperlink).

Not all properties can be changed. Some properties are **read-only**, which means that you can read the property value, but you can't modify it. One such property is the appVersion property of the navigator object, which identifies the version number of your Web browser. Although it would be convenient to quickly upgrade your version of Netscape Communicator with a simple JavaScript command, you're not allowed to change this value. Figure 8-9 shows how you would use JavaScript to display other read-only information about your browser.

Figure 8-9 ◄
Displaying read-
only properties
of the browser

browser properties ———

navigator
(browser) object ———

application
code name ———

application name ———

application version ———

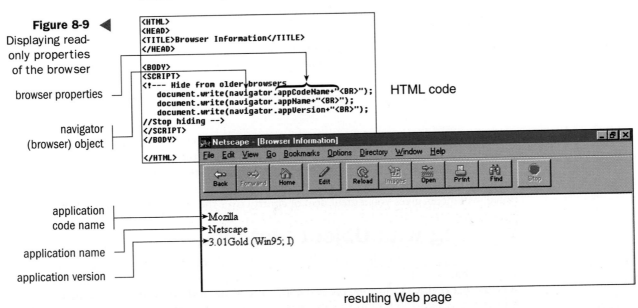

resulting Web page

In this example, the values of the appCodeName, appName, and appVersion properties are used to display the application code name, name, and version on the Web page. You might use this information when creating pages that involve HTML extensions supported by specific browsers or browser versions. Your JavaScript program might first test to see whether the user has one of those browsers before inserting the tags into the Web page.

Assigning a Property to a Variable

Although you cannot change the value of read-only properties, you can assign that value to a variable in your JavaScript program. The syntax for assigning a property to a variable is:

```
variable = object.property
```

where *variable* is the variable name, *object* is the name of the object, and *property* is the name of its property. The following are examples of property values being assigned to JavaScript variables:

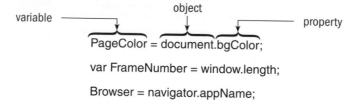

```
PageColor = document.bgColor;

var FrameNumber = window.length;

Browser = navigator.appName;
```

The first example shows how to use JavaScript to determine the background color of the page and then assign that value to a variable named PageColor. In the second example, the variable FrameNumber is given the value of the number of frames in the window (refer back to Figure 8-7 if you're having difficulty understanding the object and property references). Note that by using the "var" keyword, this command both creates the FrameNumber variable and assigns it a value. The final example shows how you would determine the name of the browser being used to read your Web page.

Using Properties in Conditional Expressions

A final situation in which you might need to work with properties is a conditional statement that changes how the page behaves based on the value of an object property. You'll use this technique later when adding form validation to Dr. Paulson's registration form. The following JavaScript code shows how you could incorporate object properties into a simple conditional expression:

```
if(document.bgColor=="black") {
   document.fgColor="white";
} else {
   document.fgColor="black";
}
```

In this example, JavaScript first checks the background color of the Web page. If the background color is black, then JavaScript changes the color of the text on the page to white (using the fgColor property of the page). On the other hand, if the background color is not black, then the text color is changed to black. As you can see, using objects, properties, and conditional statements gives you a great deal of control over the appearance of your Web page.

Working with Object Methods

Another way of controlling your Web page is with methods. Recall that methods are actions that objects can perform, or actions that you can apply to objects. Figure 8-10 shows a list of JavaScript objects and some of the methods associated with them.

Figure 8-10 ◀
JavaScript objects and their methods

Object Name	Method Name	Description
window	alert(*message*)	Displays a dialog box with a message in the window
	close()	Closes the window
	prompt(*message, default_text*)	Displays a dialog box prompting the user for information
	scroll(*x, y*)	Scrolls to the (x,y) coordinate in the window
frame	alert(*message*)	Displays a dialog box with a message in the frame
	close()	Closes the frame
	prompt(*message, default_text*)	Displays a dialog box prompting the user for information
history	back()	Returns to the previous page in the history list
	forward()	Goes to the next page in the history list
location	reload()	Reloads the current page
document	write()	Writes text and HTML tags to the current document
	writeln()	Writes text and HTML tags to the current document on a new line
form	reset()	Resets the form
	submit()	Submits the form

REFERENCE
window

WORKING WITH OBJECT METHODS

- To apply a method to an object, use the syntax:
  object.method()
  where *object* is the object name, and *method* is the name of a JavaScript method that applies to the object.

The syntax for applying a method to an object is:

```
object.method();
```

where *object* is the name of the object, and *method*() is the method to be applied. One of the most common uses of a method is the write() method applied to the document object, which is used to send text to the Web page. The following are examples of objects and methods:

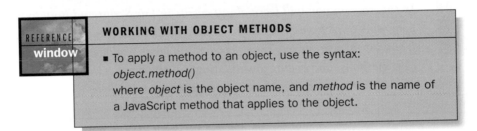

```
object                          method
       history.back();

       form.submit();

       document.write("Thank you");
```

The first example shows how to use the history object to cause the browser to go back to the previously viewed Web page. In the second example, the submit() method is applied to a form in order to send it to a CGI script. The final example, one that should be familiar to you by now, uses the write() method to send text to the Web page.

Some methods, such as the write() method, contain **parameters**, which are values that control how the method is applied to the object. In the case of the write() method, the text within parentheses is the parameter indicating what characters or tags should be sent to the document. Other methods do not require parameters. The back() method, for example, does not require a parameter; it is simply used to go back to the previous page in the history list.

A more complete list of objects, properties, and methods is included in Appendix D. For now, you have a sufficient understanding of JavaScript's object-based design to see how useful it can be in manipulating your Web pages and controlling your Web browser.

Quick Check

1 What is the difference between server-side validation and client-side validation?

2 Define the following terms: object, property, and method.

3 What object reference would you use for a check box named JOIN located in a form named ENROLL?

4 What command would change the text color on a Web page to blue?

5 What command would assign the value of the page's text color to a variable named "tcolor"?

6 What command would you use to reset a form named ENROLL?

You've studied the basic principles of JavaScript's object-oriented programming language. In the next session you'll learn how JavaScript can be used to respond to user-initiated events, and you'll apply what you've learned to modifying Dr. Paulson's registration form.

SESSION 8.2

In this session you will learn about events in JavaScript and how to run JavaScript programs in response to specific events. You'll also learn how to initiate these events from within a program. Then you'll apply what you've learned about objects, properties, methods, and events to validating a Web page form. You'll see how to prompt the user for information and how to alert the user when mistakes have been made.

Managing Events

To begin working on Dr. Paulson's Web page form, you first need to understand the concept of events. An **event** is a specific action that triggers the browser to run a block of JavaScript commands. Up to now, your JavaScript programs have run exclusively when the Web page is loaded by the browser. But in Dr. Paulson's form, some of the programs must run in response to what the user is doing to the form.

JavaScript supports several different kinds of events, many of which are associated with forms and form fields. Each event has a unique name. A list of these events is shown in Figure 8-11.

Figure 8-11 ◀
JavaScript events

Event	Description
Abort	Occurs when the user cancels the loading of an image
Blur	Occurs when the user leaves a form field (either by clicking outside of the field or pressing the Tab key)
Click	Occurs when the user clicks a field or a hyperlink with the mouse
Change	Occurs when the value of a form field is changed by the user
Error	Occurs when the browser encounters an error in running a JavaScript program
Focus	Occurs when a window or form field is made active (usually by moving the cursor into the field or by clicking the object with the mouse)

Events can take place in rapid succession. Consider the example shown in Figure 8-12. A user presses the Tab key to enter an input field, changes the field's value, and leaves the field by pressing the Tab key. The first event that the browser recognizes in this scenario is the Focus event as the input field becomes the active field in the form. After the user changes the value in the field and leaves the field, the Change event is triggered as the browser notes that the value of the field has been changed. Finally, the Blur event occurs as the focus leaves the field and goes to a different field on the form.

Figure 8-12 ◀
Events initiated
by the user
during data
entry

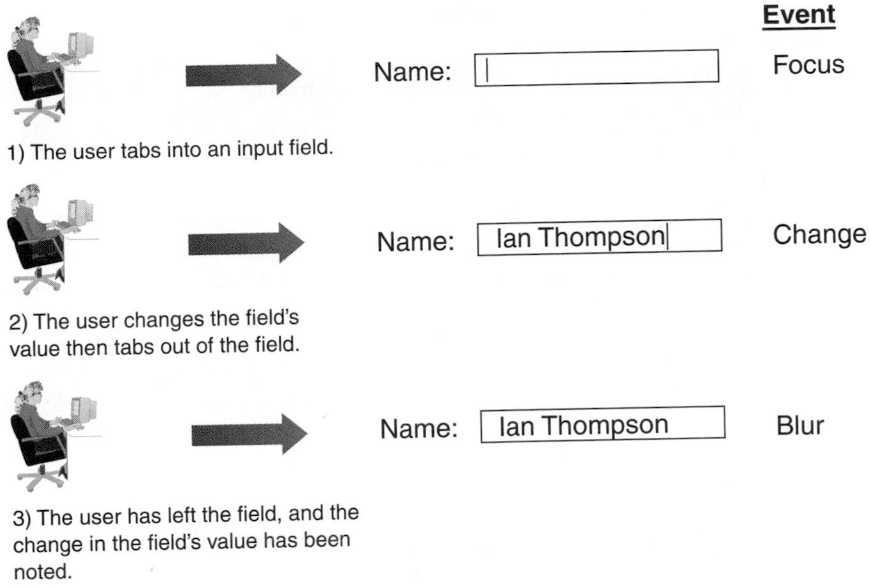

Event

Name: [|]   Focus

1) The user tabs into an input field.

Name: [Ian Thompson|]   Change

2) The user changes the field's
value then tabs out of the field.

Name: [Ian Thompson   ]   Blur

3) The user has left the field, and the
change in the field's value has been
noted.

Using Event Handlers

With so many different events associated with your Web objects, you need some way of telling the browser how to run a set of commands whenever a specific event occurs. This is where an event handler becomes important. An **event handler** is code added to an HTML tag that is run whenever a particular event occurs. The syntax for invoking an event handler is:

```
<HTML_tag Properties event_handler ="JavaScript commands;">
```

where *HTML_tag* is the name of the tag, *Properties* are properties associated with the tag, *event_handler* is the name of an event handler, and *JavaScript commands* are the set of commands or, more often, a single command that calls a JavaScript function to be run when the event occurs.

REFERENCE
window

CALLING AN EVENT HANDLER

■ To invoke an event handler, use the JavaScript syntax:
  <HTML_tag Properties event_handler ="JavaScript commands;">
  where *HTML_tag* is an HTML tag (usually an <INPUT> tag),
  Properties are properties associated with the tag, *event_handler*
  is the name of an event handler, and *JavaScript commands* are
  either a set of JavaScript commands, separated by semicolons,
  or a single command that calls a JavaScript function.

Different HTML tags have different event handlers. Figure 8-13 lists some of the names of event handlers available in JavaScript and the objects with which they are associated.

Figure 8-13 ◄
JavaScript
event handlers

Object	Names of Event Handlers
button	onClick
check box	onClick
document	onLoad, onUnload, onError
form	onSubmit, onReset
frames	onBlur, onFocus
hyperlink	onClick, onMouseOver, onMouseOut
image	onLoad, onError, onAbort
image map hotspot	onMouseOver, onMouseOut
input box	onBlur, onChange, onFocus, onSelect
radio button	onClick
reset button	onClick
selection list	onBlur, onChange, onFocus
submit button	onClick
text area box	onBlur, onChange, onFocus, onSelect
window	onLoad, onUnload, onBlur, onFocus

In the example shown in Figure 8-14, the onClick event handler is used with radio buttons to change the page's background color to red, blue, or green in response to the user clicking one of the three options. Note that the JavaScript commands invoked in this way do not require <SCRIPT> tags, but they do have to be placed within a pair of single or double quotation marks in the tag. You can enter several commands in this way, separating one command line from another with a semicolon; however, when you have several JavaScript commands to run, the standard practice is to place them in a function, which can then be called using a single command line.

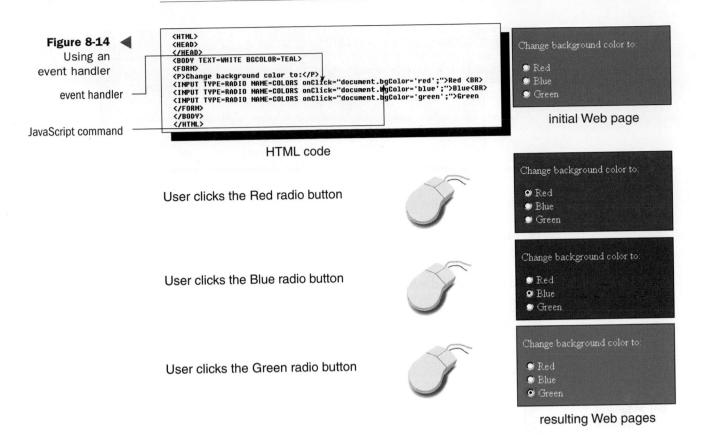

Figure 8-14
Using an
event handler

event handler

JavaScript command

```
<HTML>
<HEAD>
</HEAD>
<BODY TEXT=WHITE BGCOLOR=TEAL>
<FORM>
<P>Change background color to:</P>
<INPUT TYPE=RADIO NAME=COLORS onClick="document.bgColor='red';">Red <BR>
<INPUT TYPE=RADIO NAME=COLORS onClick="document.bgColor='blue';">Blue<BR>
<INPUT TYPE=RADIO NAME=COLORS onClick="document.bgColor='green';">Green
</FORM>
</BODY>
</HTML>
```

HTML code

initial Web page

User clicks the Red radio button

User clicks the Blue radio button

User clicks the Green radio button

resulting Web pages

Using the onLoad Event Handler

Now that you've learned about objects, properties, methods, and events, you are ready to start modifying Dr. Paulson's form. As shown in the following list of changes you need to make to the form, your first task is to set up the form so that the current date is entered automatically into the FORMDATE field whenever the browser opens the page.

☐ 1) Automatically enter the current date in the FORMDATE field and move to the next field in the form.

☐ 2) If "Other" is selected from the Physician selection list box, prompt for the name of the physician; otherwise go to the APGAR component fields.

☐ 3) Automatically calculate the total APGAR score.

☐ 4) Check that valid APGAR component scores have been entered.

☐ 5) Check that parental consent has been obtained before submitting the form.

RUNNING A JAVASCRIPT PROGRAM WHEN LOADING A PAGE

- To run a JavaScript program when your Web page loads, modify the <BODY> tag to use the onLoad event handler as follows:
  <BODY onLoad="*JavaScript Command;*">
  where *JavaScript Command* is either a function or a set of commands run by the onLoad event handler when the page is loaded by the browser.

The event handler for the opening of a Web page is called **onLoad**. Because this handler is associated with the document object, you must place it in the <BODY> tag of the HTML file. You'll begin your work on the form by adding this event handler to the Study.htm document now.

To add the onLoad event handler to Dr. Paulson's form:

1. Start your text editor and open the **Study.htm** file from the Tutorial.08 folder on your Student Disk.

2. Type **onLoad="StartForm();"** in the <BODY> tag of the HTML file. See Figure 8-15.

Figure 8-15 ◀
Inserting the
onLoad event
handler

event handler ——

custom function ——

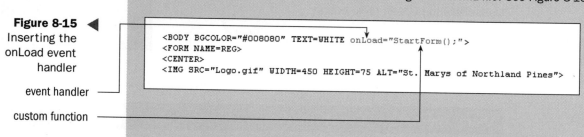

```
<BODY BGCOLOR="#008080" TEXT=WHITE onLoad="StartForm();">
<FORM NAME=REG>
<CENTER>
<IMG SRC="Logo.gif" WIDTH=450 HEIGHT=75 ALT="St. Marys of Northland Pines">
```

Note that this event handler runs the function StartForm() when the page is initially loaded into the browser. StartForm() is a user-defined function that you'll create in the next set of steps.

3. Save your changes to the Study.htm file.

Now you have to create the StartForm() function. This function will have two purposes: first it will enter the current date into the Date field, and then it will move the cursor to the next field in the form. Because users are not expected to enter the current date themselves, this function provides a way of avoiding the Date field during data entry.

User-defined functions are usually collected together between a set of <SCRIPT> tags located in the HEAD section of the file. One user-defined function, named DateToday(), has already been put in place for you in the Study.htm file. The code for the DateToday() function is as follows:

```
function DateToday() {
   var Today=new Date();
   var ThisDay=Today.getDate();
   var ThisMonth=Today.getMonth()+1;
   var ThisYear=Today.getYear();
   return ThisMonth+"/"+ThisDay+"/"+ThisYear;
}
```

This function contains JavaScript commands that you are, by now, familiar with. It uses the date object and extracts the current day, month, and year, and then combines those values in a text string, which it then returns to the user. StartForm() will call the DateToday() function to retrieve a text string containing the current date, and then it will place that text in the Date field in the registration form. The code for the StartForm() function is as follows:

```
function StartForm() {
    document.REG.FORMDATE.value=DateToday();
}
```

Before you enter this function into the Study.htm file, take a moment to examine the code. The command uses the document.REG.FORMDATE object reference for the form's first field (see Figure 8-6), which is the Date field. The property of this particular object is the "value" property, which is simply the value entered into the input field. The value in this case is whatever text string is returned from the DateToday() function—which should be the current date. Other properties and methods associated with input boxes are shown in Figure 8-16.

Figure 8-16 ◀
Properties and
methods of
input boxes

Property	Description
defaultValue	The default value of the input box
name	The name of the input box
type	The type of the input box
value	The current value of the input box

Method	Description
focus()	Makes the input box active
blur()	Leaves the input box
select()	Selects the text in the input box

Next, you need to add the StartForm() function to the Study.htm file so that it can retrieve the current date from the DateToday() function and place it in the Date field.

To add the StartForm() function to the Study.htm file:

1. Go to the <SCRIPT> tag in the Study.htm file.

2. Below the closing bracket of the DateToday() function, enter the following commands:

```
function StartForm() {
    document.REG.FORMDATE.value=DateToday();
}
```

Your file should look like Figure 8-17.

Figure 8-17 ◄
Creating the
StartForm()
function

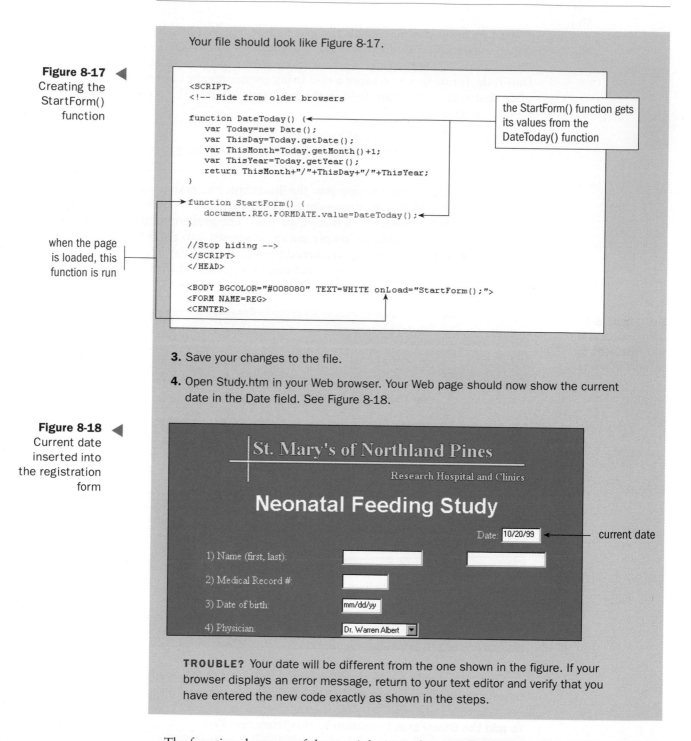

```
<SCRIPT>
<!-- Hide from older browsers

function DateToday() {
    var Today=new Date();
    var ThisDay=Today.getDate();
    var ThisMonth=Today.getMonth()+1;
    var ThisYear=Today.getYear();
    return ThisMonth+"/"+ThisDay+"/"+ThisYear;
}

function StartForm() {
    document.REG.FORMDATE.value=DateToday();
}

//Stop hiding -->
</SCRIPT>
</HEAD>

<BODY BGCOLOR="#008080" TEXT=WHITE onLoad="StartForm();">
<FORM NAME=REG>
<CENTER>
```

the StartForm() function gets its values from the DateToday() function

when the page is loaded, this function is run

3. Save your changes to the file.

4. Open Study.htm in your Web browser. Your Web page should now show the current date in the Date field. See Figure 8-18.

Figure 8-18 ◄
Current date
inserted into
the registration
form

St. Mary's of Northland Pines

Research Hospital and Clinics

Neonatal Feeding Study

Date: 10/20/99 ◄———— current date

1) Name (first, last):

2) Medical Record #:

3) Date of birth: mm/dd/yy

4) Physician: Dr. Warren Albert ▼

TROUBLE? Your date will be different from the one shown in the figure. If your browser displays an error message, return to your text editor and verify that you have entered the new code exactly as shown in the steps.

The function does one of the two jobs it needs to—it displays the date in the Date field. The function must also jump to the next field in the form. To accomplish this, you have to learn how to make JavaScript not only respond to an event, but also initiate one.

Emulating Events

When you use JavaScript to emulate an event, you are causing the Web page to perform an action for the user. To emulate an event, you apply an event method to an object on your Web page. Figure 8-19 displays the event methods that can be associated with various objects in your browser.

Figure 8-19 ◀
Event methods

Object	Event Methods
button	click()
check box	click()
document	clear()
form	reset(), submit()
frames	blur(), close(), focus()
input box	focus(), blur(), select()
radio button	click()
reset button	click()
submit button	click()
text area box	focus(), blur(), select()
window	blur(), close(), focus()

The following are examples of JavaScript commands that emulate events. The examples are based on a Web page that contains a form named ORDERS and an input box named PRODUCT.

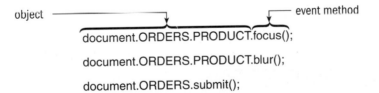

object ——————————┐   ┌—— event method

document.ORDERS.PRODUCT.focus();

document.ORDERS.PRODUCT.blur();

document.ORDERS.submit();

In the first example, the PRODUCT input box is given the focus, which means that the user's cursor is positioned in that particular input box, making it ready for data entry. In the second example, the focus is removed from the PRODUCT input box using the blur() method. In the final example, the entire ORDERS form is submitted (presumably to a CGI script running on a Web server). This method emulates the action of clicking a Submit button on the form.

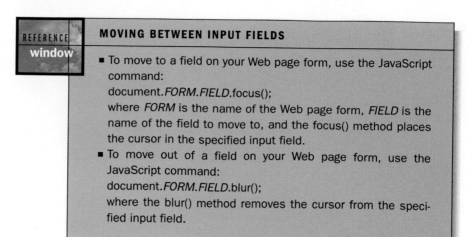

REFERENCE
window

MOVING BETWEEN INPUT FIELDS

- To move to a field on your Web page form, use the JavaScript command:

  document.*FORM.FIELD*.focus();

  where *FORM* is the name of the Web page form, *FIELD* is the name of the field to move to, and the focus() method places the cursor in the specified input field.
- To move out of a field on your Web page form, use the JavaScript command:

  document.*FORM.FIELD*.blur();

  where the blur() method removes the cursor from the specified input field.

In the StartForm() function in your file, you need to add a command that places the cursor in the next field in the REG form, which is the field used for entering the first name of the infant. The field's name is FIRST, so the command to move the cursor to this field is:

```
document.REG.FIRST.focus();
```

You'll insert this command into the StartForm() function now.

To add the focus() method to the StartForm() function:

1. Return to the Study.htm file in your text editor.

2. Locate the StartForm() function at the beginning of the file, and then add the following command to the end of the command block:

   document.REG.FIRST.focus();

   See Figure 8-20.

Figure 8-20 ◀
Moving the
focus to the
FIRST field

move to the
FIRST field

```
function StartForm() {
    document.REG.FORMDATE.value=DateToday();
    document.REG.FIRST.focus();
}
```

3. Save your changes to the Study.htm file, and then reload the file in your Web browser.

   TROUBLE? If you're using Netscape Navigator or Netscape Communicator, you might have to reopen the file. Simply clicking the Reload button might not invoke the changes you've made to the JavaScript program.

   When the page is reopened, the Name field should be selected. You can verify this by typing some text. The characters should appear in this field.

You've completed the first task on your list for Dr. Paulson. The next few fields in the form don't require any modifications. However, Dr. Paulson does want you to change the behavior of the Physician selection list.

☑ 1) Automatically enter the current date in the FORMDATE field and move to the next field in the form.

☐ 2) If "Other" is selected from the Physician selection list box, prompt for the name of the physician; otherwise go to the APGAR component fields.

☐ 3) Automatically calculate the total APGAR score.

☐ 4) Check that valid APGAR component scores have been entered.

☐ 5) Check that parental consent has been obtained before submitting the form.

Working with a Selection Object

Dr. Paulson wants the form to evaluate the option chosen by the user from the Physician selection list. If the user selects one of the seven physicians in the list, the cursor should go to the field for the APGAR Activity score. On the other hand, if the user selects "Other," the form should prompt the user to enter that physician's name before continuing.

You need to create another function to handle this task. The function, which you'll name CheckOther(), should run whenever the user leaves the Physician selection list. This means that the associated event handler is the onBlur() event. You'll add this event handler to the <SELECT> tag for the Physician selection list now.

To add the onBlur() event handler to the tag:

1. Return to your text editor and the Study.htm file.

2. Locate the <SELECT> tag for the Physician selection list, and then insert the following code into the tag:

onBlur="CheckOther();"

See Figure 8-21.

Figure 8-21 ◄
Adding the
onBlur event
handler to the
<SELECT> tag

onBlur event handler

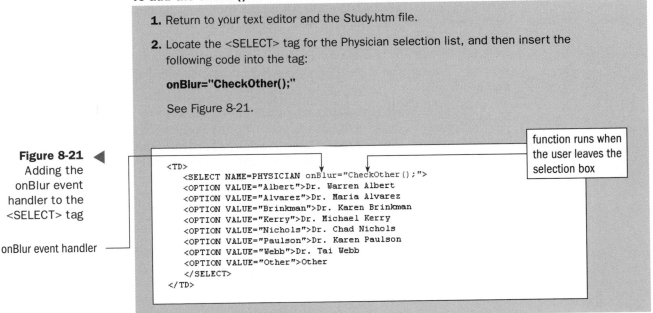

```
<TD>
    <SELECT NAME=PHYSICIAN onBlur="CheckOther();">
    <OPTION VALUE="Albert">Dr. Warren Albert
    <OPTION VALUE="Alvarez">Dr. Maria Alvarez
    <OPTION VALUE="Brinkman">Dr. Karen Brinkman
    <OPTION VALUE="Kerry">Dr. Michael Kerry
    <OPTION VALUE="Nichols">Dr. Chad Nichols
    <OPTION VALUE="Paulson">Dr. Karen Paulson
    <OPTION VALUE="Webb">Dr. Tai Webb
    <OPTION VALUE="Other">Other
    </SELECT>
</TD>
```

function runs when the user leaves the selection box

Now you have to create the CheckOther() function. To do so, you need to learn a little about how JavaScript works with selection lists and their options. JavaScript treats a selection list as an array of option values. In the case of Dr. Paulson's form, the tags that define the Physician selection list are:

```
<SELECT NAME=PHYSICIAN>
    <OPTION VALUE="Albert">Dr. Warren Albert
    <OPTION VALUE="Alvarez">Dr. Maria Alvarez
    <OPTION VALUE="Brinkman">Dr. Karen Brinkman
    <OPTION VALUE="Kerry">Dr. Michael Kerry
    <OPTION VALUE="Nichols">Dr. Chad Nichols
    <OPTION VALUE="Paulson">Dr. Karen Paulson
    <OPTION VALUE="Webb">Dr. Tai Webb
    <OPTION VALUE="Other">Other
</SELECT>
```

Two of the properties associated with selection lists are the value and text properties. Each option in the selection list has a value property that corresponds to the VALUE property entered into the <OPTION> tag. For the Physician selection list, the following are the JavaScript objects and properties for each option value:

```
document.REG.PHYSICIAN.options[0].value="Albert"
document.REG.PHYSICIAN.options[1].value="Alvarez"
document.REG.PHYSICIAN.options[2].value="Brinkman"
document.REG.PHYSICIAN.options[3].value="Kerry"
document.REG.PHYSICIAN.options[4].value="Nichols"
document.REG.PHYSICIAN.options[5].value="Paulson"
document.REG.PHYSICIAN.options[6].value="Webb"
document.REG.PHYSICIAN.options[7].value="Other"
```

Each option in the selection list belongs to a hierarchy of object names. In this case, the hierarchy starts with the document object, goes to the REG form within the document, then goes to the PHYSICIAN field within the form and, finally, goes to each individual option within the selection list. Note that the array of selection options starts with an index value of 0, not 1.

Similarly, the text that is actually displayed in the selection list is specified by the text property. For options in the Physician selection list, this results in the following objects and properties:

```
document.REG.PHYSICIAN.options[0].text="Dr. Warren Albert"
document.REG.PHYSICIAN.options[1].text="Dr. Maria Alvarez"
document.REG.PHYSICIAN.options[2].text="Dr. Karen Brinkman"
document.REG.PHYSICIAN.options[3].text="Dr. Michael Kerry"
document.REG.PHYSICIAN.options[4].text="Dr. Chad Nichols"
document.REG.PHYSICIAN.options[5].text="Dr. Karen Paulson"
document.REG.PHYSICIAN.options[6].text="Dr. Tai Webb"
document.REG.PHYSICIAN.options[7].text="Other"
```

Figure 8-22 shows some of the other properties and methods associated with selection lists and selection options.

Figure 8-22 ◀
Properties and
methods of
selection lists

Properties of Selection Lists	Description
length	The number of options in the list
name	The name of the selection list
selectedIndex	The index value of the currently selected option in the list

Properties of Options in the List	Description
defaultSelected	A Boolean value indicating whether the option is selected by default
index	The index value of the option
selected	A Boolean value indicating whether the option is currently selected
text	The text associated with the option displayed in the browser
value	The value of the option

Methods of Selection Lists	Description
focus()	Makes the selection list active
blur()	Leaves the selection list

REFERENCE window

REFERENCING VALUES IN A SELECTION LIST

- To reference the currently selected option value in a selection list, use the object and property:
  document.*FORM*.*FIELD*.options[*index*].value
  where *FORM* is the name of the Web page form, *FIELD* is the name of the selection field, and *index* is the index number of the currently selected option.
- To reference the currently selected option text (the text displayed in the selection box) in a selection list, use the object and property:
  document.*FORM*.*FIELD*.options[*index*].text
- To determine the index number of the currently selected option, use the JavaScript command:
  IndexVariable = document.*FORM*.*FIELD*.selectedIndex;
  where *IndexVariable* is a variable that will contain the value of the currently selected index.

The first task the CheckOther() function should perform is to determine whether the user has chosen the option "Other" from the Physician selection list. The option the user selects is stored in the selectedIndex property. For example, if the user selects "Other" from the selection list, the following object has a value of 7, because "Other" has an index value of 7 in the array of selection options:

```
document.REG.PHYSICIAN.selectedIndex
```

If the user selects "Other" from the list of physicians, you want the CheckOther() function to prompt the user for the physician's name before going on to the next field in the form (the APGAR Activity score). However, if the user selects one of the physicians in the list, then the form should proceed to the APGAR Activity field without prompting. The code for the CheckOther() function, therefore, is as follows:

```
function CheckOther() {
    if(document.REG.PHYSICIAN.selectedIndex==7) {
    //Prompt for the name of the physician
}
    document.REG.ACT.focus();
}
```

The second line of the function is only a comment right now. You don't know how to prompt the user for information yet—that topic will be covered shortly. For now, you'll enter this function as shown into the Study.htm file.

To add the CheckOther() function to the Study.htm file:

1. Go to the <SCRIPT> tag in the Study.htm file.

2. Below the StartForm() function, enter the following commands:

```
function CheckOther() {
    if(document.REG.PHYSICIAN.selectedIndex==7) {
    //Prompt for the name of the physician
}
    document.REG.ACT.focus();
}
```

Your file should look like Figure 8-23.

Figure 8-23
Inserting the CheckOther() function

checks whether the user has selected "Other" from the list

```
function StartForm() {
    document.REG.FORMDATE.value=DateToday();
    document.REG.FIRST.focus();
}

function CheckOther() {
    if(document.REG.PHYSICIAN.selectedIndex==7) {
    //Prompt for the name of the physician
}
    document.REG.ACT.focus();
}

//Stop hiding -->
</SCRIPT>
```

Prompting the User for Input

To prompt the user for input, JavaScript provides the prompt() method. The **prompt() method** creates a dialog box containing a message and an input field into which the user can type a value or text string. The syntax for the prompt() method is:

```
prompt("Message", "Default_text");
```

where *Message* is the message that will appear in the dialog box, and *Default_text* is the default text that appears in the dialog box's input field. Figure 8-24 shows an example of the JavaScript prompt() method.

Figure 8-24 ◀
Prompt dialog
box as it
appears in
two browsers

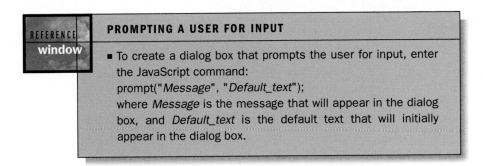

JavaScript command

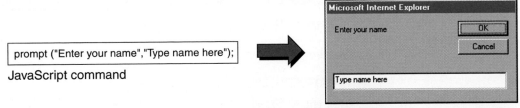

Internet Explorer prompt dialog box

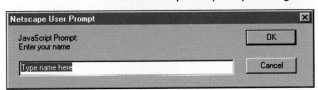

Netscape Navigator prompt dialog box

REFERENCE window	**PROMPTING A USER FOR INPUT**
	▪ To create a dialog box that prompts the user for input, enter the JavaScript command: prompt("*Message*", "*Default_text*"); where *Message* is the message that will appear in the dialog box, and *Default_text* is the default text that will initially appear in the dialog box.

The prompt() method also returns a result that can be stored in a variable or placed in an object. For example, the following JavaScript command will place whatever text the user enters in the dialog box into the UserName variable:

```
UserName=prompt("Enter your name","Type name here");
```

You can use the prompt() method in the CheckOther() function to prompt the user for the name of the physician, and then insert the response into the OTHERNAME field. The command to do this is:

```
document.REG.OTHERNAME.value=prompt("Enter name of
physician","Name");
```

You'll replace the comment in the CheckOther() function with this command now.

To add the prompt() method to the CheckOther() function:

1. Go to the CheckOther() function in the Study.htm file.

2. Replace the comment (//Prompt for the name of the physician) in the function with the following line (make sure to type this text all on one line):

   document.REG.OTHERNAME.value=prompt("Enter name of physician","Name");

   Figure 8-25 shows the revised code for the CheckOther() function.

Figure 8-25
Creating
a prompt
dialog box

prompt message

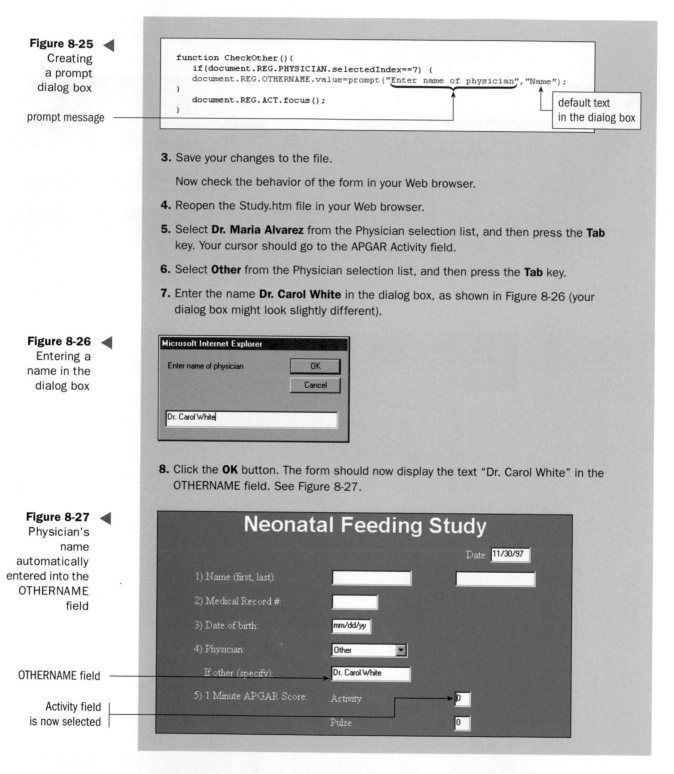

```
function CheckOther(){
    if(document.REG.PHYSICIAN.selectedIndex==7) {
    document.REG.OTHERNAME.value=prompt("Enter name of physician","Name");
    }
    document.REG.ACT.focus();
}
```

default text
in the dialog box

3. Save your changes to the file.

Now check the behavior of the form in your Web browser.

4. Reopen the Study.htm file in your Web browser.

5. Select **Dr. Maria Alvarez** from the Physician selection list, and then press the **Tab** key. Your cursor should go to the APGAR Activity field.

6. Select **Other** from the Physician selection list, and then press the **Tab** key.

7. Enter the name **Dr. Carol White** in the dialog box, as shown in Figure 8-26 (your dialog box might look slightly different).

Figure 8-26
Entering a
name in the
dialog box

Microsoft Internet Explorer

Enter name of physician   OK

Cancel

Dr. Carol White

8. Click the **OK** button. The form should now display the text "Dr. Carol White" in the OTHERNAME field. See Figure 8-27.

Figure 8-27
Physician's
name
automatically
entered into the
OTHERNAME
field

Neonatal Feeding Study

Date: 11/30/97

1) Name (first, last):

2) Medical Record #:

3) Date of birth: mm/dd/yy

4) Physician: Other

OTHERNAME field ——— If other (specify): Dr. Carol White

5) 1 Minute APGAR Score: Activity   0

Activity field
is now selected

Pulse   0

One of the advantages of using a dialog box rather than simply moving the cursor to the OTHERNAME field is that it alerts the user that something specific must be entered.

Quick Check

1. Define the following terms: event, event handler, and event method.

2. How would you modify your HTML file to run the function Welcome() whenever the page is loaded into the browser?

3 How would you modify the following tag so that it runs the function CheckCredit() whenever the user exits the input field?

```
<INPUT NAME=CreditNumber>
```

Use the following HTML tags to answer Quick Checks 4 through 6:

```
<FORM NAME=PRODUCT>
    <SELECT NAME=MODEL>
            <OPTION VALUE="P220">Pentium 220
            <OPTION VALUE="P300">Pentium 300
            <OPTION VALUE="P500">Pentium 500
    <SELECT>
</FORM>
```

4 What JavaScript command would you enter to change the value of the first option in the selection list to "P250"?

5 What JavaScript command would you enter to change the text of the first option in the selection list to "Pentium 250"?

6 What JavaScript command would you enter to store the index of the option the user selected in a variable named ModelNumber?

7 What JavaScript command would create a dialog box prompting the user with the message "Enter a new model" and provide an input box for the user to enter the new value?

You've learned how to work with events and event handlers, and you've used JavaScript to insert text automatically into a form field and to control the movement of the cursor in Dr. Paulson's form. In the next session you'll learn how to create a calculated field and how to alert users when they enter unacceptable values into the form.

SESSION

8.3

In this session you will learn how to create a calculated field and how to perform validation checks on values that the user enters. You'll learn how to notify the user when mistakes have been made. You'll also learn how to perform a final validation check when the form is submitted.

Creating Calculated Fields

At this point you've completed the first two tasks in your list for Dr. Paulson's registration form.

☑ 1) Automatically enter the current date in the FORMDATE field and move to the next field in the form.

☑ 2) If "Other" is selected from the Physician selection list box, prompt for the name of the physician; otherwise go to the APGAR component fields.

☐ 3) Automatically calculate the total APGAR score.

☐ 4) Check that valid APGAR component scores have been entered.

☐ 5) Check that parental consent has been obtained before submitting the form.

Your next task is to calculate the total APGAR score automatically and store this value in the TOTAL field. The APGAR score is a measure of the general health of the baby and is composed of the five components: activity, pulse, grimace, appearance, and respiration. The formula for the total APGAR score is simply:

```
TOTAL = ACTIVITY + PULSE + GRIMACE + APPEARANCE + RESPIRATION
```

In Dr. Paulson's form, you need to create a function named APGAR() that will recalculate the total APGAR value every time the focus leaves one of the five component fields. The first thing you'll do is add the onBlur() event handler to call the APGAR() function to the <INPUT> tags for those five fields.

To enter the onBlur() event handler to the five APGAR fields:

1. If you took a break after the previous session, start your text editor and reopen the Study.htm file from the Tutorial.08 folder of your Student Disk.

2. Go to the <INPUT> tag for the Activity field and insert the line:

   onBlur="APGAR();"

   See Figure 8-28.

Figure 8-28 ◀
Using the onBlur event handler to call the APGAR() function

```
<!--- Activity component of the APGAR score --->
<TR>
   <TD ROWSPAN=6 VALIGN=TOP>
      5) 1 Minute APGAR Score:
   </TD>
   <TD>
      Activity
   </TD>
   <TD>
      <INPUT NAME=ACT VALUE=0 SIZE=1 MAXLENGTH=1 onBlur="APGAR();">
   </TD>
</TR>
```

3. Add this same line of code to the <INPUT> tags of the other four component fields (but *not* to the TOTAL field). You might want to use the Copy and Paste functions of your text editor.

4. Save your changes to the Study.htm file.

Next, you need to create the APGAR() function. This function will add up the values entered into each of the component fields; however, because JavaScript treats these values as text, you must first convert them from the text format to the number format so that the APGAR() function can add them together. You can do this with the eval() function.

REFERENCE window	**CONVERTING A TEXT VALUE TO A NUMBER VALUE**
	▪ To change a text value into a numeric value, use the eval() function as follows: *NumberVariable* = eval(*TextValue*); where *NumberVariable* is a variable that will contain the number value, and *TextValue* is a text string or text variable. For example, eval("55") produces the numeric value 55.

The **eval()** function takes a number that is represented as a text string and converts it to a number. For example, the following command takes the text string "10," converts it to the number 10, and stores that value in the variable TOTAL:

```
TOTAL = eval("10");
```

Converting the text values to numbers is important; otherwise, JavaScript will simply append one text string to the other. For example, consider the following command:

```
"10" + "5"
```

This command results in the text string "105". However, the following command results in the numeric value 15:

```
eval("10") + eval("5")
```

Using the eval() function, you would enter the APGAR() function as follows:

```
function APGAR() {
    var A = eval(document.REG.ACT.value);
    var P = eval(document.REG.PULSE.value);
    var G = eval(document.REG.GRIMACE.value);
    var AP = eval(document.REG.APP.value);
    var R = eval(document.REG.RESP.value);
    document.REG.TOTAL.value = A + P + G + AP + R;
}
```

This function takes the values from each of the five component fields, stores them in the variables indicated, and then adds the variables together. The result is placed directly into the TOTAL field. You'll add the APGAR() function to the Study.htm file now.

To create the APGAR() function:

1. Locate the CheckOther() function at the top of the Study.htm file and insert the following lines of code below it.

```
function APGAR() {
    var A = eval(document.REG.ACT.value);
    var P = eval(document.REG.PULSE.value);
    var G = eval(document.REG.GRIMACE.value);
    var AP = eval(document.REG.APP.value);
    var R = eval(document.REG.RESP.value);
    document.REG.TOTAL.value = A + P + G + AP + R;
}
```

Figure 8-29 shows the revised file.

Figure 8-29 ◀
Inserting the
APGAR()
function

```
function CheckOther() {
    if(document.REG.PHYSICIAN.selectedIndex==7) {
    document.REG.OTHERNAME.value=prompt("Enter name of physician","Name");
}

    document.REG.ACT.focus();
}

function APGAR() {
    var A = eval(document.REG.ACT.value);
    var P = eval(document.REG.PULSE.value);
    var G = eval(document.REG.GRIMACE.value);
    var AP = eval(document.REG.APP.value);
    var R = eval(document.REG.RESP.value);
    document.REG.TOTAL.value = A + P + G + AP + R;
}

//Stop hiding -->
</SCRIPT>
```

2. Save your changes to the Study.htm file, and then reopen the file in your Web browser. Notice that each APGAR component field has a default value of O.

Next, you'll check the function by entering some test values.

3. Enter the following APGAR component values:

2 in the Activity field

0 in the Pulse field

1 in the Grimace field

2 in the Appearance field

2 in the Respiration field

Each time you enter a component value and press the Tab key to leave the field, triggering the onBlur() event handler, the form should run the APGAR() function, and the value in the TOTAL field should change. Figure 8-30 shows the final result after you tab out of the Respiration field.

Figure 8-30 ◀
Calculating
the total
APGAR score

total result is
automatically
calculated

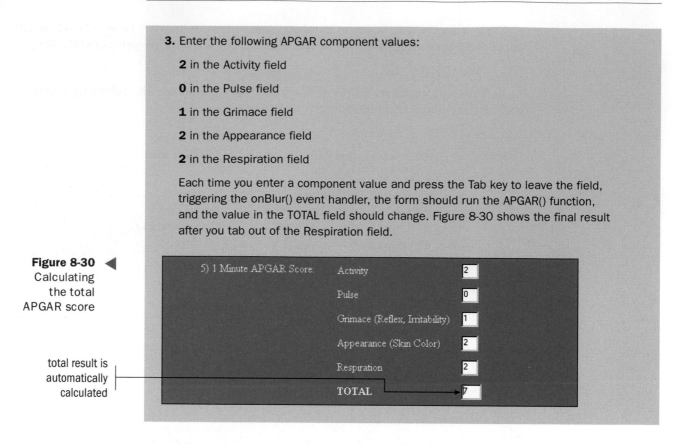

By using the onBlur() event handler and the APGAR() function, you've created a field that is automatically calculated for the user. In its current form, the APGAR() function will accept any value for each of the components; however, as indicated on your task list, the function must also make sure that only valid APGAR component scores are entered.

☑ 1) Automatically enter the current date in the FORMDATE field and move to the next field in the form.

☑ 2) If "Other" is selected from the Physician selection list box, prompt for the name of the physician; otherwise go to the APGAR component fields.

☑ 3) Automatically calculate the total APGAR score.

☐ 4) Check that valid APGAR component scores have been entered.

☐ 5) Check that parental consent has been obtained before submitting the form.

Validating User Input

Dr. Paulson wants the form to allow only the values 0, 1, and 2 to be entered into the APGAR component fields. Therefore, you have to include some way of checking the user's entries in these fields to make sure that they are valid. If the user enters an incorrect value in one of the component fields, two things must happen:

1. The browser should display a dialog box informing the user of the mistake.

2. The cursor should be positioned back in the field in which the user entered the incorrect value, preventing the user from leaving the field until a valid value has been entered.

This presents a problem in the registration form. Five different component fields could be accessing the APGAR() function at any time. How do you know which field is the one in which the user entered an incorrect value? To make this work, you have to pass information to the function, indicating which field is using it. You do this with the "this" keyword.

The "this" Keyword

The **this** keyword is a word reserved by JavaScript to refer to the currently selected object (whatever that might be). For example, if the Pulse field is the current field, the following two commands produce the same action (changing the value of the Pulse field to 2):

```
document.REG.PULSE.value = 2;
this.value = 2;
```

You can also use the "this" keyword to pass information about the currently selected field to a function. For example, you have two input boxes, PULSE and RESP, both of which will use the same function, SetVal(), as shown in the following lines of code:

```
<SCRIPT>
function SetVal(field) {
    field.value = 2;
}
</SCRIPT>

<INPUT NAME = PULSE onFocus="SetVal(this);">
<INPUT NAME = RESP onFocus="SetVal(this);">
```

When the PULSE input box receives the focus, it calls the SetVal() function, including the "this" keyword, as a parameter. Because the PULSE input box is the currently selected object, the SetVal() function creates a variable named "field" that refers to the PULSE input box. Because "field" now refers to the PULSE input box, the command "field.value = 2;" changes the value of the input box to 2. When the RESP input box receives the focus, the same thing occurs: the "this" keyword is included as a parameter value, and the SetVal() function uses that information to determine that it must change the value of the RESP field.

In the same way, you can modify the <INPUT> tags for the five APGAR component fields to include information, through the "this" keyword, to tell the APGAR() function which field is currently selected. You'll add the "this" keyword to the onBlur event handler for each of the APGAR component fields now.

To add the "this" keyword to the onBlur() event handlers:

1. Return to the Study.htm file in your text editor and go to the <INPUT> tag for the Activity field.

2. In the code onBlur="APGAR();" type the word **this** within the parentheses.

3. Repeat Step 2 in the <INPUT> tags for the remaining four components of the APGAR score.

4. Save your changes.

Now that you've added the "this" keyword to the event handler that calls the APGAR() function, you need to make several changes to the function itself. First, the function must store the value of the active field in a variable. Then it needs to test whether or not the value of that variable is equal to 0, 1, or 2. If it is, the function can calculate the total APGAR score as before; if not, the function should alert the user that a mistake has been made and return the cursor to the appropriate field so that the user can enter the correct value.

The revised APGAR() function is as follows:

```
function APGAR(field) {
    var score = field.value;
    if(score==0 || score==1 || score==2) {
        var A = eval(document.REG.ACT.value);
        var P = eval(document.REG.PULSE.value);
        var G = eval(document.REG.GRIMACE.value);
        var AP = eval(document.REG.APP.value);
        var R = eval(document.REG.RESP.value);
        document.REG.TOTAL.value = A + P + G + AP + R;
    } else {
        //alert the user
        field.focus();
    }
}
```

Figure 8-31 illustrates how this function works.

Figure 8-31
Testing an
APGAR
component
value

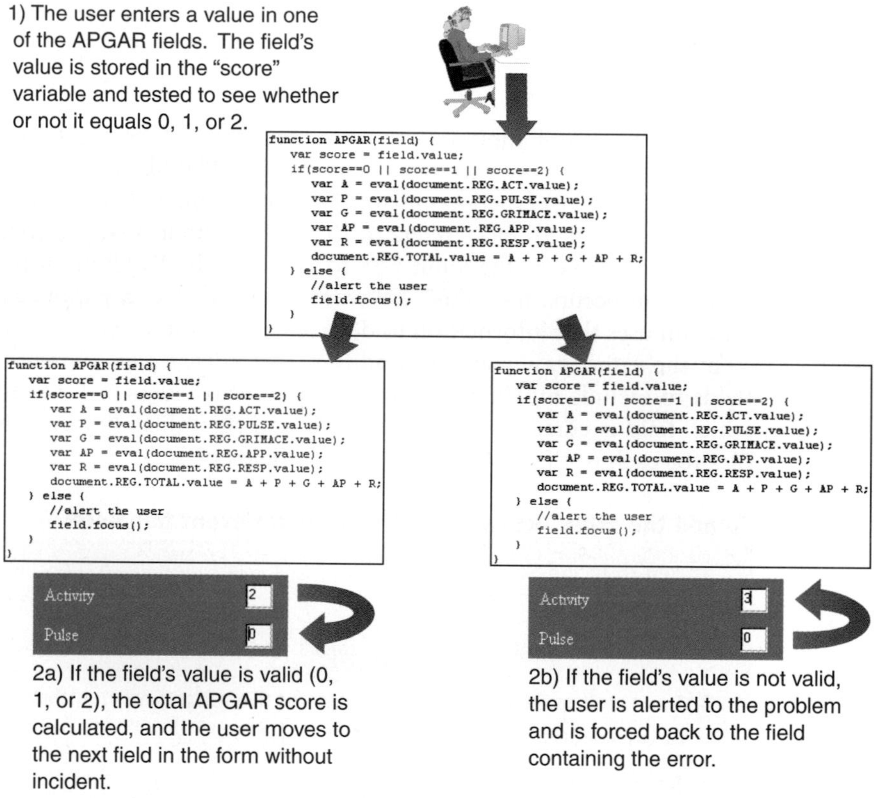

1) The user enters a value in one of the APGAR fields. The field's value is stored in the "score" variable and tested to see whether or not it equals 0, 1, or 2.

2a) If the field's value is valid (0, 1, or 2), the total APGAR score is calculated, and the user moves to the next field in the form without incident.

2b) If the field's value is not valid, the user is alerted to the problem and is forced back to the field containing the error.

The new version of the APGAR() function has a single parameter, "field," which stores information about which field called the function. The function then stores the current value of this field in a variable named "score." Then the function tests whether score equals 0 *or* score equals 1 *or* score equals 2 (remember that the ‖ symbols represent the "or" logical operator). If this is the case, the function calculates the total APGAR score as before, and the user continues on to the next field in the form. However, if the user enters a value other than 0, 1, or 2, the function alerts the user that a mistake has been made and returns the user to the original field. As with the prompt() method earlier, the command for alerting the user is inserted as a comment at this point. In the next section, you'll learn how to create a dialog box that alerts the user to an error.

Now, you need to revise the APGAR() function to include the new commands.

To revise the APGAR() function:

1. Locate the APGAR() function at the top of the Study.htm file.

2. In the line "function APGAR() {" type the word **field** within the parentheses.

3. Add the following two lines below the function statement (indented three spaces to make the code easier to follow):

```
var score = field.value;
if(score==0 || score==1 || score==2) {
```

TROUBLE? The | symbol is often located above the \ symbol on your keyboard. You can type it by pressing the \ key while holding down the Shift key.

4. Insert the following commands *above* the last line (the closing brace }) of the function (indented three spaces):

```
} else {
   //alert the user
   field.focus();
}
```

Figure 8-32 shows the entire APGAR() function as it should appear in your text editor.

Figure 8-32 ◀
Revised
APGAR()
function

retrieves the value of
the current field and
stores it in the
"score" variable

commands run
if a valid APGAR
value is entered

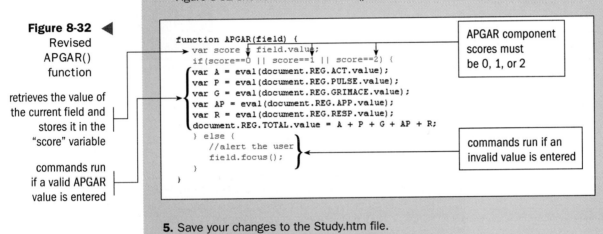

```
function APGAR(field) {
   var score = field.value;
   if(score==0 || score==1 || score==2) {
      var A = eval(document.REG.ACT.value);
      var P = eval(document.REG.PULSE.value);
      var G = eval(document.REG.GRIMACE.value);
      var AP = eval(document.REG.APP.value);
      var R = eval(document.REG.RESP.value);
      document.REG.TOTAL.value = A + P + G + AP + R;
   } else {
      //alert the user
      field.focus();
   }
}
```

APGAR component scores must be 0, 1, or 2

commands run if an invalid value is entered

5. Save your changes to the Study.htm file.

Notifying the User with Alert and Confirm Dialog Boxes

If the user enters an incorrect value for one of the APGAR components, the form should display a dialog box informing the user of the error. To accomplish this, you can use the alert() method. The **alert() method** operates in the same way as the prompt() method, except that it does not provide an input box in which the user can type a response. Instead, it simply displays a dialog box containing a message. The syntax for the alert() method is:

```
alert("Message");
```

where *Message* is the message that will appear in the dialog box. An example of an alert dialog box is shown in Figure 8-33. (Note that different browsers will display slightly different dialog boxes.)

Figure 8-33 ◀
Alert dialog box
as it appears in
two browsers

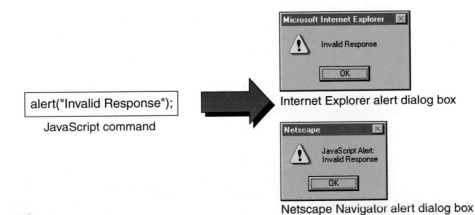

alert("Invalid Response");

JavaScript command

Microsoft Internet Explorer

Invalid Response

OK

Internet Explorer alert dialog box

Netscape

JavaScript Alert:
Invalid Response

OK

Netscape Navigator alert dialog box

JavaScript provides another method called the confirm() method, which works in the same way as the prompt() and alert() methods. The **confirm() method** displays a message in a dialog box that is similar to the alert dialog box, except that it includes both an OK button and a Cancel button. If the user clicks the OK button, the value "true" is returned. If the user clicks the Cancel button, the value "false" is returned. Figure 8-34 shows an example of using the confirm() method to create a dialog box. You would use the confirm() method in situations that require a "yes" (OK) or "no" (Cancel) response from the user.

Figure 8-34 ◀
Confirm dialog
box as it
appears in
two browsers

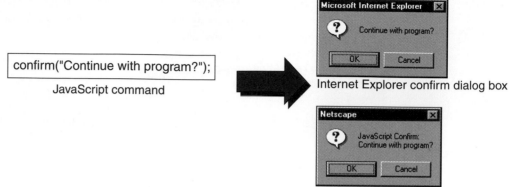

confirm("Continue with program?");

JavaScript command

Internet Explorer confirm dialog box

Netscape Navigator confirm dialog box

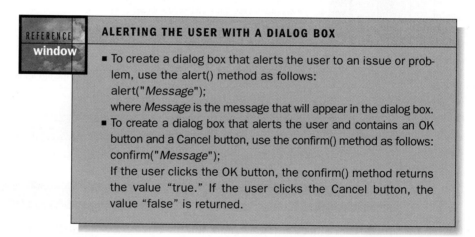

REFERENCE
window

ALERTING THE USER WITH A DIALOG BOX

- To create a dialog box that alerts the user to an issue or problem, use the alert() method as follows:
  alert("*Message*");
  where *Message* is the message that will appear in the dialog box.
- To create a dialog box that alerts the user and contains an OK button and a Cancel button, use the confirm() method as follows:
  confirm("*Message*");
  If the user clicks the OK button, the confirm() method returns the value "true." If the user clicks the Cancel button, the value "false" is returned.

In your program, you need to use the alert() method. You'll replace the comment line in the APGAR() function with a command to alert the user that only values of 0, 1, and 2 are allowed.

To add the alert() method to the APGAR() function:

1. In the APGAR() function, replace the comment "//alert the user" with the following line of code:

   alert("You must enter a 0, 1, or 2");

   Figure 8-35 shows the final version of the APGAR() function.

Figure 8-35 ◀
Final APGAR()
function

```
function APGAR(field) {
    var score = field.value;
    if(score==0 || score==1 || score==2) {
    var A = eval(document.REG.ACT.value);
    var P = eval(document.REG.PULSE.value);
    var G = eval(document.REG.GRIMACE.value);
    var AP = eval(document.REG.APP.value);
    var R = eval(document.REG.RESP.value);
    document.REG.TOTAL.value = A + P + G + AP + R;
    } else {
        alert("You must enter a 0, 1, or 2");
        field.focus();
    }
}
```

creates an
alert dialog box ⟶

2. Save your changes, and then reopen the file in your Web browser.

   To test the revised APGAR() function, you'll attempt to enter an incorrect value in the Activity field.

3. Click the **Activity** input box and change its value from the default of 0 to **3**, and then press the **Tab** key. Your Web browser should display a dialog box similar to the one shown in Figure 8-36.

Figure 8-36 ◀
Alerting the
user to an
invalid entry

alert dialog box ⟶

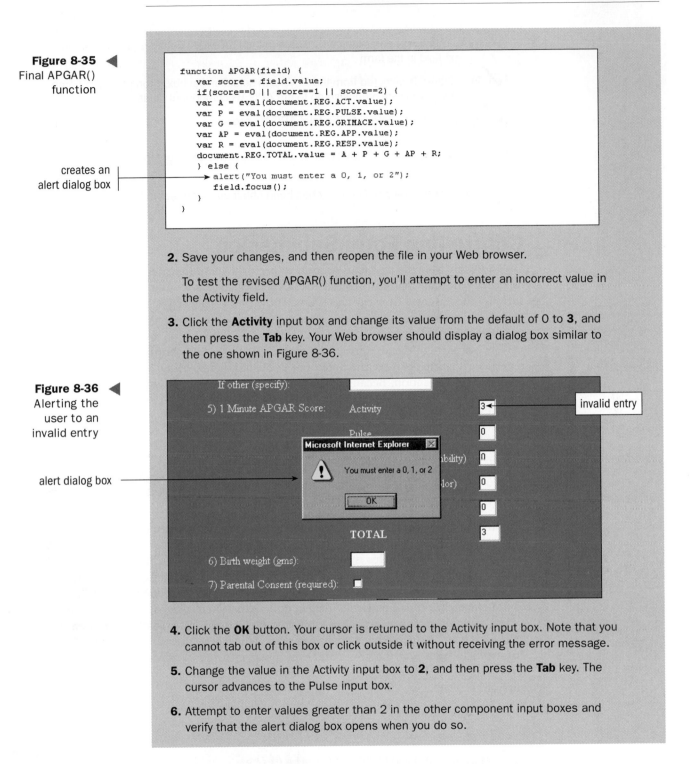

4. Click the **OK** button. Your cursor is returned to the Activity input box. Note that you cannot tab out of this box or click outside it without receiving the error message.

5. Change the value in the Activity input box to **2**, and then press the **Tab** key. The cursor advances to the Pulse input box.

6. Attempt to enter values greater than 2 in the other component input boxes and verify that the alert dialog box opens when you do so.

You've finished modifying the necessary fields on the registration form. The next task on your list is to provide one final validity check before the form is submitted to a CGI script running on the hospital's Web server.

☑ 1) Automatically enter the current date in the FORMDATE field and move to the next field in the form.

☑ 2) If "Other" is selected from the Physician selection list box, prompt for the name of the physician; otherwise go to the APGAR component fields.

☑ 3) Automatically calculate the total APGAR score.

☑ 4) Check that valid APGAR component scores have been entered.

☐ 5) Check that parental consent has been obtained before submitting the form.

Controlling Form Submission

Dr. Paulson wants the registration form to perform a validity check to determine whether or not a parental consent form has been filled out. This is indicated on the registration form by the Parental Consent check box. If the box is checked, then it is assumed that the consent form has been filled out. This validity check must be performed when the user tries to submit the form.

When a user completes a form and then clicks the Submit button, a Submit event is initiated. JavaScript provides the onSubmit event handler to allow you to run a program in response to this action. Because the Submit event is associated with the form object, you must place the event handler in the <FORM> tag, as shown in the following example:

```
<SCRIPT>
function goodbye() {
    alert("Thank you for your time");
}
</SCRIPT>
<FORM onSubmit="goodbye();">
```

In this example, the goodbye() function is run automatically when the user clicks the Submit button located elsewhere in the HTML file, and a dialog box with the message "Thank you for your time" is displayed. This is a simple example in which the function does not actually perform any validation; it just displays a message. The form in this example will be submitted to the CGI script as soon as the user clicks the OK button in the alert dialog box. When you need to validate the form or a particular field in it, the situation is a bit more complicated.

For validation you need a function that will return a Boolean value, either true or false—a "true" value if the form passes your validation criteria, and a "false" value if it does not. In addition, the command you insert into the <FORM> tag must include the *return* keyword. For example, if the function you're running is named Check_Data(), the correct HTML tag is:

```
<FORM onSubmit="return Check_Data();">
```

and *not*:

```
<FORM onSubmit="Check_Data();">
```

By adding the *return* keyword to the command, you're applying whatever value is calculated by the Check_Data() function to the onSubmit event handler. So if Check_Data() returns the value "false," the submission is canceled. If it returns the value "true," the form is submitted. If you don't include the "return" keyword, the Check_Data() function will still run, but it will not have any impact on the event handler. In the case of Dr. Paulson's form, omitting the "return" keyword would cause the form to be submitted regardless of whether or not parental consent has been obtained—which is not what you want. So you must include the "return" keyword with the event handler.

With this in mind, you'll next add the onSubmit event handler to the <FORM> tag, using the function name Check_Data(). You haven't created this function yet, but you will do so in the next set of steps.

To add the Check_Data() function to the onSubmit event handler:

1. Return to the Study.htm file in your text editor and go to the <FORM> tag.

2. In the <FORM> tag, insert the following command (see Figure 8-37):

onSubmit="return Check_Data();"

Figure 8-37 ◄
Using the
onSubmit event
handler

command runs when
the form is submitted

```
<BODY BGCOLOR="#008080" TEXT=WHITE onLoad="StartForm();">
<FORM NAME=REG onSubmit="return Check_Data();">
<CENTER>
<IMG SRC="Logo.gif" WIDTH=450 HEIGHT=75 ALT="St. Marys of Northland Pines">
```

3. Save your changes to the file.

Now you need to create the Check_Data() function, whose purpose is to determine whether or not the Parental Consent check box has been checked. You can tell whether a check box object has been checked using the "checked" property. This property is a Boolean value, either true or false. In Dr. Paulson's form, the Parental Consent check box has the field name CONSENT. The following JavaScript command will assign the value "true" to the "parents_agree" variable if the check box is checked, and "false" if it is not:

```
var parents_agree=document.REG.CONSENT.checked;
```

Other properties and methods of check box objects are shown in Figure 8-38.

Figure 8-38 ◄
Properties and
methods of
check boxes

Property	Description
checked	A Boolean value indicating whether or not the check box has been checked
defaultChecked	A Boolean value indicating whether or not the check box is checked by default
name	The name of the check box
value	The value associated with the check box when it is checked

Method	Description
click()	Clicks the check box
focus()	Makes the check box active

Once the value of the parents_agree variable is known, Dr. Paulson wants the form to take one of two actions: it should indicate that the form has been submitted if parents_agree is "true," or it should alert the user that a mistake has been made if parents_agree is "false." You can accomplish this using the following commands:

```
if(parents_agree) {
   alert("Form submitted successfully");
} else {
   alert("You still need parental consent");
}
```

Note that because parents_agree is a Boolean variable with a value of either "true" or "false," it is sufficient to place it alone in the conditional expression for the If statement. JavaScript will simply use the value of parents_agree to determine how to proceed.

The final part of the Check_Data() function should return the value of the parents_agree variable. Remember, this value will determine whether or not the form is submitted. The complete text of the Check_Data() function, therefore, is:

```
function Check_Data() {
    var parents_agree=document.REG.CONSENT.checked;
    if(parents_agree) {
       alert("Form submitted successfully");
    } else {
       alert("You still need parental consent");
    }
    return parents_agree;
}
```

You'll add this function to the Study.htm file now.

To create the Check_Data() function:

1. Below the APGAR() function at the top of the Study.htm file, insert the following lines:

```
function Check_Data() {
    var parents_agree=document.REG.CONSENT.checked;
    if(parents_agree) {
       alert("Form submitted successfully");
    } else {
       alert("You still need parental consent");
    }
    return parents_agree;
}
```

Figure 8-39 shows the new function as it appears in your file.

Figure 8-39 ◀
Inserting the
Check_Data()
function

```
function Check_Data() {
   var parents_agree=document.REG.CONSENT.checked;
   if(parents_agree) {
      alert("Form submitted successfully");
   } else {
      alert("You still need parental consent");
   }
   return parents_agree;
}


//Stop hiding -->
</SCRIPT>
</HEAD>

<BODY BGCOLOR="#008080" TEXT=WHITE onLoad="StartForm();">
<FORM NAME=REG onSubmit="return Check_Data();">
```

2. Save your changes to Study.htm, and then reopen the file in your Web browser.

Next, you'll test the Check_Data() function by trying to submit the form without first checking the Parental Consent check box.

3. Click the **Register** button on the form. A dialog box similar to the one shown in Figure 8-40 is displayed.

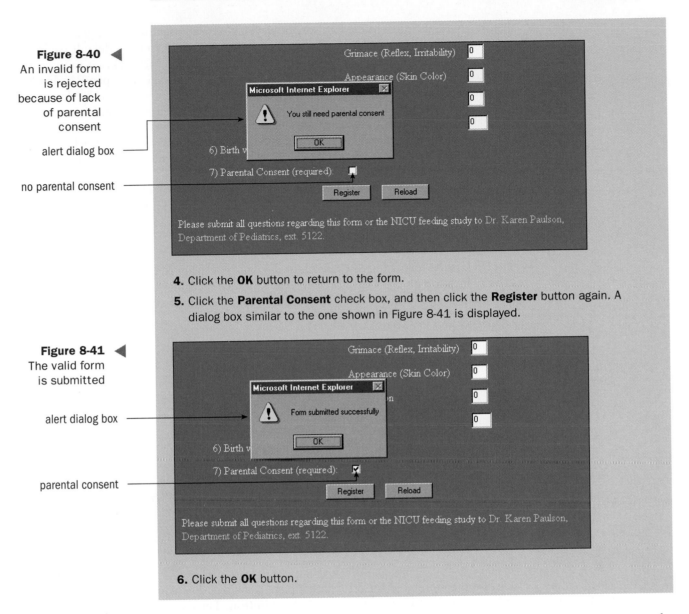

Figure 8-40
An invalid form
is rejected
because of lack
of parental
consent

alert dialog box

no parental consent

4. Click the **OK** button to return to the form.

5. Click the **Parental Consent** check box, and then click the **Register** button again. A dialog box similar to the one shown in Figure 8-41 is displayed.

Figure 8-41
The valid form
is submitted

alert dialog box

parental consent

6. Click the **OK** button.

In a more advanced version of this page, you might add other validation criteria to the Check_Data() function. For example, you might check whether or not a name and medical record number have been entered for the patient. You might double-check the values of each APGAR component to verify that they are still valid, and so forth. However, this example gives you an idea of how a final validation check would work, and of the importance of including validity checks in your form.

Reloading a Page

You've completed the tasks on your list for Dr. Paulson's registration form.

☑ 1) Automatically enter the current date in the FORMDATE field and move to the next field in the form.

☑ 2) If "Other" is selected from the Physician selection list box, prompt for the name of the physician; otherwise go to the APGAR component fields.

☑ 3) Automatically calculate the total APGAR score.

☑ 4) Check that valid APGAR component scores have been entered.

☑ 5) Check that parental consent has been obtained before submitting the form.

Before giving the form to Dr. Paulson, however, you need to modify the behavior of the Reset button. The Reset button will reset all fields in the form to their default values. Is this what you want? Not exactly; recall that the first action this form takes is to insert the date into the FORMDATE field. This action runs whenever the page is loaded. Unfortunately, resetting a form is not the same as reloading the page, so the date value would not be entered automatically if you simply included a Reset button for the user to click. Instead, your form should include a Reload button that will completely reload the page. This button will activate the onLoad event handler as well as reset all fields to their default values. In this way, the form will be in the correct condition for each user who enters a record in the form.

To reload a page, you use the location object. The **location object** contains information about the current location of the Web page. If you want to load a particular page in your browser, you can do so with the command:

```
location = URL;
```

where *URL* is the text string of the URL of the page you want to load. One of the properties of the location object is the "href" property, which identifies the URL of the currently loaded page. If you want to reload the current page, you can do so with the command:

```
location = location.href;
```

Note that you could also use the command "location.reload()," but this particular method is not supported by Internet Explorer version 3.0.

REFERENCE window	**LOADING A WEB PAGE**
	■ To load a Web page in your browser, use the JavaScript command: location = *URL* where *URL* is a text string containing the URL of the page you want to load. ■ To reload the current page in your Web browser, use the command: location = location.href;

Because the command for reloading a page is a single-line command, you can enter it directly into the <INPUT> tag for the Reload button. The command should be activated whenever the button is clicked, so you'll use the onClick event handler in the tag.

To insert the command to reload the page:

1. Return to the Study.htm file in your text editor, and go to the <INPUT> tag for the Reload button at the bottom of the form. This tag is located in the section "Form registration and reset buttons."

2. Insert the following command into the <INPUT> tag:

```
onclick="location=location.href;"
```

See Figure 8-42.

Figure 8-42 ◀
Reloading the
page with the
location object

```
<!--- Form registration and reset buttons --->
<TR>
    <TD COLSPAN=3 ALIGN=CENTER>
        <INPUT TYPE=SUBMIT VALUE="Register">  
        <INPUT TYPE=BUTTON VALUE="Reload" onClick="location=location.href;">
    </TD>
</TR>
</TABLE>
</CENTER>
```

command runs when
the Reload button
is clicked

3. Save your changes to the Study.htm file, and then reopen the file in your Web browser.

4. Enter some text in the form, and then click the **Reload** button. Verify that the page reloads properly, all fields display their default values, the current date is inserted into the FORMDATE field, and the cursor is placed in the First Name input box.

5. Close your Web browser and your text editor.

DESIGN
window

FORM VALIDATION TIPS

- Include descriptions with your input fields so that users know ahead of time what values are appropriate to enter in each field.
- Use check boxes, selection lists, and radio buttons as often as possible to control which values the users are allowed to enter.
- Create JavaScript functions that test values entered into your input boxes. If a value should be entered only within a defined range, create a function that rejects values outside that range.
- Make sure that any alert or prompt dialog boxes you create are clear and precise, informing the user exactly of the error that was made.
- Perform a second validation at the time at which the form is submitted to confirm that appropriate data values have been entered in all fields.

Quick Check

1. Why must you use the eval() function when adding input box values together?

2. If the input field WEIGHT in the STUDY form contains the value 50, and the WEIGHT input field contains the value 25, what value would be returned by the following expression?

    ```
    document.STUDY.WEIGHT.value + document.STUDY.WEIGHT2.value;
    ```

3. What does the "this" keyword refer to?

4. What command will create a dialog box containing the message "Weight Invalid" and an OK button?

5. What command will create a dialog box containing the message "Accept weight value?" along with an OK button and a Cancel button?

6. What should you add to the following tag so that it runs the form validation function CheckIt() when the user clicks the Submit button?

    ```
    <FORM NAME=STUDY>
    ```

7. In Quick Check 6, what must the CheckIt() function return in order for it to prohibit invalid forms from being submitted to a CGI script?

In developing Dr. Paulson's form, you learned about the object-based nature of the JavaScript language. You also learned how to run scripts in response to events that might occur in your own Web pages. Finally, you learned a little about form validation and its importance in ensuring the accuracy of data entered in a form.

You give the Study.htm file to Dr. Paulson for her evaluation. She will take the Web page you created and place it on the hospital's Web server. Before making it available to her clinical study, she'll test it to verify that the form validation commands you inserted work properly and that the form correctly places data into the hospital database via a CGI script running on the Web server. Dr. Paulson will get back to you with any changes she would like you to make.

Tutorial Assignments

After reviewing your form, Dr. Paulson made a few changes to it. She also has some additional modifications she wants you to make. The following is the list of changes and additions Dr. Paulson would like you to complete:

- Revise the APGAR function so that if the current field is the Respiration input box, the function will jump past the APGAR TOTAL input box to the Birth Weight input box. This will help prevent users from inadvertently entering data into the APGAR TOTAL input box.

- Another eligibility criterion is that patients must have a birth weight of 1200 grams or more. The form should alert users of this whenever a birthweight of less than 1200 grams is entered in the BWGT field.

- Revise the form so that it prohibits the user from submitting the form without parental consent or for an infant whose birth weight is less than 1200 grams.

Dr. Paulson gives you her updated file for you to work on, to make the changes noted. To revise Dr. Paulson's form:

1. Start your text editor and open the Studtxt2.htm file in the TAssign folder of the Tutorial.08 folder on your Student Disk, and then save the file as Study2.htm in the same folder.

2. Go to the APGAR() function. Below the line that calculates the total APGAR score, insert a nested If command block. The block should test whether or not the name of the current field is equal to RESP. If so, it should set the focus to the BWGT field.

3. Revise the BWGT field so that the CheckWgt() function is run whenever the focus leaves the field.

4. Create the CheckWgt() function, inserting it between the APGAR() and CheckData() functions in the HEAD section of the document.

5. Have the CheckWgt() function create a variable named "wgt" that contains the value of the BWGT field.

6. In the CheckWgt() function, if wgt is less than 1200, display an alert dialog box with the message "Patients with birth weights less than 1200 grams are ineligible."

7. Go to the <FORM> tag and insert an event handler that will return the value of the CheckData() function when the form is submitted.

EXPLORE

8. Go to the CheckData() function. Using what you know about JavaScript commands, provide a line-by-line interpretation of the function, indicating what each command does and what the overall result of the function is.

9. Save your changes to the file.

10. Load Study2.htm in your Web browser. Verify that pressing the Tab key in the Respiration field jumps you past the APGAR TOTAL field.

11. Try to submit the form under the following conditions:

   - birth weight = 1000 grams/parental consent
   - birth weight = 1800 grams/no parental consent
   - birth weight = 1200 grams/parental consent

   What happens under each condition?

12. Print a copy of your HTML and JavaScript code.

13. Close your Web browser and your text editor.

1. Creating an Online Order Form for UB Computing UB Computing is one of the leading manufacturers of PCs in the United States. Primarily a mail-order company, UB Computing has created a Web site where customers can purchase its products. Dale Crawford, the supervisor of Web Sales, has asked you to work on a Web page order form for the PS300 computer, a PC marketed for small businesses.

Customers can select different options for processor speed, memory, hard disk size, and monitor size. They can also add additional components such as modems and network cards. Because of this, the order form has to calculate the total cost of the PS300 under each possible configuration. The configuration options and their costs are shown in Figure 8-43.

Figure 8-43 ◀

Base Price of PS300 system = $2300	
Initial configuration: 300 MHz CPU, 4 GB hard drive, 32 MB memory, 15" monitor	
Other Configurations	
CPU	350 MHz (add $400)
Hard drive	8 GB (add $300)
Memory	16 MB (subtract $50); 64 MB (add $200); 128 MB (add $400)
Monitor	17" (add $300); 19" (add $500); 21" (add $700)
Modem	add $150
Network card	add $150

Dale gives you a Web page with the order form already created, as shown in Figure 8-44. Your job is to create a JavaScript function named TotalCost() that will calculate the total cost based on what the user has selected in the order form. The function will run whenever the user clicks the Calculate Total button at the bottom of the order form.

Figure 8-44 ◄

To create the UB Computing order form:

1. Start your text editor and open the file PSText.htm in the Cases folder of the Tutorial.08 folder on your Student Disk, and then save the file as PS300.htm in the same folder.

2. Within the <SCRIPT> tags at the top of the PS300.htm file, create the function TotalCost() (no parameters are needed).

3. Within the TotalCost() function, write JavaScript commands to perform the actions listed in Steps 4 through 12.

4. Declare the following variables with the indicated initial values:

   - CPUCost (the initial cost of the CPU) set to 0
   - HDCost (the initial cost of the hard drive) set to 0
   - MEMCost (the initial cost of the computer memory) set to 0
   - MONCost (the initial cost of the monitor) set to 0
   - MODEMCost (the initial cost of the modem) set to 0
   - ECARDCost (the initial cost of the Ethernet card) set to 0
   - BASE (the base price of the system) set to 2300

5. Determine which Processor Speed radio button the user has selected in the form. Individual radio buttons in the CPU field of the ORDER form are referred to using the following object property references:

   document.ORDER.CPU[0] for the first radio button (300 MHz CPU)

   document.ORDER.CPU[1] for the second radio button (350 MHz CPU)

Use an If statement to determine whether or not the following expression is true:

document.ORDER.CPU[1].checked

If so, change the value of CPUCost to 400.

6. Determine which Hard Drive radio button the user has selected in the form, using the same techniques you used in Step 5. If the user has selected the second option button (corresponding to an 8 GB hard drive), increase the value of the HDCost variable to 300.

7. Create a variable named MEMIndex that contains the index value of the selected option from the Memory selection list.

8. Set the value of the MEMCost variable to the value of the selected option. *Hint*: The value of the selected option is equal to:

eval(document.ORDER.MEM.options[MEMIndex].value)

9. Create a variable named MONIndex that contains the index value of the option selected from the Monitor selection list, and then use the same techniques you employed in Step 8 to set the value of the MONCost variable to the value of the selected option.

10. Determine whether or not the Modem check box has been selected; if so, change the value of the MODEMCost variable to 150.

11. Determine whether or not the Ethernet Card check box has been selected; if so, change the value of the ECARDCost variable to 150.

12. Set the value of the Total input box to the sum of each of the six configuration options plus the value of the BASE variable.

13. Add an event handler to the Calculate Total button so that it runs the TotalCost() function when clicked.

14. Add an event handler to the Reload button so that it reloads the Web page when clicked.

15. Save and print the PS300.htm file.

16. Load the page in your Web browser and print the Web page for each of the following configurations:

   - CPU=350 MHz, hard drive = 8 GB, memory = 32 MB, monitor = 15", 56K modem
   - CPU=300 MHz, hard drive = 4 GB, memory = 64 MB, monitor = 19", 56K modem, Ethernet card
   - CPU=350 MHz, hard drive = 8 GB, memory = 128 MB, monitor = 21", Ethernet card

17. Close your Web browser and your text editor.

2. Creating a Hyperlink Selection List for the Monroe Public Library The Monroe Public Library has added Web access for its patrons. In order to make it easier for new users to access particular pages, the library has employed you to create custom Web pages for different topics. One of these pages contains links to various government Web sites.

Because there are so many hyperlinks, your supervisor, Denise Kruschev, thinks the best approach is for the list of hyperlinks to be contained within selection list boxes. Denise envisions users clicking a site within a selection list, which would then open up the Web page automatically.

Denise has already created the Web page shown in Figure 8-45. Now you have to use JavaScript to open up the Web pages indicated by the options in the selection lists.

Figure 8-45 ◄

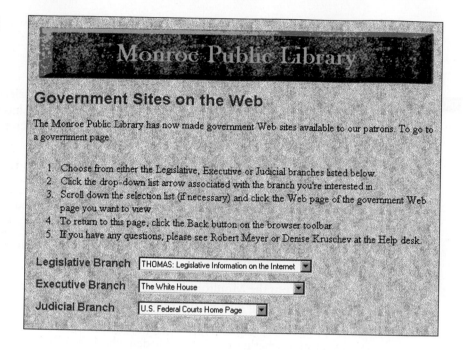

To finish the Monroe Public Library government Web page:

1. Start your text editor and open the file MPLtext.htm in the Cases folder of the Tutorial.08 folder on your Student Disk, and then save the file as MPL.htm in the same folder.

2. Scroll through the MPL.htm file and note that the values of the selection options are all URLs, and that the text displayed in the selection list consists of descriptions of the Web pages.

3. In the <SELECT> tag for each of the three selection lists, insert an event handler that will run the function JumpToList(this) whenever the value of the selection list changes.

4. Within the HEAD section of the MPL.htm file, create a JavaScript function named JumpToList(field).

5. Create a variable named URLNumber, and then set the variable equal to the value of the selectedIndex property of the "field" parameter. This variable will contain the index number of the selected option from the selection list field.

6. Create a variable named URLValue, and then set the variable equal to the value of the selected option.

7. Set the location object equal to URLValue. Briefly explain what this command will do, given what you know about the location object.

8. Save and print the MPL.htm file.

9. Open the MPL.htm file in your Web browser. Click the "Department of Education" option in the Executive Branch selection list and verify that the appropriate Web page is loaded in your browser.

10. Close your Web browser and your text editor.

3. Creating a Color Picker for WebWorld Graphics You work as a Web author at WebWorld Graphics. You want to create a simple Web page that will allow you to compare various color values for text and background colors. You decide to use JavaScript to create a Color Picker Web page. Assume that you've already created the form for the page, as shown in Figure 8-46. The form includes input boxes in which you'll place the hexadecimal color values for the red, green, and blue components for the background and foreground colors.

Figure 8-46 ◄

A Simple Color Picker

Background (enter values from '00' to 'FF')

RED: FF   GREEN: FF   BLUE: FF

Text (enter values from '00' to 'FF')

RED: 00   GREEN: 00   BLUE: 00

Apply   Reload

HAMLET:

Speak the speech, I pray you, as I pronounced it to you, trippingly on the tongue: but if you mouth it, as many of your players do, I had as lief the town-crier spoke my lines.

Your only remaining task is to create a JavaScript function that takes those values, combines them, and applies them to the page's background and foreground (text) colors. To create the Color Picker Web page:

1. Start your text editor and open the file CPtext.htm in the Cases folder of the Tutorial.08 folder on your Student Disk, and then save the file as CP.htm in the same folder.

2. Scroll through the CP.htm file and note the name of each input box in the Color Picker form.

3. Go to the Apply button at the bottom of the form and insert an event handler that will run the ApplyColor() function when this button is clicked.

4. Insert another event handler in the Reload button that will reload the Web page when this button is clicked.

5. Create the function ApplyColor() in the HEAD section of the CP.htm file. Do not include any parameters for the function. The ApplyColor() function should perform the actions specified in the steps that follow.

6. Create the following variables with the following values:
   - BCR equal to the value of the BackRed input box
   - BCG equal to the value of the BackGreen input box
   - BCB equal to the value of the BackBlue input box
   - TCR equal to the value of the TextRed input box
   - TCG equal to the value of the TextGreen input box
   - TCB equal to the value of the TextBlue input box

7. Create a variable named BackColor equal to the pound symbol (#) joined with the values of the BCR, BCG, and BCB variables.

8. Create a variable named TextColor equal to the pound symbol (#) joined with the values of the TCR, TCG, and TCB variables.

9. Set the background color of the document equal to BackColor.

10. Set the foreground color of the document equal to TextColor.

11. Save your changes to the CP.htm file.

12. Print the ApplyColor() function.

13. Open the CP.htm file in your browser and test your page for the following color combinations (note, some versions of Netscape do not support changing the foreground color once the page has been opened by the browser.)
    - Background = "#CC33CC" Foreground="#FFFFFF"
    - Background = "#3300CC" Foreground ="#FFCCCC"
    - Background = "#333300" Foreground = "#FFFFCC"

14. Click the Reload button and verify that it reloads your Web page and resets the colors to your browser's default values.

15. Close your Web browser and your text editor.

4. Creating a Mortgage Calculator for Frontier Savings and Loan You've been asked to create a mortgage calculator for the Frontier Savings and Loan Web site as a service to the bank's customers. Your manager, Lisa Drummond, explains that the page should contain a form in which the customer enters the loan amount, the number of monthly payments, and the yearly interest rate, and then clicks a button to see what the monthly payment and total payments for the loan would be. You need JavaScript to accomplish this task. A function named Monthly(), which is used to calculate the monthly payment, is shown below:

```
function Monthly(I, N, S) {
    // I = yearly interest rate;
    // N = number of monthly payments;
    // S = loan amount;
    return (S*I/12*Math.pow(I/12+1,N))/(Math.pow(I/12+1,N)-1);
}
```

The Monthly() function takes three parameter values: the yearly interest rate (I), the total number of monthly payments (N), and the amount of the loan (S). With these parameters the function returns the value of the monthly payment needed to pay off the loan.

Note that this function uses the Math.pow() method, which calculates the value of a base value raised to an exponent; for example:

$$\text{Math.pow}(a, n) = a^n$$

Once you know the value of the monthly payment, the total amount paid is simply the monthly payment multiplied by the total number of payments. Using the Monthly() function, you'll complete the rest of the Web page for Frontier Savings and Loan.

To create the mortgage calculator Web page:

1. Start your text editor and create a file named Mortgage.htm in the Cases folder of the Tutorial.08 folder on your Student Disk.

2. Create a form that contains the following fields (the layout of the form is up to you):

   - Five input fields used for the loan amount, yearly interest rate, number of payments, monthly payment amount, and total payment.
   - Two buttons: one labeled Calculate (used to calculate the monthly and total payments) and the other labeled Reset (used to reset the form).

3. Within the HEAD section of the Mortgage.htm file, insert the Monthly() function shown earlier.

4. Create a function named ShowVal() that extracts the values in the interest rate, number of payments, and loan amount fields and calls the Monthly() function with those values to determine the monthly payment. (*Hint:* Don't forget to use the "eval" function when extracting field values.) Use the results of the Monthly() function to determine the total amount of payments to the bank. Place the results of your two calculations in the appropriate fields on your form.

5. Add an event handler to the Calculate button that runs the ShowVal() function when this button is clicked.

6. The Monthly() function requires that the interest rate be a number between 0 and 1. Create a function named CheckInterest() that checks to see if the interest rate is greater than 0 and less than 1. If it is not, the CheckInterest() function should display a message to the user and return the user to the interest rate field.

7. Add an event handler to the interest rate field that calls the CheckInterest() function whenever the user leaves the field.

8. At the top of the Web page, before the calculator, insert the <H2> heading "Mortgage Calculator" along with a paragraph describing the purpose of the Web page and how to use the calculator you created.

9. Save your changes to Mortgage.htm, and then print the HTML code and JavaScript commands you created.

10. Open the Mortgage.htm file in your Web browser. Test your mortgage calculator with the following values, and print the resulting Web pages:

    - loan = 100000, interest rate = 0.085, number of payments = 300
    - loan = 100000, interest rate = 0.10, number of payments = 300
    - loan = 100000, interest rate = 0.085, number of payments = 360

11. Close your Web browser and your text editor.

Creating a Multimedia Web Page

Enhancing a Page with Sound, Video, and Java Applets

OBJECTIVES

In this tutorial you will:

- Work with external and embedded multimedia files

- Learn about the principles of sound and video clips

- Work with the <EMBED> tag to enhance a Web page with sound and video

- Provide tags for browsers that do not support embedded objects

- Learn how to create background sound with Internet Explorer

- Use the <APPLET> tag to add a Java applet to a Web page

- Create a scrolling marquee with the <MARQUEE> tag

LAB Multimedia

CASE

The Mount Rainier Newsletter

Mount Rainier dominates the skyline of the state of Washington, and Mount Rainier National Park is a popular vacation spot for travelers to the Northwest. The park publishes a monthly newsletter, *Mount Rainier News*, which is handed out to visitors at the entrance gate. The newsletter contains information on upcoming events, tips on park trails and enjoying nature, and information on campsites and lodging. In recent years, the newsletter has also been published on the World Wide Web so that travelers can receive park news before they arrive. The Web page contains all the information available in the printed version as well as links to other sites on the Web about Mount Rainier and the surrounding communities of Sunrise, Longmire, and Paradise.

Tom Bennett, the supervisor of *Mount Rainier News*, has been looking at other newsletter sites on the Web and has noticed how multimedia elements like sound, video, and animation have been used to add interest and information to those pages. Tom has asked you to add these elements to the *Mount Rainier News* Web page to make it more appealing. The current page features stories on an upcoming folk festival and a new attraction at the Paradise visitors' center. Tom would like you to locate sound and video clips that can be used to enhance those stories.

SESSION

9.1

In this session you will learn about the properties of external and embedded media. You'll examine how sound waves can be saved in a sound file, and learn how to reduce the size of your sound file. You'll create a hyperlink to a sound clip and also embed the sound clip within a Web page. Finally, you'll see how Internet Explorer allows you to specify a background sound for your Web page.

Working with Multimedia

One of the most popular and useful features of the World Wide Web is the ability to transfer information through the use of sound and video. In creating Web pages that feature these elements, you have to consider several factors, not the least of which is the issue of bandwidth. **Bandwidth** is a measure of the amount of data that can be sent through a communications circuit each second. Bandwidth values range from slow connections—such as phone lines, which transfer data at a rate of 28.8 kbps—to high-speed direct network connections capable of transferring data at several megabytes per second. Large sound and video files cause the most trouble for users with low bandwidth connections. One of the goals when you use multimedia is to create media clips that are compact in size without sacrificing quality.

As shown in Figure 9-1, multimedia can be added to a Web page in one of two ways: as external media or inline media. With **external media**, the sound or video file is accessed through a hyperlink. **Inline media** clips are placed into the Web page itself as embedded objects. The advantage of using an external file is that users can choose whether or not to retrieve the multimedia clip. This is useful in situations where the user has a low bandwidth connection and wants the choice of not taking the time to download a large multimedia file. An embedded media clip works like an inline image and can be played within the Web page itself. Because the clip appears within the Web page, you can supplement it with other material on the page. For example, descriptive text can appear alongside an embedded video clip. The downside of inline media is that the user is forced to wait for the clip to be retrieved by the browser. If the user has a low bandwidth connection, this could be a long wait.

Figure 9-1 ◀
Inline and
external media

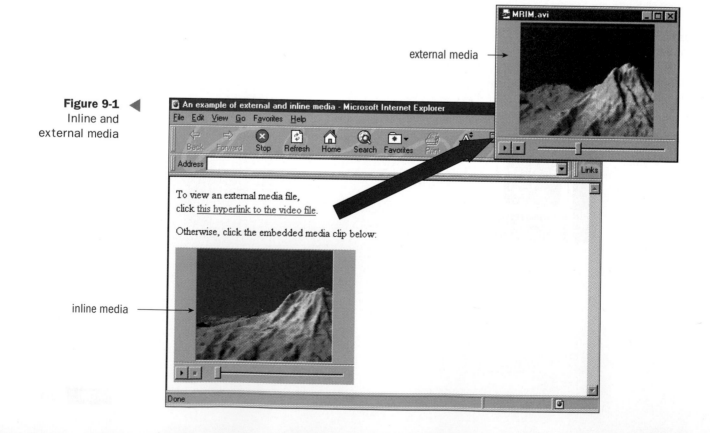

Tom asks you to create two versions of the *Mount Rainier News* Web page—one with external media, and the other with inline media. The first page, named Rainier.htm, will use external media and will be posted on the Web server for users with low bandwidth Internet connections, such as phone lines. The second page, Rainier2.htm, will be made available to users at the park headquarters. Because this page will be accessed directly with a high-speed connection, it will use inline media.

The version of the newsletter that you'll be working with is shown in Figure 9-2. In addition to a table of links to other Web sites, the page contains three news articles. One is the current weather forecast, located at the top of the page. The second is an article about the upcoming folk festival at Sunrise. The third article describes MRIM, the Mount Rainier Interactive Map, recently installed at the Paradise visitors' center.

Figure 9-2 ◀
The *Mount Rainier News* Web page

Other Web Pages

About Mount Rainier
Mt. Rainier Natn'l Park
Mt. Rainier Associates
Visitor Centers
Campgrounds
Picnic Areas
Food & Lodging
Climbing Information
Winter Recreation

Visiting the Park
Longmire
Paradise
Ohanapecosh
Sunrise
Mowich Lake

Current News
Weather Forecast
Road Conditions
Trail Conditions

TODAY'S WEATHER FORECAST

TODAY...Partly sunny.
TONIGHT...Partly cloudy. Showers with snow level lowering to 4000.

Autumn Folk Festival

Folk singers, Joan Adams and Shannon Davis

From September 10th - 12th, come to Sunrise for the annual autumn folk festival. The Sunrise Festival is quickly becoming one of the Northwest's top folk events, with its intimate performances from world-famous troubadours. Camping spots are still available at Sunrise campground, but they're going fast.

In addition to the intimate song sharing in the campground every evening during the festival, there'll be workshops, great food and craft vendors. Call Maria Thompson at 555-9011 for camping information. Call Ted Cashman (555-8122) to sign up for one of the workshops.

Visitors Set to Meet MRIM

Want to see what it's like to hover over Columbia Crest at 14,400 feet, or ski down the Ingraham Glacier without fear of falling? Then visit **MRIM**, the Mount Rainier Interactive Map now available at the Paradise visitors' center.

MRIM uses state-of-the-art computer animation combined with data from geological satellites to help you explore places you might never visit on foot. The results of your journey are displayed on a large screen monitor - perfect for group presentations or individual explorations. Contact Doug LeCourt at Paradise for more information.

Your first task is to add a sound clip to the article on the Sunrise Folk Festival. Before doing that, you'll learn a little more about sound files.

Working with Sound Files

It is easier to work with sound clips if you understand some of the issues involved in converting a sound from an analog form to a digital form, suitable for saving as a sound file. Consider the simple sound wave shown in Figure 9-3. There are two components to the sound wave: amplitude and frequency. The **amplitude** is the height of the sound wave, and it relates to the loudness of the sound—the higher the amplitude, the louder the sound. The **frequency** is the speed at which the sound wave moves, and it relates to the sound pitch. Sounds with high frequency are produced at higher pitches.

Figure 9-3 ◀
A simple
sound wave

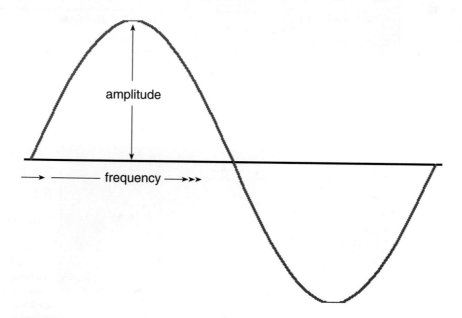

amplitude

frequency ──▶▶▶

Sampling Rate and Sample Resolution

A sound wave is a continuous event. To convert it to a form that can be stored in a sound file, your computer must record measurements of the sound at discrete moments in time. Each measurement is called a **sample**. The number of samples taken per second is called the **sampling rate**. Sampling rate is measured in kilohertz (KHz). The most commonly used sampling rates are 11 KHz, 22 KHz, and 44 KHz. A higher sampling rate means that more samples are taken per second, which results in a sound file that more closely matches the original sound wave (Figure 9-4). The trade-off in increasing the sampling rate is that it increases the size of the sound file.

Figure 9-4
Approximating
a sound wave
with different
sampling rates

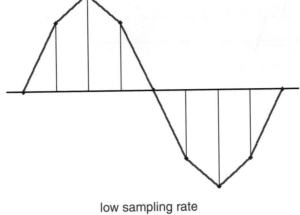

low sampling rate

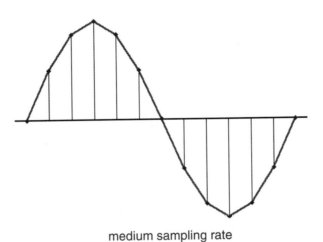

medium sampling rate

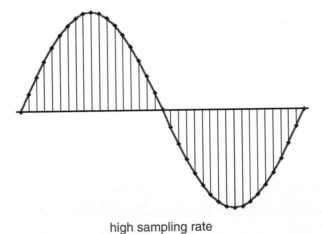

high sampling rate

A second factor in converting a sound to digital form is the sample resolution. **Sample resolution** indicates the precision in measuring the sound within each sample. There are two sample resolution values, 8-bit and 16-bit. As shown in Figure 9-5, increasing the resolution creates a sound file that represents the sound wave in greater detail. However, a 16-bit sound file is twice the size of an 8-bit sound file. Generally you should save your files at the 16-bit resolution because the improved sound quality is worth the increased file size.

Figure 9-5 ◄
Approximating
a sound wave
at different
sample
resolutions

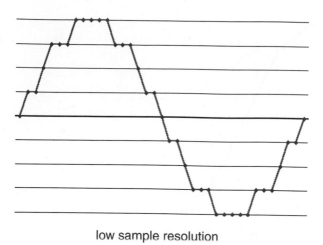

low sample resolution

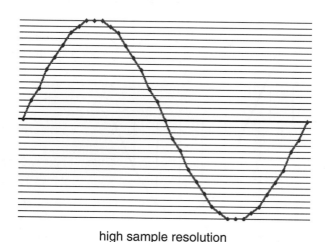

high sample resolution

A final choice you'll have to make with your sound files is determining the number of channels to use. This choice is typically between using stereo or monaural (mono) sound, although in some situations you might want to add extra channels. Stereo provides a richer sound than monaural, but at the expense of approximately doubling the size of the sound file.

Figure 9-6 shows how sampling rate, sample resolution, and channel size relate to sound quality in terms of everyday objects. Your telephone provides the poorest sound quality, as reflected in the low sampling rate and sample resolution as well as the monaural sound. A CD player provides much higher sound quality at a higher sampling rate and sample resolution. The CD player also supports stereo sound (and, in some cases, additional sound channels).

Figure 9-6 ◄
Sampling rate
and sample
resolution as
related to
sound quality

Sampling Rate and Sample Resolution	Sound Quality
8 KHz, 8-bit, mono	Telephone
22 KHz, 16-bit, stereo	Radio
44 KHz, 16-bit, stereo	CD

If you want to create a sound file, you need a computer with a sound card, speakers, a microphone, and sound-editing software. There are several sound editors available on the Web. In addition to modifying the sampling rate, sample resolution, and number of channels, these sound editors also allow you to add special sound effects, remove noise, and copy and paste sounds between files. Figure 9-7 lists some of the sound editors you can access on the Web.

Figure 9-7 ◀
Sound-editing
software
available on
the Web

Title	URL	Platform
CoolEdit	http://www.syntrillium.com	Windows 95
Sound Gadget Pro	http://www.compsoc.man.ac.uk/~nigel/software/sgpro/index.html	Windows 95
SoundHack	http://www.shareware.com	Macintosh
Sound Machine	http://www.shareware.com	Macintosh

Sound File Formats

Several different competing sound formats are in use on the Web. The various formats are used by different operating systems and provide varying levels of sound quality and sound compression (the ability to reduce the size of the sound file). Figure 9-8 lists some of the common sound file formats that might be used for the Sunrise Folk Festival sound clip.

Figure 9-8 ◀
Sound file
formats

Format	Description
AU	Also called μlaw (mu-law) format. Sound files with this format usually have an .au filename extension. One of the more common sound formats, it's available on most operating systems. AU sound files have 8-bit sample resolutions, use a sampling rate of 8 KHz, and are recorded in mono.
AIFF/AIFC	Audio Interchange File Format. Sound files with this format usually have an .aiff or .aif filename extension. AIFF was developed by Apple and is primarily used on the Macintosh operating system. AIFF sound files can be either 8-bit or 16-bit, mono or stereo, and can be recorded at several different sampling rates.
SND	The SND format is used on the Macintosh operating system for creating system sounds. This format is not widely used on the Web.
WAVE	WAVE sound files were developed for the Windows operating environment. Sound files with this format are identified with a .wav filename extension. WAVE files can be recorded in either 8-bit or 16-bit sample resolutions, stereo or mono, and under a wide range of sampling rates. There are also several different compression schemes for WAVE files.
MPEG	Moving Pictures Expert Group. A format primarily used for video clips designed for good compression.
RealAudio	A format designed for real-time retrieval of sound over low to high bandwidth connections. RealAudio files tend to be much smaller than AU or WAVE files, but the sound quality is usually not as good.

WAVE (or WAV) files are the most commonly used formats on the Web because of the dominance of the Windows operating system and the fact that support for WAVE files is built into Windows. If your users are primarily working on Macintoshes, you should consider AIFF or SND files.

RealAudio sound files are also popular on the Web because the format enables the user to play the sound file as it is being downloaded by the server, rather than wait for the entire file to be downloaded and then played. This makes RealAudio ideal for broadcasting up-to-the-minute news and sporting events. To play RealAudio files, your browser must have the

RealAudio player installed. You can find out more about RealAudio and the RealAudio player at http://www.real.com.

If you don't want to create your own sound clips, many sites on the Web maintain an archive of sound clips that you can download. A few of these sites are listed in Figure 9-9. Be aware that some sound clips have copyright restrictions.

Figure 9-9 ◀
Sound archives
on the Web

Title	URL
Sound America	http://www.soundamerica.com
Historic sound clips	http://www.webcorp.com/sounds/index.htm
Index of sounds	http://sunsite.sut.ac.jp/multimed/sounds/
MSU Voice Library	http://web.msu.edu/vincent/index.html
Sound Site	http://www.niagara.com/~ndp/soundsite/
Yahoo!'s list of sound archives	http://www.yahoo.com/Computers_and_Internet/Multimedia/Sound/Archives/

Because of the popularity of the WAVE format, Tom saved the Sunrise Folk Festival sound clip in this format. He has already used a sound editor to experiment with different values for the sampling rate, sample resolution, and stereo versus monaural sound. As shown in Figure 9-10, the size of Tom's various sound files ranged from 111 kilobytes to more than 3 megabytes.

Figure 9-10 ◀
File size of the
Sunrise Folk
Festival sound
clip under
various
resolutions
and rates

Sampling Rate	Sample Resolution			
	Monaural		Stereo	
	8-bit	16-bit	8-bit	16-bit
6 KHz	111 k	223 k	223 k	447 k
8 KHz	149 k	298 k	298 k	596 k
11 KHz	205 k	410 k	410 k	821 k
22 KHz	410 k	821 k	821 k	1643 k
44 KHz	821 k	1643 k	1643 k	3286 k

Tom doesn't want to overwhelm users with a huge sound file, but he also doesn't want a sound file that poorly represents the folk festival. After listening to the sound clip under each combination, Tom decided on a monaural recording with a 16-bit sample resolution and a sampling rate of 6 KHz. The size of this file is only 223 kilobytes, and its sound quality is satisfactory. Tom saved the sound file for you as AF98-1.wav.

Linking to a Sound File

Now that you know the format for the sound clip, and the clip has been saved in a file, you're ready to create the Rainier.htm file and insert a hyperlink to the AF98-1.wav file. Recall that Rainier.htm is the page that will be accessed by users with low bandwidth connections and will use hyperlinks to external media files. Because media clips tend to be large, it's a good idea to include information about their size in your Web page. This will give users some idea of how long it will take to retrieve the clip before they initiate the download. You'll create the Rainier.htm file and add a hyperlink to the sound clip now.

To create a link to the AF98-1.wav sound file:

1. Start your text editor.

2. Open the file **Raintxt.htm** from the Tutorial.09 folder on your Student Disk, and then save the file as **Rainier.htm** in the same folder.

3. Locate the last paragraph of the article on the Sunrise Folk Festival.

4. Directly above the <HR> tag, insert the following text (indented to make your code easier to read):

```
<P>Listen to the sounds of <I>Adams & Davis</I> from the 1998 festival:</P>
    <BLOCKQUOTE>
      <A HREF="AF98-1.wav">Wild Mountain Thyme (223K — WAV format)</A><BR>
    </BLOCKQUOTE>
```

Note that this code uses the <BLOCKQUOTE> tag, which indents a block of text. You can read more about the <BLOCKQUOTE> tag in the Tag Reference appendix.

TROUBLE? In case your browser or operating system does not support the WAV format, the file AF98-1.au has also been placed on your Student Disk. You can use that file in these steps. If you use this file, change the hyperlink text to indicate that the size of the file is 112K and the sound format is AU.

Figure 9-11 displays the revised text of the Rainier.htm file.

Figure 9-11 ◀
Inserting a
hyperlink to the
AF98-1.wav file

sound format

sound file description

sound file

file size

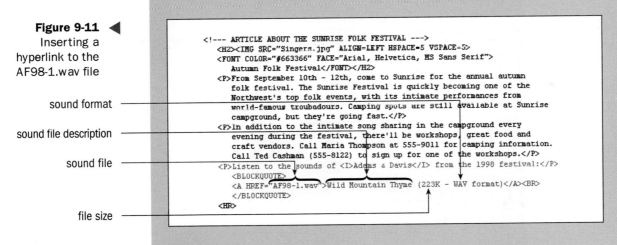

5. Save the changes to the file.

Now that you've inserted a hyperlink to the sound clip, you're ready to test the link. What happens when you do so depends on how your system and browser have been configured. When your browser encounters a link to an external file, such as a sound file, it checks to see if there is any program installed on the system designed to handle those types of files. Such programs are called **helper applications** because they help the browser to interpret and present the file. Different users will have different helper applications installed on their systems. As you saw earlier, there are many different brands of sound editors, and, similarly, there are many different kinds of sound players. Some browsers, such as Netscape Navigator or Communicator, include a sound player with the browser. In the case of Netscape, the sound player is called LiveAudio. If the file type does not have a helper application already installed on the system, the browser might display an error message and prompt you to download a helper application from the browser's Web site.

In the following steps you'll test your newly created hyperlink. These steps assume that you have the Microsoft Media Player installed on your system and that it is set up to handle WAV files. However, you might have a completely different helper application installed on your system. If so, you should use that instead. If necessary, check with your instructor or technical support person to determine which player is installed on your system. If no player has been installed, you will have to download and install a player if you want to hear the sound clip.

To test the hyperlink to the AF98-1.wav file:

1. Open the Rainier.htm file in your Web browser.

2. Click the hyperlink **Wild Mountain Thyme (223K - WAV format)** located on the page. As shown in Figure 9-12, the browser should access a helper application. You might have to click a play button to start playing the sound clip.

Figure 9-12 ◄
Playing the
AF98-1.wav
sound clip

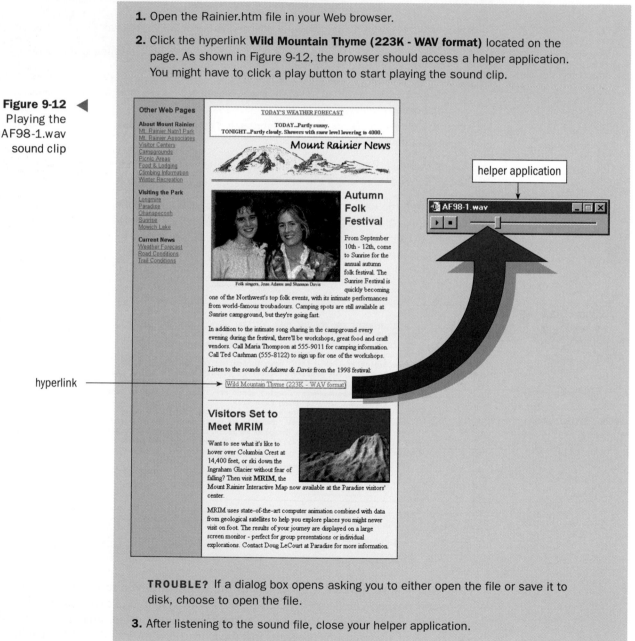

TROUBLE? If a dialog box opens asking you to either open the file or save it to disk, choose to open the file.

3. After listening to the sound file, close your helper application.

Now that you've created a hyperlink to the AF98-1 sound clip, you'll repeat this process to create the second version of the page. But this time, instead of creating a hyperlink to the sound file, you'll embed the clip in the Web page.

Embedding a Sound File

A sound clip placed directly into a Web page is one example of an embedded object. An **embedded object** is any media clip, file, program, or other object that can be run or viewed from within the Web page. To use embedded objects, the browser must support them, and it must have access to software called plug-ins. **Plug-ins**, also called **add-ons**, are applications that enable the browser to work with an embedded object. When the browser encounters an embedded object, it will load the appropriate plug-in plus any controls needed to manipulate the object. For example, a sound file plug-in might place controls on the Web page that enable the user to play the sound clip, pause it, rewind it, or change the volume. Because the object is embedded, these controls appear as part of the Web page.

One problem with plug-ins is that they require the user to download and install additional software before being able to view your page. Many users will choose not to view the page rather than take the time to do this.

There are many plug-ins available for embedded sound clips. Netscape Navigator and Communicator provide the LiveAudio sound player. Internet Explorer provides the ActiveX controls, including the ActiveMovie media player. Since sound has become such a useful feature on the Web, your Web browser probably supports one of these plug-ins.

Using the <EMBED> Tag

To embed a sound clip into a Web page, you use the <EMBED> tag. The syntax for this tag is:

```
<EMBED SRC=URL WIDTH=value HEIGHT=value>
```

where *URL* is the URL or filename of the embedded object, and the HEIGHT and WIDTH properties define the size of the embedded object on the Web page. You might think it strange to define the width and height of an embedded sound clip, but these properties refer to the size of the object and the object's controls. You need to define a size large enough to display the necessary controls for the user to play the media clip. Depending on the object type and the plug-in used by the browser, you might have to set additional properties. For example, Netscape supports the use of the AUTOSTART property for embedded sound clips. Specifying AUTOSTART= "true" will cause the sound clip to be played automatically when the page is loaded. Another property is the VOLUME property, which is used to set the volume of the sound clip. (This can also be done by the user with the sound player controls displayed on the Web page.) You can use these properties in your Web page, but they might be ignored by other browsers using different plug-ins. Check the documentation for the plug-in to determine which properties you can set.

REFERENCE window

EMBEDDING A MEDIA CLIP

- To embed a sound or video clip on your Web page, use the following HTML tags:
  <EMBED SRC=URL WIDTH=value HEIGHT=value>
  where *URL* is the name of the sound or video file to be embedded, and the WIDTH and HEIGHT properties define the size of the embedded object on your Web page.
- To start the media clip automatically when the page loads, use the following property within the <EMBED> tag:
  AUTOSTART="true"

Having learned how to create an embedded object, you'll now create the Rainier2.htm file with the embedded Sunrise Folk Festival sound clip. Once again, you'll use the AF98-1.wav file. (If you used the AF98-1.au file in the previous set of steps, use that file again here.) Remember that the Rainier2 page is the page that will be installed at the visitors' center and accessed directly by the user through a high-speed connection.

To embed the AF98-1.wav sound file:

1. Return to your text editor and reopen the **Raintxt.htm** file from the Tutorial.09 folder on your Student Disk. Save the file as **Rainier2.htm** in the same folder.

2. Directly above the <HR> tag at the end of the Sunrise Folk Festival article, insert the following text (substitute the AF98-1.au file if your system supports that format):

```
<P>Listen to the sounds of <I>Adams & Davis</I> from the 1998 festival:</P>
     <BLOCKQUOTE>
     <EMBED SRC="AF98-1.wav" WIDTH=145 HEIGHT=60><BR>
     </BLOCKQUOTE>
```

See Figure 9-13.

Figure 9-13 ◀
Inserting an
embedded
sound clip

size of the embedded
object on the
Web page

embedded sound file

```
<!--- ARTICLE ABOUT THE SUNRISE FOLK FESTIVAL --->
 <H2><IMG SRC="Singers.jpg" ALIGN=LEFT HSPACE=5 VSPACE=5>
 <FONT COLOR="#663366" FACE="Arial, Helvetica, MS Sans Serif">
 Autumn Folk Festival</FONT></H2>
 <P>From September 10th - 12th, come to Sunrise for the annual autumn
   folk festival. The Sunrise Festival is quickly becoming one of the
   Northwest's top folk events, with its intimate performances from
   world-famous troubadours. Camping spots are still available at Sunrise
   campground, but they're going fast.</P>
 <P>In addition to the intimate song sharing in the campground every
   evening during the festival, there'll be workshops, great food and
   craft vendors. Call Maria Thompson at 555-9011 for camping information.
   Call Ted Cashman (555-8122) to sign up for one of the workshops.</P>
 <P>Listen to the sounds of <I>Adams & Davis</I> from the 1998 festival:</P>
   <BLOCKQUOTE>
   <EMBED SRC="AF98-1.wav" WIDTH=145 HEIGHT=60><BR>
   </BLOCKQUOTE>
 <HR>
```

Note that in inserting the embedded sound clip you did not need to specify the clip's size, as you did earlier with the hyperlink. This is because the sound clip will be downloaded automatically to the user's browser, whether the user wants it or not. The height and width values were determined for you. When you embed your own media clips in the future, you'll probably have to test various height and width values to find a size that looks right.

3. Save your changes to the file.

4. Open the Rainier2.htm file in your Web browser. As shown in Figure 9-14, the page loads with the controls for the embedded sound clip displayed on the page. (The controls on your screen might look different from those in the figure.)

Figure 9-14 ◀
Using an
embedded
sound clip

Other Web Pages

About Mount Rainier
Mt. Rainier Natn'l Park
Mt. Rainier Associates
Visitor Centers
Campgrounds
Picnic Areas
Food & Lodging
Climbing Information
Winter Recreation

Visiting the Park
Longmire
Paradise
Ohanapecosh
Sunrise
Mowich Lake

Current News
Weather Forecast
Road Conditions
Trail Conditions

TODAY'S WEATHER FORECAST

TODAY...Partly sunny.
TONIGHT...Partly cloudy. Showers with snow level lowering to 4000.

Mount Rainier News

Autumn Folk Festival

Folk singers, Joan Adams and Shannon Davis

From September 10th - 12th, come to Sunrise for the annual autumn folk festival. The Sunrise Festival is quickly becoming one of the Northwest's top folk events, with its intimate performances from world-famous troubadours. Camping spots are still available at Sunrise campground, but they're going fast.

In addition to the intimate song sharing in the campground every evening during the festival, there'll be workshops, great food and craft vendors. Call Maria Thompson at 555-9011 for camping information. Call Ted Cashman (555-8122) to sign up for one of the workshops.

embedded sound clip ────

Listen to the sounds of *Adams & Davis* from the 1998 festival:

controls for the Media
Player plug-in

Visitors Set to Meet MRIM

Want to see what it's like to hover over Columbia Crest at 14,400 feet, or ski down the Ingraham Glacier without fear of falling? Then visit **MRIM**, the Mount Rainier Interactive Map now available at the Paradise visitors' center.

MRIM uses state-of-the-art computer animation combined with data from geological satellites to help you explore places you might never visit on foot. The results of your journey are displayed on a large screen monitor - perfect for group presentations or individual explorations. Contact Doug LeCourt at Paradise for more information.

TROUBLE? If you do not see controls for the sound clip on your Web page, it could be because your browser does not support embedded objects. You might also have mistyped the name of the sound file. Return to your text editor and verify that your code matches the code shown in Figure 9-13.

5. If necessary, click the **play** button on the embedded object to start playing the sound clip.

TROUBLE? If necessary, consult the documentation for your browser or plug-in to learn how to work with the sound clip, or ask your instructor or technical support person for assistance.

Using the <BGSOUND> Tag

In version 3.0, Internet Explorer introduced a tag for playing background sounds on your Web page. The syntax of the <BGSOUND> tag is:

```
<BGSOUND SRC=URL LOOP=value>
```

where *URL* is the URL or location of the sound file, and the LOOP property defines how many times the sound clip will be played in the background. LOOP can either be an integer (1, 2, 3, ...) or INFINITE if you want the sound clip to be played continuously. The default LOOP value is 1. For example, to set the AF98-1.wav file to play once in the background when the Rainier2.htm page is loaded, you could add the following tag anywhere in the file:

```
<BGSOUND SRC="AF98-1.wav" LOOP=1>
```

Because this is a background sound, no control or object appears on the Web page; therefore, the user cannot stop the sound from playing, pause it, or rewind it. Because the user has no control over the sound, you should use the <BGSOUND> tag with caution. You should also set the LOOP value to 1 or to a small number. Having a sound clip played over and over again can be extremely irritating to users.

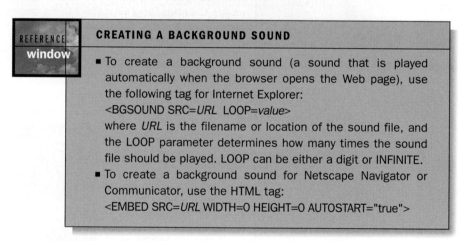

REFERENCE window

CREATING A BACKGROUND SOUND

- To create a background sound (a sound that is played automatically when the browser opens the Web page), use the following tag for Internet Explorer:
  <BGSOUND SRC=*URL* LOOP=*value*>
  where *URL* is the filename or location of the sound file, and the LOOP parameter determines how many times the sound file should be played. LOOP can be either a digit or INFINITE.
- To create a background sound for Netscape Navigator or Communicator, use the HTML tag:
  <EMBED SRC=*URL* WIDTH=0 HEIGHT=0 AUTOSTART="true">

The <BGSOUND> tag is not supported by Netscape Navigator or Communicator and will be ignored by those browsers. You should keep this in mind when deciding whether or not to use the <BGSOUND> tag on your Web page. You can create a similar effect to the <BGSOUND> tag by inserting an embedded sound clip on your Web page, setting its width and height properties to 0, and having the clip start automatically when loaded. For example, to insert a background sound clip with Netscape, use the following HTML tag:

```
<EMBED SRC="AF98-1.wav" WIDTH=0 HEIGHT=0 AUTOSTART="true">
```

The sound clip will start automatically, but because its size is 0, it will not appear on the Web page. (The sound clip might appear on the page for some versions of Internet Explorer.)

Quick Check

1. Describe the two ways of adding sound to your Web page.

2. Define the following terms: bandwidth, sampling rate, and sample resolution.

3. What sound file formats would you use for an intranet composed exclusively of Macintosh computers?

4. What tag would you enter to allow users to access the sound file Music.wav as an external sound clip?

5. What is an embedded object? What two requirements must a browser meet in order to use an embedded object?

6. What tag would you enter to allow users to access the sound file Music.wav as an embedded object?

7. What tag would you enter to have the Music.wav file played once in the background when the page is loaded by Internet Explorer? What code would you enter to accomplish the same thing in Netscape Navigator?

You've finished adding sound to the Mount Rainier newsletter page. You show your work to Tom, and he approves of both of the files you've created. In the next session you'll learn about various video file formats and how to insert them into your Web pages.

SESSION

9.2

In this session you will work with external and inline video. You'll learn about different video formats and how to use them to control the size of your video clips. You'll also work with the <EMBED> tag to embed a video clip in the Rainier2.htm page. Finally, you'll learn about an extension to the <IMG> tag that allows you to create inline images that also work as inline video clips.

Working with Video Files

Tom's next task for you is to add a video clip to the Web page taken from the Mount Rainier Interactive Map, which was recently installed at the Paradise visitors' center. This video clip shows a simulated flyby of Mount Rainier.

Displaying video is one of the most popular uses of the Web. Video files can be exciting and can provide a great deal of information. However, video files can be very large and difficult to work with. Depending on the format, a single video clip, no more than 30 seconds in length, can be as large as 10 megabytes.

A video file translates a continuous stream of images into digital format. You can create video files with a video capture board installed on your computer to record images from a camcorder, television, or VCR. You can also create video clips using computer animation software. In either case, creating a video file can be a time-consuming process as you try to balance the desire to create an interesting and visually attractive clip against the need to create a file that is compact in size.

To create and work with video files, you can install some of the video editors listed in Figure 9-15.

Figure 9-15 ◀
Video-editing
software
available on
the Web

Title	URL	Platform
VidEdit	http://www.earthstation1.simplenet.com/software.html	Windows 95
Main Actor	http://www.mainconcept.de/html/products.html	Windows 95
Personal AVI editor	http://www.shareware.com	Windows 95
Quick Editor	http://www.shareware.com	Macintosh

Frame Rates and Codecs

A video file is composed of frames, and each **frame** is an individual image. When the video file is played, each frame is displayed in sequence, giving the illusion of motion. The number of frames displayed in each unit of time is called the **frame rate** and is expressed in frames per second (fps). Working with the frame rate is one way you can control the size and quality of your video file. A video file with a high frame rate will have a smooth playback, but at the expense of taking up a lot of space on your hard drive. For comparison, a VCR renders video at the speed of 30 fps. Video files that try to match this speed are usually quite large in size. You can reduce the frame rate to reduce the size of the file. When you do so, you're not slowing down the video; instead, you're reducing the number of frames displayed each second, thereby reducing the total number of frames in the file. For example, instead of using 30 frames in one second of video, you might be using only 15. The overall duration of the video clip remains the same. The downside of reducing the frame rate is that the video playback might appear ragged.

Another way of controlling the size of the video file is by compressing each individual frame. The image is compressed when stored in the file. Then, as the video clip is played, the image is decompressed and displayed. The technique of compressing and decompressing video frames is a called a **codec** (for compression/decompression). There are many different types of codecs, each with its own advantages and disadvantages. Your video editor will usually allow you to choose the codec for your video file. You'll have to experiment to determine which codec provides the best file compression without sacrificing video quality. Different codecs perform better on different files.

You can also reduce the size of your video files by simply reducing the size of the video frames. A frame size of 160 pixels wide by 120 pixels high is considered standard on the Web, but you can reduce this size if you find your video file is too large. Changing the video from color to grayscale can also reduce the size of the file. If your video clip contains a sound track, you can reduce the sampling rate, the sample resolution, or the number of channels to further reduce the size of the video file. Each of these techniques should be available to you in your video-editing software.

Video File Formats

Video on the Web typically appears in one of three formats: AVI, MPEG, or QuickTime. Figure 9-16 describes these three formats.

Figure 9-16
Video file
formats

Format	Description
AVI	Also known as Video for Windows (VfW). The standard video format supported by Windows. Video files with this format are identified by the .avi extension. AVI files are not widely supported on other operating systems.
MPEG	Moving Pictures Expert Group. MPEG video files have either the .mpg or .mpeg file extension. MPEG videos compress very well, but can suffer from slowback due to decompression. Some MPEG formats require an MPEG board to be installed on the system. MPEG players exist for all operating systems.
QuickTime	Developed for the Macintosh, QuickTime video files have either the .qt or (more commonly) the .mov file extension. QuickTime players exist for all operating systems, making QuickTime, along with AVI videos, one of the most widely used formats on the Web.

Which format should you use for your Web page? The answer depends, in part, on who you think your audience will be. The QuickTime format was developed for the Macintosh, but QuickTime players exist for other operating systems (such as QuickTime for Windows). Therefore, QuickTime might be the format with the most cross-platform support. Few video players exist for AVI files outside the Windows environment. On the other hand, support for AVI is built into Windows, and cross-platform support might not be a consideration, given that the Windows platform controls 80% of the computer market. Video players for MPEG files are also available for all operating systems, but MPEG files are not as prevalent as AVI or QuickTime videos. Given the current situation, many developers advise that Web authors provide both QuickTime and AVI video clips to their users, if they want to provide maximum coverage. You'll follow that recommendation in your work on the *Mount Rainier News* Web page.

Tom has an excerpt from the Mount Rainier Interactive Map—a three-second video clip simulating a flyby of the summit at 14,000 feet. Using video-editing software, Tom saved the video clip in AVI format under a variety of sizes and frame rate settings (Figure 9-17).

Figure 9-17
File sizes of the
MRIM video clip
under different
frame sizes and
frame rates

| Frame Rate | Frame Size (in pixels) | |
	200 x 167	400 x 334
5 fps	187 k	595 k
10 fps	371 k	719 k
15 fps	671 k	745 k
20 fps	890 k	974 k
25 fps	917 k	969 k

The size of this video clip ranges from just under 1 megabyte down to 187 kilobytes. As you can see from the figure, there is no easy way of predicting what the size of the video clip will be under varying conditions. Reducing the frame rate from 25 fps to 20 fps actually increased the file size for the 400 × 334 video clip. You must experiment to find the best setting for your needs. After viewing the different clips, Tom decided to use the smallest video clip, at 187 kilobytes in size. Tom saved the clip under the filename MRIM.avi. Tom also used his video editor to convert this file to QuickTime format and saved the file as MRIM.mov. The size of this file is 215 kilobytes. Tom gives you both of these clips; your job is to add hyperlinks to the Rainier.htm file that point to the two video files.

Linking to a Video File

You follow the same procedure to link to a video clip as you did to link to a sound clip. Once again, you should include information about the size of each video file so that users can determine whether or not they want to retrieve the clip. You'll place the hyperlinks to the video clip files at the bottom of the Rainier.htm file.

To create hyperlinks to the MRIM.avi and MRIM.mov files:

1. If you took a break after the previous session, start your text editor and reopen the Rainier.htm file from the Tutorial.09 folder of your Student Disk.

2. Locate the last paragraph of the article on the Mount Rainier Interactive Map.

3. Directly above the </TD> tag, insert the following code:

```
<P>Preview a clip from the Mount Rainier Interactive Map</P>
    <BLOCKQUOTE>
    <A HREF="MRIM.avi">Summit Flyby (187K - AVI format)</A><BR>
    <A HREF="MRIM.mov">Summit Flyby (215K - QuickTime format)</A>
    </BLOCKQUOTE>
```

The revised code is shown in Figure 9-18.

Figure 9-18 ◀
Inserting
hyperlinks
to the MRIM
video files

video file
video file description
file size
video format

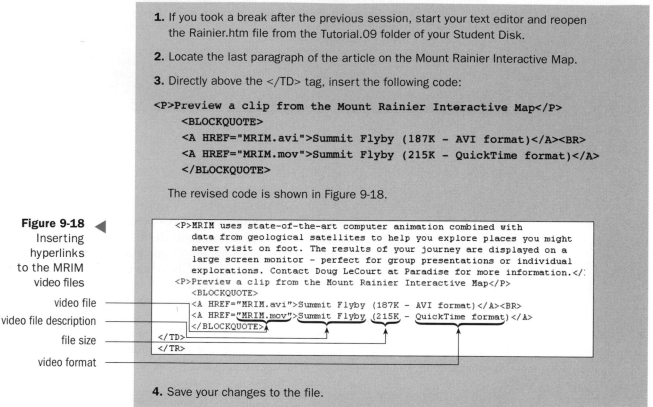

4. Save your changes to the file.

As you discovered earlier with sound files, different browsers will respond in different ways to hyperlinks to video clips. Both Internet Explorer and Netscape Navigator or Communicator are capable of displaying AVI and MOV files directly within the browser without the use of plug-ins. In this case, when a user clicks a hyperlink for a video file, the clip is displayed on its own Web page. The user can start the clip either by clicking a control that appears with the clip or by clicking the image if no controls appear. If there are no controls, the user can also right-click the image to view a shortcut list of commands, such as pause, stop, and rewind.

On other browsers, a plug-in will be activated when the user clicks the hyperlink, making the video clip play in a separate window. With this in mind, you'll test the hyperlinks you just created to learn if your browser supports video files and, if so, how it supports them.

To test your video file hyperlinks:

1. Open the Rainier.htm file in your browser.

2. Click the hyperlinks to the AVI and MOV files you just created. Depending on their configurations, your computer and browser might be able to display only one of the video files. If so, verify that the video clip works. Figure 9-19 shows a sample of how one user might access the MRIM.avi video clip.

Figure 9-19 ◀
Playing the
MRIM video clip

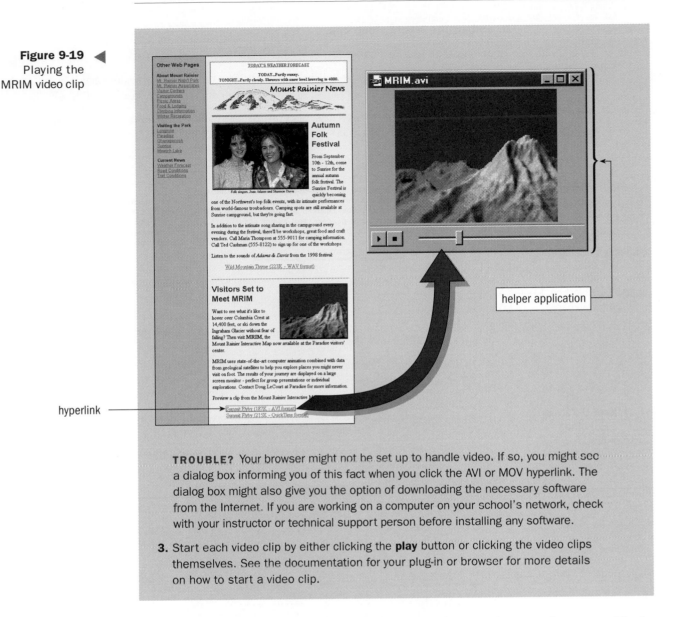

hyperlink

helper application

TROUBLE? Your browser might not be set up to handle video. If so, you might see a dialog box informing you of this fact when you click the AVI or MOV hyperlink. The dialog box might also give you the option of downloading the necessary software from the Internet. If you are working on a computer on your school's network, check with your instructor or technical support person before installing any software.

3. Start each video clip by either clicking the **play** button or clicking the video clips themselves. See the documentation for your plug-in or browser for more details on how to start a video clip.

Now that you've created hyperlinks to the video clips, your next task is to modify the Rainier2 Web page by placing the video clip within the page itself.

Embedding a Video File

To embed a video file, you can use the <EMBED> tag, just as you did to embed the sound file in the previous session. As before, you must specify a source for the embedded video clip with the SRC property and a size for the clip using the HEIGHT and WIDTH properties. The object's height and width should be large enough to display any controls needed to operate the clip. You usually have to decide the size by trial and error. In addition to these properties, you can also specify whether or not you want the clip to start automatically when the page is loaded by entering AUTOSTART="true" within the <EMBED> tag (the default is to not start the clip automatically).

In this case, you'll embed the MRIM.avi video clip in the Rainier2.htm file. (If your browser supports only QuickTime files, you can substitute the MRIM.mov file.) The size of this clip is 200 pixels wide by 167 pixels high. You'll increase the value of the HEIGHT property to 200 to accommodate the embedded object's video clip controls. Also, Tom does not want the clip to start automatically, so you will not set the AUTOSTART property.

To embed the MRIM video clip:

1. Return to your text editor and open the Rainier2.htm file.

2. Insert the following code at the end of the article on the Mount Rainier Interactive Map (use MRIM.mov instead of MRIM.avi if your browser supports only QuickTime videos):

```
<P>Click the image below for a preview of the Mount Rainier Interactive Map.</P>
    <EMBED SRC="MRIM.avi" WIDTH=200 HEIGHT=200>
```

Figure 9-20 shows the revised code.

Figure 9-20 ◀
Inserting
an embedded
video clip

embedded video file ──

size of the
embedded object on
the Web page ──

```
    <P>MRIM uses state-of-the-art computer animation combined with
        data from geological satellites to help you explore places you might
        never visit on foot. The results of your journey are displayed on a
        large screen monitor - perfect for group presentations or individual
        explorations. Contact Doug LeCourt at Paradise for more information.</P>
    <P>Click the image below for a preview of the Mount Rainier Interactive Map.</P>
        <EMBED SRC="MRIM.avi" WIDTH=200 HEIGHT=200>
</TD>
</TR>
```

3. Save your changes to the file.

4. Open the Rainier2.htm file in your Web browser. As shown in Figure 9-21, the page loads with the embedded video clip.

Figure 9-21 ◀
Running
the embedded
video clip

embedded video clip ──

video controls ──

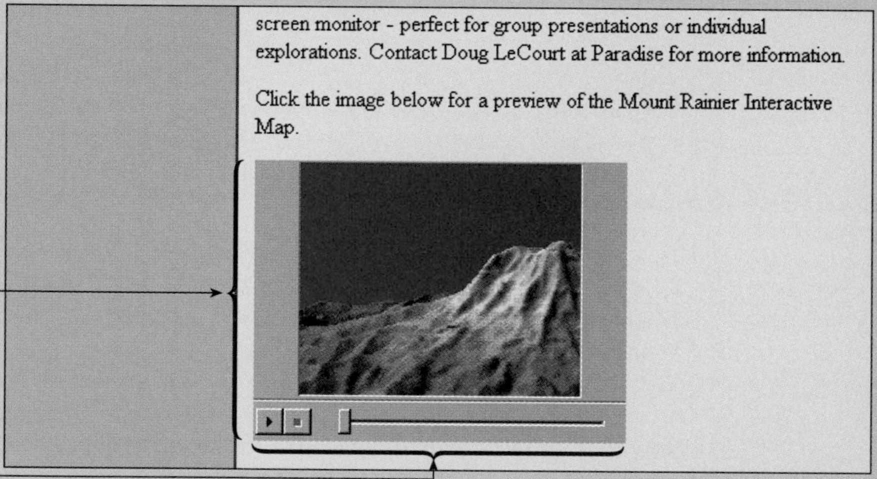

TROUBLE? Depending on your browser and its configuration, your page might look different from the one shown in Figure 9-21. The size of the embedded clip might be different, and the clip might not have the controls shown in the figure.

5. Start the video clip by either clicking the **play** button or clicking the video clip itself. See the documentation for your plug-in or browser for more details on how to start the clip.

Using the <NOEMBED> Tag

As you might have noticed, embedded objects can dramatically increase the size of your Web page and the time required for the browser to load it. What if your browser doesn't support the embedded object? It should notify you that this object has been placed on the page and, perhaps, give you the option of downloading the appropriate software for it. What if you're using an older browser that doesn't even have that capability? That's when you need the <NOEMBED> tag.

REFERENCE window

SUPPORTING BROWSERS THAT DO NOT RECOGNIZE EMBEDDED OBJECTS

■ To support browsers that don't recognize the <EMBED> tag, use the <NOEMBED> tag with the following syntax:
<EMBED SRC=*URL* HEIGHT=*value* WIDTH=*value*>
<NOEMBED>
      HTML tags recognized by older browsers
</NOEMBED>
where the text and tags placed between the <NOEMBED> and </NOEMBED> tags will be rendered by older browsers and ignored by browsers that recognize the <EMBED> tag.

The <NOEMBED> tag works like the <NOFRAME> tag for framed presentations. It provides a way of supporting older browsers that don't recognize the <EMBED> tag. The general syntax of the <NOEMBED> tag is:

```
<EMBED SRC=URL HEIGHT=value WIDTH=value>
<NOEMBED>
    HTML tags recognized by older browsers
</NOEMBED>
```

A newer browser that recognizes the <EMBED> tag will embed the object on the Web page. It will also recognize the <NOEMBED> tags and will ignore any text that lies within them. An older browser, on the other hand, will ignore the <EMBED> and <NOEMBED> tags because it doesn't recognize them, but it will run whatever tags are entered between the <NOEMBED> tags.

For example, if you wanted to provide support for both new and older browsers with the MRIM.avi movie clip, you could enter the following HTML code:

```
<P>Preview a clip from the Mount Rainier Interactive Map</P>
<EMBED SRC="MRIM.avi" WIDTH=200 HEIGHT=200>
<NOEMBED>
    <A HREF="MRIM.avi">Summit Flyby (187K - AVI format)</A>
</NOEMBED>
```

In this case, new browsers would see only the embedded video clip, while older browsers would see only the hyperlink to the video file.

Using the DYNSRC Property

If your users have Internet Explorer, you can take advantage of some additional properties for the <IMG> tag supported by Internet Explorer version 3.0 and above. One of these is the DYNSRC property, which stands for "dynamic source." This property allows you to specify a video clip that is associated with an inline image. For example, the MRIM article contains an inline image using the following <IMG> tag:

```
<IMG SRC="MRIM.jpg" ALIGN=RIGHT HSPACE=5 VSPACE=1>
```

You could replace this tag with the following:

```
<IMG DYNSRC="MRIM.avi" SRC="MRIM.jpg" ALIGN=RIGHT
HSPACE=5 VSPACE=1>
```

The result of the new tag is that Internet Explorer will display the MRIM.jpg graphic as an inline image, but if the user clicks the image, the browser will play the MRIM.avi file. Using this tag allows you to display a GIF or JPEG graphic as a preview of the inline video clip, but to play the video clip itself whenever the user clicks the image.

There are other properties you can use along with the DYNSRC property. These include the CONTROLS property, to specify whether to include VCR-like controls below the video clip (including the word CONTROLS in the <IMG> tag inserts the controls, and omitting this word removes them); and the LOOP property, to specify the number of times the video will be played. LOOP can either be a digit or the word "INFINITE" (to allow the clip to be played without stopping). You can also control how the video clip is started by using the START property. Entering START=FILEOPEN in the <IMG> tag starts the clip automatically when the browser opens the file. Specifying START=MOUSEOVER starts the clip when the user moves the mouse over the image. Omitting the START property causes the clip to start when the image is clicked by the user.

Because the DYNSRC property and associated properties are supported only by Internet Explorer, if you use these properties you will probably have to supplement your HTML code with the <EMBED> tag to allow other browsers to use the embedded video clip.

If you want to use the DYNSRC property despite its limitations, you can create a JavaScript program to test whether the user is running Internet Explorer and, if so, you can have JavaScript insert an <IMG> tag with the DYNSRC property. If the user is not running Internet Explorer, JavaScript will insert an <EMBED> tag. Sample code for doing this is shown below:

```
<SCRIPT>
<!--- Hide from non-JavaScript browsers
var btype = navigator.appName;
if (btype == "Microsoft Internet Explorer") {
    document.write('<IMG SRC="MRIM.jpg" DYNSRC="MRIM.avi">');
} else {
    document.write('<EMBED SRC="MRIM.avi">');
}
//Stop hiding --->
</SCRIPT>
```

Note that this code uses the navigator object, which refers to the current browser, and the appName property, which contains the name of the current browser. You could supplement this code by adding the HEIGHT, WIDTH, and other properties to the tags created by the document.write() methods.

DESIGN window

TIPS FOR USING MULTIMEDIA IN YOUR WEB PAGE

- Avoid embedding large files on your Web page if the page will be accessed by users with slow Internet connections. Use hyperlinks instead.
- Always indicate the size of the media clip when creating a hyperlink to it, so that your users know how large the file is before committing to retrieving it.
- Provide different media formats to your users. Provide both AVI and QuickTime versions of your video files. Provide both WAV and AU versions of your audio files.
- Test your media clips on different browsers and browser versions.

Quick Check

1. Define the following terms: frame, frame rate, and codec.

2. Name three ways of reducing the size of a video file.

3. What are the three main video file formats used on the Web? Which would you use in a network primarily composed of computers running Windows 95?

4. What tag would you enter to allow users to access the Movie.mov video clip as an external video clip?

5   What tag would you enter to allow users to access the Movie.mov video clip as an embedded object?

6   What HTML tag would you enter to run the tag you created in Quick Check 4 for older browsers and the tag you created in Quick Check 5 for new browsers?

7   If your users are running Internet Explorer, how would you modify the tag <IMG SRC="Movie.jpg"> to allow it to run the video file "Movie.mov" whenever the user places the mouse over the inline image?

8   What are the limitations of the tag you created in Quick Check 7?

This concludes your work with external and embedded video clips. You've learned about the various video formats and the issues involved in working with video files. You'll show Tom the two versions of the Rainier page to get his feedback. In the next session you'll supplement the Rainier2 page by adding a Java applet to display a scrolling window of current news and reports.

SESSION

9.3

In this session you will work with Java applets to create a scrolling marquee. You'll learn how Java applets are stored in .class files and how to access those files from your Web page. You'll also learn to control how your Java applet works by sending parameter values to it. Finally, you'll learn how to create a scrolling marquee using one of the HTML extensions supported by Internet Explorer.

Introducing Java Applets

Tom has reviewed your work with sound and video and has only one more task for you to complete. The top of the *Mount Rainier News* Web page contains a table that shows the current weather forecast. Tom would like to expand the forecast to include two-day predictions. Doing so presents a problem, however. Including more text in the table will increase the table size and push the articles further down the page. Tom would like to avoid this because he thinks it would ruin the page layout. The best solution would be to retain the current size of the table, but have the text automatically scroll, as it does in theater marquees. Tom has seen scrolling text in other Web pages and knows that it might require the use of a Java applet. Because adding a Java applet will increase the size of the Web page, Tom suggests that you add this feature to the Rainier2 page. The Rainier page is designed for users with low bandwidth connections to the park's Web server, and Tom doesn't want to add more files to it. Therefore, you'll modify only the Rainier2 page.

Understanding Applets and .class Files

As you learned earlier in Tutorial 7, the Java computing language was developed to allow users to run programs from within their Web browsers rather than on the Web server. Each Java program is called an **applet**. Unlike JavaScript, a Java applet is not inserted into your HTML file; rather, it is an external file that is downloaded and executed by your browser. The applet itself usually appears as an embedded object on your Web page in an area called an **applet window**. You can specify the size and position of the applet window as it appears on your Web page. Some applets, however, might appear outside of your browser as separate applications that can be resized, minimized, and placed on the desktop. In the example that follows, you'll work with an applet that is embedded within the Rainier2 Web page.

To create a Java applet, you need a Java Developer's Kit (JDK). You can download a free copy of the Java Developer's Kit at the Sun Microsystems Java page located at http://www.java.sun.com. Commercial JDKs also exist that provide easy-to-use graphical tools and menus to help you create your Java applets quickly and easily. Once you have the JDK, be prepared to learn more about the Java computing language. It is somewhat similar to JavaScript, but it is a more advanced and powerful language.

After you write the code for a Java program using one of the JDKs, you need to save the source code as a file with the four-letter extension ".java." You then need to use the JDK to change the file into an executable file (a file that runs by itself without requiring additional software) in a process called **compiling**. The executable file has the filename extension ".class" and is called a **.class file**. A single Java applet may require more than one .class file to work properly. A .class file is different from the other program files you have on your computer. Unlike .exe or .com files, which are run by your operating system, a .class file can be run only from within a Java Interpreter. In most cases, the Java Interpreter is your Web browser. This feature is what allows the same Java applet to be run under a Windows 95 machine or a Macintosh, as long as the browser supports Java.

Many Java applets are available on the Web. Figure 9-22 lists a few of the more popular sources for applets. You can find Java applets for stock market tickers, games, animations, and other utilities.

Figure 9-22 ◀
Java applet
archives on
the Web

Title	URL
Applets from Sun	http://java.sun.com/applets/
Gamelan	http://www.gamelan.com/
Java Boutique	http://www.javaboutique.com/
Java Rating Service	http://www.jars.com/
Yahoo!'s list of Java applets	http://www.yahoo.com/Computers_and_Internet/Programming_Languages/Java/Applets/

Working with the <APPLET> and <PARAM> Tags

To use a Java applet in your Web page, you need the <APPLET> tag. The <APPLET> tag identifies the .class file used by the applet and allows you to specify any parameters needed to run the .class file. The general syntax of the <APPLET> tag is:

```
<APPLET CODE=file.class WIDTH=value HEIGHT=value>
    <PARAM>
    <PARAM>
 . . .
    <PARAM>
</APPLET>
```

where *file.class* is the filename of the .class file, and WIDTH and HEIGHT specify the size of the applet window in pixels. Each <PARAM> tag is used for special parameters required by the applet. The <PARAM> tag is optional. Documentation is usually supplied with the applet to specify which parameters, if any, are required. The syntax of the <PARAM> tag is:

```
<PARAM NAME=text VALUE=value>
```

where *text* is a text string identifying the name of the parameter (as specified in the documentation for the applet), and *value* is the value that is passed from the Web page to the applet.

REFERENCE window

INSERTING A JAVA APPLET

- To insert a Java applet, use the following syntax:
  ```
  <APPLET CODE=file.class WIDTH=value HEIGHT=value>
  <PARAM>
  <PARAM>
  ...
  <PARAM>
  </APPLET>
  ```
  where *file.class* is the name of the applet that is called by the browser, and the WIDTH and HEIGHT properties define the size of the applet window as it appears on the Web page.
- If the applet requires some parameters in order to function, enter the parameter values with the following syntax:
  ```
  <PARAM NAME=text VALUE=value>
  ```
  where the NAME property is the name of the particular parameter, and the VALUE property is the value that you want to assign to it.
- To access a Java applet located in a different folder from the one that contains the current HTML file, insert the following property in the <APPLET> tag:
  ```
  CODEBASE=URL
  ```
  where *URL* is the location of the *file.class* file.

Figure 9-23 shows some of the other properties supported by the <APPLET> tag.

Figure 9-23 ◄
Properties
of the
<APPLET> tag

Property	Description
ALT=*text*	Where *text* is a text string that should be displayed in place of the applet (used during the time before the applet has finished loading)
CODEBASE=*URL*	Where *URL* is the location of the .class file, if different from the Web page calling the applet
CODE=*file*.class	The name of the .class file
HEIGHT=*value*	The height of the applet as it appears on the Web page, in pixels
HSPACE=*value*	Where *value* is the horizontal space between the applet window and the surrounding text
NAME=*text*	Where *text* is the name of the applet
VSPACE=*value*	Where *value* is the vertical space between the applet window and the surrounding text
WIDTH=*value*	The width of the applet as it appears on the Web page, in pixels

The CODEBASE property enables you to run an applet placed in a different location from your Web page. This allows you to maintain only one copy of your applet, which you can then access from many different Web pages located in different folders. Web authors often place all of their applets in a single folder so that they can better manage them. Another aspect of the CODEBASE property is that it allows you to run *someone else's* Java applet off that person's Web server. However, this practice is discouraged and, in some cases, is a violation of a copyright. If you want to use someone else's Java applet in your own Web page, you should first obtain permission, retrieve the .class file, and place it on your own Web server.

You might run into problems when trying to run a .class file locally on your computer. In some situations, Internet Explorer 3.0 and 4.0 will restrict the ability to work with a .class file locally. This restriction is part of Internet Explorer's security measures, designed to limit how applets interact with the local hard drive. You can overcome this problem by downloading a patch from http://www.microsoft.com/java/vm/dl_x86.htm. Otherwise, you might have to relocate the applet to your Web server and access it remotely using the CODEBASE property. Netscape Navigator and Communicator do not have this restriction.

Notice that Java applets require an opening <APPLET> and closing </APPLET> tag. In addition to inserting <PARAM> tags between these two tags, you can also insert other HTML tags and text. You would do this for older browsers that don't support Java applets. Older browsers will ignore the <APPLET> and <PARAM> tags and will, instead, display the text you specify. New browsers that support Java applets will ignore that text, however. Consider the following structure in your HTML file:

```
<APPLET CODE=file.class>
    <PARAM>
    <PARAM>
...
<H3>To enjoy this page, upgrade your browser to supportJava</H3>
</APPLET>
```

With this code, the browser will display the applet; or, if it is an older browser, it will display the message about upgrading.

Inserting a Java Applet into a Web Page

Tom has located a Java applet for you to use in the Rainier2.htm file. The applet allows you to specify several lines of text that can be scrolled vertically through a window, like movie credits. The name of the .class file is CreditRoll.class, and it is located on your Student Disk. The CreditRoll.class file uses the parameters shown in Figure 9-24.

Figure 9-24 ◄
Parameters of
the CreditRoll
applet

Parameter Name	Description
BGCOLOR	The background color of the applet window, expressed as a color value
FADEZONE	The text in the applet window will fade in and out as it scrolls. This parameter sets the size of the area in which the text fades (in pixels).
TEXTCOLOR	The color value of the text in the applet window
FONT	The font used for the scrolling text in the applet window
TEXT*x*	Each line of text in the applet window requires a separate TEXT*x* parameter, where *x* is the line number. For example, the parameter TEXT1 sets the text for the first line in the applet window, TEXT2 sets the text for the second line in the applet window, and so forth.
URL	If the applet window is clicked, it will open the Web page specified in this URL parameter.
REPEAT	Specifies whether the text in the applet window is repeated. Setting this parameter's value to "yes" causes the text to scroll continuously.
SPEED	The speed at which the text scrolls, expressed in pixels per $\frac{1}{100}$ of a second
VSPACE	The space between each line of text, in pixels
FONTSIZE	The point size of the text in the applet window

After considering how he wants the weather information to appear, Tom asks you to use the parameter values shown in Figure 9-25. These values will create a marquee box with dark purple text on a white background. The box will include eight lines of text (including two blank lines) forecasting the weather for the next two days. The text is set to scroll continuously.

Figure 9-25 ◄

Values for the CreditRoll applet

Parameter Name	Parameter Value
BGCOLOR	FFFFFF (white)
FADEZONE	20
TEXTCOLOR	663366 (dark purple)
FONT	ARIAL
TEXTx	TODAY'S WEATHER FORECAST TODAY...Partly sunny. TONIGHT...Partly cloudy. Showers with sleet. TUESDAY...Rain heavy at times. Snow likely. WEDNESDAY...Clearing. Click to view the Weather Page.
URL	http://www.nps.gov/mora/weather.htm
REPEAT	yes
SPEED	100
VSPACE	3
FONTSIZE	12

The size of the applet window will be 400 pixels wide by 60 pixels high. This will roughly match the size of the box containing the weather report currently displayed on the Rainier2 Web page. Now that you know the size of the applet window and the value of the parameters, you are ready to replace the box containing the weather information with a window containing the CreditRoll applet. Because there is a lot of text involved in inserting this applet, the CRoll.txt file, which contains the text and parameter values for the applet, has been created for you and placed on your Student Disk. You'll copy the contents of the CRoll.txt file and paste them in the Rainier2.htm file.

To insert the CreditRoll applet:

1. If you took a break after the previous session, start your text editor and open the **CRoll.txt** file in the Tutorial.09 folder of your Student Disk.

2. Copy all of the text in the file, and then close the file.

3. Open the Rainier2.htm file in your text editor.

4. Locate the <!---WEATHER REPORT---> comment tag located midway through the file.

5. Delete all of the text between the <!---WEATHER REPORT---> and <!---END OF REPORT---> comment tags.

6. Paste the text you copied from the CRoll.txt file between the <!---WEATHER REPORT---> and <!---END OF REPORT---> comment tags. (You should indent the text to make your code easier to follow.)

The revised code in the Rainier2.htm file should appear as shown in Figure 9-26. Take some time to study the HTML code you just inserted. Note that blank lines are indicated in the values for the TEXT2 and TEXT7 parameters by the empty space allotted to those values.

Figure 9-26 ◀
Inserting the CreditRoll applet and applet parameters

Java .class file

applet parameters

parameter name
parameter value

dimensions of the applet window

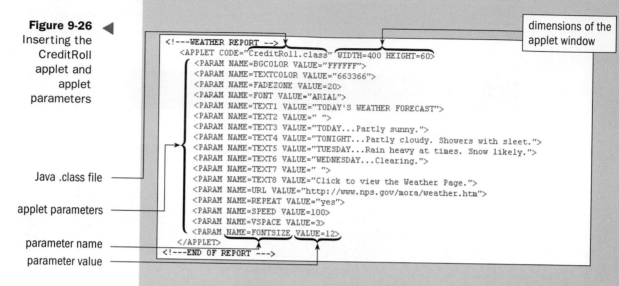

```
<!---WEATHER REPORT -->
    <APPLET CODE="CreditRoll.class" WIDTH=400 HEIGHT=60>
        <PARAM NAME=BGCOLOR VALUE="FFFFFF">
        <PARAM NAME=TEXTCOLOR VALUE="663366">
        <PARAM NAME=FADEZONE VALUE=20>
        <PARAM NAME=FONT VALUE="ARIAL">
        <PARAM NAME=TEXT1 VALUE="TODAY'S WEATHER FORECAST">
        <PARAM NAME=TEXT2 VALUE=" ">
        <PARAM NAME=TEXT3 VALUE="TODAY...Partly sunny.">
        <PARAM NAME=TEXT4 VALUE="TONIGHT...Partly cloudy. Showers with sleet.">
        <PARAM NAME=TEXT5 VALUE="TUESDAY...Rain heavy at times. Snow likely.">
        <PARAM NAME=TEXT6 VALUE="WEDNESDAY...Clearing.">
        <PARAM NAME=TEXT7 VALUE=" ">
        <PARAM NAME=TEXT8 VALUE="Click to view the Weather Page.">
        <PARAM NAME=URL VALUE="http://www.nps.gov/mora/weather.htm">
        <PARAM NAME=REPEAT VALUE="yes">
        <PARAM NAME=SPEED VALUE=100>
        <PARAM NAME=VSPACE VALUE=3>
        <PARAM NAME=FONTSIZE VALUE=12>
    </APPLET>
<!---END OF REPORT --->
```

7. Save your changes to Rainier2.htm.

8. Open the Rainier2.htm file in your Web browser. Because of the large number of embedded objects and the Java applet, the page will take longer to load. Figure 9-27 shows the CreditRoll applet as it appears on the Web page.

Figure 9-27 ◀
The CreditRoll applet in action

text fades as it exits the applet window

text scrolls vertically

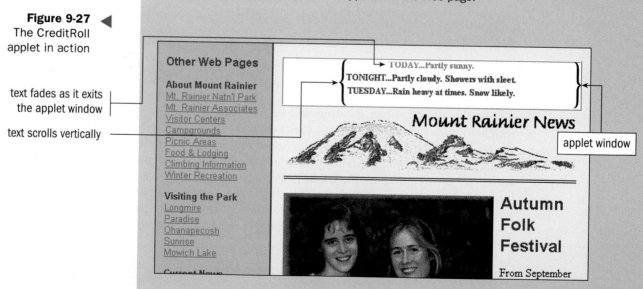

applet window

TROUBLE? If your browser has trouble accessing the CreditRoll applet, check the <APPLET> and <PARAM> tags for any errors or misspellings. If you are still having problems with the applet after fixing any errors, your browser might be preventing you from running the applet locally. Return to the Rainier2.htm file and insert the following property in the <APPLET> tag: CODEBASE="http://www.course.com". This should allow you to access the CreditRoll.class file on the Course Technology Web server. You will have to be connected to your Internet Service Provider for this to work. Ask your instructor or technical support person for assistance, if necessary.

Using Internet Explorer's <MARQUEE> Tag

If you don't want to use an applet to create a box with scrolling text, and you know that users accessing your Web page will be using Internet Explorer 3.0 or above, you can take advantage of the Internet Explorer <MARQUEE> tag to create a theater-style marquee. The general syntax of the <MARQUEE> tag is:

> <MARQUEE>*Marquee Text*</MARQUEE>

where *Marquee Text* is the text that will appear in the marquee box. Browsers that do not support the <MARQUEE> tag, such as Netscape Navigator or Communicator, will simply display the marquee text without any scrolling.

REFERENCE
window

CREATING A MARQUEE WITH INTERNET EXPLORER

- To create a marquee (a box of scrolling text) for the Internet Explorer browser, without using a Java applet, use the following HTML tag:
  <MARQUEE>*Marquee Text*</MARQUEE>
  where *Marquee Text* is the text that will scroll from right to left across the box.
- To control the appearance and size of the marquee, insert the following properties into the <MARQUEE> tag:
  BGCOLOR=*color* WIDTH=*value* HEIGHT=*value*
  where the BGCOLOR property controls the background color of the marquee box, and the WIDTH and HEIGHT properties define the box's dimensions.
- To control the placement of the marquee with the surrounding text, use the properties:
  HSPACE=*value* VSPACE=*value* ALIGN=*alignment*
  where the HSPACE and VSPACE properties define the amount of horizontal and vertical space around the box (in pixels), and the ALIGN property determines the alignment of the box with the surrounding text. (See the <IMG> tag for information on ALIGN values.)
- To control the behavior of text within the marquee, use the properties:
  BEHAVIOR=*item* DIRECTION=*item* LOOP=*value*
  where BEHAVIOR is either SCROLL (to continuously scroll the text across the box), SLIDE (to slide the text across the box and then stop), or ALTERNATE (to bounce the text back and forth across the box). The DIRECTION property is either LEFT or RIGHT, defining in which direction the text moves. The LOOP value determines how often the text moves across the box, and is either a digit or INFINITE.
- To control the speed of the text within the marquee, use the properties:
  SCROLLAMOUNT=*value* SCROLLDELAY=*value*
  where SCROLLAMOUNT is the amount of space (in pixels) that the text moves each time it advances across the page, and SCROLLDELAY is the amount of time, in milliseconds, between text advances.

Modifying the Marquee's Appearance

By default, the marquee will be placed within a box that is a single line high, extending the entire width of the Web page (or in the case of tables, the entire width of the table cell). The box's background color is transparent, displaying whatever color or background image you've selected for the page. You can modify the appearance of the marquee using the BGCOLOR, HEIGHT, and WIDTH properties. The syntax for these properties is:

<MARQUEE BGCOLOR=*value* HEIGHT=*value* WIDTH=*value*>

where BGCOLOR is the box's background color, expressed either as a color value or color name, and HEIGHT and WIDTH are the box's height and width expressed in pixels. Figure 9-28 shows a sample <MARQUEE> tag and its appearance in Internet Explorer.

Figure 9-28
Creating scrolling text with the <MARQUEE> tag

box dimensions

marquee text

text moves from the right to the left

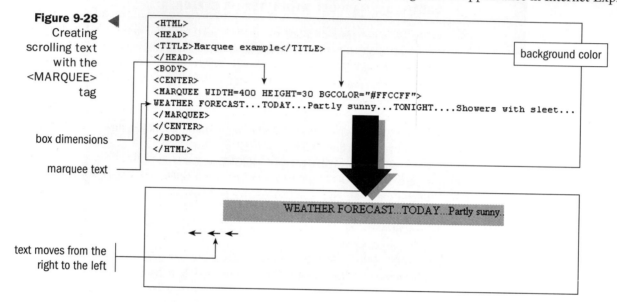

Because the marquee appears within a box, Internet Explorer provides properties similar to those used with inline images to control the placement of the box with the surrounding text. The syntax for controlling the layout of the marquee is:

<MARQUEE HSPACE=*value* VSPACE=*value* ALIGN=*alignment*>

where the HSPACE and VSPACE properties are used to specify the amount of horizontal and vertical space, in pixels, around the marquee box. The ALIGN property controls how the surrounding text is aligned with the box. The ALIGN property can have the value TOP, MIDDLE, or BOTTOM, which align the surrounding text with the top, middle, or bottom of the marquee box, respectively. You cannot control the alignment of the text within the box. That text is always aligned with the top of the box.

Modifying the Marquee's Behavior

Text within the marquee scrolls continuously at a predefined rate from the right side of the box to the left. The <MARQUEE> tag provides properties to allow you to alter the direction of the scrolling, the speed of the scrolling, and the number of times the text scrolls. The syntax for changing the marquee's behavior is:

<MARQUEE BEHAVIOR=*item* DIRECTION=*item* LOOP=*value*>

where the BEHAVIOR property controls how the text moves across the box, the DIRECTION property controls the direction of the text, and the LOOP property defines the number of times the text scrolls by.

The BEHAVIOR property has three possible values: SCROLL, SLIDE, or ALTERNATE. The default value is SCROLL, which causes the text to scroll across the box. Specifying a value of SLIDE for the BEHAVIOR property will cause the text to slide from the box's right edge to the left and then stop there. The ALTERNATE value will cause the text to bounce back and forth between the left and right edges of the box.

The DIRECTION property has two values: LEFT or RIGHT. The default value is RIGHT, which causes the text to start from the right edge of the box. LEFT causes the text to start from the box's left edge. The LOOP parameter can have either an integer value or the value INFINITE (the default) for continuous scrolling.

Two other properties, SCROLLAMOUNT and SCROLLDELAY, control the speed at which the text moves across the marquee. The syntax for these properties is:

```
<MARQUEE SCROLLAMOUNT=value SCROLLDELAY=value>
```

The SCROLLAMOUNT property specifies the amount of space, in pixels, that the text moves each time it advances across the page. Increasing the SCROLLAMOUNT value increases the speed of the marquee. The SCROLLDELAY property defines the amount of time, in milliseconds, between text advances. A low SCROLLDELAY value will cause the text to move quickly across the screen. You will need to experiment with these two properties to arrive at a marquee speed that you like.

You should show restraint in using the <MARQUEE> tag. Like animated GIFs, marquees can distract your users from other elements on your Web page. Also, a continuous marquee can quickly become a nuisance.

Because the <MARQUEE> tag is supported only by Internet Explorer, Tom decides against using it in the Rainier2.htm file. Tom is pleased with the results of your work. For now, you can close your text editor and your browser.

To close your work:

1. Close your Web browser.

2. Return to your text editor, and then close the Rainier2.htm file.

Quick Check

1. What is compiling?

2. How does a .class file differ from other executable files you might find on your computer?

3. What tag would you enter to insert the Java applet StockTicker.class in your Web page?

4. What tag would you enter to use the applet StockTicker.class if it is located at the URL http://www.wstreet.com?

5. The StockTicker.class applet has two parameters. The URL parameter identifies the URL of a Web resource containing stock data, and the TIME parameter specifies the time lag, in seconds, between stock market updates. If URL="http://www.stockinfo.com" and TIME=60, what HTML tags would you add to use these values?

6. In Internet Explorer, what tag would you enter to create a scrolling marquee containing the text "Stock Information" in white letters on a black background?

7. What property or properties would you add to the tag in Quick Check 6 to cause the text to scroll once from the left side of the marquee to the right and then stop?

Satisfied with the condition of both the Rainier.htm and Rainier2.htm pages, you present them to Tom for his approval. He examines the CreditRoll applet and is pleased with how it allows him to enter an almost unlimited amount of weather information without altering the layout of the newsletter page. He wants to examine the pages a little more closely and will contact you with any changes later.

Tutorial Assignments

Tom has returned with some additional multimedia clips he would like you to add to the *Mount Rainier News* Web page. One is a sound clip containing some more music from the previous year's Sunrise Folk Festival. The sound file has been saved in both the WAV format (as AF98-2.wav) and the AU format (as AF98-2.au). The other clip is a video clip with some more excerpts from the Mount Rainier Interactive Map. You have two video files—MRIM2.avi and MRIM2.mov. You'll modify both of the pages you created in the tutorial, creating two versions of the newsletter: one with hyperlinks to external files and the other with embedded media clips. Tom also wants you to add a background sound to the Web page with embedded media clips. The background sound is based on a short sound file that welcomes users to Mount Rainier.

Tom would also like you to modify the behavior of the CreditRoll applet. He wants you to add an additional line to the applet with the long-range forecast. He thinks that the text scrolls a little too slowly and would like you to speed up the scrolling. He wants the fadezone area reduced and would like to have the text of the applet window changed to black.

Tom gives you two new files to work on.

To make Tom's changes to the *Mount Rainier News* Web page:

1. Start your text editor and open the Raintxt3.htm file in the TAssign folder of the Tutorial.09 folder on your Student Disk, and then save the file as Rainier3.htm in the same folder.

2. Below the hyperlink for the *Wild Mountain Thyme* sound file, insert a hyperlink to the AF98-2 file (either the WAV file or the AU file, depending on your operating system). In the hyperlink include the name of the piece *À la Claire Fontaine* and the size of the sound file.

3. Below the hyperlinks for the MRIM video files, insert two more hyperlinks to the MRIM2 video files (both the AVI and MOV file). Include information on the size of each video clip and the description "Mount Rainier flyby - East ridge."

4. Save your changes to the Rainier3.htm file.

5. Open the Rainier3.htm file in your browser and verify that all of the hyperlinks work correctly.

6. Print a copy of the Rainier3.htm file in your browser and text editor.

7. Open the Raintxt4.htm file from the TAssign folder of the Tutorial.09 folder on your Student Disk, and then save the file as Rainier4.htm in the same folder.

8. Below the embedded sound clip for the AF98-1.wav (or AF98-1.au) file, insert an embedded sound clip for the AF98-2 file (either WAV or AU format). Set the size of the embedded object to 145 pixels wide by 60 pixels high.

9. Below the embedded MRIM video clip, insert a video clip for the MRIM2 video file. Use either the AVI or QuickTime version, depending on your operating system and browser. Set the size of the embedded video clip to 208 by 208.

10. In the HEAD section of the file, insert a tag to play a background sound. Use the file Welcome.wav (or Welcome.au, if that is the sound format supported by your system). Set the sound to play only once.

11. Locate the CreditRoll applet tag and make the following changes:

   - Insert a new TEXT parameter after TEXT6 (name it TEXT7) with the forecast: "LONGTERM...Warmer and drier." Change the original TEXT7 parameter to TEXT8, and then update the remaining TEXT parameters accordingly.
   - Increase the value of the SPEED parameter to 120.
   - Set the FADEZONE value to 1.
   - Change the TEXTCOLOR parameter to black. (You will have to use black's color value, not its color name.)

12. Save your changes to the Rainier4.htm file.

13. Open the Rainier4.htm file in your browser and verify that the embedded links and Java applet work correctly. If you are using Internet Explorer, verify that the background sound tag plays correctly.

14. Print a copy of the Rainier4.htm file from both the browser window and your text editor.

15. Close your browser and your text editor.

Case Problems

1. Adding Multimedia to the Lincoln Museum of Natural History Web Page Maria Kalski is the Director of Public Relations for the Lincoln Museum of Natural History, located in Lincoln, Iowa. Maria wants to disprove the notion that museums are boring, stuffy places, so she has asked you to help enliven the museum's Web page. Maria has already added some fun graphics and text fonts to the page. Now she would like you to add some video and sound clips. She gives you a couple of files that she wants added to the Web site. She wants you to create a hyperlink to the video file (a clip of a dinosaur coming to life in a museum), and she wants the sound file to be added to the page's background, to be played whenever the page is loaded by the browser.

The final version of your Web page is shown in Figure 9-29.

Figure 9-29 ◀

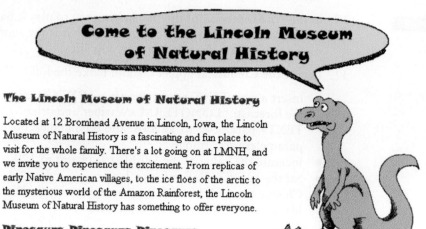

To create the Lincoln Museum of Natural History Web page:

1. Start your text editor and open the file LMNHtext.htm in the Case1 folder of the Tutorial.09 folder on your Student Disk, and then save the file as LMNH.htm in the same folder.

2. Locate the word "movie" in the final paragraph of the page. Change this text to a hyperlink pointing to either the Dino.avi or Dino.mov file (depending on which video format your system supports).

3. Include in the hyperlink the type of video format you chose in Step 2, as well as the size of the video file.

4. Go to the bottom of the file and, directly below the image map, insert <SCRIPT> tags for a JavaScript program.

5. Using the JavaScript program presented earlier in the tutorial as a model, write a program that uses the appName property to determine which browser is displaying the LMNH page.

EXPLORE

6. If the browser is Microsoft Internet Explorer, use the document.write() method to create a background sound using Internet Explorer's <BGSOUND> tag. Use the Dino.wav file as the sound source (use Dino.au instead, if that is what your system supports).

EXPLORE

7. If the browser is *not* Internet Explorer, use the document.write() method to create an embedded sound clip with Dino.wav (or Dino.au) as the source. Set the dimensions of the embedded sound clip to 0 by 0, and have the sound clip played automatically when the page is loaded by the browser.

8. Save your changes to LMNH.htm and print the file. Close your text editor.

9. Open the LMNH page in your browser and verify that the hyperlink displays the video clip and that the sound clip plays automatically when the page loads.

EXPLORE

10. If you have access to both Netscape and Internet Explorer, open the page in both browsers and verify that the background sound is played each time.

11. Close your Web browser.

2. Creating the Robert Frost Web Page Professor Debra Li of the Madison State College English Department has asked you to help her create a page devoted to the works of the poet Robert Frost. Debra has already created a page with a short biography of the poet and the complete text of two of his works. She would like to add interest to the page by inserting sound clips of the two poems, so that her students can listen to Frost's poetry as well as read it.

Debra also wants you to create hyperlinks to some other Frost pages on the Web. She's located a Java applet that creates a set of graphical buttons that act as hyperlinks, and she thinks this applet would also make her page more interesting. The Java applet uses the button.class file and has the parameters shown in Figure 9-30 (parameter names are in lowercase and should be enclosed in double quotation marks).

Figure 9-30 ◀

Parameter Name	Description
"buttons"	The number of buttons in the set
"color"	The color of all the buttons in the set
"direction"	The orientation of the set of buttons (0=vertical orientation, 1=horizontal orientation)
"border width"	The width of the borders of the buttons, in pixels
"f_size"	The point size of the text labels on each button
"f_color"	The color value of the button labels
"f_color2"	The color value of the button labels when the mouse passes over the button or when the button is clicked
"f_offset"	The space between the button labels and the button borders, in pixels
"font"	The font face of the button labels; can be either TimesRoman, Helvetica or Courier
"label x"	The label for each button; use the "label 0" parameter for the first button's label, "label 1" for the second button's label, and so forth
"link x"	The URL that each button links to; use the "link 0" parameter for the first button's hyperlink, "link 1" for the second button's hyperlink, and so forth

A preview of the page you'll create for Debra is shown in Figure 9-31.

Figure 9-31 ◀

The Robert Frost Web Page

Robert Frost was born in San Francisco on March 26, 1874. When Frost was a young man, his father died, causing the family to move to Massachusetts. Frost attended Dartmouth College for less than a semester, after which he moved back to Massachusetts to teach and work as a reporter for a local newspaper. Frost returned to college in 1897 to attend Harvard, but he did not graduate. Frost was essentially a self-educated man.

After Harvard, Frost married and sold the farm he had inherited. With the proceeds of the sale, he moved his family to England, where he wrote for ten years without success. His first works were published by a London publisher in 1913.

Frost's works, once printed, met immediate acclaim. His collection of poems *A Further Place* won the Pulitzer Prize in 1937. Though he is sometimes cast as a pastoral poet, Frost was also a fierce intellectual with a decidedly dark view of himself and the world. Frost would use rural settings as a metaphor for his philosophical views. Robert Frost is one of the best-known and most loved of American poets. He died in Boston on January 29, 1963.

Two of Frost's poems are included below. Click the sound icon located next to each poem's title to download a sound clip of the poem. The sound files are 383K and 181K in size.

Fire and Ice

Some say the world will end in fire,
Some say in ice.
From what I've tasted of desire
I hold with those who favor fire.
But if it had to perish twice,
I think I know enough of hate
To say that for destruction ice
Is also great
And would suffice.

Devotion

The heart can think of no devotion
Greater than being shore to the ocean—
Holding the curve of one position,
Counting an endless repetition.

Click the buttons below to view other Robert Frost sites on the Web.

| Frost in Cyberspace | Robert Frost. Three Volumes | A Frost Bouquet |

To create the Robert Frost Web page:

1. Start your text editor and open the file RFtext.htm in the Case2 folder of the Tutorial.09 folder on your Student Disk, and then save the file as RF.htm in the same folder.

2. Locate the title of the "Fire and Ice" poem in the table at the bottom of the page.

3. Below the title, insert the inline graphic Sound.gif. Align the graphic with the bottom of the surrounding text, and set the horizontal space to 3 pixels and the image border to 0 pixels.

4. Change the Sound graphic to a hyperlink that points to the FireIce.wav file (or FireIce.au, if your browser does not support the WAV format).

5. Repeat Steps 3 and 4 for the "Devotion" poem located in the first row and second column of the table. Have the Sound graphic point to the Devotion.wav (or Devotion.au) file.

6. Indicate the size of the two sound files at the end of the last paragraph before the table.

7. At the bottom of the RF.htm file, within the <P ALIGN=CENTER> and </P> tags, insert the Java applet that calls the button.class file. Set the size of the applet to 600 pixels wide by 26 pixels high.

8. Use the following parameter values in the applet:

   - The number of buttons is 3.
   - The color value of the buttons is "C0C0C0".
   - The buttons are oriented horizontally on the page.
   - The button border width is 3 pixels.
   - The font size of the button labels is 13.
   - The color of the button labels is "000000" ("FFFFFF" when clicked).
   - There are 4 pixels between the button labels and the button borders.
   - The font face is Helvetica.
   - The label of the first button is "Frost in Cyberspace" and it points to "http://www.libarts.sfasu.edu/Frost/Frost.html."
   - The second button label is "Robert Frost. Three Volumes" and it points to "http://www.columbia.edu/acis/bartleby/frost/."
   - The third button label is "A Frost Bouquet" and it points to "http://www.lib.virginia.edu/exhibits/frost/home.html."

9. Print the HTML tags for the Java applet, and then save and close the RF.htm file.

10. View the page in your Web browser and test the three links to the other Frost pages as well as the links to the two sound clips. (*Note:* If you have problems running the button.class applet with Internet Explorer, you might have to upgrade your version of the browser, using software from http://www.microsoft.com/java/vm/dl_x86.htm. If this happens, check with your instructor before accessing this Web site.)

11. Print a copy of the Web page.

12. Close your Web browser and your text editor.

3. Creating a Page About Fractals Fractals are geometric objects, recently discovered by mathematicians, that closely model the sometimes chaotic world of nature. Douglas Hefstadt teaches mathematics at Franklin High School in Monroe, Illinois. He has just begun a unit on fractals for his senior math class. Douglas has constructed a Web page on the topic and needs your help to complete the page before placing it on the school's network. He has a video clip of a fractal that he wants placed on the page, as well as a Java applet that allows students to interactively explore the Mandelbrot Set (a type of fractal object). Douglas wants your assistance in putting these two objects on the Web page. A preview of the page you'll create is shown in Figure 9-32.

Figure 9-32 ◀

Exploring the World of Fractals

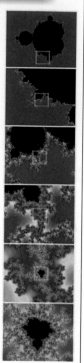

A *fractal* is a geometric object that retains its complexity under any level of magnification. Many fractals are *self-similar* in that the fractal image is infinitely repeated on a smaller scale as one "zooms" into the object. The most famous of the fractal objects is the *Mandelbrot Set* named after its discoverer, Benoit B. Mandelbrot. As you can see in the accompanying images, the Mandelbrot Set, a bug-shaped object, appears again and again as one magnifies the image.

Fractals are not simply an abstract geometric concept. Fractals appear everywhere in nature: from the irregular shape of a coastline to the outlines of trees, clouds and mountains. The application of fractal geometry to science and physics has allowed mathematicians and physicists to describe phenomena that had, until recently, eluded description.

Fractals have also been used in image processing. Mathematician Michael F. Barnsley has applied fractal mathematics to the compression of digital photographs and video images. Because of their beauty, fractals are a popular source of computer art as well.

Links to other pages on fractals
- Exploring Fractals
- Fractory
- Fractals and Fractal Art
- Fractals on the Web
- Fractals

To travel into the Mandelbrot Set, run the video clip below.

Ready to explore your own fractals? Great. Use the Java applet below. To improve the resolution of the fractal image, change the value in the drop-down list box (a value of 1 is the most precise; 10 is the least), and click the *Redraw* button. To magnify a particular section of the fractal, click the *Zoom In* button, and drag a rectangle over the section you want to magnify. To switch between the Mandelbrot Set and the Julia Set (another type of fractal, closely related to the Mandelbrot Set) click the *Switch [M <-> J]* button and then click a spot on the Mandelbrot Set.

This applet is generously provided by James Henstridge.

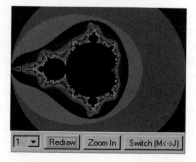

To create the Fractal page:

1. Start your text editor and open the file Fractext.htm in the Case3 folder of the Tutorial.09 folder on your Student Disk, and then save the file as Fractal.htm in the same folder.

2. Below the paragraph inviting the user to run the video clip, insert an embedded video clip between the <P ALIGN=CENTER> and </P> tags. The source of the video clip is Mandel.avi (substitute Mandel.mov if your system requires this format).

3. Set the size of the embedded object to 104 pixels wide by 120 pixels high.

EXPLORE

4. Below the embedded video clip, use the <NOEMBED> tags to insert a hyperlink to the Mandel.avi (or Mandel.mov) file in order to provide support for older browsers that cannot display embedded objects. Be sure to indicate the size of the video file alongside the hyperlink.

5. At the bottom of the file, between the <P ALIGN=CENTER> and </P> tags, insert a Java applet that uses the Mandel.class file.

6. Set the size of the applet to 250 pixels wide by 210 pixels high.

EXPLORE

7. Insert the statement "Your browser does not support Java applets" into the Fractal.htm file, so that it will be displayed only by older browsers that do not recognize applets.

8. Print a copy of the new HTML tags you entered into this document.

9. Save and close the Fractal.htm file.

10. Open the page in your Web browser and play the video clip to verify that it works. Test the Fractal applet.

11. Print a copy of your Web page, and then close your Web browser.

EXPLORE

4. Creating Your Own Multimedia Web Page In this Case Problem, you'll download a media file (sound or video, or both) from the Web and create a Web page based on the media clip(s) you downloaded. If it is a clip from a movie, create a Web page that describes and advertises the movie. If it is a sports or music clip, create a Web page that describes that topic. The subject matter, content, and layout of the page are up to you. Note that you should use caution in posting your Web page on the World Wide Web for public consumption. Doing so might violate the copyright privileges of the person or organization that created the original media clip.

To create your multimedia Web page:

1. Create a file named MyMedia.htm in the Case4 folder of the Tutorial.09 folder on your Student Disk.

2. Embed the media clip (or clips) that you have chosen on the Web page.

3. Insert text that describes the clip (or clips).

4. Provide support for older browsers that don't support embedded objects, by including a hyperlink to your multimedia file. Use the <NOEMBED> tag so that this hyperlink appears only in older browsers.

5. Use the CreditRoll.class applet located in the Case4 folder of the Tutorial.09 folder to add a scrolling window to your page. The window can contain information about you or the media clip, or both.

6. Print a copy of the HTML code and the page itself.

7. Close your Web browser and your text editor.

Lab Assignment

This Lab Assignment is designed to accompany the interactive Course Lab called Multimedia. To start the Multimedia Course Lab, click the Start button on the Windows 95 taskbar, point to Programs, point to Course Labs, point to New Perspectives Applications, and click Multimedia. If you do not see Course Labs on your Programs menu, see your instructor or technical support person.

Multimedia Multimedia brings together text, graphics, sound, animation, video, and photo images. In this Lab you will learn how to apply multimedia and then have the chance to see what it might be like to design some aspects of multimedia projects.

1. Click the Steps button to learn about multimedia development. As you proceed through the Steps, answer the Quick Check questions. After you complete the Steps, you will see a Quick Check Report. Follow the instructions on the screen to print this report.

2. In Explore, browse through the STS-79 Multimedia Mission Log. How many videos are included in the Multimedia Mission Log? The image on the Mission Profile page is a vector drawing, what happens when you enlarge it?

3. Listen to the sound track on Day 3. Is this a WAV file or a MIDI file? Why do you think so? Is this a synthesized sound or a digitized sound? Listen to the sound track on page 8. Can you tell if this is a WAV file or a MIDI file?

4. Suppose you were hired as a multimedia designer for a multimedia series on targeting fourth- and fifth-grade students. Describe the changes you would make to the Multimedia Mission Log so it would be suitable for these students. Also, include a sketch showing a screen from your revised design.

5. When you view the Mission Log on your computer, do you see palette flash? Why or why not? If you see palette flash, list the images that flash.

6. Multimedia can be effectively applied to projects such as encyclopedias, atlases, and animated storybooks; to computer-based training for foreign languages, first aid, or software applications; for games and sports simulations; for business presentations; for personal albums, scrapbooks, and baby books; for product catalogs and Web pages.

Suppose you were hired to create one of these projects. Write a one-paragraph description of the project you would be creating. Describe some of the multimedia elements you would include. For each of the elements indicate its source and whether you would need to obtain permission for its use. Finally, sketch a screen or two showing your completed project.

Answers to Quick Check Questions

SESSION 6.1

1   A CGI script is any program or set of commands running on the Web server that receives data from the Web page and then acts upon that data to perform a certain task.

2   The <FORM> tag identifies the beginning and end of a form.

3   <INPUT NAME=Phone>

4   <INPUT NAME=Phone SIZE=10>

5   <INPUT NAME=Phone SIZE=10 MAXLENGTH=10>

6   <INPUT NAME=Subscribe VALUE="Yes">

7   Set the value of the TYPE property to PASSWORD.

SESSION 6.2

1   <SELECT NAME=State>
   <OPTION>California
   <OPTION>Nevada
   <OPTION>Oregon
   <OPTION>Washington
</SELECT>

2   Change the <SELECT> tag to <SELECT MULTIPLE>.

3   <OPTION SELECTED>Oregon

4   <INPUT TYPE=RADIO NAME=State VALUE=California>California
<INPUT TYPE=RADIO NAME=State VALUE=Nevada>Nevada
<INPUT TYPE=RADIO NAME=State VALUE=Oregon>Oregon
<INPUT TYPE=RADIO NAME=State VALUE=Washington>Washington

5   <INPUT TYPE=RADIO NAME=State VALUE=1>California
<INPUT TYPE=RADIO NAME=State VALUE=2>Nevada
<INPUT TYPE=RADIO NAME=State VALUE=3>Oregon
<INPUT TYPE=RADIO NAME=State VALUE=4>Washington

6   <INPUT TYPE=CHECKBOX>California
A value of "on" is sent to the CGI script.

7   <TEXTAREA ROWS=5 COLS=30 NAME=Memo>Enter notes here.</TEXTAREA>

8   WRAP=PHYSICAL or WRAP=HARD

SESSION 6.3

1 <INPUT TYPE=SUBMIT VALUE="Send Form">

2 <INPUT TYPE=RESET VALUE="Cancel Form">

3 <INPUT TYPE=IMG NAME=Sites SRC="Sites.gif" VALUE="GotoPage">

4 Sites.42, GotoPage.21

5 <INPUT TYPE=HIDDEN NAME=Subject VALUE="Form Responses">

6 <FORM METHOD=GET ACTION="http://www.j_davis.com/cgi-bin/post-query">

7 multipart/form-data

8 <FORM ACTION="mailto:walker@j_davis.com">
This action might not be supported by all browsers.

SESSION 7.1

1 A client-side program is a program that is run on the user's computer, usually within the user's Web browser. A server-side program is run off of the Web server.

2 Java can be more difficult to learn than JavaScript. Java requires a developer's kit to create executable applets, whereas JavaScript does not. Java programs must be compiled; JavaScript programs are scripts that can be run without compiling. Java is the more powerful of the two languages.

3 A JavaScript program is run by the Web browser either in the process of rendering the HTML file or in response to an event, such as the user clicking a Submit button or positioning the mouse on a hyperlink.

4 <SCRIPT> and </SCRIPT>

5 to prevent older browsers, which do not support JavaScript, from displaying the JavaScript commands on the Web page

6 document.write("<H1>Avalon Books</H1>")

SESSION 7.2

1 number, string, Boolean, and null values

2 var Now = new Date();

3 var Tdate = Now.getDate();

4 the month number starts at 0 and goes to 11, rather than starting at 1 and going to 12

5 An expression is a JavaScript command that assigns a value to a variable. An operator is an element that performs an action within an expression. A binary operator works on two elements in an expression. A unary operator works on only a single expression element.

6   y = x + 1;
     y = x++;

7   The = operator is used to assign a value to an element. The == operator is used to compare two values.

8   function *function_name(parameters)*{
     JavaScript commands
     }

SESSION 7.3

1   An array is an ordered collection of values referenced by a single variable name.
     var Colors = new Array();

2   Colors[1]="Red";
     Colors[2]="Green";
     Colors[3]="Blue";
     Colors[4]="Black";
     Colors[5]="White";
     There are six elements in this array.

3   A loop is a set of instructions that are executed repeatedly. There are two types of loops: loops that repeat a set number of times before quitting (For loops), and loops that repeat until a certain condition is met (While loops).

4   for(i=1; i<=5; i++) {
     document.write("News Flash!
");
     }

5   5, 10, 15, 20, 25

6   if(Month=="September") {
     document.write("Welcome back to school!");
     }

7   if(Month=="September") {
     document.write("Welcome back to school!");
   } else {
     document.write("Today's headlines");
     }

8   if(Month=="September") {
     document.write("Welcome back to school!");
   } else {
     if(Month="June") {
      document.write("Summer's here!")
     } else {
       document.write("Today's headlines");
     }
   }

SESSION 8.1

1. In server-side validation, the user input is checked on the Web server, usually via a CGI script. In client-side validation, user input is checked within the Web browser on the user's computer.

2. An object is an item that exists in a defined space, such as a Web page, Web browser, form, or table. A property describes an object's appearance, purpose, or behavior. A method is an action that can be performed with an object or to an object.

3. document.ENROLL.JOIN

4. document.fgColor="blue";

5. document.fgColor=tcolor;

6. document.ENROLL.reset();

SESSION 8.2

1. An event is a specific action that triggers the browser to run a block of JavaScript commands. An event handler is code added to an HTML tag that is run whenever a particular event occurs. An event method is a method applied to a JavaScript object to emulate the occurrence of an event.

2. Edit the <BODY> tag to read: <BODY onLoad="Welcome();">.

3. <INPUT NAME=CreditNumber onBlur="CheckCredit();">

4. document.PRODUCT.MODEL.options[0].value=P250;

5. document.PRODUCT.MODEL.options[0].text="Pentium 250";

6. var ModelNumber = document.PRODUCT.MODEL.selectedIndex;

7. prompt("Enter a new model");

SESSION 8.3

1. Because input box values are stored as text strings, you must use the eval() function to convert the text strings into numbers.

2. 5025

3. the currently selected object

4. alert("Weight Invalid");

5. confirm("Accept weight value?");

6. <FORM NAME=STUDY onSubmit="return CheckIt();">

7. a boolean value, either true or false

SESSION 9.1

1 You can add sound by either embedding a sound clip into the Web page or by providing a hyperlink to a sound file.

2 Bandwidth is a measure of the amount of data that can be sent through a communications circuit each second. The number of samples taken per second from a sound source is called the sampling rate. Sample resolution indicates the precision in measuring the sound within each sample.

3 AIFF, AIFC, or SND

4 <A HREF="Music.wav">

5 An embedded object is any media clip, file, program, or other object that can be run or viewed from within the Web page. The browser must be able to support the <EMBED> tag and it must have a plug in or add-on installed to work with the object.

6 <EMBED SRC="Music.wav">

7 <BGSOUND SRC="Music.wav" LOOP=1>
In Netscape, you can use the tag:
<EMBED SRC="MUSIC.wav" WIDTH=0 HEIGHT=0 AUTOSTART="true">

SESSION 9.2

1 A frame is an individual image in a video file. The number of frames displayed in each unit of time is called the frame rate. The technique of compressing and decompressing video frames is called a codec (for compression/decompression).

2 changing the size of each frame, reducing the frame rate, compressing the file via the codec, reducing the size of the sound track by changing the sample size or sampling rate, or reducing the color depth of the images in the video file

3 AVI, MPEG, and QuickTime. You would use AVI files on a Windows 95 network.

4 <A HREF="Movie.mov">

5 <EMBED SRC="Movie.mov">

6 <EMBED SRC="Movie.mov">
<NOEMBED>
  <A HREF="Movie.mov">
</NOEMBED>

7 <IMG SRC="Movie.jpg" DYNSRC="Movie.mov" START=MOUSEOVER>

8 It might not be supported by browsers other than Internet Explorer.

SESSION 9.3

1 Compiling is a process that changes a file into an executable file (that is, a file that runs by itself without requiring additional software).

2 It must be run within a Java interpreter, such as your Web browser.

3 <APPLET CODE="StockTicker.class">

4 <APPLET CODE="StockTicker.class" CODEBASE="http://www.wstreet.com">

5 <PARAM NAME=URL VALUE="http://www.stockinfo.com">
<PARAM NAME=TIME VALUE=60>

6 <FONT COLOR="#FFFFFF">
<MARQUEE BGCOLOR="#000000">Stock Information</MARQUEE>
</FONT>

7 DIRECTION=LEFT BEHAVIOR=SLIDE

Creating a Company Web Site

OBJECTIVES

In this case you will:

- Paste text into a Web page formatted with tables

- Create hyperlink anchors and link to anchors on other Web pages

- Insert a registered trademark symbol, using a special character code

- Create form elements for a product order form

- Create a JavaScript program to calculate the total cost of the order

CASE

FrostiWear Winter Clothes

FrostiWear is a retail mail-order company that specializes in winter clothing and gear. Recently, the company created a Web site to advertise its wares on the World Wide Web. Part of the Web site will allow customers to order products online.

You've been asked by Susan Crawford, the director of the company's Internet Advertising Division, to create Web pages for the company's line of gloves and mittens. In order to start you out slowly, she's given you a short list of four popular products that she would like you to add to the company's Web site. Later on, if she approves your work, she'll ask you to add the complete company line (over 35 styles of gloves and mittens).

Susan wants the pages you create to fit in with the established style of the company's Web site. She gives you a file, Frosti.txt, containing one of the standard page layouts. You'll use this layout as a template for two of the pages she wants you to create. These are:

- Gloves.htm: a page containing an overview of FrostiWear's glove and mitten products

- GProduct.htm: a page with specific information on the four products that Susan wants you to add to the site

Susan also wants you to create a third page, GOrder.htm, which contains an order form for the company's glove and mitten products. This page should be based on the company's standard form stored in the Order.txt file.

Your form should automatically calculate the total cost of the order, based on the price of the brand and the quantity ordered by the customer. In addition, FrostiWear provides a 5% discount (rounded to the nearest dollar) for customers who have a FrostiWear Club card. Therefore, your form should automatically calculate the discount, if the customer has a card, and subtract it from the total. If the customer is not a FrostiWear Club member, the form should display a message inviting the customer to join.

To complete these pages, Susan gives you graphics files of the glove products and text files containing product specifications and descriptions. Figure AC1-1 and Figure AC1-2 list the files you'll be working with.

Figure AC1-1 ◀
Text files for
the FrostiWear
Web site

Filename	Description
Arctic.txt	Description of the ArcticBlast glove
FLG.txt	Description of the Fingerless Glove
Frosti.htm	FrostiWear home page
Frosti.txt	Basic layout of all FrostiWear Web pages
Gloves.txt	Overview of the line of FrostiWear gloves and mittens
GMitt.txt	Description of the Glomitt glove/mitt combination product
Order.txt	Standard layout for FrostiWear's online order forms
PFM.txt	Description of the PolyFleece mitt

Figure AC1-2 ◀
Graphics files
for the
FrostiWear
Web site

Filename	Description
ArcticB.jpg	Graphic of the ArcticBlast glove
Blueline.gif	Background image, to be used on all Web pages except the online order form page
FLess.jpg	Graphic of the Fingerless Glove
FLogo.gif	FrostiWear company logo, to be included on all Web pages
Glomitt.jpg	Graphic of the Glomitt glove/mitt combination product
Gloves.gif	Graphic to be used in the Glove Overview Web page
PolyFlce.jpg	Graphic of the PolyFleece mitt
Sweaters.jpg	Graphic displayed on the FrostiWear home page

To create Web pages for the FrostiWear Web site:

1. Start your text editor and open the file Frosti.txt in the Case1 folder of the Tutorial.add folder on your Student Disk, and then save the file as Gloves.htm in the same folder. Change the title of the Web page to "FrostiWear Gloves."

2. Insert within the second table cell, where indicated, the Gloves.gif inline image, aligned with the right cell margin.

3. Below the inline image, but within the table cell, insert the contents of the Gloves.txt file (you might want to use the copy and paste features of your text editor to do this). Format the paragraph title with the H1 header style and make it blue in color. Separate one paragraph from another, using paragraph marks.

4. Insert the registered trademark symbol ® after every occurrence of the words: PolyFleece, ArcticBlast, and Gore-Tex.

5. Change the following text to hypertext (each item, except the last, appears in the second paragraph; the last item appears in the third paragraph):
   - "Fingerless Gloves" linked to the FLess anchor in the GProduct.htm file
   - "PolyFleece mitt" linked to the PolyF anchor in the GProduct.htm file
   - "Glomitt" linked to the Glomitt anchor in the GProduct.htm file
   - "ArcticBlast Gore-Tex mitts" linked to the ArcticBlast anchor in the GProduct.htm file
   - "online order form" linked to the GOrder.htm file

6. Save the Gloves.htm file and preview it in your Web browser. Your page should appear similar to the one shown in Figure AC1-3 (your browser might render the page slightly differently). Print your Web page.

Figure AC1-3 ◀
The Gloves and
Mitts page

FROSTIWEAR™

Home Page   **Online Store**   **Contacting Us**   **Corporate Info**

Home Page

Online Store
  Rainwear
  Insulated Jackets
  Insulated Clothes
  Hats and Headwear
  Gloves and Mitts
  Insulated Underwear

Contacting Us
  Phone
  E-mail
  Fax
  Shipping

Corporate Info
  Philosophy
  Financial Statement
  Stock
  Year-end Report

Gloves and Mitts

FrostiWear provides several brands of gloves and mitts to keep your fingers warm in even the coldest weather. No matter what your activity, you can find the glove or mitt you need.

For mild days in which you need to have free use of fingers (for such activities as photography), choose our Fingerless Gloves. For colder days of hiking, snowshoeing, or simple winter walks, choose the PolyFleece® mitts. To enjoy the best of both worlds, purchase a Glomitt, a fingerless glove with a wool hood that slips back for added protection against the cold. Finally, for the serious outdoorsman, consider our ArcticBlast® Gore-Tex® mitts with ultra-protection against severe cold.

You can order your gloves or mitts using the online order form, or if you prefer, talk to one of our sales representatives at 1-888-555-5421. Remember, you can get a 5% discount by using your FrostiWear Club card.

7. Return to your text editor, print the HTML code for the Gloves.htm file, and then save the file.

8. Reopen the Frosti.txt template file in your text editor and save it as GProduct.htm. Change the Web page title to "FrostiWear Glove Products."

9. In the second table cell insert the FLess.jpg graphic, aligned with the right cell margin.

10. Below the graphic, insert the contents of the FLG.txt file, which describes the Fingerless Glove.

11. Format the text you inserted by displaying the paragraph title in blue, using the H1 heading style. Insert an anchor named "FLess" at the beginning of the H1 header you created.

12. Below the paragraph, insert the product specification table shown in Figure AC1-4. Create a row of table headers and set the width of the first table column to 150 pixels and the second column's width to 300 pixels. Set the border width of the table to 2 pixels.

Figure AC1-4 ◀
Table of Fingerless Gloves product specifications

Specification	Description
Product ID	G725
Color	Burgundy, Red, Black, Gray
Size	Small, Medium, Large, XLarge
Price	$28.00

13. Below the table, enter sections containing content from the text files for the three remaining products. Format those sections in the same way you formatted the Fingerless Gloves section, and include the appropriate inline image and product information table for each item. Make the following changes to each section:

For PolyFleece mitts:

- Insert an anchor named "PolyF" at the beginning of the section.
- In the product specification table, the Product ID is G726, and the price is $38.00.

For Glomitts:

- Insert an anchor named "Glomitt" at the beginning of the section.
- The Product ID is G727, and the price is $18.00.

For ArcticBlast mitts:

- Insert an anchor named "ArcticBlast" at the top of the section.
- The Product ID is G728, and the price is $98.00.

 EXPLORE

14. Insert the registered trademark symbol after every occurrence of the words: PolyFleece, ArcticBlast, and Gore-Tex on the page.

15. Link the text "Order online." to GOrder.htm (each of the four times this text occurs on the page).

16. Open the page in your Web browser. Your page should look similar to the one shown in Figure AC1-5.

Figure AC1-5 ◄
The Glove
Products page

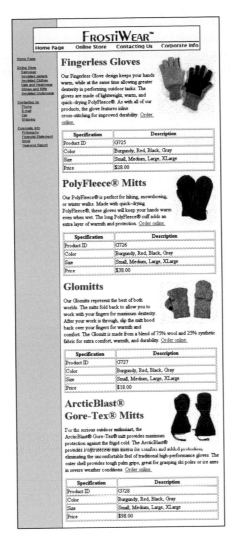

17. Verify that each of the four product hyperlinks you created jumps to the appropriate location in the GProduct.htm page. Print a copy of your page as it appears in your Web browser.

18. Return to your text editor, print the HTML code for the GProduct.htm file, and then save the file.

19. Open the Order.txt file and save it as GOrder.htm.

20. Change the text "Product Order Form" in the page's title and heading to "Gloves and Mitts Order Form." Change the text "Product page" in the initial paragraph to "Gloves and Mitts page," and link it to the Gloves.htm file.

21. Within the Order form, change the Brand selection list so that it displays the names of the four glove brands along with their prices. Set the value of each of the four options in the selection list to the price of the glove or mitt.

22. Enter options for the Size and Color selection lists, based on the table entries in the GProduct.htm page.

23. Within the HEAD section of the GOrder.htm file, create a JavaScript function named "Calculate()." The Calculate() function should do the following:

- Determine the value (price) of the selected brand (*Hint*: first determine the selected index in the Brand selection list, and then use this information to determine the value of the option corresponding to that index).
- Multiply the brand's price by the quantity ordered. Store this value in a variable named "Subtotal."

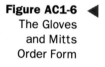

- Determine the customer discount and store it in a variable named "Discount." The discount should be either 0 or, if the customer is a FrostiWear card holder, it should be equal to Math.round(0.05*Subtotal).
- Subtract Discount from Subtotal and store the result in a variable named "Total."
- Store the Subtotal value in the SUBTOTAL input box, the Discount value in the DISCOUNT input box, and the Total value in the TOTAL input box.

24. Modify the Calculate Total button so that it runs the Calculate() function when clicked.

25. Modify the form so that if the customer is not a FrostiWear Club member, an alert box is displayed containing the text "You can enjoy additional savings with a FrostiWear Club card" when the customer submits the order.

26. Go to your Web browser and open the GOrder.htm page. Your page should appear similar to the one shown in Figure AC1-6.

Figure AC1-6 ◀
The Gloves
and Mitts
Order Form

FrostiWear™
Home Page   Online Store   Contacting Us   Corporate Info

Gloves and Mitts Order Form

Go to the Gloves and Mitts page to learn more about our products and styles.

1) I am a FrostiWear Club Member* ☐ Club ID: `FC-#####`
2) Brand: `Fingerless Gloves ($28)` ▾
3) Sex: `Male` ▾
4) Size: `Small` ▾
5) Color: `Burgundy` ▾
6) Quantity: `0`

Subtotal: `0`
Discount: `0`

Total: `0`

[Calculate Total] [Add to Shopping Cart] [Reset Form]

*FrostiWear Club members receive a 5% discount on all merchandise (rounded to the nearest dollar amount).

27. Print a copy of the Web page showing the total order cost for the following values:
- FrostiWear Club Member = yes, Brand = Glomitt, Quantity = 3
- FrostiWear Club Member = no, Brand = Fingerless Gloves, Quantity = 4
- FrostiWear Club Member = yes, Brand = ArcticBlast, Quantity = 1
- FrostiWear Club Member = no, Brand = PolyFleece Mitts, Quantity = 3

28. Return to your text editor and print a copy of the HTML code. Close your text editor.

29. Open the Gloves.htm page and verify that all of the hyperlinks you created between the three pages work properly. (Links to Web pages other than the FrostiWear home page will not work.) Close your Web browser.

Creating the Web Site for Mayer Photography

OBJECTIVES

In this case you will:

■ Create a Web page using tables to control the text layout

■ Insert an animated GIF to provide support for older browsers that do not support applets

■ Create and use an image map involving polygonal hotspots

■ Create text of different colors, sizes, and font faces

■ Insert an embedded video clip and provide support for older browsers that do not support inline media

CASE

Mayer Photography

Mayer Photography is a family-owned photography studio founded by Ted and Jane Mayer in 1972. They've managed to create a successful business in Elmridge, New Hampshire, and the neighboring communities. Ted Mayer approaches you to create a Web site for his service.

Ted envisions four Web pages for his Web site: a home page that describes the company and provides contact information for customers, a page describing the company's wedding services, a page devoted to the company's portrait services, and a final page that will describe monthly specials offered by the company. You'll name these pages Mayer.htm, Weddings.htm, Portrait.htm, and Special.htm, respectively.

Ted has also collected four testimonials from former Mayer Photography customers. He would like to include these comments on each of the four Web pages. He provides text files containing these comments as well as the general text that he wants you to place on his Web site. He also gives you graphics files containing samples of his company's work. Because Mayer Photography has lately been involved in providing video services for weddings, he has also provided a video clip (in AVI and QuickTime format) that he would like you to add to the Web page describing the company's wedding services. Figure AC2-1 shows the files you'll place on each Web page.

Figure AC2-1 ◀
Files for
the Mayer
Photography
Web site

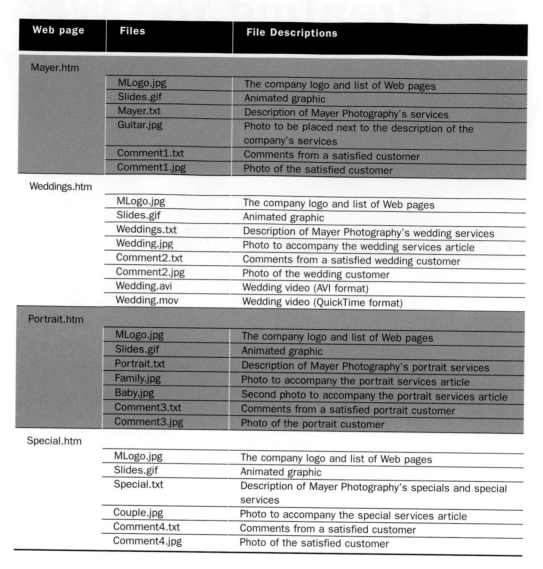

Web page	Files	File Descriptions
Mayer.htm		
	MLogo.jpg	The company logo and list of Web pages
	Slides.gif	Animated graphic
	Mayer.txt	Description of Mayer Photography's services
	Guitar.jpg	Photo to be placed next to the description of the company's services
	Comment1.txt	Comments from a satisfied customer
	Comment1.jpg	Photo of the satisfied customer
Weddings.htm		
	MLogo.jpg	The company logo and list of Web pages
	Slides.gif	Animated graphic
	Weddings.txt	Description of Mayer Photography's wedding services
	Wedding.jpg	Photo to accompany the wedding services article
	Comment2.txt	Comments from a satisfied wedding customer
	Comment2.jpg	Photo of the wedding customer
	Wedding.avi	Wedding video (AVI format)
	Wedding.mov	Wedding video (QuickTime format)
Portrait.htm		
	MLogo.jpg	The company logo and list of Web pages
	Slides.gif	Animated graphic
	Portrait.txt	Description of Mayer Photography's portrait services
	Family.jpg	Photo to accompany the portrait services article
	Baby.jpg	Second photo to accompany the portrait services article
	Comment3.txt	Comments from a satisfied portrait customer
	Comment3.jpg	Photo of the portrait customer
Special.htm		
	MLogo.jpg	The company logo and list of Web pages
	Slides.gif	Animated graphic
	Special.txt	Description of Mayer Photography's specials and special services
	Couple.jpg	Photo to accompany the special services article
	Comment4.txt	Comments from a satisfied customer
	Comment4.jpg	Photo of the satisfied customer

A preview of the first page you'll create, Mayer.htm, is shown in Figure AC2-2.

To create Web pages for the Mayer Photography Web site:

1. Start your text editor and create a new file named Mayer.htm in the Case2 folder of the Tutorial.add folder on your Student Disk. Specify the title "Mayer Photography: Home Page" for the Web page. Set the page's background color to white and the text color to black. Set the color of all links, followed links, and activated links that you'll create on the Web page, to brown.

2. At the top of the page, insert the MLogo.jpg file. Set the border width to 0 pixels and specify "Mayer Photography" as the alternate text. Create an image map for the logo with the following polygonal hotspot coordinates:

   - (3,83)(20,69)(40,66)(60,69)(81,83)(60,97)(40,100)(20,97) pointing to the Mayer.htm file
   - (103,83)(120,69)(140,66)(160,69)(181,83)(160,97)(140,100)(120,97) pointing to the Weddings.htm file
   - (203,83)(220,69)(240,66)(260,69)(281,83)(260,97)(240,100)(220,97) pointing to the Portrait.htm file
   - (303,83)(320,69)(340,66)(360,69)(381,83)(360,97)(340,100)(320,97) pointing to the Special.htm file

Figure AC2-2
The Mayer.htm
Web page

Who Are We?

Mayer Photography is a family-owned business of professional photographers, providing our customers with the highest-quality images and services. We specialize in portraits, senior class photos and weddings. If your special day is approaching, pay us a visit and we'll show you how Mayer Photography can help you preserve your memories forever.

A Family Business

Ted and Jane Mayer started Mayer Photography in 1972 after graduating from the New England School of Photography. Their work has won numerous awards in competitions across the country. Joining the business in 1992, their sons, Jason and Andrew, uphold the family tradition of excellence in photography.

Contact us at:

Mayer Photography
8911 Bronte Avenue
Elmridge, NH 79112
603-555-8121

"We had Mayer Photography do an album for our family reunion. Everyone was so pleased with their work, that they've handled all of the weddings in our family since."

Kris Thomson, Grovedale

Home   Weddings   Portraits   Specials

3. Directly to the right of the logo, insert the animated GIF "Slides.gif."

4. Insert a horizontal line below the logo and animated GIF, and then center these three elements on the Web page (as shown in Figure AC2-2).

5. Below the horizontal line, create a centered table that is 600 pixels wide, with the space between and within the table cells equal to 5 pixels. The table should have a single row with two columns. The width of the first column should be 170 pixels, and the second column should be 430 pixels wide.

6. For the first column, insert the Comment1.jpg graphic, centered horizontally and aligned with the top of the table cell. Below the image, insert the contents of the Comment1.txt file. Italicize the name of the customer and the customer's home town in a paragraph below the comment text. Change the color of the table cell to brown, and change the text in the table cell to white, 2 pixels in size, with either an Arial, Helvetica, or Sans Serif font face.

7. At the top of the second table column, insert the contents of the Mayer.txt file. Format the titles of each paragraph to display an H2 heading, using brown text and either an Arial, Helvetica, or Sans Serif font. Indent the address information at the bottom of the column, using block quotes. Insert the Guitar.jpg graphic between the first and second articles, aligned with the right cell margin. Set the horizontal distance between the graphic and the surrounding text to 5 pixels.

8. Within the first article (titled "Who Are We?"), link the text "portraits, senior class photos" to the Portrait.htm file. Link the text "weddings" in the same sentence to the Weddings.htm file.

9. Below the two-column table you just created, insert another horizontal line, followed by another table that extends across the width of the Web page. The table should have one row and four table headers, each one 25% of the width of the table. Within the four table cells, insert the following centered text: "Home," "Weddings," "Portraits," and "Specials," and link that text to the files Mayer.htm, Weddings.htm, Portrait.htm, and Special.htm, respectively.

10. Save your changes to Mayer.htm. Print a copy of the HTML code, and then open the page in your Web browser and print a copy of the page as it appears in the browser.

11. Create the Weddings.htm page with your text editor, using the same layout you applied to the Mayer.htm page. Once again, the left column should contain a graphic and a testimonial from a satisfied customer, and the right column should contain information on how Mayer Photography handles weddings. Use the Comment2.txt file along with the Comment2.jpg graphic for the testimonial. Use the Weddings.txt file along with the Wedding.jpg graphic for the column containing wedding information. The Wedding.jpg image should be aligned with the right cell column margin, alongside the text of the first paragraph of wedding information.

12. Use a different color scheme for the Weddings.htm page. Instead of brown, use the color value 9966FF (a lavender color) for text links, paragraph headings, and the background of the left column.

13. Italicize the words *Draybeck Video Services* in the paragraph on wedding videos.

14. Within the right column, directly below the wedding videos paragraph, insert a centered embedded video clip using either the Wedding.avi or Wedding.mov file (depending on which video format your computer supports).

15. If the customer's browser does not support inline video, have the Wedding.htm page display hyperlinks to the Wedding.avi and Wedding.mov files instead. Include information on the size and format of each video clip along with the linked text.

16. Save the Wedding.htm file. Your page should appear as shown in Figure AC2-3. Print a copy of the HTML code you used to create your page, and print your page as it appears in the Web browser.

Figure AC2-3 ◄
The Mayer
Photography
wedding page

17. Create the Portrait.htm page shown in Figure AC2-4. Apply the same layout choices you used in the two other pages. Use the Comment3.txt file for the Greer family testimonial, along with the Comment3.jpg graphic. Use the Portrait.txt file for the information on Mayer Photography portraits, along with the Family.jpg and Baby.jpg graphics. The color value of the left column background, text links, and paragraph headings should be 006699. Print a copy of the HTML code for this file, along with the page as it appears in your Web browser.

Figure AC2-4 ◀
The Mayer
Photography
portraits page

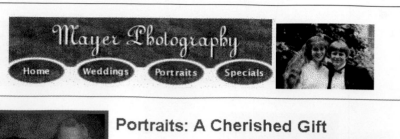

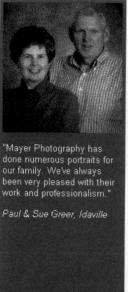

Portraits: A Cherished Gift

A well-crafted portrait is a gift you'll cherish forever. At Mayer Photography, we understand this and we strive to create portraits of unsurpassed quality. We work with you to create the portrait you deserve. You can choose between

a formal studio setting or, if the mood strikes you, we can go to locations that highlight your personality and interests.

"Mayer Photography has done numerous portraits for our family. We've always been very pleased with their work and professionalism."

Paul & Sue Greer, Idaville

For Any Occasion

Whether you're interested in large group photos, family portraits, or Senior class pictures; Mayer Photography is the place to go for portraits. We offer competitive group rate pricing for organizations, businesses and students. Our highly-trained and experienced staff is ready to serve you.

Home   Weddings   Portraits   Specials

18. Create the Special.htm page shown in Figure AC2-5. Use the Comment4.txt file for the testimonial from Barbara Lee, along with the Comment4.jpg graphic. Insert the text from the Special.txt file into the right column, along with the Couple.jpg graphic. The color value of the left column background, text links, and paragraph headings should be 006600.

19. Indent the e-mail address, using block quotes, and change the e-mail address itself into hypertext pointing to the specified address.

20. Print both the Web page and the corresponding HTML code you created.

Figure AC2-5
The Mayer
Photography
specials page

Special Prices, Special People

During the month of May, Mayer Photography is reducing the price of its family portraits by 15%. If you've delayed creating that special photo, don't delay any longer, and get it at a special price. As always, Mayer Photo will offer competitive discounts for large groups and organizations.

Digital Photography

As you can see from our Web site, Mayer Photography is not shy about jumping into the computer age. If you have a PC or Macintosh, look into our scanning services. We can take your photos and convert them into graphics files suitable for desktop wallpaper or the World Wide Web. We can also use our imaging software to enhance your photos with special effects. Call us for details. You can also e-mail us at:

DigitPhotos@MayerPhoto.com

"I'm so pleased with their work. I call Mayer Photography on almost every special occasion."

Barbara Lee, Whitenburg

Home   Weddings   Portraits   Specials

21. Test the hyperlinks you created for this Web site, both at the bottom of the page and within the Mayer Photography logo. Verify that the links allow you to open each of the four pages you created.

22. Close your Web browser and your text editor.

Creating an Online Newsletter

In this case you will:

- Design and create an online newsletter incorporating several Web pages

- Format your newsletter using tables, special fonts, and other layout features

- Create an image map containing hotspots to each page in the Web site

- Create a JavaScript program that displays the current date

- Insert a scrolling banner Java applet that displays a list of events

- Create an online survey form containing several form elements

Twin Life Magazine*   EXPLORE

Twin Life is a magazine created for parents of twins, triplets, and other multiple-birth children. Recently the company has decided to go online and publish parts of its monthly magazine on the World Wide Web. You've been asked by Elise Howard, the magazine's editor, to create a Web site for the contents of *Twin Life*. You've been handed a disk containing text files of the articles she wants you to add and graphics files of the images she wants to have placed on the site.

Elise envisions a total of five Web pages for the site: a front page, a news page, a monthly features page, a page of special articles, and a customer survey page. Figure AC3-1 lists the files that you should use for each page of the Web site.

Please note: All of Additional Case 3 is an Exploration Exercise.

Figure AC3-1 ◀
Files for
the *Twin Life*
Web site

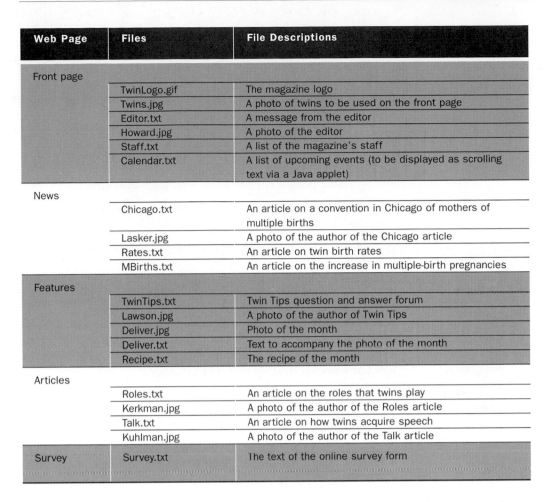

Web Page	Files	File Descriptions
Front page		
	TwinLogo.gif	The magazine logo
	Twins.jpg	A photo of twins to be used on the front page
	Editor.txt	A message from the editor
	Howard.jpg	A photo of the editor
	Staff.txt	A list of the magazine's staff
	Calendar.txt	A list of upcoming events (to be displayed as scrolling text via a Java applet)
News		
	Chicago.txt	An article on a convention in Chicago of mothers of multiple births
	Lasker.jpg	A photo of the author of the Chicago article
	Rates.txt	An article on twin birth rates
	MBirths.txt	An article on the increase in multiple-birth pregnancies
Features		
	TwinTips.txt	Twin Tips question and answer forum
	Lawson.jpg	A photo of the author of Twin Tips
	Deliver.jpg	Photo of the month
	Deliver.txt	Text to accompany the photo of the month
	Recipe.txt	The recipe of the month
Articles		
	Roles.txt	An article on the roles that twins play
	Kerkman.jpg	A photo of the author of the Roles article
	Talk.txt	An article on how twins acquire speech
	Kuhlman.jpg	A photo of the author of the Talk article
Survey	Survey.txt	The text of the online survey form

The actual layout of the pages in the Web site is up to you, but it should incorporate the following features:

- Each Web page should have a title and you need to specify the colors of the page's background, text, and linked text.

- The front page should display a message with the current date: for example, "Today is 11/4/99."

- The site should show at least one example of a font that uses the Arial, Helvetica, or Sans Serif face and is a different color from the surrounding text.

- The magazine's logo (TwinLogo.gif) should include an image map linking to the five Web pages in the Web site. (You will have to determine the coordinates for each hotspot using either your graphics software or an image map editor.) In addition, each page in the site should have text links to all five pages, in order to provide support for browsers that cannot display client-side image maps.

- The pages should use tables to format the layout of the different articles in the newsletter. There should be at least one example of an article that has a different background color from the rest.

- The list of upcoming events (found in the Calendar.txt file) should be displayed in a scrolling window, using the CreditRoll.class Java applet. You need to determine the values of each parameter in the applet, aside from the TEXTx parameters.

- Any text in one article that refers to the contents of another article should be changed to a hyperlink pointing to that article.

- A Submit button and a Reset button should be included with the online survey form.

To create Web pages for the *Twin Life* Web site:

1. Using your text editor, create HTML files named TwinLife.htm, News.htm, Feature.htm, Articles.htm, and Survey.htm.

2. Using the list of files shown in Figure AC3-1, insert the appropriate text and graphics into each of these Web pages (you can copy the text using the copy and paste functions of your text editor). Format the pages with an attractive layout.

3. Open the TwinLife.htm file in your Web browser and test each of the hyperlinks you created. When satisfied with the behavior and appearance of the Web site, print a copy of each Web page as it appears in your Web browser.

4. Return to your text editor and print the HTML code for each of the five Web pages.

5. Close your Web browser and your text editor.

Lab Assignment

Web Pages & HTML

To start this Lab, click the Start button on the taskbar, point to Programs, point to Course Labs, point to New Perspectives Applications, and click Web Pages and HTML.

Web Pages & HTML It's easy to create your own Web pages. There are many software tools to help you become a Web author. In this Lab you'll experiment with a Web authoring wizard that automates the process of creating a Web page. You'll also try your hand at working directly with HTML code.

1. Click the Steps button to activate the Web authoring wizard and learn how to create a basic Web page. As you proceed through the Steps, answer all of the Quick Check questions. After you complete the Steps, you will see a Quick Check summary Report. Follow the instructions on the screen to print this report.

2. In Explore, click the File menu, then click New to start working on a new Web page. Use the wizard to create a Home page for a veterinarian who offers dog day-care and boarding services. After you create the page, save it on drive A or C, and print the HTML code. Your site must have the following characteristics:
   a. Title: Dr. Dave's Dog Domain
   b. Background color: Gold
   c. Graphic: Dog.jpg
   d. Body text: Your dog will have the best care day and night at Dr. Dave's Dog Domain. Fine accommodations, good food, playtime, and snacks are all provided. You can board your pet by the day or week. Grooming services also available.
   e. Text link: "Reasonable rates" links to www.cciw.com/np3/rates.htm
   f. E-mail link: "For more information:" links to **daveassist@drdave.com**

3. In Explore, use the File menu to open the HTML document called Politics.htm. After you use the HTML window (not the wizard) to make the following changes, save the revised page on Drive A or C, and print the HTML code. Refer to the HTML Tag Reference at the end of this book for a list of HTML tags you can use.
   a. Change the title to Politics 2000
   b. Center the page heading
   c. Change the background color to FFE7C6 and the text color to 000000
   d. Add a line break before the sentence "What's next?"
   e. Add a bold tag to "Additional links on this topic:"
   f. Add one more link to the "Additional links" list. The link should go to the site **http://www.elections.ca** and the clickable link should read "Elections Canada".
   g. Change the last graphic to display the image "next.gif"

4. In Explore use the Web authoring wizard and the HTML window to create a Home page about yourself. You should include at least a screenful of text, a graphic, an external link, and an e-mail link. Save the page on drive A, then print the HTML code. Turn in your disk and printout.

Appendix A HTML Extended Color Names

COLOR NAME	HEXADECIMAL VALUE	PREVIEW

Extended Color Names

The following is a list of extended color names and their corresponding hexadecimal triplets supported by most Web browsers. To view these colors, you must have a video card and monitor capable of displaying up to 256 colors. As with other aspects of Web page design, you should test these color names on a variety of browsers before committing to their use. Different browsers may render these colors differently, or not at all.

COLOR NAME	HEXADECIMAL VALUE	PREVIEW
ALICEBLUE	#F0F8FE	
ANTIQUEWHITE	#FAEBD7	
AQUA	#00FFFF	
AQUAMARINE	#70DB93	
AZURE	#F0FFFF	
BEIGE	#F5F5DC	
BLACK	#000000	
BLUE	#0000FF	
BLUEVIOLET	#9F5F9F	
BRASS	#B5A642	
BRIGHTGOLD	#D9D919	
BRONZE	#8C7853	
BROWN	#A52A2A	
CADETBLUE	#5F9F9F	
CHOCOLATE	#D2691E	
COOLCOPPER	#D98719	
COPPER	#B87333	

Appendix A **HTML Extended Color Names**

COLOR NAME	HEXADECIMAL VALUE	PREVIEW
CORAL	#FF7F00	
CORAL	#FF7F50	
CRIMSON	#DC143C	
CYAN	#00FFFF	
DARKBLUE	#00008B	
DARKBROWN	#5C4033	
DARKCYAN	#008B8B	
DARKGOLDENROD	#B8860B	
DARKGRAY	#A9A9A9	
DARKGREEN	#006400	
DARKKHAKI	#BDB76B	
DARKMAGENTA	#8B008B	
DARKOLIVEGREEN	#4F4F2F	
DARKORANGE	#FF8C00	
DARKORCHID	#9932CD	
DARKPURPLE	#871F78	
DARKSALMON	#E9967A	
DARKSLATEBLUE	#6B238E	
DARKSLATEGRAY	#2F4F4F	
DARKTAN	#97694F	

Appendix A HTML Extended Color Names

COLOR NAME	HEXADECIMAL VALUE	PREVIEW
DARKTURQUOISE	#7093DB	
DARKVIOLET	#9400D3	
DARKWOOD	#855E42	
DIMGRAY	#545454	
DUSTYROSE	#856363	
FELDSPAR	#D19275	
FIREBRICK	#8E2323	
FORESTGREEN	#238E23	
GOLD	#CD7F32	
GOLDENROD	#DBDB70	
GRAY	#C0C0C0	
GREEN	#00FF00	
GREENCOPPER	#527F76	
GREENYELLOW	#93DB70	
HOTPINK	#FF69B4	
HUNTERGREEN	#215E21	
INDIANRED	#4E2F2F	
INDIGO	#4B0082	
IVORY	#FFFFF0	
KHAKI	#9F9F5F	

Appendix A **HTML Extended Color Names**

COLOR NAME	HEXADECIMAL VALUE	PREVIEW
LAVENDER	#E6E6FA	
LIGHTBLUE	#C0D9D9	
LIGHTCORAL	#F08080	
LIGHTCYAN	#E0FFFF	
LIGHTGRAY	#A8A8A8	
LIGHTGREEN	#90EE90	
LIGHTPINK	#FFB6C1	
LIGHTSTEELBLUE	#8F8FBD	
LIGHTWOOD	#E9C2A6	
LIME	#00FF00	
LIMEGREEN	#32CD32	
MAGENTA	#FF00FF	
MANDARINORANGE	#E47833	
MAROON	#8E236B	
MEDIUMAQUAMARINE	#32CD99	
MEDIUMBLUE	#3232CD	
MEDIUMFORESTGREEN	#6B8E23	
MEDIUMGOLDENROD	#EAEAAE	
MEDIUMORCHID	#9370DB	
MEDIUMSEAGREEN	#426F42	

Appendix A **HTML Extended Color Names**

COLOR NAME	HEXADECIMAL VALUE	PREVIEW
MEDIUMSLATEBLUE	#7F00FF	
MEDIUMSPRINGGREEN	#7FFF00	
MEDIUMTURQUOISE	#70DBDB	
MEDIUMVIOLETRED	#DB7093	
MEDIUMWOOD	#A68064	
MIDNIGHTBLUE	#2F2F4F	
MINTCREAM	#F5FFFA	
MISTYROSE	#FFE4E1	
NAVYBLUE	#23238E	
NEONBLUE	#4D4DFF	
NEONPINK	#FF6EC7	
NEWMIDNIGHTBLUE	#00009C	
NEWTAN	#EBC79E	
OLDGOLD	#CFB53B	
OLIVE	#808000	
ORANGE	#FF7F00	
ORANGERED	#FF2400	
ORCHID	#DB70DB	
PALEGOLDENROD	#EEE8AA	
PALEGREEN	#8FBC8F	

Appendix A HTML Extended Color Names

COLOR NAME	HEXADECIMAL VALUE	PREVIEW
PALETURQUOISE	#AFEEEE	
PINK	#BC8F8F	
PLUM	#EAADEA	
POWDERBLUE	#B0E0E6	
PURPLE	#800080	
QUARTZ	#D9D9F3	
RED	#FF0000	
RICHBLUE	#5959AB	
ROYALBLUE	#4169E1	
SADDLEBROWN	#8B4513	
SALMON	#6F4242	
SANDYBROWN	#F4A460	
SCARLET	#8C1717	
SEAGREEN	#238E68	
SIENNA	#8E6B23	
SILVER	#E6E8FA	
SKYBLUE	#3299CC	
SLATEBLUE	#007FFF	
SNOW	#FFFAFA	
SPICYPINK	#FF1CAE	

COLOR NAME	HEXADECIMAL VALUE	PREVIEW
SPRINGGREEN	#00FF7F	
STEELBLUE	#236B8E	
SUMMERSKY	#38B0DE	
TAN	#DB9370	
TEAL	#008080	
THISTLE	#D8BFD8	
TOMATO	#FF6347	
TURQUOISE	#ADEAEA	
VERYDARKBROWN	#5C4033	
VERYDARKGRAY	#CDCDCD	
VIOLET	#4F2F4F	
VIOLETRED	#CC3299	
WHEAT	#D8D8BF	
WHITE	#FFFFFF	
YELLOW	#FFFF00	
YELLOWGREEN	#99CC32	

Appendix B **HTML Special Characters**

CHARACTER	CODE	CODE NAME	DESCRIPTION

The following table lists the extended character set for HTML, also known as the ISO Latin-1 Character set. Characters in this table can be entered either by code number or code name. For example, to insert the registered trademark symbol, ®, you would use either &reg or &#174.

Not all code names are recognized by all browsers. Some older browsers that support only the HTML 2.0 standard will not recognize the code name &times, for instance. Code names that may not be recognized by older browsers are marked with an asterisk. If you are planning to use these symbols in your document, you may want to use the code number instead of the code name.

CHARACTER	CODE	CODE NAME	DESCRIPTION
	&#00 - &#08		Unused
	&#09		Tab
	&#10		Line feed
	&#11 - &#31		Unused
	&#32		Space
!	&#33		Exclamation mark
"	&#34	&quot	Double quotation mark
#	&#35		Pound sign
$	&#36		Dollar sign
%	&#37		Percent sign
&	&#38	&amp	Ampersand
'	&#39		Apostrophe
(	&#40		Left parenthesis
)	&#41		Right parenthesis
*	&#42		Asterisk
+	&#43		Plus sign
,	&#44		Comma
-	&#45		Hyphen
.	&#46		Period
/	&#47		Forward slash
0 - 9	&#48 - &#57		Numbers 0 - 9
:	&#58		Colon
;	&#59		Semicolon
<	&#60	&lt	Less than sign

Appendix B HTML Special Characters

CHARACTER	CODE	CODE NAME	DESCRIPTION
=	&#61		Equals sign
>	&#62	&gt	Greater than sign
?	&#63		Question mark
@	&#64		Commercial at
A - Z	&#65 - &#90		Letters A - Z
[	&#91		Left square bracket
\	&#92		Back slash
]	&#93		Right square bracket
^	&#94		Caret
_	&#95		Horizontal bar
`	&#96		Grave accent
a - z	&#97 - &#122		Letters a - z
{	&#123		Left curly brace
|	&#124		Vertical bar
}	&#125		Right curly brace
~	&#126		Tilde
	&#127 - &#129		Unused
,	&#130		Low single comma quotation mark
ƒ	&#131		Function sign
„	&#132		Low double comma quotation mark
…	&#133		Ellipses
†	&#134		Dagger
‡	&#135		Double dagger
ˆ	&#136		Caret
‰	&#137		Per mile sign
Š	&#138		Capital S with hacek
<	&#139		Less than sign
Œ	&#140		Capital OE ligature

Appendix B **HTML Special Characters**

CHARACTER	CODE	CODE NAME	DESCRIPTION
	&#141 - &#144		Unused
'	&#145		Single beginning quotation mark
'	&#146		Single ending quotation mark
"	&#147		Double beginning quotation mark
"	&#148		Double ending quotation mark
•	&#149		Middle dot
–	&#150		En dash
—	&#151		Em dash
~	&#152		Tilde
™	&#153	&trade*	Trademark symbol
š	&#154		Small s with hacek
›	&#155		Greater than sign
œ	&#156		Small oe ligature
	&#157 - &#158		Unused
Ÿ	&#159		Capital Y with umlaut
		*	Non-breaking space
¡	&#161	&iexcl*	Inverted exclamation point
¢	&#162	&cent*	Cent symbol
£	&#163	&pound*	Pound sterling
¤	&#164	&curren*	General currency symbol
¥	&#165	&yen*	Yen sign
¦	&#166	&brvbar*	Broken vertical bar
§	&#167	&sect*	Section sign
¨	&#168	&uml*	Umlaut
©	&#169	&copy*	Copyright symbol
ª	&#170	&ordf*	Feminine ordinal
«	&#171	&laquo*	Left angle quotation mark
¬	&#172	&not*	Not sign

Appendix B HTML Special Characters

CHARACTER	CODE	CODE NAME	DESCRIPTION
	&#173	&shy*	Soft hyphen
®	&#174	&reg*	Registered trademark
¯	&#175	&macr*	Macron
°	&#176	&deg*	Degree sign
±	&#177	&plusmn*	Plus/minus symbol
²	&#178	&sup2*	Superscript 2
³	&#179	&sup3*	Superscript 3
´	&#180	&acute*	Acute accent
µ	&#181	&micro*	Micro symbol
¶	&#182	&para*	Paragraph sign
·	&#183	&middot*	Middle dot
¸	&#184	&cedil*	Cedilla
¹	&#185	&sup1*	Superscript 1
º	&#186	&ordm*	Masculine ordinal
»	&#187	&raquo*	Right angle quotation mark
¼	&#188	&frac14*	Fraction one-quarter
½	&#189	&frac12*	Fraction one-half
¾	&#190	&frac34*	Fraction three-quarters
¿	&#191	&iquest*	Inverted question mark
À	&#192	&Agrave	Capital A, grave accent
Á	&#193	&Aacute	Capital A, acute accent
Â	&#194	&Acirc	Capital A, circumflex accent
Ã	&#195	&Atilde	Capital A, tilde
Ä	&#196	&Auml	Capital A, umlaut
Å	&#197	&Aring	Capital A, ring
Æ	&#198	&Aelig	Capital AE ligature
Ç	&#199	&Ccedil	Capital C, cedilla
È	&#200	&Egrave	Capital E, grave accent

Appendix B **HTML Special Characters**

CHARACTER	CODE	CODE NAME	DESCRIPTION
É	&#201	&Eacute	Capital E, acute accent
Ê	&#202	&Ecirc	Capital E, circumflex accent
Ë	&#203	&Euml	Capital E, umlaut
Ì	&#204	&Igrave	Capital I, grave accent
Í	&#205	&Iacute	Capital I, acute accent
Î	&#206	&Icirc	Capital I, circumflex accent
Ï	&#207	&Iuml	Capital I, umlaut
Ð	&#208	&ETH*	Capital ETH, Icelandic
Ñ	&#209	&Ntilde	Capital N, tilde
Ò	&#210	&Ograve	Capital O, grave accent
Ó	&#211	&Oacute	Capital O, acute accent
Ô	&#212	&Ocirc	Capital O, circumflex accent
Õ	&#213	&Otilde	Capital O, tilde
Ö	&#214	&Ouml	Capital O, umlaut
×	&#215	&times*	Multiplication sign
Ø	&#216	&Oslash	Capital O slash
Ù	&#217	&Ugrave	Capital U, grave accent
Ú	&#218	&Uacute	Capital U, acute accent
Û	&#219	&Ucirc	Capital U, circumflex accent
Ü	&#220	&Uuml	Capital U, umlaut
Ý	&#221	&Yacute	Capital Y, acute accent
Þ	&#222	&THORN	Capital THORN, Icelandic
ß	&#223	&szlig	Small sz ligature
à	&#224	&agrave	Small a, grave accent
á	&#225	&aacute	Small a, acute accent
â	&#226	&acirc	Small a, circumflex accent
ã	&#227	&atilde	Small a, tilde
ä	&#228	&auml	Small a, umlaut

Appendix B HTML Special Characters

CHARACTER	CODE	CODE NAME	DESCRIPTION
å	&#229	&aring	Small a, ring
æ	&#230	&aelig	Small AE ligature
ç	&#231	&ccedil	Small C, cedilla
è	&#232	&egrave	Small e, grave accent
é	&#233	&eacute	Small e, acute accent
ê	&#234	&ecirc	Small e, circumflex accent
ë	&#235	&euml	Small e, umlaut
ì	&#236	&igrave	Small i, grave accent
í	&#237	&iacute	Small i, acute accent
î	&#238	&icirc	Small i, circumflex accent
ï	&#239	&iuml	Small i, umlaut
ð	&#240	&eth	Small ETH, Icelandic
ñ	&#241	&ntilde	Small N, tilde
ò	&#242	&ograve	Small o, grave accent
ó	&#243	&oacute	Small o, acute accent
ô	&#244	&ocirc	Small o, circumflex accent
õ	&#245	&otilde	Small o, tilde
ö	&#246	&ouml	Small o, umlaut
÷	&#247	&divide*	Division sign
ø	&#248	&oslash	Small o slash
ù	&#249	&ugrave	Small u, grave accent
ú	&#250	&uacute	Small u, acute accent
û	&#251	&ucirc	Small u, circumflex accent
ü	&#252	&uuml	Small u, umlaut
ý	&#253	&yacute	Small y, acute accent
þ	&#254	&thorn	Small thorn, Icelandic
ÿ	&#255	&yuml	Small y, umlaut

Appendix C
Putting a Document on the World Wide Web

Once you've completed your work on your HTML file, you're probably ready to place it on the World Wide Web for others to see. To make a file available to the World Wide Web, you have to transfer it to a computer connected to the Web called a **Web server**.

Your **Internet Service Provider** (**ISP**)—the company or institution through which you have Internet access—usually has a Web server available for your use. Because each Internet Service Provider has a different procedure for storing Web pages, you should contact your ISP to learn its policies and procedures. Generally you should be prepared to do the following:

- Extensively test your files under a variety of browsers and under different display conditions. Weed out any errors and design problems before you place the page on the Web.
- If your HTML documents have a three-letter "HTM" extension, rename those files with the four-letter extension "HTML." Some Web servers will require the four-letter extension for all Web pages.
- Check the hyperlinks and inline objects in each of your documents to verify that they point to the correct filenames. Verify the filenames with respect to upper and lower cases. Some Web servers will distinguish between a file named "Image.gif" and one named "image.gif." To be safe, match the uppercase and lowercase letters.
- If your hyperlinks use absolute pathnames, change them to relative pathnames.
- Find out from your ISP the name of the folder into which you'll be placing your HTML documents. You may also need a special user name and password to access this folder.
- Use **FTP**, a program used on the Internet that transfers files, or e-mail to place your pages in the appropriate folder on your Internet Service Provider's Web server. Some Web browsers, like Internet Explorer and Netscape Navigator, have this capability built in, allowing you to transfer your files with a click of a toolbar button.
- Decide on a name for your site on the World Wide Web (such as "http://www.jackson_electronics.com"). Choose a name that will be easy for customers and interested parties to remember and return to.
- If you select a special name for your Web site, you may have to register it. Registration information can be found at http://www.internic.net. This is a service your ISP may also provide for a fee. Registration is necessary to ensure that any name you give to your site is unique and not already in use by another party. Usually you will have to pay a yearly fee to keep control of a special name for your Web site.
- Add your site to the indexes of search pages on the World Wide Web. This is not required, but it will make it easier for people to find your site. Each search facility has different policies regarding adding information about Web sites to its index. Be aware that some will charge a fee to include your Web site in their list.

Once you've completed these steps, your work will be available on the World Wide Web in a form that is easy for users to find and access.

HTML Tag Reference

The following is a list of the major HTML tags and properties. The three columns at the right indicate the earliest HTML, Netscape and Internet Explorer versions which started supporting these tags. For example a version number of "3.0" for Internet Explorer indicates that versions of Internet Explorer 3.0 *and above* will support the tag or attribute. Both opening and closing tags are displayed where they are required (e.g. <TABLE> ... </TABLE>). A single tag means that no closing tag is needed.

You can view more detailed information about the latest HTML specifications at http://www.w3.org. Additional information about browser support for different HTML tags is available at http://www.htmlcompendium.org/.

Since the World Wide Web is always in a constant state of change, you should check this information against the current browser versions.

Properties are of the following types.

- *Color*   A recognized color name or color value.
- *CGI Script* The name of a CGI script on the Web server.
- *Document*   The file name or URL of file.
- *List*   List of items separated by commas. Usually enclosed in double quotes.
- *Options*   Limited to a specific set of values (values are shown below the property).
- *Text*   Any text string.
- *URL*   The URL for a Web page or file.
- *Value*   A number, usually an integer.

Block-Formatting Tags

Block-Formatting tags are tags that are used to format the appearance of large blocks of text.

TAGS AND PROPERTIES	DESCRIPTION	HTML	NETSCAPE	IE
<ADDRESS> ... </ADDRESS>	The <ADDRESS> tag is used for information such as addresses, authorship and so forth. The text is usually italicized and in some browsers it is indented.	2.0	1.0	1.0
<BASEFONT>	The <BASEFONT> tag specifies the default font size, in points, for text in the document. The default value is 3.	3.2	1.0	2.0
SIZE=*Value*	*Value* is the size (in points) of the text font.	3.2	1.1	2.0
<BLOCKQUOTE> ... </BLOCKQUOTE>	The <BLOCKQUOTE> tag is used to set off long quotes or citations by usually indenting the enclosed text on both sides. Some browsers italicize the text as well.	2.0	1.0	2.0
 	The tag forces a line break in the text.	2.0	1.0	2.0
CLEAR=*Option* (LEFT I RIGHT I ALL I NONE)	Causes the next line to start at the spot in which the specified margin is clear.	3.0	1.0	2.0
<CENTER> ... </CENTER>	The <CENTER> tag centers the enclosed text or image horizontally.	3.2	1.1	2.0
<DFN> ... </DFN>	The <DFN> tag is used for the defining instance of a term, i.e. the first time the term is used. The enclosed text is usually italicized.	2.0		2.0
<DIV> ... </DIV>	The <DIV> tag is to set the text alignment of blocks of text or images. Supported by older browsers, it has been made obsolete by newer tags.	3.0	2.0	3.0

HTML Tag Reference

TAGS AND PROPERTIES	DESCRIPTION	HTML	NETSCAPE	IE
\<HR\>	The \<HR\> tag creates a horizontal line.	1.0	1.0	2.0
ALIGN=*Option* (LEFT | CENTER | RIGHT)	Alignment of the horizontal line. The default in CENTER.	3.2	1.1	2.0
COLOR=*Color*	Specifies a color for the line.			3.0
NOSHADE	Removes 3D shading from the line.	3.0	1.1	3.0
SIZE=*Value*	The size (height) of the line in pixels.	3.2	1.1	2.0
WIDTH=*Value*	The width (length) of the line either in pixels or as a percentage of the display area.	3.2	1.1	2.0
\<H1\> ... \</H1\> **\<H2\> ... \</H2\>** **\<H3\> ... \</H3\>** **\<H4\> ... \</H4\>** **\<H5\> ... \</H5\>** **\<H6\> ... \</H6\>**	The six levels of text headings ranging from the largest (\<H1\>) to the smallest (\<H6\>). Text headings appear in a bold face font.	1.0	1.0	1.0
ALIGN=*Option* (LEFT | RIGHT | CENTER)	The alignment of the heading.	3.0	4.0	2.0
\<LISTING\> ... \</LISTING\>	The \<LISTING\> tag displays text in a fixed width font resembling a typewriter or computer printout. This tag has been rendered obsolete by some newer tags.	2.0		3.0
\<NOBR\> ... \</NOBR\>	The \<NOBR\> tag prevents line breaks for the enclosed text. This tag is not often used.		1.1	2.0
\<P\> ... \</P\>	The \<P\> tag defines the beginning and ending of a paragraph of text.	1.0	1.0	1.0
ALIGN=*Option* (LEFT | CENTER | RIGHT)	The alignment of the text in the paragraph.	1.0	1.1	3.0
\<PLAINTEXT\> ... \</PLAINTEXT\>	The \<PLAINTEXT\> tag displays text in a fixed width font. An obsolete tag which authors should avoid using. It is supported by some earlier versions of Netscape, but in an erratic way.	2.0	4.0	2.0
\<PRE\> ... \</PRE\>	The \<PRE\> tag retains the preformatted appearance of the text in the HTML file, including any line breaks or spaces. Text is usually displayed in a fixed width font.	1.0	1.0	1.0
\<WBR\> ... \</WBR\>	The \<WBR\> tag overrides other tags that may preclude the creation of line breaks and directs the browser to insert a line break if necessary. Used in conjunction with the \<NOBR\> tag. This tag is not often used.		1.1	2.0
\<XMP\> ... \</XMP\>	The \<XMP\> tag displays blocks of text in a fixed width font. The tag is obsolete and should not be used.	3.2		5.0

HTML Tag Reference

TAGS AND PROPERTIES	DESCRIPTION	HTML	NETSCAPE	IE
Character Tags	Character tags modify the appearance of individual characters, words or sentences from that of the surrounding text. Character tags usually appear nested within Block-Formatting tags.			
\<ABBR\> ... \</ABBR\>	The \<ABBR\>tag indicates text in an abbreviated form (e.g. WWW, HTTP, URL, etc.).	4.0		
\<ACRONYM\> ... \</ACRONYM\>	The \<ACRONYM\> tag indicates a text acronym (e.g. WAC, radar, etc.).	4.0		4.0
\<B\> ... \</B\>	The \<B\> tag displays the enclosed text in bold type.	1.0	1.0	1.0
\<BIG\> ... \</BIG\>	The \<BIG\> tag increases the size of the enclosed text. The exact appearance of the text depends on the browser and the default font size.	3.0	2.0	3.0
\<BLINK\> ... \</BLINK\>	The \<BLINK\> tag causes the enclosed text to blink on and off.		1.0	
\<CITE\> ... \</CITE\>	The \<CITE\> tag is used for citations and is usually displayed in italics.	1.0	1.0	2.0
\<CODE\> ... \</CODE\>	The \<CODE\> tag is used for text taken from the code for a computer program. It is usually displayed in a fixed width font.	1.0	1.0	1.0
\<EM\> ... \</EM\>	The \<EM\> tag is used to emphasize text. The enclosed text is usually displayed in italics.	1.0	1.0	2.0
\<FONT\> ... \</FONT\>	The \<FONT\> tag is used to control the appearance of the text it encloses.	3.0	1.1	2.0
COLOR=*Color*	The color of the enclosed text.	3.0	2.0	2.0
FACE=*List*	The font face of the text. Multiple font faces can be specified, separated by commas. The browser will try to render the text in the order specified by the list.	3.0	3.0	2.0
SIZE=*Value*	Size of the font in points, it can be absolute or relative. Specifying SIZE=5 sets the font size to 5 points. Specifying SIZE=+5 sets the font size 5 points larger than that specified in the \<BASEFONT\> tag.	3.0	4.0	2.0
\<I\> ... \</I\>	The \<I\> tag italicizes the enclosed text.	1.0	1.0	1.0
\<KBD\> ... \</KBD\>	The \<KBD\> tag is used for text made to appear as if it came from a typewriter or keyboard. Text is displayed with a fixed width font.	1.0	1.0	2.0
\<SAMP\> ... \</SAMP\>	The \<SAMP\> tag displays text in a fixed width font.	1.0	1.0	2.0

HTML Tag Reference

TAGS AND PROPERTIES	DESCRIPTION	HTML	NETSCAPE	IE
<SMALL> ... </SMALL>	The <SMALL> tag decreases the size of the enclosed text. The exact appearance of the text depends on the browser and the default font size.	3.0	2.0	3.0
<STRIKE> ... </STRIKE>	The <STRIKE> tag displays the enclosed text with a horizontal line striking through it. Note: future revisions to HTML may be phase out STRIKE in favor of the more concise S tag from HTML 3.0	3.2	3.0	2.0
<STRONG> ... </STRONG>	The <STRONG> tag is used to strongly emphasize the enclosed text, usually in a bold font.	1.0	1.0	1.0
_{...}	The <SUB> tag displays the enclosed text as a subscript.	1.0	2.0	3.0
^{...}	The <SUP> tag displays the enclosed text as a superscript.	1.0	2.0	3.0
<TT> ... </TT>	The <TT> tag displays text in a fixed width, teletype style font.	1.0	1.0	1.0
<U> ... </U>	The <U> tag underlines the enclosed text. The <U> tag should be avoided because it will confuse users with hypertext, which is typically underlined.	1.0	3.0	2.0
<VAR> ... </VAR>	The <VAR> tag is used for text that represents a variable is usually displayed in italics.	1.0	1.1	1.0

Document Tags

TAGS AND PROPERTIES	DESCRIPTION	HTML	NETSCAPE	IE
	Document tags are tags that specify the structure of the HTML file or control its operations and interactions with the Web server.			
<!>	The <!> tag is used for comments in documenting the features of your HTML file.	1.0	1.0	1.0
<BASE>	The <BASE> tag allows you to specify the URL for the HTML document. It is used by some browsers to interpret relative hyperlinks.	1.0	1.0	2.0
HREF=URL	Specifies the URL from which all relative hyperlinks should be based.	1.0	4.0	2.0
TARGET=Text	Specifies the default target window or frame for every hyperlink in the document.	4.0	2.0	3.0
<BODY> ... </BODY>	The <BODY> tag encloses all text, images and other elements that will be visible to the user on the Web page.	1.0	1.0	1.0
ALINK=Color	Color of activated hypertext links, which are links the user has pressed with the mouse button but have not yet released.	1.0	1.1	2.0
BACKGROUND=Document	The graphic image file used for the Web page background.	1.0	1.1	2.0
BGCOLOR=Color	The color of the Web page background.	3.2	1.1	2.0

HTML Tag Reference

TAGS AND PROPERTIES	DESCRIPTION	HTML	NETSCAPE	IE
BGPROPERTIES=FIXED	Keeps the background image fixed so that it does not scroll with the Web page.			2.0
LEFTMARGIN=*Value*	Indents the left margin of the page the number of pixels specified in *value*.			2.0
LINK=*Color*	Color of all unvisited links.	1.0	1.1	2.0
TEXT=*Color*	Color of all text in the document.	1.0	1.1	2.0
TOPMARGIN=*Value*	Indents the top margin of the page the number of pixels specified in *value*.			2.0
VLINK=*Color*	Color of previously visited links.	1.0	1.1	2.0
<HEAD> ... </HEAD>	The <HEAD> tag encloses code that provides information about the document.	1.0	1.0	1.0
<HTML> ... </HTML>	The <HTML> tag indicates the beginning and end of the HTML document.	1.0	1.0	1.0
<ISINDEX>	The <ISINDEX> tag identifies the file as a searchable document.	1.0	1.0	2.0
ACTION=*CGI Program*	Sends the submitted text to the program identified by *CGI Program*.			2.0
PROMPT=*Text*	The text that should be placed before the index's text-input field.	3.0	1.1	2.0
<LINK>	The <LINK> tag specifies the relationship between the document and other objects.	1.0	3.0	2.0
HREF=*URL*	The URL of the LINK tag, hotlinks the user to the specified document.	1.0		2.0
ID=*Text*	The file, URL or text that acts as a hypertext lik to another document.	1.0	3.0	3.0
REL=*URL*	Directs the browser to link forward to the next page in the document.	1.0		2.0
REV=*URL*	Directs the browser to go back to the previous link in the document.	2.0		2.0
TITLE=*Text*	The title of the document named in the link.	1.0		2.0
<META>	The <META> tag is used to insert information about the document not defined by other HTML tags and properties. It can include special instructions for the Web server to perform.	1.0	1.0	1.0
CONTENT=*Text*	Contains information associated with the NAME or HTTP-EQUIV properties.	1.0	1.1	2.0
HTTP-EQUIV=*Text*	Directs the browser to request the server to perform different HTTP operations.	2.0	1.1	2.0
NAME=*Text*	The type of information specified in the CONTENT property.	2.0	1.1	2.0
<TITLE> ... </TITLE>	The <TITLE> tag is used to specify the text that appears in the Web browser's title bar.	2.0	1.1	2.0

Form Tags

	Form tags are used to create user-entry forms.			
<BUTTON> ... </BUTTON>	Buttons created with the <BUTTON> tag, function just like buttons created with the <INPUT> tag, but they offer richer rendering possibilities. For example, the BUTTON element may have content.	4.0	4.0	4.0

HTML Tag Reference

TAGS AND PROPERTIES	DESCRIPTION	HTML	NETSCAPE	IE
NAME=*Text*	Specifies the button name.	4.0		5.0
VALUE=*Text*	Specifies the initial value of the button.	4.0		5.0
TABINDEX=*Value*	Specifies the tab order in the form.	4.0		5.0
TYPE=*Option* (SUBMIT | RESET | BUTTON)	Specifies the type of button. Setting the type to "BUTTON" creates a push button for use with client-side scripts.	4.0		4.0
<FIELDSET> ... </FIELDSET>	<The FIELDSET> tag allows authors to group form controls and labels. Grouping controls makes it easier for users to understand their purpose while simultaneously facilitating moving between fields.	4.0		4.0
ALIGN=*Option* (TOP | BOTTOM | MIDDLE | LEFT | RIGHT)	Specifies the alignment of the legend with respect to the field set (see the <LEGEND> tag for more information.)	4.0		4.0
<FORM> ... </FORM>	The <FORM> tag marks the beginning and end of a Web page form.	1.0	1.0	1.0
ACTION=*URL*	Specifies the URL to which the contents of the form are to be sent.	1.0	2.0	2.0
ENCTYPE=*Text*	Specifies the encoding type used to submit the data to the server.	2.0	2.0	2.0
METHOD=*Option* (POST | GET)	Specifies the method of accessing the URL indicated in the ACTION property.	2.0	2.0	2.0
TARGET=*Text*	The frame or window that displays the form's results.	4.0	2.0	3.0
<INPUT> ... </INPUT>	The <INPUT> tag creates an input object for use in a Web page form.	1.0	1.0	2.0
ALIGN=*Option* (LEFT | RIGHT | TOP | TEXTTOP | MIDDLE | ABSMIDDLE | BASELINE | BOTTOM | ABSBOTTOM)	Specifies the alignment of an input image. Similar to the ALIGN option with the <IMG> tag.	1.0	1.1	2.0
CHECKED	Specifies that an input checkbox or input radio button is selected.	1.0	2.0	2.0
MAXLENGTH=*Value*	Specifies the maximum number of characters inserted into an input text box.	1.0	2.0	2.0
NAME=*Text*	The label given to the input object.	1.0	2.0	2.0
SIZE=*Value*	The visible size, in characters, of an input text box.	1.0	2.0	2.0
SRC=*Document*	The source file of the graphic used for an input image object.	1.0	2.0	2.0
TABINDEX=*Value*	Specifies the tab order in the form.	4.0		4.0
TYPE=*Option* (CHECKBOX | HIDDEN | IMAGE | PASSWORD | RADIO | RESET | SUBMIT | TEXT | TEXTAREA)	Specifies the type of input object. CHECKBOX creates a checkbox. HIDDEN creates a hidden object. IMAGE creates an image object. PASSWORD creates a text box which hides the text as the user enters it. RADIO creates a radio button. RESET creates a button that resets the form's fields when pressed. SUBMIT creates a button that submits the form when pressed. TEXT creates a text box. TEXTAREA creates a text box with multiple line entry fields.	1.0	2.0	2.0

HTML Tag Reference

TAGS AND PROPERTIES	DESCRIPTION	HTML	NETSCAPE	IE
USEMAP=#*Map_Name*	Identifies the input image as an image map. Similar to the USEMAP property used with the <IMG> tag.	1.0	2.0	2.0
VALUE=*Value*	Specifies the information that is initially displayed in the input object.	2.0	2.0	2.0
VSPACE=*Value*	The amount of space above and below the image, in pixels.	1.0	2.0	2.0
WIDTH=*Value*	The width of the input image in pixels.	1.0	2.0	2.0
<LEGEND> ... </LEGEND>	The <LEGEND> tag allows authors to assign a caption to a FIELDSET (see the <FIELDSET> tag above.)	4.0		4.0
ALIGN=*Option* (TOP | BOTTOM | LEFT | RIGHT)	Specifies the position of the legend with respect to the field set.	4.0		4.0
<OPTION> ... </OPTION>	The <OPTION> tag is used for each item in a selection list. This tag must be placed within <SELECT> tags.	1.0	1.0	1.0
SELECTED	The default or selected option in the selection list.	1.0	2.0	2.0
VALUE=*Value*	The value returned to the server when the user selects this option.	2.0	2.0	2.0
<SELECT> ... </SELECT>	The <SELECT> tag encloses a set of <OPTION> tags for use in creating selection lists.	1.0	2.0	2.0
MULTIPLE	Allows the user to select multiple options from the selection list.	2.0	2.0	2.0
NAME=*Text*	The name assigned to the selection list.	1.0	2.0	2.0
SIZE=*Value*	The number of visible items in the selection list.	2.0	2.0	2.0
TABINDEX=*Value*	Specifies the tab order in the form.	4.0		4.0
<TEXTAREA> ... </TEXTAREA>	The <TEXTAREA> tag creates a text box.	1.0	1.0	2.0
COLS=*Value*	Specifies the height of the text box in characters.	1.0	2.0	2.0
NAME=*Text*	Specifies the name assigned to the text box.	1.0	1.0	2.0
ROWS=*Value*	Specifies the width of the text box in characters.	1.0	2.0	2.0
TABINDEX=*Value*	Specifies the tab order in the form.	4.0		4.0
WRAP=*Option* (OFF | VIRTUAL | PHYSICAL)	Specifies how text should be wrapped within the text box. OFF turns off text wrapping. VIRTUAL wraps the text, but sends the text to the server as a single line. PHYSICAL wraps the text and sends the text the server as it appears in the text box.		2.0	2.0

Frame Tags

Frame tags are used for creating and formatting frames.

<IFRAME> ... </IFRAME>	The <IFRAME> tag allows authors to insert a frame within a block of text. Inserting an inline frame within a section of text allow you to insert an HTML document in the middle of another, and they may both be aligned with surrounding text.	4.0		3.0

HTML Tag Reference

TAGS AND PROPERTIES	DESCRIPTION	HTML	NETSCAPE	IE
ALIGN=*Option* (LEFT | RIGHT | MIDDLE | JUSTIFY)	Specifies the alignment of the floating frame.	4.0		3.0
HEIGHT=*Value*	Specifies the height of the floating frame, in pixels.	4.0		4.0
MARGINHEIGHT=*Value*	Specifies the amount of space above and below the frame object and the frame borders.	4.0		3.0
MARGINWIDTH=*Value*	Specifies the amount of space to the left and right of the frame object, in pixels.	4.0		3.0
NAME=*Text*	Label assigned to the frame.	4.0		3.0
SCROLLING=*Option* (YES | NO | AUTO)	Specifies whether scroll bars are visible. AUTO (the default) displays scroll bars only as needed.	4.0		3.0
SRC=*Document*	Specifies the document or URL of the object to be displayed in the frame.	4.0		3.0
WIDTH=*Value*	Specifies the width of the floating frame, in pixels.	4.0		3.0
<FRAME>	The <FRAME> tag defines a single frame within a set of frames.	4.0	2.0	3.0
BORDERCOLOR=*Color*	Specifies the color of the frame border.		3.0	4.0
FRAMEBORDER=*Option* (YES | NO)	Specifies whether the frame border is visible.	4.0	3.0	3.0
FRAMESPACING=*Value*	Specifies the amount of space between frames, in pixels.			3.0
MARGINHEIGHT=*Value*	Specifies the amount of space above and below the frame object and the frame borders.	4.0	2.0	3.0
MARGINWIDTH=*Value*	Specifies the amount of space to the left and right of the frame object, in pixels.	4.0	2.0	3.0
NAME=*Text*	Label assigned to the frame.	4.0	2.0	3.0
NORESIZE	Prevents users from resizing the frame.	4.0	2.0	3.0
SCROLLING=*Option* (YES | NO | AUTO)	Specifies whether scroll bars are visible. AUTO (the default) displays scroll bars only as needed.	4.0	2.0	3.0
SRC=*Document*	Specifies the document or URL of the object to be displayed in the frame.	4.0	2.0	3.0
<FRAMESET> ... </FRAMESET>	The <FRAMESET> tag marks the beginning and the end of a set of frames.	4.0	2.0	3.0
BORDER=*Value*	The size of the borders, in pixels.		3.0	3.0
BORDERCOLOR	The color of the frame borders.		3.0	3.0
COLS=*List*	The size of each column in set of frames. Columns can be specified either in pixels, as a percentage of the display area or with an asterisks (*) indicating that any remaining space be allotted to that column. e.g.COLS="40,25%,*"	4.0	2.0	3.0
ROWS=*List*	The size of each row in set of frames. Rows can be specified either in pixels, as a percentage of the display area or with an asterisks (*) indicating that any remaining space be allotted to that column. e.g.ROWS="40,25%,*"	4.0	2.0	3.0
<NOFRAMES> ... </NOFRAMES>	Enclosing body tags to be used by browsers which do not support frames.	4.0	2.0	3.0

HTML Tag Reference

Graphic and Link Tags

Graphic and Link tags are used for hypertext links and inline images.

TAGS AND PROPERTIES	DESCRIPTION	HTML	NETSCAPE	IE
<A> ... </A>	The <A> tag marks and the beginning an end of a hypertext link.	1.0	1.0	1.0
HREF=*URL*	Indicates the target, file name or URL that the hypertext points to.	1.0	1.0	1.0
NAME=*Text*	Specifies a name for the enclosed text, allowing it to be a target of a hyperlink.	1.0	1.0	2.0
REL=*Text*	Specifies the relationship between the current page and the link specified by the HREF property.	1.0		2.0
REV=*Text*	Specifies a reverse relationship between the current page and the link specified by the HREF property.	1.0		2.0
TABINDEX=*Value*	Specifies the tab order in the form.	4.0		4.0
TARGET=*Text*	Specifies the default target window or frame for the hyperlink.	4.0	1.0	3.0
TITLE=*Text*	Provides a title for the document whose address is given by the HREF property.	1.0		2.0
<AREA>	The <AREA> tag defines the type and coordinates of a hotspot within an image map.	3.2	1.0	2.0
COORDS–*Value 1, value 2...* Rectangle: COORDS=*x_left, y_upper, x_right, y_lower* CIRCLE: COORDS= *x_center, y_center, radius* POLYGON: COORDS= $x_1, y_1, x_2, y_2, x_3, y_3, ...$	The coordinates of the hotspot. The coordinates depend upon the shape of the hotspot:	3.2	1.0	2.0
HREF=*URL*	Indicates the target, file name or URL that the hotspot points to.	3.2	1.0	2.0
SHAPE=*Option* (RECT | CIRCLE | POLY)	The shape of the hotspot.	3.2	1.0	2.0
TABINDEX=*Value*	Specifies the tab order in the form.	4.0		4.0
TARGET=*Text*	Specifies the default target window or frame for the hotspot.	4.0	2.0	3.0
<IMG>	The <IMG> tag is used to insert an inline image into the document.	1.0	1.0	2.0
ALIGN=*Option* (LEFT | RIGHT | TOP | TEXTTOP | MIDDLE | ABSMIDDLE | BASELINE | BOTTOM | ABSBOTTOM)	Specifies the alignment of the image. Specifying an alignment of LEFT or RIGHT aligns the image with the left or right page margin. The other alignment options align the image with surrounding text.	1.0	1.1	2.0
ALT=*Text*	Text to display if the image cannot be displayed by the browser.	2.0	1.1	2.0
BORDER=*Value*	The size of the border around the image in pixels.	3.2	1.1	2.0
CONTROLS	Display VCR-like controls under moving images. Used in conjunction with the DYNSRC property.			2.0
DYNSRC=*Document*	Specifies the file of a video, AVI clip or VRML worlds displayed inside the page.			2.0

HTML Tag Reference

TAGS AND PROPERTIES	DESCRIPTION	HTML	NETSCAPE	IE
HEIGHT=*Value*	The height of the image in pixels.	3.0	1.1	2.0
HSPACE=*Value*	The amount of space to the left and right of the image, in pixels.	3.0	1.1	2.0
ISMAP	Identifies the graphic as an image map. For use with server-side image maps.	3.0	2.0	2.0
LOOP=*Value*	Specifies the number of times a moving image should be played. The value must be either a digit or INFINITE.			2.0
LOWSRC=*Document*	A low-resolution version of the graphic that the browser should initially display before loading the high resolution version.		1.0	4.0
SRC=*Document*	The source file of the inline image.	1.0	1.0	2.0
START=*Item* (FILEOPEN | MOUSEOVER)	Tells the browser when to start displaying a moving image file. FILEOPEN directs the browser to start when the file is open. MOUSEOVER directs the browser to start when the mouse moves over the image.			2.0
USEMAP=#*Map_Namet*	Identifies the graphic as an image map and specifies the name of image map definition to use with the graphic. For use with client-side image maps.	3.2	2.0	2.0
VSPACE=*Value*	The amount of space above and below the image, in pixels.	3.2	1.1	2.0
WIDTH=*Value*	The width of the image in pixels.	3.0	1.1	2.0
<MAP> ... </MAP>	The <MAP> specifies information about a client-side image map. (Note that it must enclose <AREA> tags.)	3.2	1.0	2.0
NAME=*Text*	The name of the image map.	3.2	2.0	2.0

List Tags

List tags are used to create a variety of different kinds of lists.

TAGS AND PROPERTIES	DESCRIPTION	HTML	NETSCAPE	IE
<DD>	The <DD> tag formats text to be used as relative definitions in a <DL> list.	1.0	1.0	2.0
<DIR> ... </DIR>	The <DIR> tag encloses an unordered list of <LI> items, formatted in narrow columns.	1.0	1.0	2.0
TYPE=*Option* (CIRCLE | DISC | SQUARE)	Specifies the type of bullet used for displaying each <LI> item in the <DIR> list.		2.0	
<DL> ... </DL>	The <DL> tag encloses a definition list in which the <DD> definition term, is left aligned and the <DT> relative definition, is indented.	1.0	1.0	2.0
<DT>	The <DT> tag is used to format the definition term in a <DL> list.	1.0	1.0	2.0
<LI>	The <LI> tag identifies list items in a <DIR>, <MENU>, <OL> or <UL> list.	1.0	1.0	2.0
<MENU> ... </MENU>	The <MENU> tag encloses an unordered list of items, similar to a <UL> or <DIR> list.	1.0	1.0	2.0

HTML Tag Reference

TAGS AND PROPERTIES	DESCRIPTION	HTML	NETSCAPE	IE
<OL> ... </OL>	The <OL> tag encloses an ordered list of <LI> items. Typically ordered lists are rendered as numbered lists.	1.0	1.0	1.0
START=*Value*	The *value* of the starting number in the ordered list.	3.2	2.0	2.0
TYPE=*Option* (A | a | I | i | 1)	Specifies how ordered items are to be marked. A = uppercase letters. a = lowercase letters. I = uppercase Roman numerals. i = lowercase Roman numerals. 1 = Digits. The default is 1.	3.2	2.0	2.0
<UL>	The <UL> tag encloses an unordered list of <LI> items. Typically unordered lists are rendered as bulleted lists.	1.0	1.0	1.0
Type=*Option* (CIRCLE | DISK | SQUARE)	Specifies the type of bullet used for displaying each <LI> item in the <UL> list.	3.2	2.0	

Miscellaneous Tags

Miscellaneous tags do not fit into any specific category. These tags are currently only supported by Internet Explorer 3.0 and above.

TAGS AND PROPERTIES	DESCRIPTION	HTML	NETSCAPE	IE
<BGSOUND>	The <BGSOUND> is used to play a background sound clip when the page is first opened.			2.0
LOOP=*Value*	Specifies the number of times the sound clip should be played. LOOP can either be a digit or INFINITE.			3.0
SRC=*Document*	The sound file used for the sound clip.			2.0
<MARQUEE> ... </MARQUEE>	The <MARQUEE> tag is used to create an area containing scrolling text.			2.0
ALIGN=*Option* (TOP | MIDDLE | BOTTOM)	The alignment of the scrolling text within the marquee.			2.0
BEHAVIOR=*Option* (SCROLL | SLIDE | ALTERNATE)	Controls the behavior of the text in the marquee. SCROLL causes the text to repeatedly scroll across the page. SLIDE causes the text to slide onto the page and stop at the margin. ALTERNATE causes the text to bounce from margin to margin.			2.0
BGCOLOR=*Color*	The background color of the marquee.			2.0
DIRECTION=*Option* (LEFT | RIGHT)	The direction that the text scrolls on the page.			2.0
HEIGHT=*Value*	The height of the marquee in either pixels or as a percentage of the display area.			2.0
HSPACE=*Value*	The amount of space to the left and right of the marquee, in pixels.			2.0
LOOP=*Value*	The number of times the marquee will be scrolled, can be either a digit or INFINITE			2.0
SCROLLAMOUNT=*Value*	The amount of space between successive draws of the text in the marquee.			2.0
SCROLLDELAY=*Value*	The amount of time between scrolling actions, in milliseconds.			2.0
VSPACE=*Value*	The amount of space above and below the marquee, in pixels.			2.0

HTML Tag Reference

TAGS AND PROPERTIES	DESCRIPTION	HTML	NETSCAPE	IE
WIDTH=*Value*	The width of the marquee in either pixels or as a percentage of the display area.			2.0
Script and Applet Tags	Script tags are used for client-side scripts, including JavaScript and VBScript. Applet tags are used for Java applets.			
<APPLET> ... </APPLET>	The <APPLET> tag, supported by all Java-enabled browsers, allows designers to embed a Java applet in an HTML document. It has been deprecated in favor of the <OBJECT> tag in HTML 4.0.	3.2	2.0	3.0
ALIGN=*Option* (TOP | BOTTOM | MIDDLE | LEFT | RIGHT)	Specifies the alignment of the applet with the surrounding text.	3.2	2.0	3.0
ALT=*Text*	Specifies alternate text to be displayed in place of the Java applet.	3.2	3.0	3.0
ARCHIVE=*List*	List of archives containing classes and other resources that will be "preloaded" for use with the Java applet.	4.0	3.0	
CODEBASE=*URL*	Specifies the base URL for the applet. If not specified, the browser assumes the same location as the current document.	3.2	2.0	3.0
CODE=*Text*	Specifies the name of the CLASS file that contains the Java applet.	3.2	2.0	3.0
HEIGHT=*Value*	Specifies the height of the applet, in pixels.	3.2	2.0	3.0
HSPACE=*Value*	Specifies the horizontal space around the applet, in pixels.	3.2	2.0	3.0
NAME=*Text*	The name assigned to the Java applet.	3.2	2.0	3.0
OBJECT=*Text*	Specifies a resource containing a serialized representation of an applet's state. It is interpreted relative to the applet's codebase. The serialized data contains the applet's class name but not the implementation. The class name is used to retrieve the implementation from a class file or archive.	4.0		
VSPACE=*Value*	Specifies the vertical space around the applet, in pixels.	3.2	2.0	3.0
WIDTH=*Value*	The width of the applet, in pixels.	3.2	2.0	3.0
<NOSCRIPT> ... </NOSCRIPT>	The <NOSCRIPT> tag is used to enclose HTML tags for browsers that do not support client-side scripts.	4.0	3.0	3.0
<OBJECT> ... </OBJECT>	Most user browsers have built-in mechanisms for rendering common data types such as text, GIF images, colors, fonts, and a handful of graphic elements. To render data types they don't support natively, user agents generally run external applications. The <OBJECT> tag allows authors to control whether data should be rendered externally or by some program, specified by the author, that renders the data within the user agent.	2.0	1.1	1.0

HTML Tag Reference

TAGS AND PROPERTIES	DESCRIPTION	HTML	NETSCAPE	IE
ALIGN=*Option* (TOP | BOTTOM | MIDDLE | LEFT | RIGHT)	Specifies the alignment of the embedded object relative to the surrounding text.	4.0	2.0	3.0
BORDER=*Value*	Specifies the width of the embedded object's border, in pixels.	4.0		3.0
CLASSID=*URL*	Specifies the URL of the embedded object.	4.0		3.0
CODEBASE=*URL*	Specifies the base path used to resolve relative references within the embedded object.	4.0	2.0	3.0
CODETYPE=*Text*	Specifies the type of data object.	4.0		3.0
DATA=*URL*	Specifies the location of data for the embedded object.	4.0	2.0	3.0
HEIGHT=*Value*	Specifies the height of the embedded object, in pixels.	4.0	2.0	3.0
HSPACE=*Value*	Specifies the horizontal space around the embedded object, in pixels.	4.0		3.0
NAME=*Text*	Specifies the name of the embedded object.	4.0		3.0
STANDBY=*Text*	Specifies a message the browser should display while rendering the embedded object.	4.0		3.0
TABINDEX=*Value*	Specifies the tab order of the object when it is placed within a form.	4.0		4.0
TYPE=*Text*	Specifies the type of data object.	4.0	2.0	3.0
VSPACE=*Value*	Specifies the vertical space around the embedded object, in pixels.	4.0		3.0
WIDTH=*Value*	Specifies the width of the embedded object, in pixels.	4.0	2.0	3.0
<PARAM> ... </PARAM>	<PARAM> tags specify a set of values that may be required by an object at run-time. Any number of PARAM elements may appear in the content of an <OBJECT> or <APPLET> tag, in any order, but must be placed at the start of the content of the enclosing <OBJECT> or <APPLET> tag.	3.2	1.0	3.0
NAME=*Text*	Specifies the name of the parameter.	3.2	2.0	3.0
VALUE=*Text*	Specifies the value of the parameter.	3.2	2.0	3.0
VALUETYPE=*Option* (DATA | REF | OBJECT)	Specifies the type of the value attribute.	4.0		3.0
<SCRIPT> ... </SCRIPT>	The <SCRIPT> tag places a client-side script within a document. This element may appear any number of times in the HEAD or BODY of an HTML document.	3.2	3.0	3.0
LANGUAGE=*Text*	Specifies the language of the client-side script.	4.0	3.0	3.0
SRC=*URL*	Specifies the source of the external script file.	4.0	3.0	3.0
TYPE=*Text*	Specifies the type of scripting language.	4.0	3.0	3.0

Table tags

Table tags are used to define the structure and appears of graphical tables.

TAGS AND PROPERTIES	DESCRIPTION	HTML	NETSCAPE	IE
<CAPTION> ... </CAPTION>	The <CAPTION> tag encloses the table caption.	3.0	1.1	2.0
ALIGN=*Option* (LEFT | RIGHT | CENTER | TOP | BOTTOM)	Specifies the alignment of the caption with respect to the table. The LEFT, RIGHT and CENTER options are only supported by Internet Explorer 3.0	3.0	2.0	2.0

HTML Tag Reference

TAGS AND PROPERTIES	DESCRIPTION	HTML	NETSCAPE	IE
VALIGN=*Option* (TOP | BOTTOM)	Specifies the vertical alignment of the caption with respect to the table.			2.0
<COL> ... </COL>	The <COL> tag specifies the default settings for a column or group of columns.	3.0		4.0
ALIGN=*Option* (CENTER | JUSTIFY | LEFT | RIGHT)	Specifies the horizontal alignment of text within a column.	4.0		4.0
SPAN=*Value*	Specifies the columns modified by the <COL> tag.	4.0		4.0
VALIGN=*Option* (TOP | MIDDLE | BOTTOM)	Specifies the vertical alignment of text within a column.	4.0		4.0
<COLGROUP> ... <COLGROUP>	The <COLGROUP> tag encloses a group of <COL> tags, grouping columns together to set their alignment properties.	3.0		4.0
ALIGN=*Option* (CENTER | JUSTIFY | LEFT | RIGHT)	Specifies the horizontal alignment of text within a column group.	4.0		4.0
SPAN=*Value*	Specifies the columns within the column group.	4.0		4.0
VALIGN=*Option* (TOP | MIDDLE | BOTTOM)	Specifies the vertical alignment of text within a column group.	4.0		4.0
<TABLE> ... </TABLE>	The <TABLE> tag is used to specify the beginning and ending of the table.	1.0	1.1	1.0
ALIGN=*Option* (LEFT | CENTER | RIGHT)	Specifies the horizontal alignment of the table on the page. Only LEFT and RIGHT are supported by Netscape 3.0 and Internet Explorer 3.0.	3.0	2.0	3.0
BACKGROUND=*Document*	Specifies a background image for the table.			4.0
BGCOLOR=*Color*	Specifies a background color for the table.	4.0	3.0	2.0
BORDER=*Value*	Specifies the width of the table border in pixels.	3.0	2.0	2.0
BORDERCOLOR=*Color*	Specifies the color of the table border.			2.0
BORDERCOLORDARK=*Color*	Specifies the color of the shaded edge of the table border.			2.0
BORDERCOLORLIGHT=*Color*	Specifies the color of the unshaded edge of the table border.			2.0
CELLPADDING=*Value*	Specifies the space between table cells in pixels.	3.2	2.0	2.0
CELLSPACING=*Value*	Specifies the space between cell text and the cell border in pixels.	3.2	2.0	2.0
FRAME=*Option* (ABOVE | BELOW | BOX | HSIDES | LHS | RHS | VOID | VSIDES)	Specifies the display of table borders. ABOVE = Top border only. BELOW = Bottom border only. BOX = Borders on all four sides. HSIDES = Top and bottom borders. LHS = Left side border. RHS = Right side border. VOID = No borders. VSIDES = Left and right side borders.	3.0		3.0
HEIGHT=*Value*	The height of the table in pixels or as a percentage of the display area.		4.0	4.0

HTML Tag Reference

TAGS AND PROPERTIES	DESCRIPTION	HTML	NETSCAPE	IE
RULES=*Option* (ALL | COLS | NONE | ROWS)	Specifies the display of internal table borders. ALL = Borders between every row and column. COLS = Border between every column. NONE = No internal table borders. ROWS = Borders between every row.	3.0		3.0
WIDTH=*Value*	The width of the table in pixels or as a percentage of the display area.	3.0	2.0	2.0
<TBODY> ... </TBODY>	The <TBODY> tag identifies text that appears in the table body as opposed to text in the table header (<THEAD> tag) or the table footer (TBODY tag).	3.0		4.0
HALIGN=*Option* (LEFT | CENTER |RIGHT)	The horizontal alignment of text in the cells of the table body.	4.0		4.0
VALIGN=*Option* (TOP | MIDDLE | BOTTOM)	The vertical alignment of text in the cells in the table body.	4.0		4.0
<TD> ... </TD>	The <TD> tag encloses the text that will appear in an individual table cell.	1.0	1.1	2.0
ALIGN=*Option* (LEFT | CENTER | RIGHT)	Specifies the horizontal alignment of cell text.	1.0	2.0	2.0
BACKGROUND=*Document*	Specifies a background image for the cell.			4.0
BGCOLOR=*Color*	Specifies a background color for the cell.	4.0	3.0	2.0
BORDERCOLOR=*Color*	Specifies the color of the cell border.			2.0
BORDERCOLORDARK=*Color*	Specifies the color of the shaded edge of the cell border.			2.0
BORDERCOLORLIGHT=*Color*	Specifies the color of the unshaded edge of the cell border.			2.0
COLSPAN=*Value*	Specifies the number of columns the cell should span.	3.2	2.0	2.0
HEIGHT=*Value*	The height of the cell in pixels or as a percentage of the display area.	3.2	2.0	2.0
NOWRAP	Prohibits the browser from wrapping text in the cell.	3.0	2.0	2.0
ROWSPAN=*Value*	Specifies the number of rows the cell should span.	3.2	2.0	2.0
VALIGN=*Option* (TOP | MIDDLE | BOTTOM)	Specifies the vertical alignment of cell text.	3.0	2.0	2.0
WIDTH= *Value*	The width of the cell in pixels or as a percentage of the width of the table.	3.2	2.0	2.0
<TFOOT> ... </TFOOT>	The <TFOOT> tag encloses footer information that will be displayed in the table footer when the table is printed on multiple pages.	4.0		4.0
ALIGN=*Option* (LEFT | CENTER |RIGHT)	The horizontal alignment of the table footer.	4.0		4.0
VALIGN=*Option* (TOP | MIDDLE | BOTTOM)	The vertical alignment of the table footer.	4.0		4.0
<TH> ... </TH>	The <TH> tag encloses the text that will appear in an individual table header cell.	1.0	1.1	2.0
ALIGN=*Option* (LEFT | CENTER | RIGHT)	Specifies the horizontal alignment of header cell text.	1.0	2.0	2.0
BACKGROUND=*Document*	Specifies a background image for the header cell.			4.0

HTML Tag Reference

| --- | --- | --- | --- | --- |
BGCOLOR=*Color*	Specifies a background color for the header cell.	4.0	3.0	2.0
BORDERCOLOR=*Color*	Specifies the color of the header cell border.			2.0
BORDERCOLORDARK=*Color*	Specifies the color of the shaded edge of the header cell border.			3.0
BORDERCOLORLIGHT=*Color*	Specifies the color of the unshaded edge of the header cell border.			3.0
COLSPAN=*Value*	Specifies the number of columns the header cell should span.	1.0	2.0	2.0
HEIGHT=*Value*	The height of the header cell in pixels or as a percentage of the display area.	3.2	2.0	2.0
NOWRAP	Prohibits the browser from wrapping text in the header cell.	3.0	2.0	2.0
ROWSPAN=*Value*	Specifies the number of rows the header cell should span.	3.0	2.0	2.0
VALIGN=*Option* (TOP | MIDDLE | BOTTOM)	Specifies the vertical alignment of header cell text.	3.0	2.0	2.0
WIDTH= *Value*	The width of the header cell in pixels or as a percentage of the width of the table.	3.2	2.0	2.0
<THEAD> ... </THEAD>	The <THEAD> tag encloses header information that will be displayed in the table header when the table is printed on multiple pages.	3.0		3.0
ALIGN=*Option* (LEFT | CENTER |RIGHT)	The horizontal alignment of the table header.	3.0		3.0
VALIGN=*Option* (TOP | MIDDLE | BOTTOM)	The vertical alignment of the table header.	3.0		3.0
<TR> ... </TR>	The <TR> tag is encloses table cells within a single row.	3.0	1.1	2.0
ALIGN=*Option* (LEFT | CENTER | RIGHT)	Specifies the horizontal alignment of text in the row.	3.0	2.0	2.0
BGCOLOR=*Color*	Specifies a background color for the header cell.	4.0	3.0	2.0
BORDERCOLOR=*Color*	Specifies the color of the header cell border.			2.0
BORDERCOLORDARK=*Color*	Specifies the color of the shaded edge of the header cell border.			2.0
BORDERCOLORLIGHT=*Color*	Specifies the color of the unshaded edge of the header cell border.			2.0
VALIGN=*Option* (TOP | MIDDLE | BOTTOM)	The vertical alignment of the text in the table row.	3.0	2.0	2.0

OBJECTS, PROPERTIES, METHODS, AND EVENT HANDLERS	DESCRIPTIONS AND EXAMPLES

The following are some of the more important JavaScript objects, properties, and methods.

button	A push button in an HTML form Buttons can be referred to using their button names. For example, to emulate the action of clicking a button named "RUN," use the following expression: RUN.click();
Properties	
name	The name of the button element
value	The value of the button element
Methods	
click()	Emulates the action of clicking the button
Event Handlers	
onClick	Used to run JavaScript code when the button is clicked

checkbox	A check box in an HTML form Check boxes can be referred to using their field names. For example, to emulate the action of clicking a check box named "SUBSCRIBE," use the following expression: SUBSCRIBE.click();
Properties	
checked	A Boolean value that indicates whether or not the check box is checked.
defaultChecked	A Boolean value that indicates whether or not the check box is selected by default
name	The name of the check box element
value	The value of the check box element
Methods	
click()	Emulates the action of clicking the check box
Event Handlers	
onClick	Used to run JavaScript code when the check box is clicked

Appendix D
JavaScript Objects, Properties, Methods, and Event Handlers

date

An object containing information about a specific date or the current date. Here are two examples of assigning a date object to a variable named "Someday":

SomeDay = new Date("June, 15, 1995, 14:35:00");
SomeDay = new Date(1997, 5, 15, 14, 35, 0);

You can also create a variable containing the current date and time by removing the date and time values. For example:
Today = new Date();

Methods

getDate()	Returns the day of the month from 1 to 31
getDay()	Returns the day of the week from 0 to 6 (Sunday = 0, Monday =1, ...)
getHours()	Returns the hour in military time from 0 to 23
getMinutes()	Returns the minute from 0 to 59
getMonth()	Returns the value of the month from 0 to 11 (January = 0, February =1, ...)
getSeconds()	Returns the seconds
getTime()	Returns the date as an integer representing the number of milliseconds since January 1st, 1970 at 00:00:00
getTimesoneOffset()	Returns the difference between the local time and Greenwich Mean Time in minutes
getYear()	Returns the number of years since 1900 (in other words, 1996 is represented by "96.") This value method is inconsistently applied past the year 1999.
setDate(*date*)	Sets the day of the month to the value specified in *date*
setHours(*hour*)	Sets the hour to the value specified in *hour*
setMinutes(*minutes*)	Sets the minute to the value specified in *minutes*
setMonth(*month*)	Sets the month to the value specified in *month*
setSeconds(*seconds*)	Sets the second to the value specified in *seconds*
setTime(*time*)	Sets the time using the value specified in *time*, where *time* is a variable containing the number of milliseconds since January 1st, 1970 at 00:00:00
setYear(*year*)	Sets the year to the value specified in *year*
toGMTString()	Converts the date to a text string in Greenwich Mean Time

Appendix D
JavaScript Objects, Properties, Methods, and Event Handlers

OBJECTS, PROPERTIES, METHODS, AND EVENT HANDLERS	DESCRIPTIONS AND EXAMPLES
toLocaleString()	Converts a date object's date to a text string, using the date format that the Web browser is set up to use
UTC()	Returns the date in the form of the number of milliseconds since January 1st, 1970, 00:00:00
document	**An HTML document**

Properties

alinkColor	The color of active hyperlinks in the document
anchors	An array of anchors within the document. Use anchors[0] to refer to the first anchor, anchors[1] to refer to the second anchor, and so forth.
bgColor	The background color used in the document
cookie	A text string containing the document's cookie values
fgColor	The text color used in the document
form	A form within the document (the form itself is also an object)
forms	An array of forms within the document. Use forms[0] to refer to the first form, forms[1] to refer to the second form, and so forth.
lastModified	The date the document was last modified
linkColor	The color of hyperlinks in the document
links	An array of links within the document. Use links[0] to refer to the first hyperlink, links[1] to refer to the second hyperlink, and so forth.
location	The URL of the document
referrer	The URL of the document containing the link that the user accessed to get to the current document
title	The title of the document
vlinkColor	The color of followed hyperlinks

Methods

clear()	Clears the contents of the document window
close()	Closes the document stream
open	Opens the document stream

OBJECTS, PROPERTIES, METHODS, AND EVENT HANDLERS	DESCRIPTIONS AND EXAMPLES
write()	Writes to the document window
writeln()	Writes to the document window on a single line (used only with preformatted text)
elements	**Elements within an HTML form**
Properties	
length	The number of elements within the form
form	**An HTML form within a document** **You can refer to a specific form using that form's name. For example, for a form named "REG," you can apply the submit method with the following expression:** **REG.submit();**
Properties	
action	The location of the CGI script that receives the form values
elements	An array of elements within the form (including input boxes, check boxes, buttons, and other fields). Use elements[0] to refer to the first element, elements[1] to refer to the second element, and so forth. Use the field name of the element to work with a specific element.
encoding	The type of encoding used in the form
method	The type of method used when submitting the form
target	The name of the window into which CGI output should be directed
Methods	
submit()	Submits the form to the CGI script
Event Handlers	
onSubmit	Used to run JavaScript code when the form is submitted by the browser
frame	**A frame window within the Web browser**
Properties	
frames	An array of frames within the frame window. Use frames[0] to refer to the first frame, frames[1] to refer to the second frame and so forth.
parent	The name of the window that contains the frame
self	The name of the current frame window

Appendix D
JavaScript Objects, Properties, Methods, and Event Handlers

OBJECTS, PROPERTIES, METHODS, AND EVENT HANDLERS	DESCRIPTIONS AND EXAMPLES
top	The name of the topmost window in the hierarchy of frame windows
window	The name of the current frame window
Methods	
alert(*message*)	Displays the text contained in *message* in a dialog box
clearTimeout(*name*)	Cancels the time out whose value is *name*
close()	Closes the window
confirm(*message*)	Displays the text contained in *message* in a dialog box along with OK and Cancel buttons
prompt(*message*, *default_text*)	Displays the text contained in *message* in a dialog box with a text entry box into which the user can enter a value or text string. The default value or text is specified by the value of *default_text*.
setTimeout(*expression*, *time*)	Evaluates the value of *expression* after the number of milliseconds specified in the value of *time* has passed
hidden	**A hidden field on an HTML form** **Hidden fields can be referred to using their field names. For example, to change the value of the hidden field "PWORD" to "newpassword," use the expression:** **PWORD.value = "newpassword"**
Properties	
name	The name of the hidden field
value	The value of the hidden field
history	**An object containing information about the Web browser's history list**
Properties	
length	The number of items in the history list
Methods	
back()	Goes back to the previous item in the history list
forward()	Goes forward to the next item in the history list
go(*location*)	Goes to the item in the history list specified by the value of *location*. The *location* variable can be either an integer or the name of the Web page.

Appendix D
JavaScript Objects, Properties, Methods, and Event Handlers

OBJECTS, PROPERTIES, METHODS, AND EVENT HANDLERS	DESCRIPTIONS AND EXAMPLES
image	An embedded image within the document (available only in Netscape Navigator 3.0 or higher)
Properties	
border	The value of the BORDER property of the <IMG> tag
complete	A Boolean value that indicates whether or not the image has been completely loaded by the browser
height	The height of the image in pixels
hspace	The horizontal space around the image in pixels
lowsrc	The value of the LOWSRC property of the <IMG> tag
src	The source of the inline image
vspace	The vertical space around the image in pixels
width	The width of the image in pixels
link	A link within an HTML document
Properties	
target	The target window of the hyperlinks
location	An object that contains information about the location of a Web document
Properties	
hash	The location's anchor name
host	The location's hostname and port number
href	The location's URL
pathname	The path portion of the location's URL
port	The port number of the location's URL
protocol	The protocol used with the location's URL

OBJECTS, PROPERTIES, METHODS, AND EVENT HANDLERS	DESCRIPTIONS AND EXAMPLES
math	A JavaScript object used for advanced mathematical calculations For example, to calculate the square root of 27 and store this value in the variable "SQ27," use the following JavaScript expression: var SQ27 = math.sqrt(27);

Properties

E	The value of the base of natural logarithms (2.7182...)
LN10	The value of the natural logarithm of 10
LN2	The value of the natural logarithm of 2
PI	The value of pi (3.1416...)

Methods

abs(*number*)	Returns the absolute value of *number*
acos(*number*)	Returns the arc cosine of *number* in radians
asin(*number*)	Returns the arc sine of *number* in radians
atan(*number*)	Returns the arc tangent of *number* in radians
ceil(*number*)	Rounds *number* up to the next highest integer
cos(*number*)	Returns the cosine of *number*, where *number* is an angle expressed in radians
exp(*number*)	Raises the value of E (2.7182...) to the value of *number*
floor(*number*)	Rounds *number* down to the next lowest integer
log(*number*)	Returns the natural logarithm of *number*
max(*number1*, *number2*)	Returns the greater of *number1* and *number2*
min(*number1*, *number2*)	Returns the lesser of *number1* and *number2*
pow(*number1*, *number2*)	Returns the value of *number1* raised to the power of *number2*
random()	Returns a random number between 0 and 1
round(*number*)	Rounds *number* to the closest integer
sin(*number*)	Returns the sine of *number*, where *number* is an angle expressed in radians
tan(*number*)	Returns the tangent of *number*, where *number* is an angle expressed in radians

Appendix D
JavaScript Objects, Properties, Methods, and Event Handlers

OBJECTS, PROPERTIES, METHODS, AND EVENT HANDLERS	DESCRIPTIONS AND EXAMPLES
navigator	An object representing the Web browser currently in use
Properties	
appCodeName	The code name of the Web browser
appName	The name of the Web browser
appVersion	The version of the Web browser
userAgent	The user-agent text string sent from the client to the Web server
option	An option from a selection list
Properties	
defaultSelected	A Boolean value indicating whether or not the option is selected by default
index	The index value of the option
selected	A Boolean value indicating whether or not the option is currently selected
text	The text of the option as displayed on the Web page
value	The value of the option
password	A password field in an HTML form You can refer to a specific password field using the field name. For example, for a password field named "PWORD," you can apply the focus() method with the following expression: PWORD.submit();
Properties	
defaultValue	The default value of the password
name	The name of the password field
value	The value of the password field
Methods	
blur()	Emulates the action of leaving the text area box
focus()	Emulates the action of moving into the text area box
select()	Emulates the action of selecting the text in a text area box

OBJECTS, PROPERTIES, METHODS, AND EVENT HANDLERS	DESCRIPTIONS AND EXAMPLES
radio	An array of radio buttons on an HTML form Use the name of the radio button set to refer to individual buttons. For example if the name of the radio button set is "Products," use Products[0] to refer to the first radio button, Products[1] to refer to the second radio button, and so forth.
Properties	
checked	A Boolean value indicating whether or not a specific radio button has been checked
defaultChecked	A Boolean value indicating whether or not a specific radio button is checked by default
length	The number of radio buttons in the set
name	The name of a set of radio buttons
value	The value of a specific radio button
Methods	
click()	Emulates the action of clicking the radio button
Event Handlers	
onClick	Used to run JavaScript code when the radio button is clicked
reset	A Reset button in an HTML form You can refer to a specific Reset button using the button's name. For a Reset button named "RELOAD," you can apply the click() method with the following expression: RELOAD.click();
Properties	
name	The name of the Reset button
value	The value of the Reset button
Methods	
click()	Emulates the action of clicking the Reset button
Event Handlers	
onClick	Used to run JavaScript code when the Reset button is clicked

Appendix D
JavaScript Objects, Properties, Methods, and Event Handlers

OBJECTS, PROPERTIES, METHODS, AND EVENT HANDLERS	DESCRIPTIONS AND EXAMPLES
select	A selection list in an HTML form You can refer to a specific selection list using the selection list's name. For example, to determine the number of options in a selection list named "PRODUCT," use the following expression: PRODUCT.length;
Properties	
length	The number of options in the selection list
name	The name of the selection list
options	An array of options within the selection list. Use options[0] to refer to the first option, options[1] to refer to the second option, and so forth. See the options object for more information on working with individual selection list options.
selectedIndex	The index value of the selected option from the selection list
Event Handlers	
onBlur	Used to run JavaScript code when the user leaves the selection list
onChange	Used to run JavaScript code when the user changes the selected option in the selection list
onFocus	Used to run JavaScript code when the user enters the selection list
string	An object representing a text string or string of characters For example to italicize the text string "Order Today!", use the following expression: "Order Today!".italics();
Properties	
length	The number of characters in the string
Methods	
anchor(*name*)	Turns the text string into a hyperlink anchor with a name value set to *name*
big()	Modifies the text string to display big characters (similar to the effect of applying the <BIG> tag)
blink()	Modifies the text string to display blinking characters (similar to the effect of applying the <BLINK> tag)
bold()	Modifies the text string to display characters in bold (similar to the effect of applying the <B> tag)
charAt(*index*)	Returns the character in the text string at the location specified by *index*

OBJECTS, PROPERTIES, METHODS, AND EVENT HANDLERS	DESCRIPTIONS AND EXAMPLES
fixed()	Modifies the text string to display fixed-width characters (similar to the effect of applying the <FIXED> tag)
fontColor(*color*)	Modifies the text string to display text in a color specified by *color* (similar to applying the <FONT> tag to the text along with the COLOR property)
fontSize(*value*)	Modifies the text string to display text in the font size specified by the *value* parameter (similar to applying the <FONT> tag to the text along with the SIZE property)
indexOf(*string, start*)	Searches the text string and returns the index value of the first occurrence of the text string *string*. The search starts at the character indicated by the value of *start*.
italics()	Modifies the text string to display characters in italics (similar to the effect of applying the <I> tag)
lastIndexOf(*string, start*)	Searches the text string and locates the index value of the last occurrence of the text string *string*. The search starts at the character indicated by the value of *start*.
link(*href*)	Turns the text string into a hyperlink pointing to the URL contained in *href*
small()	Modifies the text string to display small characters (similar to the effect of applying the <SMALL> tag)
strike()	Applies the strikeout character to the text string (similar to the effect of applying the <STRIKE> tag)
sub()	Modifies the text string to display subscript characters (similar to the effect of applying the <SUB> tag)
substring(*first, last*)	Returns a substring of characters from the text string, starting with the character at the index number *first* and ending with the character at the index number *last*
sup()	Modifies the text string to display superscript characters (similar to the effect of applying the <SUP> tag)
toLowerCase()	Changes all of the characters in the text string to lowercase
toUpperCase()	Changes all of the characters in the text string to uppercase
submit	A Submit button in an HTML form You can refer to a specific Submit button using the button's name. For a Submit button named "SAVE," you can apply the click() method with the following expression: SAVE.click();

Properties

name	The name of the Submit button
value	The value of the Submit button

Appendix D
JavaScript Objects, Properties, Methods, and Event Handlers

OBJECTS, PROPERTIES, METHODS, AND EVENT HANDLERS	DESCRIPTIONS AND EXAMPLES
Methods	
click()	Emulates the action of clicking the Submit button
Event Handlers	
onClick	Used to run JavaScript code when the user clicks the Submit button
text	An input box from an HTML form You can refer to an input box using the box's name. For example, to move the cursor to an input box named "ADDRESS," use the following expression: ADDRESS.focus();
Properties	
defaultValue	The default value of the input box
name	The name of the input box
value	The value of the input box
Methods	
blur()	Emulates the action of leaving the input box
focus()	Emulates the action of moving into the input box
select()	Emulates the action of selecting the text in an input box
Event Handlers	
onBlur	Used to run JavaScript code when the user leaves the input box
onChange	Used to run JavaScript code when the user changes the value of the input box
onFocus	Used to run JavaScript code when the user enters the input box
onSelect	Used to run JavaScript code when the user selects some or all of the text in the input box
textarea	A text area box in an HTML form You can refer to a specific text area box using the box's name. For example, to move the cursor out of a text area box named "COMMENTS," use the expression: COMMENTS.blur();
Properties	
defaultValue	The default value of the text area box
name	The name of the text area box

OBJECTS, PROPERTIES, METHODS, AND EVENT HANDLERS	DESCRIPTIONS AND EXAMPLES
value	The value of the text area box
Methods	
blur()	Emulates the action of leaving the text area box
focus()	Emulates the action of moving into the text area box
select()	Emulates the action of selecting the text in a text area box
Event Handlers	
onBlur	Used to run JavaScript code when the user leaves the text area box
onChange	Used to run JavaScript code when the user changes the value of the text area box
onFocus	Used to run JavaScript code when the user enters the text area box
onSelect	Used to run JavaScript code when the user selects some or all of the text in the text area box
window	The document window contained within the Web browser
Properties	
defaultStatus	The default text string displayed in the window's status bar
frames	An array of frames within the window. Use frames[0] to refer to the first frame, frames[1] to refer to the second frame, and so forth. See the frames object for properties and methods that can be applied to individual frames.
length	The number of frames in the parent window
name	The name of the window
parent	The name of the window containing this particular window
self	The name of the current window
status	The text string displayed in the window's status bar
top	The name of the topmost window in a hierarchy of windows
window	The name of the current window
Methods	
alert(*message*)	Displays the text contained in *message* in a dialog box
clearTimeout(*name*)	Cancels the time out whose value is *name*

OBJECTS, PROPERTIES, METHODS, AND EVENT HANDLERS	DESCRIPTIONS AND EXAMPLES
close()	Closes the window
confirm(*message*)	Displays the text contained in *message* in a dialog box along with OK and Cancel buttons
prompt(*message, default_text*)	Displays the text contained in *message* in a dialog box with a text entry box into which the user can enter a value or text string. The default value or text is specified by the value of *default_text*.
setTimeout(*expression, time*)	Evaluates the value of *expression* after the number of milliseconds specified in the value of *time* has passed
Event Handlers	
onLoad	Used to run JavaScript code when the window or frame finishes loading
onUnload	Used to run JavaScript code when the window or frame finishes unloading

Appendix E **JavaScript Operators**

OPERATORS	DESCRIPTION

The following are some operators used in JavaScript expressions.

Assignment	Assignment operators are used to assign values to variables.
=	Assigns the value of the variable on the right to the variable on the left (x=y)
+=	Adds the two variables and assigns the result to the variable on the left (x+=y is equivalent to x=x+y)
–=	Subtracts the variable on the right from the variable on the left and assigns the result to the variable on the left (x–=y is equivalent to x=x–y)
*=	Multiplies the two variables together and assigns the result to the variable on the left (x*=y is equivalent to x=x*y)
/=	Divides the variable on the left by the variable on the right and assigns the result to the variable on the left (x/=y is equivalent to x=x/y)
%=	Divides the variable on the left by the variable on the right and assigns the remainder to the variable on the left (x%=y is equivalent to x=x%y)

Arithmetic	Arithmetic operators are used for arithmetic functions.
+	Adds two variables together (x+y)
–	Subtracts the variable on the right from the variable on the left (x–y)
*	Multiplies two variables together (x*y)
/	Divides the variable on the left by the variable on the right (x/y)
%	Calculates the remainder after dividing the variable on the left by the variable on the right (x%y)
++	Increases the value of a variable by 1 (x++ is equivalent to x=x+1)
--	Decreases the value of a variable by 1 (x-- is equivalent to x=x–1)
–	Changes the sign of a variable (–x)

Logical	Logical operators are used for evaluating true and false expressions.
&&	Returns true only if both expressions are true (also known as an AND operator)
||	Returns true when either expression is true (also known as an OR operator)
|	Returns true if the expression is false, and false if the expression is true (also known as a *negation* operator)

Appendix E JavaScript Operators

OPERATORS	DESCRIPTION
Comparison	Comparison operators are used for comparing expressions
==	Returns true when the two expressions are equal (x==y)
!=	Returns true when the two expressions are not equal (x!=y)
>	Returns true when the expression on the left is greater than the expression on the right (x > y)
<	Returns true when the expression on the left is less than the expression on the right (x < y)
>=	Returns true when the expression on the left is greater than or equal to the expression on the right (x >= y)
<=	Returns true when the expression on the left is less than or equal to the expression on the right (x <= y)
Conditional	Conditional operators determine values based on conditions that are either true or false
(condition) ? value1 : value2	If condition is true, then this expression equals value1, otherwise it equals value2.